THE
HISTORY
OF
CHILDHOOD

Lloyd deMause, Editor

A CONDOR BOOK
SOUVENIR PRESS (E & A) LTD

Contents

Foreword

The direction of human affairs has never been confided to children, and historians, who have concerned themselves primarily with political and military affairs and at most with the intrigues and rivalries of royal courts, have paid almost no attention to the ordeals of childhood. Even the students of education have, on the whole, devoted themselves to the organization and curricula of schools, and with the theories of education, with only occasional reference to what happened to the pupils at home and in the world at large.

Yet it seems clear that the history of childhood must be of major importance to any study of human society, for if, as it is said, the child is father to the man, it should be possible, with an understanding of any individual's or any group's past, to form a more intelligent judgment of their performance as adults. For that reason the present experiment in reviewing systematically the attitudes and practices of parents towards their children is to be warmly welcomed. Whatever the findings of the scholars contributing to this pioneer volume, they will all substantially add to our knowledge of mankind's past and so deepen our understanding of changing attitudes and reactions.

Unhappily the results of these investigations are most depressing. They tell a long and mournful story of the abuse of children from the earliest times even to the present day. We need not assume that the generalizations here advanced apply to all people at all times. No one can doubt that there have always been parents who loved and cherished their children and that such mistakes as they may have made in the upbringing were due to ignorance rather than to ill-will. As a matter of fact, while in our own day cases of battered children are shockingly common, it must be said that ever since the eighteenth century a more humanitarian attitude gradually emerged. Parenthetically one is reminded of the fact that in England societies for the prevention of cruelty to animals sprang up at least as early as societies for the prevention of cruelty to children.

Possibly the heartless treatment of children, from the practice of infanticide and abandonment through to the neglect, the rigors of swaddling, the purposeful starving, the beatings, the solitary confinement, and so on, was and is only one aspect of the basic aggressiveness and cruelty of human nature, of the inbred disregard of the rights and feelings of others. Children, being physically unable to resist aggression, were the victims of forces over which they had no control, and they were abused in many imaginable and some almost unimaginable ways by way of expressing conscious or more commonly unconscious motives of their elders.

There may well have been yet another facet to the problem—one which can never be proved, but for which there are many indicators. Humans, like all animals and plants, have an almost infinite reproductive potential. More babies have always been born than society could provide room or employment for. Hence the widespread practice of infanticide in one form or another, the chief victims always being the female infants who would eventually produce yet more souls. Hence probably also the notion, prevalent at least in the Christian world, that sex relations were sinful and that the resultant offspring was, from the moment of birth, evil. How else is one to explain the cruel practices designed to exorcise the evil and make children less of a nuisance than they were? Countless women felt that they had too many children. The well-to-do upper classes, it is true, were frequently concerned to ensure themselves of an heir to the estate, and in some parts of the world it is even now true that peasant families desire large families so as to provide for their old age. But in the Western world, when life expectancy at birth was thirty years or less, this was not a controlling factor. Peasant women who had to work all day in the fields tended to regard young children as an encumbrance and took any and every means to discipline and quiet them. That children were put to work at a very early age is no news, but even at work they were often treated more as slaves than as humans. In short, children were not uncommonly looked upon as a real burden, and often called forth resentment and hostility.

The present volume abounds in evidence of all kinds, from all periods and all peoples. The story is monotonously painful, but it is high time that it should be told and that it should be taken into account not only by psychiatrists and sociologists, but also by historians. So large and crucial a segment of human existence should not forever remain veiled and neglected by those whose mission it is to recover man's past.

William L. Langer
Archibald Cary Coolidge Professor of History, Emeritus
Harvard University
Past President, American Historical Association

December, 1973

Editor's Preface

What was it like to have been a child in colonial America, or in Renaissance Italy? Did parents always act much the same as they do today? Did they love and care for their children in similar ways, or has child care changed substantially over the centuries? How did parents feel about their children, what did they say to them, what were their private fantasies about them, and how did these affect growing up in the past?

These are the kinds of questions the ten of us who are the authors of this book asked ourselves five years ago as we embarked upon the major research project of writing a history of childhood in the West, to be conducted under the auspices of the Association for Applied Psychoanalysis. What we found was a fascinating story in its own right, but it is also a story which cannot help but have a major effect on our understanding of history and of how we got to where we are today. If perspective is all, it is surely most important in our crucial task of raising the next generation who will run the world we leave them.

Despite the psychoanalytic origin of our project, we are all historians first, and have considered it our central task to examine the sources objectively in order to reconstruct how parents and children related to each other in different time periods and different countries. Joint investigations are rare in the study of history; ours has been a particularly close and fruitful collaboration, with each new bibliographic discovery made by one of us quickly communicated to the others. We have had several meetings in these five years, and we were connected by a series of Project Bulletins, yet finally each contribution was written independent of the others. We have not attempted to disguise our differences of interpretation wherever they occur, for our differences like our omissions will prove our best clues to future research.

That this book is only a beginning we freely admit. Childhood history is not the easiest of historical fields in which to specialize. It has often seemed, after sifting through dozens of difficult manuscripts in order to discover a single golden nugget about childhood, that our field is the extreme instance of the historian's rule that "the things that really matter are hardly ever committed to paper." Yet in the end we found the reconstruction of childhood in the past a thoroughly fascinating enterprise, well worth our best efforts. We think you will agree with us.

Lloyd deMause

Contributors

Lloyd deMause
History of Childhood Quarterly:
The Journal of Psychohistory
2315 Broadway
New York, New York 10024

Richard B. Lyman, Jr.
Professor of History
Simmons College
300 The Fenway
Boston, Massachusetts 02115

Mary Martin McLaughlin
Box 247, Route 1
Valley Farm Road
Millbrook, New York 12545

James Bruce Ross
2801 New Mexico Avenue
Washington, D.C. 20007

M. J. Tucker
Professor of History
State University of New York at Buffalo
233 Diefendorf Hall
Buffalo, New York 14214

Elizabeth Wirth Marvick
Professor of Government
Claremont Graduate School
Claremont, California 91711

Joseph E. Illick
Professor of History
California State University, San Francisco
1600 Holoway Avenue
San Francisco, California 94132

John F. Walzer
Professor of History
California State University, Long Beach
6101 East Seventh Street
Long Beach, California 90840

Patrick P. Dunn
Professor of History
The University of Wisconsin—La Crosse
La Crosse, Wisconsin 54601

Priscilla Robertson
12627 Osage Road North
Anchorage, Kentucky 40223

CHAPTER 1

The Evolution of Childhood

LLOYD
DEMAUSE

Do ye hear the children weeping,
Oh my brothers . . .
The Cry of the Children
Elizabeth Barrett Browning

The history of childhood is a nightmare from which we have only recently begun to awaken. The further back in history one goes, the lower the level of child care, and the more likely children are to be killed, abandoned, beaten, terrorized, and sexually abused. It is our task here to see how much of this childhood history can be recaptured from the evidence that remains to us.

That this pattern has not previously been noticed by historians is because serious history has long been considered a record of public not private events. Historians have concentrated so much on the noisy sandbox of history, with its fantastic castles and magnificent battles, that they have generally ignored what is going on in the homes around the playground. And where historians usually look to the sandbox battles of yesterday for the causes of those today, we instead ask how each generation of parents and children creates those issues which are later acted out in the arena of public life.

At first glance, this lack of interest in the lives of children seems odd. Historians have been traditionally committed to explaining continuity and change over time, and ever since Plato it has been known that child-hood is a key to this understanding. The importance of parent-child re-lations for social change was hardly discovered by Freud; St. Augustine's cry, "Give me other mothers and I will give you another world," has been echoed by major thinkers for fifteen centuries without affecting historical writing. Since Freud, of course, our view of childhood has acquired a new dimension, and in the past half century the study of childhood has become routine for the psychologist, the sociologist, and the anthropologist. It is only beginning for the historian. Such deter-mined avoidance requires an explanation.

Historians usually blame the paucity of the sources for the lack of serious study of childhood in the past. Peter Laslett wonders why the "crowds and crowds of little children are strangely missing from the written record. . . . There is something mysterious about the silence of all these multitudes of babes in arms, toddlers and adolescents in the statements men made at the time about their own experience. . . . We cannot say whether fathers helped in the tending of infants. . . . No-thing can as yet be said on what is called by the psychologists toilet training. . . . It is in fact an effort of mind to remember all the time that children were always present in such numbers in the traditional world, nearly half the whole community living in a condition of semi-oblitera-tion."[1] As the family sociologist James Bossard puts it: "Unfortunately, the history of childhood has never been written, and there is some doubt whether it ever can be written [because] of the dearth of his-torical data bearing on childhood."[2]

This conviction is so strong among historians that it is not surprising that this book began not in the field of history at all but in applied psychoanalysis. Five years ago, I was engaged in writing a book on a psychoanalytic theory of historical change, and, in reviewing the results of half a century of applied psychoanalysis, it seemed to me that it had failed to become a science mainly because it had not become evolu-tionary. Since the repetition compulsion, by definition, cannot explain historical change, every attempt by Freud, Roheim, Kardiner, and others to develop a theory of change ultimately ended in a sterile chicken-or-egg dispute about whether child-rearing depends on cultural traits or the other way around. That child-rearing practices are the basis for adult personality was proven again and again. Where they originated stumped every psychoanalyst who raised the question.[3]

In a paper given in 1968 before the Association for Applied Psycho-analysis, I outlined an evolutionary theory of historical change in parent-child relations, and proposed that since historians had not as yet begun the job of writing childhood history, the Association should sponsor a team of historians who would dig back into the sources to uncover the major stages of child-rearing in the West since antiquity. This book is the outcome of that project.

The "psychogenic theory of history" outlined in my project proposal began with a comprehensive theory of historical change. It posited that the central force for change in history is neither technology nor economics, but the "psychogenic" changes in personality occurring because of successive generations of parent-child interactions. This theory involved several hypotheses, each subject to proof or disproof by empirical historical evidence:

1. That the evolution of parent-child relations constitutes an independent source of historical change. The origin of this evolution lies in the ability of successive generations of parents to regress to the psychic age of their children and work through the anxieties of that age in a better manner the second time they encounter them than they did during their own childhood. The process is similar to that of psychoanalysis, which also involves regression and a second chance to face childhood anxieties.

2. That this "generational pressure" for psychic change is not only spontaneous, originating in the adult's need to regress and in the child's striving for relationship, but also occurs independent of social and technological change. It therefore can be found even in periods of social and technological stagnation.

3. That the history of childhood is a series of closer approaches between adult and child, with each closing of psychic distance producing fresh anxiety. The reduction of this adult anxiety is the main source of the child-rearing practices of each age.

4. That the obverse of the hypothesis that history involves a general improvement in child care is that the further back one goes in history, the less effective parents are in meeting the developing needs of the child. This would indicate, for instance, that if today in America there are less than a million abused children,[4] there would be a point back in history where most children were what we would now consider abused.

5. That because psychic structure must always be passed from generation to generation through the narrow funnel of childhood, a society's child-rearing practices are not just one item in a list of cultural traits. They are the very condition for the transmission and development of all other cultural elements, and place definite limits on what can be achieved in all other spheres of history. Specific childhood experiences must occur to sustain specific cultural traits, and once these experiences no longer occur the trait disappears.

Now it is obvious that any evolutionary psychological theory as ambitious as this one is cannot really be tested in a single book, and our goal in this book has been the more modest one of reconstructing from what evidence remains what it felt like to be a child and a parent in the past. Whatever evidence there is for actual evolutionary patterns for childhood in the past will only emerge as we set forth the fragmentary and often confusing story we have uncovered of the lives of children during the past two thousand years in the West.

PREVIOUS WORKS ON CHILDREN IN HISTORY

Although I think this book is the first to examine seriously the history of childhood in the West, historians have undeniably been writing about children in past ages for some time.[5] Even so, I think that the study of the history of childhood is just beginning, since most of these works so badly distort the facts of childhood in the periods they cover. Official biographers are the worst offenders; childhood is generally idealized, and very few biographers give any useful information about the subject's earliest years. The historical sociologists manage to turn out theories explaining changes in childhood without ever bothering to examine a single family, past or present.[6] The literary historians, mistaking books for life, construct a fictional picture of childhood, as though one could know what really happened in the nineteenth-century American home by reading *Tom Sawyer*.[7]

But it is the social historian, whose job it is to dig out the reality of social conditions in the past, who defends himself most vigorously against the facts he turns up.[8] When one social historian finds widespread infanticide, he declares it "admirable and humane."[9] When another describes mothers who regularly beat their infants with sticks while still in the cradle, she comments, without a shred of evidence, that "if her discipline was stern, it was even and just and leavened with kindness."[10] When a third finds mothers who dunk their infants into ice water each morning to "strengthen" them, and the children die from the practice, she says that "they were not intentionally cruel," but simply "had read Rousseau and Locke."[11] No practice in the past seems anything but benign to the social historian. When Laslett finds parents regularly sending their children, at age seven, to other homes as servants, while taking in other children to serve them, he says it was actually kindness, for it "shows that parents may have been unwilling to submit children of their own to the discipline of work at home."[12] After admitting that severe whipping of young children with various instruments "at school and at home seems to have been as common in the seventeenth century as it was later," William Sloan feels compelled to add that "children, then as later, sometimes deserved whipping."[13] When Philippe Ariès comes up with so much evidence of open sexual molesting of children that he admits that "playing with children's privy parts formed part of a widespread tradition,"[14] he goes on to describe a "traditional" scene where a stranger throws himself on a little boy while riding in a train, "his hand brutally rummaging inside the child's fly," while the father smiles, and concludes: "All that was involved was a game whose scabrous nature we should beware of exaggerating."[15] Masses of evidence are hidden, distorted, softened, or ignored. The child's early years are played down, formal educational content is endlessly examined, and emotional content is avoided by stressing child legislation and avoiding the home. And if the nature of the author's book is such that the ubiquity of unpleasant facts cannot be ignored, the theory is invented that "good parents leave no traces in the records." When, for instance, Alan Valentine examines 600 years of letters from fathers to sons, and of 126 fathers is unable to find one who isn't insensitive, moralistic, and thoroughly self-centered, he concludes: "Doubtless an infinite number of fathers have written to their sons letters that would warm and lift our hearts, if we only could find them. The happiest fathers leave no history, and it is the men who are not at their best with their children who are likely to write the heart-rending letters that survive."[16] Likewise, Anna Burr, covering 250 autobiographies, notes there are no happy memories of childhood, but carefully avoids drawing any conclusions.[17]

Of all the books on childhood in the past, Philippe Ariès's book *Centuries of Childhood* is probably the best known; one historian notes the frequency with which it is "cited as Holy Writ."[18] Ariès's central thesis is the opposite of mine: he argues that while the traditional child was happy because he was free to mix with many classes and ages, a special condition known as childhood was "invented" in the early modern period, resulting in a tyrannical concept of the family which destroyed friendship and sociability and deprived children of freedom, inflicting upon them for the first time the birch and the prison cell.

To prove this thesis, Ariès uses two main arguments. He first says that a separate concept of childhood was unknown in the early Middle Ages. "Medieval art until about the twelfth century did not know childhood or did not attempt to portray it" because artists were "unable to depict a child except as a man on a smaller scale."[19] Not only does this leave the art of antiquity in limbo, but it ignores voluminous evidence that medieval artists could, indeed, paint realistic children.[20] His etymological argument for a separate concept of childhood being unknown is also untenable.[21] In any case, the notion of the "invention of childhood" is so fuzzy that it is surprising that so many historians have recently picked it up.[22] His second argument, that the modern family restricts the child's freedom and increases the severity of punishment, runs counter to all the evidence.

Far more reliable than Ariès is a quartet of books, only one of them written by a professional historian: George Payne's *The Child in Human Progress*, G. Rattray Taylor's *The Angel Makers*, David Hunt's *Parents and Children in History*, and J. Louise Despert's *The Emotionally Disturbed Child—Then and Now*. Payne, writing in 1916, was the first to examine the wide extent of infanticide and brutality toward children in the past, particularly in antiquity. Taylor's book, rich in documentation, is a sophisticated psychoanalytic reading of childhood and personality in late eighteenth-century England. Hunt, like Ariès, centers mostly on the unique seventeenth-century document, Héroard's diary of the childhood of Louis XIII, but does so with great psychological sensitivity and awareness of the psychohistorical implications of his findings. And Despert's psychiatric comparison of child mistreatment in the past and present surveys the range of emotional attitudes toward children since antiquity, expressing her growing horror as she uncovers a story of unremitting "heartlessness and cruelty."[23]

Yet despite these four books, the central questions of comparative childhood history remain to be asked, much less answered. In the next two sections of this chapter, I will cover some of the psychological principles that apply to adult-child relations in the past. The examples I use, while not untypical of child life in the past, are not drawn equally from all time periods, but are chosen as the clearest illustrations of the psychological principles being described. It is only in the three succeeding sections, where I provide an overview of the history of infanticide, abandonment, nursing, swaddling, beating, and sexual abuse, that I begin to examine how widespread the practice was in each period.

PSYCHOLOGICAL PRINCIPLES OF CHILDHOOD HISTORY: PROJECTIVE AND REVERSAL REACTIONS

In studying childhood over many generations, it is most important to concentrate on those moments which most affect the psyche of the next generation: primarily, this means what happens when an adult is face to fáce with a child who needs something. The adult has, I believe, three major reactions available: (1) He can use the child as a vehicle for projection of the contents of his own unconscious (projective reaction); (2) he can use the child as a substitute for an adult figure important in his own childhood (reversal reaction); or (3) he can empathize with the child's needs and act to satisfy them (empathic reaction).

The projective reaction is, of course, familiar to psychoanalysts under terms which range from "projection" to "projective identification," a more concrete, intrusive form of voiding feelings into others. The psychoanalyst, for instance, is thoroughly familiar with being used as a "toilet-lap"[24] for the massive projections of the patient. It is this condition of being used as a vehicle for projections which is usual for children in the past.

Likewise, the reversal reaction is familiar to students of battering parents.[25] Children exist only to satisfy parental needs, and it is always the failure of the child-as-parent to give love which triggers the actual battering. As one battering mother put it: "I have never felt loved all my life. When the baby was born, I thought he would love me. When he cried, it meant he didn't love me. So I hit him."

The third term, empathic reaction, is used here in a more limited sense than the dictionary definition. It is the adult's ability to regress to the level of a child's need and correctly identify it without an admixture of the adult's own projections. The adult must then be able to maintain enough distance from the need to be able to satisfy it. It is an ability identical to the use of the psychoanalyst's unconscious called "free-floating attention," or, as Theodor Reik terms it, "listening with the third ear."[26]

Projective and reversal reactions often occurred simultaneously in parents in the past, producing an effect which I call the "double image," where the child was seen as both full of the adult's projected desires, hostilities, and sexual thoughts, and at the same moment as a mother or father figure. That is, it is both bad and loving. Furthermore, the further back in history one goes, the more "concretization" or reification one finds of these projective and reversal reactions, producing progressively more bizarre attitudes toward children, similar to those of contemporary parents of battered and schizophrenic children.

The first illustration of these closely interlocking concepts which we will examine is in an adult-child scene from the past. The year is 1739, the boy, Nicolas, is four years old. The incident is one he remembers and has had confirmed by his mother. His grandfather, who has been rather attentive to him the past few days, decides he has to "test" him and says, "Nicolas, my son, you have many faults, and these grieve your mother. She is my daughter and has always obliged me; obey me too and correct these, or I will whip you like a dog which is being trained. Nicolas, angry at the betrayal "from one who has been so kind to me," throws his toys into the fire. The grandfather seems pleased.

> "Nicholas . . . I said that to test you. Did you really think that a grandpapa, who had been so kind to you yesterday and the day before, could treat you like a dog today? I thought you were intelligent . . ." "I am not a beast like a dog." "No, but you are not as clever as I thought, or you would have understood that I was only teasing. It was just a joke . . . Come to me." I threw myself

into his arms. "That is not all," he continued, "I want to see you friends with your mother; you have grieved, deeply grieved her . . . Nicolas, your father loves you; do you love him?" "Yes, grandpapa!" "Suppose he were in danger and to save him it was necessary to put your hand in the fire, would you do it? Would you put it . . . there, if it was necessary?" "Yes grandpapa." "And for me?" "For you? . . . yes, yes." "And for your mother?" "For mamma? Both of them, both of them!" "We shall see if you are telling the truth, for your mother is in great need of your little help! If you love her, you must prove it." I made no answer; but, putting together all that had been said, I went to the fireplace and, while they were making signs to each other, put my right hand into the fire. The pain drew a deep sigh from me."[27]

What makes this sort of scene so typical of adult-child interaction in the past is the existence of so many contradictory attitudes on the adult's part without the least resolution. The child is loved and hated, rewarded and punished, bad and loving, all at once. That this puts the child in a "double bind" of conflicting signals (which Bateson[28] and others believe underlie schizophrenia), goes without saying. But the conflicting signals themselves come from adults who are striving to demonstrate that the child is both very bad (projective reaction) and very loving (reversal reaction). It is the child's function to reduce the adult's pressing anxieties; the child acts as the adult's defense.

It is also the projective and reversal reactions which make guilt impossible in the severe beatings which we so often encounter in the past. This is because it is not the actual child who is being beaten. It is either the adult's own projections ("Look at her give you the eye! That's how she picks up men—she's a regular sexpot!" a mother says of her battered daughter of two), or it is a product of reversal ("He thinks he's the boss—all the time trying to run things—but I showed him who is in charge around here!" a father says of his nine-month-old boy whose skull he has split).[29] One can often catch the merging of beaten and beater and therefore lack of guilt in the historical sources. An American father (1830) tells of horsewhipping his four-year-old boy for not being able to read something. The child is tied up naked in the cellar:

With him in this condition, and myself, the wife of my bosom, and the lady of my family, all of us in distress, and with hearts sinking within us, I commenced using the rod . . . During this most unpleasant, self denying and disagreeable work, I made frequent stops, commanding and trying to persuade, silencing excuses, answering objections . . . I felt all the force of divine authority and express command that I ever felt in any case in all my life . . . But under the all controlling influence of such a degree of angry passion and obstinacy, as my son had manifested, no wonder he thought he "should beat me out," feeble and tremulous as I was; and knowing as he did that it made me almost sick to whip him. At that time he could neither pity me nor himself.[30]

It is this picture of the merging of father and son, with the father complaining that he himself is the one beaten and in need of pity, which we will encounter when we ask how beating could have been so widespread in the past. When a Renaissance pedagogue says you should tell the child when beating him, "you do the correction against your mind, compelled thereunto by conscience, and require them to put you no more unto such labour and pain. For if you do (say you) you must suffer part of the pain with me and therefore you shall now have experience and proof what pain it is unto both of us" we will not so easily miss the merging and mislabel it hypocrisy.[31]

Indeed, the parent sees the child as so full of portions of himself that even real accidents to the child are seen as injuries to the parent. Cotton Mather's daughter Nanny fell into the fire and burned herself badly, and he cried out, "Alas, for my sins the just God throws my child into the fire!"[32] He searched everything he himself had recently done wrong, but since he believed he was the one being punished, no guilt toward his child could be felt (say, for leaving her alone), and no corrective action could be taken. Soon two other daughters were badly burned. His reaction was to preach a sermon on "What use ought parents to make of disasters befallen their children."

This matter of "accidents" to children is not to be taken lightly, for in it lies hidden the clue to why adults in the past were such poor parents. Leaving aside actual death wishes, which will be discussed later, accidents occurred in great numbers in the past because little children were so often left alone. Mather's daughter Nibby would have been burned to death but for "a person accidentally then passing by the window,"[33] because there was no one there to hear her cries. A colonial Boston experience is also typical:

"After they had supped, the mother put two children to bed in the room where they themselves did lie, and they went out to visit a neighbor. When they returned . . . the mother [went] to the bed, and not finding her youngest child (a daughter about five years of age), and after much search she found it drowned in a well in her cellar . . ."[34]

The father blames the accident on his having worked on a holy day. The point is not only that it was common to leave little children alone right up to the twentieth century. More important is that parents cannot be concerned with preventing accidents if guilt is absent because it is the adult's own projections that they feel have been punished. Massive projectors don't invent safety stoves, nor often can they even see to it that their children are given the simplest of care. Their projection, unfortunately, insures repetition.

The use of the child as a "toilet" for adult projections is behind the whole notion of original sin, and for eighteen hundred years adults were in general agreement that, as Richard Allestree (1676) puts it, "the newborn babe is full of the stains and pollution of sin, which it inherits from our first parents through our loins . . ."[35] Baptism used to include actual exorcism of the Devil, and the belief that the child who cried at his christening was letting out the Devil long survived the formal omission of exorcism in the Reformation.[36] Even where formal religion did not stress the devil, it was there; here is a picture of a Polish Jew teaching in the nineteenth century:

> He derived an intense joy from the agonies of the little victim trembling and shivering on the bench. And he used to administer the whippings coldly, slowly, deliberately . . . he asked the boy to let down his clothes, lie across the bench . . . and pitched in with the leathern thongs . . . "In every person there is a Good Spirit and an Evil Spirit. The Good Spirit has its own dwelling-place— which is the head. So has the Evil Spirit—and that is the place where you get the whipping."[37]

The child in the past was so charged with projections that he was often in danger of being considered a changeling if he cried too much or was otherwise too demanding. There is a large literature on changelings,[38] but it is not generally realized that it was not only deformed children who were killed as changelings, but also those who, as St. Augustine puts it, "suffer from a demon . . . they are under the power of the Devil . . . some infants die in this vexation . . ."[39] Some church fathers declared that if a baby merely cried it was committing a sin.[40] Sprenger and Krämer, in their bible of witchhunting, *Malleus Maleficarum* (1487), contend that you can recognize changelings because they "always howl most piteously and even if four or five mothers are set on to suckle them, they never grow." Luther agrees: "That is true: they often take the children of women in childbed and lay themselves down in their place and are more obnoxious than ten children with their crapping, eating, and screaming."[41] Guibert of Nogent, writing in the twelfth century, considers his mother saintly because she put up with the crying of an infant she had adopted:

> . . . the baby so harassed my mother and all her servants by the madness of its wailing and crying at night—although by day it was very good, by turns playing and sleeping—that anyone in the same little room could get scarcely any sleep. I have heard the nurses whom she hired say that night after night they could not stop shaking the child's rattle, so naughty was he, not through his own fault, but made so by the Devil within, and that a woman's craft

failed entirely to drive him out. The good woman was tormented by extreme pain; amid those shrill cries no contrivance relieved her aching brow.... Yet she never shut the child out of her house....[42]

The belief that infants were felt to be on the verge of turning into totally evil beings is one of the reasons why they were tied up, or swaddled, so long and so tightly. One feels the undertone in Bartholomaeus Anglicus (c. 1230): "And for tenderness the limbs of the child may easily and soon bow and bend and take diverse shapes. And therefore children's members and limbs are bound with lystes [bandages], and other covenable bönds, that they be not crooked nor evil shapen ..."[43] It is the infant full of the parent's dangerous, evil projections that is swaddled. The reasons given for swaddling in the past are the same as those of present-day swaddlers in Eastern Europe: the baby has to be tied up or it will tear its ears off, scratch its eyes out, break its legs, or touch its genitals.[44] As we shall see shortly in the section on swaddling and restraints, this often includes binding up children in all kinds of corsets, stays, backboards, and puppet-strings, and even extends to tying them up in chairs to prevent them from crawling on the floor "like an animal."

Now if adults project all their own unacceptable feelings into the child, it is obvious that severe measures must be taken to keep this dangerous "toilet-child" under control once swaddling bands are outgrown. I shall later examine various methods of control used by parents down through the centuries, but here I want to illustrate only one control device—frightening the child with ghosts—in order to discuss its projective character.

The number of ghost-like figures used to frighten children throughout history is legion, and their regular use by adults was common until quite recently. The ancients had their Lamia and Striga, who, like their Hebrew prototype Lilith, ate children raw, and who, along with Mormo, Canida, Poine, Sybaris, Acco, Empusa, Gorgon, and Ephialtes, were "invented for a child's benefit to make it less rash and ungovernable," according to Dio Chrysostom.[45] Most ancients agreed that it was good to have the images of these witches constantly before children, to let them feel the terror of waiting up at night for ghosts to steal them away, eat them, tear them to pieces, and suck their blood or their bone marrow. By medieval times, of course, witches and devils took front stage, with an occasional Jew thrown in as a cutter of babies' throats, along with hoards of other monsters and bogies "such as those [with] which nurses love to terrify them."[46] After the Reformation, God himself, who "holds you over the pit of hell, much as one holds a spider, or some loathsome insect, over the fire,"[47] was the major bogeyman used to terrify children, and tracts were written in baby talk describing the tortures God had in store for children in Hell: "The little child is in this red-hot oven. Hear how it screams to come out . . . It stamps its little feet on the floor . . ."[48]

When religion was no longer the focus of the terrorizing campaign, figures closer to home were used: the werewolf will gulp you down, Blue Beard will chop you up, Boney (Bonaparte) will eat your flesh, the black man or the chimney sweep will steal you away at night.[49] These practices came under attack only in the nineteenth century. One English parent said in 1810 that "the custom once prevalent of terrifying young minds with stories of ghosts, is now universally reprobated, in consequence of the increasing stock of national good sense. But many yet living can place fears of supernatural agency, and of darkness, among the real miseries of childhood. . . ."[50] Yet even today, in many villages of Europe, children continue to be threatened by parents with the *loup-garou* (werewolf), the *barbu* (bearded man), or the *ramoneur* (chimney sweep), or told they will be put in the basement to let the rats gnaw on them.[51]

This need to personify punitive figures was so powerful that, following the principle of "concretization," adults actually dressed up Katchina-like dummies to use in frightening children. One English writer, in 1748, while explaining how terror originated with nurses who frightened infants with stories of "raw-head and bloody-bones," said:

> The nurse takes a fancy to quiet the peevish child, and with this intent, dresses up an uncouth figure, makes it come in, and roar and scream at the child in ugly disagreeable notes, which grate upon the tender organs of the ear, and at the same time, by its gesture and near approach, makes as if it would swallow the infant up.[52]

These fearful figures were also the favorites of nurses who wanted to keep children in bed while they went off at night. Susan Sibbald remembered ghosts as a real part of her eighteenth-century childhood:

> Ghosts making their appearance were a very common occurence . . . I remember perfectly when both the nursery maids at Fowey wished to leave the nursery one evening . . . we were silenced by hearing the most dismal groanings and scratchings outside the partition next the stairs. The door was thrown open, and oh! horrors, there came in a figure, tall and dressed in white, with fire coming out of its eyes, nose and mouth it seemed. We were almost thrown into convulsions, and were not well for days, but dared not tell.[53]

The terrorized children were not always as old as Susan and Betsey. One American mother in 1882 told of a friend's two-year-old girl whose nurse, wanting to enjoy herself for the evening with the other servants while the parents were out, assured herself she wouldn't be disturbed by telling the little girl that a horrible Black Man . . . was hidden in the room to catch her the moment she left her bed or made the slightest noise . . . to make double sure that she should not be interrupted during the evening's enjoyment. She made a huge figure of a black man with frightful staring eyes and an enormous mouth, and placed it at the foot of the bed where the little innocent child was fast asleep. As soon as the evening was over in the servant's hall, the nurse went back to her charge. Opening the door quietly, she beheld the little girl sitting up in her bed, staring in an agony of terror at the fearful monster before her, and both hands convulsively grasping her fair hair. *She was stone dead!*[54]

There is some evidence that this use of masked figures to frighten children goes back to antiquity.[55] The subject of children being frightened by masks is a favorite of artists from the Roman frescos to the prints of Jacques Stella (1657), but since these early traumatic events were subject to the deepest repression, I have not yet been able to establish their precise ancient forms. It was said by Dio Chrysostom that "terrifying images deter children when they want food or play or anything else unseasonable" and theories were discussed on their most effective use: "I believe each youngster fears some bogey peculiar to himself and is wont to be terrified by this—of course, lads who are naturally timid cry out no matter what you produce to scare them. . . ."[56]

Now when infants are terrorized with masked figures when they merely cry, want food, or want to play, the amount of projection, and the adult's need to control it, has reached massive proportions only found in overtly psychotic adults today. The exact frequency of use of such concrete figures in the past cannot as yet be determined, although they were often spoken of as common. Many forms, however, can be shown to be customary. For instance, in Germany until recently there would appear in shops before Christmas time stacks of stick brooms, tied in the middle, and making a stiff brush at both ends. These were used to beat children; during the first week in December, adults would dress up in terrifying costumes and pretend to be a messenger of Christ, called the *Pelz-nickel,* who would punish children and tell them if they would get Christmas presents or not.[57]

It is only when one sees the struggle which parents go through to give up this practice of concretizing frightening images that the strength of their need to do so is revealed. One of the earliest defenders of childhood in nineteenth-century Germany was Jean Paul Richter. In his popular book *Levanna,* he condemned parents who kept children in order "by images of terror," claiming medical evidence that they "frequently fall victims to insanity." Yet his own compulsion to repeat the traumas of his own childhood was so great that he was forced to invent lesser versions for his own son:

As a person can be terrified only once by the same thing, I think it possible to spare children the reality by sportive representations of alarming circumstances. For instance: I go with my little nine-year-old Paul to walk in the thick wood. Suddenly three blackened and armed ruffians rush out and fall upon us, because I had hired them for the adventure with a small thieves' premium the day before. We two are only provided with sticks, but the band of robbers are armed with swords and a pistol without bullets . . . I turn away the pistol, so that it may miss me, and strike the dagger out of one of the thieves' hand with my stick . . . But (I add in this second edition) all such games are of doubtful advantage . . . although similar cloak and dagger pieces . . . might be tried advantageously in the night, in order to bring the fancies, inspired by a belief in ghosts, to common everyday light.[58]

Another whole area of concretization of this need to terrorize children involves the use of corpses. Many are familiar with the scenes in Mrs. Sherwood's novel, *History of the Fairchild Family*,[59] in which the children are taken on visits to the gibbet to inspect rotting corpses hanging there, while being told moral stories. What is not often realized is that these scenes are taken from real life and formed an important part of childhood in the past. Classes used to be taken out of school to hangings, and parents would often take their children to hangings and then whip them when they returned home to make them remember what they had seen.[60] Even a humanist educator such as Mafio Vegio, who wrote books to protest the beating of children, had to admit that "to let them witness a public execution is sometimes not at all a bad thing."[61]

The effect on the children of this continuous corpse-viewing was of course massive. One little girl, after her mother showed her the fresh corpse of her nine-year-old friend as an example, went around saying "They will put daughter in the deep hole, and what will mother do?"[62] Another boy woke at night screaming after seeing hangings, and "practiced hanging his own cat."[63] Eleven-year-old Harriet Spencer recorded in her diary seeing dead bodies everywhere on gibbets and broken on the wheel. Her father took her to see hundreds of corpses which had been dug up to make room for more.

. . . Papa says it is foolish and superstitious to be afraid of seeing dead bodies, so I followed him down a dark narrow steep staircase that wound round and round a long way, till they opened a door into a great cavern. It was lit by a lamp hanging down in the middle, and the friar carried a torch in his hand. At first I could not see, and when I could I hardly dared look, for on every side there were horrid black ghastly figures, some grinning, some pointing at us, or seeming in pain, in all sorts of postures, and so horrid I could hardly help screaming, and I thought they all moved. When Papa saw how uncomfortable I was, he was not angry but very kind, and said I must conquer it and go and touch one of them, which was very shocking. Their skin was all dark brown and quite dried up on the bones, and quite hard and felt like marble.[64]

This picture of the kindly father helping his daughter overcome her fear of corpses is an example of what I term "projective care," to distinguish it from true empathic care which is the result of the empathic reaction. Projective care always requires the first step of projection of the adult's own unconscious into the child, and can be distinguished from empathic care by being either inappropriate or insufficient to the child's actual needs. The mother who responds to her child's every discomfort by nursing it, the mother who gives great attention to her infant's clothes as she sends it away to the wet-nurse, and the mother who takes a full hour to tie up a child properly in swaddling clothes are all examples of projective care.

Projective care is, however, sufficient to raise children to adulthood. Indeed, it is what is often called "good care" by anthropologists studying primitive childhood, and it is not until a psychoanalytically-trained anthropologist re-studies the same tribe that one can see that projection and not true empathy is being measured. For example, studies of the Apache[65] always give them the highest ratings on the "oral satisfaction" scale so important for the development of feelings of security. The Apache, like many primitive tribes, feeds on demand for two years, and this is what the rating was based upon. But only when psychoanalytic anthropologist L. Bryce Boyer visited them was the true projective basis of this care revealed:

The care afforded infants by Apache mothers nowadays is startlingly inconsistent. They are usually very tender and considerate in the physical relationships with their babies. There is much bodily contact. Nursing times are generally determined by the baby's cry, and every distress is greeted first by the nipple of a breast or a bottle. At the same time, mothers have a very limited sense of responsibility so far as child care is concerned, and the impression gained is that the mother's tenderness for her baby is based upon her bestowing upon the infant care she herself desires as an adult. A great many mothers abandon or give away children —babies they had been nursing lovingly only a week before. Apaches very accurately name this practice "throwing the baby away." Not only do they feel scant conscious guilt for this behavior, but at times they are overtly delighted to have been able to rid themselves of the burden. In some instances, mothers who have given children away, "forget" they ever had them. The usual

Apache mother believes physical care is all an infant requires. She has little or no compunction about leaving her baby with just anyone at all while she impulsively leaves to gossip, shop, gamble or drink and "fool around." Ideally, the mother entrusts her baby to a sister or older female relative. In aboriginal times, such an arrangement was almost always possible.[66]

Even such a simple act as empathizing with children who were beaten was difficult for adults in the past. Those few educators who, prior to modern times, advised that children should not be beaten generally argued that it would have bad consequences rather than that it would hurt the child. Yet without this element of empathy, the advice had no effect whatsoever, and children continued to be beaten as before. Mothers who sent their infants to wet-nurses for three years were genuinely distressed that their children then didn't want to return to them, yet they had no capacity to locate the reason. A hundred generations of mothers tied up their infants in swaddling bands and impassively watched them scream in protest because they lacked the psychic mechanism necessary to empathize with them. Only when the slow historical process of parent-child evolution finally established this faculty through successive generations of parent-child interaction did it become obvious that swaddling was totally unnecessary. Here is Richard Steele in *The Tatler* in 1706 describing how he thought an infant felt after being born:

> I lay very quiet; but the witch, for no manner of reason or provocation in the world, takes me and binds my head as hard as she possibly could; then ties up both my legs and makes me swallow down an horrid mixture. I thought it an harsh entrance into life, to begin with taking physic. When I was thus dressed, I was carried to a bedside where a fine young lady (my mother, I wot) had like to have me hugged to death . . . and threw me into a girl's arms that was taken in to tend me. The girl was very proud of the womanly employment of a nurse, and took upon her to strip and dress me anew, because I made a noise, to see what ailed me; she did so and stuck a pin in every joint about. I still cried, upon which, she lays me on my face in her lap; and, to quiet me, fell to nailing in all the pins, by clapping me on the back and screaming a lullaby. . . .[67]

I have not found a description with this degree of empathy in any century prior to the eighteenth. It was not long thereafter that two thousand years of swaddling came to an end.

One imagines that there would be all kinds of places to look to find this missing empathic faculty in the past. The first place to look, of course, is the Bible; certainly here one should find empathy toward children's needs, for isn't Jesus always pictured holding little children? Yet when one actually reads each of the over two thousand references to children listed in the *Complete Concordance to the Bible,* these gentle images are missing. You find lots on child sacrifice, on stoning children, on beating them, on their strict obedience, on their love for their parents, and on their role as carriers of the family name, but not a single one that reveals any empathy with their needs. Even the well-known saying, "Suffer little children, and forbid them not, to come unto me" turns out to be the customary Near Eastern practice of exorcising by laying on of hands, which many holy men did to remove the evil inherent in children: "Then there were brought unto him little children, that he should put his hands on them, and pray . . . he laid his hands on them, and departed thence." (Mat. 19.13.)

All of this is not to say that parents didn't love their children in the past, for they did. Even contemporary child-beaters are not sadists; they love their children, at times, and in their own way, and are sometimes capable of expressing tender feelings, particularly when the children are non-demanding. The same was true for the parent in the past; expressions of tenderness toward children occur most often when the child is non-demanding, especially when the child is either asleep or dead. Homer's "as a mother drives away a fly from her child when it lies in sweet sleep" can be paired with Martial's epitaph:

Let not the sod too stiffly stretch its girth
Above those tender limbs, erstwhile so free;
Press lightly on her form, dear mother Earth,
Her little footsteps lightly fell on thee.[68]

It is only at the moment of death that the parent, unable to empathize before, cries out to himself, with Morelli (1400): "You loved him but never used your love to make him happy; you treated him more like a stranger than a son; you never gave him an hour of rest . . . You never kissed him when he wanted it; you wore him out at school and with many harsh blows."[69]

It is, of course, not love which the parent of the past lacked, but rather the emotional maturity needed to see the child as a person separate from himself. It is difficult to estimate what proportion of today's parents achieve with any consistency the empathic level. Once I took an informal poll of a dozen psychotherapists and asked them how many of their patients at the beginning of analysis were able to sustain images of their children as individuals separate from their own projected needs; they all said that very few had that ability. As one, Amos Gunsberg, put it: "This doesn't occur until some way along in their analysis, always at a specific moment—when they arrive at an image of themselves as separate from their own all-enveloping mother."

Running parallel to the projective reaction is the reversal reaction, with the parent and child reversing roles, often producing quite bizarre results. Reversal begins long before the child is born—it is the source of the very powerful desire for children one sees in the past, which is always expressed in terms of what children can give the parent, and never what the parent can give them. Medea's complaint before committing infanticide is that by killing her children she won't have anyone to look after *her:*

> What was the purpose, children, for which I reared you?
> For all my travail, and wearing myself away?
> They were sterile, those pains I had in the bearing of you.
> Oh surely once the hopes I had, poor me,
> Were high ones; you would look after me in old age,
> And when I died would deck me well with your own hands;
> A thing which all would have done. Oh but it is gone,
> That lovely thought.[70]

Once born, the child becomes the mother's and father's own parent, in either positive or negative aspect, totally out of keeping with the child's actual age. The child, regardless of sex, is often dressed in the style of clothes similar to that worn by the *parent's mother,* that is, not only in a long dress, but in one out of date by at least a generation.[71] The mother is literally reborn in the child; children are not just dressed as "miniature adults" but quite clearly as miniature *women,* often complete with décolleté.

The idea that the grandparent is actually reborn in the baby is a common one in antiquity,[72] and the closeness between the word "baby" and the various words for grandmother (baba, Babe) hints at similar beliefs.[73] But evidence exists for more concrete reversals in the past, ones that are virtually hallucinatory. For instance, the breasts of little infants were often kissed or sucked on by adults. Little Louis XIII often had both his penis and nipples kissed by people around him. Even though Héroard, his diarist, always made him the active one (at thirteen months "he makes M. de Souvré, M. de Termes, M. de Liancourt, and M. Zamet kiss his cock")[74], it later becomes evident that he was being passively manipulated: "He never wants to let the Marquise touch his nipples, his nurse had said to him: 'Sir, do not let anyone touch your nipples or your cock; they'll cut them off.' "[75] Yet the adults still couldn't keep their hands and lips off his penis and nipples. Both were the mother's breast returned.

Another instance of the "infant as mother" was the common belief that infants had milk in their breasts which had to be expelled. The fourteenth-century Italian *balia* (wet-nurse) was instructed to "be sure and press his breasts often—to get out any milk there because it bothers him."[76] There actually is a slight rationalization for this belief, since a newborn will on rare occasions show a drop of milky fluid on its breasts as a result of a carryover of female hormone from the mother. Yet there was a difference between this and "the unnatural but common practice of forcibly squeezing the delicate breasts of a newborn infant, by rough hand of the nurse, which is the most general cause of inflammation in these parts," as the American pediatrician Alexander Hamilton still had to write in 1793.[77]

Kissing, sucking, and squeezing the breast are but a few of the uses to which the "child as breast" is put; one finds a variety of practices such as the one this pediatrician warned of at the beginning of the nineteenth century:

> But a practice of the most injurious and disgusting nature, is that of many nursery maids, aunts and grandmothers, who suffer the child to suck their lips. I had an opportunity of observing the decay of a blooming infant, in consequence of having sucked the lips of its sickly grandmother for upwards of half a year.[78]

I have even found several references to parents "licking children.' This, for instance, may be what George du Maurier was speaking of when he said of his newborn: "The Nurse brings her to me every morning in bed, that I may lick it with 'the basting tongue'—I enjoy the operation so much that I shall perservere till it reaches the age of discretion."[79]

One receives the impression that the perfect child would be one who literally breast-feeds the parent, and the ancients would agree. Whenever children were discussed, the story of Valerius Maximus was certain to come up, describing a "perfect" child. As Pliny tells it:

> Of filial affection there have, it is true, been unlimited instances all over the world, but one at Rome with which the whole of the rest could not compare. A plebeian woman of low position who had just given birth to a child, had permission to visit her mother who had been shut up in prison as a punishment, and was always searched in advance by the doorkeeper to prevent her carrying in any food. She was detected giving her mother sustenance from her own breasts. In consequence of this marvel the daughter's pious affection was rewarded by the mother's release and both were awarded maintenance for life; and the place where it occurred was consecrated to the Goddess concerned, a temple dedicated to Filial Affection . . . [80]

The story was repeated throughout the ages as an object lesson. Peter Charron (1593) called it "turning the stream back again up to the fountainhead,"[81] and the theme was the topic of paintings by Rubens, Vermeer, and others.

Often the need to act out the image of "the child as mother" becomes overpowering; here, in a typical incident, is a "joke" played on a six-year-old girl in 1656 by Cardinal Mazarin and other adults:

One day as he made sport with her about some gallant that she
said she had; at last he began to chide her, for being with child
... They straightened her clothes from time to time, and made
her believe that she was growing big. This continued as long as it
was thought necessary to persuade her to the likelihood of her
being with child ... The time of her lying-in came, she found
betwixt her sheets in the morning a child newborn. You cannot
imagine the astonishment and grief she was in at this sight. "Such
a thing," said she, "never happened to any but to the Virgin Mary
and myself, for I never felt any kind of pain." The queen came to
console her, and offered to be Godmother; many came to gossip
with her, as newly brought to bed.[82]

Children have always taken care of adults in very concrete ways.
Ever since Roman times, boys and girls waited on their parents at table,
and in the Middle Ages all children except royalty acted as servants,
either at home or for others, often running home from school at noon
to wait on their parents.[83] I will not discuss here the whole topic of
children's work, but it should be remembered that children did much of
the work of the world long before child labor became such an issue in
the nineteenth century, generally from the age of four or five.

The reversal reaction is shown most clearly, however, in the emotional interaction between child and adult. Present day social workers
who visit "battering" mothers are often astonished at how responsive
little children are to the needs of their parents:

I remember watching an eighteen month old soothe her mother,
who was in a high state of anxiety and tears. First she put down
the bottle she was sucking. Then she moved about in such a way
that she could approach, then touch, and eventually calm her
mother down (something I had not been able to begin to do).
When she sensed her mother was comfortable again, she walked
across the floor, lay down, picked up her bottle, and started
sucking it again.[84]

This role was frequently assumed by children in the past. One child
was "never known to cry or be restless ... frequently, when a babe in
her mother's arms, at these seasons, would reach up her little hand and
wipe the tears from her mother's cheek ..."[85] Doctors used to try to
entice mothers into nursing their infants themselves instead of sending
them out to wet-nurse by promising that "in recompence whereof, he
endeavors to show her a thousand delights ... he kisses her, strokes her
hair, nose and ears, he flatters her ..."[86] Along the same theme, I have
catalogued over five hundred paintings of mothers and children from
every country, and found that the paintings showed the child looking
at, smiling at and caressing the mother at a date prior to the ones show-

ing the mother looking at, smiling at and caressing the child, rare actions for a mother in any painting.

The child's facility in mothering adults was often its salvation. Mme. de Sévigné, in 1670, decided not to take her eighteen-month-old granddaughter along with her on a trip which could have proven fatal to the child.

> Mme. du Puy-du-Fou does not want me to take my grandchild. She says it would be exposing her to danger, and at last I surrender; I should not like to imperil the little lady—I am very fond of her. . . . she does a hundred and one little things—she talks, fondles people, hits them, crosses herself, asks forgiveness, curtsies, kisses your hand, shrugs her shoulders, dances, coaxes, chucks you under the chin: in short, she is altogether lovely, I amuse myself with her for hours at a time. I do not want her to die.[87]

The need of the parent for mothering placed an enormous burden on the growing child. It was sometimes even the cause of its death. One of the more frequent reasons given for infant death was "overlaying," or suffocation in bed, and although this was often just an excuse for infanticide, pediatricians admitted that when it was genuine it was due to the mother's refusal to put the child in a separate bed when she went to sleep; "not wanting to let go of the child, [she] holds him even tighter as she sleeps. Her breast closes off the nose of the child."[88] It was this reversal image of the child-as-security-blanket that was the reality behind the common medieval warning that parents must be careful not to coddle their children "like the ivy that certainly kills the tree encircled by it, or the ape that hugs her whelps to death with mere fondness."[89]

PSYCHOLOGICAL PRINCIPLE: THE DOUBLE IMAGE

The continuous shift between projection and reversal, between the child as devil and as adult, produces a "double image" that is responsible for much of the bizarre quality of childhood in the past. We have already seen how this shift from the adult image to the projected image is a precondition for battering. But we can see a richer picture of the double image by examining in some detail an actual childhood in the past. The most complete record of childhood prior to modern times is the diary of Héroard, doctor of Louis XIII, with almost daily entries about what he saw the child and those around him do and say. The diary often allows us to glimpse the shifting double image as it occurs in Héroard's own mind, as his picture of the baby shifts between projective and reversal images.

The diary opens with the dauphin's birth in 1601. Immediately, his adult qualities appear. He came out of the womb holding his umbilical cord "with such force that she had trouble getting it back from him." He was described as "strongly muscled," and his cry was so loud that "he didn't sound at all like a child." His penis was carefully examined, and he was declared "well provided for."[90] Since he was a dauphin, one skips over these first projections of adult qualities as simple pride in a new king, but soon the images begin piling up, and the double image of his being both an adult and a voracious child grows.

The day after his birth . . . his cries in general sound not at all like an infant's cries and they never did, and when he sucks at the breast it was with such mouthfuls, and he opens his jaws so wide, that he takes at one time as much as others do in three. Consequently, his nurse was almost always dry . . . He was never satisfied.[91]

The image of the week-old dauphin as alternately an infant Hercules, who strangled the snakes, and a Gargantua, who needed 17,913 cows to nurse him, is totally at odds with the actual sickly, weak, swaddled infant who emerges from Héroard's record. Despite the dozens of people who were assigned to care for him, no one was able to provide for his simplest needs for food and rest. There were constant unnecessary changes in wet-nurses and continuous outings and long trips.[92] By the time the dauphin was two months old he was close to death. Héroard's anxiety increased, and as a defense against the anxiety his reversal reaction became more pronounced:

Being asked by the wet-nurse, "Who is that man?" responds in his jargon and with pleasure, "Erouad!" [Héroard] One can see that his body is no longer developing or being nourished. The muscles in his chest are totally consumed, and the large fold that he had had before on his neck was now nothing but skin."[93]

When the dauphin was almost ten months old, leading-strings were tied to his robe. Leading-strings were supposed to be used to teach the infant to walk, but they were more often used to manipulate and control the child like a puppet. This, combined with Héroard's projective reactions, makes it difficult to understand what was actually happening, and what is being manipulated by those around little Louis. For instance, when he was eleven months old he was said to enjoy fencing with Héroard, and liked it so much that "he pursues me laughing through the whole chamber." But a month later Héroard reported that he "begins to move along with sturdiness, held under the arms."[94] It is obvious he was being carried or swung along on leading-strings earlier when he was said to "pursue" Héroard. Indeed, since he could not speak sentences until much later, Héroard was actually hallucinating when he reports that someone came to see the fourteen-month-old dauphin, who "turns around and looks at all those who are lined up at the balustrade, goes to choose him and holds out his hand to him, which the prince then kisses. M. d'Haucourt enters and says he has come to kiss the robe of the dauphin; he turns around and says to him it isn't necessary to do that."[95]

During this same time he was pictured as being extremely active sexually. The projective basis of ascribing adult sexual behavior to the child is apparent in Héroard's descriptions: "the dauphin [at twelve months] calls the page back and with a 'Ho!' lifts up his shirt to show him his cock . . . he makes everyone kiss his cock . . . in the company of the little girl, he pulls up his shirt, shows her his cock with such ardor that he is completely beside himself."[96] And it is only when one remembers that the following is really a fifteen-month-old baby who is probably being manipulated by leading strings, that this scene can be untangled from Héroard's massive projections:

> The dauphin goes after Mlle. Mercier, who screams because M. de Montglat hit her on her buttocks with his hand; the dauphin screamed too. She fled to the bedside; M. de Montglat followed her, and wanted to smack her rear, she cries out very loudly; the dauphin hears it, takes to screaming loudly too; enjoys this and shakes his feet and his whole body with joy . . . they make his women come; he makes them dance, plays with the little Marguerite, kisses her, embraces her; throws her down, casts himself on her with quivering body and grinding teeth . . . nine o'clock . . . He strives to hit her on the buttocks with a birch rod. Mlle. Bélier asks him: "Monsieur, what did M. de Montglat do to Mercier?" He began suddenly to clap his hands together with a sweet smile, and warm himself in such a way that he was transported with joy, having been a good half-to-quarter hour laughing and clapping his hands, and throwing himself headlong on her, like a person who had understood the joke.[97]

Only rarely did Héroard reveal that the dauphin was actually passive in these sexual manipulations: "The marquise often puts her hand under his jacket; he has himself put into his bed by the nurse where she plays with him, often putting her hand under his coat."[98] More often, he was simply depicted as being stripped, taken to bed with the King, the Queen, or both, or with various servants, and involved in sexual manipulations from the time he was an infant until he was at least seven years old.

Another example of the double image was in circumcision. As is well known, Jews, Egyptians, Arabs, and others circumcised the foreskin of boys. The reasons given for this are manifold, but all of them can be covered by the double image of projection and reversal. To begin with, such mutilations of children by adults always involve projection and punishment to control projected passions. As Philo put it in the first century, circumcision was for "the excision of passions, which bind the mind. For since among all passions that of intercourse between man and woman is greatest, the lawgivers have commended that that instrument, which serves this intercourse, be mutilated, pointing out, that these powerful passions must be bridled, and thinking not only this, but all passions would be controlled through this one."[99] Moses Maimonides agrees:

> I believe one of the reasons for circumcision was the diminution of sexual intercourse and the weakening of the sexual organs; its purpose was to restrict the activities of this organ and to leave it at rest as much as possible. The true purpose of circumcision was to give the sexual organ that kind of physical pain as not to impair its natural function or the potency of the individual, but to lessen the power of passion and of too great desire.[100]

The reversal element in circumcision can be seen in the glans-as-nipple theme embedded in the details of one version of the ritual. The infant's penis is rubbed to make it erect, and the foreskin is split, either by the mohel's fingernail or with a knife, and then torn all around the glans. Then the mohel sucks the blood off the glans.[101] This is done for the same reason that everyone kissed little Louis's penis—because the penis, and more particularly the glans, is the mother's nipple returned, and the blood is her milk.[102] The idea of the child's blood as having magic-milk qualities is an old one, and underlies many sacrificial acts, but rather than examine this complex problem here I would like to concentrate on the main idea of circumcision as the coming-out of the glans-as-nipple. It is not generally known that the exposure of the glans was a problem for more than just the circumcising nations. To the Greeks and Romans, the glans was considered sacred; the sight of it "struck terror and wonder in the heart of man,"[103] and so they either tied up the prepuce with a string, which was called *kynodesme,* or else pinned it closed with a *fibula,* a clasp, which was called infibulation.[104] Evidence of infibulation, both for "modesty" and "to restrain lust," can also be found in the Renaissance and modern times.[105]

When the foreskin wasn't sufficiently long to cover the glans, an operation was sometimes performed whereby the skin was cut around the base of the penis and the skin drawn forward.[106] In ancient art, the glans was usually shown covered, either with the penis coming to a point, or else clearly showing the tied foreskin, even when erect. I have only found two cases where the glans showed: either when it was meant to inspire awe, as in the representations of the phallus which were used to hang in doorways, or when the penis was shown being used in fellatio.[107]

Thus, to Jew and Roman alike, the image of reversal was imbedded in their attitude toward the glans-as-nipple.

INFANTICIDE AND DEATH WISHES TOWARD CHILDREN

In a pair of books rich in clinical documentation, the psychoanalyst Joseph Rheingold examined the death wishes of mothers[108] toward their children, and found that they are not only far more widespread than is commonly realized, but also that they stem from a powerful attempt to "undo" motherhood in order to escape the punishment they imagine their own mothers will wreak upon them. Rheingold shows us mothers giving birth and begging their own mothers not to kill them, and traces the origin of both infanticidal wishes and post-partum depression states as not due to hostility toward the child itself, but rather to the need to sacrifice the child to propitiate their own mothers. Hospital staffs are well aware of these widespread infanticidal wishes, and often allow no contact between the mother and child for some time. Rheingold's findings, seconded by Block, Zilboorg, and others,[109] are complex and have far-reaching implications; here we can only point out that filicidal impulses of contemporary mothers are enormously widespread, with fantasies of stabbing, mutilation, abuse, decapitation, and strangulation common in mothers in psychoanalysis. I believe that the further back in history one goes, the more filicidal impulses are acted out by parents.

The history of infanticide in the West has yet to be written, and I shall not attempt it here. But enough is already known to establish that, contrary to the usual assumption that it is an Eastern rather than a Western problem, infanticide of both legitimate and illegitimate children was a regular practice of antiquity, that the killing of legitimate children was only slowly reduced during the Middle Ages, and that illegitimate children continued regularly to be killed right up into the nineteenth century.[110]

Infanticide during antiquity has usually been played down despite literally hundreds of clear references by ancient writers that it was an accepted, everyday occurrence. Children were thrown into rivers, flung into dung-heaps and cess trenches, "potted" in jars to starve to death, and exposed on every hill and roadside, "a prey for birds, food for wild beasts to rend" (Euripides, *Ion*, 504). To begin with, any child that was not perfect in shape and size, or cried too little or too much, or was otherwise than is described in the gynecological writings on "How to Recognize the Newborn That is Worth Rearing,"[111] was generally killed. Beyond this, the first-born was usually allowed to live,[112] especially if it was a boy. Girls were, of course, valued little, and the instructions of Hilarion to his wife Alis (1 B.C.) are typical of the open way these things were discussed: "If, as may well happen, you give birth to a child, if it is a boy let it live; if it is a girl, expose it."[113] The result was a large imbalance of males over females which was typical of the West until well into the Middle Ages, when the killing of legitimate children was probably much reduced. (The killing of illegitimate children does not affect the sex ratio, since both sexes are generally killed.) Available statistics for antiquity show large surpluses of boys over girls; for instance, out of 79 families who gained Milesian citizenship about 228-220 B.C., there were 118 sons and 28 daughters; 32 families had one child, 31 had two. As Jack Lindsay puts it:

> Two sons are not uncommon, three occur now and then, but more than one daughter was practically never reared. Poseidippos stated, "even a rich man always exposes a daughter" . . . Of 600 families from second-century inscriptions at Delphi, one per cent raised two daughters.[114]

The killing of legitimate children even by wealthy parents was so common that Polybius blamed it for the depopulation of Greece:

> In our own time the whole of Greece has been subject to a low birth-rate and a general decrease of the population, owing to which cities have become deserted and the land has ceased to yield fruit, although there have neither been continuous wars nor epidemics . . . as men had fallen into such a state of pretentiousness, avarice and indolence that they did not wish to marry, or if they married to rear the children born to them, or at most as a rule but one or two of them . . .[115]

Until the fourth century A.D., neither law nor public opinion found infanticide wrong in either Greece or Rome. The great philosophers agreed. Those few passages which classicists consider as a condemnation of infanticide seem to me to indicate just the opposite, such as Aristotle's "As to exposing or rearing the children born, let there be a law that no deformed child shall be reared; but on the ground of number of children, if the regular customs hinder any of those born being exposed, there must be a limit filed to the procreation of offspring." Similarly, Musonius Rufus, sometimes called "The Roman Socrates," is often quoted as opposing infanticide, but his piece "Should Every Child That Is Born Be Raised?" quite clearly only says that since brothers are very useful they should not be killed.[116] But more ancient writers openly approved of infanticide, saying, like Aristippus, that a man could do what he wants with his children, for "do we not cast away from us our spittle, lice and such like, as things unprofitable, which nevertheless are engendered and bred even out of our own selves."[117] Or like Seneca, they pretend only sickly infants are involved:

> Mad dogs we knock on the head; the fierce and savage ox we slay; sickly sheep we put to the knife to keep them from infecting the flock; unnatural progeny we destroy; we drown even children who at birth are weakly and abnormal. Yet it is not anger, but reason that separates the harmful from the sound.[118]

The theme of exposure loomed large in myth, tragedy, and the New Comedy, which is often built around the subject of how funny infanticide is. In Menander's *Girl from Samos*, much fun is made of a man trying to chop up and roast a baby. In his comedy *The Arbitrants*, a shepherd picks up an exposed infant, considers raising it, then changes his mind, saying, "What have I to do with the rearing of children and the trouble." He gives it to another man, but has a fight over who got the baby's necklace.[119]

It must be noted, however, that infanticide was probably common since prehistoric times. Henri Vallois, who tabulated all the prehistoric fossils dug up from the Pithecanthropines to the Mesolithic peoples, found a sex ratio of 148 to 100 in favor of men.[120] The Greeks and Romans were actually an island of enlightenment in a sea of nations still in an earlier stage of sacrificing children to gods, a practice which the Romans tried in vain to stop. The best documented is Carthaginian child sacrifice, which Plutarch describes:

> ... with full knowledge and understanding they themselves offered up their own children, and those who had no children would buy little ones from poor people and cut their throats as if they were so many lambs or young birds; meanwhile the mother stood by without a tear or moan; but should she utter a single moan or let fall a single tear, she had to forfeit the money, and her child was sacrificed nevertheless; and the whole area before the statue was filled with a loud noise of flutes and drums so that the cries of wailing should not reach the ears of the people.[121]

Child sacrifice is, of course, the most concrete acting out of Rheingold's thesis of filicide as sacrifice to the mother of the parents. It was practiced by the Irish Celts, the Gauls, the Scandinavians, the Egyptians, the Phoenicians, the Moabites, the Ammonites, and, in certain periods, the Israelites.[122] Thousands of bones of sacrificed children have been dug up by archeologists, often with inscriptions identifying the victims as first-born sons of noble families, reaching in time all the way back to the Jericho of 7,000 B.C.[123] Sealing children in walls, foundations of buildings, and bridges to strengthen the structure was also common from the building of the wall of Jericho to as late as 1843 in Germany.[124] To this day, when children play "London Bridge is Falling Down," they are acting out a sacrifice to a river goddess when they catch the child at the end of the game.[125]

Even in Rome, sacrifice of children led an underground existence. Dio said Julianus "killed many boys as a magic rite;" Suetonius said because of a portent the Senate "decreed that no male born that year

should be reared;" and Pliny the Elder spoke of men who "seek to secure the leg-marrow and the brain of infants."[126] More frequent was the
practice of killing your enemy's children, often in great numbers,[127] so
that noble children not only witnessed infanticide in the streets but
were themselves under continual threat of death depending on the
political fortunes of their fathers.

Philo was the first person I have found who spoke out clearly against
the horrors of infanticide:

> Some of them do the deed with their own hands; with monstrous
> cruelty and barbarity they stifle and throttle the first breath
> which the infants draw or throw them into a river or into the
> depths of the sea, after attaching some heavy substance to make
> them sink more quickly under its weight. Others take them to be
> exposed in some desert place, hoping, they themselves say, that
> they may be saved, but leaving them in actual truth to suffer the
> most distressing fate. For all the beasts that feed in human flesh
> visit the spot and feast unhindered on the infants, a fine banquet
> provided by their sole guardians, those who above all others
> should keep them safe, their fathers and mothers. Carnivorous
> birds, too, come flying down and gobble up the fragments . . .[128]

Although in the two centuries after Augustus, some attempts were
made to pay parents to keep children alive in order to replenish the
dwindling Roman population,[129] it was not until the fourth century
that real change was apparent. The law began to consider killing an
infant murder only in 374 A.D.[130] Yet even the opposition to infanticide by the Church Fathers often seemed to be based more on their
concern for the parent's soul than with the child's life. This attitude
can be seen in Saint Justin Martyr's statement that the reason a Christian shouldn't expose his children is to avoid later meeting them in a
brothel: "Lest we molest anyone or commit sin ourselves, we have been
taught that it is wicked to expose even newly-born children, first because we see that almost all those who are exposed (not only girls, but
boys) are raised in prostitution."[131] When the Christians themselves
were accused of killing babies in secret rites, however, they were quick
enough to reply: "How many, do you suppose, of those here present
who stand panting for the blood of Christians—how many, even, of you
magistrates who are so righteous against us—want me to touch their
consciences for putting their own offspring to death?"[132]

After the Council of Vaison (442 A.D.), the finding of abandoned
children was supposed to be announced in church, and by 787 A.D.,
Dateo of Milan founded the first asylum solely for abandoned infants.[133]
Other countries followed much the same pattern of evolution.[134] Despite much literary evidence, however, the continued existence of wide-

spread infanticide in the Middle Ages is usually denied by medievalists, since it is not evident in church records and other quantitative sources. But if sex ratios of 156 to 100 (c. 801 A.D.) and 172 to 100 (1391 A.D.) are any indication of the extent of the killing of legitimate girls,[135] and if illegitimates were usually killed regardless of sex, the real rate of infanticide could have been substantial in the Middle Ages. Certainly, when Innocent III began the hospital of the Santo Spirito in Rome at the end of the twelfth century he was fully aware of the number of women throwing their babies into the Tiber. As late as 1527, one priest admitted that "the latrines resound with the cries of children who have been plunged into them."[136] Detailed studies are just beginning, but it is possible that infanticide may have been only sporadically punished prior to the sixteenth century.[137] Certainly when Vincent of Beauvais wrote in the thirteenth century that a father was always worrying about his daughter "suffocating her offspring," when doctors complained of all the children "found in the frost or in the streets, cast away by a wicked mother," and when we find that in Anglo-Saxon England the legal presumption was that infants who died had been murdered if not proved otherwise, we should take these clues as a signal for the most vigorous sort of research into medieval infanticide.[138] And just because formal records show few illegitimate births, we certainly shouldn't be satisfied with assuming that "in traditional society people remained continent until marriage," since many girls managed to hide their pregnancies from their own mothers who slept beside them,[139] and they certainly can be suspected of hiding them from the church.

What is certain is that when our material becomes far fuller, by the eighteenth century,[140] there is no question that there was high incidence of infanticide in every country in Europe. As more foundling homes were opened in each country, babies poured in from all over, and the homes quickly ran out of room. Even though Thomas Coram opened his Foundling Hospital in 1741 because he couldn't bear to see the dying babies lying in the gutters and rotting on the dung-heaps of London, by the 1890s dead babies were still a common sight in London streets.[141] Late in the nineteenth century Louis Adamic described being brought up in an Eastern European village of "killing nurses," where mothers sent their infants to be done away with "by exposing them to cold air after a hot bath; feeding them something that caused convulsions in their stomachs and intestines; mixing gypsum in their milk, which literally plastered up their insides; suddenly stuffing them with food after not giving them anything to eat for two days . . ." Adamic was to have been killed as well, but for some reason his nurse spared him. His account of how he watched her do away with the other babies she received provides a picture of the emotional reality behind all those centuries of infanticide we have been reviewing.

In her own strange, helpless way, she loved them all . . . but when
the luckless infants' parents or the latter's relatives could not or
did not pay the customary small sum for their keep . . . she disposed of them. . . . One day she returned from the city with an
elongated little bundle . . . a horrible suspicion seized me. The
baby in the cradle was going to die! . . . when the baby cried, I
heard her get up, and she nursed it in the dark, mumbling, "Poor,
poor little one!" I have tried many times since to imagine how
she must have felt holding to her breast a child she knew was fated
to die by her hand . . . "You poor, poor little one!" She pur-
posely spoke clearly so I would be sure to hear. ". . . fruit of sin
through no fault of your own, but sinless in yourself . . . soon you
will go, soon, soon, my poor one . . . and, going now, you will not
go to hell as you would if you lived and grew up and became a
sinner." . . . The next morning the child was dead . . . [142]

Once the infant in the past was born, he was regularly surrounded by
the aura of death and counter-measures against death. Since ancient
times, exorcisms, purifications, and magic amulets have been thought
necessary to rout the host of death-dealing powers felt to lurk about
the child, and cold water, fire, blood, wine, salt, and urine were used on
the baby and its surroundings.[143] Isolated Greek villages even today retain this atmosphere of warding off death:

> The new-born child sleeps tightly swaddled in a wooden rocking
> cradle which is enveloped from end to end in a blanket, so that
> he lies in a kind of dark airless tent. Mothers are fearful of the ef-
> fects of cold air and evil spirits . . . the hut or house after dark is
> like a city under siege, with windows boarded, the door barred,
> and salt and incense at strategic points such as the threshold to
> repel any invasion of the Devil.[144]

Old women, symbols, according to Rheingold, of the grandmother
whose death wishes were warded off, were thought to have an "evil
eye," under whose gaze the child would die. Amulets, generally in the
form of a penis or of phallus-shaped coral, are given the infant to ward
off these death wishes.[145] As the child grew up, death wishes toward it
kept breaking through. Epictetus said, "What harm is there if you
whisper to yourself, at the very moment you are kissing your child, and
say 'Tomorrow you will die?' "[146] An Italian during the Renaissance
would say, when a child does something clever, "that child is not meant
to live."[147] Fathers of every age tell their sons, with Luther, "I would
rather have a dead son than a disobedient one."[148] Fenelon says to ask a
child questions such as, "Would you let your head be cut off in order
to get into heaven?"[149] Walter Scott said his mother confessed she was
"under a strong temptation of the Devil, to cut my throat with her
scissors, and bury me in the moss."[150] Leopardi said of his mother,

"When she saw the death of one of her infants approaching, she experienced a deep happiness, which she attempted to conceal only from those who were likely to blame her."[151] The sources are full of similar examples.

Urges to mutilate, burn, freeze, drown, shake, and throw the infant violently about were continuously acted out in the past. The Huns used to cut the cheeks of newborn males. Robert Pemell tells how in Italy and other countries during the Renaissance parents would "burn in the neck with a hot iron, or else drop a burning wax candle" on newborn babies to prevent "falling sickness."[152] In early modern times, the string underneath the newborn's tongue was usually cut, often with the midwife's fingernail, a sort of miniature circumcision.[153] The mutilation of children throughout the ages has excited pity and laughter in adults, and was the basis for the widespread practice in every age of mutilating children for begging,[154] going back to Seneca's "Controversy," which concludes that mutilating exposed children was not wrong:

> Look on the blind wandering about the streets leaning on their sticks, and those with crushed feet, and still again look on those with broken limbs. This one is without arms, that one has had his shoulders pulled down out of shape in order that his grotesqueries may excite laughter . . . Let us go to the origin of all those ills—a laboratory for the manufacture of human wrecks—a cavern filled with the limbs torn from living children . . . What wrong has been done to the Republic? On the contrary, have not these children been done a service inasmuch as their parents had cast them out?[155]

Throwing the swaddled child about was sometimes practiced. A brother of Henri IV, while being passed for amusement from one window to another, was dropped and killed.[156] The same thing happened to the little Comte de Marle: "One of the gentlemen-in-waiting and the nurse who was taking care of him amused themselves by tossing him back and forth across the sill of an open window . . . Sometimes they would pretend not to catch him . . . the little Comte de Marle fell and hit a stone step below."[157] Doctors complained of parents who break the bones of their children in the "customary" tossing of infants.[158] Nurses often said that the stays children were encased in were necessary because otherwise they could not "be tossed about without them. And I remember an eminent surgeon say a child was brought to him with several of its ribs crushed inward by the hand of the person who had been tossing it about without its stays."[159] Doctors also denounced the customary violent rocking of infants, "which puts the babe into a dazed condition, in order that he may not trouble those that have the care of him."[160] This was the reason that cradles began to be attacked in the eighteenth century; Buchan said he was against cradles because of the common "ill-tempered nurse, who, instead of soothing the accidental uneasiness or indisposition to sleep of her baby, when laid down to rest, is often worked up to the highest pitch of rage; and, in the excess of her folly and brutality, endeavors, by loud, harsh threats, and the impetuous rattle of the cradle, to drown the infant's cries, and to force him into slumber."[161]

Infants were also sometimes nearly frozen through a variety of customs, ranging from baptism by lengthy dipping in ice-water and rolling in the snow, to the practice of the plunge-bath, which involved regular plunging of the infant over and over again in ice cold water over its head "with its mouth open and gasping for breath."[162] Elizabeth Grant remembers in the early nineteenth century that a "large, long tub stood in the kitchen court, the ice on the top of which often had to be broken before our horrid plunge into it . . . How I screamed, begged, prayed, entreated to be saved . . . Nearly senseless I have been taken to the housekeeper's room . . ."[163] Going back to the ancient custom of the Germans, Scythians, Celts, and Spartans (though not Athenians, who used other hardening methods),[164] dipping in cold rivers used to be common, and cold water dipping has since Roman times been considered therapeutic for children.[165] Even the putting of children to bed wrapped in cold wet towels was sometimes used both to harden and as therapy.[166] It is not surprising that the great eighteenth-century pediatrician William Buchan said "almost one half of the human species perish in infancy by improper management or neglect."[167]

ABANDONMENT, NURSING AND SWADDLING

Although there were many exceptions to the general pattern, up to about the eighteenth century, the average child of wealthy parents spent his earliest years in the home of a wet-nurse, returned home to the care of other servants, and was sent out to service, apprenticeship, or school by age seven, so that the amount of time parents of means actually spent raising their children was minimal. The effects of these and other institutionalized abandonments by parents on the child have rarely been discussed.

The most extreme and oldest form of abandonment is the outright sale of children. Child sale was legal in Babylonian times, and may have been quite common among many nations in antiquity.[168] Although Solon tried to restrict the right of child sale by parents in Athens, it is unclear how effective the law was.[169] Herodas showed a beating scene where a boy was told "you're a bad boy, Kottalos, so bad that none could find a good word for you even were he selling you."[170] The church tried for centuries to stamp out child sale. Theodore, Archbishop of Canterbury in the seventh century, ruled a man might not sell his son into slavery after the age of 7. If Giraldus Cambrensis is to be believed, in the twelfth century the English had been selling their children to the Irish for slaves, and the Norman invasion was a punishment from God for this slave traffic.[171] In many areas, child sale continued sporadically into modern times, not being outlawed in Russia, for instance, until the nineteenth century.[172]

Another abandonment practice was the use of children as political hostages and security for debts, which also went back to Babylonian times.[173] Sidney Painter describes its medieval version, in which it was "quite customary to give young children as hostages to guarantee an agreement, and equally so to make them suffer for their parents' bad faith. When Eustace de Breteuil, the husband of a natural daughter of Henry I, put out the eyes of the son of one of his vassals, the king allowed the enraged father to mutilate in the same way Eustace's daughter whom Henry held as hostage."[174] Similarly, John Marshall gave up his son William to King Stephen, saying he "cared little if William were hanged, for he had the anvils and hammers with which to forge still better sons," and Francis I, when taken prisoner by Charles V, exchanged his young sons for his own freedom, then promptly broke the bargain so that they were thrown in jail.[175] Indeed, it was often hard to distinguish the practice of sending one's children to serve as pages or servants in another noble household from the use of children as hostages.

Similar abandonment motives were behind the custom of fosterage, which was common among all classes of Welsh, Anglo-Saxons, and Scandinavians, wherein an infant was sent to another family to be reared to age 17, and then returned to the parents. This continued in Ireland until the seventeenth century, and the English often sent their children to be fostered by the Irish in medieval times.[176] Actually, this was just an extreme version of the medieval practice of sending noble children at the age of seven or earlier into the homes of others or to monasteries as servants, pages, ladies-in-waiting, oblates, or clerks, practices still common in early modern times.[177] As with the equivalent lower class practice of apprenticeship,[178] the whole subject of the child as laborer in the homes of others is so vast and so poorly studied that it unfortunately cannot be much examined here, despite its obvious importance in the lives of children in the past.

Besides institutionalized abandonment practices, the informal abandoning of young children to other people by their parents occurred quite often right up to the nineteenth century. The parents gave every kind of rationalization for giving their children away: "to learn to speak" (Disraeli), "to cure timidness" (Clara Barton), for "health" (Edmund Burke, Mrs. Sherwood's daughter), or as payment for medical services rendered (patients of Jerome Cardan and William Douglas). Sometimes they admitted it was simply because they were not wanted (Richard Baxter, Johannes Butzbach, Richard Savage, Swift, Yeats,

Augustus Hare, and so on). Mrs. Hare's mother expresses the general casualness of these abandonments: "Yes, certainly, the baby shall be sent as soon as it is weaned; and, if anyone else would like one, would you kindly recollect that we have others."[179] Boys were of course preferred; one eighteenth-century woman wrote her brother asking for his next child: "If it is a boy, I claim it; if a girl, I will be content to stay for the next."[180]

However, it was the sending of children to wet-nurse which was the form of institutionalized abandonment most prevalent in the past. The wet-nurse is a familiar figure in the Bible, the Code of Hammurabi, the Egyptian papyri, and Greek and Roman literature, and they have been well organized ever since Roman wet-nurses gathered in the Colonna Lactaria to sell their services.[181] Doctors and moralists since Galen and Plutarch have denounced mothers for sending their children out to be wet-nursed rather than nursing them themselves. Their advice had little effect, however, for until the eighteenth century most parents who could afford it, and many who couldn't, sent their children to wet-nurse immediately after birth. Even poor mothers who could not afford sending their children out to nurse often refused to breast-feed them, and gave them pap instead. Contrary to the assumptions of most historians, the custom of not breast-feeding infants at all reaches back in many areas of Europe at least as far as the fifteenth century. One mother, who had moved from an area in northern Germany where nursing infants was more common, was considered "swinish and filthy" by Bavarian women for nursing her child, and her husband threatened he would not eat if she did not give up this "disgusting habit."[182]

As for the rich, who actually abandoned their children for a period of years, even those experts who thought the practice bad usually did not use empathic terms in their treatises, but rather thought wet-nursing bad because "the dignity of a newborn human being [is] corrupted by the foreign and degenerate nourishment of another's milk."[183] That is, the blood of the lower-class wet-nurse entered the body of the upper-class baby, milk being thought to be blood frothed white.[184] Occasionally the moralists, all men of course, betrayed their own repressed resentment against their mothers for having sent them out to wet-nurse. Aulus Gellius complained: "When a child is given to another and removed from its mother's sight, the strength of maternal ardour is gradually and little by little extinguished . . . and it is almost as completely forgotten as if it had been lost by death."[185] But usually repression won and the parent was praised. More important, repetition was assured. Though it was well known that infants died at a far higher rate while at wet-nurse than at home, parents continued to mourn their children's death, and then helplessly handed over their next infant as though the wet-nurse were a latter-day avenging goddess who required yet another sacrifice.[186] Sir Simonds D'Ewes had already lost several sons at wet-nurse, yet he sent his next baby for two years to "a poor woman who had been much misused and almost starved by a wicked husband, being herself also naturally of a proud, fretting and wayward disposition; which together in the issue conduced to the final ruin and destruction of our most sweet and tender infant . . ."[187]

Except in those cases where the wet-nurse was brought in to live, children who were given to the wet-nurse were generally left there from 2 to 5 years. The conditions were similar in every country. Jacques Guillimeau described how the child at nurse might be "stifled, over-laid, be let fall, and so come to an untimely death; or else may be devoured, spoiled, or disfigured by some wild beast, wolf or dog, and then the nurse fearing to be punished for her negligence, may take another child into the place of it."[188] Robert Pemell reported the rector in his parish told him it was, when he first came to it, "filled with suckling infants from London and yet, in the space of one year, he buried them all except two."[189] Yet the practice continued inexorably until the eighteenth century in England and America, the nineteenth century in France, and into the twentieth century in Germany.[190] England was, in fact, so far in advance of the continent in nursing matters that quite wealthy mothers were often nursing their children as early as the seventeenth century.[191] Nor was it simply a matter of the amorality of the rich; Robert Pemell complained in 1653 of the practice of "both high and low ladies of farming out their babies to irresponsible women in the country," and as late as 1780 the police chief of Paris estimated that of the 21,000 children born each year in his city, 17,000 were sent into the country to be wet-nursed, 2,000 or 3,000 were placed in nursery homes, 700 were wet-nursed at home and only 700 were nursed by their mothers.[192]

The actual length of nursing varied widely in every age and region. Table 1 lists the references I have been able to locate so far.

If this chart is any indication of general trends, it is possible that by early modern times, perhaps as a result of a reduction of projective care, very long nursing was becoming less common. It is also true that statements about weaning became more accurate as children were less often relegated to the wet-nurse; Roesslin, for example, says: "Avicen advices to give the child suck two years/how be it among us most commonly they suck but one year . . ."[194] Surely Alice Ryerson's statement that the "age of weaning was drastically reduced in actual practice in the period just preceding 1750" is too sweeping.[195] Although wet-nurses were expected to refrain from intercourse while nursing, they rarely did so, and weaning usually preceded the birth of the next child. Therefore, nursing for as much as two years might always have been exceptional in the West.

TABLE 1
AGE IN MONTHS AT FULL WEANING

Source[193]	Months at Weaning	Approx. Date	Nationality
Wet-nurse Contract	24	367 B.C.	Greek
Soranus	12-24	100 A.D.	Roman
Macrobius	35	400	Roman
Barberino	24	1314	Italian
Metlinger	10-24	1497	German
Jane Grey	18	1538	English
John Greene	9	1540	English
E. Roesslin	12	1540	German
Sabine Johnson	34	1540	English
John Dee	8-14	1550	English
H. Mercurialis	15-30	1552	Italian
John Jones	7-36	1579	English
Louis XIII	25	1603	French
John Evelyn	14	1620	English
Ralph Joesslin	12-19	1643-79	English
John Pechey	10-12	1697	English
James Nelson	3-4	1753	English
Nicholas Culpepper	12-48	1762	English
William Cadogan	4	1770	English
H. W. Tytler	6	1797	English
S. T. Coleridge	15	1807	English
Eliza Warren	12	1810	English
Caleb Tickner	10-12	1839	English
Mary Mallard	15	1859	American
German Statistical Study	1-6	1878-82	German

Feeding vessels of all kinds have been known since 2,000 B.C.; cows'
and goats' milk were used when available, and often the infant would
be put right to the teat of the animal to suck.[196] Pap, generally made of
bread or meal mixed with water or milk, supplemented or replaced nursing from the earliest weeks, and sometimes was crammed down the
child's throat until it vomited.[197] Any other food was first chewed by
the wet-nurse, then given to the infant.[198] Opium and liquor were regularly given to infants throughout the ages to stop them from crying.
The Ebers Papyrus says of the effectiveness for children of a mixture of
poppy-seeds and fly-dung: "It acts at once!" Dr. Hume complained in
1799 of thousands of infants killed every year by nurses "forever pour-
ing Godfrey's Cordial down their little throats, which is a strong opiate
and in the end as fatal as arsenic. This they pretend they do to quiet the
child—thus indeed many are forever quieted . . ." And daily doses of
liquor were often "poured down the throat of a little being who is in-

capable of declining the portion, but who exhibit an abhhorence by struggling efforts and wry faces . . ."[199]

There are many indications in the sources that children as a general practice were given insufficient food. Children of the poor, of course, have often been hungry, but even children of the rich, especially girls, were supposed to be given very meager allowances of food, and little or no meat. Plutarch's description of the "starvation diet" of Spartan youth is well known, but from the number of references to scanty food, nursing babies only two or three times a day, fasts for children, and deprivation of food as discipline, one suspects that, like parents of contemporary child abusers, parents in the past found it hard to see to it that their children were adequately fed.[200] Autobiographies from Augustine to Baxter have confessed to the sin of gluttony for stealing fruit as a child; no one has ever thought to ask if they did so because they were hungry.[201]

Tying the child up in various restraint devices was a near-universal practice. Swaddling was the central fact of the infant's earliest years. As we have noted, restraints were thought necessary because the child was so full of dangerous adult projections that if it were left free it would scratch its eyes out, tear its ears off, break its legs, distort its bones, be terrified by the sight of its own limbs, and even crawl about on all fours like an animal.[202] Traditional swaddling is much the same in every country and age; it "consists in entirely depriving the child of the use of its limbs, by enveloping them in an endless length bandage, so as to not unaptly resemble billets of wood; and by which, the skin is sometimes excoriated; the flesh compressed, almost to gangrene; the circulation nearly arrested; and the child without the slightest power of motion. Its little waist is surrounded by stays . . . Its head is compressed into the form the fancy of the midwife might suggest; and its shape maintained by properly adjusted pressure . . ."[203]

Swaddling was often so complicated it took up to two hours to dress an infant.[204] Its convenience to adults was enormous—they rarely had to pay any attention to infants once they were tied up. As a recent medical study of swaddling has shown, swaddled infants are extremely passive, their hearts slow down, they cry less, they sleep far more, and in general they are so withdrawn and inert that the doctors who did the study wondered if swaddling shouldn't be tried again.[205] The historical sources confirm this picture; doctors since antiquity agreed that "wakefulness does not happen to children naturally nor from habit, i.e., customarily, for they always sleep," and children were described as being laid for hours behind the hot oven, hung on pegs on the wall, placed in tubs, and in general, "left, like a parcel, in every convenient corner."[206] Almost all nations swaddled. Even in ancient Egypt, where it is claimed children were not swaddled because paintings showed them naked, swaddling may have been practiced, for Hippocrates said the Egyptians swaddle, and occasional figurines showed swaddling clothes.[207] Those few areas where swaddling was not used, such as in ancient Sparta and in the Scottish highlands, were also areas of the most severe hardening practices, as though the only possible choice were between tight swaddling or being carried about naked and made to run in the snow without clothes.[208] Swaddling was so taken for granted that the evidence for length of swaddling is quite spotty prior to early modern times. Soranus says the Romans unswaddled at from 40 to 60 days; hopefully, this is more accurate than Plato's "two years."[209] Tight swaddling, often including strapping to carrying-boards, continued throughout the Middle Ages, but I have not yet been able to find out for how many months.[210] The few source references in the sixteenth and seventeenth century, plus a study of the art of the period, suggest a pattern of total swaddling in those centuries for between one to four months; then the arms were left free and the body and legs remained swaddled for between six to nine months.[211] The English led the way in ending swaddling, as they did in ending outside wet-nursing. Swaddling in England and America was on its way out by the end of the eighteenth century, and in France and Germany by the nineteenth century.[212]

Once the infant was released from its swaddling bands, physical restraints of all kinds continued, varying by country and period. Children were sometimes tied to chairs to prevent their crawling. Right into the nineteenth century leading strings were tied to the child's clothes to control it and swing it about. Corsets and stays made of bone, wood, or iron were often used for both sexes. Children were sometimes strapped into backboards and their feet put in stocks while they studied, and iron collars and other devices were used to "improve posture," like the one Francis Kemble described: "a hideous engine of torture of the backboard species, made of steel covered with red morocco, which consisted of a flat piece placed on my back, and strapped down to my waist with a belt and secured at the top by two epaulets strapped over my shoulders. From the middle of this there rose a steel rod or spine, with a steel collar which encircled my throat and fastened behind."[213] These devices seemed to be more commonly used in the sixteenth to nineteenth centuries than in medieval times, but this could be due to the paucity of earlier sources. Two practices, however, were probably common to every country since antiquity. The first is the general scantiness of dress for "hardening" purposes; the second is the use of stool-like devices which were supposed to assist walking, but in fact were used to prevent crawling, which was considered animal-like. Felix Würtz (1563) describes the use of one version:

... there are stools for children to stand in, in which they can turn around any way, when mothers or nurses see them in it, then they care no more for the child, let it alone, go about their own business, supposing the child to be well provided, but they little think on the pain and misery the poor child is in ... the poor child ... must stand maybe many hours, whereas half an hour standing is too long ... I wish that all such standing stools were burned ...[214]

TOILET TRAINING, DISCIPLINE, AND SEX

Although chairs with chamber pots underneath have existed since antiquity, there is no evidence for toilet training in the earliest months of the infant's life prior to the eighteenth century. Although parents often complained, like Luther, of their children's "befouling the corners," and although doctors prescribed remedies, including whipping, for "pissing in the bed" (children generally slept with adults), the struggle between parent and child for control in infancy of urine and feces is an eighteenth-century invention, the product of a late psychogenic stage.[215]

Children, of course, have always been identified with their excrements; newborn infants were called ecrême, and the Latin merda, excrement, was the source of the French merdeux, little child.[216] But it was the enema and the purge, not the potty, which were the central devices for relating to the inside of the child's body prior to the eighteenth century. Children were given suppositories, enemas, and oral purges in sickness and in health. One seventeenth-century authority said infants should be purged before each nursing so the milk wouldn't get mixed up with the feces.[217] Héroard's diary of Louis XIII is filled with minute descriptions of what goes into and comes out of Louis's body, and he was given literally thousands of purges, suppositories, and enemas during his childhood. The urine and feces of infants were often examined in order to determine the inner state of the child. David Hunt's description of this process clearly reveals the projective origin for what I have termed the "toilet-child":

The bowels of children were thought to harbor matter which spoke to the adult world insolently, threateningly, with malice and insubordination. The fact that the child's excrement looked and smelled unpleasant meant that the child himself was somewhere deep down inside badly disposed. No matter how placid and cooperative he might appear, the excrement which was regularly washed out of him was regarded as the insulting message of an inner demon, indicating the "bad humors" which lurked within.[218]

It was not until the eighteenth century that the main focus moved from the enema to the potty. Not only was toilet training begun at an earlier age, partly as a result of diminished use of swaddling bands, but the whole process of having the child control its body products was invested with an emotional importance previously unknown. Wrestling with an infant's will in his first few months was a measure of the strength of involvement by parents with their children, and represented a psychological advance over the reign of the enema.[219] By the nineteenth century, parents generally began toilet training in earnest in the earliest months of life, and their demands for cleanliness became so severe by the end of the century that the ideal child was described as one "who cannot bear to have any dirt on his body or dress or in his surrounding for even the briefest time."[220] Even today, most English and German parents begin toilet training prior to six months; the average in America is more like nine months, and the range is greater.[221]

The evidence which I have collected on methods of disciplining children leads me to believe that a very large percentage of the children born prior to the eighteenth century were what would today be termed "battered children." Of over two hundred statements of advice on child-rearing prior to the eighteenth century which I have examined, most approved of beating children severely, and all allowed beating in varying circumstances except three, Plutarch, Palmieri, and Sadoleto, and these were addressed to fathers and teachers, and did not mention mothers.[222] Of the seventy children prior to the eighteenth century whose lives I have found, all were beaten except one: Montaigne's daughter. Unfortunately, Montaigne's essays on children are so full of inconsistencies that one is uncertain whether to believe even this one statement. He is most famous for his claim that his father was so kind to him that he hired a musician to play an instrument every morning to awaken him so that his delicate brain wouldn't be startled. If true, this unusual home life could only have lasted two or three years, however, for he was actually sent at birth to a wet-nurse in another village, and kept there for several years, and was sent to school in another town from age 6 to 13 because his father found him "sluggish, slow and unretentive." When he made the statement that his daughter was "over six years old now, and has never been guided or punished for her childish faults . . . by anything but words . . .," she was, in fact, 11 years old. He elsewhere admitted of his children, "I have not willingly suffered them to be brought up near me."[223] So perhaps we ought to reserve judgment on this, our one unbeaten child. (Peiper's extensive survey of the literature on beating reaches similar conclusions to mine.)[224]

Beating instruments included whips of all kinds, including the cat-o'-nine-tails, shovels, canes, iron and wooden rods, bundles of sticks, the *discipline* (a whip made of small chains), and special school instruments like the flapper, which had a pear-shaped end and a round hole to raise blisters. Their comparative frequency of use may be indicated by the categories of the German schoolmaster who reckoned he had given 911,527 strokes with the stick, 124,000 lashes with the whip, 136,715 slaps with the hand, and 1,115,800 boxes on the ear.[225] The beatings described in the sources were generally severe, involved bruising and bloodying of the body, began early, and were a regular part of the child's life.

Century after century of battered children grew up and in turn battered their own children. Public protest was rare. Even humanists and teachers who had a reputation for great gentleness, like Petrarch, Ascham, Comenius, and Pestalozzi, approved of beating children.[226] Milton's wife complained she hated to hear the cries of his nephews when he was beating them, and Beethoven whipped his pupils with a knitting needle and sometimes bit them.[227] Even royalty was not exempt from battering, as the childhood of Louis XIII confirms. A whip was at his father's side at table, and as early as 17 months of age, the dauphin knew enough not to cry when threatened with the whip. At 25 months regular whippings began, often on his bare skin. He had frequent nightmares about his whippings, which were administered in the morning when he awakened. When he was king he still awoke at night in terror, in expectation of his morning whipping. The day of his coronation, when he was eight, he was whipped, and said, "I would rather do without so much obeisance and honor if they wouldn't have me whipped."[228]

Since infants who were not swaddled were in particular subjected to hardening practices, perhaps one function of swaddling was to reduce the parent's propensity for child abuse. I have not yet found an adult who beat a swaddled infant. However, the beating of the smallest of infants out of swaddling clothes occurred quite often, a sure sign of the "battering" syndrome. Susannah Wesley said of her babies: "When turned a year old (and some before), they were taught to fear the rod, and to cry softly." Giovanni Dominici said to give babies "frequent, yet not severe whippings. . . ." Rousseau said that babies in their earliest days were often beaten to keep them quiet. One mother wrote of her first battle with her 4-month-old infant: "I whipped him til he was actually black and blue, and until I *could not* whip him any more, and he never gave up one single inch." The examples could easily be extended.[229]

One curious method of punishment, which was inflicted on the early medieval ecclesiastic Alcuin when he was an infant, was to cut or prick the soles of the feet with an instrument which resembled a cobbler's knife. This reminds one of the Bishop of Ely's habit of pricking his young servants with a goad which he always held in one hand. When Jane Grey complained of her parents giving her "nips and bobs," and Thomas Tusser complained of "touzed ears, like baited bears,/ what bobbed lips, what jerks, what nips" it may have been the goad which was used. Should further research show that the goad was also used on children in antiquity, it would put a different light on Oedipus's killing of Laius on that lonely road, for he was literally "goaded" into it—Laius having struck him "full on the head with his two-pointed goad."[230]

Although the earliest sources are quite sketchy on the precise severity of discipline, there seems to be evidence of visible improvement in every period in the West. Antiquity is full of devices and practices unknown to later times, including shackles for the feet, handcuffs, gags, three months in "the block," and the bloody Spartan flagellation contests, which often involved whipping youths to death.[231] One Anglo-Saxon custom suggests the level of thought about children in earliest times. Thrupp says: "It was customary when it was wished to retain legal testimony of any ceremony, to have it witnessed by children, who then and there were flogged with unusual severity; which it was supposed would give additional weight to any evidence of the proceedings . . ."[232]

References to detailed modes of discipline are even harder to find in the Middle Ages. One thirteenth-century law brought child-beating into the public domain: "If one beats a child until it bleeds, then it will remember, but if one beats it to death, the law applies."[233] Most medieval descriptions of beating were quite severe, although St. Anselm, as in so many things, was far in advance of his time by telling an abbot to beat children gently, for "Are they not human? Are they not flesh and blood like you?"[234] But it is only in the Renaissance that advice to temper childhood beatings began in earnest, although even then it was generally accompanied by approval for beatings judiciously applied. As Bartholomew Batty said, parents must "keep the golden mean," which is to say they should not "strike and buffet their children about the face and head, and to lace upon them like malt sacks with cudgels, staves, fork or fire shovel," for then they might die of the blows. The correct way was to "hit him upon the sides . . . with the rod, he shall not die thereof."[235]

Some attempts were made in the seventeenth century to limit the beating of children, but it was the eighteenth century which saw the biggest decrease. The earliest lives I have found of children who may not have been beaten at all date from 1690 to 1750.[236] It was not until the nineteenth century that the old-fashioned whipping began to go out of style in most of Europe and America, continuing longest in Germany, where 80% of German parents still admit to beating their children, a full 35% with canes.[237]

As beatings began to decrease, substitutes had to be found. For instance, shutting children up in the dark became quite popular in the eighteenth and nineteenth centuries. Children were put in "dark closets, where they were sometimes forgotten for hours." One mother shut her 3-year-old boy up in a drawer. Another house was "a sort of little Bastille, in every closet of which was to be found a culprit—some were sobbing and repeating verbs, others eating their bread and water . . ." Children were sometimes left locked in rooms for days. One 5-year-old French boy, in looking at a new apartment with his mother, told her, "Oh no, mama, . . . it's impossible; there's no dark closet! Where could you put me when I'm naughty."[238]

The history of sex in childhood presents even more difficulty than usual in getting at the facts, for added to the reticence and repression of our sources is the unavailability of most of the books, manuscripts, and artifacts which form the basis for our research. Victorian attitudes towards sex still reign supreme among most librarians, and the bulk of works which relate to sex in history remain under lock and key in library storerooms and museum basements all over Europe, unavailable even to the historian. Even so, there is evidence enough in the sources so far available to us to indicate that the sexual abuse of children was far more common in the past than today, and that the severe punishment of children for their sexual desires in the last two hundred years was the product of a late psychogenic stage, in which the adult used the child to restrain, rather than act out, his own sexual fantasies. In sexual abuse, as in physical abuse, the child was only an incidental victim, a measure of the part it played in the defense system of the adult.

The child in antiquity lived his earliest years in an atmosphere of sexual abuse. Growing up in Greece and Rome often included being used sexually by older men. The exact form and frequency of the abuse varied by area and date. In Crete and Boeotia, pederastic marriages and honeymoons were common. Abuse was less frequent among aristocratic boys in Rome, but sexual use of children was everywhere evident in some form.[239] Boy brothels flourished in every city, and one could even contract for the use of a rent-a-boy service in Athens. Even where homosexuality with free boys was discouraged by law, men kept slave boys to abuse, so that even free-born children saw their fathers sleeping with boys. Children were sometimes sold into concubinage; Musonius Rufus wondered whether such a boy would be justified in resisting being abused: "I knew a father so depraved that, having a son conspicuous for youthful beauty, he sold him into a life of shame. If, now, that lad who was sold and sent into such a life by his father had refused and would not go, should we say that he was disobedient . . ."[240] Aristotle's main objection to Plato's idea that children should be held in common was that when men had sex with boys they wouldn't know if they were their own sons, which Aristotle says would be "most unseemly."[241] Plutarch said the reason why freeborn Roman boys wore a gold ball around their necks when they were very young was so men could tell which boys it was not proper to use sexually when they found a group in the nude.[242]

Plutarch's statement was only one among many which indicate that the sexual abuse of boys was not limited to those over 11 or 12 years of age, as most scholars assume. Sexual abuse by pedagogues and teachers of smaller children may have been common throughout antiquity. Although all sorts of laws were passed to try to limit sexual attacks on school children by adults, the long heavy sticks carried by pedagogues and teachers were often used to threaten them. Quintillian, after many years of teaching in Rome, warned parents against the frequency of sexual abuse by teachers, and made this the basis of his disapproval of beating in schools:

> When children are beaten, pain or fear frequently have results of which it is not pleasant to speak and which are likely to be a source of shame, a shame which unnerves and depresses the mind and leads the child to shun and loathe the light. Further, if inadequate care is taken in the choices of respectable governors and instructors, I blush to mention the shameful abuse which scoundrels sometimes make of their right to administer corporal punishment or the opportunity not infrequently offered to others by the fear thus caused in the victims. I will not linger on this subject; it is more than enough if I have made my meaning clear.[243]

Aeschines quotes some of the Athenian laws which attempted to limit sexual attacks on schoolchildren:

> . . . consider the case of the teachers . . . it is plain that the lawgiver distrusts them . . . He forbids the teacher to open the schoolroom, or the gymnastics trainer the wrestling school, before sunrise, and he commands them to close the doors before sunset; for he is exceeding suspicious of their being alone with a boy, or in the dark with him.[244]

Aeschines, when prosecuting Timarchus for having hired himself out as a boy prostitute, put several men on the stand who admitted having paid to sodomize Timarchus. Aeschines admitted that many, including himself, were used sexually when they were children, but not for pay, which would have made it illegal.[245]

The evidence from literature and art confirms this picture of the sexual abuse of smaller children. Petronius loves depicting adults feeling the "immature little tool" of boys, and his description of the rape of a seven-year-old girl, with women clapping in a long line around the bed, suggests that women were not exempt from playing a role in the process.[246] Aristotle said homosexuality often becomes habitual in "those who are abused from childhood." It has been assumed that the small nude children seen on vases waiting on adults in erotic scenes are servants, but in view of the usual role of noble children as waiters, we should consider the possibility that they may be children of the house. For, as Quintillian said about noble Roman children: "We rejoice if they say something over-free, and words which we should not tolerate from the lips even of an Alexandrian page are greeted with laughter and a kiss ... they hear us use such words, they see our mistresses and minions; every dinner party is loud with foul songs, and things are presented to their eyes of which we should blush to speak."[247]

Even the Jews, who tried to stamp out adult homosexuality with severe punishments, were more lenient in the case of young boys. Despite Moses's injunction against corrupting children, the penalty for sodomy with children over 9 years of age was death by stoning, but copulation with younger children was not considered a sexual act, and was punishable only by a whipping, "as a matter of public discipline."[248]

It must be remembered that widespread sexual abuse of children can only occur with at least the unconscious complicity of the child's parents. Children in the past were under the fullest control of their parents, who had to agree to give them over to their abusers. Plutarch muses on how important this decision was for fathers:

> I am loathe to introduce the subject, loathe too to turn away from it ... whether we should permit the suitors of our boys to associate with them and pass their time with them, or whether the opposite policy of excluding them and shooing them away from intimacy with our boys is correct. Whenever I look at blunt-spoken fathers of the austere and astringent type who regard intimacy with lovers as an intolerable outrage upon their sons, I am circumspect about showing myself a sponsor and advocate of the practice. [Yet Plato] declares that men who have proven their worth should be permitted to caress any fair lad they please. Lovers who lust only for physical beauty, then, it is right to drive away; but free access should be granted to lovers of the soul.[249]

Like the adults we have previously seen around little Louis XIII, the Greeks and Romans couldn't keep their hands off children. I have only turned up one piece of evidence that this practice extended, like Louis's abuse, back into infancy. Suetonius condemned Tiberius because he "taught children of the most tender years, whom he called his *little fishes,* to play between his legs while he was in his bath. Those which had not yet been weaned, but were strong and hearty, he set at fellatio ..." Suetonius may or may not have made up the story, yet he obviously had reason to think his readers would believe him. So, apparently, did Tacitus, who told the same story.[250]

The favorite sexual use of children, however, was not fellatio, but anal intercourse. Martial said one should, while buggering a boy, "refrain from stirring the groin with poking hand . . . Nature has separated the male: one part has been produced for girls, one for men. Use your own part." This, he said, was because the masturbating of boys would "hasten manhood," an observation Aristotle made some time before him. Whenever a pre-pubertal boy was shown being used sexually on erotic vases, the penis was never shown erect.[251] For men of antiquity were not really homosexuals as we know them today, but a much lower psychic mode, which I think should be termed "ambisexual" (they themselves used the term "ambidextrous"). While the homosexual runs to men as a retreat from women, as a defense against the oedipal conflict, the ambisexual has never really reached the oedipal level, and uses boys and women almost without distinction.[252] In fact, as psychoanalyst Joan McDougall observes, the main purpose of this kind of perversion is to demonstrate that "there is no difference between the sexes." She says that it is an attempt to control childhood sexual traumata by reversal, with the adult now putting another child in the helpless position, and also an attempt to handle castration anxiety by proving that "castration does not hurt and in fact is the very condition of erotic arousal."[253] This well describes the man of antiquity. Intercourse with castrated children was often spoken of as being especially arousing, castrated boys were favorite "voluptates" in imperial Rome, and infants were castrated "in the cradle" to be used in brothels by men who liked buggering young castrated boys. When Domitian passed a law prohibiting castration of infants for brothels, Marial praised him: "Boys loved thee before . . . but now infants, too, love thee, Caesar."[254] Paulus Aegineta described the standard method used in castrating small boys:

> Since we are sometimes compelled against our will by persons of high rank to perform the operation . . . by compression [it] is thus performed; children, still of a tender age, are placed in a vessel of hot water, and then when the parts are softened in the bath, the testicles are to be squeezed with the fingers until they disappear.

The alternative, he said, was to put them on a bench and cut their testicles out. Many doctors in antiquity mentioned the operation, and Juvenal said they were often called upon to perform it.[255]

Signs of castration surrounded the child in antiquity. In every field and garden he saw a Priapus, with a large erect penis and a sickle, which was supposed to symbolize castration. His pedagogue and his teacher might be castrated, castrated prisoners were everywhere, and his parents' servants would often be castrated. St. Jerome wrote that some people had wondered whether letting young girls bathe with eunuchs was a wise practice. And although Constantine passed a law against castrators, the practice grew so rapidly under his successors that soon even noble parents mutilated their sons to further their political advancement. Boys were also castrated as a "cure" for various diseases and Ambroise Paré complained how many unscrupulous "Gelders," greedy to get children's testicles for magical purposes, persuaded parents to let them castrate their children.[256]

Christianity introduced a new concept into the discussion—childhood innocence. As Clement of Alexandria said, when Christ advised people to "become as little children" in order to enter into Heaven, one should "not foolishly mistake his meaning. We are not little ones in the sense that we roll on the floor or crawl on the ground as snakes do." What Christ means was that people should become as "uncontaminated" as children, pure, without sexual knowledge.[257] Christians throughout the Middle Ages began to stress the idea that children were totally innocent of all notions of pleasure and pain. A child "has not tasted sensual pleasures, and has no conception of the impulses of manhood . . . one becomes as a child in respect of anger; and is as the child in relation to his grief, so that sometimes he laughs and plays at the very time that his father or mother or brother is dead . . ."[258] Unfortunately, the idea that children are innocent and cannot be corrupted is a common defense by child molesters against admitting that their abuse is harming the child, so the medieval fiction that the child is innocent only makes our sources less revealing, and proves nothing about what really went on. Abbot Guibert of Nogent said children were blessed to be without sexual thoughts or capacities; one wonders what he then was referring to when he confessed to "the wickedness I did in childhood. . . ."[259] Mostly, servants are blamed for abusing children; even a washerwoman could "work wickedness." Servants often "show lewd tricks . . . in the presence of children [and] corrupt the chief parts of infants." Nurses should not be young girls, "for many such have aroused the fire of passion prematurely as true accounts relate and, I venture to say, experience proves."[260]

Giovanni Dominici, writing in 1405, tried to set some limits to the convenient "innocence" of childhood; he said children after the age of three years shouldn't be allowed to see nude adults. For in a child "granted that there will not take place any thought or natural movement before the age of five, yet, without precaution, growing up in such acts he becomes accustomed to that act of which later he is not ashamed . . ." That parents themselves are often doing the molesting can be seen in the language he used:

He should sleep clothed with a night shirt reaching below the knee, taking care as much as possible that he may not remain uncovered. Let not the mother nor the father, much less any other person, touch him. Not to be tedious in writing so fully of this, I simply mention the history of the ancients who made full use of this doctrine to bring up children well, not slaves of the flesh.[261]

That some change in the sexual use of children was going on in the Renaissance can be seen not only in the rising number of moralists who warned against it (Jean Gerson, like Louis XIII's nurse, said it was the *child's* duty to prevent others from molesting him), but also in the art of the time. Not only were Renaissance paintings full of nude *putti*, or cupids taking off blindfolds in front of nude women, but in addition real children were shown more and more often chucking the chin of the mother, or slinging one of their legs over hers, both conventional iconographic signs for sexual love, and the mother was often painted with her hand very near the genital area of the child.[262]

The campaign against the sexual use of children continued through the seventeenth century, but in the eighteenth century it took an entirely new twist: punishing the little boy or girl for touching its own genitals. That this, like early toilet-training, was a late psychogenic stage is suggested by the fact that prohibitions against childhood masturbation are found in none of the primitive societies surveyed by Whiting and Child.[263] The attitude of most people toward childhood masturbation prior to the eighteenth century can be seen in Fallopius's counsel for parents to "be zealous in infancy to enlarge the penis of the boy."[264] Although mastrubation in adults was a minor sin, medieval penitentials rarely extended the prohibition to childhood; adult homosexuality, not masturbation, was the main obsession of pre-modern sexual regulation. As late as the fifteenth century Gerson complains how adults tell him they never heard that masturbation was sinful, and he instructs confessors to ask adults directly: "Friend, do you touch or do you rub your rod *as children have the habit of doing?*"[265]

But it was not until the beginning of the eighteenth century, as a climax of the effort to bring child abuse under control, that parents began severely punishing their children for masturbation, and doctors began to spread the myth that it would cause insanity, epilepsy, blindness, and death. By the nineteenth century, this campaign reached an unbelievable frenzy. Doctors and parents sometimes appeared before the child armed with knives and scissors, threatening to cut off the child's genitals; circumcision, clitoridectomy, and infibulation were sometimes used as punishment; and all sorts of restraint devices, including plaster casts and cages with spikes, were prescribed. Circumcision became especially widespread; as one American child psychologist put it, when a child of two rubs his nose and can't be still for a moment, only circumcision works. Another doctor, whose book was the bible of many an American nineteenth-century home, recommended that little boys be closely watched for signs of masturbation, and brought in to him for circumcision without anaesthetic, which invariably cured them. Spitz's graphs on different advice given for masturbation, based on 559 volumes surveyed, show a peak in surgical intervention in 1850-1879, and in restraint devices in 1880-1904. By 1925, these methods had almost completely died out, after two centuries of brutal and totally unnecessary assault on children's genitals.[266]

Meanwhile, sexual use of children after the eighteenth century was far more widespread among servants and other adults and adolescents than among parents, although when one reads of the number of parents who continued to let their children sleep with servants after previous servants had been found abusing them sexually, it is obvious that the conditions for child abuse still remained within the control of the parents. Cardinal Bernis, remembering being sexually molested as a child, warned parents that "nothing is so dangerous for morals and perhaps for health as to leave children too long under the care of chambermaids, or even of young ladies brought up in the châteaux. I will add that the best among them are not always the least dangerous. They dare with a child that which they would be ashamed to risk with a young man."[267] A German doctor said nursemaids and servants carried out "all sorts of sexual acts" on children "for fun." Even Freud said he was seduced by his nurse when he was two, and Ferenczi and other analysts since his time have thought unwise Freud's decision in 1897 to consider most reports by patients of early sexual seductions as only fantasy. As psychoanalyst Robert Fleiss puts it, "No one is ever made sick by his fantasies," and a large number of patients in analysis even today report using children sexually although only Fleiss builds this fact into his psychoanalytic theory. When one learns that as late as 1900 there were still people who believed venereal disease could be cured "by means of sexual intercourse with children," one begins to recognize the dimensions of the problem more fully.[268]

It goes without saying that the effects on the child in the past of such severe physical and sexual abuse as I have described were immense. I would here like to indicate only two effects on the growing child, one psychological and one physical. The first is the enormous number of nightmares and hallucinations by children which I have found in the sources. Although written records by adults which indicate anything at all about a child's emotional life are rare at best, whenever discovered they usually reveal recurring nightmares and even outright hallucinations. Since antiquity, pediatric literature regularly had sections on how to cure children's "terrible dreams," and children were sometimes beaten for having nightmares. Children lay awake nights terrorized by imaginary ghosts, demons, "a witch on the pillow," "a large black dog under the bed," or "a crooked finger crawling across the room".[269] In addition, the history of witchcraft in the West is filled with reports of children's convulsive fits, loss of hearing or speech, loss of memory, hallucination of devils, confession of intercourse with devils, and accusations of witchcraft against adults, including their parents. And finally, even further back in the Middle Ages, we encounter children's dancing mania, children's crusades and child-pilgrimages, subjects which are simply too vast to discuss here.[270]

A final point I wish only to touch upon is the possibility that children in the past were actually retarded physically as a result of their poor care. Although swaddling by itself usually does not affect the physical development of primitive children, the combination of tight swaddling, neglect, and general abuse of children in the past seemed often to have produced what we would now regard as retarded children. One index of this retardation is that while most children today begin to walk by 10-12 months, children in the past generally walked later. The ages of first walking in Table 2 are all those I have found in the sources so far.

TABLE 2
AGE OF FIRST WALKING

Reference[271]	Age of First Walking in Months	Approx. Date	Nationality
Macrobius	28	400 A.D.	Roman
Federico d'Este	14	1501	Italian
James VI	60	1571	Scottish
Anne of Denmark	108	1575	Danish
Anne Clifford's child	34	1617	English
John Hamilton	14	1793	American
Augustus Hare	17	1834	English
Marianne Gaskell	22	1836	English
H. Taine's son	16	1860	French
Tricksy du Maurier	12	1865	English
W. Preyer's son	15	1880	German
Franklin Roosevelt	15	1884	American
G. Dearborn's daughter	15	1900	American
Amer. Inst. Child Life	12-17	1913	American
Univ. of Minn.—23 babies	15	1931	American

PERIODIZATION OF MODES OF PARENT-CHILD RELATIONS

Since some people still kill, beat, and sexually abuse children, any attempt to periodize modes of child rearing must first admit that psychogenic evolution proceeds at different rates in different family lines, and that many parents appear to be "stuck" in earlier historical modes. There are also class and area differences which are important, especially since modern times, when the upper classes stopped sending their infants to wet-nurses and began bringing them up themselves. The periodization below should be thought of as a designation of the modes of parent-child relations which were exhibited by the psychogenically most advanced part of the population in the most advanced countries, and the dates given are the first in which I found examples of that mode in the sources. The series of six modes represents a continuous sequence of closer approaches between parent and child as generation after generation of parents slowly overcame their anxieties and began to develop the capacity to identify and satisfy the needs of their children. I also believe the series provides a meaningful taxology of contemporary child-rearing modes.

1. *Infanticidal Mode (Antiquity to Fourth Century A.D.):* The image of Medea hovers over childhood in antiquity, for myth here only reflects reality. Some facts are more important than others, and when parents routinely resolved their anxieties about taking care of children by killing them, it affected the surviving children profoundly. For those who were allowed to grow up, the projective reaction was paramount, and the concreteness of reversal was evident in the widespread sodomizing of the child.

2. *Abandonment Mode (Fourth to Thirteenth Century A.D.):* Once parents began to accept the child as having a soul, the only way they could escape the dangers of their own projections was by abandonment, whether to the wet nurse, to the monastery or nunnery, to foster families, to the homes of other nobles as servants or hostages, or by severe emotional abandonment at home. The symbol of this mode might be Griselda, who so willingly abandoned her children to prove her love for her husband. Or perhaps it would be any of those pictures so popular up to the thirteenth century of a rigid Mary stiffly holding the infant Jesus. Projection continued to be massive, since the child was still full of evil and needed always to be beaten, but as the reduction in child sodomizing shows, reversal diminished considerably.

3. *Ambivalent Mode (Fourteenth to Seventeenth Centuries):* Because the child, when it was allowed to enter into the parents' emotional life, was still a container for dangerous projections, it was their task to mold it into shape. From Dominici to Locke there was no image more popular than that of the physical molding of children, who were seen as soft wax, plaster, or clay to be beaten into shape. Enor-

mous ambivalence marks this mode. The beginning of the period is approximately the fourteenth century, which shows an increase in the number of child instruction manuals, the expansion of the cults of Mary and the infant Jesus, and the proliferation in art of the "close-mother image."

4. *Intrusive Mode (Eighteenth Century):* A tremendous reduction in projection and the virtual disappearance of reversal was the accomplishment of the great transition for parent-child relations which appeared in the eighteenth century. The child was no longer so full of dangerous projections, and rather than just examine its insides with an enema, the parents approached even closer and attempted to conquer its mind, in order to control its insides, its anger, its needs, its masturbation, its very will. The child raised by intrusive parents was nursed by the mother, not swaddled, not given regular enemas, toilet trained early, prayed with but not played with, hit but not regularly whipped, punished for masturbation, and made to obey promptly with threats and guilt as often as with other methods of punishment. The child was so much less threatening that true empathy was possible, and pediatrics was born, which along with the general improvement in level of care by parents reduced infant mortality and provided the basis for the demographic transition of the eighteenth century.

5. *Socialization Mode (Nineteenth to Mid-twentieth Centuries):* As projections continued to diminish, the raising of a child became less a process of conquering its will than of training it, guiding it into proper paths, teaching it to conform, socializing it. The socializing mode is still thought of by most people as the only model within which discussion of child care can proceed, and it has been the source of all twentieth-century psychological models, from Freud's "channeling of impulses" to Skinner's behaviorism. It is most particularly the model of sociological functionalism. Also, in the nineteenth century, the father for the first time begins to take more than an occasional interest in the child, training it, and sometimes even relieving the mother of child-care chores.

6. *Helping Mode (Begins Mid-twentieth Century):* The helping mode involves the proposition that the child knows better than the parent what it needs at each stage of its life, and fully involves both parents in the child's life as they work to empathize with and fulfill its expanding and particular needs. There is no attempt at all to discipline or form "habits." Children are neither struck nor scolded, and are apologized to if yelled at under stress. The helping mode involves an enormous amount of time, energy, and discussion on the part of both parents, especially in the first six years, for helping a young child reach its daily goals means continually responding to it, playing with it, tolerating its regressions, being its servant rather than the other way around, interpreting its emotional conflicts, and providing the objects specific to its evolving interests. Few parents have yet consistently attempted this

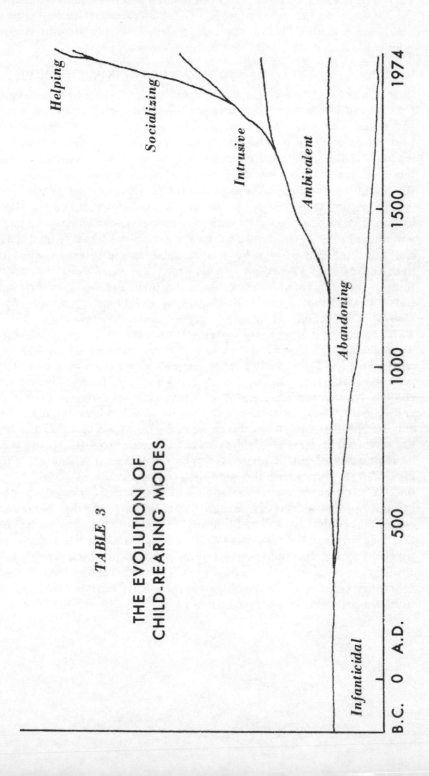

TABLE 3

THE EVOLUTION OF
CHILD-REARING MODES

Helping

Socializing

Intrusive

Ambivalent

Abandoning

Infanticidal

B.C.   0   A.D.   500   1000   1500   1974

kind of child care. From the four books which describe children brought up according to the helping mode,[272] it is evident that it results in a child who is gentle, sincere, never depressed, never imitative or group-oriented, strong-willed, and unintimidated by authority.

PSYCHOGENIC THEORY: A NEW PARADIGM FOR HISTORY

Psychogenic theory can, I think, provide a genuinely new paradigm for the study of history.[273] It reverses the usual *"mind as tabula rasa,"* and instead considers the *"world as tabula rasa,"* with each generation born into a world of meaningless objects which are invested with meaning only if the child receives a certain kind of care.[274] As soon as the mode of care changes for enough children, all the books and artifacts in the world are brushed aside as irrelevant to the purposes of the new generation, and society begins to move in unpredictable directions. How historical change is connected with changing child-care modes we have yet to spell out. In this book, we have carefully refrained from discussing this topic, but will not be so abstemious in the future. Most of us have already begun work on articles which will extend our childhood findings into the broader area of psychohistory, and we have even initiated a new scholarly journal, *History of Childhood Quarterly: The Journal of Psychohistory,* in which to publish our future studies.

If the measure of a theory's vitality is its ability to generate interesting problems, childhood history and psychogenic theory should have an exciting future. There is still a lot to learn about what growing up in the past was really like. One of our first tasks will be to investigate why childhood evolution proceeds at different rates in different countries and different class and family lines. Yet we already know enough to be able for the first time to answer some major questions on value and behavior change in Western history. First to benefit from the theory will be the history of witchcraft, magic, religious movements, and other irrational mass phenomena. Beyond this, psychogenic theory should eventually contribute to our understanding of why social organization, political form, and technology change in specific times and directions and not in others. Perhaps the addition of the childhood parameter to history may even end the historian's century-long Durkheimian flight from psychology, and encourage us to resume the task of constructing a scientific history of human nature which was envisioned so long ago by John Stuart Mill as a "theory of the causes which determine the type of character belonging to a people or to an age."[275]

REFERENCES

I wish to express my sincerest thanks for comments on this paper to my wife Gladys, to John Benton, Edward Shorter, Henry Ebel, Rudolph Binion, William Dresden, and of course to each of my collaborators in this volume.

1. Peter Laslett, *The World We Have Lost* (New York, 1965), p. 104.
2. James H. S. Bossard, *The Sociology of Child Development* (New York, 1948), p. 598.
3. Geza Roheim, "The Study of Character Development and The Ontogenetic Theory of Culture," in *Essays Presented to C. G. Seligman*, E. E. Evans-Pritchard, et al., eds. (London, 1934), p. 292; Abram Kardiner, ed., *The Individual and His Society* (New York, 1939), p. 471; in *Totem and Taboo*, Freud side-stepped the problem by positing an "inheritance of psychic dispositions;" Sigmund Freud, *The Standard Edition of the Complete Psychological Works of Sigmund Freud*, vol. 13, James Strachey, ed. (London, 1955), p. 158.
4. Enid Nemy, "Child Abuse: Does It Stem From the Nation's Ills and Its Culture?" *New York Times*, August 16, 1971, p. 16; some estimates reach as high as 2.5 million abused children, see Vincent J. Fontana, *Somewhere a Child is Crying* (New York, 1973), p. 38.
5. An evaluation of some of the most recent works can be found in John C. Sommerville, "Towards a History of Childhood and Youth," *Journal of Interdisciplinary History*, 3 (1972), 438-47; and Edward Saveth, "The Problem of American Family History," *American Quarterly*, 21 (1969), 311-29.
6. See especially Neil J. Smelser, *Social Change in the Industrial Revolution: An Application of Theory of the British Cotton Industry* (Chicago, 1959); Fred Weinstein and Gerald Platt, *The Wish to Be Free: Society, Psyche, and Value Change* (Berkeley and Los Angeles, 1969); and Talcott Parsons and Robert F. Bales, *Family, Socialization, and Interaction Process* (New York, 1955).
7. See Peter Coveney, *The Image of Childhood: The Individual and Society: A Study of the Theme in English Literature* (Baltimore, 1967); Gillian Avery, *Nineteenth Century Children: Heroes and Heroines in English Children's Stories 1780-1900* (London, 1965); F. J. Harvey Darton, *Children's Books in England: Five Centuries of Social Life* (Cambridge, 1966); and Paul Hazard, *Books, Children & Men* (Boston, 1944).
8. The best childhood histories include: Grace Abbott, *The Child and the State*, 2 vols. (Chicago, 1938); Abt-Garrison, *History of Pediatrics* (Philadelphia, 1965; Philippe Ariès, *Centuries of Childhood: A Social History of Family Life* (New York, 1962); Sven Armens, *Archetypes of the Family in Literature* (Seattle, 1966); David Bakan, *Slaughter of the Innocents* (San Francisco, 1971); Howard Clive Barnard, *The French Tradition in Education* (Cambridge, 1922); Rosamond Bayne-Powell, *The English Child in the Eighteenth Century* (London, 1939); Frederick A. G. Beck, *Greek Education: 450-350 B.C.* (London, 1964); Jessie Bedford (pseud., Elizabeth Godfrey), *English Children in the Olden Time* (London, 1907); H. Blumner, *The Home Life of the Ancient Greeks*, Alice Zimmern, trans. (New York, 1966); Bossard, *Sociology;* Robert H. Bremner et al., eds., *Children and Youth in America: A Documentary History*, 3 vols., (Cambridge, Massachusetts, 1970); Elizabeth Burton, *The Early Victorians at Home 1837-1861* (London, 1972); M. St. Clare Byrne, *Elizabethan Life in Town and Country* (London, 1961); Ernest Caulfield, *The Infant Welfare Movement in the Eighteenth Century* (New York, 1931); Oscar Chrisman, *The Historical Child* (Boston, 1920); Phillis Cunnington and Anne Boch, *Children's Costume in England: From the Fourteenth to the End of the Nineteenth Century* (New York, 1965); John Demos, *A Little Commonwealth: Family*

Life in Plymouth Colony (New York, 1970); J. Louise Despert, *The Emotionally Disturbed Child–Then and Now* (New York, 1967); George Duby, *La Société aux XIᵉ et XIIᵉ Siècles dans la Région Maconnaise* (Paris, 1953); Alice Morse Earle, *Child Life in Colonial Days* (New York, 1899); Jonathan Gathorne-Hardy, *The Rise and Fall of the British Nanny* (London, 1972); Willystine Goodsell, *A History of Marriage and the Family* (New York, 1934); Sister Mary Rosaria Gorman, *The Nurse in Greek Life: A Dissertation* (Boston, 1917); E. H. Hare, "Masturbatory Insanity: The History of an Idea," *Journal of Mental Science,* 108 (1962); 2-25; Edith Hoffman, *Children in the Past* (London, n.d.); Christina Hole, *English Home-Life, 1450 to 1800* (London, 1947); David Hunt, *Parents and Children in History* (New York, 1970); Anne L. Kuhn, *The Mother's Role in Childhood Education: New England Concepts 1830-1860* (New Haven, 1947); W. K. Lacey, *The Family in Classical Greece* (Ithaca, New York, 1968); Marion Lochhead, *Their First Ten Years: Victorian Childhood* (London, 1956); Alan Macfarlane, *The Family Life of Ralph Josselin: A Seventeenth-Century Clergyman* (Cambridge, 1970); Morris Marples, *Princes in the Making: A Study of Royal Education* (London, 1965); H. I. Marrou, *A History of Education in Antiquity* (New York, 1956); Roger Mercer, *L'enfant dans la société du XVIIIᵉ siècle* (Dakar, 1951); Edmund S. Morgan, *The Puritan Family: Religion & Domestic Relations in Seventeenth-Century New England* (New York, 1966); George Henry Payne, *The Child in Human Progress* (New York, 1916); Lu Emily Pearson, *Elizabethans at Home* (Stanford, California, 1957); Albrecht Peiper, *Chronik der Kinderheilkunde* (Leipzig, 1966); Henricus Pecters, *Kind en juegdige in het begin van de modern tijd* (Antwerpen, 1966); Ivy Pinchbeck and Margaret Hewitt, *Children in English Society,* Vol. 1: *From Tudor Times to the Eighteenth Century* (London, 1969); Chilton Latham Powell, *English Domestic Relations, 1487-1653* (New York, 1917); F. Gordon Roe, *The Georgian Child* (London, 1961); F. Gordon Roe, *The Victorian Child* (London, 1959); John Ruhrah, ed., *Pediatrics of the Past: An Anthology* (New York, 1925); Alice Ryerson, "Medical Advice on Child Rearing," Ed.D. thesis, Harvard University Graduate School of Education, 1960; Paul Sangster, *Pity My Simplicity: The Evangelical Revival and the Religious Education of Children 1738-1800* (London, 1963); Levin L. Schücking, *The Puritan Family* (London, 1969); Rene A. Spitz, "Authority and Masturbation: Some Remarks on a Bibliographical Investigation," *The Psychoanalytic Quarterly,* 21 (1952), 490-527; George Frederic Still, *The History of Paediatrics* (London, 1931); Karl Sudhoff, *Erstlinge der Pädiatrischen Literatur: Drei Wiegendrucke über Heilung und Pflege des Kindes* (Munich, 1925); Gordon Rattray Taylor, *The Angel-Makers: A Study in the Psychological Origins of Historical Change 1750-1850* (London, 1958); Bernard Wishy, *The Child and the Republic: The Dawn of Modern American Child Nurture* (Philadelphia, 1968).

9. Charles Seltman, *Women in Antiquity* (London, 1956), p. 72.
10. Daniel R. Miller and Guy E. Swanson, *The Changing American Parent: A Study in the Detroit Area* (New York, 1958), p. 10.
11. Bayne-Powell, *English Child,* p. 6.
12. Laslett, *World,* p. 12; E. S. Morgan agrees that Puritan parents sent their children away at a young age only because they were "afraid of spoiling them by too great affection," *Puritan Family,* p. 77.
13. William Sloane, *Children's Books in England and America in the Seventeenth Century* (New York, 1955), p. 19.
14. Ariès, *Centuries of Childhood,* p. 103.
15. *Ibid.,* p. 105.
16. Alan Valentine, ed., *Fathers to Sons: Advice Without Consent* (Norman, Oklahoma, 1963), p. xxx.

17. Anna Robeson Burr, *The Autobiography: A Critical and Comparative Study* (Boston, 1909); also see Emma N. Plank, "Memories of Early Childhood in Autobiographies," *The Psychoanalytic Study of the Child*, vol. 8 (New York, 1953).
18. Frank E. Manuel, "The Use and Abuse of Psychology in History," *Daedalus*, 100 (1971), 203.
19. Ariès, *Centuries of Childhood*, pp. 33, 10.
20. An enormous bibliography and many examples of paintings of the child in early medieval art can be found in Victor Lasareff, "Studies in the Iconography of the Virgin," *Art Bulletin*, 20 (1938), pp. 26-65.
21. Natalie Z. Davis, "The Reasons of Misrule," *Past and Present*, 50 (1971), 61-62. Frank Boll, *Die Lebensalter: Ein Beitrag zur antiken Ethologie und zur Geschichte der Zahlen* (Leipzig and Berlin, 1913) has the best bibliography on "Ages of Man"; for all the variations in Old English on the word "child," see Hilding Back, *The Synonyms for "Child," "Boy," "Girl" in Old English* (London, 1934).
22. Richard Sennett, *Families Against the City* (Cambridge, Massachusetts, 1970); Joseph F. Kett, "Adolescence and Youth in Nineteenth-Century America," *The Journal of Interdisciplinary History*, 2 (1971), 283-99; John and Virginia Demos, "Adolescence in Historical Perspective," *Journal of Marriage and the Family*, 31 (1969), 632-38.
23. Despert, *Emotionally Disturbed Child*, p. 40.
24. Donald Meltzer, *The Psycho-Analytical Process* (London, 1967); Herbert A. Rosenfield, *Psychotic States: A Psychoanalytical Approach* (New York, 1965).
25. Brandt F. Steele, "Parental Abuse of Infants and Small Children," in E. James Anthony and Therese Benedek, eds., *Parenthood: Its Psychology and Psychopathology* (Boston, 1970); David G. Gil, *Violence Against Children: Physical Child Abuse in the United States* (Cambridge, Massachusetts, 1970); Brandt F. Steele and Carl B. Pollock, "A Psychiatric Study of Parents Who Abuse Infants and Small Children," in Ray E. Helfer and C. Henry Kempe, eds., *The Battered Child* (Chicago, 1968), pp. 103-45; Richard Galdston, "Dysfunctions of Parenting: The Battered Child, the Neglected Child, the Exploited Child," in John G. Howells, ed., *Modern Perspectives in International Child Psychiatry* (New York, 1971), pp. 571-84.
26. Theodor Reik, *Listening With the Third Ear* (New York, 1950); also see Stanley L. Olinick, "On Empathy, and Regression in Service of the Other," *British Journal of Medical Psychology*, 42 (1969), 40-47.
27. Nicholas Restif de la Bretonne, *Monsieur Nicolas; or, The Human Heart Unveiled*, Vol. 1, R. Crowder Mathers, trans. (London, 1930), p. 95.
28. Gregory Bateson, *Steps to an Ecology of Mind* (New York, 1972).
29. Barry Cunningham, "Beaten Kids, Sick Parents," *New York Post*, February 23, 1972, p. 14.
30. Samuel Arnold, *An Astonishing Affair!* (Concord, 1830), pp. 73-81.
31. Powell, *Domestic Relations*, p. 110.
32. Cotton Mather, *Diary of Cotton Mather*, vol. 1 (New York, n.d.), p. 283.
33. *Ibid.*, p. 369.
34. Carl Holliday, *Woman's Life in Colonial Boston* (Boston, 1922), p. 25.
35. Richard Allestree, *The Whole Duty of Man* (London, 1766), p. 20.
36. Keith Thomas, *Religion and the Decline of Magic* (New York, 1971), p. 479; Beatrice Saunders, *The Age of Candlelight: The English Social Scene in the 17th Century* (London, 1959), p. 88; Traugott K. Oesterreich, *Possession, Demoniacal and Other Among Primitive Races, in Antiquity, the Middle Ages, and Modern Times* (New York, 1930); Grünewald's "St. Cyriakus" shows a girl being exorcised, her mouth being forced open to let the devil out.
37. Shmarya Levin, *Childhood in Exile* (New York, 1929), pp. 58-59.

38. Carl Haffter, "The Changeling: History and Psychodynamics of Attitudes to Handicapped Children in European Folklore." *Journal of the History of the Behavioral Sciences*, 4 (1968), 55-61 contains the best bibliography; see also Bayne-Powell, *English Child*, p. 247; and Pearson, *Elizabethans*, p. 80.
39. St. Augustine, *Against Julian* (New York, 1957), p. 117.
40. William E. H. Lecky, *History of the Rise and Influence of the Spirit of Rationalism in Europe* (New York, 1867), p. 362.
41. Haffter, *Changeling*, p. 58.
42. Abbot Guibert of Nogent, *Self and Society in Medieval France: The Memoirs of Abbot Guibert of Nogent*, John F. Benton, ed. (New York, 1970), p. 96.
43. G. G. Coulton, *Social Life in Britain: From the Conquest to the Reformation* (Cambridge, 1918), p. 46.
44. Ruth Benedict, "Child Rearing in Certain European Countries," *American Journal of Orthopsychiatry*, 19 (1949), 345-46.
45. Dio Chrysostom, *Discourses*, J. W. Cohoon, trans. (London, 1932), p. 36.
46. Maffio Vegio, "De Educatione Liberorum," in Maria W. Fanning, ed. *Maphei Vegii Laudensis De Educatione Liberorum Et Eorum Claris Moribus Libri Sex* (Washington, D.C., 1933), p. 642.
47. Carl Holliday, *Woman's Life in Colonial Boston* (New York, 1960), p. 18.
48. Brigid Brophy, *Black Ship to Hell* (New York, 1962), p. 361.
49. Marc Soriano, "From Tales of Warning to Formulettes: the Oral Tradition in French Children' Literature," *Yale French Studies*, vol. 43 (1969), p. 31; Melesina French, *Thoughts on Education by a Parent* (Southampton, not published, 181-?), p. 42; Roe, *Georgian Child*, p. 11; Jacob Abbott, *Gentle Measures in the Management and Training of the Young* (New York, 1871), p. 18; James Mott, *Observations on the Education of Children* (New York, 1816), p. 5; W. Preyer, *The Mind of the Child*, (New York, 1896), p. 164; William Byrd, *Another Secret Diary*, (Richmond, 1942), p. 449; Francis Joachim de Pierre de Bernis, *Memoirs and Letters* (Boston, 1901), p. 90.
50. French, *Thoughts*, p. 43; see also Enos Hitchcock, *Memoirs of the Bloomsgrove Family*, vol. 1 (Boston, 1790), p. 109; Iris Origo, *Leopardi: A Study in Solitude* (London, 1953), p. 24; Hippolyte Adolphe Taine, *The Ancient Regime* (Gloucester, Massachusetts, 1962), p. 130; Vincent J. Horkan, *Educational Theories and Principles of Maffeo Veggio* (Washington, D.C., 1953), p. 152; Ellen Weeton, *Miss Weeton: Journal of a Governess*, Edward Hall, ed. (London, 1936), p. 58.
51. Laurence Wylie, *Village in the Vaucluse* (New York, 1957), p. 52.
52. *Dialogues on the Passions, Habits and Affections Peculiar to Children* (London, 1748), p. 31; Georg Friedrich Most, *Der Mensch in den ersten sieben Lebensjahren* (Leipzig, 1839), p. 116.
53. Francis P. Hett, ed., *The Memoirs of Susan Sibbald 1783-1812*, p. 176.
54. Rhoda E. White, *From Infancy to Womanhood: A Book of Instruction for Young Mothers* (London, 1882), p. 31.
55. Strabo, *The Geography*, vol. 1, Horace L. Jones, trans. (Cambridge, Massachusetts, 1960), p. 69; Epictetus, *The Discourses as Reported by Arrian*, vol. 1, W. A. Oldfather, trans. (Cambridge, Massachusetts, 1967), pp. 217, 243 and vol. 2, p. 169.
56. Dio Chrysostom, *Discourses*, vol. 1, p. 243; and vol. 5, p. 107.
57. Anna C. Johnson, *Peasant Life in Germany* (New York, 1858), p. 353. Several informants have told me this continued into the twentieth century.
58. John Paul Friedrich Richter, *Levana; or the Doctrine of Education* (Boston, 1863), p. 288.
59. Mrs. Mary Sherwood, *The History of the Fairchild Family* (London, n.d.).
60. Taylor, *Angel-Makers*, p. 312; Most, *Mensch*, p. 118; Frances Ann Kemble,

Records of a Girlhood (New York, 1879), p. 27; Horkan, *Educational Theories,* p. 117; Dr. Courtenay Dunn, *The Natural History of the Child* (New York, 1920), p. 300; E. Mastone Graham, *Children of France* (New York, n.d.), p. 40; Hett, Memoirs, p. 10; Ivan Bloch, *Sexual Life in England* (London, 1958), p. 361; Harriet Bessborough, *Lady Bessborough and Her Family Circle* (London, 1940), pp. 22-24; Sangster, *Pity,* pp. 33-34.

61. Maffio Vegio, "De Educatione Liberorum," p. 644.
62. *Memoir of Elizabeth Jones* (New York, 1841), p. 13.
63. C. S. Peel, *The Stream of Time: Social and Domestic Life in England 1805-1861* (London, 1931), p. 40.
64. Bessborough, *Bessborough Family,* pp. 23-24.
65. John W.M. Whiting and Irvin L. Child, *Child Training and Personality: A Cross-Cultural Study* (New Haven, 1953), p. 343.
66. L. Bryce Boyer, "Psychological Problems of a Group of Apaches: Alcoholic Hallucinosis and Latent Homosexuality Among Typical Men," in *The Psychoanalytic Study of Society,* vol. 3 (1964), p. 225.
67. Asa Briggs, ed., *How They Lived,* vol. 3 (New York, 1969), p. 27.
68. Horace E. Scudder, *Childhood in Literature and Art* (Boston, 1894), p. 34.
69. Giovanni di Pagalo Morelli, *Ricordi,* V. Branca, ed. (Florence, 1956), p. 501.
70. Euripides, *The Medea,* 1029-36; Jason, too, pities only himself, 1325-7.
71. Ariès, *Centuries of Childhood,* p. 57; Christian Augustus Struve, *A Familiar Treatise on the Physical Education of Children* (London, 1801), p. 299.
72. Agnes C. Vaughan, *The Genesis of Human Offspring: A Study in Early Greek Culture* (Menasha, Wisconsin, 1945), p. 107; James Hastings, ed., *A Dictionary of Christ and the Gospels* (New York, 1911), p. 533.
73. Kett, *Adolescence,* pp. 35, 230.
74. E. Soulié and E. de Barthélemy, eds., *Journal de Jean Héroard sur l'Enfance et la Jeunesse de Louis XIII,* vol. 1 (Paris, 1868), p. 35.
75. *Ibid.,* p. 76.
76. Francesco da Barberino, *Reggimento e costume di donne* (Torino, 1957), p. 189.
77. Alexander Hamilton, *The Family Female Physician: Or, A Treatise on the Management of Female Complaints, and of Children in Early Infancy* (Worcester, 1793), p. 287.
78. Struve, *Treatise,* p. 273.
79. Albrecht Peiper, *Chronik,* p. 120; Daphne Du Maurier, ed., *The Young George du Maurier: A Selection of His Letters 1860-67* (London, 1951), p. 223.
80. Pliny, *Natural History,* H. Rockham, trans. (Cambridge, Massachusetts, 1942), p. 587.
81. Sieur Peter Charron, *Of Wisdom,* 3rd ed., George Stanhope, trans. (London, 1729), p. 1384.
82. St. Evremond, *The Works of Monsieur de St. Evremond,* vol. 3 (London, 1714), p. 6.
83. W. Warde Fowler, *Social Life at Rome in the Age of Cicero* (New York, 1926), p. 177; Edith Rickert, ed., *The Babee's Book: Medieval Manners for the Young* (London, 1908) p. xviii; Mrs. E. M. Field, *The Child and His Book* (London, 1892), reprint (Detroit, 1968), p. 91; Frederick J. Furnivall, ed., *Early English Meals and Manners* (1868), reprint (Detroit, 1969), p. 229; Pearson, *Elizabethans,* p. 172.
84. Elizabeth L. Davoren, "The Role of the Social Worker," in Ray E. Helfer and C. Henry Kempe, eds., *The Battered Child* (Chicago, 1968), p. 155.
85. Ruby Ann Ingersoll, *Memoir of Elizabeth Charlotte Ingersoll Who Died September 18, 1857 Aged 12 Years* (Rochester, New York, 1858), p. 6.
86. Jacques Guillimeau, *The Nursing of Children* (London, 1612), p. 3.
87. H. T. Barnwell, ed., *Selected Letters of Madame de Sévigné* (London, 1959),

p. 73.
88. Most, *Mensch*, p. 74
89. Charron, *Wisdom*, p. 1338; Robert Cleaver, *A godlie forme of household government* . . . (London, 1598), p. 296.
90. Soulié, *Héroard*, pp. 2-5.
91. *Ibid.*, pp. 7-9.
92. *Ibid.*, p. 11.
93. *Ibid.*, pp. 14-15
94. *Ibid.*, pp. 32.34.
95. *Ibid.*, p. 36.
96. *Ibid.*, pp. 34, 35.
97. *Ibid.*, pp. 42-43.
98. *Ibid.*, p. 45. This sexual use of the dauphin cannot be solely to imbibe his royal charisma, since the king and queen also participate.
99. Felix Bryk, *Circumcision in Man and Woman: Its History, Psychology and Ethnology* (New York, 1934), p. 94.
100. *Ibid.*, p. 100.
101. *Ibid.*, pp. 57, 115.
102. Even present day self-cutters experience the flow of blood as milk; see John S. Kafka, "The Body as Transitional Object: A Psychoanalytic Study of a Self-Mutilating Patient," *British Journal of Medical Psychology*, 42 (1969), p. 209.
103. Eric J. Dingwall, *Male Infibulation* (London, 1925), p. 60; and Thorkil Vanggaard, *Phallos: A Symbol and its History in the Male World* (New York, 1969), p. 89.
104. Dingwall, *Infibulation*, p. 61; Celsus, De Medicina, vol. 3, W. B. Spencer, trans. (Cambridge, 1938), p. 25; Augustin Cabanes, *The Erotikon* (New York, 1966), p. 171; Bryk, *Circumcision*, pp. 225-27; Soranus, *Gynecology* (Baltimore, 1956), p. 107; Peter Ucko, "Penis Sheaths: A Comparative Study," *Proceedings of the Royal Anthropological Institute of Great Britain and Ireland for 1969* (London, 1970), p. 43.
105. *Ibid.*, pp. 27, 56-58; Count de Buffon, *A Natural History*, vol. 1, William Smellie, trans. (London, 1781), p. 217.
106. Paulus Aegineta, *The Seven Books of Paulus Aegineta*, 3 vols, Francis Adams, trans. (London, 1844-47), vol. 1, p. 346; Celsus, *Medicina*, p. 421.
107. Otto J. Brendel, "The Scope and Temperament of Erotic Art in the Greco-Roman World," *Studies in Erotic Art*, Theodore Bowie and Cornelia V. Christenson, eds. (New York, 1970), plates 1, 17, 18, 20.
108. Joseph C. Rheingold, *The Fear of Being a Woman: A Theory of Maternal Destructiveness* (New York, 1964); and Rheingold, *The Mother, Anxiety, and Death: The Catastrophic Death Complex* (Boston, 1967).
109. Dorothy Bloch, "Feelings That Kill: The Effect of the Wish for Infanticide in Neurotic Depression," *The Psychoanalytic Review*, 52 (1965); Bakan, *Slaughter;* Stuart S. Asch, "Depression: Three Clinical Variations," in *Psychoanalytic Study of the Child*, vol. 21 (1966) pp. 150-71; Morris Brozovsky and Harvey Falit, "Neonaticide: Clinical and Psychodynamic Considerations," *Journal of Child Psychiatry*, 10 (1971); Wolfgang Lederer, *The Fear of Women* (New York, 1968); Galdston, *"Dysfunctions,"* and the bibliography in Rheingold.
110. For bibliographies, see, Abt-Garrison, *History of Pediatrics;* Bakan, *Slaughter;* William Barclay, *Educational Ideas in the Ancient World* (London, 1959), Appendix A; H. Bennett, "Exposure of Infants in Ancient Rome," *Classical Journal*, 18 (1923), pp. 341-45; A. Cameron, "The Exposure of Children and Greek Ethics," *Classical Review*, 46 (1932), 105-14; Jehanne Charpentier, *Le Droit de l'enfance Abandoneé* (Paris, 1967); A. R. W. Harrison, *The*

Law of Athens: The Family and Property (Oxford, 1968); William L. Langer, "Checks on Population Growth: 1750-1850," *Scientific American* (1972), 93-99; Francois Lebrun, "Naissances illégitimes et abandons d'enfants en Anjou au XVIIIe siècle," *Annales: Economies, Sociétiés, Civilisations,* 27 (1972); A. J. Levin, "Oedipus and Sampson, the Rejected Hero-Child," *International Journal of Psycho-Analysis,* 38 (1957), 103-10; John T. Noonan, Jr., *Contraception: A History of Its Treatment by the Catholic Theologians and Canonists* (Cambridge, Massachusetts, 1965); Payne, *Child;* Juha Pentikainen, *The Nordic Dead-Child Traditions* (Helsinki, 1968); Max Raden, "Exposure of Infants in Roman Law and Practice," *Classical Journal,* 20 (1925), 342-43; Edward Shorter, "Illegitimacy, Sexual Revolution, and Social Change in Modern Europe," *The Journal of Interdisciplinary History* 2 (1971), 237-72; Edward Shorter, "Infanticide in the Past," *History of Childhood Quarterly: The Journal of Psychohistory* 1 (1973), 178-80; Edward Shorter, "Sexual Change and Illegitimacy: The European Experience," in *Modern European Social History,* ed., Robert Bezucha (Lexington, Massachusetts, 1972), pp. 231-69; John Thrupp, *The Anglo-Saxon Home: A History of the Domestic Institutions and Customs of England. From the Fifth to the Eleventh Century* (London, 1862); Richard Trexler, "Infanticide in Florence," *History of Childhood Quarterly: The Journal of Psychohistory,* 1 (1973), 98-117; La Rue Van Hook, "The Exposure of Infants at Athens," *American Philogical Association Transactions and Proceedings,* 51, (1920), pp. 36-44; Oscar H. Werner, *The Unmarried Mother in German Literature* (New York, 1966); G. Glotz, *L'Exposition des Enfants, Études Sociales et Juridiques sur l'antiquité grecque* (Paris, 1906); Y.-B. Brissaud, "L'infanticide à la fin du moyen age, ses motivations psychologiques et sa répression," *Revue historique de droit français et étranger,* 50 (1972), 229-56; M. de Gouroff (Antoine J. Duguer), *Essai sur l'histoire des enfants trouvés* (Paris, 1885); William L. Langer, "Infanticide: A Historical Survey," *History of Childhood Quarterly: The Journal of Psychohistory* 1 (1973), 353-67.

111. Soranus, *Gynecology,* p. 79.
112. Lacey, *Family,* p. 164.
113. John Garrett Winter, *Life and Letters in the Papyri* (Ann Arbor, Michigan, 1933); p. 56; Naphtali Lewis and Meyer Reinhold, *Roman Civilization: Source Book 2* (New York, 1955), p. 403; *Gunnlaugs saga ormstungu* in M. H. Scargill trans., *Three Icelandic Sagas* (Princeton, 1950), pp. 11-12.
114. Jack Lindsay, *The Ancient World* (London, 1968), p. 168.
115. Polybius, *The Histories,* vol. 6, W. R. Paton, trans. (London, 1927), p. 30.
116. Cora E. Lutz, "Musonius Rufus 'The Roman Socrates'" in Alfred R. Bellinger, ed., *Yale Classical Studies,* vol. 10 (New Haven, 1947), p. 101; although his pupil, Epictetus, seems more opposed to infanticide in Epictetus, *Discourses,* chapter 23. Also see legal approval of infanticide in *The Gortyna Law Tables,* IV:21, 23, R. Dareste Ed., *Recueil des Inscriptions Juridiques Grecques* (Paris, 1894), p. 365.
117. Bartholomew Batty, *The Christian Mans Closet,* William Lowth, trans. (1581), p. 28.
118. Seneca, *Moral Essays,* John W. Basore, trans. (Cambridge, Massachusetts, 1963), p. 145.
119. Menander, *The Principal Fragments,* Frances G. Allinson, trans. (London, 1921), p. 33; Philip E. Slater, *The Glory of Hera: Greek Mythology and the Greek Family* (Boston, 1968).
120. Henri V. Vallois, "The Social Life of Early Man: The Evidence of Skeletons,"

in *Social Life of Early Man,* Sherwood L. Washburn, ed. (Chicago, 1961), p. 225.

121. Plutarch, *Moralia,* Frank C. Babbitt, trans. (London, 1928), p. 493.

122. E. Wellisch, *Isaac and Oedipus* (London, 1954), pp. 11-14; Payne, *Child,* pp. 8, 160; Robert Seidenberg, "Sacrificing The First You See," *The Psychoanalytic Review,* 53 (1966), 52-60; Samuel J. Beck, "Abraham's Ordeal: Creation of a New Reality," *The Psychoanalytic Review,* 50 (1963), 175-85; Theodore Thass-Thienemann, *The Subconscious Language* (New York, 1967), pp. 302-6; Thomas Platter, *Journal of a Younger Brother,* Jean Jennett, trans. (London, 1963), p. 85; Tertullian, "Apology," *The Anti-Nicene Fathers,* Vol. 3 (New York, 1918), p. 25; P. W. Joyce, *A Social History of Ancient Ireland,* Vol. 1, 3rd ed. (London, 1920), p. 285; William Burke Ryan, M.D., *Infanticide: Its Law, Prevalence, Prevention, and History* (London, 1862), pp. 200-20; Eusebius Pamphili, *Eclesiastical History* (New York, 1955), p. 103; J. M. Robertson, *Pagan Christs* (New York, 1967), p. 31; Charles Picard, *Daily Life in Carthage,* A. E. Foster, trans. (New York, 1961), p. 671; Howard H. Schlossman, "God the Father and His Sons," *American Imago,* 29 (1972), 35-50.

123. William Ellwood Craig, "Vincent of Beauvais, On the Education of Noble Children," University of California at Los Angeles, Ph.D. thesis, 1949, p. 21; Payne, *Child,* p. 150; Arthur Stanley Riggs, *The Romance of Human Progress* (New York, 1938), p. 284; E. O. James, *Prehistoric Religion* (New York, 1957), p. 59; Nathaniel Weyl, "Some Possible Genetic Implications of Carthaginian Child Sacrifice," *Perspectives in Biology and Medicine,* 12 (1968), 69-78; James Hastings, ed., *Encyclopedia of Religion and Ethics,* Vol. 3 (New York, 1951), p. 187; Picard, *Carthage,* p. 100.

124. H. S. Darlington, "Ceremonial Behaviorism: Sacrifices For the Foundation of Houses," *The Psychoanalytic Review,* 18 (1931); Henry Bett, *The Games of Children: Their Origin and History* (London, 1929), pp. 104-5; Joyce, *Social History,* p. 285; Payne, *Child,* p. 154; Anon., "Foundations Laid in Human Sacrifice," *The Open Court,* t. 23 (1909), 494-501.

125. Henry Bett, *Nursery Rhymes and Tales; Their Origin and History* (New York, 1924), p. 35.

126. *Dio's Roman History,* Vol. 9, Earnest Cary, trans. (London, 1937), p. 157; Suetonius, *The Lives of the Twelve Caesars,* Joseph Gavorse, ed. (New York, 1931), p. 108; Pliny, *Natural History,* vol. 8, H. Rockham, trans. (Cambridge, Massachusetts, 1942), p. 5.

127. Suetonius, *Caesars,* p. 265; Livy, *Works,* vol. 12, Evan T. Sage, trans. (Cambridge, Massachusetts, 1938), p. 9; Tacitus, *The Annals of Tacitus,* Donald R. Dudley, trans. (New York, 1966), pp. 186, 259.

128. Philo, *Works,* Vol. 7, F. H. Colson, trans. (Cambridge, Massachusetts, 1929), p. 549; also see Favorinus in J. Foote, "An Infant Hygiene Campaign of the Second Century," *Archives of Pediatrics,* 37 (1920), p. 181.

129. Lewis and Reinhold, *Roman Civilization,* pp. 344, 483.

130. Noonan, *Contraception,* p. 86.

131. St. Justin Martyr, *Writings* (New York, 1949), p. 63; also Dio Chrysostom, *Discourses,* p. 151; Tertullian, *Apology,* p. 205; Lactantius, *The Divine Institutes,* Books 1-8 (Washington, D.C. 1964), p. 452.

132. Tertullian, *Apologitical Works* (New York, 1950), p. 31.

133. Hefele-Leclercq, *Histoire des conciles,* t.II, pt. 1 (Paris, 1908), pp. 459-60; St. Magnebode (606-654) may have established an earlier foundling hospital, according to Leclercq.

134. *Dictionnaire d'archéologie chrétienne et de liturgie* (Paris, 1907-1951), tome I, article on "Alumni" by H. Leclercq, pp. 1288-1306; Thrupp, *Anglo-*

Saxon Home, p. 81.

135. Emily R. Coleman, "Medieval Marriage Characteristics: A Neglected Factor in the History of Medieval Serfdom," *The Journal of Interdisciplinary History*, 2 (1971); 205-20; Josiah Cox Russell, *British Medieval Population* (Albuquerque, New Mexico, 1948), p. 168.

136. Trexler, "Infanticide," p. 99; Brissaud, "L'infanticide," p. 232.

137. *Ibid.*, p. 100; F. G. Emmison, *Elizabethan Life and Disorder* (Chelmsford, England, 1970), pp. 7-8, 155-7; Pentikainen, *Dead-Child:* Werner, *Mother*, pp. 26-29; Ryan, *Infanticide*, pp. 1-6; Barbara Kellum, "Infanticide in England in the Later Middle Ages", *History of Childhood Quarterly: The Journal of Psychohistory*, 1 (1974) 367-88; Brissaud, "L'infanticide," pp. 243-56.

138. Craig, "Vincent of Beauvais," p. 368; Thomas Phayer, *The Regiment of Life, including the Boke of Children* (1545); Thrupp, *Anglo-Saxon Home*, p. 85; William Douglass, *A Summary, Historical and Political, of the First Planting, Progressive Improvements, and Present State of the British Settlements in North America*, vol. 2 (London, 1760), p. 202.

139. John Brownlow, *Memoranda: Or Chronicles of the Foundling Hospital* (London, 1847), p. 217.

140. Shorter, "Sexual Change"; Bakan, *Slaughter;* Shorter, "Illegitimacy"; Shorter, "Infanticide"; Charpentier, *Droit;* Robert J. Parr, *The Baby Farmer* (London, 1909); Lebrun, *Naissances;* Werner, *Mother;* Brownlow, *Memoranda;* Ryan, *Infanticide*, Langer, "Checks," and an enormous bibliography Langer has to support this article, but which is only in mimeograph form, although it is partially reproduced in his article "Infanticide: A Historical Survey," *History of Childhood Quarterly: The Journal of Psychohistory*, 1 (1974), 353-65.

141. C. H. Rolph, "A Backward Glance at the Age of 'Obscenity,' " *Encounter*, 32 (June, 1969), 23.

142. Louis Adamic, *Cradle of Life: The Story of One Man's Beginnings* (New York, 1936), pp. 11, 45, 48.

143. Royden Keith Yerkes, *Sacrifice in Greek and Roman Religions and Early Judaism* (New York, 1952), p. 34; Ernest Jones, *Essays in Applied Psycho-Analysis*, vol. 2 (New York, 1964), pp. 22-109; Gorman, *Nurse*, p. 17.

144. J. K. Campbell, *Honour, Family and Patronage* (Oxford, 1964), p. 154.

145. Walton B. McDaniel, *Conception, Birth and Infancy in Ancient Rome and Modern Italy* (Coconut Grove, Florida, 1948), p. 32; J. Stuart Hay, *The Amazing Emperor Heliogabalus* (London, 1911), p. 230; Pelper, *Chronik*, p. 95; *Juvenal and Persius*, G. G. Ramsay, trans. (Cambridge, Massachusetts, 1965), pp. 249, 337; Barberino, *Reggimento*, p. 188; Raphael Patai, *The Hebrew Goddess* (New York, 1967), p. 210; Alan Macfarlane, *Witchcraft in Tudor and Stuart England* (New York, 1970), p. 163; Hole, *English Home-Life*, p. 41; children have been associated with the iconography of death since antiquity.

146. Epictetus, *Discourses*, vol. 2, p. 213.

147. Iris Origo, *The Merchant of Prato* (London, 1957), p. 163.

148. Ewald M. Plass, comp., *What Luther Says: An Anthology*, 2 vols. (St. Louis, 1959), p. 145.

149. H. C. Barnard, ed., *Fenelon On Education* (Cambridge, 1966), p. 63.

150. Edward Wagenknecht, *When I Was a Child* (New York, 1946), p. 5.

151. Origo, *Leopardi*, p. 16.

152. Margaret Deanesly, *A History of Early Medieval Europe* (London, 1956), p. 23; Robert Pemell, *De Morbis Puerorum, or, A Treatise of the Diseases of Children* . . . (London, 1653), p. 8, a practice reminding one of the Japanese

practice of burning children's skin with moxa, which is still used for health as well as disciplinary purposes; see Edward Norbeck and Margaret Norbeck, "Child Training in a Japanese Fishing Community," in Douglas C. Haring, ed., *Personal Character and Cultural Milieu* (Syracuse, 1956), pp. 651-73.

153. Hunt, *Parents and Children,* p. 114; Robert Cleaver, *A godlie Form of householde government . . .* (New York, 1598), p. 253; Hamilton, *Female Physician,* p. 280.

154. See bibliography in Abt-Garrison, *History of Pediatrics,* p. 69.

155. Payne, *Child,* pp. 242-3.

156. Graham, *Children,* p. 110.

157. Nancy Lyman Roelker, *Queen of Navarre: Jeanne d'Albret* (Cambridge, Massachusetts, 1969), p. 101.

158. Ruhrah, *Pediatrics,* p. 216; Bayne-Powell, *English Child,* p. 165; William Buchan, *Advice to Mothers* (Philadelphia, 1804), p. 186; *The Mother's Magazine,* 1 (1833), 41; Paxton Hibben, *Henry Ward Beecher: An American Portrait* (New York, 1927), p. 28.

159. James Nelson, *An Essay on the Government of Children* (Dublin, 1763), p. 100; Still, *History of Paediatrics,* p. 391.

160. W. Preyer, *Mental Development in the Child* (New York, 1907), p. 41; Thomas Phaire, *The Boke of Chyldren* (Edinburgh, 1965), p. 28; Pemell, *De Morbis,* p. 23; Most, *Mensch,* p. 76; Dr. Heinrich Rauscher, "Volkskunde des Waldviertels," *Das Waldviertel,* 3 Band (Volkskunde), Verlag Zeitschrift "Deutsches Vaterland," (Vienna, n.d.), 1-116.

161. Buchan, *Advice,* p. 192; Hamilton, *Female Physician,* p. 271.

162. Scevole de St. Marthe, *Paedotrophia; or The Art of Nursing and Rearing Children,* H. W. Tytler, trans. (London, 1797), p. 63; John Floyer, *The History of Cold-Bathing,* Sixth ed. (London, 1732); William Buchan, *Domestic Medicine,* revised by Samuel Griffitts (Philadelphia, 1809), p. 31; Ruhrah, *Pediatrics,* p. 97; John Jones, M.D., *The arts and science of preserving bodie and soule in healthe* (1579), Univ. Microfilms, 14724, p. 32; Alice Morse Earle, *Customs and Fashions in Old New England* (Detroit, 1968), orig. published 1893, p. 2; *The Common Errors in the Education of Children and Their Consequences* (London, 1744), p. 10; William Thomson, *Memoirs of the Life and Gallant Exploits of the Old Highlander Serjeant Donald Macleod* (London, 1933), p. 9; Morton Schatzman, *Soul Murder: Persecution in the Family* (New York, 1973), p. 41; Hitchcock, *Memoirs,* p. 271.

163. Elizabeth Grant Smith, *Memoirs of a Highland Lady* (London, 1898), p. 49.

164. Aristotle, *Politics,* H. Rackham, trans. (Cambridge, Massachusetts, 1967), p. 627; Robert M. Green, trans., *A Translation of Galen's 'Hygiene' (De Sanitate Tuenda)* (Springfield, Illinois, 1951), p. 33; Peiper, *Chronik,* p. 81.

165. Horace, *Satires, Epistles, Ars Poetica,* H. Rushton Fairclough, trans. (Cambridge, Massachusetts, 1961), p. 177; Floyer, *Cold-Bathing;* Jean Jacques Rousseau, *Emile,* Barbara Foxley, trans. (London, 1911), p. 27; Earle, *Child Life,* p. 25; Richter, *Levana,* p. 140; Dorothy Canfield Fisher, *Mothers and Children* (New York, 1914), p. 113; Marian Harland, *Common Sense in the Nursery* (New York, 1885), p. 13; Earle, *Customs,* p. 24; Mary W. Montagu, *The Letters and Works of Lady Mary Wortley Montagu,* vol. 1 (London, 1861), p. 209; Nelson, *Essay,* p. 93.

166. Isaac Deutscher, *Lenin's Childhood* (London, 1970), p. 10; Yvonne Kapp, *Eleanor Marx, vol. 1—Family Life* (London, 1972), p. 41; John Ashton, *Social Life in the Reign of Queen Anne* (Detroit, 1968), p. 3.

167. Buchan, *Domestic,* p. 8.

168. Robert Frances Harper, trans., *The Code of Hammurabi King of Babylon*

about 2250 B.C. (Chicago, 1904), p. 41; Payne, *Child,* pp. 217, 279-91; Bossard, *Sociology,* pp. 607-8; Aubrey Gwynn, *Roman Education: From Cicero to Quintillian* (Oxford, 1926), p. 13; Fustel de Coulanges, *The Ancient City* (Garden City, New York, n.d.), pp. 92, 315.

169. Harrison, *Law,* p. 73.
170. Herodas, *The Mimes and Fragments* (Cambridge, 1966), p. 117.
171. Thrupp, *Anglo-Saxon Home,* p. 11; Joyce, *History,* pp. 164-5; William Andrews, *Bygone England: Social Studies in Its Historic Byways and Highways* (London, 1892), p. 70.
172. John T. McNeill and Helena M. Gamer, *Medieval Handbooks of Penance* (New York, 1938), p. 211; a late American child sale auction is described in Grace Abbott, *The Child and the State,* vol. 2 (Chicago, 1938), p. 4.
173. Georges Contenau, *Everyday Life in Babylon and Assyria* (New York, 1966), p. 18.
174. Sidney Painter, *William Marshall: Knight-Errant, Baron, and Regent of England* (Baltimore, 1933), p. 16.
175. *Ibid.,* p. 14; Graham, *Children,* p. 32.
176. Joyce, *History,* vol. 1, pp. 164-5; vol. 2, pp. 14-19.
177. Marjorie Rowling, *Everyday Life in Medieval Times* (New York, 1968), p. 138; Furnivall, *Meals and Manners,* p. xiv; Kenneth Charlton, *Education in Renaissance England* (London, 1965), p. 17; Macfarlane, *Family Life,* p. 207; John Gage, *Life in Italy at the Time of the Medici* (London, 1968), p. 70.
178. O. Jocelyn Dunlop, *English Apprenticeship and Child Labour* (London, 1912); M. Dorothy George, *London Life in the Eighteenth Century* (New York, 1964).
179. Augustus J. C. Hare, *The Story of My Life,* vol. 1 (London, 1896), p. 51.
180. Betsy Rodgers, *Georgian Chronicle* (London, 1958), p. 67.
181. Harper, *Code of Hammurabi;* Winter, *Life and Letters;* I. G. Wickes, "A History of Infant Feeding," *Archives of Disease in Childhood,* 28 (1953), p. 340; Gorman, *Nurse;* A Hymanson, "A Short Review of the History of Infant Feeding," *Archives of Pediatrics,* 51 (1934), 2.
182. Green, *Galen's Hygiene,* p. 24; Foote, "Infant Hygiene," p. 180; Soranus, *Gynecology,* p. 89; Jacopo Sadoleto, *Sadoleto On Education* (London, 1916), p. 23; Horkan, *Educational Theories,* p. 31; John Jones, *The art and science of preserving bodie and soule in healthe* (London, 1579), p. 8, Juan de Mariana, *The King and the Education of the King* (Washington, D.C., 1948), p. 189; Craig R. Thompson, trans., *The Colloquies of Erasmus* (Chicago, 1965), p. 282; St. Marthe, *Paedotrophia,* p. 10; Most, *Mensch,* p. 89; John Knodel and Etienne Van de Walle, "Breast Feeding, Fertility and Infant Mortality: An Analysis of Some Early German Data," *Population Studies* 21 (1967), pp. 116-20.
183. Foote, "Infant Hygiene," p. 182.
184. Clement of Alexandria, *The Instructor,* Ante-Nicene Christian Library, vol. 4 (Edinburgh, 1867), p. 141; Aulus Gellius, *The Attic Nights of Aulus Gellius,* vol. 2 (Cambridge, Massachusetts, 1968), p. 357; Clement of Alexandria, *Christ the Educator* (New York, 1954), p. 38.
185. Aulus Gellius, *Attic,* p. 361.
186. Morelli, *Riccordi,* pp. 144, 452.
187. James O. Halliwell, ed., *The Autobiography and Correspondence of Sir Simonds D'Ewes* (London, 1845), p. 108; see also William Bray, ed., *The Diary of John Evelyn,* vol. 1 (London, 1952), pp. 330, 386; Henry Morley, *Jerome Cardan: The Life of Girolamo Cardano of Milan, Physician,* 2 vols. (London, 1854), p. 203.

188. Guillimeau, *Nursing,* p. 3.
189. Wickes, "Infant Feeding," p. 235.
190. Hitchcock, *Memoirs,* pp. 19, 81; Wickes, "Infant Feeding," p. 239; Bayne-Powell, *English Child,* p. 168; Barbara Winchester, *Tudor Family Portrait* (London, 1955), p. 106; Taylor, *Angel-Makers,* p. 328; Clifford Stetson Parker, *The Defense of the Child by French Novelists* (Menasha, Wisconsin, 1925), pp. 4-7; William Hickey, *Memoirs of William Hickey* (London, 1913), p. 4; Jacques Levron, *Daily Life at Versailles in the Seventeenth and Eighteenth Centuries,* Elxiane Engel, trans. (London, 1968), p. 131; T. G. H. Drake, "The Wet Nurse in the Eighteenth Century," *Bulletin of the History of Medicine,* 8 (1940), 934-48; Luigi Tansillo, *The Nurse, A Poem,* William Roscoe, trans. (Liverpool, 1804), p. 4; Marmontel, *Autobiography,* vol. 4 (London, 1829), p. 123; Th. Bentzon, "About French Children," *Century Magazine,* 52 (1896), 809; Most, *Mensch,* pp. 89-112; John M. S. Allison, ed., *Concerning the Education of a Prince: Correspondence of the Princess of Nassau-Saarbruck 13 June-15 November, 1758* (New Haven, 1941), p. 26; Mrs. Alfred Sidgwick, *Home Life in Germany* (Chatauqua, New York, 1912), p. 8.
191. Lucy Hutchinson, *Memoirs of Colonel Hutchinson* (London, 1968), p. 13-15; Macfarlane, *Family Life,* p. 87; Lawrence Stone, *The Crisis of the Aristocracy: 1558-1641* (Oxford, 1965), p. 593; Kenneth B. Murdock, *The Sun at Noon* (New York, 1939), p. 14; Marjorie H. Nicolson, ed., *Conway Letters* (New Haven, 1930), p. 10; Countess Elizabeth Clinton, *The Countesse of Lincolness Nurserie* (Oxford, 1622).
192. Wickes, "Infant Feeding," p. 235; Drake, "Wet Nurse," p. 940.
193. Hymanson, "Review," p. 4; Soranus, *Gynecology,* p. 118; William H. Stahl, trans., *Macrobius: Commentary on the Dream of Scipio* (New York, 1952), p. 114; Barberino, *Reggimento,* p. 192; Ruhrah, *Pediatrics,* p. 84; Pearson, *Elizabethans,* p. 87; Macfarlane, *Family Life,* p. 87; Euch Roesslin, *The byrth of mankynde* (London, 1540), p. 30; Winchester, *Tudor,* p. 106; MacFarlane, *Family Life,* p. 87; Still, *History of Paediatrics,* p. 163; Jones, *Arts,* p. 33; Soulié, *Héroard,* p. 55; John Evelyn, *The Diary and Correspondence of John Evelyn,* ed., William Bray, n.d., p. 3; Macfarlane, *Family Life,* p. 87; John Peckey, *A General Treatise of the Diseases of Infants and Children* (London, 1697), p. 11; Nelson, *Essay,* p. 20; Nicholas Culpepper, *A Directory for Midwives: or, a guide for women in their conception, bearing, and suckling their children* (London, 1762), p. 131; Still, *History of Paediatrics,* p. 390; St. Marthe, *Paedotrophia,* p. 98; Valentine, *Fathers,* p. 93; Eliza Warren, *How I Managed My Children From Infancy to Marriage,* p. 20; Caleb Tickner, *A Guide for Mothers and Nurses in the Management of Young Children* (New York, 1839), p. 37; Robert M. Myers, ed., *The Children of Pride* (New Haven, 1972), p. 508; Knodel, "Breast Feeding," p. 118.
194. Roesslin, *Byrth,* p. 30.
195. Ryerson, "Medical Advice," p. 75.
196. Wickes, "Infant Feeding," pp. 155-8; Hymanson, "Review," pp. 4-6; Still, *History of Paediatrics,* pp. 335-6; 459; Mary Hopkirk, *Queen Over the Water* (London, 1953), p. 1305; Thompson, *Colloquies,* p. 282.
197. *The Female Instructor; or Young Woman's Companion* (Liverpool, 1811), p. 220.
198. W. O. Hassal, *How They Lived: An Anthology of Original Accounts Written Before 1485* (Oxford, 1962), p. 105.
199. Cyril P. Bryan, *The Papyrus Ebers* (New York, 1931), p. 162; Still, *History of Paediatrics* (London, 1931), p. 466; Douglass, *Summary,* p. 346;

Rauscher, "Volkskunde," p. 44; John W. Dodds, *The Age of Paradox: A Biography of England 1841-1851* (New York, 1952), p. 157; Abt-Garrison, *History of Pediatrics*, p. 11; John B. Beck, "The effects of opium on the infant subject," *Journal of Medicine*, (New York, 1844); Tickner, *Guide*, p. 115; *Friendly Letter to Parents and Heads of Families Particularly Those Residing in the Country Towns and Villages in America* (Boston, 1828), p. 10; Buchan, *Domestic*, p. 17; Pinchbeck, *Children*, p. 301.

200. John Spargo, *The Bitter Cry of the Children* (Chicago, 1968), Xenophon, *Minor Writings*, E. C. Marchant, trans. (London, 1925), p. 37; Hopkirk, *Queen*, pp. 130-5; Plutarch, *Moralia*, p. 433; St. Basil, *Ascetical Works* (New York, 1950), p. 266; Gage, *Life in Italy*, p. 109; St. Jerome, *The Select Letters of St. Jerome*, F. A. Wright, trans. (Cambridge, Massachusetts, 1933), pp. 357-61; Thomas Platter, *The Autobiography of Thomas Platter: A Schoolmaster of the Sixteenth Century*, Elizabeth A. McCoul Finn, trans. (London, 1847), p. 8; Craig, "Vincent of Beauvais," p. 379; Roesslin, *Byrth*, p. 17; Jones, *Arte*, p. 40; Taine, *Ancient Regime*, p. 130; D. B. Horn and Mary Ranson, eds., *English Historical Documents, vol. 10, 1714-1783* (New York, 1957), p. 561; Lochhead, *First Ten Years*, p. 34; Eli Forbes, *A Family Book* (Salem, 1801), pp. 240-1; Leontine Young, *Wednesday's Children; A Study of Child Neglect and Abuse* (New York, 1964), p. 9.

201. St. Augustine, *Confessions* (New York, 1963); Richard Baxter, *The Autobiography of Richard Baxter* (London, 1931), p. 5; Augustine previously mentioned having to steal food from the table, p 18.

202. Hassall, *How They Lived*, p. 184; Benedict, "Child Rearing," p. 345; Geoffrey Gorer and John Rickman, *The People of Great Russia: A Psychological Study*, p. 98; Peckey, *Treatise*, p. 6; Ruhrah, *Pediatrics*, p. 219; Green, *Galen's Hygiene*, p. 22; François Mauriceau, *The Diseases of Women With Child, and in Child-Bed*, Hugh Chamberlin, trans. (London, 1736), p. 309.

203. William P. Dewees, *A Treatise on the Physical and Medical Treatment of Children* (Philadelphia, 1826), p. 4; for further bibliography on swaddling, see Wayne Dennis, "Infant Reactions to Restraint: an Evaluation of Watson's Theory," *Transactions New York Academy of Science*, Ser. 2, vol. 2 (1940); Erik H. Erikson, *Childhood and Society* (New York, 1950); Lotte Danziger and Liselotte Frankl, "Zum Problem der Functions-reifung," *A. fur Kinderforschung*, 43 (1943); Boyer, "Problems," p. 225; Margaret Mead, "The Swaddling Hypothesis: Its Reception," *American Anthropologist*, 56 (1954); Phyllis Greenacre, "Infant Reactions to Restraint," in Clyde Kluckholm and Henry A. Murray, eds., *Personality in Nature, Society and Culture*, 2nd ed. (New York, 1953), pp. 513-14; Charles Hudson, "Isometric Advantages of the Cradle Board: A Hypothesis," *American Anthropologist*, 68 (1966), pp. 470-4.

204. Hester Chapone, *Chapone on the Improvement of the Mind* (Philadelphia, 1830), p. 200.

205. Earle L. Lipton, Alfred Steinschneider, and Julius B. Richmond, "Swaddling, A Child Care Practice: Historical Cultural and Experimental Observations," *Pediatrics*, Supplement, 35, part 2 (March, 1965), 521-67.

206. Turner Wilcox, *Five Centuries of the American Costume* (New York, 1963), p. 17; Rousseau, *Emile*, p. 11; Christian A. Struve, *A Familiar View of the Domestic Education of Children* (London, 1802), p. 296.

207. *Hippocrates*, trans. W. H. S. Jones (London, 1923), p. 125; Steffen Wenig, *The Woman in Egyptian Art* (New York, 1969), p. 47; Erich Neumann, *The Great Mother: An Analysis of the Archetype* (New York, 1963), p. 32.

208. James Logan, *The Scotish Gael; or, Celtic Manners, As Preserved Among the*

Highlanders (Hartford, 1851), p. 81; Thompson, *Memoirs*, p. 8; Marjorie Plant, *The Domestic Life of Scotland in the Eighteenth Century* (London, 1952), p. 6.

209. Soranus, *Gynecology*, p. 114; Plato, *The Laws* (Cambridge, Massachusetts, 1926), p. 7.
210. Dorothy Hartley, *Mediaeval Costume and Life* (London, 1931), pp. 117-19.
211. Cunnington, *Children's Costume*, pp. 35, 53-69; Macfarlane, *Family Life*, p. 90; Guillimeau, *Nursing*, p. 23; Lipton, "Swaddling," p. 527; Hunt, *Parents and Children*, p. 127; Peckey, *Treatise*, p. 6; M. St. Clare Byrne, ed., *The Elizabethan Home Discovered in Two Dialogues by Claudius Hollyband and Peter Erondell* (London, 1925), p. 77. It is interesting to note that over a century before Candogan's campaign against swaddling, mothers began to reduce the age of unbinding, and that early doctors like Glisson were opposed to this change, tending to confirm its psychogenic origin in the family itself.
212. Cunnington, *Children's Costume*, pp. 68-69; Magdelen King-Hall, *The Story of the Nursery* (London, 1958), pp. 83, 129; Chapone, *Improvement*, p. 199; St. Marthe, *Paedotrophia*, p. 67; Robert Sunley, "Early Nineteenth-Century Literature on Child Rearing," in *Childhood in Contemporary Cultures*, Margaret Mead and Martha Wolfenstein, eds. (Chicago, 1955), p. 155; Kuhn, *Mother's Role*, p. 141; Wilcox, *Five Centuries;* Alice M. Earle, *Two Centuries of Costume in America*, vol. 1 (New York, 1903), p. 311; Nelson, *Essay*, p. 99; Lipton, "Swaddling," pp. 529-32; Culpepper, *Directory*, p. 305; Hamilton, *Female Physician*, p. 262; Morwenna Rendle-Short and John Rendle-Short, *The Father of Child Care: Life of William Cadogan [1711-1797)* (Bristol, 1966), p. 20; Caulfield, *Infant Welfare*, p. 108; Ryerson, "Medical Advice," p. 107; Bentzon, "French Children," p. 805; Most, *Mensch*, p. 76; Struve, *View*, p, 293; Sidgwick, *Home Life*, p. 8; Peiper, *Chronik*, p. 666.
213. Cunnington, *Children's Costume*, pp. 70-128; Tom Hastie, *Home Life*, p. 33; Preyer, *Mind*, p. 273; Earle, *Costume*, pp. 316-17; Mary Somerville, *Personal Recollections, From Early Life to Old Age, of Mary Somerville* (London, 1873), p. 21; Aristotle, *Politics*, p. 627; Schatzman, *Soul Murder;* Earle, *Child Life*, p. 58; Burton, *Early Victorians*, p. 192; Joanna Richardson, *Princess Mathilde* (New York, 1969), p. 10; Bentzon, "French Children," p. 805; Stephanie de Genlis, *Memoirs of the Countess de Genlis*, 2 vols. (New York, 1825), p. 10; Kemble, *Records*, p. 85.
214. Xenophon, *Writings*, p. 7; Horkan, *Educational Theories*, p. 36; Earle, *Child Life*, p. 26; Nelson, *Essay*, p. 83; Ruhrah, *Pediatrics*, p. 220; Soranus, *Gynecology*, p. 116. For a similar belief, see Gregory Bateson and Margaret Mead, *Balinese Character: A Photographic Analysis*, vol. 2, Special Publications of the New York Academy of Sciences (1942).
215. T. B. L. Webster, *Everyday Life in Classical Athens* (London, 1969), p. 46; J. T. Muckle, trans., *The Story of Abelard's Adversities: Historia Calamitatum* (Toronto, 1954), p. 30; Roland H. Bainston, *Women of the Reformation in Germany and Italy* (Minneapolis, 1971), p. 36; Pierre Belon, *Les Observations, de plusieurs singularitez et choses memorables trouvées en Grèce, Judée, Egypte, Arabie, et autres pays estranges* (Antwerp, 1555), pp. 317-18; Phaire, *Boke*, p. 53; Pemell, *De Morbis*, p. 55; Peckey, *Treatise*, p. 146; Elizabeth Wirth Marvick, "Héroard and Louis XIII," *Journal of Interdisciplinary History*, in press; Guillimeau, *Nursing*, p. 80; Ruhrah, *Pediatrics*, p. 61; James Benignus Bossuet, *An Account of the Education of the Dauphine, In a Letter to Pope Innocent XI* (Glasgow, 1743), p. 34.
216. Thass-Thienemann, *Subconscious*, p. 59.

217. Hunt, *Parents and Children*, p. 144. Hunt's section on purges is his most perceptive.
218. *Ibid.*, pp. 144-5.
219. Nelson, *Essay*, p. 107; Chapone, *Improvement*, p. 200; Ryerson, "Medical Advice," p. 99.
220. Stephen Kern, "Did Freud Discover Childhood Sexuality?", *History of Childhood Quarterly: The Journal of Psychohistory*, 1 (Summer, 1973), p. 130; Preyer, *Mental Development*, p. 64; Sunley, "Literature," p. 157.
221. Josephine Klein, *Samples From English Cultures*, vol. 2, *Child-rearing Practices* (London, 1965), pp. 449-52; David Rodnick, *Post War Germany: An Anthropologist's Account* (New Haven, 1948), p. 18; Robert R. Sears, et al., *Patterns of Child Rearing* (New York, 1957), p. 109; Miller, *Changing American Parent*, pp. 219-20.
222. Plutarch, "The Education of Children," in Moses Hadas, trans., *Plutarch: Selected Essays on Love, the Family, and the Good Life* (New York, 1957), p. 113; F. J. Furnivall, ed., *Queen Elizabethes Achademy*, Early English Text Society Extra Series no. 8 (London, 1869), p. 1; William Harrison Woodward, *Studies in Education During the Age of the Renaissance 1400-1600* (Cambridge, Massachusetts, 1924), p. 171.
223. Michel de Montaigne, *The Essays of Michel de Montaigne*, trans., George B. Ives (New York, 1946), pp. 234, 516; Donald M. Frame, *Montaigne: A Biography* (New York, 1965), pp. 38-40, 95.
224. Peiper, *Chronik*, pp. 302-345.
225. Preserved Smith, *A History of Modern Culture*, vol. 2 (New York, 1934). p. 423.
226. Morris Bishop, trans. *Letters From Petrarch* (Bloomington, Ind., 1966), p. 149; Charles Norris Cochrane, *Christianity and Classical Culture* (London, 1940), p. 35; James Turner, "The Visual Realism of Comenius," *History of Education*, 1 (June, 1972), p. 132; John Amos Comenius, *The School of Infancy* (Chapel Hill, N.C., 1956), p. 102; Roger DeGuimps, *Pestalozzi: His Life and Work* (New York, 1897), p. 161; Christian Bec, *Les marchands écrivains: affaires et humanisme à Florence 1375-1434* (Paris, 1967), pp. 288-97; Renée Neu Watkins, trans., *The Family in Renaissance Florence* (Columbia, S.C., 1969), p. 66.
227. Christina Hole, *The English Housewife in the Seventeenth Century* (London, 1953), p. 149; Editha and Richard Sterba, *Beethoven and His Nephew* (New York, 1971), p. 89.
228. Soulié, *Héroard*, pp. 44, 203, 284, 436; Hunt, *Parents and Children*, pp. 133ff.
229. Giovanni Dominici, *On The Education of Children*, Arthur B. Cote, trans. (Washington, D.C., 1927), p. 48; Rousseau, *Emile*, p. 15; Sangster, *Pity*, p. 77.
230. Thrupp, *Anglo-Saxon Home*, p. 98; Furnivall, *Meals and Manners*, p. vi; Roger Ascham, *The Scolemaster* (New York, 1967), p. 34; H. D. Traill and J. S. Mann, *Social England* (New York, 1909), p. 239; Sophocles, *Oedipus The King*: 808.
231. Herodas, *Mimes*, p. 117; Adolf Erman, *The Literature of the Ancient Egyptians* (London, 1927), pp. 189-91; Peiper, *Chronik*, p. 17; Plutarch, *Moralia*, p. 145; Plutarch, *The Lives of the Noble Grecians and Romans*, John Dryden, trans. (New York, n.d.), p. 64; Galen, *On the Passions and Errors of the Soul*, Paul W. Harkins, trans., Ohio State University Press p. 56.

232. Thrupp, *Anglo-Saxon Home*, p. 100.
233. Peiper, *Chronik*, p. 309.
234. Eadmer, R. W. Southern, trans. *The Life of St. Anselm—Archbishop of Canterbury* (Oxford, 1962), p. 38.
235. Batty, *Christian*, pp. 14-26; Charron, *Wisdom*, pp. 1334-9; Powell, *Domestic Relations*, passim; John F. Benton, ed., *Self and Society in Medieval France: The Memoirs of Abbot Guibert of Nogent* (New York, 1970), pp. 212-41; Luella Cole, *A History of Education: Socrates to Montessori* (New York, 1950), p. 209; Comenius, *School*, p. 102; Watkins, *Family*, p. 66.
236. Bossuet, *Account*, pp. 56-7; Henry H. Meyer, *Child Nature and Nurture According to Nicolaus Ludwig von Zinzindorf* (New York, 1928), p. 105; Bedford, *English Children*, p. 238; King-Hall, *The Story of the Nursery*, pp. 83-11; John Witherspoon, *The Works of John Witherspoon, D.D.* Vol. 8 (Edinburgh, 1805), p. 178; Rev. Bishop Fleetwood, *Six Useful Discourses on the Relative Duties of Parents and Children* (London, 1749).
237. See the final chapter in this book for bibliography on England and France; see Lyman Cobb, *The Evil Tendencies of Corporal Punishment as a Means of Moral Discipline in Families and Schools* (New York, 1847), and Miller, *Changing American Parent*, pp. 13-14, for American Conditions; see Walter Havernick, *Schläge als Strafe* (Hamburg, 1964), for Germany today.
238. Smith, *Memoirs*, p. 49; Richard Heath, *Edgar Quinet: His Early Life and Writings* (London, 1881), p. 3; Lord Lindsay, *Lives of the Lindsays: or, a Memoir of the Houses of Crawford and Barcarros*, vol. 2 (London, 1849), p. 307; L. H. Butterfield, ed., *Letters of Benjamin Rush, vol. 1: 1761-1792* (Princeton, 1951), p. 511; Bentzon, "French Children," p. 811; Margaret Blundell, *Cavalier: Letters of William Blundell to his Friends, 1620-1698* (London, 1933), p. 46.
239. For bibliographies, see Hans Licht, *Sexual Life in Ancient Greece* (New York, 1963); Robert Flaceliere, *Love in Ancient Greece*, James Cleugh, trans. (London, 1960); Pierre Grimal, *Love in Ancient Rome*, Arthur Train, Jr., trans. (New York, 1967); J. Z. Eglinton, *Greek Love* (New York, 1964); Otto Kiefer, *Sexual Life in Ancient Rome* (New York, 1962); Arno Karlen, *Sexuality and Homosexuality: A New View* (New York, 1971); Vanggaard, *Phallos;* Wainwright Churchill, *Homosexual Behavior Among Males: A Cross-Cultural and Cross-Species Investigation* (New York, 1967).
240. Lutz, "Rufus," p. 103.
241. Aristotle, *Politics*, p. 81.
242. Grimal, *Love*, p. 106; Karlen, *Sexuality*, p. 33; Xenophon, *Writings*, p. 149.
243. Quintilian, *Institutio Oratoria*, H. E. Butler, trans. (London, 1921), p. 61; Karlen, *Sexuality*, pp. 34-5; Lacey, *Family*, p. 157.
244. Aeschines, *The Speeches of Aeschines*, Charles Darwin Adams, trans. (London, 1919), pp. 9-10.
245. *Ibid.*, p. 136.
246. Petronius, *The Satyricon and The Fragments* (Baltimore, 1965), p. 43.
247. Aristotle, *The Nicomachean Ethics* (Cambridge, 1947), p. 403; Quintilian, *Institutio*, p. 43; Ove Brusendorf and Paul Henningsen, *A History of Eroticism* (New York, 1963), plate 4.
248. Louis M. Epstein, *Sex Laws and Customs in Judaism* (New York, 1948), p. 136.
249. Plutarch, "Education," p. 118.
250. Suetonius, *Caesars*, p. 148; Tacitus, *The Annals of Tacitus* (New York, 1966), p. 188.
251. Martial, *Epigrams*, vol. 2, Walter C. A. Kerr, trans. (Cambridge, Massachusetts, 1968), p. 255; Aristotle, *Historia Animalium*, trans. R. Cresswell

(London, 1862), p. 180.
252. Vanggaard, *Phallos,* pp. 25, 27, 43; Karlen, *Sexuality,* pp. 33-34; Eglinton, *Greek Love,* p. 287.
253. Joyce McDougall, "Primal Scene and Sexual Perversion," *International Journal of Psycho-Analysis,* 53 (1972), p. 378.
254. Hans Licht, *Sexual Life in Ancient Greece* (New York, 1963), p. 497; Peter Tomkins, *The Eunuch and the Virgin* (New York, 1962), pp. 17-30; Vanggaard, *Phallos,* p. 59; Martial, *Epigrams,* pp. 75, 144.
255. Paulus Aegineta, *Aegeneta,* pp. 379-81.
256. Martial, *Epigrams,* p. 367; St. Jerome, *Letters,* p. 363; Tomkins, *Eunuch,* pp. 28-30; Geoffrey Keynes, ed., *The Apologie and Treatise of Ambroise Paré* (London, 1951), p. 102.
257. Clement of Alexandria, *Christ,* p. 17.
258. Origen, "Commentary on Mathew," *The Ante-Nicene Fathers,* vol. 9, Allan Menzies, ed. (New York 1925), p. 484.
259. Benton, *Self,* pp. 14, 35.
260. Craig, "Vincent of Beauvais," p. 303; Cleaver, *Godlie,* pp. 326-7; Dominici, *Education,* p. 41.
261. *Ibid.*
262. Ariès, *Centuries of Childhood,* pp. 107-8; Johannes Butzbach, *The Autobiography of Johannes Butzbach: A Wandering Scholar of the Fifteenth Century* (Ann Arbor, 1933), p. 2; Horkan, *Educational Theories,* p. 118; Jones, *Arts,* p. 59; James Cleland, *The Instruction of a Young Nobleman* (Oxford, 1612), p. 20; Sir Thomas Elyot, *The Book Named the Governor* (London, 1962), p. 16; Erwin Panofsky, *Studies in Iconology: Humanistic Themes in the Art of the Renaissance* (New York, 1972), pp. 95-166; Leo Steinberg, "The Metaphors of Love and Birth in Michelangelo's Pietàs," *Studies in Erotic Art,* Theodore Bowie and Cornelia V. Christenson, eds. (New York, 1970), pp. 231-339; Josef Kunstmann, *The Transformation of Eros* (London, 1964), pp. 21-23.
263. Whiting, *Child-Training,* p. 79.
264. Gabriel Falloppius, "De decoraturie trachtaties," cap. 9, *Opera Omnia,* 2 vols. (Frankfurt, 1600), pp. 336-37; Soranus, *Gynecology,* p. 107.
265. Michael Edward Goodich, "The Dimensions of Thirteenth Century Sainthood," Ph.D. dissertation, Columbia University, 1972, pp. 211-12; Jean-Louis Flandrin, "Mariage tardif et vie sexuelle: Discussions et hypothèses de recherche," *Annales: Economies Sociétés Civilisations* 27 (1972) 1351-78.
266. Hare, "Masturbatory Insanity," pp. 2-25; Spitz, "Authority and Masturbation," pp. 490-527; *Onania, or the Heinous Sin of Self-Pollution,* 4th ed. (London, n.d.), pp. 1-19; Simon Tissot, "L'Onanisme: Dissertation sur les maladies produites par la masturbation," (Lausanne, 1764), G. Rattray Taylor, *Sex in History* (New York, 1954), p. 223; Taylor, *Angel-Makers,* p. 327; Alex Comfort, *The Anxiety Makers: Some Curious Preoccupations of the Medical Profession* (London, 1967); Ryerson, "Medical Advice," pp. 305ff; Kern, "Freud;" pp. 117-141; L. Deslander, M.D., *A Treatise on the Diseases Produced by Onanism, masturbation, self-pollution, and other excesses,* trans. from the French (Boston, 1838); Mrs. S. M. I. Henry, *Studies in Home and Child Life* (Battle Creek, Michigan, 1897), p. 74; George B. Leonard, *The Transformation* (New York, 1972), p. 106; John Duffy, "Masturbation and Clitoridectomy: A Nineteenth Century View," *Journal of the American Medical Association,* 186 (1963), p. 246; Dr. Yellowlees, "Masturbation," *Journal of Mental Science,* 22 (1876), p. 337; J. H. Kellogg, *Plain Facts for Old and Young* (Burlington, 1881), pp. 186-497; P. C. Remondino, M.D., *History of Circumcision from the Earliest Times to the*

Present (Philadelphia, 1891), p. 272.

267. Restif de la Bretonne, *Monsieur Nicolas*, pp. 86, 88, 106; *Common Errors*, p. 22; Deslander, *Treatise*, p. 82; Andre Parreaux, *Daily Life in England in the Reign of George III*, Carola Congreve, trans. (London, 1969), pp. 125-26; Bernard Perez, *The First Three Years of Childhood* (London, 1885), p. 58; *My Secret Life*, (New York, 1966), pp. 13-15, 61; Gathorne-Hardy, *Rise and Fall*, p. 163; Henri E. Ellenberger, *The Discovery of the Unconscious* (New York, 1970), p. 299; Joseph W. Howe, *Excessive Venery, Masturbation and Continence* (New York, 1893), p. 63; C. Gasquoine Hartley, *Motherhood and the Relationships of the Sexes* (New York, 1917), p. 312; Bernis, *Memoirs*, p. 90.

268. Dr. Albert Moll, *The Sexual Life of Children* (New York, 1913), p. 219; Max Schur, *Freud: Living and Dying* (New York, 1972), pp. 120-32; Robert Fleiss, *Symbol, Dream and Psychosis* (New York, 1973), pp. 205-29.

269. Mrs. Vernon D. Broughton, ed., *Court and Private Life in the Time of Queen Charlotte: Being the Journals of Mrs. Papendiek, Assistant Keeper of the Wardrobe and Reader to Her Majesty* (London, 1887), p. 40; Morley, *Cardan*, p. 35; Origo, *Leopardi*, p. 24; Kemble, *Records*, p. 28; John Greenleaf Whittier, ed., *Child Life in Prose* (Boston, 1873), p. 277; Walter E. Houghton, *The Victorian Frame of Mind, 1830-1870* (New Haven, 1957), p. 63; Harriet Martineau, *Autobiography*, vol. 1 (Boston, 1877), p. 11; John Geninges, *The Life and Death of Mr. Edmund Geninges, Priest* (1614), p. 18; Thompson, *Religion*, p. 471.

270. Chadwick Hansen, *Witchcraft at Salem* (New York, 1970); Ronald Seth, *Children Against Witches* (London, 1969); H. C. Erik Midelfort, *Witch Hunting in Southwestern Germany* (Stanford, 1972), p. 109; Carl Holliday, *Woman's Life in Colonial Days* (Boston, 1922), p. 60; Jeffrey Burton Russell, *Witchcraft in the Middle Ages* (Ithaca, New York, 1972), p. 136; George A. Gray, *The Children's Crusade* (New York, 1972).

271. Stahl, *Macrobius*, p. 114; Julia Cartwright Ady, *Isabella D'Este: Marchioness of Mantua, 1474-1539 A Study of the Renaissance* (London, 1903), p. 186; Mary Ann Gibbs, *The Years of the Nannies* (London, 1960), p. 23; Agnes Strickland, *Lives of the Queens of England*, 6 vols. (London, 1864), p. 2; Lady Anne Clifford, *The Diary of Lady Anne Clifford* (London, 1923), p. 66; Allan McLane Hamilton, *The Intimate Life of Alexander Hamilton* (London, 1910, p. 224; Hare, *Story*, p. 54; Elizabeth Cleghorn Gaskell, *"My Diary": the early years of my daughter Marianne* (London, 1923), p. 33; Mrs. Emily Talbot, ed., *Papers on Infant Development* (Boston, 1882), p. 30; Du Maurier, *Young Du Maurier*, p. 250; Preyer, *Mind*, p. 275; James David Barber, *The Presidential Character: Predicting Performance in the White House* (Englewood Cliffs, New Jersey, 1972), p. 212; George V. N. Dearborn, *Motor-Sensory Development: Observations on the First Three Years of a Child* (Baltimore, 1910), p. 160; William B. Forbush, *The First Year in a Baby's Life* (Philadelphia, 1913), p. 11; Mary M. Shirley, *The First Two Years: A Study of Twenty-Five' Babies* (Minneapolis, 1931), p. 40. See also Sylvia Brody, *Patterns of Mothering: Maternal Influence During Infancy* (New York, 1956), p. 105; and Sidney Axelrad, "Infant Care and Personality Reconsidered," *The Psychoanalytic Study of Society*, 2 (1962), pp. 99-102, for similar retardation patterns in Albanian swaddled infants.

272. A. S. Neill, *The Free Child* (London, 1952); Paul Ritter and John Ritter, *The Free Family: A Creative Experiment in Self-Regulation for Children* (London, 1959); Michael Deakin, *The Children on the Hill* (London, 1972);

and my own book on my son, which is not yet in press.

273. Despite the single line of evolution described, the psychogenic theory of history is not uni-linear but multi-linear, for conditions outside the family also affect to some extent the course of parent-child evolution in each society. There is no claim here for reducing all other sources of historical change to the psychogenic. Rather than being an example of psychological reductionism, psychogenic theory is actually an intentional application of "methodological individualism," as described by F. A. Hayek, *The Counter-Revolution of Science* (Glencoe, Illinois, 1952); Karl R. Popper, *The Open Society and Its Enemies* (Princeton, 1950); J. W. N. Watkins, "Methodological Individualism and Non-Hempelian Ideal Types," in Leonard I. Krimerman, ed., *The Nature and Scope of Social Science* (New York, 1969), pp. 457-72. See also J. O. Wisdom, "Situational Individualism and the Emergent Group Properties," *Explanation in the Behavioral Sciences,* Robert Borger and Frank Cioffi, eds. (Cambridge, Massachusetts, 1970), pp. 271-96.

274. The quotes are from Calvin S. Hall, "Out of a Dream Came the Faucet," *Psychoanalysis and the Psychoanalytic Review,* 49 (1962).

275. See Maurice Mandelbaum, *History, Man and Reason: A Study in Nineteenth Century Thought* (Baltimore, 1971), chapter 11, for Mill's abortive attempt to invent a historical science of human nature.

CHAPTER 2

Barbarism and Religion : Late Roman and Early Medieval Childhood

RICHARD B.
LYMAN, JR.

Such are the times, then, into which your Pactula has been born. Slaughter and death are the toys of her childhood. She will know tears before laughter, sorrow before joy. Scarcely arrived on the stage of this world, soon she must exit. That the world was always like this—what else can she believe? Of the past she knows nothing; from the present she flies; she longs only for the future.

Jerome, 413 A.D.

This essay covering the patristic and early medieval ages (roughly 200 A.D.–800 A.D.) will venture the unexpected opinion that much information on childhood exists even in an apparently bleak period. While it may never be possible to construct a formal history of parent-child relations for this half-millennium, a preliminary search of materials reveals considerable data in relatively conventional historical sources. This chapter is presented as an early exploration, essentially historiographic and exemplifying in intent. It will demonstrate that material exists, and that the evidence is susceptible to familiar methods of location and analysis by historians who care to join the search for it.

"THE CAUSES CANNOT BE ASSUMED": A WORD ON METHOD

Material examined thus far suggests certain shifts in key elements of parent-child relations in this epoch. First, the range of social classes covered by our sources appears to have broadened slightly by the end of the period. With a few notable exceptions, those parents and children we know in the Roman period before Constantine are aristocratic and wealthy. By the early middle ages, we have some clues about individuals who are slightly below this group, although, as always in early records, the common folk largely escape us. Second, ideals about childhood underwent substantial change. In some measurable ways, the official and formal expectations about the treatment of children seem gentler to us after the fourth century. In literature and saints' lives, parental love becomes more important particularly from Augustine's generation forward. Third, in the area of actual behavior, it looks as if this shift in ideals had minor but practical effects. The coming of Christianity certainly did not signal the end of the "dark ages" for children, yet it may well have meant the beginning of a slightly less grim outlook.

As elsewhere in history, the influence of ideas on daily lives is informal, slow, and hard to pin down. In any event, there are important variables beyond Christianity. One of these variables is the slow decay in the West. Though greeted with resignation and a sense of doom by most pagans and not a few Christians, nevertheless the "decline and fall" can be regarded as less than a disaster for many individuals as well as the long-range hopes of humanity.[1] For example, it may have been less necessary, and even counter-productive, to expose or dispose of children (as excess or non-producing food consumers) in times of precarious life expectancy and short labor supply. The converse argument from the same evidence, however, also has some plausibility; times of severe dislocation and difficulty may have heightened individual parents' tensions and fears and caused them to seek psychological relief in projection of these concerns onto the least defended humans in their midst. Arguments based on general social conditions, asserting what parent-child relations should—or must—have been like, are therefore on a shifting substratum. A second important variable which helps explain these alleged shifts is the incorporation into the Mediterranean world of large numbers of "barbarians". Although it is exceedingly difficult, if not outright impossible, to acquire an accurate picture of these tribes before their contacts with Roman civilization, a few fragments of evidence hint at a less brutal and destructive attitude toward children than was the case with Rome. Thus, in parent-child relations, we may soon be able to begin to argue that we "have described the triumph of barbarism and religion" over the worst abuses of children in antiquity.[2]

These major variables—Christianity, difficult times, barbarians—should make us exceedingly cautious of looking to one magical matrix of causes for whatever shifts can be firmly documented. "In a word, in history, as elsewhere, the causes cannot be assumed. They are to be looked for. . . ."[3]

For one attempting to show broad patterns and continuities in social life, the sources of this period offer formidable obstacles. Owing to both the nature and condition of source materials, even the most enterprising and innovative researcher frequently comes up against dead ends. Discoveries are usually heavily based on isolated sources, and are therefore somewhat random and potentially unsystematic.[4] The choice is simple. It is to accept these limiting conditions, or to say nothing at all. To the history of childhood, therefore, the contribution of this chapter can be only to allow contrasts and comparisons with richer periods, and, by means of isolated pieces of evidence, to permit suggestions of continuities with the much fuller evidence from earlier and later periods, the classical and the high middle ages.

A number of specific methodological issues need stating as well. First of all, childhood in these ages is generally not newsworthy in its own right. Comments about children, parents, and especially infancy, are usually incidental to other topics. Second, there is rarely much precision about age; the term "child" seems to refer to anyone, depending on context and literary convention, from infancy to old age. Third, these are doubtless very violent centuries at certain times and in certain places, and one must be careful to avoid attributing rare and bestial attitudes to parents who themselves are subject to grim scenes and brutalizing events. While it may well be argued that "social conditions" do not much comfort an exposed infant, still a critical historian will want to know what conditions—physical as well as psychological—may have helped drive a parent to such an act. The interplay between public pressures and personal motives is constant and complex, and is especially difficult to measure in view of the uncertain raw material.

With few exceptions, the most traditional historical sources prove quite barren for this topic. From Tacitus to Bede, a search through dozens of histories and chronicles was disappointing. As is not unusual with classicists and medievalists, I found myself driven to a very ecumenical attitude toward all sorts of sources. This approach, however, has some inherent problems. For instance, there are long-standing and much-studied literary conventions and traditions. When Ausonius recounts a Cupid story in the fourth century, how much psychological interpretation should this standard story cycle be asked to bear?[5] How far should attitudes expressed in the poem be attributed to new psychological conditions and how much to the standard plot? Therefore, I have tried to be impressed only by frequent repetition of a single motif, by unusually vivid or protracted description, or by abnormally recurrent attention to a particular literary convention.

A similar difficulty is encountered in the study of plastic arts and paintings. It clearly is not safe to attribute infancy to all small creatures. Not infrequently they are intended to depict servants, slaves, wives, souls, demons, or angels.[6] One major artistic approach is to study scenes of the Holy Family.[7] The continuity and conventionality of themes can be appreciated by comparing a frieze of Isis suckling Horus (third century Coptic) and Mary suckling Jesus (tombstone from Fayum, Egypt, fifth or sixth century).[8] In both, the mother is staring outward, cradling the infant in her left hand, offering a breast with the right. Neither infant is cuddled by the mother, nor is either showing much interest in the breast. Horus seems considerably happier than Jesus. What conclusions may be drawn from this comparison? Perhaps few, except that artistic styles seem to be interchangeable between religions, especially in the same geographic region. The technical difficulties of pursuing this line of inquiry are further revealed by considering a Virgin and Child from the Book of Kells (eighth century?).[9] The face of the Virgin is still looking forward, out past the right shoulder of the viewer. The Virgin's arms are now more substantially enfolding the child, who is reaching perhaps toward a well-covered breast. The face of the mother is positively oriental, and highly stylized. The infant, however, has a long pointed nose, perhaps a cleft chin, and long wavy red hair. Obviously, there are limits to the conclusions which can be drawn from these observations, and in their relative isolation they are analogous to a handful of pottery sherds or individual coins. More promising is an illustration for Psalm 50, from the Utrecht Psalter (Reims, ca. 820).[10] This illustration seems rather clearly to show a naked child held by one adult, buttocks up, for another who will administer a spanking. The two adults are turned to hear a shepherd, speaking verse 17 (". . . you hate discipline") or perhaps 21 (". . . I will correct you"). Another illustration from this same psalter, this one for Psalm 88, clearly shows naked infants being whipped by angels.[11]

Another illustration of the pitfalls awaiting impetuous historians of childhood in the early middle ages is in the area of hagiography. This much studied field has enabled historians to reconstruct with tolerable accuracy the lives and careers of many individual saints, and to strip away the accretions of conventional holiness. The historian of childhood hoping to find a rich lode of biographical materials will instead encounter idealized patterns of birth, infancy, and youth. These are not useless in themselves, but are less revealing than standard biographies in modern times. Here are three examples of infancy accounts, which suggest some of the recurrent patterns and themes.

> Martin, then, was born at the town of Sabaria, in Pannonia, but was brought up in Italy, at Pavia. His parents were somewhat above the lowest grade in worldly dignity, but were pagans. His father had begun life as a common soldier and rose to be a military tribune.[12]

Parentage and place are important, as one would expect in any essentially aristocratic literature. Another theme, that of magical portent and powers, shows in this passage:

> Ambrose, then, was born when his father Ambrose held the office of Prefect of Gaul. When he was a baby, he was sleeping in his cradle with his mouth open, in the courtyard of the governor's palace, when suddenly a swarm of bees came and so covered his face and mouth that they kept on going in and out of his mouth in continuous succession. His father was taking a walk near by, with his mother and their daughter, and told the girl who was employed to suckle the babe not to drive the bees away, for he was afraid of their injuring him; and with a father's solicitude he waited to see how the marvel would end. And presently the bees flew off and soared to such a height in the air that it was impossible for human eyes to see them. It frightened his father. "If that little one lives," he said, "he will become something very big." ... That swarm of bees was generating for us the honeycombs of his writings...[13]

The willingness both to distort a possibly natural event and to allegorize freely are characteristic of saints' lives. But one also should notice the hired wet-nurse, as well as the proximity of the parents to the child. Between the early fifth century, when this life was written, and the early eighth, when the life of Saint Guthlac was composed, there is little structural change. In this later biography, parentage and good stock are still important, as is the "maidenly modesty" of the mother. However, there is now more interest in physical details of birth and infancy. Substantial attention is paid to the process of birth itself, with emphasis on "the violent pains of labor" and "suffering". The moment of birth is marked by the appearance of a miraculous "gold-red" hand reaching down from the clouds toward a cross before the natal house. After eight days, the infant is brought to baptism. As he grows, he displays a set of qualities which may fairly be taken as an early medieval ideal:

> And as the time of his infancy passed and he tried to speak in his childish way, he never was troublesome to his parents or nurses or to the bands of children of his own age. He did not imitate the impudence of the children nor the nonsensical chatter of the matrons, nor the empty tales of the common people, nor the foolish shouts of the rustics, nor the lying triflings of flatterers

nor the different cries of the various kinds of birds as children of
that age are wont to do; but possessing remarkable wisdom, he
showed a cheerful face, a pure mind, a gentle spirit, a frank
countenance; he was dutiful to his parents, obedient to his elders,
affectionate to his foster brothers and sisters, leading none astray,
chiding none, causing none to stumble, recompensing no man
evil for evil, always even-tempered.[14]

Having considered these methodological issues, I shall next proceed
somewhat chronologically, with reviews of issues and materials in the
Roman, patristic, and early medieval periods.

"TO RESTRAIN THE HANDS OF PARENTS":
A ROMAN PRELUDE

Although the history of childhood in Roman times remains to be
written, it is clear that much material is available to interested historians.[15] Sprinkled throughout the biographies, literature, laws, and
histories are frequent pieces of evidence about children. Searchers
should avoid prejudgments about the utility of sources. For instance,
tidbits are common in literature, such as that with which Arrowsmith
ends his translation of Petronius: "When Scipio captured Numantia, the
Romans found a number of mothers cuddling the half-eaten bodies of
their children in their laps. . ."[16]

Romans, especially in the eastern regions of the empire, made substantial contributions to pediatric knowledge, and these works should
be at the core of future studies about Roman children. Celsus (d. 50)
mainly compiled Greek writings on the subject, and relied heavily on
Hippocrates. Soranus of Ephesus (d. 138) wrote a detailed study of
gynecology, based on his own observations, including much information on infancy. Galen (d. 201) wrote extensively, sometimes following
Soranus, about infancy, nutrition, and discipline. Oribasius (d. 403) followed Aristotle's lost observations on the eight month child, and provided information on such topics as choosing a nurse and the quality of
milk. The royal physician to Justinian, Aetius Amidenus (d. 575), wrote
an extensive "Tetrabiblion" following Galen, which includes extensive
information on pediatric medicine and child-rearing.

In addition to biographies, miscellaneous literature, educational literature (such as Cicero and Quintilian), and pediatrics, historians of
Roman childhood have available much material in poetry. Lucretius and
Juvenal, as two examples, frequently used images from infancy for their
artistic purposes. A closer examination of these writers will illustrate
some basic themes. Lucretius speaks of slow growth to maturity as
natural:

> . . . if things could come from nothing, time
> Would not be of the essence, for their growth,
> Their ripening to full maturity.
> Babies would be young men, in the blink of an eye, . . .
> And full-grown forest come leaping out from the ground.

> Ridiculous! We know that all things grow
> Little by little, as indeed they must
> From their essential nature.[17]

Later, he speaks of the sadness with which an adult male contemplates his own death:

> No longer will you happily come home
> To a devoted wife, or children dear
> Running for your first kisses, while your heart
> Is filled with sweet unspoken gratitude.[18]

These two elements—tolerance for slow growth, and enjoyment of children as integral to family life—are among the positive contributions of the Romans to perceptions of childhood in the subsequent ages. As developed by the church fathers, these ideals help to justify exhortations for gentler child care. However, another attitude, more suggestive of actual practice, hinting that children are really something of a bother, creeps into Book IV:

> . . . Kids wet the bed
> Soaking not only sheets, but also spreads,
> Magnificent Babylonian counterpanes,
> Because it seemed that in their dreams they stood
> Before a urinal or chamber pot
> With lifted nightgowns.[19]

Those qualities of resignation and fatalism so characteristic of Lucretius, and the thinking of antiquity more generally, are applied to children as well:

> When nature, after struggle, tears the child
> Out of its mother's womb to the shores of light,
> He lies there naked, lacking everything,
> Like a sailor driven wave-battered to some coast,
> And the poor little thing fills all the air
> With lamentation—but that's only right
> In view of all the griefs that lie ahead
> Along his way through life. The animals
> Are better off, the tame ones and the wild,
> They grow, they don't need rattles, they don't need
> The babbling baby-talk of doting nurses, . . .[20]

Still, Lucretius' irritation is tempered with some sympathy that infants too share the pointless pattern of life and death, and the terrors of the night.

And just as children, fearing everything,
Tremble in darkness, we, in the full light,
Fear things that really are not one bit more awful
Than what poor babies shudder at in darkness,
The horrors they imagine to be coming.[21]

Obviously, each poet's writings will yield slightly different details, but I believe that similar contradictions emerge even in a poet reputed to be partial to children.[22] Juvenal, especially in the Fourteenth Satire, is explicit about parental motives: "So, shun damnable deeds. For this there's at least one good reason— / Lest our children repeat the crimes we have taught them." (14.39-40) Having an infant son *(filius infans)* should convince an adult to behave more honorably, for if the son in later life should be found to have followed the parent's example, "treading deeper in vice, you will—oh, of course!—be indignant, / Rail with bitter noise, and make a new will." (14.53-54) Surely, these are parent-centered sentiments, revealing that the essential purpose of the child (son) is to bring pleasure and honor to the parent (father). In Satire Six, Juvenal directly criticizes abortion (6.593-601), "the children set out to die from exposure" (6.602), and murders of stepsons and adopted sons (6.627-643). A different passage corroborates that Juvenal indeed condemns these common features of his society: "You owe the utmost reverence to a child." (14.47)[23]

Indeed, Juvenal is explicitly credited with a gentle attitude toward children by Gilbert Highet, in contrast with "his earlier bitterness about the cost of filling slaves' bellies".[24] The passage Highet cites (11.152-55) seems to me more polemical than gentle, proving little about Juvenal's attitude toward children. In the passage, a country boy, "natural, simple, and modest", is preferred to "an exhibitionist loudmouth" from the city. In similar manner Juvenal's contemporary Tacitus, in *Germania,* compared the degenerate Romans with the virtuous wild Germans. Tacitus' bias usually is taken to reveal more about his attitudes toward Romans than to provide facts about the moral fiber of the Germans. Is not Juvenal merely using a rustic boy's innocence in an analogous manner?

Perhaps the clearest passage in Juvenal revealing tenderness toward children is in the Fifteenth Satire (15.134-40), especially "We sigh at Nature's command, when earth closes over a baby / Too young for the funeral pyre . . ." There is substantial reason to believe, however, that the ancients had little trouble being tender toward a dead (or sleeping) child, and this gentle sympathy may well be hardly more than a convention revealing little about Juvenal's personal attitudes.[25] Thus, it is arguable that Juvenal, like Lucretius, is capable of positive feelings toward children in particular situations, but that their essential use for the poet is to serve as illustrations of larger themes (futility of life,

purity of the countryside, and the like) having little to do with actual
or ideal parent-child relations.

Many discussions relating to children in Roman historical studies
derive from the ancients' concern with fertility, the power of the father,
and educational patterns.[26] Often these issues were raised because of
adult-centered interest in social and economic reform. Thus, Augustan
legislation on adultery clearly had more to do with the birth rate of the
upper classes than with sympathy for the plight of infants born out of
wedlock, and Columella's first-century discussions of slave offspring reflect the long-standing effort to revive and regulate economically sound
farming in Italy.[27] With Quintilian (d. ca. 100), however, the argument
is specifically made that infants should be regarded from birth as
possessed of full capacity for growth.

> For there is absolutely no foundation for the complaint that but
> few men have the power to take in the knowledge that is im-
> parted to them . . . Those who are dull and unteachable are as ab-
> normal as prodigious births and monstrosities and are but few in
> number. A proof of what I say is to be found in the fact that
> boys commonly show promise of many accomplishments, and
> when such promise dies away as they grow up, this is plainly due
> not to the failure of natural gifts but to lack of requisite atten-
> tion. . . .[28]

From this idea that each infant has an intellect worth developing, it is a
short step to the conviction that each has a soul to save. Neither of
these positions, however, necessarily dictates specific child-rearing practices.

That older habits continued is revealed in regulations and laws from
throughout the imperial period. One which has caught the attention of
many is a papyrus from Egypt dated to 150/161.[29] Children must share
equally with a widowed mother, but only if they had been born by the
time of the bequest. Children even of convicted murderers can inherit a
tenth. However,

> If an Egyptian rears a child exposed on a dung heap and adopts
> him, a fourth of his estate is confiscated at death. . .
> A child who has been exposed on a dung heap may not become
> a priest.

Here again the basic pattern of ambivalence is revealed. Children are
useful for determining the right of a widow to inherit, have the right to
share an inheritance with a widowed mother under certain circumstances, but exposed children are a positive liability to foster parents.[30]
What was their social class before, and after, exposure? In the middle
imperial period many laws deal with problems associated with citizenship, legitimacy of soldier's offspring, and maintenance of the caste sys-

tem. It is difficult to establish that these laws represent self-conscious enlightened intentions toward children, even when the side effects may have been to mitigate some conditions under which children are born and grow. That regulatory imperial edicts had minor direct effect on children can be shown by two laws in the Theodosian Code. The first is dated 322.

> We have learned that provincials suffering from scarcity of food and lack of sustenance are selling or pledging their children. . . . It is repugnant to our customs to allow any person to be destroyed by hunger or rush forth to the commission of a shameful deed.[31]

And from the same time span (315/329):

> A law shall be written on bronze or waxed tablets or on linen cloth, and posted throughout all the municipalities of Italy, to restrain the hands of parents from infanticide and turn their hopes to the better. . . .if any parent should report that he had offspring which on account of poverty he is unable to rear, there shall be no delay in issuing food and clothing, since the rearing of a new-born infant can not tolerate delay. . . .[32]

It is significant that these laws, demonstrating the continuity of harsh and desperate measures against children, should come as late as the early fourth century. They should make it difficult for anyone to sustain the naive and pious hope that the growth of Christianity automatically made things better for children. Only in 374, for instance, was infanticide declared a capital offense, which of course did not end the practice as Christianity became the state religion.

In the next section of this chapter, I shall suggest some approaches of the Church Fathers to childhood. Deep beneath the surface of a decaying civilization, fundamental changes were occurring, which, culminating in Augustine, produced a new view of the nature of man.[33] These changes necessarily influenced theories about parent-child relations, but, as is always the case, the conservation of old customs and belief systems is a powerful, tenacious, and resourceful force.

"HEAVENLY MILK": CHILDHOOD IN THE AGE OF
THE CHURCH FATHERS

The ambivalence of the non-Christian Roman world toward children persists in the Roman Christian era, with many contradictions and incongruities.

One of the first things to strike a reader of early Christian writings is the vivid description of bodily functions connected with birth and infancy. Of course, an immediate reaction is that churchmen were concerned to explain theologically the nature of the Virgin Birth and the human infancy of the Messiah. Ought we not also ask why there developed in this particular period such an intense concern with mothers, fathers, flowing breasts, semen, and birth-pangs? After all, these topics receive relatively scant attention in the material canonized as the New Testament. A few illustrations demonstrate that this attention is indeed intense. Zeno, Bishop of Verona (d. ca. 372), wrote an address to be given to candidates for baptism just before the actual ceremony.

> Now the saving warmth of the eternal fount of salvation invites you, now our Mother adopts you that she may bring you forth, but not by the law by which *your* mothers bore, when they gave you, as prisoners, to this world, groaning with the pain of giving birth, while you were weeping, filthy, wrapped in filthy rags. . . . she brings you up not from stinking cradles but from sanctuaries . . . Fly to the ever flowing womb of the Ever Virgin Mother. . . . Admirable and truly divine, most holy birth, in which she who gives birth does not groan and he who is born again knows no tears. . . .[34]

Tertullian (d. ca. 222) had earlier addressed himself directly to issues of birth:

> Surely Christ loved man, the man that is hardened in a womb in the midst of uncleanness and comes forth through the parts of shame, the man who must grow up through all the indignity of being a baby. . . . In loving man He loved his flesh and his process of being born. . . . He remakes our birth by a new heavenly birth. . . .[35]

Tertullian's contemporary, Clement of Alexandria (d. ca. 211/215), in the "Hymn to the Savior" of the *Paedagogus*, seems especially concerned with maternal milk.

> Christ Jesus! heavenly milk—your Wisdom's grace—
> From a young bride's sweetest bosom. We tender babes
> Drink with innocent lips as it is pressed forth,
> Filled with the draught of the Spirit from a mystic breast.[36]

Elsewhere in the *Paedagogus* (1.6.41-43), Clement elaborates.

> And this solitary mother [the Church] had no milk, for she alone was not woman, but she was at once both virgin and mother— loving as a mother, inviolate as a virgin—and gathering her babes, she suckles them with her holy milk, . . . "Eat my flesh", He says "and drink my blood.". . . The infants lack nothing that will help them grow. What a paradoxical mystery![37]

In another tract, Clement elaborates further on this "paradoxical mystery".

> Contemplate the mysteries of love, and then you will behold the
> bosom of the Father . . . Insofar as he is ineffable He is Father,
> and insofar as He loves us He is Mother. For the Father became a
> woman by his love; and a proof of this is the One He begot from
> himself, for the fruit that is born of love is love. . .[38]

Such vivid imagery surely cannot merely be dismissed as rhetoric. What
anxieties about parental love are so lightly veiled herein? How many
babies failed to receive sufficient nourishment from their own mothers'
breasts? Is not the obsession with the pains and dangers of childbirth a
mirror to widely held concern? In view of the several views on sexuality
in the Bible, why does the narrowest and most restrictive seem so popular among early Christian apologists?

Radical asceticism is an important part of early Christianity. At first
glance the fourth century "Desert Fathers" certainly seem to be in head-
long flight from, among other things, family responsibilities and the
cares of parent-child relations. The energies of these earliest anchorites
were mainly expended on resisting adult temptations, such as lust and
gluttony. Furthermore, most of their biographies begin either in adolescence or upon adult conversion to the ascetic way of life, ignoring infancy and upbringing totally.[39] Children are hardly ever mentioned in
any context whatsoever, not even as figures of speech ("my son", "my
daughter").[40] With Jerome (d. 420) and by the second and third generation of this movement, however, asceticism definitely had softened
enough to allow concern for children. Phrases often refer to children
("With tender soothing words, much like a child's, . . ."), even though
the context may be unrelated to childhood.[41] Jerome seems especially
concerned to spread the faith, and a general asexuality obviously would
reduce the production of new humans who might be saved. His long
letter to Eustochium (384) wrestles with this problem.

> To prefer chastity is not to disparage matrimony. . . . Married
> ladies can be proud to come after nuns, for God Himself told
> them to be fruitful, multiply and replenish the earth. . . . a child
> born from marriage is virgin flesh. . . . I praise matrimony. But
> only because it produces virgins.[42]

Children, then, are not evil; rather, as virgins and potential new recruits,
they clearly have a useful role in the Christian world. Yet unmistakably
preferable to any natural birth is that experience

> when we are born again in Christ. . . . Let us consider our Nepotian
> to be a crying infant, our innocent child born fresh from the
> waters of Jordan. . . . We may approve of Nepotian's early mili-
> tary service: it was the swaddling-clothes of an infant faith.[43]

If one turns from Jerome to other leading church figures, a number
of these themes remain, despite a marked difference in personal and re-

ligious styles. Ambrose, the Bishop of Milan (d. 397), was interested enough in children to effect a miraculous cure in Florence in 394 of an infant boy.

> He found him on his bed, and, out of pity for the mother and having in mind her faith, he laid himself like Eliseus over the baby's body and prayed, and was privileged to restore to the mother, alive, one he had found dead. He also wrote a little book for the child, so that he might learn through reading what he could not take in as an infant.[44]

In view of later evidence of "overlain" infants, this passage hints at possible early practice of this form of "accidental" infanticide. The holy man, through his magic and by contact of flesh to flesh, could somehow undo a child's death by means of a sanctified form of "overlaying".[45]

In that same time period, John Chrysostom delivered in Antioch in 388 "An Address on Vainglory and the Right Way for Parents to Bring Up Their Children".[46] Although the main point of this treatise is that the parents are responsible for the moral upbringing of the child, it also contains some considerable information on attitudes toward very young children. An infant boy should not be decked out in "fine raiment and golden ornaments"; rather he should have a "strict tutor", who will keep him from growing long hair. A father should train the boy in virtue, for

> If good precepts are impressed on the soul while it is yet tender, no man will be able to destroy them when they have set firm, even as does a waxen seal. The child is still trembling and fearful and afraid in look and speech and in all else. Make use of the beginning of his life as thou shouldst. Thou wilt be the first to benefit, if thou has a good son, and then God. Thou dost labor for thyself.[47]

It is notable that the prime benefit is to the parent, even before God. But children are born with the capacity for growth, and the responsibility is the father's for the sound upbringing of the son. The child should not be beaten too much with rod or blows, lest he come to disregard or despise them. Rather, threats and promises are more effective.

> . . . punish him, now with a stern look, now with incisive, now with reproachful, words; at other times win him with gentleness and promises. . . . Let him rather at all times fear blows but not receive them . . . our human nature has some need for forbearance.[48]

No doubt is left that the father is in charge, for he "is arbiter at all times. . . . Even so God rules the world with the fear of Hell and the promise of His Kingdom. So must we too rule our children."[49]

Thus, it may be demonstrated that by the generation which came to maturity at the end of the fourth century, a number of ideas were in the air about the proper relations of parents and children. The chief ornament of that generation was Augustine (d. 430), a central figure for this discussion as for so many others. There are two obvious divisions to the study of Augustine's attitudes on childhood. First of all, his *Confessions* provide major insight into parent-child attitudes. While it may be doubted that there is sufficient quantity or quality of data to permit full-blown psychoanalytic assessment of Augustine, that has not prevented some from trying it,[50] nor should it prevent us from mining his writings for the fullest available insight into his infancy and upbringing. A second line of inquiry which promises rich dividends is to consider expressions by Augustine about the topic elsewhere in his voluminous writings. Although some fine studies have considered this material, it seems a line of inquiry still wide open. I shall merely point out some main lines of his thought on the subject, leaving to future work more detailed exposition.

Despite his strong ties to his mother, Augustine stressed that one's true family was not the natural one. This important idea is a key concept in approaching Christian parent-child relations. If one's ultimate loyalty is to that family which will help one be born again, then the whole matrix of relations in one's natural family recede in importance. "We should have no such connections as are contingent upon birth and death. . . . Our real selves are not bodies."[51] This statement is consistent with his attitudes toward asceticism,[52] and may be regarded as continuing the line of Christian thought going back to Mark 3:31-35. However, there are other passages in Augustine which show a strong concern for children. For instance, in his tract "On Christian Doctrine", written in two periods (396/427), he argues that the old folk customs which hurt children should be discontinued.

> The custom of kicking a stone, as if it were a destroyer of friendship, is less obnoxious than that of hitting an innocent child with the fist if he runs between two people walking together.[53]

Children's judgment is not trustworthy, for children will place greater weight on a pet's life than a man's.[54] Nonetheless, children are educable, and relatively guiltless, so Augustine is vexed by the death of infants. Although he may not be able to rationalize their suffering and early death, he is sure that all creatures, including babies, have a place in God's plan:

> In view of the encompassing network of the universe and the whole creation—a network that is perfectly ordered in time and place, where not even one leaf of a tree is superfluous—it is not possible to create a superfluous man.[55]

The baptism of infants too young to know what is happening to them is justifiable because it aids the faith of the parents, and that faith will help the infants live again even should they die young. We should not question the suffering of infants, for God works good from apparently evil events. Of the suffering experienced by the adults who watch their children in affliction, however, we can be more certain. It may goad them to live sounder Christian lives; if not, they will have no excuses for having failed to correct their ways after such a warning. In either event, the faith, the life, and the suffering of the parents are central. As for the infants, God will perhaps reserve some reward for them "in the secret place of his judgment".[56] Further, we should not assume that children are truly innocent at birth; they are self-centered and grasping, and have merely not had as much opportunity to sin.[57] Therefore, we should not be surprised that there is suffering in the world, and that it extends to infants.

In other ways Augustine showed that he was a close observer of infancy and its needs. In his commentaries on the Psalms, he sometimes used the image of infancy to make his theological points. In discussion of Psalm 130, he commented at length about weaning.

> The weakling in his earliest infancy, ... if perchance he is deprived of [his mother's] milk, he perishes. ... Be fearful, lest anyone be weaned from milk before his time.[58]

In a commentary on Psalm 57, he makes the analogy between the womb and the church quite explicit.

> It is good that being formed they should come forth, so that they perish not by a miscarriage. Let the mother bear thee, not miscarry. ... If by thy impatience thou hast shaken the sides of thy mother, she expelleth thee with pain indeed, but more to thy loss than to hers.[59]

Augustine does not seem able to blame a mother—natural or spiritual— for anything. If there is a miscarriage, it was the fault of the impatient foetus. Indeed, Augustine frequently idealizes the role of the mother.

> Because the mother loves to nourish her little one, she does not on that account want him to remain little. She holds him in her lap, fondles him with her hands, soothes him with caresses, feeds him with her milk, does everything for the little one; but she wants him to grow, so that she may not always have to do these things.[60]

Here we may well be passing into the realm of Augustine's idiosyncratic outlook on maternal nurture. Although these apparent gains in mother-child affection may be relegated to relative insignificance, nonetheless it remains clear that Augustine crystallized a new attitude, long in development, which places the infant and the child under the protection of the Lord.

> ... some tired with age, others in the vigour of youth, some of them boys, others grown men, others women—God is equally present to all.[61]

It remains to be seen what effect all these theoretical modifications had on actual social practice. It is very difficult, although tempting, to establish clear lines of influence, and much remains to be done. Nonetheless, the Imperial legislation from the fourth century onward suggests that the worst abuses of children were increasingly coming under the purview of governmental officials. The recurrence of legislation indicates how deeply ingrained were the practices of infanticide and child sale, and how futile it was merely to decree the abolition of these customs.

A long series of edicts against infanticide and the abandonment of children finally had taken up the admonition of Barnabas (ca. 130): "Never do away with an unborn child, or destroy it after its birth."[62] That these practices had continued after the conversion of Constantine is testified both by the necessity for continuous additional legislation and also by the repeated condemnation of infanticide by church figures and synodal meetings.[63] Lactantius (d. ca. 340) had argued that strangling newborn infants was very wrong, "for God breathes into their souls for life, not for death. . . . It is as wicked to expose as it is to kill."[64] A series of church councils inveighed against the practice and provided for aid to abandoned children.[65] That the problem indeed remained serious and substantial is also attested by several pieces of direct evidence. In 449 parents in Italy and Gaul reportedly sold their children through middlemen to the Vandals.[66] The laws of the Germanic tribes, codified generally in the sixth and seventh centuries, prohibited child murder.[67] As late as 787, Datheus, Archbishop of Milan, founded an asylum to care for and raise to age eight those children who were "exposed at the door of a church".[68]

In summary, Church Fathers, building on certain ideas in classical thought, progress in compassion for children by asserting that children had souls, were important to God, could be taught, should not be killed, maimed, or abandoned, and that they were very useful to the self-image of the parents. This is not to assert that children's conditions improved automatically. However, the Church began to bring serious pressure on the State in the fourth century to legislate an end to the life-endangering practices. The barbarian tribes, both as a result of their own customs and under the influence of Christian teachings, legislated against infanticide. Yet no one could claim that the life of a new-born child was very secure by 500 A.D., or that empathy was yet part of the psychological equipment of parents. To carry this sketch into the early middle ages, I shall show in conclusion how some of these theological and legal positions were translated into more popular idioms.

"TERRORS IN THE NIGHT": THE EARLY MIDDLE AGES

The late imperial period is rich in pagan and Christian poets, many of whom have been substantially neglected until recently. In many of these poems, we may well be able to witness a mixture of emotions concerning treatment of children. As abuses continued in the face of pleas by churchmen, the need to deal with and deflect the responsibility of the adult became more intense. The choices of particular literary conventions, as well as the ways they are elaborated, suggest what was on the mind—and in the conscience—of that age.

Consider the long poem by Claudian, probably written ca. 395-397, called "The Rape of Proserpine."[69] A daughter (Proserpine) is sent away to be brought up elsewhere, and the mother (Ceres) goes through an elaborate speech in which she relieves her guilt by hoping that the child will be better off; certainly there Proserpine would be safe from those suitors whom she feared because of her "innocence and modesty". But it turned out badly, for Ceres "saw her daughter locked up in a dark prison and bound with chains. The child had not looked like that when she left." Have we not here the plaint of any parent who, for reasons which seemed good enough to the parent, sent out into a dangerous world a daughter to be brought up by strangers? These regretful sentiments are intermingled with positive comments about the joys of parenthood, the desire for children, the devotion of the mother, and the pleasure to be found in children. Yet in practice it was an old nurse (Electra) who had brought up Proserpine, as a direct consequence of the mother's "concern" for the child. The nurse treated her as should a mother:

> Ceres found Electra, Proserpine's nurse, who loved her daughter like a mother. It was the nymph, Electra, who carried the child to her father, Jove, and let her play on the divine knee. She was the girl's companion, guardian, and almost, mother.

With an unfulfilled search for the daughter, the unfinished poem ends with the mother berating herself.

> It was I who deserted you; I left you there at the mercy of your foes; I was too concerned with the noise of Cybele's shrine. . . . my womb beats within me trying to forget that once it carried you inside my body.

How many mothers of the late fourth century who read this poem felt as did Ceres? May not this poem be used as a suggestive evidence for a shift to a stronger sense of maternal responsibility?

Prudentius (d. ca. 405) provides us with a different view of children. In his "Passion of St. Cassian of Forum Cornelii", from his *Peristephanon,* he describes a school teacher murdered by his pupils.[70] The boys in his charge killed him by "stabbing and piercing his body with the little styles with which they used to run over their wax tablets". Since "childhood never takes kindly to training", the boys resented the teacher. When the teacher got into trouble with the authorities for "scornfully refus[ing] to worship at the altars", he was turned over to the boys for punishment. First he was stripped and tied, then battered with classroom supplies, then scratched and pierced with many a stylus. Slow tortures were mixed with deep thrusts. Their violent relief in the attack is explicit, leading to their exhaustion and his death. This poem offers a vivid insight into the repression and hostility which must have marked schoolboys' psychological lives, theologians and theoreticians notwithstanding.

In another poem ("The Twelfth Hymn For the Epiphany"), Prudentius describes a popular Biblical scene, the slaughter of the innocents.[71] We may see in this vivid poetry some of the revulsion from infanticide starting to work its way into general consciousness.

The bodies were so tiny
that there was almost no space
for the gaping wounds; the blade
was much larger than the throat.
A barbarous thing to see!
A head was broken on stones
and the milk white brains splashed out
as the eyes fell from their pits.
A child's quivering body
was thrown in the raging stream
where, in his constricted throat,
water and air caused spasms.

One last poem from this generation, this by Ausonius (d. 394), "The Crucifixion of Cupid", pictures rather appalling parent-child brutality.[72] The women are all angry with the boy-god, and crowd about him with weapons individually chosen. "One comes with her noose, another her ghostly sword, / another shows him bottomless rivers, pointed / rocks, a white surf, and the quiet depths of the sea." Many tortures were used. Then his mother (Venus) approaches. She is furious with him "for all her troubles, / for her shame when she and Mars were snared together". But as the accusations of the angry mother mount up,

Speech alone is not enough:
after lashing him with words, golden Venus beats him with her
wreath until he cried, fearing harsher torture. His broken body

colours the roses with a redness that becomes brighter and brighter.

The other women, realizing that the mother has gone too far and, "shocked by a mother's display of hatred" try to calm her down. Venus then "becomes again a loving mother". But the boy-god has suffered more than a few bruises.

These visions and idle fears come from the darkness even now to disturb his sleep. When he suffers through the night with terror he escapes from his gloom by fleeing through the gate of ivory to the gods above.

When we turn from these "last poets of imperial Rome" to some other evidences from the early medieval period, it becomes clear that many basic patterns continue in their established tracks. Some of these have been discussed as methodological examples above. The church continued to try to regulate abortions, but with understanding and sympathy. In a Frankish penitential of ca. 830,[73] a woman who "slays those who are born or attempts to commit abortion" should be excommunicated, but priests "may mitigate somewhat in practice" and impose penance for a decade instead. And later on in the same document: "If anyone intentionally brings about abortion, he shall do penance for three years, one year on bread and water." The penalty for abortion has become identical with that for usury, or cutting "off any of his own members".

Another idea which continues into the early medieval period is that children are less capable than older people and should be "strengthened" to learn how to be moral. Gregory the Great (d. 604) recommends different admonitions for young and old; "for the most part severity of admonition directs [young men] to improvement, while kind remonstrance disposes the [old] to better deeds."[74]

A third pattern, already established in the first section of this chapter and during this half-millennium is the tendency to idealize the infancies of future saints. A characteristic infancy account shows the baby Willibald (d. after 730) as a model child.

When he was a baby in the cradle, a lovable little creature, he was cherished fondly by those who nursed him, especially by his parents, who lavished their affection on him and brought him up with great solicitude until he reached the age of three.[75]

He then became ill until he was offered to the Church. At age 5 he "began to show the first signs of spiritual understanding", whereupon the vow was kept and he was entered into a local monastery. He was a model novice and grew steadily into sainthood. We can be sure that here we are in the presence of an ideal, but there is essentially no way to determine the social reality from such materials. A major difference over the half-millennium studied in this chapter is that parental love, such as that which the baby Willibald received, is regarded as normal by its end.[76]

Close and careful research into early medieval sources must precede conclusions about the availability of more extensive material on parent-child relations in the "dark" ages. Some familiar material, however, suggests that such a search will not be entirely barren. Saints lives, discussed above, contain patterns and norms. A familiar poem, *Beowulf,* has many possibilities for Freudian analysis.[77] Grendel, dark male monster of the night, is killed when Beowulf, the young man-hero-son, rips Grendel's arm and shoulder from his body and hangs it—grisly trophy—high on the rafters. This act of violence, however, brings on the wrath of Grendel's mother, who lives in a "murky cold lake". To conquer this monster-mother, Beowulf must descend deep into the dark wet, where his sword fails him. But

> Then he saw, hanging on the wall, a heavy
> Sword, hammered by giants, strong
> And blessed with their magic, the best of all weapons
> But so massive that no ordinary man could lift
> Its carved and decorated length. He drew it
> From its scabbard, broke the chain on its hilt,
> And then, savage, now, angry
> And desperate, lifted it high over his head
> And struck with all the strength he had left,
> Caught her in the neck and cut it through,
> Broke bones and all. Her body fell
> To the floor, lifeless, the sword was wet
> With her blood, and Beowulf rejoiced at the sight.

By the ninth and tenth centuries, substantial material becomes available,[78] but the earlier period is not totally barren. Fortunatus (d. ca. 605), for example, continued the close anatomical interest evident above in discussions of the Virgin Birth.

> . . . wearing skin he then proceeded out of the womb of the untouched Maid.
> He wailed his woe inside a manger, a baby hidden in its bowels;
> The Virgin-Mother wrapped him with a swath of swaddling clothes;
> His hands, his feet, his legs she bound with bands that held him tight.[79]

In the Carolingian period itself, a famous biography provides some insight into parent-child relations.[80] Einhard's *Life of Charlemagne* may well be so heavily modelled on Suetonius' "Life of Augustus" as to be seriously unreliable, yet there are in it a number of significant details.

Einhard, son of a "distinguished family", was educated as a young boy in a monastery,[81] apparently a normal activity for the period. Unfortunately, of Charlemagne's "birth and childhood, or even . . . his boyhood, . . . nothing is set down in writing about this and nobody can be found still alive who claims to have any personal knowledge of these matters".[82] Charlemagne's interest as an adult in the education of the young, which is most famous through his support of Alcuin and the Palace School, also shows up in relationships with his own children.[83] Sons, "as soon as they were old enough", were taught to ride, fight, and hunt. Female children were taught household skills, "rather than fritter away their time in sheer idleness". When these stages occur is not clear either from the text or from the context, but generally they must have been close to the end of the period we have been calling childhood. Perhaps a child's capability for good performance in learning such skills was a threshold between childhood and the subsequent stage of development. The most interesting single item in Einhard, for our purposes, is the statement that his "extraordinarily beautiful" daughters were so well loved by their father that he kept them in his household, unmarried, for his whole life, "maintaining that he could not live without them". Among the results of this confinement of the young women were several illegitimate children, whom Einhard calls "a number of unfortunate experiences".

CONCLUSION

This chapter has sought to show that research into childhood patterns of the late Roman and early medieval periods is possible, and will yield more than minor and insignificant results. It has illustrated some of the kinds of evidence and results which may be expected, and pointed the way toward further areas of study.

The gains for children in this period appear mainly theoretical, and only dimly perceived by most parents. Folk-customs are deep-seated, and repeated prohibitions by civil and religious authorities seemed to avail little against even such grim acts as infanticide, abortion, sale of children, and abandonment. The most substantial change suggested herein is in the nurturant role of the mother. The gap remains wide between the mothers appearing in Ausonius's poetry and those mentioned in Augustine's theology, but by the seventh century many pagan motifs seem to have faded, and parental love is often described as natural and forthcoming. The continued need for legislation, as well as other scattered evidence, suggests, however, that the distance between ideals and actuality had closed rather little in half a millennium. In a well-known story from the end of the period covered in this chapter, Ölver the Viking was considered "soft" because he refused to administer a life or death test to a new-born boy.[84]

REFERENCES

The quotation at the beginning of the chapter is from St. Jerome, *The Satirical Letters*, tr. by Paul Carroll (Chicago, 1956), p. 196.

1. See a forceful statement of this position by William Carroll Bark, *Origins of the Medieval World* (Stanford, 1958).
2. Edward Gibbon, of course, had a different point in mind in *The Decline and Fall of the Roman Empire* (New York, n.d.), vol. 2, ch. lxxi, p. 1443.
3. Marc Bloch, *The Historian's Craft* (New York, 1953), p. 197.
4. A fine example of what can be done under these circumstances is the work by Emily Coleman, dealing with the Polyptych of St. Irminon. "Medieval Marriage Characteristics", *The Journal of Interdisciplinary History* II (1971), pp. 205-219, and "A Note on Medieval Peasant Demography", *Historical Methods Newsletter* V (1972), pp. 53-58. A further article, "Peasant Population Control", is announced for a forthcoming issue of *Annales E.S.C.*
5. *Ausonius*, with an English translation by H. G. E. White (Cambridge, 1951), vol. 1, pp. 206-215.
6. This point is dramatically made by perusing T. S. R. Boase, *Death in the Middle Ages: Mortality, Judgment, and Remembrance* (New York, 1972).
7. Two important studies illustrating the possibilities for such an approach are Adolf Katzenellenbogen, "The Image of Christ in the Early Middle Ages", in *Life and Thought in the Early Middle Ages*, ed. by R. S. Hoyt (Minneapolis, 1967); and Victor Lasareff, "Studies in the Iconography of the Virgin", *Art Bulletin* 20 (1938), pp. 26-65.
8. Reproduced in Peter Brown, *The World of Late Antiquity, A.D. 150-750* (New York, 1971), p. 142.
9. Reproduced in James J. Sweeney, *Irish Illuminated Manuscripts of the Early Christian Period* (New York, 1965), plate 9.
10. Reproduced in John Beckwith, *Early Medieval Art* (New York, 1964), p. 46.
11. *Ibid.*, p. 44. Cf. v. 15: "I have suffered from boyhood and come near to death. I have borne thy terrors, I cower beneath thy blows."
12. Sulpicius Severus, "The Life of St. Martin, Bishop of Tours", in *The Western Fathers*, by Sulpicius Severus et al., tr. by F. R. Hoare (New York, 1965), page 12. Martin died ca. 397.
13. Paulinus the Deacon, "The Life of St. Ambrose", in *ibid.*, pp. 150-1. Ambrose died in 397.
14. From selections in Robert Brentano, ed., *The Early Middle Ages, 500-1000* (New York, 1964), pp. 216-218. The whole life is translated by Bertram Colgrave as *Felix's Life of Saint Guthlac* (Cambridge, 1956).
15. Albrecht Peiper, *Chronik der Kinderheilkunde* (Leipzig, 1966), pp. 28-57; H. Leclercq, "Alumni", *Dictionnaire d'archéologie chrétienne et de liturgie* (Paris, 1907-1951), tome 1, cols. 1288-1306. I am indebted to Professor John Benton for making the very useful Leclercq article available to me.
16. Petronius, *The Satyricon*, tr. by William Arrowsmith (New York 1959), p. 165.
17. Lucretius, *The Way Things Are*, tr. by Rolfe Humphries (Bloomington, Indiana, 1968), p. 25. Book I.185-192.
18. *Ibid.*, p. 112. Book 3. 902-905.
19. *Ibid.*, p. 148. Book 4. 1026-29. Humphries has translated as "nightgowns" the Latin *vestem*, which certainly has only a more general meaning of covering or clothing.
20. *Ibid.*, pp. 165-166. Book 5. 220-231.
21. *Ibid.*, p. 203. Book 6. 37-41.
22. *The Satires of Juvenal*, tr. by Rolfe Humphries (Bloomington, Indiana, 1958).

Passages can easily be located in this edition. Generally sound criticism is in Gilbert Highet, *Juvenal the Satirist. A Study* (New York, 1961).
23. The Latin is *Maxima debetur puero reverentia*. That this indeed refers generically to a child is confirmed by his use of the term *filius infans* two lines further on.
24. Highet, *Juvenal*, p. 237, note 20; also cf. pp. 145-148.
25. I have come across three examples of ostentatious morning for a dead child. First is a poem attributed to Diodorus (ca. 100 B.C.-100 A.D.).

> A tiny child in the villa of Diodoros
> fell headfirst from a little ladder
> and broke his neck bones fatally,
> but when he saw his much-loved master running up
> he suddenly spread out his baby arms to him.
> Earth, do not lie heavy on the bones
> of a tiny slave child.
> Be kind to Korax, who died at two.
>
> > Willis Barnstone, tr., *Greek Lyric Poetry*
> > (New York, 1972), p. 212.

Martial (d. after 98 A.D.) mourned the death of a "little servingmaid, joy and delight of my heart", who had died just before her sixth birthday:

> Now let her romp as she will. . .
> Let her lisping voice utter the sound of my name.
> Let the turf above her delicate bones lie gently;
> Rest on her lightly, O Earth, on whom her step was so light.
>
> > Martial, *Selected Epigrams*, tr. by Rolfe
> > Humphries (Bloomington, Indiana, 1963),
> > p. 60. Book V, poem xxxiv.

An inscription dated to the fourth or fifth century continued this motif, although into areas of concern to Christians:

> To Julia Florentina, sweetest and most innocent child, . . . Eighteen months and twenty-two days [old], while dying, she was [baptized], at the eighth hour of the night. She lived another four hours, so that she received communion again, . . . When both her parents were weeping for her without ceasing, at night the voice of Divine Majesty was heard, forbidding lamentation for the dead. . . .
>
> > Quoted in J. N. Hillgarth, ed., *The Conversion of Western Europe 350-750* (Englewood Cliffs, N.J., 1969), p. 13. From E. Diehl, ed., *Inscriptiones latinae christianae veteres*, I, no. 1549.

26. Cf. for instance, Jerome Carcopino, *Daily Life in Ancient Rome* (New Haven, 1940), chapter IV, "Marriage, Woman, and the Family". Carcopino cites considerable evidence from law codes and digests to suggest that the more enlightened emperors (Trajan, Hadrian) were attempting to mitigate, if not eliminate, the more brutal forms of child mistreatment. Also cf. H. I. Marrou, *A History of Education in Antiquity* (New York, 1964), especially pp. 147, 199-200, 313, 456, 510-511.
27. These, and other pertinent citations, are conveniently located in N. Lewis and M. Reinhold, ed., *Roman Civilization: Selected Readings* (New York, 1955), vol. II, "The Empire", pp. 47-52, 166-173, 253-4.
28. Quoted in *ibid.*, 287-288. See the Loeb Classical Library volumes on Quintilian for a full text.
29. Quoted in *ibid.*, 380-83. "Berlin Papyrus No. 1,210".
30. A fine article on foster-children is Leclercq, "Alumni". There are highly sug-

gestive excerpts in Lewis and Reinhold, ed., *Roman Civilization,* II, pp. 403-405, including the frequently cited comment from Oxyrhynchus Papyrus No. 744: "If you chance to bear a child and it is a boy, let it be; if it is a girl, expose it."

31. Lewis and Reinhold, ed., *Roman Civilization,* II, pp. 483-4. Code no. XI. xxvii. 2.
32. *Ibid.,* p. 483. Code no. XI. xxvii. 1.
33. Three important general studies arguing this point are Chester G. Starr, *Civilization and the Caesars: The Intellectual Revolution in the Roman Empire* (New York, 1965); E. R. Dodds, *Pagan and Christian in an Age of Anxiety: Some Aspects of Religious Experience from Marcus Aurelius to Constantine* (New York, 1965); and C. N. Cochrane, *Christianity and Classical Culture* (New York, 1957). Also cf. the important biography by Peter Brown, *Augustine of Hippo: A Biography* (Berkeley, 1969), and Peter Brown, "Approaches to the religious crisis of the third century A.D.", *English Historical Review* 83 (1968), pp. 542-558.
34. The problems connected with baptism in the early church have been much studied, and are of considerable relevance to childhood history. Cf. J. Jeremias, *Infant Baptism in the First Four Centuries* (London, 1960); Kurt Aland, *Did the Early Church Baptize Infants?* (London, 1962); J. Jeremias, *The Origins of Infant Baptism* (Naperville, Illinois, n.d.); J. D. C. Fisher, *Christian Initiation: Baptism in the Medieval West* (London, 1965); and Ernest Evans, *Tertullian's Homily on Baptism* (London, n.d.). The particular quote comes from Hillgarth, *The Conversion of Western Europe,* p. 11.
35. Tertullian, "On the Flesh of Christ", 4. 3-4, in Herbert A. Musurillo, *The Fathers of the Primitive Church* (New York, 1966), p. 156. Cf. also the detailed attention to this issue by Leo I at Chalcedon in 451; "The Tome of Leo" in J. B. Russell, ed., *Religious Dissent in the Middle Ages* (New York, 1971), pp. 27-30.
36. Musurillo, *Primitive Church,* p. 190.
37. *Ibid.,* 190-191.
38. "Who is the Rich Man Who is Saved?", in *ibid.,* 192.
39. An exception is the "Life of St. Anthony" by Athanasius.
40. Cf. Helen Waddell, tr., *The Desert Fathers* (London, 1936).
41. Letter to Heliodorus, 374, in Paul Carroll, tr., *The Satirical Letters of St. Jerome* (Chicago, 1956), p. 2.
42. *Ibid.,* 36-37. Is Jerome so driven by his psychological need to talk about virginity and childbirth that he has neglected the theological implications of Original Sin?
43. Letter to Heliodorus, 396, in *ibid.,* p. 178-179.
44. "Life of Saint Ambrose" by Paulinus, XXVIII, in Sulpicius Severus, *Western Fathers,* p. 170. The boy's age is indicated by the phrase "then quite a little thing."
45. Eliseus is a Greek form of Elisha. The Biblical model for the Ambrose story is in 2 Kings 4:31-37. The nominal cause of death was "an evil spirit" which had temporarily been driven out by Ambrose through "repeated prayers and his laying on of hands. But some days later this baby was seized with a sudden illness and passed away." Of course, the cause of death may have been natural. What I am driving at is that the form of cure used by Ambrose suggests not only a general familiarity with adult "overlaying", but also continuing concern by many parents for reversal of a regretted childhood death. Cf. footnote 25 for comparisons.
46. M. L. W. Laistner, *Christianity and Pagan Culture in the Later Roman Empire* (Ithaca, 1951). The text is translated as an appendix, pp. 75-122.

47. *Ibid.*, p. 95.
48. *Ibid.*, 99-100.
49. *Ibid.*, 113.
50. Joseph McCabe, *St. Augustine* (New York, 1903); Charles Kligerman, "A Psychoanalytic Study of the Confessions of St. Augustine", *Journal of the American Psychoanalytic Association* 6 (1957), 469-484; E. R. Dodds, "Augustine's Confessions: A Study of Spiritual Maladjustment", *Hibbert Journal* 26 (1927-8), pp. 459-473; B. Legewie, *Augustinus: Eine Psychographie* (1925); Rebecca West, *St. Augustine* (1933). Cf. also Robert J. O'Connell, *St. Augustine's Early Theory of Man 386-391* (Cambridge, 1968).
51. St. Augustine, *Of True Religion,* tr. by J. H. S. Burleigh (Chicago, 1959). Paragraphs 88-89, pp. 84-85.
52. F. Van der Meer, *Augustine the Bishop: Church and Society at the Dawn of the Middle Ages* (New York, 1961), chapter 8 generally, and especially pp. 214-215; Gerhart B. Ladner, *The Idea of Reform: Its Impact on Christian Thought and Action in the Age of the Fathers* (New York, 1967), Revised Edition, Part Three, "Monasticism as a Vehicle of the Christian Idea of Reform in the Age of the Fathers", pp. 319-426. Also cf. Augustine's letter to Proba and Juliana in St. Augustine, *Select Letters,* tr. by James Houston Baxter (Cambridge, 1953), p. 269. (Loeb Classical Library edition)
53. Saint Augustine, *On Christian Doctrine,* tr. by D. W. Robertson, Jr. (Indianapolis, 1958), paragraph XX, pp. 55-56.
54. Saint Augustine, *On Free Choice of the Will,* tr. by A. S. Benjamin and L. H. Hackstaff (Indianapolis, 1964), paragraph 62, p. 100.
55. *Ibid.*, paragraph 226, pp. 139-140.
56. *Ibid.*, paragraphs 227-231, pp. 140-141.
57. Herbert A. Deane, *The Political and Social Ideas of St. Augustine* (New York, 1966), pp. 56-59.
58. Erich Przywara, arr., *An Augustine Synthesis* (New York, 1958), p. 277.
59. *Ibid.*, p. 278.
60. *Serm.* XXIII, iii, 3, in *ibid.*, p. 292.
61. *Serm.* XLVII, xvi, 30; in *ibid.*, p. 369.
62. *The Epistle of Barnabas, 19.* In *Early Christian Writings: The Apostolic Fathers,* tr. by M. Staniforth (Baltimore, 1968), p. 217.
63. Tertullian in 200 A.D. has already noted that although laws against exposure and infanticide were on the books, "it so happens that no laws are evaded with more impunity or greater safety...". Quoted in Abt-Garrison, *History of Pediatrics* (Philadelphia, 1965), p. 56. Leclercq, "Alumni", provides additional details.
64. *Divine Institutes* 1. VI c.xx, quoted in Abt-Garrison, *History,* p. 57. Also cf. Leclercq, "Alumni", col. 1302.
65. *Ibid.*
66. George H. Payne, *The Child in Human Progress* (New York, 1916), p. 291. Cf. also Meyer and Reinhold, *Roman Civilization,* p. 483, for Theodosian Code XI. xxvii.2, A.D. 322, for African families' child sale.
67. Leclercq, "Alumni", col. 1304. Also cf. Title 24.1 of the law of the Salian Franks, "Concerning the Killing of Little Children and Women", in Brian Tierney, ed., *The Middle Ages. Volume I. Sources of Medieval History* (New York, 1970), pp. 56-57. Chapter XX of the Burgundian Code, "An edict concerning foundlings", can be found in Robert Brentano, ed., *The Early Middle Ages 500-1000* (New York, 1964), p. 153.
68. Abt-Garrison, *History,* p. 57-58;
69. In Harold Isbell, tr., *The Last Poets of Imperial Rome* (Baltimore, 1971), pp. 75-106. All quotations can be located through book and line numbers. This

is a very fine collection of poets, well translated; most of these writings, and some besides, appear in the Loeb Classical Library series. I preferred to use the more graceful and poetic translations of Isbell.

70. Prudentius, *Works,* tr. by H. J. Thompson (Cambridge, 1953), v. II. pp. 221-229.
71. Isbell, *Last Poets,* pp. 208-214.
72. *Ibid.,* pp. 65-68.
73. Paragraph 21 of Halitgar's *Roman Penitential,* found in Marshall W. Baldwin, ed., *Christianity Through the Thirteenth Century* (New York, 1970), p. 139.
74. *Pastoral Rule,* ch. 1, Admonition 2, in *ibid.,* p. 105.
75. Huneberc of Heidenheim, *The Hodoeporicon of St. Willibald,* in C. H. Talbot, tr., *The Anglo-Saxon Missionaries in Germany* (New York, 1954), p. 154.
76. Willibald, *Life of St. Boniface,* in *ibid.,* 27. This is a different Willibald than the famous saint; he wrote ca. 768. "In his very early childhood, after he had been weaned and reared with a mother's usual anxious care, his father lavished upon him more affection than upon the rest of his brothers." Cf. the substantial love credited to the father here. Parents, rather than only mothers, are presumed to love children.
77. Burton Raffel, tr., *Beowulf* (New York, 1963). The long quotation is on page 72.
78. For example, cf. the *Colloquies* of Aelfric, Abbot of Eynsham, ca. 1005; the poems of Gottschalk, d. 869; Odo of Cluny's life of Gerald of Aurillac, 930.
79. #11, *Pange, lingua,* in James J. Wilhelm, tr., *Medieval Song, An Anthology of Hymns and Lyrics* (New York, 1971), p. 39.
80. Einhard and Notker the Stammerer, *Two Lives of Charlemagne,* tr. by Lewis Thorpe (Baltimore, 1969). Also cf. the current series of studies by Emily Coleman cited in footnote 4.
81. Einhard, *Charlemagne,* p. 49. The comment is by Walahfrid Strabo, in a prologue.
82. *Ibid.,* p. 59.
83. *Ibid.,* 74-5. The remaining quotations all come from these pages.
84. O. H. Werner, *The Unmarried Mother in German Literature* (New York, 1966), p. 21. Marc Bloch, in *Feudal Society* (Chicago, 1961), p. 19, has a slightly different version.

CHAPTER 3

Survivors and Surrogates: Children and Parents from the Ninth to the Thirteenth Centuries

MARY
MARTIN
McLAUGHLIN

"In her despair, his mother wholly rejected her baby, weaning him before he had hardly begun to nurse, and refusing to hold or touch him with her own hands."

John of Lodi, *Life of St. Peter Damian,*
late eleventh century

"Yet thou knowest, Almighty One, with what purity and holiness in obedience to Thee she raised me, how greatly she provided me with the care of nurses in infancy and of masters and teachers in boyhood, with no lack even of fine clothes for my little body, so that I seemed to equal the sons of kings and counts in indulgence."

Guibert of Nogent, *Memoirs,* 1115

SOME INTRODUCTORY REFLECTIONS ON TWO ELEVENTH-CENTURY CHILDHOODS

For the period from which these voices speak, as for all but the most recent times, the realities of early life must remain a largely hidden world, accessible to us only partially and indirectly, through the recollections, portrayals and fantasies of those who were no longer children. Among such fragile if indispensable witnesses, the two works just quoted have for our period and purposes a singular importance. Offering us the fullest, the most intimate and revealing accounts of infancy and childhood in Western society during the time-span of this study, they lead us most directly into the virtually uncharted hinterland of childhood during these distant centuries.[1] To suggest that much of this terrain is still unexplored is by no means to undervalue the contributions of modern scholarship in many areas that impinge upon it. Studies concerned with the family and its changing structure, with medieval demography, law and education, with the history of medicine and especially pediatrics, with religious movements and cultural transformations, as well as essays on the "idea" and the "cult" of childhood: all of these and many others help us in some measure to recreate both the immediate and the social settings of children's lives in the remoter past.[2] Still in its own infancy, however, is the effort to approach more closely the psychic realities of these lives, to gain some understanding, however tentative and incomplete, of the experiences of childhood, the modes of rearing and the relations of parents and children, with all of their profound implications for the development of both individuals and societies.[3] Whatever may be the verdict on the various hypotheses advanced in this volume, the discovery of childhood in these and in other centuries must inevitably, like all such novel ventures, pose fresh and formidable questions that will leave almost no field of history uninvaded.

To explore many of these issues in depth is, in the present state of research, beyond the scope of this essay, although I hope that it may help to formulate them more precisely. What is presented here is, primarily, an interim report on a continuing journey of discovery through the vast body of materials from which a history of childhood in this period may eventually be constructed. Reaching occasionally backward to the ninth century and more often forward into the thirteenth, it is anchored most firmly to the time that lies between. Geographically, it is centered in those regions of Europe which were the heartlands of Western Christendom, with occasional forays into areas that were in this period the frontiers of Western expansion. Even within these rough limits it can hardly claim comprehensiveness. For if there is truth in the statement that "there was no place for children in the medieval world,"[4] it rests in the perception that children are to be found not in any well-defined and fenced-off area, such as nurseries, homes and schools, but everywhere in this society and in the sources on which our knowledge of it is based. We meet them, and the evidence of their fortunes, in almost every kind of record, from works of art and literature to manorial surveys and ecclesiastical legislation. Much of this multifarious evidence is, it is true, fragmentary and widely scattered; some of it, whether consciously or unconsciously, is falsified or distorted; and these qualities enhance the difficulties of comprehending and interpreting it.

But if the nature of our sources sets certain limits to our inquiry, they also offer the more promising, even unexpected opportunities with which it is especially concerned. Their possibilities and their limitations are most clearly exhibited in the two works, John of Lodi's life of Peter Damian and the personal reminiscences of Guibert of Nogent, which will serve as guides of our exploration. In what they do, as well as in what they do not, tell us, they bring into focus its central themes and problems. Standing at the heart of our period, they introduce us to the early development of lives and personalities that are, for this time, exceptionally well documented and, though in different ways, uncommonly significant. They thus give us vantage-points from which to examine not only the broader implications of these childhoods, but continuities and changes in the treatment of children and in attitudes towards them during these centuries as a whole.

The man whose childhood John of Lodi describes was, indeed, no ordinary person. For Peter Damian, who was born in the early eleventh century, perhaps in 1007, in the Italian city of Ravenna, to respectable but evidently far from prosperous parents, was destined to become one of the great spiritual reformers of his age and one of its most notable saints. An eloquent preacher and zealous ascetic, head of a congregation of hermits dedicated to the contemplative life, a powerful opponent of abuses and in later life a cardinal-bishop of the Roman Church, he played a major part in the most important ecclesiastical movements of the century.[5] He also wrote copiously and sometimes brilliantly on many subjects; but his writings, though variously self-revealing, contain little that is directly autobiographical.[6] For our most substantial and sequential knowledge of his life, in both its earlier and its later phases, we must turn to John of Lodi,[7] a devoted disciple of Peter Damian's last years, who wrote at the request of his fellow-monks of Fonte Avellana a biography that was, like other such works, intended above all to demonstrate the sanctity of its hero.

No doubt John's story of Peter Damian's early life reflected also his own ideas and fantasies of childhood and it is perhaps this concern, as well as the immediacy of his sources and his intense devotion to his subject, that explains the vividness, empathy and apparent veracity in which this biography markedly transcends the conventions of the medieval saint's-life.[8] Strikingly absent from it are the visions, dreams and portents that commonly attended the births of saintly children and the glorification of their parentage that was also a tradition of this genre. In keeping with its principles, however, John did wish to stress those experiences which formed and tested the heroic virtues of his subject, and so, perhaps, he did not hesitate to record a childhood of almost unrelieved misery and deprivation. Peter's adversities began, in fact, at the very moment of his birth, to a mother "worn out by child-bearing,"

into a family already so numerous and so impoverished that when this
son was born, an adolescent brother bitterly reproached their mother
for having added yet another child to an overcrowded household, to the
"throng of heirs" competing for a meagre inheritance.[9]

Enraged by this attack, the mother fell into what John of Lodi describes as "a violent fit of feminine malice" (in which we may perceive
the symptoms of postpartum depression), wringing her hands and declaring that she was utterly wretched and unworthy to live any longer.
In her despair, she wholly rejected her baby, refusing to nurse him and
"to hold or touch him with her own hands." Cast away "before he had
learned to live," disinherited from the maternal breast that was his
only possession, this tiny creature began to grow dark with hunger and
cold, and so weak that he could hardly cry; "only the barest whisper
came from his scarcely palpitating little chest." At this point, when the
baby seemed about to perish from maternal neglect, he was rescued
through the intervention of a certain priest's wife, or concubine, who
had been a domestic servant in his father's family and who had perhaps
assisted at the child's birth. Clearly hers was also an important role in
the symmetry as well as the sensibility of John's story, for she is the
"good" foil of the "bad" mother in a pairing that is later balanced by
the contrast between Peter's "good" and "bad" brothers. Appalled by
the inhuman harshness of his mother, this compassionate woman vehemently reproached her, asking how a Christian mother could behave
as no lioness or tigress would do. If these mothers faithfully nurse their
cubs, she cried, how could human mothers reject children formed in the
image of God and shaped in their own wombs? Clinching her argument
with the stern warning that to continue in this way would be to risk
being judged guilty of filicide, the priest's wife contrived to soften the
mother's heart and restore the dying child to life.

To set an example of proper maternal solicitude, in whose details
John of Lodi took evident pleasure, she freed the baby's withered limbs
from their swaddling bands, warmed the naked little body at the fire
and cured the rash or scabies that covered it by rubbing it lavishly with
oil. Then, he exclaimed, "you would have seen the tender little limbs,
wrapped in poultices soaked in melted fat, begin to grow rosy as their
vital heat returned, and the beauty of infancy flower again." So, we are
told, the compassion of a "sinful little woman" snatched a desperate
child from the jaws of death and saved his mother from "the dreadful
sin of infanticide." Indeed, restored to that maternal self and feeling
which "an alien savagery had driven out," Peter's mother from that
time on showed unstinting diligence and love in the nursing of her baby,
who flourished under this care until he was weaned.

Shortly after this, however, when he was still a very young child,
Peter was prematurely orphaned by the death of both of his parents.

Left to the care of his family, he was, unhappily, adopted by the very brother, probably the eldest, who had been so angered by his birth and who, with a wife equally harsh and cruel, now treated the little boy, according to his biographer, in a savage and "stepmotherly" fashion. Fed grudgingly with slops fit only for pigs, he was forced to go about barefoot, clad in rags, a "battered child," frequently kicked and beaten. Subjected to this brutality for some years, compelled to live "like a slave," he was eventually turned out to become a swineherd. From this period of Peter's boyhood only one episode, which John considered highly significant, is reported at length. One day the miserable boy chanced to find a gold coin and, delighted by this unexpected wealth, he reflected for a long time on what he might buy with it. After long inner debate, he was at last divinely inspired to renounce his dreams of transitory pleasure and to give up his cherished coin to a priest for a Mass to be offered for his father's soul. If to his biographer this renunciation of the ephemeral for the eternal seemed to presage his later sanctity, to us it may seem not without meaning that only his father and not his rejecting mother was included in this generous offering.[10]

Concluding his tale of childhood misery on a happier note, John reports that when Peter was perhaps twelve years old, he was delivered from his tormentors and placed in the care of another brother, as kind as the first was cruel, who lavished on the boy so much affection that "it seemed to exceed a father's love." It was to this brother, Damian, who later became an archpriest of Ravenna, that Peter owed the education that made possible his career first as a secular teacher and then as a distinguished churchman. To this brother, whose name he adopted, Peter remained deeply devoted in later life, as he was to a nephew, also called Damian, for whose education he in turn provided, and to the sisters of whom his biographer says nothing. To this last attachment Peter himself testified in a fashion that adds suggestively to our knowledge of his childhood and the lasting effect of his sufferings in it. In a letter written when he was perhaps sixty, he described an earlier visit to the deathbed of a beloved sister, who had been "like a mother" to him; as he crossed the threshold of the family house for the first time since his youth, he declared, such a "cloud of timidity" hung over his eyes that he could see almost nothing of the household during the time he spent there.[11] Although John of Lodi failed to mention this affectionate sister and her role, perhaps because her presence would have disturbed the symmetry of his story, its essential truth is supported by Peter's own revelation of the enduring anxieties aroused by this visit to the home of his childhood and the painful memories associated with it.

Unlike Peter Damian, Guibert of Nogent was neither particularly influential nor, if we may judge by his account of himself, very saintly. Born a half-century or so after Peter, in Clermont-en-Beauvaisis in northern France, into a noble family of only local importance, he was destined from the first for the monastic life, which he entered at the age of twelve or thirteen.[12] Much later, he became the abbot of a small monastery, Nogent-sous-Coucy, and also, though his role on the larger scene was never more than modest, an acute observer, recorder and critic of his turbulent society. No less fascinated by himself than by the world in which he moved, he distinguished himself most strikingly from all but a few of his contemporaries by telling his own story in his *Monodiae* or "songs for one voice," a somewhat miscellaneous collection of memoirs which has been described, with some exaggeration, as "the first comprehensive autobiography of the middle ages."[13] Although these memoirs are by no means so encompassing autobiographically as we might wish, there is no work of these centuries that gives us so immediate a sense of what at least one medieval child and childhood might have been like. Indeed, his intense, perhaps obsessive, concern with his early life reveals to us not only the young Guibert in his strangely isolated and rigorously disciplined childhood, but the child living still in the man of fifty. Remarkable as his memoirs are in their portrayal of the dramas of his world, and the wealth of insights they offer into the details of its life, the true singularity of his work lies in its major theme and inspiration, that passionate attachment to his mother which remained the central and apparently the only emotionally significant relationship of his existence.

Dominating all that is most personal in his story, this possessive and somewhat ambivalent devotion is first clearly disclosed in Guibert's uncommonly precise account of the shared dangers and deliverance of his birth. For, like Peter Damian's, Guibert's early hold on life had been extremely tenuous and his entrance into the world even more dramatic, in circumstances of great peril to both mother and child. In reporting them he took, in fact, considerable retrospective pleasure, dwelling at length on his mother's prolonged and painful labor and the dangers that led his father, in hope of a safe delivery, to promise him to the monastic life even before he had been born.[14] When at last he appeared, "a weak little being, almost an abortion," and was on that same day, Holy Saturday, brought to the baptismal font, he was, as he was often told jokingly in later years, tossed from hand to hand by "a certain woman," probably the midwife, who exclaimed: "Look at this thing! Do you think such a child can live. . . . ?"[15] After his lively picture of this important occasion, Guibert tells us disappointingly little of his very early childhood. The youngest child in a family that included at least two brothers, whom he barely mentions throughout his memoirs and for whom he apparently felt little affection, at the age of about eight months he lost his father, at a time when he had, he says, scarcely begun to cherish his rattle.[16] After his father's death, which Guibert later saw as a stroke of good fortune, his mother remained a widow, devoting herself to the rearing of this, in his view at least, her favorite child, "truest to me," he insists, "of all that she bore."

What sort of woman was this whom her son regarded throughout his life as his "sole personal possession among all the goods I had in the world"?[17] In his portrayal of her, "beautiful, yet chaste, modest, steeped in the fear of the Lord," we glimpse faintly the influences of another childhood, formative perhaps for both mother and son. And we see more clearly the effects of the marriage of which he was the offspring. For terrified from her earliest years by fears of sin and sudden death, she had been given in marriage to Guibert's father, himself a mere youth, when she was still a child, "hardly of marriageable age."[18] Probably because of their youthful ignorance and inhibitions rather than through the "bewitchments" to which Guibert attributed their failure, his parents' marriage remained unconsummated for several years. During this time the impotent young husband and his still virginal wife were subjected to heavy and humiliating pressures from their families and neighbors, until at last the "bewitchment was broken," probably, as their son suggests, by his father's successful liaison with another woman. Thereafter his mother submitted, though clearly not eagerly, to those wifely duties for which, according to Guibert, she had little taste. Still a young and handsome woman when her husband died, she resisted with formidable determination the self-interested efforts of his kinsmen to persuade her to remarry so that they might gain control of her children and property.[19] Continuing for the rest of her life in what was to her and to many other women in this period the highly desirable state of widowhood,[20] she showed herself the conventionally dutiful, efficient, extraordinarily pious, in some ways generous but, it seems emotionally inhibited woman whose image emerges from Guibert's recollections. Illiterate but practically gifted, burdened with all of the responsibilities of governing a noble household, she was evidently assiduous in her concern for the physical and spiritual welfare of her son, providing him, he says, with nurses in his infancy, dressing him in fine clothes and, when she had leisure from her household cares, teaching him how and for what to pray,[21] From his earliest years Guibert appears to have been powerfully influenced by his mother's piety and sense of sin, and particularly by her uncommonly rigid standards of sexual purity and control.[22] He was also strongly affected by her concern for his education, for as soon as this child who was destined for the monastic life had begun to learn his letters, at the age of four or five, she procured the services of a teacher who became his private tutor for at least six years, living in the household and giving his full attention to his pupil, whom he worked very hard and whose every waking moment he supervised.[23]

Between his mother and his tutor, who "guarded him as a parent not as a master," Guibert was evidently brought up with excessive, indeed, repressive care, kept, he says, from ordinary games, never allowed to leave his master's company or to eat anywhere but at home, or to accept gifts from anyone without his leave. "While others of my age wandered everywhere at will and were unchecked in the indulgence of such inclinations as were natural at their age," says Guibert, "I, hedged in by constant restraints and dressed in my clerical garb, would sit and look at the troops of players like a beast awaiting sacrifice."[24] Rarely permitted a holiday, he was constantly driven to study by an assiduous but poorly educated teacher who tried to compensate for his own deficiencies with scoldings and frequent beatings. Persuading himself, at least retrospectively, of the genuine concern, the "harsh love," underlying this rough treatment, and himself returning this love, mingled with a certain contempt, Guibert was also pleasurably aware of the rivalry for his affections between his master and his mother, who was grieved and distressed, according to her son, when she saw the evidence of excessive beating. On one occasion when, he says, "she threw off my inner garment and saw my little arms blackened and the skin of my back everywhere puffed up with the cuts from the twigs," she was "grieved to the heart" and protested bitterly, "weeping with sorrow," that he should never become a cleric or "any more suffer so much to get an education."[25] Yet when she offered to give him the arms and equipment of a knight, when he had reached the age for them, Guibert proudly refused, insisting that "if I had to die on the spot, I would not give up studying my lessons and becoming a clerk."

Different as their childhoods were in many ways, Guibert evidently shared with Peter Damian not only heavy physical punishment but also the experience, or the feeling, of maternal rejection, although Guibert's came at a much later time, when in fact, he was past twelve and his mother, in her growing obsession with her own spiritual welfare, decided to withdraw from the world and undertake the life of a recluse.[26] Regarding this decision as desertion, Guibert thought of her in putting her salvation before his well-being as, for all her devotion to him, a "cruel and unnatural mother."

> She knew that I should be utterly an orphan with no one at all on whom to depend, for great as was my wealth of kinsfolk and connections, yet there was no one to give me the loving care a little child needs at such an age; though I did not lack for the necessities of food and clothing, I often suffered from the loss of that careful provision for the helplessness of tender years that only a woman can provide.... Although she knew that I would be condemned to such neglect, yet Thy love and fear, O God, hardened her heart ... the tenderest in all the world, that it might not be tender to her own soul's harm.[27]

Clearly, as this passage suggests, what is extraordinary in Guibert's reminiscences of his childhood is his capacity to convey not only its significant details but the intense, if ambivalent, emotions that were persistently evoked by his profound attachment to his mother. Living constantly, it seems, under the scrutiny of her critical and demanding eye—for even in her retirement she continued to supervise his life and to show her anxiety about him—he never ceased to feel the sense of guilt she had apparently instilled and to long for the love and approval that were, perhaps, never fully given. Throughout his recollections he shows himself as always, essentially, the jealously possessive and dependent child to whose self-concern we owe what is certainly our fullest and most intimate account of the relationship of a medieval mother and son.[28]

Unusual, in some ways unique as they are, however, and much as they differ from one another, our two accounts of childhood also exhabit clearly certain general characteristics of the kind of records from which they are drawn, and on which this study heavily depends. These are the personal, biographical and autobiographical or self-revealing works which grew more abundant during these centuries, manifesting the rising self-awareness that Marc Bloch and many others have discerned in the culture of this age.[29] Until quite late in our period, such works were for the most part written in Latin by and for, and usually about, members of a small literate minority, almost exclusively clerical or monastic in mode of life. By and large, they are concerned with the exceptional childhoods of exceptional children who were, or who appeared to be, in later life distinguished by unusual spiritual or intellectual gifts or, in the case of autobiography, by an uncommon self-consciousness, and who, again with relatively few exceptions, had been born into families of the upper classes, who were of noble or knightly or, more rarely, bourgeois origin. Like John of Lodi's "life" of Peter Damian, many of these records are, especially in the earlier centuries of our inquiry, hagiographical in character and intent, and inhibited, therefore, by the conventions of this genre. Except in a few cases, their subjects were younger children in their families, those, that is, who were commonly destined for ecclesiastical careers or for the monastic life, and they were more often boys than girls, although here the exceptions are often significant. Of more ordinary children of different social classes, we also find glimpses in various kinds of sources, including these; Guibert, for example, has a particularly sharp eye for other children. But the uncommon child and childhood predominates and any efforts at generalization must take account of this inherent bias in our evidence.

Still another important limitation, following from the considerations just suggested, lies in the fact that in more detailed accounts of childhood and in briefer references to it, we see children and childhood through the eyes of those who had, obviously, been children but very rarely parents. Here again there are exceptions, increasing in number as we advance into a time when the literacy of laymen became more common, or as we encounter in the works of Jewish writers like Moses Maimonides the father's viewpoint on infants and children. Although we would give a good deal to hear from Guibert's mother or Peter Damian's, among many others, their truly essential side of the story, only one or two mothers speak directly and too briefly, as mothers, in these centuries: among them, in the early twelfth century, the German poet, Frau Ava, who identifies herself simply as the mother of two children, one living and one dead, and both very dear to her, for whom she asks her readers' prayers.[30] In general, parents rarely speak in their parental roles; their feelings and attitudes towards their children, their ideals and expectations, are revealed in their actions or by other witnesses, not infrequently, as in Guibert's case, by their children. Regarding the testimony offered by the sources of this period to the phases or stages of childhood, our two guides are once again suggestive. Most often stressed are infancy—the precariousness of early life and the dramas of birth and survival—and the stage of childhood from four or five years on, when children of the sort we know most about are ready to learn to read and write. This appears as a major turning-point and one most heavily emphasized. Often neglected or ignored are the years in which very young children were less open to observation and instruction by the kind of writers to whom we owe a good deal of our evidence.

In keeping with the emphases and deficiencies of the evidence, this essay assumes a fairly flexible view of the temporal limits of childhood. Encompassed here are not only "infancy," commonly regarded quite literally as the period extending from birth to the fifth year, "when some children do not speak, or if they do, do not speak well," but also much of what was in the medieval definition *pueritia*, "boyhood," the later stages of childhood to around eleven or twelve.[31] Although we may think of medieval childhood as relatively brief, as in some ways it was, in allusions to this stage of life, as to others, contemporary writers, many of whom did not, in fact, know their own ages, were often vague and sometimes very liberal. Guibert of Nogent was plainly one of those people who always think of themselves as younger than they are; but in referring to himself as still a child at the age of twelve, he shared a not uncommon notion.[32]

If his account and John of Lodi's help us to define those limitations and distortions of our evidence which may skew our perspectives on the problems of childhood in this period, these records are, though far from typical in any literal sense, also exemplary and illustrative in more positive ways. For they point to what can be learned from the varied sources of this period about the care, and the neglect, of children, about the experiences, emotions and fantasies of childhood and about attitudes towards it, and most particularly, perhaps, concerning the relations of children with parents or their substitutes. In the questions they raise and in the insights they offer, they open the paths to be explored in successive divisions of this study. But our two works also open larger perspectives, both bright and dark, on the problems with which we are concerned, and these invite at least brief comment here.

When Guibert of Nogent was born, there were as yet few palpable signs of the vast movements of change that were during the next two centuries profoundly to transform the Western society of the early middle ages. The demographic expansion that would by the late thirteenth century have doubled the population of Western Europe, the economic developments, the increased productivity and capital accumulations that fostered the growth of a more highly urbanized, though still agrarian society: these and many other changes signified that this society had embarked on the career of expansion which was, with some setbacks, to mark its development in future centuries.[33] During Guibert's lifetime these processes of change were greatly accelerated and by the time of his death their signs were already striking in some areas, most visibly perhaps in the newer religious and ecclesiastical movements which were to influence more deeply than ever before nearly every phase of life in this Christian society with which each infant sealed his contract at baptism.[34] To point, even sketchily, to such changes is to suggest that they must have altered for the better the general conditions of life during these centuries, and in the large view this was probably true, for many, if not for most, members of this society, and especially for those who were the chief agents and beneficiaries of economic and social change.[35] In an expanding population, more people, we must assume, survived those hazards of disease, famine, malnutrition, violence and poverty, the fundamental insecurities that still dominated the life of this society.[36] It is, however, this darker perspective that must seem the more compelling at those levels of human experience with which this study is concerned.

For, despite improvements, the pall of mortality continued to hang most menacingly over every life, and especially every young life throughout our period. In a time when the common expectation of life has been estimated at about thirty years, the rates of mortality in childbirth were exceedingly high and those of infant mortality higher still, something perhaps in the order of one or even two in three.[37] These facts of life and death are, indeed, strikingly illustrated by our two central sources, which suggest that with the short expectancy of life in general, those children who survived were more likely than not to be orphaned or semi-orphaned at an early age. The story of Peter Damian's childhood, moreover, confronting us starkly with the images of the "un-wanted child" and the despairing, overburdened mother, raises serious questions concerning the fate of children who were unwelcome or for whatever reason abandoned or deserted. It is against this sombre back-drop of mortality that we must approach the lives and experience of children and parents in these centuries, and its implications have sug-gested the title "survivors and surrogates," which, though it could per-haps apply as well to other chapters in this volume, seems especially fitting for a period in whose records the psychological and emotional as well as the physical impact of these harsh circumstances was for the first time so variously and consciously portrayed.[38]

TO LIVE OR TO DIE: THE DRAMAS OF BIRTH AND SURVIVAL

> Racked by pains long endured and her tortures increasing as her hour drew near, when she thought I had at last in natural course come to birth, instead I was returned within the womb. By this time my father, friends and kinsfolk were crushed with dismal sorrowing for both of us, for while the child was hastening the death of the mother; and she her child's in denying him deliv-erance, all had reason for compassion.
>
> Guibert of Nugent, *Memoirs*

Dramatic though it may seem to us, Guibert's account of his birth could hardly exaggerate the fears, hardships and hazards attending preg-nancy and parturition in a time when these and other physiological processes were for the most part and for those most directly involved veiled in ignorance and mystery, and surrounded by age-old customs and superstitions.[39] Now to us among the clichés of hagiography, the dreams, visions and portents that commonly preceded and followed the conception of the future saint were often also vivid expressions of the primitive anxieties and sense of wonder associated with these mysteri-ous if natural functions.[40] Although mothers were by far the most fre-quent recipients of these predictive signs, fathers, too, might enjoy such supernatural visitations, as did the father of St. Gerald of Aurillac, who, after a vision advising him to beget his son, later shared with his wife, shortly before the child's birth, the portentous experience of hear-ing him cry out three times from the womb, "thus signifying by that small voice," according to the biographer, "the happy fame with which he was later to fill the world."[41] Of what was actually going on within the womb during the stages of fetal development, ordinary people can have had only the vaguest impressions. Learned writers, however, had increasing access to ancient knowledge of obstetrics and gynecology, notably that deriving from its primary source, the teachings of the great second-century physician, Soranus, which were through diverse channels available in the West from the early middle ages.[42] Various medical treatises, especially from the twelfth-century onwards, offered advice, often sensible or at least unobjectionable, on the care of women in pregnancy, and its stages and symptoms are also depicted in the popular literature of this time and later.[43] Particularly emphasized in both learned and popular works were the prenatal influences which might go back to the moment of conception; hence children conceived at forbidden times in the ecclesiastical year were regarded by some stern preachers as marked from the first by these particular sins of their parents.[44] Once having conceived, expectant mothers were exhorted to think the thoughts, feel the emotions and practice the virtues that would most felicitously shape the characters of their unborn children.[45]

If Guibert gives us some sense of the emotional atmosphere surrounding childbirth, he also provides as realistic a description of this occasion as we are likely to find in any but the medical writings of this period. The reason for the lack of direct description is simple; the authors of most such works, being men, were rarely, if ever, present at the actual occasion of birth, which was customarily attended only by women.[46] Until the appearance of popular, vernacular treatises fairly late in our period, moreover, the obstetrical and pediatric knowledge available in medical works of this period, can hardly have affected more than a very small minority of mothers and children.[47] This knowledge appears in any case to have been an amalgam of theoretical learning with the customary and empirical practices which were the stock in trade of the midwives or "sages femmes" who commonly supervised labor and childbirth, and we have almost no trustworthy evidence regarding their training.[48] It was the midwife, Bartholomew of England writes in the early thirteenth century, who knew how to soften the uterus with unguents and fomentations so that the child might be delivered with less difficulty and pain.[49] It was she who received the infant from the womb, severed and tied the umbilical cord at a length of four fingers, washed or bathed the baby, rubbed it with salt and sometimes crushed rose leaves or honey "to comfort its limbs and free them of mucus," and with her finger rubbed the palate and gums with honey to clean the insides of the mouth and to stimulate the infant's appetite.[50] Bartholomew strongly recommended the frequent bathing of newborns, as well as anointing with oil of myrtle or rose and the massaging of all their limbs, especially those of boys, which should be more strenuously exercised. He also provided a rationale for what was in most regions of Europe the apparently universal practice of swaddling the limbs of newborn and young infants; this should be done, he says, not only to prevent the deformities likely to occur because of the "fluidity" and "flexibility" of infantile limbs, but also to ensure that "natural heat might be restored to the interior of the body" and aid in the digestion of food, which was further encouraged, he thought, by the gentle rocking of infants in their cradles.[51]

To the treatment of newborn infants sketched here, there is the significant exception reported in detail by Gerald of Wales (Giraldus Cambrensis) in the late twelfth century and casting further light on the cosmetic practices of traditional midwifery. According to Gerald, whose account is supported by other evidence, Irish babies certainly and probably also those of other Celtic peoples were not "carefully nursed as is usual."

> For apart from the nourishment with which they are sustained by their hard parents from dying altogether, they are for the rest abandoned to ruthless nature. They are not put in cradles and swathed; nor are their tender limbs helped by frequent baths or formed by any useful art. The midwives do not use hot water to raise the nose or press down the face or lengthen the legs. Unaided nature according to her own judgment arranges and disposes without the help of any art the limbs that she has produced. As if to prove what she can do by herself she continually shapes and moulds, until she finally forms and finishes them in their full strength with beautiful upright bodies and handsome and well complexioned faces.[52]

Despite these natural advantages, however, the Irish, being in Gerald's view a totally barbarous people, were also, he maintained, addicted to incest and adultery, to which he attributed what seemed to him the extraordinarily high incidence of birth defects among them. Never, he declared, had he seen in any other nation "so many individuals who were born blind, so many lamed, maimed or having some natural defect."[53]

Although it is highly doubtful that this people was, in fact, more prone to such deficiencies than any other, the incidence of these defects in medieval society, whether congenital or the result of birth damage, appears in general to have been extremely high.[54] It was among the duties of midwives in the infant's first bathing to examine it for marks and other defects, which may well have been in a good many cases the outcome of their own ministrations. For if these women might be reasonably adequate to the demands of a normal birth, they were hardly equipped to cope with the difficulties and hazards of an abnormal one. In cases, for example, of abnormal presentation, the midwife's chief recourse was to push the child back into the womb or to try to change its position manually.[55] If all else failed, and the mother died while the child still lived, it might be excised from her body, as in the well-known case of Purchard "the Unborn" related by Ekkehard IV of Saint-Gall.[56]

In this instance the mother having died two weeks before the expécted birth, the premature child was cut from her corpse and wrapped in the fat of a newborn pig "until his skin should grow." Such excision at birth appears to have been not uncommon, and was in fact recommended by some ecclesiastical authorities, since the technique of Caesarian section had been known since antiquity, but I have found no definite evidence of a mother's survival of the operation.[57]

Once having made the hazardous passage from the womb, the infant's survival depended upon one thing above all else: its access to breast milk of good quality. In these centuries this meant, for all but the small minority of the noble and prosperous who could afford wet-nurses, the mother's milk. For all classes the mother who nursed her own children reflected the ideal maternal image. Celebrated in contemporary representations of the *Virgo lactans,* the nursing Mother of Christ, and in the poignant Eve nursing her child portrayed on the bronze doors at Hildesheim, and later at Verona, this essential maternal function was emphasized and extolled in literary and didactic works of various kinds.[58] Praising it on both scientific and emotional grounds, Bartholomew of England explained that "while the foetus exists in the womb it is nourished on blood, but at birth nature sends that blood to the breasts to be changed into milk."[59] Its own mother's milk, therefore, was better for the newborn child than another's. Anticipating modern views on the subject, he stressed also the emotional bonds thereby strengthened; "for the mother loves her own child most tenderly, embraces and kisses it, nurses and cares for it most solicitously." Repeating these themes, another thirteenth century writer stressed also the idea that as every plant draws its strength from its roots, and maternal milk best shapes the child's nature, that mother does ill who cuts her child off from these fostering sources.[60]

If the nursing mother represented the ideal of these centuries, she was also to a very large extent the reality; for the vast majority of children, except in cases of dire necessity, must have been dependent on their mother's milk. But it also seems clear that among women of the noble classes—again, it must be emphasized, a small but highly visible minority—the practice of resorting to wet-nurses became increasingly common. What has been called perhaps over-enthusiastically the "nursing revolution" of this period may thus have made some contribution to a growing population, since the use of wet-nurses is thought to have shortened the interval between pregnancies and, in general, to have encouraged the production of more children.[61] The practice of wet-nursing was, in fact, fairly common throughout this time; in the mid-eleventh century, for example, Guibert's mother provided nurses both for her own son and for the child whom she adopted in expiation of her husband's sins.[62] As this case and many others show, however, the infant was not ordinarily, so far as I have been able to discover, sent out to nurse, after the fashion of later centuries; the wet-nurse was, rather, brought into the household to the child.[63] That the use of wet-nurses in general was resisted in some noble circles is suggested by the story, intended as exemplary, of the Blessed Ida of Boulogne, which in its most inflated version describes how violently this saintly and devoted mother of three sons, who had never permitted them to be nursed by anyone but herself, reacted to the flouting of her wishes in this matter.[64]

Whether the mother or the nurse supplied the milk, nothing was more important, in the contemporary view, than its quality, and this was all the more essential because of the general conviction that the formative influences of milk affected the character as well as the physical constitution of the infant.[65] Regarding the latter, one writer declared that bad milk was above all to be avoided because those nursed on it commonly fell prey to the worst infant diseases; these are described, with their remedies, in the most influential of medieval handbooks on the subject.[66] Since good milk was vital to the child's development, every effort was to be made to secure it and to ensure its quality, especially through the selection of a healthy nurse and control of her diet. She was, for example, to avoid strong wine and coarse food, and if medicine should be required by her nursling, it should be given to her so that it might be absorbed through her milk.[67]

Beyond such general principles and prescriptions, however, the practical details of infant-feeding become more elusive. A twelfth-century poem sums up the infant's day in simple words: "It sleeps, it cries, it suckles."[68] But how frequently babies were nursed and for how long are all but unanswerable questions.[69] Marie de France assures us that the infant Milon, swaddled in fine linen and carried in his elegant cradle with its feather pillow and its fur-lined coverlet, was fed and bathed seven times a day by the nurses who accompanied him on his long journey to his foster-mother.[70] But we may doubt that most babies of this time were so fortunate. Although a thirteenth-century preacher inveighed against the over-feeding of rich children, for whom he threatened an early demise, it was perhaps not the least of the many advantages of the rich over the poor that their children were nursed more frequently and over a longer period of time.[71] What little can be discovered about the time of weaning in these centuries suggests a variability between one and three years and, perhaps, a shorter nursing period for girls and for the children of peasants; we learn, for example, that in some peasant families of the ninth century in southern France boys were weaned around two and girls at one.[72] It appears, too, that among all classes breast-feeding was often and quite early supplemented with pap made from bread and animal milk or water.[73] There is further evidence that, despite a generally well-justified fear of animal milk, necessity must not infrequently have demanded recourse to it.[74] The use of "nursing-horns," which could hardly have contained anything but animal milk, is well attested from the early middle ages onwards; in a twelfth-century poem they were listed as standard equipment of the nurse, along with swaddling-bands and bibs.[75]

But there is more to the care of babies than nursing and here again what evidence we have points largely to the habits and practices of the noble class and to the prominent role of the nurse. By the early thirteenth century, in a work of "popular science," she was assigned the functions doubtless performed by the mother in households farther down the social scale.[76] Assuming the maternal role in nursing the baby, she also rejoiced with the child when he was happy and sympathized with his sorrows; she bathed, cleaned and changed him when he was soiled; she chewed the meat in her own mouth for the toothless child and fed him with her finger. Hers was the hand that rocked his cradle and hers the voice that soothed him with lullabies; it was she who began teaching him to speak, "lisping and repeating the same words." She was, it seems, something more like a "nanny" than a wet-nurse and by this time such nurses in some noble households remained with their charges throughout their childhood years.[77]

Whether or not it was rocked by a nurse, one accoutrement of infant life assumed a growing importance during these centuries, and this is the cradle. Although our earliest pictorial representations of the rocking-cradle date from the thirteenth century, the cradle in simpler forms must certainly have been in use very much earlier; there was, for example, a deep basket-like cradle, easily portable, in which the baby was held in place by bands, and there are many literary references to cradles of one kind or another, among them the silver cradle that figures in the life of St. Elizabeth of Hungary.[78] But if this object might be something of a "status-symbol," its use could also be regarded as a matter of life and death, as is clear from numerous injunctions of ecclesiastical authorities directed at keeping children out of the parental bed and thus avoiding the danger of "overlaying" and suffocation.[79] In a series of such exhortations extending through the thirteenth century the English bishops strongly urged that children be kept in cradles at least until the age of three.[80] Quite apart from its other implications, which will be more fully considered elsewhere, this legislation is suggestive regarding the sleeping arrangements of many parents and children in this period.[81]

Babies who spent their days playing and sleeping and their nights demanding the attention of their mothers or nurses were doubtless no less trying, if less comprehensible, in this period than in later times, and the difficulties of soothing them might even encourage thoughts of demonic possession.[82] But there are also clear signs, especially from the twelfth century onwards, of tenderness towards infants and small children, in-

terest in the stages of their development, awareness of their need for
love, and active responsiveness to that "beauty of infancy" which John
of Lodi had earlier portrayed. Hildegard of Bingen, for example, explains at length, in terms favorable to the dignity of the species, why
human infants are so slow to walk, compared with animals, and why
they must crawl or creep on hands and feet before they walk.[83] Several
poets show us, though without noting its age at this momentous advance, the child taking its first steps, holding on to benches and stools,
or standing by a table, being tempted by pieces of bread held just out
of its reach; another writer pictures a child playing "peek-a-boo", covering its eyes and thinking no one sees it.[84] There is also Caesarius of
Heisterbach's story of the affectionate nun to whom Jesus appeared as
a child of three, "just beginning to talk,"[85] and, regarding speech, Salimbene's well-known tale of the babies in Frederick II's experiment, who
all died when cut off from human speech, "because they could not live
without the petting and the joyful faces and loving words of their
foster mothers, or without those "swaddling songs" which a woman
sings to put a child to sleep and without which "it sleeps badly and has
no rest."[86]

The responsiveness of children to music and singing, because "the
spirit is so new and fresh in their little bodies," is the point also of
Adelard of Bath's charming vignette of a tiny child, not yet able to
speak, standing by the fire, listening to a music master and his pupils
play the harp, and becoming so excited by the music that he began to
move his hands and fingers with its rhythm.[87] Surely we cannot deny a
genuine and deeper empathy to St. Hugh of Lincoln, whose "purity and
innocence made him exceptionally gentle with and attractive to children," whom in turn he loved particularly "because of their complete
naturalness."[88] Wherever he found them, his biographer tells us, "he
caressed them lovingly with angelic tenderness, and even when they
could hardly talk, they made affectionate noises."

> I saw a child of about six months, who, when he made the sign of
> the cross on its forehead with the holy oil, expressed such great
> delight by the movement of its limbs, that it reminded one of the
> joy of the Baptist, leaping up in the womb. The tiny mouth and
> face relaxed in continuous chuckles, and it seemed incredible that
> at an age when babies generally yell it could laugh in this way. It
> then bent and stretched out its little arms as if it were trying to
> fly, and moved its head to and fro, as if to show that its joy was
> almost too great to bear. Next it took his hand in both its tiny
> ones, and exerting all its strength, raised it to his face. It then
> proceeded to lick it instead of kissing it. . . . Those present were
> amazed at the unusual spectacle of the bishop and the infant ab-
> solutely happy in each other's company.[89]

Appealing though this spectacle may be to us as well—and it is one of several offered by a work unusually rich in such insights—it represents, like our other examples, the response not of a parent but of one of those former children in whom the sensibilities of this age were most articulate. Among its various maternal images in art, there is, however, one more significant still in its tenderness. Nowhere is the essential bond of childhood more poignantly portrayed than in a roundel in the church of the Madeleine at Vézelay, in which a barefoot peasant mother combs, or de-louses, the hair of her small child, whose head and hands rest trustingly on her knees.[90]

But this lowly mother has, also at Vézelay, her somber counterpart, a reminder of the dark fate that menaced every child in these centuries; this is the capital which depicts a grieving peasant father holding in his arms the dead child for whom he implores from St. Benedict the miracle of resurrection.[91] Only through such interventions, which fill the saints' lives and miracle-collections of this period, could most parents hope to save their children from the countless hazards of disease and disaster, violence and brutality, that were incessant threats to their survival.[92] If they failed, they could look only to such consolations as those offered by Peter Damian, who urged the bereaved parents of an infant son to dry their tears and rejoice in the thought of the eternal felicity to which he had been so swiftly transported.[93] Since baptism alone opened the way to salvation, it is not surprising that an omnipresent mortality led the Church in the course of these centuries to depart from ancient custom and to require all infants, whether or not they seemed likely to survive, to be baptized within a few days of birth.[94] Since the ceremony of baptism also signified the infant's reception into the Christian community, this requirement and the insistence on public baptism in a church may also have been intended as a deterrent to practices aimed at ensuring the infant's failure to survive.

After birth and baptism, the best milk, the most careful nursing and, after weaning, sufficient food might, as we have seen, markedly improve the chances of survival and thus explain why, as David Herlihy puts it, "those blessed with the goods of this earth were also blessed (or burdened) with children; in contrast, the deprived, the heavily burdened, the poor left comparatively few heirs."[95] If this is true, it is probably not because the poor produced fewer children, but because they could not support them. For they were most directly and constantly at the mercy of the chronic cycles of famine, malnutrition, disease and death, and their children were by far the most common victims of the parental negligence and despair, of the abandonment, exposure and even infanticide, which must be counted among major threats to young life in this period.[96]

If all of these practices were related to the pressures, material and psychological, of á society living often at the limits of subsistence, they are related most specifically to the problem of population, or "family", control in a time when the means of limiting births were totally inadequate, if not, for practical purposes, virtually non-existent. That there were attempts at such control through contraception and abortion is evident from the records condemning these practices, as well as in works recommending the means by which they might be achieved.[97] That they were largely ineffective is demonstrated by the incidence of other practices to which the records of this period also bear substantial testimony. The problem of infanticide in Western society during this period has only very recently become the subject of the serious investigation which will doubtless increase our knowledge of what, insofar as it was a secret sin, or crime, must in large measure lie beyond our closest scrutiny.[98] As the case of Peter Damian's mother suggests, simple failure or refusal to nourish may well have been the most common form of infanticide. There is, in any case, considerable evidence, especially from the earlier medieval centuries, that wherever selective or neglective factors were at work, they were likely to work to the disadvantage of girls,[99] who were not highly valued in a predominantly military and agricultural society, and even more drastically to the disadvantage not only of the illegitimate but of the physically deformed and mentally retarded, of those children who were regarded as "changelings," the works of another powerful enemy of children, the Devil.[100]

Throughout these centuries, most of our evidence of destructive practices comes from sources, chiefly ecclesiastical, whose purpose was to discourage, prevent or suppress them, or to alleviate the sufferings of their victims, and such records cast some light both on the dimensions of the problem confronting authority and the effectiveness of various efforts to deal with it.[101] From the early middle ages there is the testimony of the law codes and the penitentials to attempts to prevent the exposure of infants and their "overlaying," whether intentional or not; with the ninth century comes the first specific prohibition against the taking of infants into the parental bed.[102] During the eleventh and twelfth centuries the campaign against these practices seems to have grown in intensity, and sheer carelessness as well as evil intent on the part of parents was perceived as a cause of unfortunate "accidents"; this is clear in an exemplary story related by Peter Abelard, who also linked this sin to poverty and exploitation and regarded its "heavy punishment" as a salutary warning to other women.[103]

To official policies, however, our most substantial and revealing body of printed evidence is the English synodal legislation of the thirteenth century, mentioned earlier, and this reflects a significantly sustained effort not only to punish the delinquent but to admonish and instruct ignorant and negligent as well as ill-intentioned parents.[104] In this legislation both the deliberate killing of infants and their negligent over-laying were included in the category of major sins, reserved to the judg-ment of the bishop.[105] In synod after synod, moreover, in every English diocese, priests were enjoined to warn the women of their parishes every Sunday not only against taking young children into their beds, but also about securing them in their cradles in such a way that they could not turn over on their faces.[106] Clerical admonitions were also to stress the sin of drunkenness as a frequent cause of parental carelessness and danger to children.[107] Although infanticide in its various forms was com-monly, when it involved the parents themselves, treated as a sin rather than a crime and dealt with by ecclesiastical authorities, the early twelfth century, also in England, had seen the first secular legislation in which the killing or accidental suffocation of another's child by a nurse or teacher was made punishable in the same way as adult homicide.[108]

If the pastoral concern of the English bishops, among whom was the great Robert Grosseteste, may be regarded as a significant effort to go beyond prohibition and punishment to what seemed identifiable causes of these ills, a similar direction is evident in earlier and more positive at-tempts to cope with the problems of abandonment and exposure. Here, it seems clear, the chief victims were perceived as the offspring of illicit, irregular and impermanent unions, the children of "unmarried mothers" and prostitutes. These were the women singled out in the earliest ef-forts to provide for orphaned and abandoned children; for in the char-ter of the first medieval foundling home in the late eighth century, Bishop Dateus of Milan specifically took unmarried mothers under the protection of his hospice and similarly in the ninth century the Frankish bishops prescribed that such women were to be invited to bring their children to the churches for adoption by the charitable faithful.[109]

Given the instabilities of marriage especially in early medieval soci-ety, and the unrestrained sexuality of many of its members, the num-bers of illegitimate children were doubtless very large indeed. Among those belonging to the noble class, whose households are said to have "swarmed with bastards," the stigma of illegitimacy might have been lightly regarded, although it was a serious bar to inheritance, in a so-ciety in which this was a paramount consideration, as it was also to ecclesiastical orders.[110] But here again the heaviest burdens, not only of shame but also of support, fell upon the poor, and both were carried by the exploited women who were far more often than not unable to provide for their children.[111] The link, in the religious perspective, be-tween infanticide and illicit sexuality is clear in a vivid twelfth-century portrayal of a mother who had slain her child burning in hell with the lustful.[112] It was in this period, too, from the late eleventh century on-wards, that both categories of victims, mothers and children, began to compel the serious attention of those powerful figures who were most active in the reforming and "evangelical" movements of the age.

"Fallen women" and their children were prominent in the crowds of the deprived and oppressed who were, at this time, attracted by such magnetic reformers as Robert of Arbrissel,[113] and a growing concern with what was, in an increasingly urban environment, an ever more visible social ill culminated in the late twelfth-century campaign of Fulk of Neuilly to provide dowries and arrange respectable marriages for these unfortunate women.[114] Even more significant were contemporary ventures, modest though they may seem, aimed at salvaging the other and more numerous victims of poverty and exploitation: abandoned and exposed as well as legitimately orphaned children.[115] Again, as earlier, foundling-homes evidently first appeared in the flourishing Italian towns; in Florence, for example, there were several such establishments before the founding of the Innocenti.[116] But most far-reaching in its effects was the work of Guy of Montpellier who founded, around 1160, the Order of the Holy Spirit, among whose purposes was the care of foundlings and orphans.[117] Spreading rapidly and widely in France and elsewhere, the order won the patronage of Pope Innocent III who, appalled at the sight of "countless" infant bodies afloat in the Tiber, called Guy to Rome, where he established the foundling-hospitals of Santo Spirito and Santa Maria in Saxia, the latter becoming eventually the mother-house of his order.[118] Strongly influenced by its work, in which sisters assumed responsibility for women and children, were the confraternities whose members in various cities participated in the charitable labors of the order.[119]

Of the care given to children in these institutions during our period we know very little; those who survived were, it seems, commonly apprenticed or hired out as servants at eight or ten.[120] Our sources are often more attentive to the charitable impulses of individuals, which were also at work in this period, and they suggest that the private adoption of orphaned and abandoned children was by no means uncommon. Often, as in Peter Damian's case, responsibility for such children passed, for good or ill, to other members of their families; by the late twelfth and thirteenth centuries we find fathers making more formal testamentary provisions for the care of their minor children.[121] But the children of strangers were also the objects of such concern; Guibert, for example, refers not only to his mother's generosity in this regard, but to another noblewoman's adoption of a Jewish child, who later became a dedicated monk.[122] The rescue of children whose lives were imperilled by the growing intolerance that accompanied the crusading movement may, indeed, have had a special appeal, since in these cases the rewards of conversion were added to those of charity.[123] If in occasional dreadful episodes of persecution Jewish parents might prefer death for their children, in other kinds of crisis Christian parents might be reduced to selling their children or delivering them into serfdom.[124] That their purchase might be in some cases a form of rescue is suggested by the story of St. Hugh of Lincoln and the boys whom he brought up in his household.[125] But, as another interesting tale in his biography shows, borrowed, purchased and even rented children were sometimes fraudulently used to secure inheritances, among other purposes; in at least one such case, however, a mother repented of her bargain and submitted to the ordeal of hot iron in order to recover her child.[126]

Even the most positive and practical of the charitable efforts noted here can only have touched the margins—they could hardly have reached the causes—of the neglect, abuse and abandonment of children during these centuries. Yet they must be counted among the early fruits of an awakened consciousness of the sufferings of the poor and the weak, and thus among the more visible signs of those great "mouvements de profondeur," the long slow processes of evangelizing and education through which more humane ideals and values gradually penetrated not only the dominant minorities in this society, but also in some measure its more silent masses.[127] To the various ways in which this "secret revolution" of conscience and sensibility may have affected the experience and treatment of children during this period, there is, however, much other testimony. It is most clearly heard perhaps in those works which, like our two accounts of childhood, offer us at least some insight into the more intimate world of feeling and relationships that is a major concern of this essay.

THE EXILES: PERSPECTIVES ON THE EXPERIENCE OF CHILDHOOD IN THE ELEVENTH AND TWELFTH CENTURIES

"Thou knowest with what pains she labored so that the sound beginning of a happy and honorable childhood ... might not be ruined by an unsound heart."

Guibert of Nogent, *Memoirs*

"So, weeping, my father gave me, a weeping child, into the care of the monk, Reginald, and sent me away into exile for love of Thee, and never saw me again."

Orderic Vitalis, *Ecclesiastical History*,
c. 1138

"Lo, brethren, let us try to understand the affection of this good
Mother ... the tenderness with which she beholds the Infant in
her arms, sees him hang on her breast, hears him cry as children
do at the little hurts of his little body, and hastens to forestall all
evils which may happen to him. . . ."

> Eadmer of Canterbury, *Concerning the*
> *Excellence of the Most Glorious* ...
> *Mother of God,* c. 1115

How are we to picture the "happy and honorable" childhood of
those whose early lives were thought in this period worthy of record or
recollection?[128] For all its values, what Guibert of Nogent tells us may
seem so personal and particular as hardly to warrant wider extension.
Yet when we compare his portrayal of his childhood with others of its
kind, such striking similarities, as well as significant differences, emerge
that we are invited to go further and draw from them a larger sketch of
the images and relationships that appear to dominate the childhoods of
which we have some knowledge.[129] To attempt this is to submit to the
limitations that were noted earlier; but it is also to exploit at least some
possibilities afforded by what is, for our purposes, the most substantial
and revealing body of writings we possess from these centuries. In our
picture the experience of a few exceptional children will be magnified
and that of their brothers and sisters obscured or only dimly perceived.
But it may bring into sharper focus not only the ideal images of parents
and children with which many of our sources confront us, but some of
the realities that shaped the powerful and changing fantasies of this
period.

Although Guibert of Nogent's relationship with his mother may seem
in its intensity, as well as in the fullness of its portrayal, very much a
special case, her qualities appear with significant frequency in other
maternal portraits drawn or sketched in our sources. Like her, the noble
mothers of these centuries are commonly depicted as the efficient ad-
ministrators of their often extensive households, prudent yet generous
and charitable to the poor, distinguished for their piety and their devotion to the physical and spiritual welfare of their children.[130] All of
these virtues, and others, were impressively displayed, according to his
biographer, by the mother of St. Bernard of Clairvaux, who combined
"gentleness with firmness" in the rearing of her seven children, six boys
and one girl, all of whom ultimately entered the monastic life.[131] "As
soon as a child was born to her," we are told, "Aleth would offer it to
the Lord with her own hands," and it was for this reason that, unlike
many mothers of her class, she refused to allow her children to be
nursed by anyone else; "for it almost seemed as though the babes were
fed with the qualities of their mother's goodness as they drew the milk

from her breast." By contrast with Guibert's mother, she offered her children, when they were older, only plain and simple fare, "never allowing them to acquire the taste and habit for elaborate and delicate dishes."[132] As in her case and many others, an active concern for the education of their children was another prominent feature of the maternal portraits of our sources: the saintly Queen Margaret of Scotland, for example, was famous for having taught her children herself, as was Countess Ida of Boulogne, who had received some training in letters.[133]

If we look for the realities behind this doubtless idealized image, Guibert's more penetrating observations concerning his mother's background and experience offer us some clues to the preparation of such women as these for the arduous responsibilities of marriage and motherhood. Illiterate, as he tells us, she had evidently received little or no education as a child, and this lack of concern for the education of daughters, unless they were destined for the monastic life, was probably more common among noble familes in the eleventh century and before than it was thereafter.[134] But even in this earlier period, a number of royal and noble ladies had learned at least enough Latin to read the Psalter, and a few of them were considerably further advanced in their learning.[135] By the twelfth century the level of literacy was probably higher among women of the nobility than it was among their husbands and brothers, unless these last were monks or clerics.[136] Illuminated Gospel books and Psalters were often prized possessions of such ladies, and their texts and illustrations were, it seems, a major channel through which the newer currents of piety circulated.[137] We may assume, therefore, that the religious devotion of our mothers and their early instruction of their children had a growing basis in reality. Some of them may, in fact, have made use of the alphabet cards and similar teaching games and devices to which Peter Damian, among others, refers.[138]

Whatever the extent of their education, early marriage was the destiny of those girls who did not enter the religious life, and in either case the choice was rarely theirs to make; the decision almost always lay with their parents, for whom practical considerations and advantages commonly outweighed the desires and feelings of their children.[139] An unusual and illuminating instance of successful resistance to parental authority is the story of Christina of Markyate, a famous English recluse of the twelfth century, whose biographer paints a picture of contemporary parents much less favorable and perhaps more realistic than that offered by many of our sources.[140] Although this girl had early shown marked signs of her spiritual vocation, conversing with God in her bed as a little child, and had later vowed herself to virginity, the determination of her rich and worldly parents to force her into a desirable marriage led to a long and often violent struggle in which she was finally victorious.[141] In explaining why they were ready to stop at nothing, from bribes and threats to beating and imprisonment, to gain their end, her biographer makes it clear that, though she was "very dear" to them, they regarded her essentially as a valuable property and "feared losing her and all they could hope to gain through her."[142]

Most parents were evidently more successful than Christina's in arranging the futures of their children and most girls were, like Guibert's mother, married off by their fathers to husbands not of their own choosing and often, as in her case, at an age when they were barely nubile, if not still children. According to canon law, the minimum ages at marriage were twelve for girls and fourteen for boys, and many, it seems, were married or at least betrothed below these ages, although a growing ecclesiastical opposition to child-marriage may have had some effect as a deterrent.[143] So also, apparently, did the emphasis of canon lawyers on consent and "marital affection" as important, if not essential, elements in a valid marriage and even more perhaps, in the long run, an increasingly powerful effort to exalt the sanctity and sacramental character of Christian marriage.[144] We need not assume that all marriages were as miserable as that of Guibert's parents seems to have been to suspect that, in the setting of feudal society, conjugal affection was more often a happy accident than a natural condition and that his mother's sexual and emotional inhibitions may have been shared by many women who came as frightened children to marriages in which physical brutality and rejection were evidently far from uncommon.[145] Whatever the realities may have been, in theory and in law the husband's power and authority were supreme.[146] Even in what his biographer regarded as the "model marriage" of St. Bernard's parents, not their mutual affection but his mother's submissiveness is emphasized; "in so far as a woman can and may who is submissive to her husband's authority and who does not even have rights over her own body, she anticipated her husband's every wish."[147] That marriage was quite widely regarded by women of this period as a state to be endured rather than enjoyed is strongly suggested by the readiness, often the determination, of many of them, once widowed, to remain in that admirable condition, and by the alacrity with which many also, like Guibert's mother, turned to the consolations and securities of the religious life.[148]

Whether widowed or not, the "good mothers" of our sources are almost without exception conspicuous for those virtues, piety, dutiful acceptance of burdens and responsibilities, devotion to the spiritual development of their children, which were highly regarded by contemporary churchmen, whose promotion of these ideals doubtless did a good deal to shape the realities.[149] What is largely missing from our sources and most others of this period is any real depiction of family life, for which, indeed, the lack of privacy in these crowded feudal households may have left little place.[150] St. Bernard, it is said, loved as a child "to stay in the quiet simplicity of his home, and little could draw him away from it."[151] But even Guibert, with all of his detail, conveys little sense of domestic intimacy.[152] That the more personal and tender relations of mothers and children are little stressed in formal works does not, of course, mean that they did not exist.[153] The conventions of our sources, after all, did not encourage the portrayal of these aspects of early life, and the saintly child was usually shown as too serious to share the play and the naughtiness of his more ordinary peers, although Ailred of Rievaulx recalled that when he was a boy: "the friendship of those around me was my greatest joy and in . . . those years I gave myself up entirely to my love for my friends, so that to love and be loved seemed the most delightful thing in the world."[154] Yet the omissions of our sources may suggest, too, that there was often little room or incentive in these maternal lives for the spontaneous expression of tenderness and affection and that many children may have suffered from a deprivation to which Guibert's story of his childhood bears striking witness.[155]

Perhaps few eleventh-century mothers were capable of the under-standing insight into a child's anxieties that St. Anselm in his later life frequently and significantly attributed to his own mother. Having begged his parents to send him to school, he was as a little boy, the story goes, entrusted to a relative who took his duties as a teacher so seriously that, like Guibert's master, he kept the child constantly at his studies and never let him out of the house to play.[156] "Almost driven out of his mind" by this imprisonment, the young Anselm was finally returned to his mother in such a state of anxiety that he turned away from her and refused to speak. In tears at the thought that she had lost her son, his mother decided on a policy of complete permissiveness, or-dering all of her servants to let the child do whatever he might wish and not to oppose him in any way; through this treatment he was restored to his former happiness. The lesson of this wise indulgence was drawn by Anselm himself, who was celebrated for sensitivity and compassion for the young.[157] For he had, he declared, always tried to behave to-wards others with the same gentleness and understanding that his mother had shown him when he was a child. It is little wonder that after her death, while he was still a youth, he felt as though "the ship of his heart had lost its anchor and drifted almost entirely among the waves of the world."[158]

Whatever the virtues and deficiencies of actual mothers may have been, there can be little doubt that, as in Guibert's case, maternal ex-ample and maternal values were dominant in the lives and ideals of those children of whose experience we have some knowledge.[159] When Bernard of Clairvaux, for instance, was still living the life of a carefree and worldly youth, "the memory of his holy mother was always in his mind, so that he seemed to see her coming to him, reproaching and upbraiding him that she had not brought him up with such love and care that he could adopt this empty kind of existence."[160] If by the standards of their time the success of these mothers was judged by the spiritual distinction of their children, we may consider remarkable, too, in view of contemporary prospects, the numbers of sons and daughters they succeeded in rearing to maturity.[161] What is still more impressive, however, is the enduring devotion that some of them seem to have inspired. To this there is in the literature of this period no more eloquent testimony, not even Guibert's, than Peter the Venerable's epistolary portrait of his dead mother, in whose lovingly depicted life and character—she was not only saintly, compassionate and incessantly anxious for her children but "always happy and gay"—are reflected every facet of the contemporary maternal ideal.[162]

By contrast with this emphasis on the maternal figure and her influence, fathers and their relations with their children assume a more modest and sometimes ambiguous place in our sources.[163] If the father was not virtually absent from the child's early life, as he frequently was in a military and expansionist society, he is often depicted as the worldlier, less admirable figure, drawing the child away from his religious vocation, or more rarely, displaying the outright hostility that drove Anselm to renounce his patrimony and his native land and to find, at length, a more satisfactory father in Lanfranc at Bec.[164] Among the records examined here, only briefly in Abelard's *Story of Calamities* and more fully in the life of St. Hugh of Lincoln is the early relationship of a father and son portrayed sympathetically and even in the latter there are distinct overtones of deprivation. For, "deprived of a mother's care" by her death, Hugh was barely eight years old when he and his father together entered a community of canons regular.[165] As he himself later reported, in "talking confidentially" with his companions: "Truly, I never tasted the joys of this world. I never knew or learnt how to play." When Hugh was "learning to read," his father divided his patrimony by lot among his children, and gave the portion that fell to this youngest son to the community which he then entered by his father's choice.[166] They evidently remained closely associated in their life there, and as his father grew old, Hugh devoted himself almost entirely to his care. According to his biographer, "he often used to relate with great pleasure how for the rest of his father's life, he used to lead him and carry him about, dress and undress him, wash him, dry him and make his bed, and, when he grew feebler and weaker, prepare his food and even feed him."[167]

Although nearly all of the children with whom we are here concerned found their way eventually, like Hugh, into some form of the religious life, they did not all enter it so early or so involuntarily or by the same route. St. Anselm, for example, was perhaps twenty-seven when he became a monk at Bec, and Peter Damian was also in his twenties at the time of his conversion, as was Bernard of Clairvaux when he renounced the pleasures of the knightly life and eventually persuaded all of his brothers to do the same.[168] Intended for a secular career, like many boys of whose childhood we know nothing, Ailred of Rievaulx, a priest's son, had served in his boyhood at the Scottish court before his conversion to the monastic life.[169] But others, like Guibert, were much younger, often destined for this life from the outset and entering it as "oblates," children offered to monasteries by their parents, usually at an early age.[170] It was such children as these who faced most acutely the separation and the exile poignantly recalled by Orderic Vitalis when as an old man he wrote the words quoted earlier, adding:

> And I, a mere boy, did not presume to oppose my father's wishes, but obeyed him in all things, for he promised me for his part that if I became a monk I should taste of the joys of Heaven with the Innocents after my death. . . . And so, a boy of ten, I crossed the English channel and came into Normandy as an exile, unknown to all, knowing no one.[171]

When Orderic entered his Norman monastery in the late eleventh century, the practice of oblation was already on the wane, and its sharp decline during the next fifty years is yet another symptom of the transformations of this time.[172] But for at least two centuries and perhaps longer, the offering of noble children by their parents had been a major, indeed, probably the principal means of monastic recruitment, and its history and the motives that inspired it are most revealing of the attitudes of parents as well as the experience of children during this period.[173] Few aspects of this experience are, as Dom Knowles observes, more repellent to modern sensibility than the rearing of children "from infancy in the cloister, without home life, or the free society of other boys and girls, and without entry into many wide areas of innocent life."[174] To us this custom may seem, in fact, the most distressing instance of child-rearing practices which, though diverse and variable over this long period, frequently involved, at least among the noble classes, the early separation of children from their parents and siblings.[175]

But these were plainly not the views of their noble parents, members of a class for whom the claims of the family, or the *lignage,* and the preservation of its patrimony far transcended the wishes and interests of its youngest members, and for whom, too, social custom as well as the instabilities of life and family fortunes, encouraged the early disposition of their children's careers.[176] To such parents, especially in the period before social change and military expansion opened larger opportunities, the monasteries offered a most satisfactory solution to the problem of providing for those of their children for whom suitable alterna-

tives were not available: usually younger sons and those physically un-
fitted for the military life and daughters who might be for various
reasons unmarriageable.[177] Parents may have wept, as Orderic's father
did, when the time of separation came, though in relatively few cases,
apparently, was the parting so final.[178] But they would almost certainly
not have doubted that they were making honorable provision for the
spiritual and social welfare of those children whom they placed among
noble companions in an environment that seemed likelier than any other
to ensure their salvation.[179]

As for the children themselves, the history of their experience of this
life remains to be written; our impressions of it have been based largely
on the monastic constitutions and customaries which, in their careful
provisions for these youngest members of masculine communities, suggest a life of almost intolerable rigor and confinement.[180] It began when
the oblate was presented to the monastery, often between the ages of
five and seven, in a solemn ceremony in which, after his parents had
promised him permanently to his monastic vocation, he was divested of
his "cloak or tippet of fur or any other smock he might be wearing,"
tonsured and clothed in the cowl.[181] Thereafter he and his fellows were
expected to participate as fully as possible in the long hours of choir
service that dominated the monastic routine. In this as in every other
aspect of their lives, awake or asleep, these children, according to the
customary prescriptions, were to be kept under the constant supervision
aimed at justifying the common boast that no king's son was more carefully reared than the least of boys in a well-ordered monastery.[182]

Entrusted to the care of masters, one of whom was to remain between every two boys wherever they went, they were always to sit apart
from one another "in such a way as to prevent any physical contact,
never making signs or speaking to anyone or rising from their places
without the master's permission." In their relations with each other
and with older monks they were not to hand anything to anyone or receive anything from anyone except the abbot, prior or masters and no
one but these was ever to "make a sign to them or smile to them."[183]
None of the other monks was to enter their school or speak to them
anywhere without the permission of the abbot or prior. In the dormi-
tories, their beds were to be separated by those of their masters and
often one of these was to keep watch throughout the night by the light
of candles or lanterns; no child was ever to visit the lavatory or the la-
trine unaccompanied by a master.[184] Since, as at least one custumal put
it, "children everywhere need custody with discipline," the children
were not only beaten in their school and elsewhere, but in their own
chapter, as the older monks were.[185]

Plainly intended, among other things, to prevent sexual activities
among the children and the development of dangerous intimacies with

their elders, this rigorous watchfulness reflected, and no doubt enhanced, fears that were evidently well-founded.[186] Testimony to the facts and fantasies of sexual temptations of every variety abounds in the monastic sources of this period, which also invite serious reflection on the impact of this environment on young minds exposed to no other experience.[187] The omnipresence of the Devil and his minions, the lurid visions and nightmares that might haunt their overcharged imaginations, are vividly described by Guibert of Nogent,[188] among many others, and with perhaps greater penetration by his older contemporary, Otloh of Saint-Emmeram. Seeking self-understanding through the recording of his temptations, dreams and hallucinations, this extraordinary monk discloses with particular clarity how deeply he had been affected by the experiences of his childhood and youth and especially by his fear of beating, which fostered his own later belief in the moderate discipline of the young, with words rather than with blows.[189]

But no criticism of the abuses affecting children in monasteries is more revealing and significant than St. Anselm's admonition to a certain abbot who had complained to him of his difficulties in controlling the obstreperous boys in his charge, declaring that "we never give over beating them day and night, and they only get worse and worse."[190] Even the barest summary of Anselm's remarkable answer may convey the import of an argument that not only underscores the weaknesses of a system, but offers an impressively positive statement of a new and more sympathetic approach to the rearing of children.[191] Pointing to the destructive effects of the use of force and "injudicious oppression" upon the personalities of their young victims, Anselm declared that "feeling no love or pity, good-will or tenderness in your attitude towards them, they have in future no faith in your goodness but believe that all your actions proceed from hatred and malice against them; they have been brought up in no true charity towards anyone, so they regard everyone with suspicion and jealousy." Then he demanded, urging his benighted colleague to greater empathy, "Are they not human? Are they not flesh and blood like you? Would you like to have been treated as you treat them, and to have become what they are now?" Finally, stressing, as did Peter Damian and others, the importance of firm but gentle molding and shaping in the rearing of the young, he insisted that they must have "the encouragement and help of fatherly sympathy and gentleness" and that teaching and discipline should be adapted to the temperaments and capacities of individuals.[192]

As Anselm's argument suggests, the evils inherent in the practice of oblation were becoming increasingly evident to his contemporaries and some of them, like Ulrich of Cluny, argued vigorously against a custom which had, for the convenience of their noble relatives, filled the monasteries with a "conscript army" among whose members were many totally unsuited to the monastic life.[193] The gradual disappearance, or at least the great decline in numbers, of the oblates was, in fact, ensured by the opposition of reformers, together with the wider opportunities and perhaps also greater freedom now open to the sons of noble families.[194] But the very problems posed by the presence of children in these communities had also produced more positive effects. For it had fostered in, or forced upon, many that sense of the distinctiveness of childhood as a stage of life with its own needs and capacities which appears most strikingly in insights such as Anselm's, but which also showed itself in other ways, among them the dietary concessions, including the permission to eat meat, and other kinds of special treatment provided for monastic children.[195]

Although our sources tend to set the less attractive aspects of their lives in sharp relief, they also remind us that there could be a considerable discrepancy between the stringent regulations of monastic custumals and the actual experiences and compensations of these "exiled" children. In the monastery they often found a new "family" that inspired their devotion, in their teachers, masters and abbots the surrogates of their absent parents, and, especially in the earlier centuries of our period, in opportunities for education a path to pleasure and achievement.[196] Though certainly remarkable, the empathetic kindness and understanding of an Anselm were by no means unique, and the familial imagery that frequently pervades descriptions of the great monastic personalities of this period suggests the extent to which some of them had assumed parental roles and had been invested with qualities not only paternal but maternal.[197] His biographer speaks of the "almost motherly affection" of Hugh of Lincoln, and in the last illness of Ailred of Rievaulx, we are told, his monks used to visit him, "lying about his bed and talking with him as a little child prattles with its mother;" it is reported that his dying words to them were "I love you as earnestly as a mother does her sons."[198]

If it is in the monastic setting, and in the words and actions of such men as Anselm, Ailred and Hugh of Lincoln, that we see early and clear signs of a new gentleness and sympathy for the young, here, too, we may first follow the evolution of the new forms of piety and devotion in which the longings, deprivations and losses of generations of children may have found a most satisfying expression.[199] Once again, Anselm, that "wonderful man," as Guibert of Nogent called him, is a key figure. For in the prayers and devotions to the Virgin Mary which he composed and, incidentally, sent to great ladies of his time, he did more than anyone else, as Southern shows, to give a new shape and power to that supreme image of maternal compassion portrayed by his disciple, Eadmer, in the words quoted at the beginning of this section.[200] Ardent propagators also of the veneration of Mary and her Son were St.

Bernard and his fellow-Cistercians, and no one voiced more eloquently than Bernard the new devotion to the Infant Jesus, with which he had been inspired during his own boyhood in a Christmas vision of the Child's birth; in his sermons and other works he offered his contemporaries a new image of the Child in His human weakness, His "tears and crying," and urged them to be converted to that little Child so that they might learn "to be a little child."[201] Spreading first in the monastic environment, the new piety, with its "mood of emotional tenderness" and its stress on the humanity of the Infant Jesus and the loving-kindness of His Mother, gradually penetrated ever widening spheres of Western society.[202]

To follow its course would be to explore in depth that great transformation of sensibility and emotion some of whose signs we have already observed. But even to note a few of the changing themes and emphases perceptible in painting and sculpture, in the liturgy and the drama that emerged from it, in vernacular preaching and literature may suggest some of the ways, subtle and still undefined as well as more obvious, in which attitudes and feelings towards children and childhood may have been affected by the new images presented for popular contemplation.[203] The dramatic enactment of the Gospel story in art and liturgy was, in fact, among the novel experiences of the late eleventh and twelfth centuries, and here a growing stress on the Infancy of Christ, and especially on such themes as the Nativity and the Adoration of the Magi, gave the images of Mother and Child a much greater prominence and often an appealing humanity.[204] Their depiction in poses of mutual affection grows more common in the twelfth century, culminating in such tender portrayals as those of the "Madonna of Dom Rupert" and the somewhat later Rood Screen at Chartres. Now, as Southern observes, the familiar representation of the Child seated as if enthroned on His Mother's knee, often holding the symbols of His power, was joined by many other forms, "the laughing Child, the Child playing with an apple or a ball, the Child caressing its Mother, or ... being fed from its Mother's breast."[205] Portraying the flight into Egypt, Gislebertus of Autun in the early twelfth century shows us the Mother firmly grasping her baby, who, touching a globe with one hand, holds tight to his Mother with the other, still a helpless child.[206]

Another popular and highly pertinent theme of this period—more important, indeed, than has sometimes been thought and asking for closer study—was the Massacre of the Innocents, often portrayed in dramatic and sometimes lurid detail, but rarely with such effective emphasis on maternal love and protective care as on the twelfth-century painted ceiling of the church of Zillis in Switzerland.[207] For here the cautionary lesson of this episode is conveyed through the pairing of a scene of the slaughter itself with one showing two devoted mothers, one offering her breast to a swaddled infant, the other affectionately embracing a child of about two.[208] The new images of maternal tenderness and childish dependence were doubtless most vividly displayed in such visual forms, among them the Psalters mentioned earlier, in which noble or at least affluent mothers and their children might contemplate the Gospel scenes that often illustrated them.[209] Even before the preaching and writing of the friars gave them still greater currency, the more novel forms of devotion were popularized in such works as these, as they were also in the collections of the Miracles of the Virgin, which from the early twelfth century began to circulate throughout Europe, and in the popular sermons which may sometimes be reflected in these miracle-collections.[210] From this time, too, the Gospel stories were told and sung to lay audiences in the vernacular languages, as in the poetic *Leben Jesu* of the German Frau Ava, herself a mother, who dwelt with special sympathy on the themes of Christ's Infancy.[211]

Assuming an ever-growing prominence in the religious art and literature of this period, above all in the image of a transcendant and universal maternal surrogate, the figure of the "good mother" takes on a larger meaning also in the secular literature of the twelfth and thirteenth centuries. Even in the mid-eleventh century, before the birth of Guibert of Nogent, the first secular romance, *Ruodlieb,* portrays the mutual devotion of the young knight, obliged to seek his fortune in distant lands, and his widowed mother, the very type of the virtuous noblewoman, caring for the family property in his absence and, at last begging him to remember his poor mother, left twice widowed, "once by your father and for the second time by you, my son."[212] Not all mothers, it is true, are so glowingly depicted or unreservedly praised, and our glimpses of maternal shortcomings and filial hostilities underscore the fundamental ambivalence that characterizes the primary relationships with which we are concerned.[213] Is it, we may ask, this ambivalence and still another reflection of the maternal image that we perceive in certain compelling themes of the new vernacular literature? Is it she who is celebrated by the courtly poets as "noble, gentle, true," whose "soul-filled glance brings Christmas every day?"[214] Is she really the "distant lady," the infinitely desired and unattainable love-object of these poets, many of them, we may add, younger and often "exiled" sons, like other articulate children of this period?[215]

This is the view proposed by Herbert Moller, who sees in this adored lady all of the aspects of a maternal figure and in the lover's relation to her a projection of disguised childlike fantasies and, above all, the fear of abandonment, rejection and loss that is the deepest anxiety of these poets.[216] However we may interpret their meaning, here and elsewhere the powerful familial images, themes and fantasies of this period clearly invite us to explore their relationships with the prevailing modes of childhood experience among the noble and articulate classes. Do they, as our evidence suggests, reflect the widely felt devotions and deprivations of noble childhood in a time when the early years were dominated by maternal figures and the father's role was frequently negligible or negative; when family life was often unstable and perhaps not fully "conjugal"; when early separation from the mother was common, leading to that enduring sense of loss and longing, that quest for surrogates, whether earthly or celestial, to which contemporary records offer abundant testimony?[217] The pattern sketched here was by no means universal, or limited to the eleventh and twelfth centuries, for it apparently prevailed in the ensuing century as well.[218] But it seems to have emerged with striking clarity in a time when the demands of military life, as well as distant pilgrimage and crusade, helped to create, as Herlihy suggests, a "woman's world at home," a world in which women played a particularly active role in the administration of feudal households and in the early rearing and training of children.[219]

To the questions raised here, with their profound implications for our understanding of the psychic structures and cultural creations of this period, firmer answers must be sought in much fuller exploration of the changing social, familial and psychological realities of these centuries. But there can be no doubt that many of the childhood themes, the emotions, experiences and relationships, that we have been pursuing appear more and more clearly in the vernacular literature of the twelfth and early thirteenth centuries.[220] They are mirrored perhaps most fully and suggestively in the early parts of one great poem of this time, the *Tristan* of Gottfried of Strassburg, who depicts the ideal relationship between mother and child with rare poignancy in his portrayal of the bond between the orphaned Tristan and his foster-mother, this surrogate who simulated pregnancy and childbirth in order to protect the adopted infant from his enemies.[221]

> She lay in with a son who held her in filial affection until they both were dead. That same sweet child had the same sweet childish craving for her that a child should have for its mother. . . . She devoted all her thoughts to him in motherly affection and was as constant in her attentions as if she had carried him under her own heart.

Throughout his early childhood this mother cared for her foster-son with such tender solicitude, "wishing to see for herself all the time if he were comfortable or not," that if she had had her way, "he would always have walked on velvet." But at seven, the time of separation came and with it what Gottfried clearly regarded as the end of the carefree and happy phase of childhood. "In the blossoming years, when the ecstasy of his springtime was about to unfold and he was just entering with joy into his prime, his best life was over."[222]

It was Tristan's father who was responsible for this separation, placing the boy in the care of a teacher with whom he was "sent away to learn foreign languages" and later to learn "riding with shield and lance," along with other skills necessary to the knightly life. But the motives of this foster-father were not merely practical, for he is portrayed from the beginning as a model of devoted and self-sacrificing paternal love, willing, after his arduous search for his abducted son, to share him with another surrogate, his maternal uncle.[223] In this stress on the paternal role and on the details of early training, Gottfried's *Tristan* exhibits attitudes now more prominently featured in contemporary works dealing with the care and instruction of children who were intended for worldly and especially noble careers. Appearing first in twelfth-century "books of manners" and "nurture," this concern is perhaps best exemplified by the Anglo-Norman *Urbain*, written in the person of a father advising his young son how to become "wise, full of sweetness, debonair and courteous," with emphasis on the importance of learning to speak French well, of polite behavior in company—one should not "lounge about and scratch oneself"—and the practical details of page service.[224]

Concern for the physical care and training of young children becomes more articulate and specific in a growing number of didactic works of the thirteenth century; such treatises, displaying often also some sense of the needs of children at different stages of development, point to ways in which, with increasing literacy among laymen, more favorable values and attitudes, as well as useful pediatric information, may have become more widely diffused, at least among the more prosperous classes. Despite the obvious limitations of these writings as mirrors of childhood realities, their popularity suggests a felt need for works offering guidance for parents, and while some of them reflect the clerical perspectives which have dominated this study, in others, more novel, parental views are directly stated.

Representing the churchman's approach, Bartholomew of England provides, in one of the earliest and most influential of popular encyclopedias, a precise description of the physical constitution, emotional qualities and habits of children, and conveys as well a now more articulate sense of early childhood as a carefree and playful stage of life.[225] Little boys (*pueri*), he tells us, echoing a common though by no means universal opinion, are so called because of their "purity," since at this age the insufficient development of their organs makes them incapable of sexual activity and they are not ashamed of their nakedness.[226] Despite their innocence, however, they are capable of guile and deceit, and so in need of discipline and teaching. Painting what will seem to many a fairly lifelike picture of small boys, he describes them as "living without thought or care, loving only to play, fearing no danger more than being beaten with a rod, always hungry and hence always disposed to various infirmities from being overfed, wanting everything they see, quick to laughter and as quick to tears, resisting their mothers' efforts to wash and comb them, and no sooner clean but dirty again." Little girls, in Bartholomew's hardly original view, are better disciplined, more careful, more modest and timid, and more graceful; because of the likeness of sex they are also, he thought, dearer to their mothers than boys.[227]

Strongly urging the careful education of girls in reading and writing, Vincent of Beauvais maintained that these pursuits would keep them busy and thus distracted from "harmful and idle thoughts."[228] They should, in his view, be trained in the "womanly arts" as well as in letters, and both boys and girls should be carefully instructed in the duties and responsibilities of marriage.[229] As a theorist of education and an adviser in the rearing of the young, this most zealous of medieval encyclopedists was not particularly original, but he drew on traditional and contemporary learning in the development of ideas that display a genuine concern for the actual needs and capacities of children at different stages of early life.[230] Like his contemporary, Master Aldobrandino of Siena, Vincent repeats with slight variations the Soranian precepts concerning the physical care of children, ideas now readily accessible in learned circles.[231] In a suggested regime for the young child, he provides for frequent baths, at least two daily, careful feeding and ample playtime;[232] to similar recommendations Aldobrandino adds the advice that the child should be given what he asks for and relieved of what displeases him.[233] When at six the child begins school, he should be taught slowly and without forcing, being allowed plenty of time for sleep and for diversion. With others among his fellow-clerics, Vincent of Beauvais advocates a moderation in instruction and discipline in which we may perceive the significant assimilation and diffusion of ideas expressed by St. Anselm and his contemporaries a century and a half earlier. Teaching without beating is the ideal commonly stated, although Vincent suggests that in the matter of discipline distinctions should be made between those children for whom physical coercion is unnecessary and disastrous and others whose temperaments seem to require it; even in this case discipline should never be sudden and unpremeditated but should spring from motives of love and foresight rather than a mistaken sense of kindness.[234] It is this attitude and this conception of the child's sensitive nature that were poetically summed up, around 1200, by Walther von der Vogelweide:

"Children won't do what they ought
If you beat them with a rod.
Children thrive, children grow
When taught by words, and not a blow. . . ."

Evil words, words unkind
Will do harm to a child's mind."[235]

In some ways less enlightened are several works representing a paternal view of child-rearing, which may in their stress on the importance
of discipline and correction provide a closer reflection of the actual
practice of parents.[236] For the elderly Philip of Novara, the infant and
small child possesses three great gifts: he loves and recognizes the person who nurses him, he expresses pleasure and affection for those who
play with him, and he inspires a natural love and sympathy in those
who rear him.[237] Like the great Jewish philosopher, Moses Maimonides,
in the preceding century, this father believed that parental love increases as children grow older, but he cautioned strongly against the
excessive and indulgent display of affection, which may encourage children to be bolder in their naughtiness.[238] They should not be permitted
to do everything they wish, but should be firmly corrected while they
are young, first with words, then if necessary, by beating, and as a last
resort by "imprisonment." Parents and their surrogates should, he advised, be especially watchful for early signs of tendencies to such vices
as theft, violence and blasphemy which may lead the child to a bad
end.[239]

Unlike the clerical writers, however, Philip was primarily concerned
with the practical preparation of the boy for his future career, in the
case of noble children for one of the two "honorable" professions,
"clergie" or "chevalerie," for which training should begin at the earliest
possible moment.[240] Since men of high rank, in his lofty view, have
more important things to do than to teach their children themselves,
teachers should be qualified to instruct noble boys in the elements of
courtesy as well as in the smattering of learning he thought desirable.
As for girls, they were to be indoctrinated from the beginning in the one
virtue that was sufficient for them, obedience; for the Lord wished
women to remain always in subjection. Unless they were to be nuns,
there was no need to teach them to read and write, since many evils
come from a feminine knowledge of these arts; instruction in sewing
and weaving was desirable, however, even for the rich.[241] His firm belief that in the rearing of girls, the parents' prime concern should be the
careful custody of their chastity was shared by his contemporaries,
among them his fellow-Italian, Bellino Bissolo, whose instructions for
his young sons offer an early example of a bourgeois rather than a
courtly approach to children and their rearing.[242]

If we now begin to gain some insight into the attitudes of middle-
class parents, we find, even earlier, a few glimpses of childhood in a
still lower class. In the early twelfth-century life of the hermit, Christian
de l'Aumône, we are shown the suffering of a peasant-child, tormented

by devils because of his sense of guilt in having offended his parents and let their cows run loose in a neighbor's field.[243] His story further suggests that, though the life of such a child might be hard, it did not usually involve the early separation from parents that was common in the noble class.[244] Closer and longer family life is reflected also, towards the close of this century, in Hartmann von Aue's *Der arme Heinrich,* the first work of vernacular literature in which a child is the central figure throughout.[245] Through the tale of its nameless heroine, a peasant child, we gain, in fact, our fullest literary insight into the relations between parents and children in, or transposed to, a class far below that from which much of our evidence has come. In reading this idealized version of the old tale of the cleansing of leprosy by human blood, we may be touched by the courageous devotion of this little girl of eight or so, a model of angelic goodness, who is eager to sacrifice herself for her young lord.[245] But what may interest us most are the somewhat more realistic details of her domestic life, sleeping at the foot of her parents' bed and bathing their feet with her tears when they refuse to permit her sacrifice, and the demonstrative love displayed by her parents, which, indeed, illustrates a contemporary opinion that the children of prosperous peasants were reared more indulgently and gently than the children of nobles.[247] In this poem, and even more in the somewhat later *Meier Helmbrecht,* we cross the threshold of the "conjugal family" whose triumph in Western society seemed now assured and whose images begin to appear more clearly also in contemporary works of art.[248]

SOME CONCLUDING REFLECTIONS

Arriving at a more or less arbitrary halt in our inquiry, we may be more than ever conscious of the still unbroken silence that conceals the fortunes of the vast majority of children, and parents, in this as in other periods. But if we look back now from the vantage-point of the thirteenth century to the two accounts of childhood with which we began, we may be heartened by the knowledge that the world they represent is by no means impenetrable, that it is, in fact, in many ways open to further exploration and discovery, if not yet to definitive mapping. We may also perceive more clearly some larger directions of change, some ways in which the centuries that we have traversed, however swiftly, represent a truly critical phase in the history of childhood, a time in which its major issues were posed more sharply and consciously than ever before, when the experiences and relationships of early life found more articulate and varied expression, together with modes of feeling towards children that were to prevail or gradually to gain in strength during succeeding centuries.

If a central issue of this history, abstractly viewed, has been the enduring conflict between destructive or rejecting and fostering attitudes, this issue was stated with extraordinary, almost prophetic clarity in John of Lodi's story of Peter Damian's early years. Throughout our period and beyond, it is true, the power of destructive forces may seem little diminished. Certainly, the fundamental menace of infant and maternal mortality continued, apparently unabated; here there was to be little substantial progress before the early years of our own century. The neglect, exploitation and abandonment of children continued also, but these practices were now more widely and consciously opposed and in efforts at control or suppression, however immeasurable their effects, may be discerned clear signs of the awakening consciences and sensibilities of this time. The idea of the child as the possession and property of its parents continued to dominate parental attitudes and actions in these, as in earlier and later centuries. But the dangers inherent in this conception had achieved wider recognition and the salutary intervention of external authorities had made some modest advances. The proprietary notion had also been joined by more favorable conceptions, by a sense of the child as a being in its own right, as a nature of "potential greatness," and by a sense of childhood as a distinctive and formative stage of life. That churchmen should have been pre-eminently active in the diffusion of more humane attitudes and ideas is, given the character of medieval society, hardly surprising. Nor is the fact that attempts to translate law and precept into 'practice were in this sphere, as in many others, faltering and often ineffective. The fostering role of churchmen as pastors and preachers, reformers and surrogates, has been noted in this study, but it deserves more coherent and critical attention, in the setting of contemporary spiritual and religious movements, than it could be given here.

Clearly, as the cases of Anselm and Hugh of Lincoln suggest, in many matters affecting the lives of children the example and influence of a few great figures may have counted for a good deal, not least in giving powerful expression to the new impulses and currents of feeling whose growing strength is displayed in numerous works of this period, among them the two with which we began. In Guibert of Nogent's recollections of his early life, a new awareness is written large; and if he offers us our fullest insight into the realities of childhood during these centuries, he also draws us most deeply into that world of ambivalence and wishful thinking which encompasses the relations of parents and children, introducing us to what appear to have been, in both fact and fantasy, certain dominant experiences of many children in this time. Among the many great changes that emerged during the century and more spanned by the lifetimes of Peter Damian and Guibert, none was more profound than the slow transformation in modes of consciousness

and expression with which the relationships and experiences of childhood were inextricably bound up. Tenderness, compassion, the capacity
to comprehend the needs and emotions of others: these are fragile and
late-maturing plants of feeling and they flowered slowly in the hard and
sometimes violent lives of this period, especially in the lives of parents
who were themselves often literally, as well as emotionally, little more
than children. Yet it is in this realm of feeling that the most deeply
rooted and fruitful developments of our centuries are likely to be found.

REFERENCES

For the helpful interest and suggestions of various friends and colleagues, my
warm thanks are due. I should like particularly to thank Professors Emily Coleman
and Lester K. Little for letting me read copies of forthcoming articles and Miss
Emily Tabuteau for bibliographical information. I am above all indebted to Dom
Jean Leclercq, who has been unfailingly generous in sharing with me his current
work and his rich knowledge and insight.

The following abbreviations are used in these notes:

AASS   *Acta Sanctorum* (Antwerp, 1643 ff.)
CC   *Corpus Christianorum, Continuatio mediaevalis* (Turnhout, 1954-   )
MGH, SS   *Monumenta Germaniae historica, Scriptores* in folio (Hanover,
            1826-1934).
PL   J. P. Migne, *Patrologia Cursus Completus, series latina* (Paris,
            1844-1864).
Councils   *Councils and Synods with Other Documents Relating to the Eng-
            lish Church*, II, ed. F. M. Powicke and C. R. Cheney (2 vols., Ox-
            ford, Clarendon Press, 1964).

1. For John of Lodi's *vita* of Peter Damian, see PL 144, 111-146; for the quotation in the epigraph, 115b. The Latin text of Guibert's *De vita sua sive
   monodiarum suarum libri tres* was edited by G. Bourgin, *Guibert de Nogent:
   Histoire de sa vie*, Collection de textes pour servir à l'étude et à l'enseignement de l'histoire (Paris, 1907). Cited in these notes as Guibert, *Memoirs*, is
   the most recent and accurate English translation, *Self and Society in Medieval France: The Memoirs of Abbot Guibert of Nogent*, edited with an introduction by J. F. Benton (New York, 1970).
2. For references to the most pertinent of such works, see notes 4, 29, 33-37,
   72, 95, 130, 176.
3. On the importance for our period of this investigation, and the obstacles to
   it, see the perceptive remarks of Georges Duby, "Histoire des mentalités," in
   L'Histoire et ses méthodes, ed. Charles Samaran, L'Encyclopedie de la
   Pléiade, XI (Paris, 1961), pp. 957-958.
4. P. Ariès, *Centuries of Childhood: A Social History of Family Life*, translated from the French by Robert Baldick (New York; Vintage Books, 1962),
   p. 33.
5. For an illuminating portrait, with references to the sources and modern
   studies, see J. Leclercq, *Saint Pierre Damien: ermite et homme d'église*,
   Uomine e dottrine, 8 (Rome, 1960). See also F. Dressler, *Petrus Damiani,
   Leben und Werk*, Studia Anselmiana, 34 (Rome, 1954) and G. Lucchesi,
   "Per una Vita di San Pier Damiani," in *San Pier Damiano nel IX centenario
   della morte* (1072-1972), 2 vols. (Cesena, 1972), 113-160.
6. In a forthcoming study, "The Personal Development of Peter Damian,"

Lester K. Little explores in depth central aspects of Peter Damian's personality as revealed in his own works and in John of Lodi's "life." On his writings, see also O. J. Blum, *St. Peter Damian: His Teaching on the Spiritual Life* (Washington, 1947); and *St. Peter Damian: Selected Writings on the Spiritual Life,* translated with an introduction by Patricia McNulty (London, 1959).

7. A well-educated priest before his conversion to the monastic life, John of Lodi became a hermit and a companion of Peter Damian at Fonte Avellana in the mid-1060's. His biography of Peter was written apparently not long after the saint's death in 1072, and thereafter John became prior of Fonte Avellana and in his last years bishop of Gubbio. For an account of his life, see F. Dressler in *New Catholic Encyclopedia*, VII, 1059.

8. John's account of the life of Peter Damian was, he carefully reports, based on what he had learned from Peter himself, as well as from one of his kinsmen, another close disciple and his own personal observation (PL 144, 114-115; and for the story paraphrased and quoted here, 115-117). On the question of his veracity, which has been variously assessed, Little's study supports the view that, although perhaps in certain ways exaggerated, this account of Peter's childhood is basically truthful and reconcilable with other evidence.

9. From John of Lodi and Peter's own writings, we know of at least five siblings: three brothers, certainly two and possibly three sisters.

10. See Little's interpretation of these early experiences in relation to Peter's continuing "quest for a father" and other aspects of his later life ("The Personal Development of Peter Damian").

11. For this letter, dated 1067, see A. Wilmart, "Une lettre de S. Pierre Damien à l'imperatrice Agnès," *Revue Bénédictine,* 44 (1932), 140-145. In it Peter also remarks that on a still earlier visit to Ravenna, he had walked at night on the street where his house was, but had not been able to enter it.

12. On the problems relating to Guibert's birth and family, see Benton's analysis of the evidence in Guibert, *Memoirs,* Appendix 1, pp. 229-236. Against the common assumption that Guibert was born in 1053, Benton argues convincingly for a later date, probably April 10, 1064. Regarding his family, Benton concludes (p. 236) that Guibert's father was a younger son of a noble family of Clermont which was itself subordinate to the lords of Clermont. His mother came from a distant region, perhaps from near Saint-Germer or from Normandy, and her family, as was not uncommonly the case in feudal marriages of this period, may have been of higher social rank than her husband's.

13. So it is described by Georg Misch, *Geschichte der Autobiographie,* III, 2 (Frankfurt am Main, 1959), 109. On Guibert's imitation of Augustine's *Confessions,* see Misch, pp. 117-121, and F. Amory, "The Confessional Superstructure of Guibert de Nogent's *Vita,*" *Classica et Mediaevalia,* 25 (1964), 224-240. Beginning as a *confessio laudis* on the Augustinian model, Guibert's work, which was written c. 1115, later develops into a kind of monastic chronicle and ends as a sensational narrative of the revolt of the commune of Laon against its bishop in 1113.

14. Guibert, *Memoirs,* pp. 41-42.

15. Regarding Guibert's birth on Holy Saturday and his immediate baptism, it may be noted that, according to ancient custom, this rite of initiation had been performed only at the Paschal and Pentecostal vigils, except when there was danger of death; by the late eleventh century, however, there was increasing pressure among churchmen for immediate baptism of infants at all seasons of the year. On the evolution of this rite and its changing relations

with other sacraments, see J. D. C. Fisher, *Christian Initiation: Baptism in the Medieval West* (London, 1965), pp. 101-140, and see below, notes 94, 105 and 208.

16. Guibert, *Memoirs,* p. 44. He says, in fact, so little of his immediate family that, as Benton observes (p. 12), we do not even know how many were in it. An elder brother, perhaps eight or ten years older, followed his father's military career and served in the castle at Clermont (pp. 50-51); another older brother was, like Guibert, a monk at Saint-Germer and later at Nogent (p. 133).

17. *Ibid.,* p. 132.

18. *Ibid.,* pp. 63-68, for Guibert's revealing story of his parents' unhappy early married life, the efforts of "certain rich men" to seduce his mother and the frequent threats of his father's kinsmen to have the marriage dissolved and "give her to another husband" or to send her away to distant relatives. For further discussion of marriage in this period, see below, notes 141, 143-148.

19. *Ibid.,* pp. 70-71. Guibert's cousin was especially active in pressing for his mother's remarriage so that he might obtain wardship of his uncle's children and control of his possessions.

20. On the advantages of widowhood and contemporary veneration of this state, see below, n. 148.

21. Guibert, *Memoirs,* p. 68.

22. *Ibid.,* pp. 68, 82-86, 92, 101, and cf. Benton's discussion of Guibert's sexual attitudes and inhibitions, pp. 13-14, 24-27.

23. *Ibid.,* pp. 45-50.

24. *Ibid.,* p. 46, but about playing, Guibert later remarks that he had been "ready for a game of ball" after his remarkable recovery from a violent illness in his boyhood (p. 228).

25. Guibert, *Memoirs,* pp. 49-50.

26. *Ibid.,* pp. 72-76. This kind of withdrawal from the world became increasingly common among pious women during this period of mounting religious enthusiasm, to which Guibert also refers more generally at various points in his work; see especially pp. 53-63. For a discussion of recluses and the appeal of their way of life at this time, see N. Huyghebaert, "Les femmes laïques dans la vie religieuse des XIe et XIIe siècles dans la province ecclesiastique de Reims," *I Laici nella "societas christiana" dei secoli XI e XII.* Atti della terza Settimana internazionale di studio, Mendola, 21-27 agosto 1965 (Milan, 1968), 356-366.

27. Guibert, *Memoirs,* pp. 74-75. Guibert goes on to say (pp. 76-77) that he was at this time completely bereft, for his teacher had followed his mother's example and had entered the monastery at Saint-Germer. Meanwhile Guibert himself had, not unnaturally, taken advantage of his newfound freedom by "running wild" for a time, detesting school, churches and everything relating to a clerical career, over-sleeping, wearing his best clothes constantly and "emulating older boys in their juvenile rowdiness."

28. Until he became abbot of Nogent at the age of forty or so, Guibert as a monk at Saint-Germer was close to his mother and constantly under her anxious and apparently dominating supervision. See Benton's discussion of their relationship, especially pp. 19, 23-25.

29. M. Bloch, *La Société féodale,* 2 vols. (Paris, 1949), I, 169; *Feudal Society,* tr. L. A. Manyon (Chicago, 1964), p. 106. On this important subject, see the recent studies of Colin Morris, *The Discovery of the Individual 1050-1200* (London: SPCK, 1972) and P. Dronke, *Poetic Individuality in the Middle Ages: New Departures in Poetry* 1000-1150 (Oxford, Clarendon Press, 1970). For further discussion of the biographical and autobiographical

works with which we are particularly concerned, see below, n. 129.

30. Little is known of this first woman poet in the German language, who wrote in the early twelfth century and was, like Guibert's mother, a recluse, beyond her brief declaration of maternal feeling at the end of one of her religious poems (*Die Dichtungen der Frau Ava*, ed. F. Maurer, Altdeutsche Textbibliotek, Nr. 66, Tübingen: Max Niemeyer, 1966), p. 68. Among other mothers who speak more or less directly is the ninth-century Dhuoda, wife of Count Bernard of Septimania, who composed or had written for her a work of counsel for her absent young son (*Le Manuel de Dhuoda*, ed. E. Bondurand [Paris, 1887]); for excerpts in French, see Pierre Riché, *De l'éducation antique à l'éducation chevaleresque* (Paris, 1968), pp. 90-92. Attributed to the tenth-century Irish princess, Gormlaith, is a moving lament for her dead son—"the child that is born of one's own fair body, that is what lives in one's mind..." (O. J. Bergin, "Poems Attributed to Gormlaith," *Miscellany Presented to Kuno Meyer*, ed. O. Bergin and C. Marstrander [Halle, 1912], pp. 359-363). Though hardly, it may seem, a model mother, the famous Heloise somewhat belatedly displayed her concern for her son and Abelard's in a letter to the abbot of Cluny (*The Letters of Peter the Venerable*, edited with introduction and notes by Giles Constable [2 vols., Cambridge, Mass.], I, Letter 167, pp. 400-401).

31. The quoted definition of "infancy" is that of William of Conches, writing in the early twelfth century (*De philosophia mundi*, PL 172, 91 bc). For Bartholomew of England, this age ended and childhood, or *pueritia*, began with weaning and lasted until puberty (*De proprietatibus rerum*, Lib. VI. *De proprietatibus aetatum*, Frankfurt, 1601, p. 238). Another thirteenth century writer, Aldobrandino of Siena, distinguishes an intermediate stage or second stage of infancy between "infancy" and "childhood," which he terms *dentium plantatura*, the "teething" stage, which lasts from the time when the teeth first come in until seven; the third age is "childhood" which lasts until thirteen, and it is followed by "adolescence" (*Le régime du corps de maître Aldobrandine de Sienne, texte français du XIIIe siècle*, ed. Louis Landouzy and Roger Pepin [Paris, 1911], p. 79).

32. Guibert, *Memoirs*, pp. 72, 79-80, where he refers to himself as still in the "tender years of childhood" at twelve or thirteen; cf. his account (p. 89) of his meeting with St. Anselm, then prior of Bec, at about this time or a little later. Concerning this view of childhood, see also J. Leclercq, "Pédagogie et formation spirituelle du VIe au IXe siècle," *La Scuola nell'occidente latino dell'alto medioevo* (Spoleto, 1972), pp. 354-355.

33. On the economic expansion that was probably the most catalytic of these changes, see the *Cambridge Economic History*, ed. M. M. Postan and H. J. Habakkuk, especially Vol. 2 (1952), *Trade and Industry in the Middle Ages*, containing R. S. Lopez's discussion of the "commercial revolution" of this period, and Vol. 3 (1963), *Economic Organization and Policies in the Middle Ages*. See also J. Le Goff *La Civilisation de l'occident médiéval* (Paris: Arthaud, 1967), pp. 307-317, with a useful summary of the evidence for demographic expansion and R. Fossier's impressive study of medieval Picardy (cited below, n. 130), I, 274-287.

34. That the profound changes discernible in almost every sphere of human activity in the period coinciding roughly with Guibert's lifetime (1064?-c. 1125) should have occurred in so short a time is, R. W. Southern remarks, "the most remarkable fact in medieval history" (*Western Society and the Church in the Middle Ages*, The Pelican History of the Church, Vol. 2, London; Pelican Books, 1970, pp. 34-36). See also his discussion of the religious and ecclesiastical movements of this period, pp. 100-133; 214-272, and

Huyghebaert's study mentioned above, n. 26.

35. For some insights and bibliographical suggestions, see the recent essay by David Herlihy, "Three Patterns of Social Mobility in Medieval Society," *Journal of Interdisciplinary History*, 3 (1973), 623-647. On the social and demographic changes of the period from the tenth to the twelfth centuries, see Christopher Brooke, *Europe in the Central Middle Ages*, 962-1154 (New York, n.d.), pp. 90-123. Revealing evidence concerning "nuptiality" and "fecundity," in medieval Spain, supporting that found in other European regions, is provided in a recent study by R. Pastor de Togneri, "Historia de las familias en Castilla y Leon (siglos X-XIV) y su relacion con la formacion de los grandes dominios eclesiasticos," *Cuadernos de Historia de España*, 43-44 (Buenos Aires, 1967), 88-118. Indicating that the general duration of marriages was brief, despite the youth of the contracting parties, because of high feminine mortality in childbirth, this study points also to a regular increase in the number of children per fecund household from 2.8 in the tenth century to 4 in the thirteenth, but even then the replacement count remains weak and the demographic equilibrium fragile.

36. For a general view of the material conditions of life in these centuries, see Le Goff, *Civilisation*, pp. 290-303. Cf. E. Patzelt, "Pauvreté et maladies," *Povertà e richezza nella spiritualità dei secoli XI e XII* (Todi, 1969), pp. 165-187, and on the recurrent famines with their attendant miseries, F. Curschmann, *Hungersnöte des Mittelalters (8.-13. Jahrhundert)*, Leipziger Studien, VI, 1 (Leipzig, 1900).

37. See Le Goff, pp. 301-303. The lack of accurate statistical evidence from this and other earlier periods makes all such estimates very rough and it is likely, as E. A. Wrigley suggests, that combinations of favorable and unfavorable circumstances could result in notable differences in expectation of life, at different times and especially in different social classes, even before the benefits of modern medical knowledge became available (*Population and History*, World University Library [London, 1969], p. 131). See Wrigley's remarks (pp. 169-170) on infant mortality, which showed no tendency to fall in most parts of western Europe until the last years of the nineteenth century, when the medical knowledge necessary for the understanding and control of infant diseases was attained. Infant mortality rates have fallen by a factor of five or more since the beginning of the twentieth century. On infant and female mortality in the middle ages, see also the discussion of T. H. Hollingsworth, *Historical Demography*, The Sources of History (London, 1969), pp. 290-292, and E. Fügedi, "Pour une analyse démographique de la Hongrie médiévale," *Annales*, 24 (1969), 1299-1312.

38. On the profound sense of insecurity, physical and psychological, that dominated the minds and sensibilities of men during this period, and for some suggestions of its varied reflections in literature, thought and art, see Le Goff, *Civilisation*, pp. 397-420.

39. See A. Peiper, *Geschichte der Kinderheilkunde* (Leipzig, 1956), especially pp. 635-662. For some examples of superstitious practices relating to pregnancy and childbirth, see Lynn Thorndike, *A History of Magic and Experimental Science*, I (rev. ed., New York, 1929), 685, 713, 726, 738, 740, 757; II (1929), 135, 329, 470, 482, 767.

40. A useful study and survey of the materials is F. Lanzoni, "Il sogno della madre incinta nella litteratura medievale e antica," *Analecta Bollandiana*, 45 (1927), 225-260.

41. Odo of Cluny, *The Life of St. Gerald of Aurillac*, translated and edited by Dom Gerald Sitwell, The Makers of Christendom (London, 1958), pp. 95-96. For the Latin text of this life, see PL 133, 639-704.

42. For a useful brief summary of the complicated transmission of Soranus's teachings, see C. H. Talbot, *Medicine in Medieval England* (London, 1967), pp. 80-82; 18-20. There is an English translation of the *Gynaecia*, with introduction, by Oswei Temkin, *Soranus' Gynecology* (Baltimore, 1956). Although the Greek text of this work was not discovered until the nineteenth century, Soranus's writings were used by several late ancient and Byzantine scholars, Oribasius, Aetius of Amida, and Paul of Aegina, and through them transmitted to Byzantine and Moslem medicine. In the West his teachings were known both through these writers and in Latin translations and paraphrases whose early history is obscure. Besides an epitome of his medical questions, which incorporated sections on gynecology, perhaps intended for midwives, other works of Soranus, including at least parts of his *Gynaecia*, were translated by the physician, Caelius Aurelianus, probably in the fifth century; parts of this version are edited by M. F. Drabkin and I. E. Drabkin, *Caelius Aurelianus "Gynaecia": Fragments of a Latin Version of Soranus' "Gynaecia" from a Thirteenth Century Manuscript* (Baltimore, 1951). This text is a compilation incorporating parts of Caelius's translation and parts of another, independent version of Soranus's work by Mustio (Muscio) in the sixth century, which drew on both the epitome and the *Gynaecia* and which exists in many manuscripts from the ninth and tenth centuries to the sixteenth; it is, in fact, among the gynecological treatises assembled in the same manuscript containing the Caelian text edited by the Drabkins. Also mentioned in certain early medieval inventories and catalogues of monastic libraries are the obstetrical and pediatric works of Oribasius and Paul of Aegina; there are passages from the latter in the tenth-century Anglo-Saxon Leechbook of Bald, which contained as well a substantial section on gynecology, of which only the chapter-headings survive (Talbot, pp. 18-19).

These ancient works, together with other fragments of the classical scientific and medical tradition (e.g., the Hippocratic Aphorisms and some pseudo-Galenic materials) appear to have been the basis of study in medicine and natural philosophy in southern Italy and especially at Salerno in the eleventh century, before the arrival of Constantinus Africanus, who introduced the Graeco-Roman tradition in a new form, as reshaped and developed by Moslem science and medicine, of which he was the first to translate a considerable body of writings. On Constantinus, see Thorndike, *Magic and Experimental Science,* I, 742-759, and on the school of Salerno, Paul Oskar Kristeller, "The School of Salerno," *Bulletin of the History of Medicine,* 17 (1945), 138-194, and "Nuovi fonti per la medicina Salernitana sel secolo XII," *Rassegna di storia salernitana,* 18 (1957), 64-74. In addition to Constantine's translations of Hippocratic and Galenic works and, most important, the *Pantegni (Liber regalis)* of Hali ibn Abbas, other Moslem works on obstetrics and pediatrics, based on Greek sources, ultimately Soranian, but making some original contributions, were translated in the twelfth century; noteworthy among these are Rhazes, *Liber Almansoris,* which contains a brief but important treatise on the diseases of childhood, remarkable for its description of measles and smallpox, and Avicenna's enormously influential *Canon* of medicine, which contains chapters on the hygiene and diseases of infancy and childhood.

Gradually penetrating Western science in the twelfth and early thirteenth centuries, the influence of the Constantinian translations and others is not discernible, despite his own claims, in Adelard of Bath's early twelfth-century *Quaestiones naturales* (ed. M. Müller, *Beiträge zur Geschichte der Philosophie des Mittelalters,* XXXI, 2, 1934), which contains, among many others, several questions concerning obstetrics and gynecology (38-42, pp.

41-43); on Adelard and Arabic science, see Brian Lawn, *The Salernitan Questions: An Introduction to the History of Medieval and Renaissance Problem-Literature* (Oxford: Clarendon Press, 1963), pp. 20-30. But this influence is evident in the Salernitan questions discussed by Lawn and in another important early twelfth-century work, the *De philosophia mundi* of William of Conches (PL 172, 39-102), which presents a group of fourteen questions (Lib. IV, c. 6-17, 88c-91c) relating to gynecology and midwifery, which are often literal transcriptions of Salernitan materials in abbreviated form. Much more strikingly dependent on the works of Constantine for his medical, specifically obstetrical and pediatric information, is Bartholomew of England (Bartholomaeus Anglicus), the early thirteenth-century encyclopedist who drew also on the works of Aristotle and Galen, *inter alia;* written apparently c. 1230, his extremely popular *De proprietatibus rerum* (cited in these notes in the edition of Frankfurt am Main, 1601, as *De prop. rer.*) represents not the most advanced scientific knowledge of his time but the kind of information regarded as desirable for the student and "general reader" to whom it was addressed, and reflects as well his own powers of direct observation. On Bartholomew and his work, see Thorndike, II, 401-435.

43. In, e.g., the late twelfth-century fabliau, *Richeut*, ed. I. C. Lecompte in *The Romanic Review*, 4 (1913), 261-305, vv. 152-153, 403, which give a lively account of these symptoms. Among more scientific writers, see Bartholomew, *De prop. rer.*, VI, 241, and for an account of fetal development, pp. 234-235; cf. the less developed description of his predecessor, William of Conches, *De phil. mundi*, IV, 15-16, 90 ad. Hildegard of Bingen also offers a long and vivid discussion of the processes of conception and generation (*Hildegardis causae et curae*, ed. P. Kaiser [Leipzig: Teubner, 1903], pp. 59-71). The gynecological treatises reflecting, or deriving from, the Soranian tradition commonly advised concerning the proper regime for pregnancy; influential works, besides those noted above, were the pseudo-Trotula, *De curis (or passionibus) mulierum* (printed as *Trotulae curandarum aegritudinem ante, in et post partum Libellus* [Leipzig, 1775]), and the so-called *Gynaecia Cleopatre*. Several of these, including the pseudo-Trotula, are contained in the well-known Bodleian manuscript of the twelfth and thirteenth centuries, Ashmole 399, which included (fol. 34-34v) among other medical drawings a now famous and controversial series, which has been interpreted as depicting a medical case history (L. D. MacKinney and Harry Bober, "A Thirteenth-Century Medical Case History in Minatures," *Speculum* 35 [1960], 251-259), but which, in Talbot's more convincing view, are probably illustrations of the text of Trotula's work, depicting the diseases of women and the symptoms of pregnancy (*Medicine in Medieval England*, pp. 81-82).

44. See, e.g., *Medieval Handbooks of Penance: A Translation of the Principal "Libri Poenitentiales" and Selections from Related Documents*, edited by John T. McNeill and Helena M. Gamer (New York, 1938), pp. 208, 216, 270, 318, 329. During this long period the times of conjugal abstinence were variously defined: by Burchard of Worms in the eleventh century as the twenty days before Christmas, all Sundays and all legitimate fasts, as well as the feasts of the Apostles and other principal feast-days (*Decretum*, XIX, 5; PL 140, 960a), and by Ivo of Chartres in the early twelfth century as the three penitential seasons, all Sundays, Wednesdays and Fridays (*Decretum*, XV, 163; PL 161, 893); cf. Gratian, *Decretum*, II, c. 33, q. 4, c. 3. See in general G. Meersseman, "I penitenti nel secoli XI e XII," *I Laici*, pp. 329-331. According to the thirteenth-century German preacher, Berthold of Regensburg, physical deformities and handicaps as well as moral defects in

many children were to be explained by their conception in the forbidden seasons, to which he adds a period of six weeks after childbirth; in his view, nobles and burghers were less prone to this sin than peasants, who were not so well instructed in such matters (*Berthold von Regensburg, Vollständige Ausgabe seiner Predigten* mit Anmerkungen von Franz Pfeiffer [2 vols., Vienna, 1862], I, 323-328). The role of astrological influences at conception and birth on the character and constitution of children was of much greater concern to many learned writers; see, for example, Hildegard of Bingen, who marvels at the fact that men who know enough not to sow crops in mid-summer or the dead of winter, beget offspring at any time without regard to the proper period in their own lives or to the "time of the moon"; defective children are the likely consequence of such heedlessness (*Causae et curae*, pp. 17-18; 77-78).

45. For examples of such exhortations, see Carl Arnold, *Das Kind in der deutschen Literatur des XI-XV Jahrhunderts* (Griefswald, 1905), pp. 22-25.

46. See Peiper, p. 113, for an illustration from the *Sachsenspiegel*, c. 1230, showing the witnessing of live birth, with male witnesses standing outside the lying-in room and pointing to their ears to signify that they have heard the child's cries.

47. That such knowledge was increasingly accessible by the thirteenth century is evident not only in influential Latin works like Bartholomew's but in a vernacular treatise such as that of Aldobrandino of Siena whose advice on obstetrics and infant care shows a larger and more explicit debt to Soranic teaching (*Régime du corps*, pp. 71-78); this work includes a chapter on "how a woman should care for herself when she is pregnant" (pp. 71-73).

48. Concerning the training of midwives and their relations with physicians and the learned tradition of obstetrics, our evidence is meagre and scattered; see, e.g., H. P. Bayon, "Trotula and the Ladies of Salerno," *Proceedings of the Royal Society of Medicine,* 33 (1930-1940), 471-475. In his *Anatomia,* the twelfth-century physician, Richard of England, reports that, after prescribing a pessary for a pregnant woman, he gave instructions to the midwife for its insertion (Talbot, *Medicine in Medieval England*, p. 61). Mustio's version of Soranus was often described in the manuscripts as a treatise of instruction for midwives and was usually illustrated, as in Ashmole 399, by drawings depicting various fetal positions, normal and abnormal presentations, the birth of twins, etc. (*ibid.*, p. 81 and Pl. IV). The activities and equipment of midwives, especially the bathing of the infant, are also portrayed in art, notably in scenes of the Nativity, an increasingly popular theme in these centuries; see, e.g., the scenes depicted in the Exultet Rolls (M. Avery, *The Exultet Rolls of South Italy,* 2 vols., Princeton, 1936, II, Pl. LXI). For other examples, see R. Müllerheim, *Die Wochenstube in der Kunst* (Stuttgart, 1904).

49. Bartholomew, *De prop. rer.,* pp. 242-243.

50. *Ibid.,* cf. Aldobrandino of Siena, *Régime du corps,* p. 74, providing more detailed advice and recommending the tying of the umbilical cord with a woolen thread and binding it with cloths until it dries up and falls off. On the salient role of honey in the care and feeding of infants, see L. Unger, *Bienhonig in der kinderärztlichen Therapie der Vergangenheit* (Rostock, 1950).

51. Bartholomew, *De prop. rer.,* pp. 237-238; Bartholomew emphasizes also, as does Aldobrandino, the importance of keeping the newborn infant in a darkened room, in order to protect its eyes from too much exposure to light. Cf. Aldobrandino (*Régime du corps,* pp. 75-76) on the methods and advantages of swaddling and the importance of the nurse's manipulations;

"children take the forms their nurses give them."

52. Gerald of Wales, *The Topography of Ireland,* translated with an introduction by J. O'Meara (Dundalk, Ireland, 1951), p. 84; this translation is based on O'Meara's new edition of the text of the earliest recension of Gerald's work, without his many later additions ("Topographia," *Proceedings of the Royal Irish Academy,* 42 [1949] , 162-190).

53. *The Topography of Ireland* in *The Historical Works of Giraldus Cambrensis,* ed. Thomas Wright (London, 1863), p. 147 (this passage does not appear in the first recension).

54. See Le Goff, *Civilisation,* pp. 302-303, 402-403, and below, n. 92.

55. See above, n. 48. The *practica chirurgica* of Roger of Salerno (c. 1210), as transmitted by Roland of Parma and later printed (1490) contains practical advice on various methods, manual and instrumental, of dealing with abnormal presentations. The manipulations of midwives doubtless increased the hazards of what is, in any case, regarded as the most dangerous day in any life.

56. Ekkehard IV, *Casus Sancti Galli* (MGH, SS, II, 119-122) (translated in G. G. Coulton, *Life in the Middle Ages,* 4 vols. in 1, New York: Macmillan, 1930, IV, 79-80). Purchard, later abbot of Saint-Gall, was taken from his nurse's breast and offered as an oblate to this monastery where because of his delicacy his masters always spared "even the rod."

57. On the technique of Caesarean section, see A. C. Crombie, *Medieval and Early Modern Science* (2 vols., New York: Anchor Books, 1959), I, 233. See also *Councils,* pp. 70, 183, 234, 441, 453, 635, for the recommendation of various thirteenth-century English synods that "if a woman has died in childbirth and this is well confirmed, the infant should be excised if it is thought to be living, so that it may be baptized." Cf. the late twelfth century synodal statutes of Eudes de Sully: PL 212, 63, no. 6. The *Tristan* of Eilhart von Oberge (c. 1180) describes the Caesarian birth of its hero after his mother's death (Arnold, *Das Kind in der deutschen Literatur,* p. 90).

58. On the history of the *Virgo lactans,* see V. Lasareff, "Studies in the Iconography of the Virgin," *Art Bulletin,* 20 (1938), 27-36. In the West this iconographical type makes an early appearance in a ninth-century Gospel cover; after the beginning of the twelfth century she appears more and more prominently in painting and sculpture, especially in Italy but also in other lands. The Madonna of Dom Rupert, Liège, c. 1170, is a most significant example (see below, n. 205); in an early thirteenth-century fresco of the Flight into Egypt, in the church of Le Petit-Quevilly near Rouen, the Virgin is shown riding on a donkey and nursing the half-recumbent Infant (Lasareff, p. 35). For the nursing Eve at Hildesheim, c. 1015, and the later Eve on the bronze doors of San Zeno in Verona, see Ernst Guldan, *Eva und Maria: Eine Antithese als Bildmotiv* (Graz-Cologne, 1966), Pl. 4 and 14.

59. Bartholomew, *De prop. rer.,* p. 241; cf. Aldobrandino of Siena, *Régime du corps,* p. 70-77.

60. Bellino Bissolo, *Liber legum moralium,* ed. V. Licitra, *Studi Medievali,* 3 ser., 6 (1965), 433, emphasizing, as do all writers on this subject, the importance of milk in forming the moral character of the child.

61. J. C. Russell has tentatively advanced the hypothesis of a "nursing-revolution," as one factor in the population expansion of this period, especially among the noble classes, whose children did evidently become more numerous from the eleventh century onwards ("Aspects démographiques des débuts de la féodalité," *Annales,* 20 [1965] , 1118-1127). Russell suggests that women of the noble classes may have been both willing and able to have more children if they could have wet-nurses and that for these women the

intervals between pregnancies were probably shortened when their children were nursed by others; it was commonly believed that the nursing mother should refrain from intercourse until the child was weaned. The use of wet-nurses may also have increased the chances of survival during that period when the child was wholly or largely dependent on milk for nourishment.

62. Guibert, *Memoirs,* pp. 68, 96. For some tenth-century examples of the use of wet-nurses, see John of Salerno, *Life of St. Odo of Cluny,* translated and edited by Dom Gerard Sitwell, The Makers of Christendom (London, 1958), pp. 59-60; *Vita S. Adelwoldi* (Pl 137, 85d); *Passio S. Adalberti* (PL 137, 865b). See also Marbod of Rennes, *Vita S. Roberti Cassae Dei* (PL 171, 1507ab) for a description of the birth and infancy of its hero, which supports the view that in this period the wet-nurse was commonly brought into the household to the child. In this case the infant Robert utterly rejected the milk of his nurse, a woman of bad character, though he freely accepted his mother's.

63. Guibert, *Memoirs,* p. 96. In the royal and grander noble households of the thirteenth century, it seems, as Margaret Labarge observes, to have been the usual practice for each child to have his own nurse or nurses (*A Baronial Household in the Thirteenth Century* [New York, 1966], p. 47).

64. The late eleventh century *vita* of the Countess Ida, the wife of Count Eustace of Boulogne and the mother of three sons, the famous crusaders, Godfrey of Bouillon and Baldwin of Jerusalem, as well as another Count Eustace, simply gives favorable emphasis to the fact that she nursed all of her children herself (*B. Idae Vita,* AA SS, April, II, 139; PL 155, 437; 449). By the twelfth or thirteenth century when this story was elaborated in *Chanson du Chevalier du Cygne et de Godefroid de Bouillon* (ed. C. Hippeau, 2 vols., Paris, 1874-1877), Ida has left her children with a maid, who called a nurse for one of them when he cried. When the Countess returned and discovered this, she was greatly distressed and, trembling with rage, she forced the infant to disgorge the alien milk and proceeded to nurse him again herself.

65. See above, notes 59 and 60 and below, n. 132.

66. Bartholomew, *De prop. rer.,* pp. 237-238. Cf. Aldobrandino, *Régime du corps, p. 76,* and the *Practica puerorum,* ed. Karl Sudhoff, *Erstlinge der pädiatrischen Literatur* (Munich, 1925); for an English translation, see John Ruhräh, *Pediatrics of the Past* (New York, 1925). This brief and popular treatise, dating at earliest from the twelfth century, offers remedies for such common infant afflictions as thrush, vomiting, diarrhoea, constipation, bladder stones and teething. On the dangers of bad milk, see also Hildegard of Bingen, *Causae et curae,* ed. Kaiser. p. 67.

67. Bartholomew, *De prop. rer.,* p. 242; cf. Aldobrandino's much more specific prescriptions for the most desirable qualities to be sought in a nurse, who should be twenty-five years old, as much like the mother as possible, strong and healthy, for "sickly nurses kill the child at once" (*Régime du corps,* pp. 76-78). She should be of good character and amiable temperament, "not angry or sad or lazy or stupid," because these qualities affect children and make them stupid and badly behaved. Particular attention should be paid to the shape of the breasts, which should be firm and not too large, lest they "smother the child when they cover his nose." It is best if a month or two has passed since she gave birth, and if her child is a son rather than a daughter; her employer should also make sure that she brought her child to full term and has not lost it "either through beating or for any other reason."

68. Walther von Rheinau, *Marienleben,* quoted in Arnold, *Das Kind in der deutschen Literatur,* p. 42, with other literary descriptions of infants and

infant care.

69. Aldobrandino says that it is sufficient to nurse the child two or three times a day and for about two years (*Régime du corps*, pp. 76, 78) and this may represent the norm, although we have little evidence by which such recommendations may be assessed. See below, n. 120.

70. Marie de France, *Milun* in *Les Lais de Marie de France*, ed. Jean Rychner (Paris, 1966), pp. 129-130.

71. Berthold of Regensburg, *Predigten*, ed. Pfeiffer, I, 433; II, 205 (translated in Coulton, *Life in the Middle Ages*, II, 64).

72. See the description of the tenants of the church of St. Mary in Marseilles, in which female children were counted from age one, and boys not until two ("Descriptio mancipiorum ecclesie massiliensis," ed. Benjamin Guérard, *Cartulaire de l'abbaye de Saint-Victor de Marseilles* [2 vols., Paris, 1857], 633-656). See also S. Weinberger, "Peasant Households in Provence, ca. 800-1100," *Speculum* 48 (1973), 247-257.

73. Peiper, pp. 93-95. For the child in process of weaning, Aldobrandino of Siena recommends porridge made of pieces of bread with honey and milk, and the giving of a little wine, also a meat broth, and when he is able to chew, "little tarts of bread and sugar made in the shape of dates" (*Régime du corps*, p. 78).

74. Peiper, p. 94; cf. Arnold, *Das Kind in der deutschen Literatur*, p. 54, on children's love of cow's milk, which is also emphasized in the thirteenth-century "peasant epic," *Meier Helmbrecht*, describing the robber-knight who steals the peasants' cows and boasts that "their children eat water-soup after I've been around" (translated in *Peasant Life in Old German Epics*, by Clair H. Bell, [New York, 1931], p. 70).

75. On artificial nursing in this period, see Peiper, pp. 443-446. The "nursing-horn" was a small polished cow's horn pierced at the small end, to which were fastened two small pieces of parchment like the fingers of a glove through which the milk in the horn could be sucked. The earliest example of its use comes from the ninth-century life of St. Liudger of Frisia, cited by Peiper (p. 445); see below, n. 99. It is also mentioned in the thirteenth-century poem, "Gute Frau," describing a child whose mother could not care for him well and who was given milk through a horn in the hospital. As a child, St. Elizabeth of Thuringia had a silver "züberlin," and there are references to the nursing-horn in the Icelandic *Heimskringla Saga* (Peiper, pp. 93-95). In the French romance, *Robert le Diable*, the hero as an infant was so diabolically "biting" and so frightening to his nurse that she fed him with a horn. On this "changeling" theme, see below, n. 100.

76. For the maternal functions of the nurse and the description paraphrased here, see Bartholomew, *De prop. rer.*, p. 242. Cf. Aldobrandino, *Régime du corps*, p. 76; both writers stress the importance of frequent bathing, two or three times a day for the infant and young child, and two or three times a week for the child of seven and older (see below, n. 233). On the nurse's role, see Arnold, *Das Kind in der deutschen Literatur*, pp. 50-52.

77. For examples, see Labarge, *A Baronial Household*, pp. 45, 47.

78. For the first pictorial representation of a rocking-cradle, in the *Sachsenspiegel* (c. 1230), see Peiper, p. 113. Representations of the basket type of cradle are earlier and more common; see, for example, the picture in the *Reuner Musterbuch*, c. 1208-18 (Vienna, Nationalbibliothek, MS 507, f. IV, reproduced in Christopher Brooke, *The Twelfth Century Renaissance*, London, 1969, p. 88). For St. Elizabeth's silver cradle, see Peiper, p. 91.

79. For some early instances of such legislation, see below, n. 102.

80. See, e.g., *Councils*, I, 234-235, and for fuller references, below, n. 106.

81. Sleeping arrangements for both parents and children naturally depended a great deal on such circumstances as station in life, prosperity and degree of refinement, but there was, in general, little privacy in ordinary medieval households, even those of the nobility. For a description of rather elaborate bed-chambers of this period, see Urban T. Holmes, *Daily Living in the Twelfth Century* (Madison, Wisc. 1962), pp. 82-86. Young children appear often to have slept with, or in the room with, their nurses if they had them, or with their parents; the little peasant heroine of *Der arme Heinrich* slept at the foot of her parents' bed (see n. 246). On this subject, the following note is also suggestive.

82. Guibert, *Memoirs,* pp. 96-97. This revealing story of the orphaned infant whom his mother adopted in expiation of her dead husband's sins gives a vivid picture of the nurses' efforts, night after night shaking his rattle, to soothe this baby who was very good by day, "playing and sleeping," but whose nocturnal crying so harassed Guibert's mother and her servants that "anyone in the same little room could get scarcely any sleep." Guibert regarded this behavior as diabolically inspired and emphasized the kindness and patience with which his mother endured this trial, never shutting the child out of her house and never showing less concern for him. As an example to the multitudes of ordinary crying infants, Walter of Rheinau in his *Marienlied* portrays the infant Jesus as never disturbing the sleep of the neighbors or the household by loud crying (Arnold, *Das Kind in der deutschen Literatur,* p. 84).

83. In her *Causae et curae* (ed. Kaiser, pp. 109-110), Hildegard explains that, although human infants can sit as well as crawl before they can stand upright, they walk later than other creatures not only because of the fragility of their flesh and bones, but because humans have their greatest power above the navel, especially, she implies, in the head, the seat of reason. For a similar view, see Bartholomew, *De prop. rer.,* p. 238. This ancient question appears regularly in the scientific "problem" literature of this period (see above, n. 42, and Lawn, *Salernitan Questions,* pp. 38, 153-154). The Salernitan *Quaestiones* offer physical reasons, depending on the distribution of innate heat in the body and the presence or absence of menstrual blood in nourishment, while Adelard of Bath gives an answer similar to Hildegard's, relating weaker, more tender limbs to the nobler rational animal (*Quaestiones naturales,* ed. Müller, qu. 38, pp. 41-42). William of Conches combines the Salernitan answer with Adelard's (*De phil. mundi,* IV, 14; PL 172, 86d).

84. See Peiper, pp. 96-97, quoting the twelfth-century German poem, *Pilatus,* and the early thirteenth-century *Wolfdietrich,* on learning to walk. The *Tristan* of Eilhart von Oberge (c. 1180) describes the child learning to control its movements by playing with other children. The picture of the child playing "peek-a-boo" is from the thirteenth-century *König Tyrol.* For similar examples, see Arnold, *Das Kind in der deutschen Literatur,* pp. 84-85 and *passim.*

85. Caesarius of Heisterbach, *The Dialogue on Miracles,* translated by H. von E. Scott and C. C. Swinton Bland, with introduction by G. G. Coulton (New York, 1929), II, 10-11.

86. Salimbene de Adam, *Cronica,* edited by Ferdinando Bernini (2 vols., Bari, 1942), I, 507; see my translation in *The Portable Medieval Reader,* edited by J. B. Ross and M. M. McLaughlin (New York, 1949), pp. 366-367. In this version of an ancient tale, Salimbene describes the failure of an experiment intended to discover what language children would speak when they grew up, if they had spoken to no one beforehand, whether Hebrew, Greek,

Latin, Arabic or the language of their parents.

87. Adelard of Bath, *De eodem et diverso* (ed. H. Willner, *Beiträge zur Geschichte der Philosophie des Mittelalters*, Bd. IV, 1, 1903), pp. 25-26. Adelard's story is also meant to demonstrate the soothing effects of music and singing on children in general, as shown by their response to the lullabies of their nurses.

88. Adam of Eynsham, *The Life of St. Hugh of Lincoln*, edited and translated with introduction and notes by Decima L. Douie and Hugh Farmer, Nelson's Medieval Texts (2 vols., Edinburgh and London, 1961-1962), I, 129-130.

89. Explaining this magnetic attraction between the bishop and the baby, the biographer adds, significantly: "What . . . made so important a person pay such attention to so small a being except a knowledge of the greatness concealed in such a tiny frame?" This episode was not unique, for Hugh himself described a similar encounter with his infant nephew, who showed his delight in the same way (p. 131).

90. For an illustration of this twelfth-century roundel, see Henry Kraus, *The Living Theater of Medieval Art* (Bloomington, Ind., 1967), p. 57, no. 34. The Ancren Riwle describes a peasant mother playing hide-and-seek with her child, and when he cries for her, "she leapeth forth lightly with outspread arms, and embraceth and kisseth him and wipeth his eyes" (quoted in Holmes, *Daily Living in the Twelfth Century*, pp. 204-205).

91. See Dom Claude Jean-Nesmy, *Vézelay* (Paris, 1970), Pl. 20 and p. 70; cf. François Salet, *La Madeleine de Vézelay* (Melun, 1948), Pl. 45, no. 20. This capital illustrating a famous episode from the *Vie de saint Benoit* (c. 32), shows on the right face the peasant carrying his child in his arms, and on the central face St. Benedict reaching out his hand to the grieving father and the dead child, which is completly wrapped in swaddling bands.

92. See Le Goff's remarks on the "innumerable maladies" of children, each with its patron saint on which parents might call for healing (*Civilisation*, p. 303). Parental helplessness and grief over the serious illness and impending death of a child, and joy over miraculous cures, are not uncommon themes in the saints' lives of these centuries; see, e.g., the stories of the restoration to health of the young saints, Dunstan and Adalbert of Prague (PL 137,418 and 865), and Gerald of Aurillac's healing of a boy born deaf and dumb (*Life of St. Gerald*, tr. Sitwell, pp. 177-178). The young Stephen Muret was restored to health through the aid of St. Nicholas of Bari and his then newly discovered relics (*Vita . . . Stephani Muretensis, Scriptores ordinis Grandimontensis*, ed. J. Becquet, CC, VIII, 105).

93. For his letter of consolation to the Roman senator, Alberic, and his wife, Ermilina, on the loss of their child, see Ep. VIII, 4 (PL 144, 468d-470a). Another kind of effort to palliate such losses is reflected in the somewhat later Irish poem, "The Little Boys Who Went to Heaven" (Kenneth Jackson, *A Celtic Miscellany* [London, 1951], p. 314.

94. See above, n. 15. An example of emphasis on public baptism is provided by the statutes of the synod of Cashel in Ireland (1172), commanding parents to present their children for baptism "at consecrated fonts in the baptistries of churches" (Gerald of Wales, *The Conquest of Ireland* in Wright, *Historical Writings of Giraldus Cambrensis*, p. 233). Extensive concern with this sacrament and its administration is evident in the English synodal legislation of the thirteenth century; see *Councils*, I, 67-68, for the general teaching on this subject and II, Index, 1405, for the numerous entries under this head.

95. D. Herlihy, "Patterns of Social Mobility," *Journal of Interdisciplinary History*, 3 (1973), 626-633, raises the question of "differing rates of natural reproduction and replacement" among different social classes in medieval so-

ciety. Although it is doubtless true, as he observes, that "welfare affected replacement," i.e., survival and successful rearing, it does not seem to me that the evidence supports the view that "welfare affected reproduction." On this point, see J. Bienvenu, "Pauvreté, misères et charité en Anjou aux XIe et XIIe siècles," *Moyen Age*, 73 (1967), 31-32 and G. Duby, *L'Economie rurale et la vie des campagnes*, I, 216-219. Noteworthy also in this connection is Berthold of Regensburg's emphasis on the "tenderness" and "indulgence" shown by prosperous parents towards their children; the "overfeeding" he deplored may have been the most important factor in their higher survival rate in contrast with the children of the poor (*Predigten*, ed. Pfeiffer, II, 205, 19, 24ff.; cf. I, 433, 32ff).

96. See Le Goff, *Civilisation*, pp. 297-300, and the article of Bienvenu cited in the preceding note. On the problem of poverty and its effects, see also the forthcoming collection of studies edited by Michel Mollat, *Les Pauvres dans la société médiévale* (Paris, 1973), pursuing inquiries undertaken or projected in his "Pauvres et pauvreté à la fin du XIIe siècle," *Revue d'ascetique et de mystique*, 41 (1965), 305-323; and "La notion de la pauvreté du moyen âge; Position de problèmes," *Revue d'histoire de l'Eglise de France*, 52 (1966), 5-23.

97. On these practices and efforts to suppress them, see John T. Noonan, *Contraception: A History of Its Treatment by the Catholic Theologians and Canonists* (Cambridge, Mass., 1965), especially pp. 143-199 (on the medieval development of law and theology regarding contraception and abortion) and pp. 200-230 (on contraceptive techniques and means of dissemination). The herbal potions or "poisons of sterility" condemned by the early medieval penitentials and other works may have had some effectiveness as contraceptives or abortifacients. But the value of such "folk" remedies as well as that of the techniques of learned medicine—potions, pessaries and ointments—was doubtless greatly diminished by the mingling of the possibly effective with the plainly magical. Knowledge of ancient contraceptive techniques increased with the growth of medical knowledge and Moslem influence from the late eleventh century onward (see above, n. 42) and here again, as in the case of childbearing and rearing, the principal fount of information for the Byzantines and the Moslems and through them the medieval West was the *Gynecology* of Soranus (see Noonan, pp. 12-18), whose recommendations, together with some Moslem additions, were disseminated in such vastly influential works as Avicenna's *Canon* of medicine, as well as in Latin versions of Soranus's treatise. How widely such knowledge was available beyond medical circles is as difficult to say as it is to assess the effectiveness of ecclesiastical prohibitions of its use; it seems clear, as Noonan concludes (p. 230), that though apparently not a large social problem, the attempt at least to practice contraception and abortion was a reality of medieval civilization. For another view of this problem, see Jean-Louis Flandrin, "Contraception, mariage et relations amoureuses dans l'occident chrétien," *Annales*, 24 (1969), 1370-1390, emphasizing the distinction, in medieval law and theory with respect to contraception, between marital and extra-marital relations and, especially in the latter, the possible significance of the practice of *coitus interruptus*, surely the most effective means of contraception before modern times.

98. The powerful, though often ineffective, impulse to secrecy and the concealment of illegitimate pregnancies is strikingly evident in the documents—royal "acts of grace" for the benefit of women condemned for the crime of infanticide in the fourteenth and fifteenth centuries—examined by Yves Brissaud in one of the most significant of the recent studies cited in this

volume ("L'infanticide à la fin du moyen âge, ses motivations psychologiques et sa repression," *Revue historique de droit francais et étranger*, 50 [1972], 229-256). What gives this study, which concerns the period immediately following that encompassed in this essay, its exceptional value is the evidence provided by these materials of the psychological pressures, the motives of shame and fear of social rejection, that led these women, most of them girls under twenty and all of humble origins, first to attempt to conceal their illegitimate pregnancies and their solitary sufferings in childbirth, and then to maintain this secrecy by killing or exposing their infants. Particularly revealing of contemporary attitudes is the fact that in nearly all cases the women declared, in extenuation of their crimes, that they had baptized the infant before killing it.

99. The possibility of female infanticide as a means of "population control" in a ninth-century peasant community is suggested by Emily Coleman in an article based on a study of the polyptych of Saint-Germain-des-Prés and forthcoming in *Annales*. For this period and later there is evidence of female infanticide in particular, as well as infanticide in general, among pagan peoples before or in process of conversion to Christianity. On the father's power of life and death over the newborn child, among barbarian peoples as in Roman antiquity, see N. Belmont, "Levana, ou comment 'élever' les enfants," *Annales*, 38 (1973), 77-89; this power might also be exercised, among Germanic peoples, by the child's grandmother and sometimes by the mother's brother. See, e.g., the life of the Frisian Saint Liudger (744-809) by his nephew Altfried, telling the story of the saint's mother, whose pagan grandmother, angry because her son's wife had so many daughters and no sons, sent servants to snatch this baby from its mother's breast before it had nursed; for according to pagan custom a child could be killed only before it had received earthly nourishment. When the servants took the baby girl to a tub of water to drown her, she clung to the rim of the tub, struggling for her life, and was mercifully rescued by a neighbor-woman, who proceeded to feed the child first with honey and then with milk through a nursing-horn, and thus prevent its death (*Altfridi vita sancti Liudgeri* in *Die Geschichtsquellen des Bistums Münster*, Bd. IV., Ed. W. Dickamp, Münster i. Westf., 1881, lib. I, esp. 6-7). See also the admonitions of the missionary bishop, Otto of Bamberg, to the heathen Pomeranians in the early twelfth century, attacking their practice of female infanticide as unnatural (Herbord, *Dialogus de vita Ottonis episcopi Babenbergensis*, 2, 18, 33, MGH, SS, 20, 733, 20-25; 741, 35-38; cf. Ebo, *Vita Ottonis*, 2, 12, MGH, SS, 12, 851ff.), and the abundant evidence of this practice in Iceland and other Nordic regions during this period (Juha Pentikäinen, *The Nordic Dead-Child Tradition: Nordic Dead-Child Beings: A Study in Comparative Religion*, FF Communications, No. 202 [Helsinki, 1968], pp. 68-76). This illuminating study is essentially concerned with Nordic fantasies and beliefs regarding "dead-child beings" as projections of collective guilt or anxiety over these rejected children.

100. On traditional attitudes towards abnormal children and treatment of them, see Carl Haffter, "The Changeling: History and Psychodynamics of Attitudes to Handicapped Children in European Folklore," *Journal of the History of the Behavioral Sciences*, 4 (1968), 55-61. The folk belief that the mentally retarded or deformed child was a supernatural substitute for the "real" child was christianized in the notion of the "changeling" as a demon-child left by the Devil who had stolen the human child; see Baudouin de Gaiffier, "Le diable voleur d'enfants. A propos de la naissance des saints Etienne, Laurent et Barthélemy," *Etudes critiques d'hagiographie et d'iconologie* (Studia

Hagiographica, 43), pp. 169-193, for the development of this idea in the legends of these saints and in other works from the eleventh century onwards (for bibliography see pp. 169-170, n. 1). See also Jeffrey B. Russell, *Witchcraft in the Middle Ages* (Ithaca, New York, 1972), pp. 117-119 and *passim*. The idea of the "changeling" led to extraordinary and often brutal practices aimed at reversing the exchange, as well as to the outright exposure or slaying of the abnormal child; for some examples, see Peiper, pp. 178-179. Multiple births, especially the birth of twins, were often regarded also with fear, suspicion or at least ambivalence because of the common belief that the mother's adultery was responsible; hence the practice of permitting the "legitimate" child to live and exposing or abandoning the other (Pentikainen, *Dead-Child Tradition*, pp. 60-61). For a sophisticated literary treatment of these powerful folk-motifs, see the twelfth-century *lai* "Fresne" ("The Lay of the Ash Tree") by Marie de France (*Lais*, ed. Rychner), pp. 44-60.

101. The possibilities offered by the excellent edition of English synodal legislation used in this study underscore the need, as a basis for further inquiry and generalization, for an intensive and systematic study of both ecclesiastical and secular legislation concerning infanticide during this period, and the efforts to enforce it, especially as revealed in the episcopal and secular court records from the twelfth century on. For the first volume of a similar French series, see Odette Pontal, *Les statuts synodaux français du XIIIe siècle, I. Les statuts de Paris et le synodal de l'Ouest*, Collection des documents inédits sur l'histoire de France, IX (Paris, 1971). See also A. Artonne, L. Guizard, O. Pontal, eds., *Répertoire des statuts synodaux des diocèses de l'ancienne France du XIIIe à la fin du XVIIIe siècle*, Documents, études, répertoires publiés par l'Institut de Recherche et d'Histoire de Textes, VIII (Paris, 1964). Useful also would be a study of the interpretation of ecclesiastical legislation on this subject by canonists and theologians of the twelfth and thirteenth centuries; severe penalties, including imprisonment, were envisaged for infanticide and for the abandonment by parents of infants or sick children, in the *Decretals* of Pope Gregory IX, compiled by Raymond of Peñaforte c. 1230 (ed. Venice, 1514), tit. X and XI. See also his *Summa de poenitentia et matrimonio cum glossis Joannis de Friburgo* (reprinted, Farnborough, England, 1967). Further light on the problem might be cast by a careful study of the treatment of this subject in the sermons, confessors' manuals and other didactic works of these centuries. The sin of infanticide is vehemently castigated, for example, in the *Praeloquia* of Bishop Rather of Verona in the tenth century (PL 136, 269ac), but I have found few references to it in later works of this kind.

102. For the legislation of the synod of Mainz, 853, see Peiper, p. 655; the punishment for the suffocation of a child in bed after baptism was forty days penance on bread, water and vegetables and abstention from intercourse for a year. For the prescriptions of earlier Germanic law codes, see MGH, Leges, Sectio I, Vol. IV, pt. 1, ed. A. Boretius (Hanover, 1962), no. 24, 1-4, pp. 89-90; see also Vol. V, pt. 1, ed. K. Lehmann (Hanover, 1885), c. XCI, p. 150; cf. Peiper, p. 177, for reference to a seventh-century law of the Spanish Visigoths which punished infanticide with death or blinding. The legislation of the early medieval penitentials is conveniently surveyed in John T. McNeill and Helena M. Gamer, *Medieval Handbooks of Penance*. From the Penitentials of Adamnan and Columban in the sixth and seventh centuries to the *Corrector* of Burchard of Worms in the eleventh century, these works show a persistent concern with the "overlaying" of infants, whether intentional or unintentional; on this distinction, see the Frankish Penitential of St. Hubert, c. 850 (p. 293) providing that "if anyone overlays an unbaptized baby, she

shall do penance for three years; if unintentionally, two years." See also pp. 141, 254, 275, 302, 340, and for Burchard's admonitions concerning abortion and contraception as well as infanticide, and summing up earlier views of poverty as an extenuating factor in such cases, *Decretum*, 19: PL 140, 972. It makes a great difference, he says, whether the guilty person is a "poor little woman" (*paupercula*) and acted on account of the difficulty of feeding or whether she acted to conceal a crime of fornication; in the former case the punishment, ten years penance on legal *feriae*, was apparently halved.

103. In his story of the poor woman who, lacking clothing for her suckling baby, takes him to herself to keep him warm with her own rags and accidentally smothers the baby whom she "clasps with utmost love," Abelard clearly had in mind involuntary infanticide. Yet he also declared that when this woman comes before the bishop, a heavy punishment is imposed on her, "not for the fault that she committed," but as a warning to her and to other women to exercise greater care (*Peter Abelard's 'Ethics'*, edited with an introduction, English translation and notes by David E. Luscombe [Oxford, 1971], pp. 38-39).

104. See *Councils*, II, 1, 70 (Salisbury I, 1217), [29]: women are to be warned to nurse their children carefully and not to take them into bed with them at night lest they overlay them, and not to leave them alone in the house where there is a fire or near water without someone watching them, and "this should be said to them every Sunday." For the reiteration of such admonitions cf. pp. 136, 183, 204-205, 214, 234-235, 274, 351, 410, 457, 520. Noteworthy is the persistent implication that the dangers against which these admonitions were directed were very common; see, e.g., pp. 204-205 (Mandates of Robert Grosseteste) and p. 520, forbidding the taking of children into bed, "propter pericula que frequentissime inde imminere noscuntur." See also Berthold of Regensburg, *Predigten*, I 268, 18, insisting that little children should have proper care and never be left unwatched.

105. *Ibid.*, 2, 1973 (Exeter II, 1287); cf. 1, 137 (Winchester I, 1224). In the prescriptions of this legislation concerning baptism, there are also frequent references to the conditional re-baptism of exposed infants (*Councils*, II, 1, 32, 70, 140-141, 183, 233-234, 453, 589-590, 634-635).

106. *Ibid.*, 1, 214 (Coventry, 1224).

107. *Ibid.*, 1, 214, referring to the dangers of drunkenness, especially the setting of fires in which the guilty are suffocated with their children. In an unpublished thirteenth-century German *Summa de sacramentis* (Munich, Clm 22 333, fol. 100ra-101ra), confessors are urged to question penitents about drunkenness, especially peasants who, "after drinking in the taverns, beat their pregnant wives and kill their unborn children."

108. See *Leges Henrici Primi*, ed. L. J. Downer (Oxford: Clarendon Press, 1972), p. 270, for the provision that if anyone should kill or overlay a child entrusted to him to be reared or taught, the penalty shall be the same as for adult homicide. A capitulary of Charlemagne three centuries earlier had in fact established the principle that infanticide should be treated as homicide, but there appears to be no evidence of its enforcement (J. D. Mansi, *Sacrorum conciliorum nova et amplissima collectio*, 31 vols., Florence and Venice, 1759-81, XVII, 2, 1060). By the thirteenth century French secular law took increasing cognizance of this offense; according to the *Etablissements de saint Louis*, in cases of involuntary infanticide the woman was subject only to the canonical penalties (imprisonment is here specified), but if she repeated her offense, she should be turned over to the secular authorities and burned (*Les Etablissements de saint Louis*, Liv. I, c. 39, 4 vols., edited by Paul Viollet [Paris, 1881-1886] II, 55). This provision was, as Brissaud notes

("L'infanticide ... ," p. 247), borrowed textually from the customs of
Anjou and Maine, compiled in the thirteenth century and in successive redac-
tions more severe in the treatment of this crime; by the fifteenth century
voluntary infanticide was punished by burning or burial alive. The customary
law of Normandy preserved the distinction between involuntary and voluntary infanticide, the former subject only to ecclesiastical penalties, and the
latter punishable by burning. Cf. Philippe de Beaumanoir, *Coutumes de
Beauvaisis,* Texte critique publié ... par A. Salmon, Collection des textes
pour servir à l'étude et à l'enseignement d'histoire (2 vols., reprinted, Paris,
1970), II, 446-420. From the late thirteenth century on, there is increasing
evidence of the application of the most severe penalties; two women were
condemned to the fire for this crime in Paris in 1291, and two more in
Aurillac in the same period (for these and other examples, see Brissaud, pp.
248-250).
109. See Peiper, p. 186; according to the charter of Bishop Dateus if these unmarried mothers could not nurse their own children, nurses were to be hired
for them. The children were to be cared for and taught a trade until the
completion of their seventh year, when they might leave and live where they
pleased.
110. For Marc Bloch's comments on the prevalence of bastards in noble households, see *La société féodale,* II, 40 (*Feudal Society,* tr. Manyon, p. 320);
cf. Le Goff's remarks on the greater shamefulness of illegitimacy among the
lower classes (*Civilisation,* p. 353). Though doubtless more burdensome and
probably more shameful among the lowly, its disadvantages for those of
higher birth as well were considerable. From the eleventh century, illegitimate birth was a bar to entering ecclesiastical orders, requiring episcopal and
eventually papal dispensation (*Dictionnaire de droit canonique* [Paris, 1924-
1965], II, 253-255); see the remarks of Guibert of Nogent regarding the case
of the bishop-elect of Laon in 1106 (*Memoirs,* p. 155). Illegitimacy was also
almost universally a bar to inheritance, although in many regions of Europe
and according to ecclesiastical law children born before the marriage of their
parents were legitimized by their subsequent marriage provided they were of
marriageable condition when the child was conceived. This was not the case
in England after the great council of Merton (1236), when the king's court
refused to recognize all such forms of legitimation as applicable to the law of
landed property (*Councils,* II, I, 198-201); cf. p. 87, for a reference to the
exclusion of bastards from both ecclesiastical and secular offices. See also
the synodal legislation prescribing that those of illegitimate birth, as well as
the sons of serfs, who had been ordained without dispensation, were to be
suspended until dispensation was received (II, 1, 60); priests were further enjoined to inquire at baptism of a child concerning its parentage so as to discover who was illegitimate or not (II, 1, 70, 228-229, 455-456). For French
custom in this matter, see, e.g., Beaumanoir, *Coutumes de Beauvaisis,* I,
578-599; II, 1377. The general condition of the illegitimate child was summed
up by the thirteenth century German preacher, Berthold of Regensburg, remarking on the shamefulness of the sin that made the child "élos und
érbélos und réhtélos," depriving it of honorable marriage, inheritance and
legal position, as well as secular and ecclesiastical honors (*Predigten,* ed.
Pfeiffer, I, 178, 13ff; 413). According to the German customary law of the
later middle ages, the illegitimate child of peasant parents was regarded as related only to the mother, having no claims on the father's family and no
rights of inheritance (H. Fehr, *Die Rechtsstellung der Frau und der Kinder
in den Weistümern,* Jena, 1912, pp. 261-271). The stigma and shame attach-
ing to illegitimacy, for both mother and child, and in various social classes,

is a recurrent theme in the narrative and literary sources of these centuries; see, among a multitude of examples, Marie de France, *Milun* (above, n. 70), Hartmann von Aue, *Gregorius* (below, n. 220), Gottfried von Strassburg, *Tristan* (below, n. 221), Caesarius of Heisterbach's story of the despair felt by the lay-brother, Henry, over his illegitimacy (*Dialogue on Miracles,* I, 229-230), and the satirical verses of the German poet, Der Stricker, on the "invisible pictures" seen only by those of legitimate birth (quoted in Arnold, *Das Kind in der deutschen Literatur,* p. 32).

111. See above, n. 102, for the common view, summed up in the *Decretum* of Burchard of Worms, of poverty as extenuating, though not justifying, practices destructive of life. On the relation between poverty, misery and the exposure or abandonment of children, see Bienvenu, "Pauvreté, misères, et charité. . . ," *Moyen Age,* 72 (1966), 398-399. For the importance of motives of shame and fear in relation to infanticide and exposure, see above, n. 98.

112. Herrad of Landsberg, *Hortus deliciarum,* ed. Walter (Strassburg, 1952), Pl. XLIV. Cf. Caesarius of Heisterbach's story of the nun who died without confessing her adultery and infanticide and who afterwards appeared to a kinswoman as condemned eternally to carry her burning child, whose fire ceaselessly tormented and devoured her (*Dialogue on Miracles,* II, 308).

113. Baudri of Dol, *Vita Roberti de Arbrisselo* (PL 162, 1055); cf. the letter of Marbod of Rennes to Robert, accusing him of permitting women to bear their children in his entourage. Robert's companions, Vital of Savigny and Bernard of Tiron, were also noted for their concern for women and orphaned or rejected children; see *Vita Bernardi* (PL 172, 1441) and Bienvenu "Pauvreté, misères et charité . . ." *Moyen Age,* 72 (1966), 389-392.   The contemporary heretical preacher, Henry of Lausanne, was reputed to have urged his followers to marry and thus rescue women of ill-fame (J. B. Russell, *Dissent and Reform in the Early Middle Ages* [Berkeley and Los Angeles, 1965], p. 71.

114. On Fulk of Neuilly, see John W. Baldwin, *Masters, Princes and Merchants: The Social Views of Peter the Chanter and His Circle* (2 vols., Princeton, 1970), I, 136-137. To Fulk's fund for these dowries, the scholars of Paris are said to have contributed 250 pounds in silver and the bourgeoisie over a thousand pounds. Contemporaneously the decretal of Pope Innocent III to all the faithful declared that those who rescued women from brothels and took them in marriage performed works meritorious for the remission of sins (PL 214, 102; 29 April 1198).

115. On this concern for orphaned and abandoned children in general, see L. Lallemand, *Histoire de la charité* (Paris: Picard, 1906), pp. 135-151, reprinting the relevant sections from his *Histoire des enfants abandonnés et delaissés* (Paris, 1885). See also Ludwig Ruland, *Das Findelhaus, seine geschichtliche Entwicklung und sittliche Bedeutung* (Berlin, 1913). A fresh study of this subject is greatly to be desired. Another late twelfth-century preacher and advocate of effective charity towards the poor, Raoul Ardent, urged that everyone who possessed special gifts and talents should offer these freely for the advantage of the poor, especially orphans and widows; rich merchants, e.g., should use their money to endow orphans or provide for their education (Gilles Couvreur, "Pauvreté et droits des pauvres à la fin du XIIᵉ siècle," *La Pauvreté; Des sociétés de penurie à la société d'abundance* in *Recherches et debats du Centre catholique des intellectuels français,* 49 [Paris, 1964], pp. 21-23).

116. In Milan, the foundation of Dateus, which disappeared, probably in the fires of 1071 or 1075, was survived or succeeded by two smaller institutions,

a *brefotrofio* at San Celso of the late tenth century and the foundling-home of Broglio, founded in 1145 (Lallemand, *Histoire de la charité*, p. 140). In Florence, Siena, Pisa and Mirandola, among others, refuges or homes for foundlings were established in the late twelfth and early thirteenth centuries (pp. 138-141). In France, from the thirteenth century, town hospitals sometimes received orphans, but they often, like the Hotel-Dieu in Troyes and in Angers, refused foundlings.

117. Lallemand, p. 142. In 1198, Pope Innocent III constituted the hospital in Montpellier the head of the order, and submitted to the jurisdiction of Guy and his successors all foundations then and in the future (PL 214, 83, 85); later, in 1228, the headship of the order was transferred to the Roman hospital of Santa Maria in Saxia.

118. On Innocent's patronage of this order and his propaganda in favor of abandoned children, see Lallemand, pp. 143-144; see also Pietro de Angelis, *L'Arcispedale de Santo Spirito in Saxia nel passato e nel presente* (Rome, 1952).

119. *Ibid.*, p. 144 and p. 146, on the confraternities within urban parishes whose members participated in the charitable activities of the order.

120. *Ibid.*, pp. 147-148. Much of the evidence concerning the treatment of these children is later than the thirteenth century. On being received, they were conditionally baptized, often even if their parents had not left a little salt on their clothing to show that they had not been baptized, and named, commonly after the saint whose feast-day coincided with their baptism. The larger institutions had resident wet-nurses, but apparently most children were put out to nurse, the length of time for wet-nursing ranging from fifteen to eighteen months; once weaned, they were returned to the hospice where they remained for varying lengths of time. Boys from eight to ten years old were apprenticed or put out as servants, while girls, it appears, were often kept longer.

121. For an earlier case much like that of Peter Damian and his brothers, see the tenth-century life of Abbot John of Saint Arnulf in Metz (PL 137, 247-248); the future abbot, the oldest son of a very elderly father and a much younger mother, after his father's death and his mother's remarriage, as an adolescent took complete charge of his younger brothers and the whole household. Regarding later testamentary provision for the care of orphans and minor children, see John H. Mundy, "Charity and Social Work in Toulouse, 1100-1250," *Traditio*, 22 (1966), pp. 256-257. In the cases here cited, from documents of the late twelfth and early thirteenth century, testators provided for minor children either by entrusting them and their property to other branches of the family (see n. 184), or by setting up something similar to modern trust funds under the direction of testamentary executors (see n. 185). See also p. 266, for testamentary clauses providing for the child's care in a monastic community and usually envisaging his eventual entry into the religious life.

122. Besides the case of his mother's adoption of an orphaned infant, who may have been Jean, later abbot of Saint-Germer (*Memoirs*, pp. 96-97, 134), Guibert also describes the rescue of a little boy, during the massacre of the Jews at Rouen at the time of the First Crusade, by the son of the countess of Eu, who took the child to his mother to be reared; he later became, according to Guibert, a devout and learned monk at Saint-Germer (pp. 134-137).

123. For the case of a Jewish boy whom an eleventh-century count of Macon had baptized with his own name and entrusted to his countess to be reared, see Georges Duby, *La société aux XIe et XIIe siècles dans la région maconnaise* (Paris, 1953), p. 121. In his autobiographical account of his conversion first

from Judaism to Christianity and later to the monastic life, Hermann of Scheda in the early twelfth century tells the story of how, after his own conversion, he kidnapped his seven-year-old half-brother so that he, too, might become a Christian. The child's mother, "wild with grief," complained to the city authorities of Mainz and after being pursued to the monastery of Flonheim, Hermann left the boy there to be instructed and fled elsewhere; he had nothing to say, however, about the boy's later fate (*Hermannus quondam Judaeus Opusculum de conversione sua*, edited by G. Niemeyer, MGH, *Quellen zur Geistesgeschichte des Mittelalters*, Bd. IV, 109, 114-116).

124. On the Jewish preference, in times of persecution, for death rather than conversion for their children, see the episodes described by Solomon bar Samson, c. 1140 (Jacob K. Marcus, *The Jew in the Medieval World: A Source Book*, 315-1781 [New York, 1960] pp. 115-120, 127-130, 131-135). Regarding the selling of children into slavery, in the ninth and tenth centuries, young boys were among the principal categories of slaves exported from France to Spain and other parts of the Moslem world in a traffic largely conducted by Jewish traders; the origins of these slave-boys are not wholly clear, but they seem to have been mainly pagan (Slavic) children captured and then castrated, chiefly at Verdun, which was, according to Liutprand of Cremona in the tenth century, the great "eunuch-factory" of the West (Charles Verlinden, *L'Esclavage dans l'Europe médiévale, t. I. Peninsule iberique-France* [Bruges, 1955], pp. 715-716). According to the prejudiced testimony of Gerald of Wales, it was a "common practice" of the Anglo-Saxons before the Norman Conquest to "send their own sons and kinsmen for sale in Ireland," a practice which, in his view, served to justify the conquest of both parties to these transactions (*The Conquest of Ireland* in *Historical Works*, ed. Wright, pp. 215-216). Caesarius of Heisterbach in the early thirteenth century refers to a little pagan (probably Slavic) girl, about ten years old, whom his aunt had bought as a slave and had baptized (*Dialogue on Miracles*, II, c. 44, p. 208). According to the thirteenth-century German *Schwabenspiegel*, the sale of children in cases of dire necessity was permissible; but they were not to be delivered to death or to the heathens or to prostitution (Peiper, p. 181). Bienvenu reports the evidently exceptional case of the giving of children into serfdom as suggesting the extremes to which economic misery could lead; in this case a certain freeman begged the abbot of Saint-Florent-de-Saumur to receive as serfs two of his children whom he could no longer feed; after resisting, the abbot finally agreed, on being assured of the concordance of the mother and the children themselves ("Pauvreté, misères, et charité . . . ," *Moyen Age*, 72 (1966), 408-409.

125. Adam of Eynsham, *Life of St. Hugh of Lincoln*, I, 132-133. Among the boys whom Hugh educated and to whom, if they were promising, he gave ecclesiastical preferment, was one, Robert of Noyon, who had been bought for a "small sum" at five or thereabouts, by Archbishop Hugh of Canterbury; on meeting Bishop Hugh, this child promptly deserted the archbishop and attached himself to Hugh "as joyfully as if he had been restored to a father." He was later sent to the nunnery of Elstow for his early education. Hugh's biographer also refers to another boy, Benedict, whom the bishop had found in Caen, and whom he adopted, reared in his household until he was a youth and then sent to the schools.

126. See P. Le Cacheux, "Une charte de Jumièges concernant l'épreuve par la fer chaud (fin du XIe siècle)," *Société de l'Histoire de Normandie, Mélanges*, (1927), pp. 205-216, for the case of a peasant mother who had sold, or rented, her infant for ten sous a year to the wife of a wealthy citizen of Bayeux, as a substitute for her own baby who had died at birth. When, after

the untimely deaths of both foster-parents, she failed to receive her money, the true mother appealed to Duke William of Normandy for the return of her child and, having successfully undergone the ordeal, recovered him, but at the price of his inheritance. The late twelfth-century case related by Adam of Eynsham (*Life of St. Hugh of Lincoln*, II, 20-25) with interesting implications regarding child-marriage, legitimacy and other issues, concerns the childless wife of an elderly Lincolnshire knight, who in order to defraud her brother-in-law of his inheritance, simulated pregnancy and passed off a peasant woman's newborn girl as hers, having hired the child's true mother as its nurse. Although Bishop Hugh excommunicated the parties to this deception, the foster-mother persisted, after her husband's death, in claiming his inheritance for this child, who at age four was given in marriage with her lands by the king to a certain youth. In defiance of the bishop's frequent constitutions forbidding the marriage of those who had not yet reached the age of discretion, this marriage uniting a peasant of unfree birth to a noble was performed, and despite all of Hugh's efforts to right the wrong, the husband was permitted to keep what he had wrongfully acquired, since according to English law, a child was regarded as legitimate whom the husband of a woman had so recognized during his lifetime. (On child-marriage and legitimacy, see notes 110 and 143.) That the substitution or "suppositio" of infants for fraudulent purposes was a not uncommon sin is suggested also by the English synodal lesiglation of the thirteenth century; see *Councils*, II, 1, 357 and 632, "de partu supposito vel exposito."

127. Cf. the remarks of Duby, "Histoire des mentalités," *L'Histoire et ses méthodes*, p. 958.

128. For the quotations in the epigraph to this section, see Guibert, *Memoirs*, p. 68; *The Ecclesiastical History of Orderic Vitalis*, edited and translated with introduction and notes by Marjorie Chibnall, Vol. II: Books III and IV, Oxford Medieval Texts (Oxford, 1969), Introd., p. xiii; Southern, *The Making of the Middle Ages*, pp. 239-240 (Southern's translation consists of phrases taken from Eadmer's *Liber de Excellentia B. Mariae*, PL 159, 557-580, especially 564-565).

129. The picture drawn and the themes developed here are based on a fairly thoroughgoing but by no means exhaustive examination of the biographical and autobiographical materials of the eleventh and twelfth centuries; largely hagiographical and semi-hagiographical, they reflect the virtues and deficiencies of their genre, concerning which the cautionary remarks of Leopold Genicot are worth noting ("L'Eremitisme du XIe siècle dans son contexte économique et social," *L'Eremitismo in Occidente nei secoli XI e XII*, Atti della seconda Settimana internazionale di studio, La Mendola, 1962 (Milan, 1965), pp. 54-58. In describing the parentage and childhood experience of their subjects, many authors of such works fall back on the usual clichés regarding noble parents, careful education, etc. but these are in themselves often revealing of contemporary ideals, and in some significant instances, especially when the biographer was close to the person and experience of his subject, his account is sufficiently expanded to permit some real insight into the images and relationships with which we are particularly concerned.

130. See, for an early example, Hermann of Reichenau's epitaph on his mother, Hiltrud, the mother of seven, who died in 1052, beloved by all as a gentle, pious peacemaker, benefactor of the poor, and practical ruler of her household (*Chronicon*, MGH, SS, 5, 130). On the basis in reality of contemporary portrayals of the administrative efficiency of the noblewoman, see David Herlihy's study of the role and position of women as landowners and land-managers during this period, "Land, Family and Women in Continental Eu-

rope, 701-1200," *Traditio,* 18 (1962), 89-120. According to Herlihy, the importance of women with regard to land and family, though varying markedly over time, became especially pronounced after 950 and reached a kind of apex in the eleventh century; a significant factor also during this period was the greater physical mobility of the population, with the husband and father more frequently absent from home and the wife assuming a more continuous supervision over the family's fixed possessions (p. 111f.). On this point, see also Marc Bloch, *La société féodale,* II, 19-21 (*Feudal Society,* tr. Manyon, pp. 307-309); Robert Fossier, *La terre et les hommes en Picardie jusqu'à la fin du XIIIe siècle* (2 vols., Paris and Louvain, 1968), I, 269-271; and Huyghebaert, "Les femmes laïques. . . ," *I Laici,* pp. 374-375; 379-386. On other aspects of the maternal image in this period, see also Martin Bernards, "Die Frau in der Welt und die Kirche während des 11. Jahrhunderts," *Sacric Erudiri,* 20 (1971), 40-100; Herbert Grundmann, "Die Frauen und die Literatur," *Archiv für Kulturgeschichte,* 26 (1935), 129-161; Marie-Louise Portmann, *Die Darstellung der Frau in der Geschichtsschreibung des früheren Mittelalters,* Basler Beiträge zur Geschichtswissenschaft, 69 (Basel and Stuttgart, 1958), pp. 52-141.

131. *Vita Prima Bernardi* (PL 185, 227-228), translated by Geoffrey Webb and Adrian Walker, *St. Bernard of Clairvaux* (Westminster, Maryland, 1960), pp. 13-14. The birth of Bernard, her third son, was preceded by the customary portentous dream, whose favorable interpretation filled his mother's heart with joy and love for her unborn son, whom she vowed most particularly to the Lord's service, planning for his education even before his birth.

132. *Vita Prima,* PL 185, 228; Webb and Walker, p. 14. Cf. Guibert, *Memoirs,* p. 72, remarking that his mother's "delicacy and customary sumptuous diet did not accord with frugality"; she was also, it appears, indulgent with her son when it came to food and clothing.

133. For St. Margaret of Scotland, see *Vita,* I, 9; 4, 27; AA SS, June, II, 329, 334; cf. *Vita B. Idae,* PL 155, 438d. St. Anselm of Canterbury was also first instructed by his mother, to whose conversation he always, as a child, "lent a ready ear" (*The Life of St. Anselm, Archbishop of Canterbury by Eadmer,* edited with introduction, notes and translation by R. W. Southern, Nelson's Medieval Texts, London, 1962, p. 4). It was St. Bernard's mother, not his father, who placed her son, as soon as he was able, in the care of teachers at the church of Chatillon-sur-Saone (*Vita prima,* c. II; PL, 185, 228; Webb and Walker, p. 16. Later in our period, the young Beatrice of Tienen, born about 1200, was instructed by her mother, not only in Christian virtues but also in reading; she began to learn to read and recite the Psalter at five (*Vita Beatricis, De autobiografie van de Z. Beatrijs Van Tienen, O. Cist.,* edited by L. Reypens, S. J. [Antwerp, 1964], pp. 23-24). I am indebted to Dom Jean Leclercq for knowledge of this interesting text.

134. See Huyghebaert, "Les femmes laïques . . . ," *I Laici,* pp. 348-349.

135. See Grundmann, "Die Frauen und die Literatur," *Archiv für Kulturgeschichte,* 26 (1935), pp. 134-135, for some examples, including that of the ninth-century Queen Judith, wife of Louis the Pious, who was apparently well-educated enough to read the biblical commentaries of Rabanus Maurus and the Latin poetry of Walahfrid Strabo, Several ladies of the Saxon dynasty in the tenth century had also received some education in letters, notable among them the learned and enterprising Hadwig, niece of Otto I, described as a "brilliant Minerva," devoted to Latin learning and the reading of Latin poetry (Portmann, *Die Darstellung der Frau,* pp. 128-130). Throughout our period, even girls not intended for the monastic life were sometimes sent to convents to be taught, like the little sisters who were, ac-

cording to a story of Caesarius of Heisterbach, sent to a Cistercian nunnery
to learn their lessons. Both were zealous and rivalrous students, but one fell
sick and, fearful of losing ground, tried to bribe the schoolmistress to hold
her sister back (*Dialogue on Miracles,* I, 222).

136. Grundmann, "Die Frauen und die Literatur," *Archiv für Kulturgeschichte,*
26 (1935), 133-134. Cf. Erich Auerbach, *Literary Language and Its Public in
Late Latin Antiquity and in the Middle Ages,* translated from the German
by Ralph Manheim, Bollingen Series, LXXIV (New York, 1965), pp. 289-
291, emphasizing the role of Anglo-Norman noblewomen as patrons of literature, among them Constance FitzGilbert of Lincolnshire, who commissioned
literary works and "read them in her room"; she is, as Auerbach notes, the
first person of whom such a statement is made. Among other examples,
Auerbach notes the description by Chrétien of Troyes (*Yvain,* 1. 5366) of a
young girl, the daughter of a knight, reading a romance to her parents in the
garden, as well as the reference in *Floire et Blancheflor* to noble children
who read Latin and French.

137. See Andre Grabar and Carl Nordenfalk, *Romanesque Painting from the
Eleventh to the Thirteenth Century* (Lausanne, 1958), pp. 170-172, on the
growing importance of ladies of the nobility as a new clientele for illuminated books, which were cherished by women of high birth as visible signs
of both their rank and their piety. The earliest example of a *de luxe* Psalter
in the possession of a pious gentlewoman is the famous Albani Psalter, now
at Hildesheim, which was originally owned by Christina of Markyate (see below, notes 140-142). By the early thirteenth century even a girl of humble
origins might aspire to possession of a Psalter, if we may believe the story
told by Thomas of Cantimpré in his *Bonum Universale de Apibus* (translated by Coulton, *Life in the Middle Ages,* I, 123), of the little girl of six
who begged her father for a Psalter, which he was too poor to buy, and who,
sent by him "to the mistress who teaches the Psalter to the daughters of
rich folk," miraculously read it at first sight, thereby so impressing the
wealthy ladies of the parish that they bought a copy for her.

138. Peter Damian, *Opusc.* XLV, 4: PL 145, 698, referring to the "literary
games" in which children learn the first elements of articulate speech; some
of these, he says, are called "abecedaries," others "syllabaries" or "nomi-
naries," and still others "calculators." On similar teaching devices, see A.
Gloria, "Volgare illustre del 1106 e proverbi volgari del 1200," *Atti del R.
Istituto Veneto,* VI, 3, 103.

139. Concerning this aspect of a vast paternal authority over minor children,
both boys and girls, see G. Lepointe, *Droit romain et ancien droit français.
Régimes matrimoniaux* (Paris, 1958), p. 133 and *passim.* After the middle
of the twelfth century paternal consent was not, as hitherto, regarded in
canon law as essential to a valid marriage for either boys or girls, but girls
were, as René Metz observes, the chief beneficiaries of this new conception,
which penetrated the matrimonial law of the Church through doctrine
rather than legislation, and which only gradually passed into practice ("La
Femme en droit canonique médiéval," in *La Femme,* Recueils de la Société
Jean Bodin, 12 [Brussels, 1962], pt. II, 86-87). On the position of the
daughter in relation to paternal authority, see the other studies in this volume, especially pp. 141, 245, 265, 303.

140. *The Life of Christina of Markyate, A Twelfth Century Recluse,* edited and
translated by C. H. Talbot (Oxford, 1959), pp. 35-75. Born probably in the
late eleventh century, Christina was the daughter of a wealthy Anglo-Saxon
family of noble rank in Huntingdon; her anonymous "life" reflects in its
frank and autobiographical tone direct contact with Christina herself.

141. From her early childhood, when she came under the influence of a pious canon called Sueno, Christina seems to have found in a series of spiritual friends and guides surrogates for the parents who were ultimately unsympathetic to her religious aspirations. For the dramatic story of her resistance to the consummation of the marriage forced on her by her parents, see pp. 45ff. In this case the mother appears to have been more relentlessly cruel than the father in her determination to compel her daughter to marriage, declaring that she "did not care who deflowered her, providing that some means could be found," and resorting to the most brutal beating and public humiliation in her efforts to achieve her goal (pp. 73-75).

142. *Ibid.*, pp. 67-69. Not only was Christina exceptionally comely and lovable, according to her biographer, but she was also so intelligent and so prudent in practical affairs that "if she had given her mind to worldly pursuits she could have enriched and ennobled not only herself and her family but also all her relatives." Her parents, moreover, hoped that she would have children who would be like her in character, and were "so keen on these advantages that they begrudged her a life of virginity."

143. According to Gratian, betrothal was forbidden before the age of seven, but he says nothing specific regarding the age of marriage (*Decretum*, C. XXX, Q. II: PL 187, 1442a). Among other examples of the opposition of churchmen to child-marriage, see Adam of Eynsham, *The Life of St. Hugh of Lincoln*, II, 23-25; cf. *Councils*, II, 1, 135, 351-352, 376, 412, 642-644. See also R. Metz, "La protection de la liberté des mineurs dans le droit matrimonial de l'Eglise," *Acta congressus internationalis iuris canonici* (Rome, 1953), pp. 174ff. That marriage or betrothal before the age of twelve (for girls) was regarded as a basis for the voiding of the marriage is shown by two interesting cases decided by the archiepiscopal court of Pisa in the early thirteenth century (Gero Dolezalek, *Das Imbreviaturbuch des erzbischöflichen Gerichtsnotars Hubaldus aus Pisa, Mai bis August 1230* [Cologne and Vienna, 1969], pp. 134, 136). In both cases women appealed successfully for the annulment of their marriages on the ground that they had been married or betrothed before the age of twelve. In one case the plaintiff argued also that her parents had used threats and physical force to compel her to marriage against her will (p. 136). Despite both ecclesiastical and individual opposition, however, the practice of youthful marriage persisted.

144. See John T. Noonan, Jr., "Marital Affection in the Canonists," *Studia Gratiana*, 12 (1966), 481-509. Gratian regularly identified marital affection, defined as the intention to take a spouse as a spouse, with willing consent to marriage (pp. 497-498) and regarded both as constituting a valid marriage; by his successors the concept was developed not only in this direction, but as a formula for use when the Church ordered estranged spouses to be reunited. Exemplifying ecclesiastical opposition to clandestine marriage and various pastoral efforts to exalt the sacrament of matrimony and to foster its dignity are many prescriptions and injunctions of the English synods of the thirteenth century (*Councils*, II, 1, especially 34, 85-88, 301-302, 367-368, 375-376, 642-644). This effort may also be perceived in the growing number of treatises on marriage in this period and in the guidance given to confessors for the instruction of penitents; see, e.g., R. Weigand, "Kanonistische Ehetraktate aus dem 12. Jahrhundert," *Monumenta Iuris Canonici*, Series C, Subsidia 4 (Vatican City, 1971), 59-79, and J. G. Ziegler, *Die Ehelehre der Pönitentialsummen von 1200-1350*, Studien zur Geschichte der katholischen Moraltheologie, Bd. IV (Regensburg, 1956).

145. Regarding physical brutality to wives and their repudiation, see Huyghebaert, "Les femmes laïques. . . ," *I Laici*, pp. 350-355, with particular refer-

ence to the cases of Guibert's mother and the eleventh-century Flemish St. Godelieve who, having fled from her brutal husband and his mother, was finally murdered on his orders; cf. Guibert, *Memoirs,* pp. 210-211, for the story of Count John of Soissons and his maltreatment of his "pretty young wife." Berthold of Regensburg in the thirteenth century strongly exhorted husbands to be gentle with their wives and restrained in their physical demands (*Predigten,* I, 323f.). See also Robert Fossier, *Histoire sociale de l'Occident médiéval* (Paris, 1970), p. 130.

146. On the marital authority of the husband in ecclesiastical and secular law, see the treatment of this theme on the various studies assembled in *La Femme,* II, especially pp. 89-91; 123-125; 170-183; 245-247; 285-302; 364-365. Although there were considerable variations in this matter according to time and region, the subordination of women to their husbands was powerfully stressed; in general, the legal and economic disabilities of the married woman were lessened in the urban environment of the Low Countries, especially from the thirteenth century onwards, and here, too, the share of the mother in parental authority over children appears to have been larger (*ibid.,* pp. 277-285; 302-306; 306-310). See also the valuable analysis of Robert Fossier, emphasizing the gradual enlargement of the woman's share in the affairs of the "conjugal" family in medieval Picardy (*La terre et les hommes en Picardie,* I, 269-273).

147. *Vita prima Bernardi,* c. II (PL 185, 230); tr. Webb and Walker, pp. 18-19. According to the commonly accepted theological and legal tradition, spouses had equal power over one another's bodies, this being, at least theoretically, one important area of conjugal equality for women; see R. Metz, "La femme en droit canonique médiéval," *La Femme,* II, 87-89, and cf., for example, Peter Abelard, *Problemata Heloissae,* XLII (PL 178, 727d-728a).

148. Although the Church never favored second marriages and refused them the nuptial blessing, their validity was never seriously questioned. But the state of widowhood, which in this period often occurred very early, was generally considered more salutary and more honorable than remarriage, and from the tenth century widows were taken under the immediate protection of the ecclesiastical courts (Metz in *La Femme,* II, 91-95, drawing on A. Rosambert, *La veuve en droit canonique jusqu'au XIVe siècle* [Paris, 1923]). The institution of the dowry, and the widow's "dower rights" in her husband's property, also served in some measure to protect her position in secular society. On the veneration shown by churchmen towards widows, and on their role as "recluses" or as nuns in the religious life of the eleventh and twelfth centuries, see Huyghebaert, "Les femmes laïques . . . ," *I Laici,* pp. 356-364, 366-375. It was not only widows who responded to the appeal of a life that, in fact, exerted a powerful attraction on women of various classes and conditions in this period; among many examples, St. Bernard's mother, though still living at home, "imitated the life of a hermit or monk," and without entering the religious life tried to make up for this by almsgiving and works of mercy (*Vita prima,* c. III; PL 185, 230; Webb and Walker, pp. 18-19). For other cases, see above, n. 26, and below, notes 162 and 170.

149. On the alliance of contemporary reforming churchmen with royal and noble ladies, and its significance for the dissemination of more elevated spiritual ideals and newer forms of piety, see Bernards, "Die Frau in der Welt und die Kirche . . . ," *Sacris Erudiri,* 20 (1971), 49-100, and Huyghebaert, "Les femmes laïques . . . ," *I Laici,* pp. 375-379. Like the maternal image in the works that we have been considering, the ideal set before noblewomen in letters and other works addressed to them often bore a strong resemblance to the model of the "pious woman" as presented by the Christian fathers centuries earlier, but it usually reflected as well the aspirations and values of

contemporary reforming movements. Noteworthy, in this context, is the influence of Robert of Arbrissel on such ladies as the Countess Ermengarde of Brittany and the mother of Peter the Venerable (Bienvenu, "Pauvreté, misères, et charité . . . ," *Moyen Age,* 73 [1967], 17, 23-24, and below, n. 162).

150. See Bloch's remarks on "la vie noble" (*La société féodale,* II, 25-45; *Feudal Society,* tr. Manyon, pp. 302ff.). For further insights into the life of the noble household with its discomforts and lack of privacy, see Holmes, *Daily Living in the Twelfth Century,* pp. 177-196, and Labarge, *A Baronial Household of the Thirteenth Century,* pp. 18-37.

151. *Vita prima,* c. II (PL 185, 229); Webb and Walker, pp. 16-17.

152. Although Guibert's early life was dominated by his close relationships with his mother and his teacher, his account conveys a stronger sense of confinement and supervision than of pleasurable intimacy. One gains a perhaps clearer sense of family life from the story of Christina of Markyate's childhood, for her parents appear to have been tender and indulgent with her until she crossed them. Gerald of Wales writes with affection of his boyhood home and its physical setting, but with little detail about life within the castle of Manorbier (*De rebus a se gestis,* edited by J. S. Brewer, Rolls Series, Vol. 22; for a partial translation, see *The Portable Medieval Reader,* pp. 344-345, and see also *The Autobiography of Giraldus Cambrensis,* translated by H. E. Butler [London, 1937]). His happy childhood at St. Albans was recalled in verse by Alexander Neckam, whose mother had nursed both her own child and the future King Richard I (Thorndike, II, 188).

153. Here the insights offered by lyric poetry and by some twelfth and early thirteenth century romances are perhaps more telling, with respect both to the association of the experience of tenderness with the mother and to the sense of longing for it. For some examples, see below, notes 213-215, 219, 223.

154. Ailred of Rievaulx, *De spiritali amicitia* (*Opera Omnia, I. Opera Ascetica,* ed. A. Hoste and C. H. Talbot, CC, I) Prol., p. 287; PL 195, 659. Ailred's biographer describes him as a little boy coming home "from the games that small boys play with their fellows" (*Walter Daniel's Life of Ailred,* translated with introduction and notes by F. M. Powicke, Nelson's Medieval Texts [London; Nelson, 1950], p. 72). The *topos* of the *puer sanctus* is among the more prominent conventions of contemporary hagiography; on this theme and others relevant to this study, see Louise Gnädinger, *Eremitica: Studien zur altfranzösischen Heiligenviten des 12. und 13. Jahrhunderts,* Beihefte zur Zeitschrift für romanische Philologie, 130 (1972), pp. 57-58 and *passim.* The often unbelievably "saintly children" of contemporary saints-lives may sometimes seem quite unattractive little prigs; for example, the young Beatrice of Tienen, who from infancy had such a loathing of bad language that if she heard it from her brothers or from servants, she would carry tales to her father and invoke his severity on the offenders (*Vita Beatricis,* ed. Reypens, pp. 22-23). Like other "holy" children, she is portrayed, in this case by herself, as holding herself aloof from the childish play of others of her age, and this familiar theme may often obscure the realities which we glimpse, for example, not only in Ailred's recollections, but in Guibert's account of the pleasures of which he was deprived (*Memoirs,* p. 46) and in Gerald of Wales's reminiscences of his childish games and the companionship of his brothers (see above, n. 152).

155. Guibert, *Memoirs,* especially pp. 74-75.

156. *The Life of Anselm, Archbishop of Canterbury, by Eadmer,* Appendix, pp. 172-173. The passage containing this story is found in only one group of

manuscripts of Eadmer's work and it is probably not by him, but is almost certainly a personal recollection by one of Anselm's friends at Bec, possibly Boso.

157. *Ibid.,* p. 173, for Anselm's remarks on this episode, and for instances of this compassion, pp. 16-24; 37-40 and below, n. 190.

158. *Ibid.,* p. 6. His mother's death apparently marked the beginning of the period of intense and irreconcilable hostility between Anselm and his father which was the prelude to his departure for France. The hostility between fathers and sons, and among brothers, is a common theme in the historical and literary works of this period; Orderic's *Ecclesiastical History,* to name but one of them, offers numerous cases (see, e.g., Book IV, ed. Chibnall, p. 357). See also Le Goff's remarks on the tensions characterizing the agnatic family, which seem also to have given a special importance to the role of the maternal uncle (*Civilisation,* pp. 353-354) and below, n. 217.

159. Until his mother's death, for example, Anselm's love and reverence for her had "kept him from turning away from study and devoting himself to worldly pursuits." For another instance of the power of maternal example, see Peter the Venerable's "Letter to his Brothers," *The Letters of Peter the Venerable,* ed. Constable, I, Letter 53, especially p. 173.

160. *Vita prima,* c. IV (PL 185, 237-238); Webb and Walker, p. 24. Their mother also appeared in a vision to Bernard's younger brother, Andrew, to show her approval of their decision to enter the monastic life (pp. 25-26).

161. With Bernard's four brothers and one sister may be compared the eight sons of Raingard, mother of Peter the Venerable (*The Letters of Peter the Venerable,* II, Appendix A, pp. 233-246). In the family of Peter Abelard, who was also devoted to his mother, at least three brothers and one sister appear to have reached maturity. Notable also for their numbers, eight, twelve, and fifteen children, are the Norman families described by Orderic Vitalis (for some figures, see Paul Rousset, "La description du monde chevaleresque chez Orderic Vital," *Moyen Age,* 77 [1970], 429, n. 4).

162. *The Letters of Peter the Venerable,* I, Letter 53, pp. 153-173. Peter's long letter, addressed to his brothers, begins with a description of his grief—as if he had been "struck on the head with a stone"—on learning of his mother's death as he was returning from a journey to Italy. In his portrayal of her life and virtues he emphasized the experiences that led to her conversion, her friendship with the reformer, Robert of Arbrissel, who encouraged her desire to withdraw from the world, the death of her husband not long after they had mutually agreed to enter the monastic life, and her refusal to remarry. Even as a nun in the Cluniac priory of Marcigny, where Peter apparently visited her frequently, her maternal concern for her children was so intense and unceasing that, he remarks (p. 168), the sisters thought it excessive.

163. This seems less true of such earlier records as the tenth-century lives of Sts. Odo of Cluny and Gerald of Aurillac, in which the father's role appears more prominent; it was Odo's father who, according to his biographer, played the most important role in his early life, dedicating him to St. Martin while he was an infant in the cradle, beginning to educate him for the ecclesiastical life, but then withdrawing him from it, and sending him as a page to the household of Count William of Aquitaine (*The Life of St. Odo of Cluny,* tr. Sitwell, pp. 7-11).

164. *The Life of St. Anselm of Canterbury,* pp. 6-7; his father's hatred of him is said to have become so keen that he persecuted the young Anselm as much, or even more, for the things he did well as for those he did badly. For Anselm's relationship with Lanfranc at Bec, see pp. 8-11.

165. Adam of Eynsham, *Life of St. Hugh of Lincoln,* I, 5. Cf. Peter Abelard, *Historia Calamitatum,* edited by Joseph T. Muckle, *Mediaeval Studies,* 12 (1950), 175-176; edited by Jacques Monfrin (Paris, 1962), p. 63. Abelard briefly notes his knightly father's concern for the education of his sons, a concern that was the more diligent in his case because he was the eldest son and therefore "dearer to the paternal heart."

166. *Life of St. Hugh of Lincoln,* I, 6-7. According to Hugh himself, he was particularly fortunate in having as his teacher and guide in this community one of the canons who was so distinguished for his piety and learning that the nobles of the region around Grenoble competed in entrusting their children to his care.

167. *Ibid.,* I, 14-15. Apropos of this interesting reversal of roles, his biographer adds that these duties had for Hugh a "taste sweeter than honey, or spiced wine for a thirsty man," and that his father "blessed him a thousand times."

168. Not without significance regarding the quality of their spiritual leadership is the fact that these men, together with other reformers of the eleventh and twelfth centuries, came to the monastic life not as oblates but as young men after a genuine experience of conversion.

169. Of "fine old English stock," son of the hereditary priest of Hexham in Northumbria, Ailred was brought up from boyhood at the court of King David of Scotland, son of the saintly Queen Margaret, with Henry, the king's son, as his closest friend and companion (*The Life of Ailred,* pp. 2-3; see above, n. 154).

170. Although he had been promised to the monastic life before his birth, Guibert was not strictly speaking an oblate, since he entered the monastery as a novice at twelve or thirteen (*Memoirs,* pp. 77-78). Hermann of Tournai, on the other hand, describes how he was offered to the monastery of Saint-Martin as a newborn infant; for not long before his birth both of his parents had decided to enter the monastic life, and shortly after he was born his mother placed her infant in his cradle on the high altar of the monastic church, while she and his sisters joined the women's community founded by St. Odo of Tournai. The case of Hermann's parents was but one of many instances in which the religious enthusiasm of this period led entire families to enter the monastic life, often in the double communities which also proliferated at this time. See Hermann, *Liber de restauratione Sancti Martini Tornacensis,* c. 63-70 (MGH, SS, 14, 303-307); cf. Huyghebaert, "Les Femmes laïques . . . ," *I Laici,* pp. 366-371.

171. *The Ecclesiastical History of Orderic Vitalis,* II, Introd., p. xiv. Orderic added that, on his arrival at Saint-Evroul, "like Joseph in Egypt I heard a language which I could not understand"; but he also found "nothing but kindness and friendship" among these strangers. From his eleventh year his entire life was spent in this monastery, whose history became the starting-point of the great work which came gradually to encompass the whole history of the Church and which is, as Miss Chibnall observes (p. xxix), in fact an unparalleled social history of the eleventh century, especially in Normandy.

172. See *The Monastic Constitutions of Lanfranc,* translated from the Latin with Introduction and notes by David Knowles, Nelson's Medieval Texts (London, 1951), Introduction, p. xiv; cf. *I Laici,* pp. 176, 180.

173. Southern, *Western Society and the Church,* pp. 224-225; 228-230.

174. *The Monastic Constitutions of Lanfranc,* Introduction, pp. xviii-xix. In spite of the disadvantages of this system for both the monasteries and the children, it is fair to add Knowles's judgment that "there must have been much in it that was apt to the social and educational conditions of the early medieval centuries" and that it is easy "to compile a long list of children of the

cloister who developed virile and many-sided characters."

175. To generalize about the child-rearing practices of various classes in medieval society during this long period is extremely difficult, not to say impossible. Among the noble classes, children of both sexes were normally kept at home under feminine, usually maternal, supervision until the age of seven or so. The practice of sending those of the sons who were destined for the military life for rearing in the households of others, often the father's overlord or the maternal uncle or other relative, was apparently common, serving, among other things, to consolidate family and feudal alliances. That it was by no means universal is evident from the sources examined here, among others. Girls, too, were sometimes sent away in this fashion and boys intended for the ecclesiastical, though not monastic, life might be reared in the household of a bishop, again often a relative. Before the appearance of the twelfth and thirteenth century treatises on manners (see below, n. 224), there is little detailed evidence of the kind of training given the child in noble households from the age of seven to twelve or so. In the Celtic societies of this period and earlier, notably in Ireland and Wales, the practice of fosterage, the placing of noble and freeborn children, both boys and girls, in the care of foster-parents at a much earlier age, sometimes shortly after birth, seems to have prevailed. See Miles Dillon and Nora Chadwick, *The Celtic Realms* (New York, 1967), pp. 100-101, and Kathleen Hughes, *The Church in Early Irish Society* (Ithaca, N.Y., 1966), pp. 6, 154; Gerald of Wales remarks that the ties of affection were stronger between foster-parents and foster-children and between foster-brothers than between those related by blood (*Topography of Ireland and Description of Wales*, ed. Wright, pp. 137, 512).

176. On the "solidarities" of family and *lignage* and on the evolution of customs of inheritance, especially primogeniture, intended to preserve the family patrimony, see Bloch, *La Société féodale*, I, 191-221; 293-324; see also Duby, *La société aux XIe et XIIe siècles dans la région maconnaise*, pp. 274-281; K. Leyser, "The German Aristocracy from the Ninth to the Early Twelfth Century," *Past and Present*, 41 (December, 1968), 25-53; Fossier, *La terre et les hommes en Picardie*, I, 262-270, and for a succinct general account, Fossier, *Histoire sociale*, pp. 124-129. Of family fortunes and their instabilities owing to death, war and other causes, Orderic Vitalis offers many examples, among them the rise and decline of the Norman family of Giroie in the tenth and eleventh centuries (*Ecclesiastical History*, II, 22-35, 125-151).

177. See Southern, *Western Society and the Church*, pp. 228-230.

178. Among many others, the case of Guibert and his mother, though not typical, suggests that monastic children were in not infrequent contact with their parents and other members of their families. In many, if not in most, cases, children were offered to monasteries in close proximity to their families and, indeed, often dominated by them.

179. For a list of medieval abbeys reserved for the sons and daughters of noble families, see U. Berlière, "Le recrutement dans les monastères bénédictins aux XIIIe et XIVe siècles," *Académie Royale de Belgique, Classe des lettres, Memoires*, XVIII, fasc. 6 (1924), 16-21.

180. On this subject in general, see the essay of Pierre Riché, "L'enfant dans la société monastique aux XIe et XIIe siècles," forthcoming in *Actes, Colloque international, Pierre Abélard-Pierre le Vénérable* (Paris, 1974). Several sets of Cluniac customs are edited in Bruno Albers, *Consuetudines monasticae* (4 vols., Monte Cassino, 1907-1911). See also *Corpus Consuetudinum Monasticarum*, edited by Kassius Hallinger (Rome, 1963-   ), of which four volumes have so far appeared, containing custumals of the eighth and

ninth centuries, as well as those of Bec, Eynsham, and Knowles's edition of Lanfranc's Constitutions for Christ Church, Canterbury. Especially influential in the later eleventh and twelfth centuries were the Cluniac customs drawn up by Bernard and Ulrich of Cluny; see *Consuetudines Bernardi,* edited by M. Herrgott in *Vetus Disciplina Monastica* (Paris, 1726) and *Consuetudines Udalrici* (PL 149, 741-747). For translations, see *The Monastic Constitutions of Lanfranc,* drawn up by Archbishop Lanfranc of Canterbury from the customs of Bec and Cluny, and the excerpts concerning oblates from the Custumal of Saint-Benigne in Dijon, translated by Coulton, *Life in the Middle Ages,* IV, 99-101.

181. For this description of the ceremony of oblation, see *The Monastic Constitutions of Lanfranc,* pp. 110-111. The parents' promise had previously been written down and witnessed; after being made orally, it was placed on the altar. There is an interesting series of acts of oblation, executed by fathers and brothers and in several cases signed by the mother, among the fragments of twelfth-century manuscripts of Saint-Rémi in Reims in Paris, B.N. lat. 13090, f. 72-77b. At this time and earlier, the promise was binding for life; later, from the twelfth century, oblates were free to leave the monastery in adolescence when final vows were taken, but as Knowles remarks (p. xviii), it is not easy to find a recorded case of such departure.

182. See, e.g., *Consuetudines Bernardi,* ed. Herrgott, I, 27, p. 210; *Consuetudines Udalrici,* III, 8 (PL 149, 747d); cf. the Cluniac custumal of Maillezais, edited by J. Becquet, "Le Coutumier Clunisien de Maillezais," *Revue Mabillon,* 54 (1964), p. 18.

183. *The Monastic Constitutions of Lanfranc,* pp. 115-116; cf. pp. 117-118, where the same custody is prescribed for older boys and novices.

184. *Ibid.,* p. 117; cf. the Custumal of Saint-Benigne, Coulton, *Life in the Middle Ages,* IV, 100. See also the story of Odo of Cluny's disregard of the injunction concerning latrines, which was considered a very serious fault at Baume in the early tenth century (*The Life of St. Odo of Cluny,* tr. Sitwell, p. 32). In Cluniac monasteries children apparently had their own places in the lavatories and latrines (*Consuetudines Udalrici,* III, 8; PL 149, 742c, 744c).

185. See the Rule of St. Benedict, c. 37, and *Consuetudines Udalrici* (PL 149, 747d). In general the prescribed "discipline" was beating with "smooth pliant osier rods" or firm plucking by the hair; children were never to be disciplined "with kicks or fists or the open palm or in any other way" (Coulton, *Life in the Middle Ages,* IV, 100). That discipline sometimes exceeded these prescriptions is evident; see the story of St. Stephen Obazine's severity in striking boys with the open hand on the face (*ibid.,* p. 179), and below, n. 190.

186. These provisions reflect a view of the sexuality of children rather more realistic than the idea expressed by Guibert of Nogent in his treatise on the incarnation that childhood is a time entirely free of sexuality (PL 156, 33; translated by Benton, *Memoirs,* p. 14); on this theme, see below, n. 226). A serious concern with the problem of clerical homosexuality was displayed by Peter Damian, whose *Liber Gomorrhianus* (PL 145, 159b-190d) is the fullest treatment of this subject in our period; see especially c. I (161d) on various "sins against nature," including masturbation, and c. XV (174d-175c) on pederasty. The punishment recommended for the seduction of a child or youth by a cleric or monk was public beating, loss of the tonsure, imprisonment in chains and irons for six months, and fasting three days a week until vespers; after this another six months of isolation in a cell under strict custody. In earlier medieval penitentials youthful sexual acts were much more lightly punished; see, e.g., the Roman Penitential, no. 67 (McNeill and Gamer, *Medieval Handbooks of Penance,* p. 309). See also, as an example

of similar tales on this subject, the story told by Peter the Venerable of the
devils who forced a certain master of a monastic school to sin with one of
his boys (*De miraculis*, PL 189, 977), and for an illustration of the general
theme, the capital at Vézelay portraying the abduction of Ganymede (Salet,
Vézelay, Pl. 31, no. 12).

187. For ample testimony on this subject, one need look no further than Guibert's
numerous stories of the sexual sins and temptations which are also reported
in great profusion in other works of these centuries. See, e.g., Otloh of
Saint-Emmeram, *Liber de suis tentationibus, varia fortuna et scriptis* (PL
146, 47-50), and in another example of Anselm's "fatherly pity," the story
of how he cured the sexual anxieties of a young monk (*The Life of St.
Anselm*, pp. 23-24).

188. See his *Memoirs*, pp. 79-81, for a particularly vivid description of his boyhood nightmares, filled with images of death and dead men, "especially
those whom I had seen or heard of as slain by swords or by some such
death," and of demons, so terrifying that only the watchful protection of
his master kept him from "going almost mad." Cf. pp. 85-86, for another
nocturnal vision in which he was carried off by two devils, and for his
stories of demonic intervention in the lives of others, see pp. 101-102, 110-
112, 137-139, 140-143. Another among many examples of childish visions
of the dead is offered by Peter the Venerable, *De miraculis*, II, 25 (PL 189,
941d-943e), concerning a child-monk's vision of his dead uncle, a former
prior of his monastery, who led him to its cemetery where he beheld a vast
assembly of the dead. On child-devils of a particularly troublesome variety,
the "little black boys" of antiquity and the middle ages, see Gregorio Pinco,
"Sopravvivenze della demonologia antica nel monachesimo medievale,"
Studia Monastica, 13 (1971), 31-36. For an interesting explanation of the
growing obsession, in a time of social and cultural change, with the Devil as
the humanized and personified power of evil and with demonology in its
varied forms, see Russell, *Witchcraft in the Middle Ages*, pp. 100-132.

189. Of special interest among Otloh's writings are his *Liber de tentationibus*
(PL 146, 29a-58c; for translated excerpts, see Coulton, *Life in the Middle
Ages*, IV, 84-92) and his *Liber visionum* (337-396), of which the first four
reflect most directly his childhood experience. For his fear of beating as a
young schoolboy in the monastery, see *De tentationibus*, 38; cf. *Liber
visionum*, III, 352-353, for the story of his experience as a young teacher at
Saint-Emmeram and how he was led to an understanding of the need for
prudence and gentleness in the discipline of the young. Cf. his *Vita S. Wolf-
gangi*, 389ff. On Otloh, see Misch, *Geschichte der Autobiographie*, III, 1,
57-107, and Morris, *Discovery of the Individual*, pp. 79-83; see also G.
Vinay, "Otlone de Sant'Emmeran ovvero l'autografia di un nevrotico," *La
Storiografia altomediaevale*, II (Spoleto, 1970), 13-38, and J. Leclercq,
"Modern Psychology and the Interpretation of Medieval Texts," *Speculum*,
48 (1973), 478-479. Although Otloh was not an oblate, he was sent in early
childhood to study at Tegernsee, and he later experienced much conflict and
many hesitations regarding his monastic vocation; he also suffered from
radical doubt concerning the existence of God and the reliability of Scriptures, and these issues appear to have been more urgent than the sexual
temptations by which, however, he was, he says, daily plagued.

190. *The Life of St. Anselm*, pp. 37-39; for Anselm's own practice of his precepts, see above, notes 156, 157, 187. At Canterbury itself, the tenth-century St. Dunstan had acquired the role of protector of boy-monks from excessive beating and the story told by Osbern in the late eleventh century of
his miraculous healing of the blind girl and its use as a warning against ex-

cessive cruelty to children was elaborated in later versions which tell of Dunstan's direct intervention, at the approach of Christmas, in helping boys to escape punishment by their masters (*Memorials of Saint Dunstan, Archbishop of Canterbury*, edited by William Stubbs, Rolls Series, 63 (1874), 140-142; cf. A. F. Leach, *The Schools of Medieval England* (reprinted, New York, 1969), pp. 81-84). Eadmer himself was responsible for one of these versions, as he was also for the life of a much earlier archbishop of Canterbury, Bregwine, who was, like Dunstan, famous as a protector of schoolboys from the anger and beatings of their masters (B. S. Schultz, "Eadmer's Life of Bregwine, Archbishop of Canterbury, 761-764," *Traditio,* 22 [1966], 124-141).

191. Though novel in the clarity and completeness of its development, Anselm's approach had a background in the ideas of certain of his patristic and especially his Carolingian predecessors, such as Alcuin and Theodulf of Orleans, who had recommended patience and the need for "maternal" affection, as well as for discipline, in the education of children, and who had seen in them "indeterminate" beings, capable of being shaped by their training (Leclercq, "Pédagogie et formation spirituelle," *La Scuola* [Spoleto, 1972], p. 287). The current of opposition to harsh discipline, and a sense of its futility, was evidently becoming stronger in the course of the eleventh century, See, e.g., the protests of Ecbert of Liège against the "more than rhadamanthine harshness" of some "stupid teachers" in their efforts to teach what they themselves do not know, and their "bloodthirsty" and "vengeful" treatment of their pupils (*Fecunda ratis*, edited by E. Voigt, [Halle, 1889], p. 179). By the similar harshness of his own master, Guibert of Nogent was convinced, as he says, of the need for restraint and moderation in the training of the young (*Memoirs*, pp. 47-48). See also below, n. 234.

192. In developing this theme, Anselm used first the simile of the "tree-shoot" and its need for freedom to put out its branches so that they may grow fruitfully, rather than becoming "twisted and knotted" by excessive confinement, and then the image of the leaf of gold or silver which the goldsmith "now presses and strikes gently with his tool and now even more gently raises it with careful pressure and gives it shape" (pp. 37-38). Similarly, Peter Damian, addressing the young, remarked "you are at the pliant age; if the clay suffers any injury in the potter's hands, this, if not corrected at once, becomes hard as stone," adding that the twig, once bent, can never be straightened ("On the Perfection of Monks," c. 20, in McNulty, *The Spiritual Writings of Peter Damian*, p. 121).

193. For Ulrich's vehement complaint that many noble parents used the monasteries as repositories, or "dumping-grounds," for their sick, deformed and otherwise handicapped children, see PL 149, 637.

194. For the opposition of the Cistercians and Carthusians to the practice of oblation, see J. Dubois, "L'institution monastique des convers," *I Laici*, p. 257; among the reforming orders of this period the Cistercians set fifteen years as the minimum age for entering the novitiate and the Carthusians, twenty. The growing emphasis on the importance of a genuine personal vocation for the monastic life, and other changes in the "mechanisms" of conversion (cf. Duby, *I Laici*, p. 176), also reduced the numbers of oblates, as did the opportunities offered to younger sons by various military and expansionist ventures from the late eleventh century. On the continuance of the practice, though on a much smaller scale, in the later middle ages, see U. Berlière, "Le récrutement dans les monastères. . . ," *Acad. Roy. de Belgique, Classe de lettres, Memoires*, XVIII, 6 (1924), citing among others the com-

plaints of Bishop William of Auvergne in the thirteenth century concerning the "deformed and incapable children thrust upon the monasteries, especially noblemen's bastards or children below the age of discretion or those whom men wish to get rid of cheaply."

195. On special provisions for the physical care of monastic children, see Gerd Zimmermann, *Ordensleben und Lebensstandard: die "cura corporis" in den Ordensvorschriften des abendländischen Hochmittelalters*, Beiträge zur Geschichte des altern Mönchtums und des Benediktinerordens, Heft 32 [Münster i. Westfalen, 1973], pp. 159-161. In monastic constitutions and customaries, a clear distinction was made between the "children," up to the age of twelve, and the novices; for the children there were commonly such dietary modifications as the alleviation of fasting and the allowing of meat-eating and special "snacks," as well as distinctions in clothing. The rigors of the monastic routine, especially of choir service, were often tempered also; if a boy fell asleep during the offices, he was usually not beaten, but was kept awake by some such means as being handed a heavy book to hold.

196. Though plainly an essential aspect of the history of childhood, and one for which an adequate general study is greatly needed, early education in this period, whether in or outside of the monastery, can only be touched on within the limits of this essay. Despite the apparently ineluctable association of teaching the corporal punishment, recollections and discussions of monastic education were not infrequently pleasurable and laudatory. See, for example, the happy reminiscences of Walahfrid Strabo of his schooldays at Reichenau in the early ninth century ("The school-life of Walahfrid Strabo," translated by James Davie Butler, *Bibliotheca Sacra*, 40 (1883), 152-172), and his poetic description of Grimald of Saint-Gall, seated in the orchard of the monastery, with his young pupils playing and picking fruit nearby (MGH, Poet., II, 335, 11. 429-444). Insight into methods of teaching Latin grammar, and a vignette of the oblate's day, is provided by Aelfric's *Colloquy* (c. 1005), written when he was master of oblates at Cerne Abbey in Dorset (translated in A. F. Leach, *Educational Charters and Documents* [Cambridge, 1911], pp. 37-41). For the most recent study of English monastic education see the relevant chapters in Nicholas Orme, *English Schools in the Middle Ages* (London, 1973), and on early medieval education, the essays in *La Scuola* (Spoleto, 1972). The character and values of monastic education are further illumined by J. Leclercq, *The Love of Learning and the Desire for God* (New York, 1962), especially pp. 116-151.

197. Of Anselm at Bec, for example, Eadmer remarks that "all loved him as if he were a very dear father, for he bore with equanimity the habits and infirmities of them all" (*The Life of St. Anselm*, p. 22). According to one of the later lives of St. Bernard, written c. 1180, his first action on returning to Clairvaux after one of his journeys was to visit the novices, so that "these young and tender sucklings might be refreshed the more abundantly with the milk of his consolation;" those among them who were troubled, he pitied "as a father pities his own children" PL 185, 422). On Bernard's concern for the young, see J. Leclercq's chapter "St. Bernard's Idea of the Role of the Young," in his *Contemplative Life* (Washington, D.C., 1973), pp. 26-35.

198. *Walter Daniel's Life of Ailred*, p. 40 and p. 58; according to the biography by Jocelyn of Furness, Ailred "exceeded his fellow prelates in patience and tenderness."

199. See Southern, *Making of the Middle Ages*, pp. 226-257, for a most perceptive discussion of the preeminent roles of St. Anselm and St. Bernard in giving impulse and expression to the new spirituality with its stress on personal

experience and self-knowledge, as well as to more affective modes of piety and devotion.

200. To Anselm's influence Guibert of Nogent is an important witness, for he was among the young men who benefited from his kindness; "while he was still prior at Bec, he admitted me to his acquaintance, and though I was a mere child of most tender age and knowledge, he readily offered to teach me to manage the inner self, how to consult the laws of reason in the government of the body" (*Memoirs,* pp. 89-90). For Anselm's prayers, see A. Castel, *Méditations et prières de saint Anselme* (Paris, 1923); see also R. W. Southern, *Saint Anselm and His Biographer,* pp. 34-47, and see above, n. 128.

201. Bernard's boyhood vision "on the night of the Lord's Nativity" is described in *Vita prima* c. II (PL 185, 228); Webb and Walker, pp. 17-18: "It was as if the boy saw re-enacted the birth of the infant Word . . . and this made young Bernard's heart overflow with a love and longing unheard of in a mere boy." His treatise "in praise of the Blessed Mother and her Son and His Holy Nativity" (*In nativitate Domini,* Sermo I-II; PL 183, 124-125), is among his earliest works; see the selections translated in *St Bernard on the Christian Year,* by a Religious of C.S.M.V. (London: Mowbray, 1954), pp. 33-37, and on imitation of the Lord's childlike qualities, pp. 116-117 (from *In conversione S. Pauli* II: PL 183, 365ab). See also *De purificatione B. Mariae,* Sermo II, *De puero, Maria et Joseph,* 369-372.

202. Southern, *The Making of the Middle Ages,* pp. 238-257. See also J. Fournée, "Les orientations doctrinales de l'iconographie mariale à la fin de l'époque romane", *Centre international d'études romanes,* II (1971), 23-60.

203. On various modes of diffusion, see Etienne Delaruelle, "La culture religieuse des laïcs en France aux XIe et XIIe siècles," *I Laici,* pp. 548-581.

204. *Ibid.,* p. 551, on the popularity of the Infancy cycle in the liturgical drama and in art. Among other examples, the transept at Saint-Savin originally contained a full cycle of scenes from the Childhood of Christ, easily viewed by the laity for whom the portion of the nave west of the transept was reserved; similar scenes were depicted in the church of Saint-Aignan at Brinay and on the vaulted ceiling in front of the apse of the church of Saint-Nicolas at Tavant (Grabar and Nordenfalk, *Romanesque Painting,* pp. 87-88; 95, 97-99). For perhaps the most familiar sculptured portrayals of this period, those of the West Portal and capitals at Chartres, see E. Houvet, *Cathedral de Chartres. Portail Occidental ou Royal* (Paris, n.d.), especially Pl. 54 and 76; see also R. Crozet, "A propos des chapiteaux de la façade occidental de Chartres," *Cahiers de civilisation médiévale,* 14 (1971).

205. Southern, *The Making of the Middle Ages,* pp. 238-240, and Pl. IV (the "Madonna of Dom Rupert"). In the portrayal of the Nativity on the roodscreen at Chartres, c. 1230-1240, the Mother is shown lying on her bed, looking down most tenderly upon, and reaching out to touch, the swaddled Child lying next to her bed in a cradle; for a reproduction, see Roberto Salvini, *Medieval Sculpture* (London, 1969), Pl. 203. On the development of newer and more varied forms of portrayal, see V. Lasareff, "Studies in the Iconography of the Virgin," *Art Bulletin,* 20 (1938), pp. 42-63.

206. Denis Grivot and George Zarnecki, *Gislebertus, Sculptor of Autun* (New York; 1961), p. 67 and Pl. 5. Here, too, as the authors note, the wheel under the donkey reminds us that the sculptor himself may have been inspired by a scene frequently enacted in one of the cycles of Christmas or "Magi" plays in which the early life of Christ was vividly and publicly enacted.

207. For illustrations and discussion of this ceiling, see *Suisse romane* (Paris, 1958), p. 259, and pp. 251-255. For a list of portrayals of the Massacre, more numerous for the twelfth century than for the thirteenth or four-

teenth, see L. Réau, *L'Iconographie de l'art chrétien* (Paris, 1955), II, 271-272. Most often stressed, with growing vividness and perhaps admonitory significance, are the brutality of the slayers and the grief of the mothers; see, e.g., the capitals of the West Portal of Chartres (Yves Delaporte, "Representations du Massacre des Innocents à la cathédrale de Chartres," *Notre Dame de Chartres*, II [1971] 10-15), and those at Saint-Sernin, Toulouse, and at Poitiers, as well as the frieze at Saint-Trophime, Arles, the bronze doors at Pisa, and the baptismal font of San Giovanni in Fonte, Verona, where the children are portrayed with exceptional realism (G. H. Crichton, *Romanesque Sculpture in Italy* [London, 1954], pp. 84-85). These motifs are most powerfully and poignantly expressed by Giovanni Pisano in the pulpit of Sant'Andrea in Pistoia (see Salvini, *Medieval Sculpture*, Pl. 268). In the late eleventh-century play of the Innocents, the *Ordo Rachelis*, one of the extensions of the "Magi" cycle, the voices of the slaughtered children and the lament of Rachel, leading the chorus of bereaved mothers, are heard, alternating with the responses of consoling angels; on this play and its versions, see Karl Young, *The Drama of the Medieval Church* (2 vols., Oxford, 1933), I, 110ff., and O. B. Hardison, Jr., *Christian Rite and Christian Drama in the Middle Ages* (Baltimore, 1969), pp. 315, 223-226.

208. In one of Abelard's hymns for the feast of the Innocents, a poetic version of Rachel's lament, the themes of maternal love, as well as maternal grief and suffering, are strongly stressed (PL 178, no. 77, 1808-1809). Perhaps it was not by chance that, by the twelfth century, the eve of "Innocents' Day" or "Childermas," had come to be celebrated as a festival for children, following by several weeks the feast of St. Nicholas, whose greatly expanding cult reached its height at this time; on these festivals, see A. F. Leach, *The Schools of Medieval England*, pp. 144-148. It seems not improbable that the development and conjunction of all of these themes may reflect positive ecclesiastical efforts to foster more protective attitudes towards children. Pertinent also, in this context, is a growing concern with their participation in the sacramental life of the Church, especially in the sacraments of confirmation and the Eucharist, now more clearly separated from baptism; a concern that prompted consideration by theologians of the capacities and the instruction of children. On these developments, see Fisher, *Christian Initiation*, pp. 101-108; 120-140, and for efforts to provide for the religious instruction of children in thirteenth-century England, *Councils*, II, 1, 265-269; the earliest instance in this period of preaching addressed directly to children appears to be that offered in the *Praeloquia* of Rather of Verona in the tenth century, with separate instructions for smaller children, older children and adolescents (PL 136, 203-204). For lively portrayals of the baptism of children, see M. Avery, *The Exultet Rolls of South Italy*, Plates CXVI-CXVII, XCIX.

209. Grabar and Nordenfalk, *Romanesque Painting*, pp. 170-172, and see above, n. 137. A striking example is the Ingeborg-Psalter of the early thirteenth century, containing numerous scenes dominated by feminine figures; here, too, the Infant Jesus is shown, on the Flight into Egypt, playing with his Mother's hands (F. Deuchler, *Der Ingeborg-Psalter* [Berlin: De Gruyter, 1967]).

210. See Southern, *The Making of the Middle Ages*, pp. 246-254, on the development and circulation of these collections, of which one of the earliest, apparently, was made by Peter Damian.

211. *Die Dichtungen der Frau Ava*, ed. F. Maurer, pp. 11-19, and see above, n. 30. For French versions, see Delaruelle, "La culture religieuse . . . ," *I Laici*, pp. 563-565.

212. *Ruodlieb,* translated by Gordon B. Ford (Leiden: Brill, 1965), especially pp. 39-40, 85-102. The relations between widowed mothers and their children are a salient feature of this revealing work; the hero ultimately marries the daughter of another devoted mother, and during his earlier adventures he had encountered a woman who, having murdered her husband, was granted her life on the plea of her stepchildren, to whom she promised to be a "true mother, not a stepmother, as before" (pp. 68-69). That the situation of Ruodlieb and his mother was well founded in contemporary reality is, as K. Leyser observes, suggested by what has been called the first German family letter, written a few decades later by another such widowed mother, requesting her brother's help in the absence of her exiled sons ("The German Aristocracy in the Early Middle Ages," *Past and Present,* 41 [1968], 38-39). Another version of these familiar themes is Hildegard of Bingen's "divinely inspired" life of the young St. Rupert, whose hostile father died when Rupert was three and whose childhood and youth were spent in close and loving companionship with his widowed mother (*Vita sancti Ruperti:* PL 197, 1083-1086).

213. A striking instance of this ambivalence is recorded by the thirteenth century friar, Salimbene, who, he tells us, never loved his mother so much again after hearing her story of how she had left him lying in his cradle during an earthquake, while she rushed his two small sisters to safety (*Cronica,* ed. Bernini, I, 46-47). Among historical mothers of this period, none displayed more implacable hostility towards a child than did the redoubtable Queen Constance of France to her eldest son, Henry (see Jean Dhondt, "Sept femmes et un trio des rois," *Miscellanea mediaevalia in memoriam J.F. Niermeyer* [Groningen, 1967], pp. 50-52). Cf. the more ambivalent relationship of the early twelfth century Spanish queen, Urraca, with her young son (*Historia Compostellana:* PL 170, 936-947). In the late twelfth-century *Richeut,* the earliest surviving *fabliau,* the heroine, a prostitute and apostatenun, is portrayed as taking a brutal revenge on her illegitimate son, who grew up to be a notorious seducer (ed. Lecompte, *Romanic Review,* 4 [1913], 261-305). A well-known example of ambiguous maternal devotion is the case of Perceval's mother, who is portrayed by Chrétien of Troyes as so selfishly anxious to keep her son from knightly pursuits that she failed to prepare him properly for life (see M.-N. Lefay-Toury, "Romans bretons et mythes courtois. L'évolution du personnage féminin dans les romans de Chrétien de Troyes," *Cahiers de civilisation médiéval,* 15 [1972], 283-284).

214. For affirmative answers to these questions, see Herbert Moller, "The Meaning of Courtly Love," *Journal of American Folklore,* 73 (1960), 39-52. Moller's emphasis on the latent content of this poetry and its profound collective appeal is by no means incompatible with other current interpretations of this courtly poetry, among them the view that it represents essentially an art of performance, which plays on the perspectives of its audience (see, e.g., Frederick Goldin, *Lyrics of the Troubadours and Trouvères: An Anthology and a History* [New York, 1973], pp. 108, 121-125). The quoted phrases are paraphrased from verses of the troubadour, Bernart de Ventadour, translated by Harvey Birenbaum in *Medieval Age,* edited by Angel Flores (New York, 1963), pp. 180-181; cf. Moller, pp. 42-43, and Goldin, pp. 139-141.

215. In his provocative analysis of the unconscious meaning of the familiar paradoxes of courtly poetry, Meiler points out (p. 41) that the venerated person or image is a woman "whose very existence in the poet's life has an assuring, exhilarating and uplifting effect," who is "absolutely unique and irreplaceable," who inspires in the poet "a ceaseless desire for her amorous at-

tention, for mutual fondling, embracing and kissing." In the dichotomy of the tender and sensual feelings reflected in much of this poetry, and its infantile or childish imagery, as well as in the striking inequality of the lovers, Moller finds further support for his hypothesis.

216. See p. 41, and pp. 44-45, on the absence in this poetry of the "threatening father-figure," the presence of "numerous minor rivals," and the "deeply ambivalent concept of the lady herself," as at once "unboundedly good and yet cruel in her displeasure."

217. Among earthly surrogates of this period none holds a more important place in both life and literature than the maternal uncle, who often appears, as G. C. Homans remarks, as a kind of "male mother" (*English Villagers of the Thirteenth Century* [New York, 1968], pp. 191-192). On the uncle-nephew relationship, as portrayed in no fewer than eighty literary works of this time, see R. Bezzola, "Les neveux," *Mélanges de langue et littérature du moyen âge et de la renaissance offerts à Jean Frappier* (2 vols., Geneva, 1970), I, 89-111. Cf. G. Duby, "Structures de parenté et noblesse: France du nord, XIe-XIIe siècles," *Miscellanea . . . J. F. Niermeyer*, p. 157.

218. See Michael Goodich's very recent study, "Childhood and Adolescence among the Thirteenth-Century Saints," *History of Childhood Quarterly,* I (1973), especially p. 298.

219. See Herlihy's perceptive conclusions regarding the "social impact of Europe's great waves of military and geographic expansion" in "Land, Family and Women . . . ," *Traditio,* 18 (1962), 110-113. This was a time also, as was suggested earlier, when preoccupation with household responsibilities and with the care of more numerous families apparently encouraged the practice of wet-nursing in many noble households and so removed many noble mothers from the closest early relationship with their infants (see above, notes 61, 64, 67).

220. The themes of abandonment, exposure, rejection and illegitimacy are significantly developed in a number of twelfth-century works, such as the *Lais* of Marie de France mentioned earlier (see notes 70 and 100). A particularly striking example, deserving of much closer study, is the *Gregorius* of Hartmann von Aue (edited by F. Maurer, Berlin, 1968), in which these themes are combined with motifs of a double incest, with clear Oedipal overtones, between a brother and sister whose child, having been reared in a monastery, later returns and, at first unrecognized, marries his mother. For a recent study, see K. C. King, "The Mother's Guilt in Hartmann's *Gregorius,*" *Mediaeval German Studies Presented to Frederick Norman* (London, 1965), pp. 84-93.

221. Quoted here is the English translation of A. T. Hatto: *Gottfried von Strassburg, "Tristan," with the "Tristan" of Thomas* (London: Penguin Classics, 1960), pp. 65-68.

222. *Ibid.,* pp. 68-69.

223. *Ibid.,* pp. 93-103; on the maternal uncle, see above, n. 217.

224. For *Urbain* and similar works, see H. Rosamond Parsons, *Anglo-Norman Books of Courtesy and Nurture* (1929), pp. 16-19 and *passim.* Another of these poems, the *Petit Traitise,* stresses the polite behavior of children to one another, urging them not to hurt their companions at play or to coerce anyone (pp. 48-49).

225. *De prop. rer.,* Lib. VI, pp. 238-239.

226. *Ibid.,* p. 238; see above, n. 186, for the view of Guibert of Nogent.

227. *De prop. rer.,* pp. 240-241.

228. For Vincent's treatise on the education of noble children, written, c. 1247-49, at the request of Queen Margaret, wife of St. Louis, see *De eruditione*

filiorum nobilium, edited by A. Steiner (Cambridge, Mass., 1938); on the education of girls, see pp. 172-219. See also Astrik L. Gabriel, *The Educational Ideas of Vincent of Beauvais* (South Bend, Ind.: University of Notre Dame Press, 1962), pp. 40-44. Much more advanced and equalitarian were the ideas on this subject of Vincent's younger contemporary, Pierre Dubois, who, as a feature of his program of French colonial expansion, advocated that girls be given the same education as boys, but with special emphasis on medicine and surgery (*De recuperatione terrae sanctae,* edited by C. V. Langlois [Paris, 1891], pp. 70-72

229. *De eruditione,* pp. 172-176; 194-197.

230. *Speculum doctrinale* in *Speculum Quadruplex, sive Speculum maius* [reprinted, Graz, 1964-1965], Lib. XII, c. 31. Cf. Gabriel, *Educational Ideas,* pp. 17-18.

231. For Aldobrandino's advice regarding infants, see above, notes 47, 49, 59. This Sienese physician, who lived in Troyes in the later thirteenth century, and evidently died before 1287, wrote his popular treatise, *Le Régime du corps,* apparently the first medical work in the French language, about 1256, at the request of Countess Beatrice of Savoy. On the Latin translations or paraphrases of Soranus, and on the dissemination of his ideas, see above, n. 42. They were well known, for example, to another thirteenth-century physician, Gilbertus Anglicus, and they are repeated in his *Compendium medicinae,* though Soranus is not mentioned by name (Talbot, *Medicine in Medieval England,* pp. 80-83).

232. Vincent, *Speculum doctrinale,* Lib. XII, c. 32; cf. Gabriel, *Educational Ideas,* pp. 17-19. An illuminated initial letter of a contemporary manuscript of Aldobrandino's work, reproduced in the printed edition (p. 74), shows a nurse, or midwife, bathing a child in a large barrel-shaped tub.

233. This should be done, according to Aldobrandino, so that the child's nature may be good-humored; this is the age when the child retains most and learns both good and bad behaviour. As soon as the child is seven, he should be forced to learn good habits, and care should be taken that nothing happens to him to anger him excessively or to age him too fast (*Régime du corps,* p. 80). His diet should also be carefully supervised, and he should be fed three times a day after intervals of play. He may be given wine diluted with water, but as little milk, fruit and cheese as possible, because they are likely to cause stones. At this age, it is well to send the child to school, to a master who teaches in an orderly way without beating and will not force him to remain in school against his will. Cf. the almost identical advice, perhaps derived from Aldobrandino, of the late thirteenth century "Dialogue of Placides and Timeo" (Langlois, *La vie en France,* III, 333).

234. Vincent, *De eruditione,* ed. Steiner, pp. 89-101.

235. This poem is translated in *An Anthology of Medieval Lyrics,* edited by Angel Flores (New York, 1962), pp. 438-439.

236. A model of paternal concern was offered by St. Louis himself, that devoted son of a devoted mother, in his *Enseignemens* addressed to his son and daughter, a version of which was inserted by Jean de Joinville in his *Memoirs* (see the edition of Natalis de Wailly, Paris, 1874). For a discussion of these texts, see Langlois, *La vie en France,* IV, 23-46. The ideal of paternal instruction of children is reflected also in another contemporary work of religious edification, the treatise entitled "C'est dou pere qui son filz enseigne et dou filz qui au pere demande ce que ile ne set," which offers, along with much else, instruction in the duties of parents and children (*ibid.,* pp. 47-65).

237. The father of at least one son, Philip of Novara, born of a noble family in the Lombard city of Novara, spent much of his life in the service of the

Ibelin in Cyprus and Syria. His last work, a moral treatise on the four ages of man, written after 1265, was edited by Marcel de Freville: Philippe de Navarre (sic), *Des .IIII. tenz d'aage d'ome* (here cited as *Les quatre ages de l'homme*), Société des anciens textes français (Paris: Didot, 1888). For Philip's description of the infant, see p. 2.

238. *Ibid.,* p. 3. For Maimonides' views on the father's love for his children, see *Guide for the Perplexed,* translated by M. Friedländer (2nd edition revised, New York: Dover Publications, 1965), pp. 378-379. Recommending very early circumcision, Maimonides argues that then the child will not have much pain and also that when he is very young, the parents "do not think much of him, because the image of the child, that leads the parents to love him, has not yet taken a firm root in their minds." That image becomes stronger by the continual sight of the child, and grows with his develop-ment; the parents' love for a newborn child is not so great as it is when the child is a year old, and the year-old child is less loved by them than when it is six. For another influential medieval Jewish father's views on children, see Saadia Gaon, *The Book of Beliefs and Opinions,* translated from the Arabic and Hebrew by Samuel Rosenblatt (New Haven: Yale University Press, 1948), pp. 381-383; reflecting on the pains, anxieties and sorrows of parenthood, Saadia concludes that "the sole reason why the love of children has been implanted in the hearts of men is in order that they might hold on to those with whom their Lord has favored them and not lose patience with them." A favorite among Salernitan questions from the thirteenth century to the seventeenth asked why parents loved their children more than the lat-ter loved them; the answer commonly depended on the physical grounds that the child has its essence from the substance of both parents, and the parents, knowing this, love the child so much the more, while the child, hav-ing nothing of his substance in the parents, loves them less (Lawn, *The Salernitan Questions,* pp. 151-153).

239. Philip of Novara, *Les quatre âges de l'homme,* p. 3-9; Philip recommended a somewhat perfunctory and superficial religious instruction as important for the instilling of good morals.

240. *Ibid.,* pp. 10-14.

241. *Ibid.,* pp. 14-21.

242. The works of this late thirteenth-century Milanese moralist are edited by Vincenzo Licitra, "Il *Liber legum moralium* e il *De regimine vite et sanitatis* di Bellino Bisolo," *Studi medievali,* 3a ser., 6 (1965), 409-454. For his ideas about children and their training, see especially pp. 420, 433-435; in the matter of discipline, he shared the views of Philip of Novara, declaring that "the father who spares the rod does not love his child" (p. 434). His *De regimine vite,* recommending frequent bathing and washing of hands and face and offering sensible and very specific advice regarding diet, reflects a concern for hygiene and cleanliness, displayed also in the *Regimen sanitatis* and other works, which was by no means uncommon in this period (see Talbot, *Medicine in Medieval England,* pp. 144-145).

243. M. Coens, "La vie de Christian de l'Aumône," *Analecta Bollandiana,* 52 (1934), p. 14; this boy of seven was delivered from these mortal attacks by confessing his sins.

244. *Ibid.,* p. 15, for the statement that Christian remained in his parents' house throughout his boyhood.

245: This poem is translated by C. H. Bell in *Peasant Life in Old German Epics: Meier Helmbrecht and Der arme Heinrich,* pp. 93-134. See also the German edition of F. Maurer (Berlin, 1968), pp. 43-85.

246. *Peasant Life,* especially pp. 101, 105, 112.

247. *Ibid.*, pp. 105-107, 110-111, 120-121; the child-heroine refers more than once to her parents' "forbearance and kindness, such as loving parents show their child in every way," and we are told that in their joy at her safe return from Salerno "three times and more her mouth they kissed." According to an anonymous thirteenth-century preacher, the rearing of young nobles, who were more strictly disciplined and "made to eat with servants," was less gentle and tender than that of peasant children, on whom their parents lavished affection when they were young and who were then put to the plow when they were grown (B. Hauréau, *Notices et extraits de quelques manuscrits de la Bibliothèque Nationale,* IV, 95). The contrast was made in another way by a contemporary physician who remarked that the children of peasants were always born beautiful, even though later, through excessive labor and lack of hygiene, they become ugly" (Talbot, *Medicine in Medieval England,* p. 95).

248. For *Meier Helmbrecht,* see Bell, *Peasant Life,* pp. 37-89. The thirteenth century German peasant family depicted in this poem consisted of the parents, two daughters and the foolishly ambitious son whom the father tried in vain to keep at home. Among a slowly increasing number of representations of the family in art from the late twelfth century may be noted the reliefs at Borgo San Donnino (Crichton, *Romanesque Sculpture in Italy,* p. 77 and Pl. 43, 44b), and the portrayal of embracing parents with their two children in the thirteenth century Reuner Musterbuch (see above, n. 78). Regarding the structure of peasant families specifically, the evidence so far examined points to the earlier prevalence of the "conjugal" family in this class in various regions of Europe, e.g., in Provence by the tenth and eleventh centuries (Weinberger, "Peasant Households ..." *Speculum,* 48 [1973], 255-256), and in Spain by the tenth century (M. B. Pontieri, "Una familia de propietarios rurales en la Liebana del siglo X," *Cuadernos de Historia de España,* 43-44 (1967), 119-132. For suggestive evidence from the tenth century in northern France, see B. Guérard, *Le polyptyque de l'abbaye de Saint-Rémi de Reims* (Paris, 1853), pp. 7-23. See also G. Duby, "Structures familiales dans le moyen âge occidental," *Rapports,* XIIIe Congrès international des sciences historiques (Moscow, 1970), and G. C. Homans, *English Villagers of the Thirteenth Century,* pp. 215-217. Fossier concludes that, at least in the areas with which he is concerned, the thirteenth century saw the expansion of a "new family structure," the conjugal family, of which the Church and the peasant and bourgeois communities appear as the champions; after a time of hesitations and reversals, the "conjugal cell" constituted the center of family association (*La terre et les hommes en Picardie,* I, 270). For another view of this process, see D. Herlihy, "Family Solidarity in Medieval Italian History," *Economy, Society and Government in Medieval Italy:* Essays in Memory of Robert L. Reynolds, edited by David Herlihy, Robert S. Lopez and Vsevolod Slessarev (Kent, Ohio: Kent State University Press, 1969), pp. 173-184.

CHAPTER 4

The Middle-Class Child in Urban Italy, Fourteenth to Early Sixteenth Century

JAMES BRUCE
ROSS

"I called to mind when, the exact hour and moment, and where and how he was conceived by me, and how great a joy it was to me and his mother; and soon came his movements in the womb which I noted carefully with my hand, awaiting his birth with the greatest eagerness. And then when he was born, male, sound, well-proportioned, what happiness, what joy I experienced; and then as he grew from good to better, such satisfaction, such pleasure in his childish words, pleasing to all, loving towards me his father and his mother, precocious for his age."

Giovanni Morelli

What was it like to be a middle-class child in the urban centers of northern and central Italy in the period of "the Renaissance", from about 1300 to the early sixteenth century? The life of the peasant child and of the proletarian urban child remains almost wholly obscure, but thanks to the articulate impulses of the mercantile and professional classes, and the remarkable number of their extant records, we can gain some understanding of the upbringing of their children. Although no voices of children reach us directly, we can hear them, faintly and imperfectly to be sure, through the media of those who controlled their lives or observed their development. Fathers of families sometimes recall their own early years and usually record with care the vital data of their offspring; moralists and preachers admonish parents in traditional Christian terms; educators create an ideal ethic of pedagogy from classical sources; physicians and artists observe and comment upon the child in particular ways. A few exceptional individuals write their own life history, transmuting their childhood experience in their old age. All of these adults draw from the accumulated wisdom of the past but reflect as well the power of prevailing custom and the peculiar strains of an aggressive and competitive society subject to physical disasters, plague, famine and flood, as well as civil violence and war.

In pursuit of evidence for this elusive subject the modern scholar must search widely, examining masses of diverse materials, published and unpublished, in order to find even a few fragments or tessera with which to construct some kind of mosaic. The shapes that emerge will be faulty, the colors dim, but perhaps the whole may make some sense to the modern student of childhood, past and present. Deeper psychological insight, more lively historical imagination, as well as the fruits of contemporary quantitative studies, will enrich and doubtless modify the tentative conclusions of this short essay, but the evidence presented, almost wholly from the sources, will, I hope, remain valuable to the future inquirer.

Because the Tuscans, and especially the Florentines, were more articulate than any other people in Italy at this time and their records richer and more accessible than those of other areas, their voices are heard most clearly in this essay. The political fragmentation of the peninsula of Italy, only a geographical expression until the mid-nineteenth century, precludes the characterization of any child as "Italian", and the uneven cultural development of the major parts makes questionable any generalization beyond the limits of a single territorial entity. It seems valid, however, to consider as a whole the experience of the middle-class child in central and northern Italy. "The City" (Rome) was distinct in every way, and "The Kingdom" (Naples, with or without Sicily) was overwhelmingly rural, retarded in social and cultural development, and therefore relatively inarticulate for our purposes.

THE FIRST TWO YEARS: Mother or Nurse?
THE *BALIA:* Ideal and Actual

What were the infant's first contacts with the world outside the womb? Birth in the parental bed, bath in the same room, and baptism in the parish church were followed almost at once by delivery into the hands of a *balia* or wet-nurse, generally a peasant woman living at a distance, with whom the infant would presumably remain for about two years or until weaning was completed. Immediate separation from its mother, therefore, was the fate of the new-born child in the middle-class families of urban Italy in the period of our study. It became wholly dependent for food, care and affection upon a surrogate, and its return to its own mother was to a stranger in an alien home, to a person with whom no physical or emotional ties had ever been established. Clearly the *balia* looms large in any discussion of the young child in Italy.

The antiquity of the institution of the wet-nurse is well known to all students of pediatrics.[1] Of interest to us here is the continuity of a body of injunctions concerning the choice of a wet-nurse and the performance of her basic functions, especially as they had been formulated by the physician Soranus of Ephesus (96-138 A.D.).[2] This core of material seems to be the source of most of the didactic treatises on the care of infants that were written in our period although the lines of transmission are not clear. Of equal interest in these Italian writings is the persistence of the advocacy of maternal feeding, but in ambivalent terms similar to those of Soranus:

> Other things being equal, it is better to feed the child with maternal milk; for this is more suited to it, and the mothers become more sympathetic towards the offspring, and it is more natural to be fed from the mother after parturition, just as before parturition. But if anything prevents it one must choose the best wet-nurse, lest the mother grow prematurely old, having spent herself through the daily suckling. . . . The mother will fare better with a view to her own recovery and to further child-bearing, if she is relieved of having her breasts distended. . . .[3]

Among the Italian writers of the fourteenth century the wet-nurse is accepted as a matter of course. For example, the mother is relegated to a minor role by the leading authority on the subject, the poet-notary, Francesco da Barberino, who urges that the wet-nurse be as much like the mother as possible, and that if she falls sick, she should take the infant to its mother,[4] "who, if she wishes and it is convenient, will be able to suckle it with fine milk; though it is true that in the beginning the milk of another is better than hers."[5] Much the same attitude is shown by the Tuscan merchant Paolo da Certaldo in his collection of moral admonitions written after 1350. Not mentioning the mother at all, he calls for great care in the choice of a wet-nurse:

> She should be prudent, well-mannered, honest, not a drinker or a drunkard, because very often children draw from and resemble the nature of the milk they suck; and therefore be careful the wet nurses of your children aren't proud and don't have other evil traits.[6]

The theme of the nursling resembling the nurse, expressed by Soranus,[7] implied by Barberino and frequently repeated, is used by the great popular preacher San Bernardino of Siena with dramatic impact in his sermons advocating maternal feeding:

> Even if you are prudent and of good customs and habits, and discreet . . . you often give your child to a dirty drab, and from her, perforce, the child acquires certain of the customs of the one who suckles him. If the one who cares for him has evil customs or is of base condition, he will receive the impress of those customs because of having sucked her polluted blood.

But even San Bernardino admits the validity of "lawful reasons" for not nursing one's own child, such as poor health and inadequate milk, while deploring the "unlawful" reason, "to procure yourself more pleasure".[8] His comments, like those of the Lombard humanist Maffeo Vegio of the next generation (c. 1407-1458), denouncing refusal to nurse one's child as the act of a monster,[9] reflect the deep-seated social resistance to maternal feeding. Recognition of this prevailing attitude leads Vegio in his florid Latin and his contemporaries writing mostly in the vernacular, to pass rapidly in their treatises from advocacy of the ideal solution to such qualifying phrases as "if the mother's health permits", and "if she has enough milk", or "if she wishes to bear more children in the near future", and occasionally, "if it offends her".

Such phrases represent the current concession to the power of custom, stronger than the authority of antiquity,[10] which forced many didactic writers of the period, such as Alberti, Palmieri and Rucellai, to take up the urgent practical problem of finding a qualified wet-nurse, and keeping her, which confronted most middle-class families.[11] Springing from a subtle interplay of social, psychological and physiological forces, the institution of the wet-nurse prevailed and became apparently a symbol of gentility.[12] It persisted for centuries among "gentle" families, and not only in the homes of the rich and princely. The Italian medical treatises on pediatrics in the sixteenth century do little more than repeat the same appeals to mothers to nurse their own children and the same advice as to the qualifications of a good wet-nurse.[13] There were, in fact, no acceptable alternatives in a society marked by high infant mortality in which concern for the perpetuation of the basic social unit, the family, dominated the social attitudes of theorists.[14] The same concern pervades the family records of the age.[15]

If the mother could not or would not nurse her own child, or was not permitted by her husband to do so, the wet-nurse was regarded as a necessity.[16] Animal milk was apparently not considered tolerable. Cow's milk is rarely mentioned and that of other beasts only as a horrid possibility since the child so nourished would resemble the source. Paolo da Certaldo speaks firmly:

Be sure that the wet-nurse has plenty of milk because if she lacks it she may give the baby the milk of a goat or sheep or ass or some other animal because the child, boy or girl, nourished on animal milk doesn't have perfect wits like one fed on women's milk, but always looks stupid and vacant and not right in the head.[17]

And the poetic Barberino warns the wet-nurse:

Don't give the infant goat's milk, if you can avoid it,
And even less, that of bitch or sow,
And avoid cow's milk; give it yours,
If not, send it away,
(But, if necessary, I'll grant you ewe's milk).[18]

Even if theoretically acceptable, the use of animal milk would have presented insoluble difficulties of transportation and preservation to urban families. In the country cottages of the wet-nurses, however, animal milk must have been used far more frequently than was acknowledged, especially in time of dire necessity. Vasari tells of a child suckled by a goat at two months when its mother died of the plague.[19]

But why not at least keep the infant near its true mother by having a resident wet-nurse? This practice was in fact strongly advocated by some, Vegio, for example, who was so nourished,[20] and was considered as a possibility by others such as Paolo da Certaldo,[21] and Barberino,[22] whose treatise is specifically written for wet-nurses both inside and outside the home. It also seems to be assumed by Alberti but actually it was restricted to more wealthy families.[23] Perhaps the social disadvantages of having a resident nurse by enlarging the numbers in the household and reducing the living space, and by increasing the burden of supervision for an over-burdened mother, probably aided by few if any servants, made the practice unacceptable to most urban families.[24]

Some examples from the sources, however, illustrate the dangers of generalization about the circumstances of the infant's first feeding. Diverse practices are apparent, and in some cases the mother nursed the child—usually briefly, either initially or intermittently, or both. While the fifteen children of the Florentine merchant, Antonio Rustichi, according to his records of 1412 to 1436, were all sent immediately after baptism to wet-nurses outside,[25] six of the seven children of Cristofano Guidini, Sienese notary who died in 1410, enjoyed their mother's milk for a short time (from two weeks to more than two months) before being sent out, and the seventh spent her brief span of one year at her mother's breast.[26]

In the Florentine family of Antella a fourteenth-century father made use of four resident wet-nurses, two of whom were slaves, none lasting more than five months, and later of three outside wet-nurses who lasted longer—all these for four children.[27] An attempt to use wet-nurses also as general servants is recorded three times by one of the Florentine Adriani who finally resorted to an outside wet-nurse.[28]

The birth of twins created special problems. Of two boys born to Guidini in 1385, "Manno" was kept by his mother two weeks, then sent out to a wet-nurse who kept him for two months (until she became pregnant), returned to his mother for eleven days until a second nurse was found with whom he stayed for sixteen months (until she became pregnant). "Gherardo" stayed with his mother for about five weeks, then went in direct succession to three wet-nurses (the first two became pregnant) for periods of six, nine and three months.[29] Twin girls in another Florentine family, in 1505, were "kept at home for some days because we suspected, in fact were certain, that they had not come to the term of nine months, rather between seven and eight." One died at home after three weeks, the other was brought back dead from the home of her second wet-nurse at fifteen months.[30]

Maffeo Vegio's mother, he says, "always nursed her own children unless she was prevented by ill-health or lack of milk, which was often the case". He and his brother were entrusted to wet-nurses, at home, and each took on characteristics of his *balia*. Lorenzo resembled his not only in manners but in physical traits so that "he seemed to have the same features, the same expression and even the same walk" but her bad milk left him with a renal malady from which he died young, while Maffeo took on the excessive modesty and reticence of his nurse "as if I had imbibed with her milk her heart and spirit".[31]

The only artist distinguished by Vasari as having enjoyed his mother's milk is Raphael (1483-1520), whose father insisted that the child "should be suckled by his own mother and should be trained in childhood in the family ways at home rather than in the houses of peasants or common people with their less gentle, indeed, their rough manners and behaviour." Michelangelo (1475-1564) was put out to nurse with the wife of a stone-cutter and therefore said jokingly to Vasari that "with my mother's milk I sucked in the hammer and chisels I use for my statues."[32]

For the foundlings or "cast-offs", illegitimate or unwanted legitimate infants left at the receiving fonts or windows of the *ospedali* or orphanages in the larger cities, the only source of milk was a wet-nurse, generally a slave-girl bought by the prior or hired from her owners for this purpose.[33]

The day of baptism at the parish church, coming normally two or three days after birth, was a momentous occasion:[34] "How much does it cost to make a child a Christian?" asks Francesco Datini, rich merchant of Prato (d. 1410); and his partner answers: "According to how much you want to do yourself honor", adding that in Florence it was customary for godparents to send two large cakes, two large boxes of spiced cookies and a bunch of candles and little torches.[35] Datini honored himself as a godparent of the child of one of his dearest friends by sending three ells of the finest cloth to the mother but cut down on the cakes as "expensive and of little value", saying "she has had so many children it isn't called for."[36]

For the infant it was a crucial moment because on this day when it entered the Christian community, received its names and its godparents, it was usually taken from its mother and handed over to a substitute for an indefinite period. The house of the *balia* was the place where the child first came into sustained contact with a "mother", a "father", other children, animals, and the world of nature. The long separation had begun.

What kind of person was sought as a wet-nurse and how was she found? The father was given the responsibility in Alberti's dialogue:

> He must think far ahead to find a good nurse, he must . . . get hold of one who will be ready in time. He must check that she is not sick or of immoral character. . . . Yet this sort of person always seems to be unavailable just when you need her most. . . . You know, too, how rare is a good nurse and how much in demand."[37]

In practice fathers seem to have made use of agents or intermediaries among whom the best known is Datini, the self-made merchant whose enormous correspondence contains letters revealing his efforts and those of his childless wife to find *balia* for their friends and clients. Margherita complains:

> They seem to have vanished from the world for none has come into my hands. And some I had at hand, whose babies were at the point of death but now they say, they are well again. . . . I have found one . . . whose milk is two months old; and she has vowed that if her babe, which is on the point of death, dies tonight, she will come, as soon as it is buried.[38]

Her efforts were sometimes matched by her husband's. In letters to a partner, he presents two candidates: one, the baker's wife because of her proximity ("almost in the house") and "even if she has recently committed a fault one shouldn't notice it; her husband is glad for her to serve you, if she can, to satisfy you and earn something". The other, an honest woman, the wife of a rich peasant, "bore a child a month ago and the creature died two days ago".[39]

It seems unlikely that any available *balia* conformed to the specifications of Barberino whose fourteenth-century ideal echoes that of Soranus centuries before and is repeated by the Italian doctors of the six-teenth-century; he prescribes a woman

> between twenty-five and thirty-five years, as much like the mother as possible, and let her have good color and a strong neck and strong chest and ample flesh, firm and fat rather than lean, but by no means too much so, her breath not bad, her teeth clean. And as for her manners, guard against the proud and wrathful and gloomy, neither fearful, nor foolish, nor coarse .... Let her breasts be between soft and hard, big but not excessive in length, the quantity of her milk moderate, and the color white and not green, nor yellow and even less black, the odor good and also the taste, not salty or bitter, but on the sweet side, and uniform throughout, but not foamy, and abundant. And note that the best is one who has her own male child. And beware of one who "goes bad" such as one whom her husband won't leave alone, and one whom you find gravid. . . .[40]

If such *balie* were hard to find, nonetheless many country girls seem to have sought the job, spurred on by their husbands, to judge by the verses of one of their carnival songs:

> Here we come, *balie* from the Casentino,
> each one looking for a baby,
> and here are our husbands
> who lead us on the way,
> whoever has a baby, show him to us,
> male or female, it doesn't matter.[41]

It was with the husbands that urban fathers made the contracts, or with their agents, fixing the monthly stipend of the wife.

It seems likely that the infant from this moment was wholly dependent upon the *balia*. There is little evidence that parents visited the child, although they are urged to do so by a moralist: "Always visit the children whom you give out of your house to a *balia*, and often, so you can see how they are; and if they're not in good shape change at once to another *balia*."[42] The comment of Lapo Mazzei, a poor notary of Prato and father of fourteen, to his patron, Datini, confirms this impression of parental indifference: "Your godson, whom I have seen only once before, has come back to me from his wet-nurse in the hills, the finest little curly badger that I have ever had."[43] Guidini notes that he went to see his first-born, a son, about three weeks after its removal and gave the *balia* two florins, probably an advance on her wages of fifty *soldi* a month.[44] A visit to a natural son, two years old, is recorded by the artist Benvenuto Cellini in his well-known memoirs.[45]

Without regular supervision what kind of care would the surrogate mother give the new-born infant? If her own infant had just died, did she resent the newcomer or find in it physical relief and emotional consolation? Or if her own nursling was alive, could she feed both infants adequately or did she face a bitter choice? And what kind of treatment would the little intruder receive from the older children of the *balia* or from her husband, the *balio,* who gained a profit from this arrangement but supposedly lost his conjugal rights for its duration? Different kinds of sources yield different evidence but one conclusion seems undeniable, that the life of a child in these first two years or so may well have been precarious and pitiable. Some excerpts from the unpublished *recordanze* (a kind of a family journal and diary) of a Florentine merchant afford a wholly objective record, in the spirit of Alberti who recommends: "As soon as the child is born, one should note in the family records and secret books, the hour, day, month, year as well as place of birth."[46]

For the years 1412 to 1436 Antonio Rustichi made meticulous entries in his journal concerning his fifteen children, including the following:[47]

> *Recordanze* that on this day, 6 March 1417, in the name of God, there was born to me a male child by my wife, Chaterina, and he was born on Saturday night at four hours and he is the first. He was baptized on the 9th day of the same month and given the name Lionardo and his godparents were the following: . . . who sent my lady Chaterina these presents: . . .

> *Recordanze* that on this day, 9 March, I sent out to wet-nurse my first child named Lionardo, and I gave him to a *balia* of Santo Ambrogio, to dame Chaterina, wife of Ambrogio, master-mason and farmer, for 5 *lire* 10 *soldi* a month, which wages I fixed with Santi di Francescho. . . . And the things I sent with the child are these, and they are all new.

The list comprises 32 items, some multiple, including a variety of garments (lined cloaks, little shirts, robes with and without sleeves, bibs, caps, etc.), 6 swaddling bands and 6 pieces of woolen cloth, a branch of coral with a silver ring, and an old cradle with coverlet and pillow.

On 24 January 1418, his second son, Stefano, was born, on 27 January baptized and on the same day given to a wet nurse, dame Caterina, wife of Amadio the baker, for 5 *lire* 10 *soldi* monthly.

> Then on 3 February 1419, I took back Stefano because the *balia* was pregnant and gave him to dame Chaterina d' Ambrogio, and took back my other son whom she had, by name, Lionardo, and so he was weaned. So in all dame Caterina d' Amadio had Stefano 12 months and 5 days, which came to 66 *lire*. In all, by agreement with Ambrogio and dame Chaterina they had the two children 31½ months at 5 *lire* and 10 *soldi* monthly which comes to 173 *lire* 5 *soldi*.

Antonio's third child, Filippa, was born 24 February 1419, baptized 26 February and on 2 March given to a *balia*, for 4 *lire* a month, with a "layette" of 23 items similar to Lionardo's, including a number of "used" objects. On 2 June 1420, she was taken from the breast because the *balia* was pregnant. The latter was paid for 15 months but kept the child another 8½ to wean at 50 *soldi* a month, making 23½ months in all. The fourth child, Costanza, was sent out on 26 March 1420, for 4 *lire* 15 *soldi* but died on 31 March, and was buried in the country. The *balia* and her husband brought back "all her equipment" and were paid for the burial "what they asked" and in addition 4 silver pennies for the milk although "it didn't amount to much". The fifteenth entry has a familiar ring for Ghostanza, born 1436, was sent out with a "layette" of 25 items including an old cradle, a branch of coral and other used objects, and was taken from her first *balia* who became pregnant.

Rustichi was an unusually conscientious father in recording family data but his contemporaries gave the basic facts with occasional additions. For example, the Florentine merchant, Gregorio Dati, notes the dates of birth, baptism, and names of godparents of each of his twenty-five children by three wives, with occasional comments on "a fine healthy boy" or "a fine little girl."[48] The Sienese notary, Guidini, records more fully, adding the names of each *balia* and her husband and the months each of his seven spent with the wet-nurse.[49]

Adjustment to not one but to several successive *balie* was apparently the fate of many infants, and it continued to be a fatal weakness of the system. The experience of Jerome Cardan (1501-1576), famous physician-gambler, reaffirms the evidence of the earlier period which could be multiplied from unpublished sources:

> I lost, in the very first month of my life, my wet-nurse on the day she fell ill, so they tell me, of the plague; and my mother returned to me. . . . When my second month was not yet run, Isidoro . . . of Pavia took me naked from a warm vinegar bath and gave me over to a wet-nurse. The latter carried me to . . . a village seven miles from Milan . . . . There my body wasted, while the belly grew hard and swollen. When the reason was known—that my nurse was pregnant—I was transferred to a better nurse, who suckled me until I was three.[50]

We have no direct communication with the *balie* themselves except through the corporate voice of their carnival songs. To continue the one quoted above:[51]

> We shall take good care of him,
> and he will be so well fed,
> that we'll soon have him standing straight
> like a proud knight.

If the baby falls sick
or is a bit run down,
we'll take such good care of him
that he will soon recover:
but we must help him out
in changing him frequently;
when he's wet, we must dry him
and wash him with a little wine.

We're fine in our way of life,
prompt and skilful in our trade,
always when the baby cries
we feel our milk returning:
acting with energy and speed,
we do our duty,
we take him out of the cradle
drying his little face.

When he's hit by the evil eye
we go clear up to Poppi:
a woman puts him on her knee
and gives him back his health,
sometimes she wants us
to take him bare for some days
behind the oven
amusing him in the "little sun".[52]

In every matter, we know what to do,
so that the baby grows up quickly;
as long as he stays straight and hard
we don't mind getting tired;
and he'll never leave us
until his nursing is finished:
so you can be quite confident
in sending him to the Casentino.

But what kind of care did the infant actually receive from the *balia?*
Another song is more specific in emphasizing feeding, swaddling and
changing, the essential offices of the nurse:[53]

With lots of good fine milk
our breasts are full.
To avoid all suspicion,
let the doctor see it,
because in it is found
the life and being of the creature,
for good milk nourishes
with no trouble and makes the flesh firm. . . .

> We're young married women,
> well experienced in our art,
> we can swaddle the baby in a flash
> and no one has to show us
> how to use the cloth and bands;
> while caring for him we arrange them carefully
> because if he catches cold,
> the baby is harmed and the *balia* blamed.
>
> We change three times a day
> the wool and linen cloths and white bands,
> and we never get tired or cross
> being with him so he won't cry. . . .

These promises are far more realistic than the elaborate directions of Barberino, but even so doubts arise. Was there ever enough milk for the little stranger? Could the complex process of swaddling ever be done "in a flash"? Were infants ever "changed" three times a day, and what actually was changed? Here, and in the layettes of Rustichi's infants, there seems to be a distinction between the *fascie* or long bands and the *pezze* or pieces of cloth. Were the latter the raw material for more bands or did they provide cloth for a "diaper" beneath the bands, or both? Did the *balia* put "little shirts" beneath the bands or a sack-like cloth enveloping the feet of wholly swaddled children?[54]

Warnings by the moralists suggest some carelessness or negligence in basic care. Paolo da Certaldo succinctly states that "the child should be kept very clean and warm and often examined and looked over, member by member", [55] and San Bernardino clearly feels it wise to remind mothers and nurses:

> When you have a little child and he cries, take him up! Is there need to unswaddle him? Do it. If there is need to suckle him, do so. When he is sleepy, so that he cries, you should lull him to sleep, and when it is necessary to clean him, you should do so,[56]

and using the figure of a man burnishing steel, he says "until he makes it bright and clean and gleaming like a baby girl."[57]

Did the *balia* when she swaddled the baby "leave free the part where the water comes out so the band won't prevent it from coming"? And was she careful "not to bind too tightly and cause the baby to cry or suffer, and yet not too loosely so that it could get its arms out and scratch its eyes"?[58] If a child wet the bed at night whose fault was it? When a woman heard that her baby, lent out to her childless friends, the Datinis, had twice pissed in his bed she sent word with irritation "that he is not in the habit of doing so, and he never does so unless he remains uncovered at night or perhaps he did not have on the band she uses to swaddle his stomach."[59]

How could an over-worked country woman find time to do more than the minimum? How could she have eased his teething, taught him his first words, guided his first steps, protected him as he began to walk from all surrounding dangers (fire, tools, animals, darkness, wells, high places, and so on)?[60] And when and why would she have dressed him up in the variety of garments sent along? In intervals between swaddlings or as the heavy swaddling was reduced and finally ended? The little coats, some fur-lined, may have been used to keep out the cold and wrapped round the swaddled infant.[61] Perhaps the fancier garments were sent more as a symbol of the parents' affluence than for use.

The fate of the child put out with a *balia* depended upon many variables including the duration of the stay. Supposedly it lasted for two years or until weaning, which was obviously abrupt in many cases; Barberino says about two years and warns against sudden weaning.[62] Actually it varied considerably, as a few examples will show. A girl child in the Florentine Sassetti family was returned in 1370 after twenty-nine months by her *balia* with whom the parents remained on good terms "although the child was in rather poor shape, but in truth more from illness than from poor care".[63] The fortunate illegitimate daughter of Datini (by a slave-girl) was taken in by his wife in 1395 and brought "home" at six years from her *balia* whose husband wrote saying that he and his wife had loved her like a daughter, and "because she is a good girl and very fearful," he hoped they would be kind to her.[64] The father of Giovanni Morelli was left by his father with a *balia* in the country until he was "ten or twelve", perhaps because his parent "had so many grown children, or because his wife being dead and he an old man, he didn't want the trouble of bringing up the child, or the expense". The grown man remembered this *balia* as "the most awful bestial woman that ever was", who had given him so many blows that the mere thought of her so enraged him that he would have killed her if he could have laid hands on her.[65] A branch of the Adriani family of Florence in 1470 received their son back from his *balia* at fifteen months and were told he had been "eight days without the breast" because she had become pregnant.[66]

In general, it seems clear that the pregnancy of the *balia* more frequently terminated the stay than the early death of the child. The causes of the latter are rarely made clear. Did illegitimate infants die more frequently and earlier than legitimate babies in the care of a *balia?*[67] Infanticide veiled as "smothering" may well have occurred more frequently than we know though there were more humane ways of disposing of unwanted children, legitimate and illegitimate. The foundling hospitals received a steady stream of the latter. But the danger of "smothering" is made clear by Barberino's injunction: "don't let the baby lie with you in such a way that you might roll over on top of him."[68] (It is worth noting that the "layettes" sent with infants by Rustichi and others included a cradle with coverlet and pillow.)[69]

Few explicit references to "smothering", however, have been found. Among the many deaths of young children noted by Morelli in his review of three generations, only one, a nephew, was thought to have been "suffocated" at the home of the *balia;*[70] the great killer in this family was the Black Death in the recurrent waves of 1363, 1374, 1400. Another instance is found in an early life of the humanist Marsiglio Ficino; his grandmother appeared to his mother in a dream, grieving, on the seventeenth day after the birth of a child, and "the next day countrymen brought back her child suffocated by her nurse."[71] And a few days after Cellini visited his natural son he received word the child was dead, "smothered" by his nurse.[72] The question arises, however, why a *balia* would deliberately "smother" a child or carelessly run the risk of doing so. The child's death would mean the end of an arrangement profitable to her and to her husband. And the penalties for infanticide might be harsh.[73]

THE RETURN OF THE NATIVE: From About Two to Seven
CHILD AND MOTHER: Care in Theory and Practice

The return of the child to its native home after some two years forced upon him another severe adjustment; now displaced from the only "mother" he had ever known he must find his true mother in the midst of a strange household, an urban "family" which might be large and complex in composition.[74] If the trend may have been towards the smaller "nuclear" family there is plenty of evidence of the persistence of the large "family" in the fourteenth and fifteenth centuries, that is, in the sense defined by Alberti as "children, wife, and other members of the household, both relatives and servants . . . . I would want all my family to live under one roof, to warm themselves at one hearth and to seat themselves at one table."[75]

A few examples of the size and composition of households may be helpful.

One of the Peruzzi, Florentine merchants, notes in his "secret book" for 1314 the expenses incurred for half of the cost of "the house and family" which he had in common with his brother; he himself had twelve children.[76] Two other merchants in the Florentine tax records of 1427 claim substantial reductions on the basis of large households, one noting a household of fifteen members, including two married sons and their families, as well as five adolescent sons, the other listing twelve dependents, wife, sister and nine children.[77] In praising his wife in the late fourteenth century another merchant, Velluti, says she is a big, beautiful woman of fifty, wise, understanding, tireless, and splendid as a nurse, "and that's not to be wondered at, considering how many she's had to manage, husbands, sons, brothers and other persons".[78] A mixed household under the roof of a widow is described in 1442 as containing her husband's two natural children, her own three sons, her daughters, the wives of two sons and three children of one of them.[79] A similar composite household is that of Paoli Niccolini, wool merchant of the mid fifteenth century; it included his children by two wives, the sons of one wife by her first husband and two of his sons by a slave whom he freed and kept in residence.[80]

Discord in such households was inevitable. San Bernardino notes what a bride might expect on arrival in her new home, such as the enmity of step-children: ". . . and she has no love for them and can scarcely bear for them to have enough to eat. And they are often so knowing as to perceive that she doesn't wish them well and would like for her to have nothing at all to eat." And if she finds another daughter-in-law in the house, "there will soon be an end to peace and concord," and if a mother-in-law, "I'll say no more!"[81] Morelli describes admiringly the way in which his sister "Mea", married at fifteen into a large, disorderly and quarrelsome household, imposed peace upon old and young by her grace and virtue.[82]

The child returning from the *balia*, therefore, might have to compete for the attention of his mother, or some adult woman, not only with his own siblings but with half-brothers and sisters, legitimate or illegitimate, some obviously of alien blood, or with cousins under the tutelage of their fathers. Illegitimate children were sometimes even brought home from overseas, as in the case of Gregorio Dati, who, in 1391 had a child by a Tartar slave in Valencia, whom he sent back to Florence to be reared at three months.[83] A member of the Velluti family brought back from Sicily in 1355 his dead brother's illegitimate daughter, age ten, although he was at first dubious about her parentage, "and I welcomed her, and I and my family . . . treated her as though she were my own daughter".[84] The numbers of children might even be augmented by little slave-servants, especially girls of eleven or twelve, Tartars, Slavs, or "Arabs", whom Datini and other merchants bought to use as household drudges or little nurses.[85] These children were distinguished from the others by looks, speech, manners and the clothes they were required to wear, marked with black,[86] as were the older slave-servants in the house.

If it was difficult for the returning child to win a place in his mother's affections in such households, perhaps he attached himself at first to an older sister or brother, to an uncle or an aunt or grandparent living in the house. When a well-known Florentine widow was looking for a bride for one of her sons, she commented favorably on a girl who was "responsible for a large family (there are twelve children, six boys and

six girls) and the mother is always pregnant and is not very compe-
tent."[87] The grandmothers in the Medici family seem to have been active in the upbringing of children in that restless clan as they moved
from city to villa, villa to villa, to escape the plague, bad weather and
other troubles.[88] In a well-known picture, Ghirlandaio conveys the feeling of intimacy which a child might develop towards a grandfather.[89]

We shall never know what impressions of his family a child actually
formed but some early adult memories, recorded in different ways, may
be helpful. A study of Leonardo da Vinci, an illegitimate child who was
successively part of several family groups, makes suggestive use of the
drawings of heads, mostly in profile, dating perhaps from as early as the
artist's sixteenth year.[90] By means of verbal portraits the Florentine
Giovanni Morelli in his private journal, written mostly in his thirties,
evokes vivid images of those whom he loved most in the family constellation, treating as shadowy figures the others. He idealizes his father,
whom he lost at three years, as a "poor abandoned boy", left at the
balia's until ten or twelve years, who never saw his father, but who by
courage and virtue triumphed over paternal neglect and fraternal indifference to become head of the family.[91] Married at twenty-eight to
Telda, "thirteen and beautiful", he sired five children before he died in
the plague of 1374, leaving four surviving children, two girls, nine and
six, and two boys, four and three, at the mercy of "a cruel mother" who
soon re-married and turned them over to her parents.[92] For a brief period an heroic young cousin served as a father figure to the child in a
large family group which fled to Bologna to escape the plague but this
admirable young man who skilfully managed the large household soon
died.[93] The child's next attachment was to his older sister, Mea, beautiful, gifted and gay, but she married at fifteen and died in childbirth at
twenty-two.[94] For Giovanni the loss of his father was irreparable, "so
great is the benefit the child receives from a living father",[95] his hourly
guidance and good counsel; his first duty should be to insure that in
case of his death the wife does not remarry and leave their children,
"for there is no mother so bad that she isn't better for her children than
any other woman".[96]

Giovanni's passionate desire to live to bring up his own children was
fulfilled but death took his beloved first-born, Alberto, at ten years.
This loss threw Giovanni into an agony of grief and probably excessive
self-reproach. His greatest joy brought him his greatest torment, he says,
speaking to himself:

> You had a son, intelligent, lively and healthy so that your anguish
> was greater at his loss. You loved him but never used your love to
> make him happy; you treated him more like a stranger than a son;
> you never gave him an hour of rest; you never looked approvingly
> at him; you never kissed him when he wanted it; you wore him

out at school and with many harsh blows. . . . You have lost him
and will never see him again in this world![97]

When, on the anniversary of Alberto's death, the boy appeared to him
in a dream, an angelic vision, the roles are reversed, the son comforts
the grieving father. Throughout these *ricordi* the father-son relationship
emerges as paramount in the life of a child.[98]

> If we bear in mind that few children of the urban middle classes were
> suckled and cared for by their own mothers in the first two years of
> life, how can we explain

the fascination, almost the obsession, with children and the
mother-child relation that is perhaps the single most important
motif in Florentine art during the first century of the Renaissance,
with its *putti,* its children and adolescents, its secularized madon-
nas, its portraits of women.[99]

This phenomenon may indicate a "keener appreciation of the values of
domestic life" related to the emergence of the conjugal family and reflected in the transformation of the Florentine "palaces" into a new
world of privacy.[100] Other lines of inquiry have considered from different points of view the representations of the madonna and child, not
only in Florence but throughout urban Italy in the period from the
fourteenth to the sixteenth century.[101]

One may ask what relation to reality these pictures and sculptures of
madonna and child bear. In general, they portray a large, sometimes
enormous, well-fed, chubby baby boy, usually nude and often active,
its masculinity displayed prominently (even if the genitals are sometimes lightly veiled over) in various positions of intimacy with its young,
beautiful, tender—if sometimes sad, and often adoring mother. He pulls
at her bosom or veil, snuggles against her, sucks vigorously, rests or
sleeps trustingly on her lap, and in dozens of playful ways and postures
reveals the close emotional bond between them.[102] Actually a child at
this age, about a year or so, was probably lying swaddled and immobile,
and often miserable and underfed, at the mercy of a wet-nurse miles
away from its mother. In the pictures, the child reigns supreme over the
mother, the sole object of her love and attention.

Could these religious pictures represent a secular fantasy of maternal
intimacy which the artists themselves probably never knew or could not
observe even in the infancy of their own children? Do they suggest an
attempt by adult males to blot out the deprivation suffered in the years
with the *balia* and to compensate for this loss by picturing in loving detail the various forms of intimacy between mother and child? And did
these pictures afford some emotional compensation for "the fellowship
in feeding" they could not or did not experience to the women whose
suckling babes were out of reach?

In Alberti's dialogue on the family, the characters, married and un-married, place upon the father the weight of responsibility for the up-bringing of children after infancy, "that tender age . . . more properly assigned to women's quiet care".[103] They debate the balance of paternal joys and sorrows and seem to ignore or denigrate the mother's role, stressing the father's love as "more unshakable, more constant, more vast, more complete" than any other.[104] Even they, however, reveal cer-tain circumstances which diminished his role and enhanced the mother's, such as his absences from home and his greater age.[105] Recent demo-graphic studies, especially of the Florentine area, have established sta-tistically a striking disparity in age between husband and wife and a consequent remoteness of the father from the child. Some social and cultural implications of the close proximity of mother and child have also been suggested.[106]

The relative closeness in age of the young mother to the child was often enhanced by frequent absences, even prolonged, of mercantile fathers, and by political exile following upon sudden reversal of party controls, such as the return of the Medici to Florence in 1434. San Bernardino sharply warns against the long absences of merchants and encourages wives to try to force them to return: "I'm not speaking of a week or two weeks or even a month . . . but to stay two years or three is not rational and hence displeasing to God."[107] Such practices, a nor-mal aspect of mercantile activity, were probably more disruptive of family life than political exile. Many young women of prominent fam-ilies, however, were made "widows" by the exile of their husbands. Vespasiano, the Florentine book-seller and biographer, pays tribute to some of these illustrious women, noting their careful administration of the household, their solicitude for their children; he admires especially those who, as real widows, remained celibate and devoted themselves wholly to their souls and their children.[108]

"Young widows" were, in fact, a common social phenomenon and concern for their welfare, fiscal and moral, and that of their children pervades many kinds of sources. The preacher-prophet of Florence, Savonarola (1452-1498), devotes a whole treatise to widowhood in which he analyzes the motives for remarrying or remaining chaste. He does not condemn those young widows who remained unmarried not for love of God but "rather for human reasons such as the love of their children", from whom they cannot bear to separate themselves.[109] San Antonino of Florence (1389-1459), in his letters of guidance to a young widow, urges her to try to be both father and mother to her children, "a father in punishing and training them, a mother in nourishing them, not with dainties or too many indulgences as do carnal mothers but not spiritual ones; for children need both bread and blows."[110] And San Bernardino, "let the widow learn to rear her family" and be especially watchful of daughters.[111]

Anxiety for the welfare of children whose widowed mothers remarry is expressed in many ways. Paolo da Certaldo urges fathers

> to avoid like fire leaving your goods and children only in the hands of your wife. . . . In many ways and for many reasons, it may happen that she'll leave your children and rob them of their patrimony or treat them badly or see someone else abuse them and remain silent. . . .[112]

The provisions of many wills contain a clause "if she remains a widow and lives with her children" qualifying legacies to daughters and wives.[113] In his history of his family, Morelli, abandoned at four by a "cruel mother", notes in every case whether a widow remarried or stayed with her children. He gives elaborate directions to his heirs how to ensure in their wills that the mother should not leave the offspring, listing several provisions which he grades in terms of the husband's confidence in his wife's devotion to their children.[114]

When the young Sienese notary Guidini fell under the influence of a holy woman and wished to leave the secular world, his mother urged him to marry, reproaching him:

> You will abandon me? I have no one left, my father is dead, and I have reared you with such labor, you who were left to me at twenty-eight months, and I never wished to remarry in order not to leave you![115]

Rucellai in his memoirs expresses profound gratitude to his remarkable mother who, being widowed at nineteen with four sons "did not choose to abandon us and put up a strong resistance to remarrying against the wishes of her brothers and mother . . . and she lived to be more than eighty which was the greatest consolation to me."[116]

Best known to us of all fifteenth-century widows is Alessandra Macinghi Strozzi, married at sixteen, who went into exile with her husband in 1434 with seven children. On his death in 1436 she returned to Florence with the bones of three, four living children, and one in the womb. In her letters to her older sons, exiled in their maturity, we see her shrewd administration of their patrimony, her solicitude for her daughters, and her love for the youngest son whose education she guided personally until at thirteen he was sent to Naples to join his brothers. She begged them not to give him blows but to use discretion with him and when he erred to reprove him gently for "he has a good nature" and "you will gain more in this way than by blows" [117] On his departure she wrote:

> Think how hard it is for me when I remember how I was left a young widow with five children, and small ones as you well know. And this Matteo was still in my body, and I have brought him up with me believing that nothing but death could take him from me.[118]

If young widows remarried, taking their dowries with them, as they had a legal right to do, the economic, as well as the emotional deprivation of the children might be serious.[119]

How well prepared was the child of about two years to face the second great adjustment, to his home and mother? Could he walk and talk, was he sturdy enough to face the new demands? We have little evidence. Barberino assumes that the *balia* will guide his first steps and words, after he is weaned at two years,[120] and two centuries later much the same advice is given by an Italian physician who believes in close supervision so that

> the health of the child will be easily safe-guarded until it comes to the age of two years or the age at which it is quite capable of walking, talking and eating on its own account.[121]

He advocates the use of a little "carriage" on wheels, or "walker", and a little chair with a hole for resting and evacuation.[122] Such equipment was probably provided by the parents after the child's return from the *balia*. The swaddling clothes have apparently been removed by this time.

The age between two and about seven was the period when the child of either sex must have known most closely the mother's care and developed its first emotional bond with her, a bond which might be enhanced by the youth of the mother, the age and absences of the father, or the widowhood of the mother. Perhaps the earlier deprivation suffered by both child and mother deepened this relationship and helps to explain the sustained devotion of many adult males to their mothers.[123] It is doubtful whether this period was at first one "full of delight and accompanied by general laughter at the child's first words", as Alberti suggests.[124] San Bernardino evokes a different kind of welcome when he attacks the odious "putting out" system: "and when he comes home to you, you say, 'I don't know whom you are like, certainly none of us!' "[125] But time tempered the strangeness on both sides, and San Bernardino shrewdly notes the different qualities with which a mother looks at her own children ("with the eye of the heart"), those of her neighbor ("with pleasant mien"), and those of her enemies ("with a stern eye and scowl").[126]

The predominant role of the mother is implicit in the treatise of the Dominican Giovanni Dominici (c. 1356 to c. 1420), himself the son of a widow, written for a lady who was "almost a widow", to advise her about the daily life of the child as well as its moral training: "one can effectively control children until they are grown up to about the age of twelve, then they begin to throw off the maternal yoke."[127] The mother should adorn the house with pictures and statues "pleasing to childhood", such as "a good representation of Jesus nursing, sleeping in

His mother's lap or standing courteously before Her", or one in which "he sees himself mirrored in the Holy Baptist . . . a little child who enters the desert, plays with birds" or "of Jesus and the Baptist pictured together. . . ."[128] She should dress both sexes simply, in decent attire and modest colors; "from three years on" the son is to

> know no distinction between male and female other than dress
> and hair. From then on let him be a stranger to being petted, em-
> braced and kissed by you until after the twenty-fifth year. Granted
> that there will not take place any thought or natural movement
> before the age of five . . . do not be less solicitous that he be
> chaste and modest always and, in every place, covered as modestly
> as if he were a girl.[129]

As for sleeping, she should not allow him after three years to "sleep on one bed or on one pillow with his sisters or romp too much with them during the day". Rear them separately if possible. "He should sleep clothed with a night shirt reaching below the knees. . . . Let not the mother nor the father, much less any other person, touch him."[130]

"Do not forbid them to play games. . . . Growing nature makes the child run and jump." As long as they play these simple games "you play with them and let them win". If they hurt one another, chide the wrongdoer but moderately so the injured one won't delight in revenge.[131]

To prepare them for adversity the mother should inure them to hardships, putting the boy to sleep sometimes dressed, "once a week on a couch, occasionally on a chest, and with the windows open", treating him "somewhat as if he were the son of a peasant." And "accustom them to eat bitter things, such as peachstones, horehound, strong herbs and fritters" and occasionally "certain harmless little remedies like purgatives" to prepare them for future sickness.[132] And in anticipation of poverty, "children should be accustomed to eat coarse food, to wear cheap and common clothing, to go on foot. . . ."[133]

From other kinds of sources it is clear that Dominici's prescriptions reflect religious attitudes and sexual fears more than the secular reality he observes and deplores:

> At present how much you work and strive to lead them about the
> whole day, to hug and kiss them, to sing them songs, to tell them
> foolish stories, to scare them with a dozen bogies, to deceive
> them, to play hide and seek with them and to take pains in mak-
> ing them beautiful, healthy, cheerful, laughing and wholly con-
> tent according to the sensual!"[134]

His advice raises many questions, few of which can be answered. How was it possible to separate boys and girls at such an age, to prevent them from seeing and touching one another as they romped in the confines of an urban house and courtyard? The everyday garment of both sexes in the early years seems to have been a short tunic of wool, loose or belted, with little underneath.[135]

Close relations between the sexes in childhood are evident in some sources, for example, in Morelli's account of trying to marry a young girl whom he had wanted for a wife from the time she was a tiny child.[136] Also, a member of the Valori family in 1452 chose as his wife the one of two sisters whom he knew well "because up to the age of twelve we had been brought up almost together."[137] A mixed group of lively children is pictured in a letter of Piero, age eight, to his father, Lorenzo de' Medici, in 1479:

> We are all well and studying. Giovanni [four] is beginning to spell. . . Giuliano [the baby] laughs and thinks of nothing else, Lucrezia [nine] sews, sings and reads. Maddalena [six] knocks her head against the wall. . . . Luisa [two] begins to say a few little words. Contessina [over a year] fills the house with her noise.[138]

Spontaneous play by young children is recognized as natural even by the austere Dominici who sees no good in toys, such as "little wooden horses, attractive cymbals, imitation birds, gilded drums, and a thousand different kinds of toys, all accustoming them to vanity".[139] In pictures of the period, little children playing spontaneously are most often shown in the persons of the Christ Child and little St. John, reaching out to each other, sometimes embracing, sometimes with a lamb, lively and responsive.[140] They are also represented in dozens of ways, singly, in two's and larger groups, as tiny "angel-children", called *putti* or *amorini*, usually winged, nude, appealing.[141] One of the most playful groups is that of the very young and chubby, winged male *amori* by Agostino di Duccio who are frantically engaged in a variety of activities on land and sea, shooting, boating, swimming on sea monsters, playing musical instruments.[142] More realistic, perhaps, is the representation of seven nude *putti* in a drawing by Raphael who are acting out with glee a specific game, "judge and prisoner".[143]

But all these *putti* are ideal, not real, infants inspired clearly by classical forms though doubtless influenced by observation of living children; their robust forms, angelic faces, fantastic activities, can hardly be considered as typical of actual children. And the same is true of the most famous examples of older children, some adolescent, on the two singers' pulpits created for the cathedral in Florence.[144] The grace and dignity of the classically clad, almost sexless children of Luca della Robbia in their dancing and music-making convey the character of a heavenly, not earthly, choir, though the faces may resemble those of Tuscan boys, then and now. And the almost Bacchic abandon of the winged wreath dancers in Donatello's frieze seems even more remote from the homes and streets of Italian cities.[145] What did these ideal children mean to those who created them or those who looked at them, children and adults? What were real children doing at these ages in the home, or school or shop? About the homely activities of the child, where and how he ate, slept, defecated, played, we know very little. Even surviving domestic architecture reveals little about the use of living space for intimate purposes.[146]

The moralists tell us little, the *ricordi* almost nothing. Paolo da Certaldo is succinct, as always: "Feed the boy well and dress him as well as you can, I mean in good taste and decently.... Dress the girl well but as for eating, it doesn't matter as long as it keeps her alive; don't let her get fat."[147]

And Dominici, with future poverty in mind:

Children should be accustomed to eat coarse food, to wear cheap and common clothes.... They should also learn to wait on themselves, and to use as little as possible the services of maid or servant, setting and clearing the table, dressing and undressing themselves, putting on their own shoes and clothes and so forth.[148]

Did children eat, standing up, scraps from the table, while serving or later? (Seated children are generally seen only in school-room scenes.) Filarete, the humanist-architect, writing in the 1460's about an "ideal school", warns that children should not eat too much; let them be given tough meat so they won't bolt their food, and, up to the age of twenty, stand to eat while one child reads aloud. They should not sleep more than six to eight hours.[149] If one may judge from the slender young children in the family portraits of the age, even the children of the rich were not over-fed; though well-formed they look less amply fed than the chubby babies or the plump *putti* of the artists.[150]

In general, the didactic treatises of the humanist educators, inspired by classical authorities, call for a regime of austerity tempered by reason and concern for the individual.[151] The most celebrated teacher of the age, Vittorino da Feltre (1378-1446), wrote no treatises but put the prevailing principles of classical-Christian education into effect in his boarding school for children of the ruling family of Mantua and other deserving children of varying ages, some as young as six or seven. "The Pleasant House" was governed by the ever-watchful ascetic eye of the celibate master who permitted no coddling in habits of eating, clothing or sleeping, obviously guided by sexual fears.[152] Few mothers of busy households could have supervised the daily habits of the children as effectively as Vittorino.

It has often been noted that Tuscan fathers dreaded the birth of daughters because of the steadily rising size of dowries and that many surplus girls were put early into nunneries.[153] The carnival song of the involuntary nuns frankly attacks the fathers responsible for their lot:

> It was not our intention
> to wear this black . . .
> we had little knowledge
> when we put on these robes
> but now that we're grown up
> we know our error . . .
> I curse my father
> who wanted me held here.[154]

Other sources offer evidence, however, of a wide range of attitudes towards having daughters and bringing them up. Obviously boys were considered more desirable. The barren wife of Datini, writing to console a friend who had just borne another girl, notes that

> the father is such a good and wise and reasonable man that he is fond of girls as well as of boys. However, it would be a great consolation for you to have boys so that the memory of your good name won't fade as soon as it will without sons, because, as you well know, girls do not make families but rather "unmake" them.

She sends along a small keg of malmsey wine from Venice, said to be good in "making" male children.[155] One of Datini's partners pokes fun at another who is moaning about having a girl child and doesn't want to see her, "though it's only one; think how he'll feel when he has four or six!"[156] Datini comforts another partner on the birth of a girl: "be of good cheer and don't worry about the dowry; if she's as pretty as her mother you can marry her off without a dowry, just as a gift!"[157]

A more affirmative attitude is shown by another associate of Datini:

> We have three girls and one boy . . . and Beatrice is pregnant and says it will be a girl. I'm counting on sharing with you, half and half, when I have enough. . . . By my faith, girls give me just as great pleasure as boys. May it please God to give your wife a half-dozen.[158]

In 1464 Rucellai at seventy speaks with pride of his "fine family, seven children, two sons and five daughters, all well married", but only a very rich man could have afforded that many dowries.[159] When a daughter was born to the poet Pietro Aretino he consoled himself by thinking how much more of a comfort she would be to him in his old age than a son who at twelve or so "begins to break away from the paternal yoke". And when the child at eleven was absent for a week he begged to have her back "because neither daughter without father nor father without daughter can be happy."[160]

The moralists give a grim picture of the home life of the little girl. Paolo da Certaldo urges parents to teach her all the house-hold tasks, to bake bread, wash the fowl, sift flour, cook and wash, make beds and spin and weave "French purses", and embroider in silk and cut out linen and woolen clothes and resole hose and all such things.[161]

San Bernardino is explicit about motive:

Make your daughter into a little drudge . . . oh, but there is a maid servant! This may be, but make her work not because there is need of it but to keep her busy. Make her tend the children, wash the swaddling bands and all else". If you do, "she won't wait at the windows or be giddy-pated."[162]

Above all, the mother must never leave the daughter alone, at home, in any room, or outside the house:

See that she may not know how to be without you . . . that she never has anything to do with pages or servants. Never trust her in the house of your kinsmen . . . . And see to it that they don't sleep with their own brothers when they have arrived at a certain age. Hardly trust her even to her own father, when she is of an age to take a husband.[163]

A member of the Alberti family speaks disparagingly of "the frivolous mannerisms, the habit of tossing the hands about, the chattering that some little girls do all day, in the house, at the door, and wherever they go."[164] Vespasiano repeats many of the usual admonitions and praises as a model for the upbringing of a young girl "the case of a child who was seldom seen either at the window or at the door".[165]

Such frequent references to doors and windows make clear that little girls, though restricted in their activities, resisted these efforts at segregation, clearly based on fears for their chastity, and saw quite a lot of what actually went on. It seems likely that any effective separation of boys and girls in the daytime did not begin until the boys went off to primary school. Paolo da Certaldo makes a sharp distinction at this time:

At six or seven put him to learn to read, and then set him either to study or to that craft he most enjoys. If the child is a girl, set her to cooking and not to reading for it isn't suitable for a girl to learn to read unless you want her to become a nun.[166]

One of the most vivid pictures of what a fortunate little girl's life might be like is contained in the Datini correspondence where we see the illegitimate child of a slave-girl being lovingly cared for and taught to read, dressed up and indulged by both parents and finally married off in style.[167] When she was brought home from the *balia* she found another child, Tina, the niece of Margherita, Datini's childless wife, who had been "borrowed" for long intervals from her parents, at first when only seven, "though it seemed hard to her mother." Her father wrote:

> We have laughed at your accounts of Tina's ways and manners
> and we think you and Margherita are beguiled by love of her. But
> if God and nature have made her pleasing, it's good. . . . [and on
> her return] You've made Tina so self-confident I don't wonder
> she likes someone who's dressed her up in such fine clothes, and
> she talks of nothing but going back to you.

During another long stay of Tina, now ten, with the Datinis, her father
wrote:

> It pleases me that Tina is eager to read. I beg you to correct and
> punish her for I think she needs it. And when she errs, remind her
> of her promises to me and tell her if I hear she disobeys in any
> way I'll come for her and bring her home on horse-back.

The parents had trouble in persuading the Datinis to return their child.[168]

The maternal pride, and feminine vanity, exhibited in "dressing up"
little girls (and boys) such as Ginevra and Tina was deplored by Dominici, especially since girls, "on account of their less perfect nature" are
all the more eager for such things.

> How much time is wasted in the frequent combing of children's
> hair; in keeping the hair blond if they are girls or perhaps having
> it curled! How much care is taken to teach them how to have a
> good time, to make courtesies and bows; how much inanity and
> expense in the making of embroidered bonnets, ornamented
> capes, fancy petticoats, carved cradles, little colored shoes and
> fine hose![169]

The relatively open life of girl children in the Datini household is a
far cry from the ideal prescribed by Dominici for both sexes, according
to which children were supposed to show the utmost humility and
reverence towards their parents and abject obedience to their will. One
cannot generalize from single cases but it is clear that there was often a
great discrepancy between theory and actuality. The rigid and austere
upbringing of girls in certain famous families of the fifteenth century,
so much admired, and doubtless exaggerated, by Vespasiano, contrasts
with the apparently easy-going regime of the Medici household in the
same period.

The idéal little girl of this period is well represented in a favorite religious theme, that of the young Virgin ascending the steps of the
Temple, innocent, beautiful, modest in her long robe, sometimes looking back trustingly towards her admiring mother and other adults below, sometimes a bit fearfully at the High Priest above waiting to receive her.[170] It was in this virginal state that parents were determined to
hand over their daughters of thirteen to sixteen years to their mature
bridegrooms, perhaps twice their age.

FROM FATHER TO MASTER: The Father's Role
DISCIPLINE AND INSTRUCTION

During the younger years of the child the father's responsibility seems to have been limited primarily to periods of illness and disaster except where the poor health of the mother or poverty made his attention indispensable.[171] One of the married Alberti family members speaks of the anguish of the father during the first period of life which "seems to be almost nothing but attacks of smallpox, measles, and rose rash. It is never free of stomach trouble, and there are always periods of debility."[172] These and dozens of other kinds of diseases of children are described in the Italian medical treatises of the sixteenth century but few are clearly identified in the sources. In the *ricordi* the fact of death is usually simply stated and dated by the father, especially with reference to cases of very early mortality at the home of the *balia*.

Morelli, in reviewing his own life, notes his "illness" at four years, "long serious illness" at seven, "smallpox" at nine, and a grave illness and fever at twelve.[173] He describes much more fully the mortal illness of his son, Alberto, in 1406:

He fell ill with a flow of blood from the nose. It happened . . . three times before we noticed that he had fever, and then Monday morning when he was at school, the fever seized him, the blood burst from his nose and stomach and body, and, as it pleased God, he lived sixteen days . . . in great torment and agony. . . .[174]

Further details of the child's suffering make it clear that Alberto's father rarely, if ever, left the child during this time; he includes his wife, however, in this account and in the description of their common grief that followed.

Strenuous efforts to keep alive a baby of six months, the illegitimate son of Datini, were made by his friends in Prato in communication with the father in Florence. The child, afflicted by "seizures", perhaps due to the "humidity", and fever, died after a few days despite the use of medicines, ointments and "incantations", the "beaver's fat" sent from Florence by his father arrived too late. He had been removed from the house of his *balia* so that he might receive better care.[175] Lapo Mazzei writes to Datini that he took his little son afflicted with epilepsy into his own bed with him.[176]

The harsh treatment received by the young Cardan from both parents perhaps intensified the night terrors and sweats from which he suffered, as well as the hallucinations he experienced from four to seven and found agreeable while resting in bed until his father permitted him to get up.[177] His treatment of his own children seems to have been little better; his older son was given out to a dissolute *balia* and barely survived the illnesses of his third and fourth years.[178]

Italian physicians were pioneers in writing treatises on the diseases of children, but their works were largely compendia of the medical lore of antiquity which was widely disseminated after the invention of printing.[179] Little clinical observation was included in the pediatric treatises of the sixteenth century.[180] Only two pediatric cases are given by the celebrated Ugo Benzi,[181] and only a few are noted by the eccentric physician, Cardan, in his autobiography.[182]

The mass death of children from the Black Death made a far deeper impression on parents and children than the occasional though frequent deaths attributed to the "Lord of giving and taking" and accepted as such. After the first impact in central Italy in 1348 the dread of its recurrence added to the other elements of insecurity in society. The diverse reactions to this mysterious visitation are well known from Boccaccio's *Decameron,* and his contemporaries shared in the resort to flight as the only recourse.[183]

Morelli in his *Ricordi* (1398-1421) includes a retrospective account of the first blow in 1348 but more illuminating are his dates of deaths in his family in the successive waves of 1363, 1374, 1400, his account of the family flight in a group of about twenty to Bologna in 1374 (when he was three), and his elaborate advice to his descendents as to how they should behave and respond to the danger in diet, medication, exercise and habits. Above all, "I encourage or recommend early flight", especially in the spring, and not to the country but to a city where good doctors and medicines are available. Take care of the children, don't economize at such a time, keep the family happy, lead a good life, drive out melancholy![184]

Many families followed his advice and that of Alberti: "The father should flee, the son should flee . . . all should flee, because there is no help against this great poison, this great curse, except flight."[185] In 1400, after participating in public penance and making his will, Datini set out with his wife, Ginevra, servants, partners and others, for Bologna where he stayed for fourteen months.[186] Rustichi in 1424 notes the death and burial of his first-born Lionardo, age seven, in a small town "to which I had fled with all my household."[187] Some stayed in town but moved from house to house, like Gregorio Dati who in 1420 moved his family three times but lost members of his ménage in each house, five children, a man-servant and a slave-girl.[188]

The poorer ones simply stayed at home, cared for their own, and accepted their fate, like Lapo Mazzei, the pious friend of the rich Datini:

I have seen my two sons, the older and the middle one die in my arms, in a few hours. God knows what my hopes were for the first, who was already a companion to me and a father with me to the others, and what progress he had made . . . and God knows how he never failed, night and morning, to say his prayers on his knees in his room . . . and how he behaved in the face of death, giving words of admonition . . . and preparing himself to obey what was asked of him. . . . And at the same time in one bed were Antonia sick unto death and the other boy who died. Think how my heart broke, seeing the little ones suffer and their mother not well or strong, and hearing the words of the older one. And to think of three dead![189]

How the children who survived reacted to the horror of death all around them we do not know. They must have been accustomed in general to the impact of death, and doubtless even the terrors of the plague were more tolerable if children were close to their parents. Pictures of the flight into Egypt of the Holy Family showing the close relationship of parents and child and tender solicitude for the infant at this fearful moment must have met an emotional need and perhaps strengthened the courage of parents not to abandon their dying infants as some did, according to Boccaccio.[190]

Another subject of particular meaning may have been the Slaughter of the Innocents, representing the mass death of infants mown down by ruthless soldiers. Especially realistic is the detail in one picture of a young blond mother clad in red, her arms raised in shock as she views her child of about a year, clad in a little blue tunic, lying bleeding to death, or dead, stretched out on her knees, while behind her the cruel slaughter goes on.[191] These pictures seem to represent the alternatives faced by parents, flight from an implacable foe or death.[192]

In theory the father was considered to be directly responsible for the son's education but even the members of the Alberti family agree that "if the father is not himself capable of teaching, or is too busy with more important tasks (if anything is more important than the care of one's children)," let him find a tutor.[193] Seven is often termed the suitable age at which to begin formal education but Palmieri, and similarly Rucellai, suggest starting earlier to teach the child his letters at home, making use of little devices such as forming letters in fruits and sweetmeats and giving them to him if he can recognize S, O, C and other letters.[194] Dominici also mentions the value of little inducements or rewards, such as new shoes, an inkstand, a slate and so on.[195] Vegio stresses parental responsibility in the early years of schooling, proposing the use of a relative or older brother as a mentor and the participation of the parents in hearing the child recite what he has supposedly learned.[196]

Most middle-class children first encountered formal instruction at the age of seven or earlier in the schools of the commune.[197] These "common schools" were deplored by Dominici as places where "a multitude of wicked, dissolute persons assemble, facile in evil or difficult to control"; all the parents could do was to fortify the child morally.[198] Vegio sees a positive advantage in sending the child out of the home for his schooling, among his peers and away from women and servants, but the parents should get to know the teachers, pay them well and beware of over-crowded classrooms and frequent changes of teachers.[199]

Some records of actual experience may prove useful. A succinct account of his education is given by a member of the Valori family of Florence, born 1354:

> In 1363, when the plague stopped, I Bartolomeo, was put to learn grammar at the school of Master Manovello and I stayed there up to 1367 through the month of May. And then in June of the same year I was put to learn abacus to know how to keep accounts, with Master Tomaso ... , and I stayed there up to February, 1368. And on the same day I was sent to the bank of Bernardo ....[200]

Though his schooling was delayed by the plague, this boy went through the three stages which were the normal progression in a mercantile society, learning to read, learning to do accounting and then apprenticeship in a bank or shop.

Morelli, without a father's guidance, went to school at five where he suffered "many blows and frights" in subjection to his master. At eight he was put under a master in the house whose discipline by day and night he found "displeasing to childish freedom". And at eleven to twelve after a severe case of smallpox, he suffered from a master of unusual harshness.[201] His little son, Alberto, was more precocious; at four he wanted to go to school, as six he knew "Donatus" (primary Latin grammar), and at eight the Psalter, at nine he studied Latin and learned to read mercantile letters.[202] The father reproaches himself bitterly after the child's death for having "worn him out at school and with many and frequent harsh blows."[203]

Antonio Rustichi recorded the early education of his sons as conscientiously as their births. He sent Lionardo at five and Stefano at four to primary school in 1422, changed them to a second master in 1423, and soon shifted to a master in the house, who was given his keep but "no salary, or shoes or clothes". The latter lasted only a few weeks, going off to Pisa to study. In 1425 Antonio sent Stefano (seven), and Marabottino (four) to a teacher at Or San Michele "to learn to read", adding a third son in 1427. But he shifted all three to another master in 1428 because the teacher "was not instructing them well". They were moved again "to learn to read" in 1431, and in 1432 sent to learn the abacus.[204] And so on. This over-burdened father clearly tried to find not only the most economical way of educating his sons, sending them in groups and experimenting with a house tutor, but was also determined that they should be well taught. The frequent changes of teachers recall the similar shifts of *balia*'s from which his children had suffered earlier.

Vegio's conventional humanistic pedagogy contains some elements drawn from his own experience as a child. His first school master was "harsh, rigid, wrathful" who from excessive diligence resorted too frequently to cruel punishments even when unnecessary. "He frightened me with threats, oppressed me with fear, drove me into isolation, never allowed my spirit to breathe." When the boy, not yet eleven, was by chance transferred to another master, humane and benevolent, "It was like liberation from prison", and it was a marvel how his spirit rose, how he gave himself up wholly to the study of literature and spontaneously undertook any task without compulsion. "So much it meant to me to have a master who was kind, gentle, inclined to praise and appreciate my intelligence as it really was."[205]

Another child in northern Italy, Jerome Cardan, had a wholly different education, one markedly out of the ordinary, as he recognizes:

> My father, in my earliest childhood, taught me the rudiments of arithmetic, and about that time made me acquainted with the arcana; whence he had come by this learning, I know not. This was about my ninth year. Shortly after, he instructed me in the elements of the astrology of Arabia, meanwhile trying to instill in me some system of memorizing. . . . After I was twelve years old he taught me the first six books of Euclid. . . . This is the knowledge I was able to acquire and learn without any elementary schooling, and without a knowledge of the Latin tongue.[206]

What discipline accompanied this home instruction by a father in his sixties we do not know for "when I was just seven years old . . . and really justly deserved an occasional whipping, they decided to refrain from this punishment." His father forced the child at seven to accompany him daily as his page "in spite of my tender age and frail little body." Only dysentery and fever spared him for a while but at ten he had to resume the role, a kind of apprenticeship, which most boys entered at about this age.[207]

The little Saint Augustine's first day in school, as painted by Benozzo Gozzoli (1420-c. 1497), epitomizes the momentous transference of authority and discipline from father to master. At the left stand the parents, the sad-eyed Monica lightly resting her left hand on the boy's head, the stern father raising his hands as if to project the child into the eager hands of the black-clad master who is about to seize the boy by the neck. The child, whose head is thus between three sets of hands, stands proudly, arms crossed, but fixes an uneasy eye, not on the master but on one of the big boys to the right, who holds a small bare-backed boy on his own back to receive the blows of a rod held aloft by another master, accompanied by a good little boy reading a book.

Within the arcaded, crowded schoolroom in the background, confusion reigns; some little faces look out curiously at the newcomer.[208] All of the elements of the schoolroom are here, with emphasis upon the rod, and this was advocated by the traditional moralists of our period although its use was to be seriously challenged by the humanist educators, as for example by Guarino of Verona (1434-1460), one of the most influential:

> The master must not be prone to flogging as an inducement to learning. It is an indignity to a free-born youth, and its infliction renders learning itself repulsive, and the mere dread of it provokes to unworthy evasions on the part of timorous boys. The scholar is thus morally and intellectually injured, the master is deceived, and the discipline altogether fails of its purpose. The habitual instrument of the teacher must be kindness, though punishment should be retained as it were in the background as a final resource.[209]

No scruples troubled the mind of the Dominican friar Dominici:

> Because of the need to hold in check this age inclined to evil and not to good, often take occasion to discipline the little children, but not severely. Frequent yet not severe whippings do them good.... Double the punishment if they deny or excuse their fault or if they do not submit to punishment.... And this should continue not only while they are three, four, or five years old but as long as they have need of it up to the age of twenty-five.[210]

The merchant-moralist Paolo of Certaldo understands better the relation of father and son:

> The man who does not correct his children does not love them. Therefore if you have sons always punish and admonish them, but moderately and in proportion to their fault.... Reprove another person gently and cautiously ... have regard to time and place, and do it without pride or anger. This does not apply to little children but to men and big boys who have outgrown childish punishments, that is, with whip or rod.[211]

As a penetrating study has pointed out, the pedagogy of the articulate Florentine "merchant-writers", based upon experience rather than theory, tended to coincide and interact with the ethic of the scholar-humanists in recognizing the individuality and dignity of the child, in stressing reason and persuasion rather than force as the most successful method, and in respecting the child's inclinations and aptitudes in selecting a vocation for him.[212]

Some fathers recognize the high spirits of school boys as natural. Lapo Mazzei writing to Datini about his son Piero:

I tell you it's more reasonable than not for boys, when they're real boys, to let off steam at school and to act a bit crazy at times. Don't you think that if you had to buy a colt, you'd sooner trust the advice of a simple man who had broken in fourteen of them, like me, than some wise-acre who's never had any?[213]

But it seems clear that both fear and blows often prevailed in the classroom. Petrarch's scathing comments on teacher and classroom together with the fresco of Saint Augustine's first day in school are probably more true to life than the relief symbolizing "grammar" of Luca della Robbia showing a benign master seated before two handsome docile boys with book in hand.[214]

How did a child react to such treatment? With fear and anger, as we have seen in some cases. But what could he do? One remarkable case of passive resistance is recorded by Morelli who tells how his father, a big boy of ten to twelve years when finally brought back from the *balia,* took care of himself:

Impelled by his good character he went to school of his own accord to learn to read and write. . . . When he had received many blows from his teacher he left and wouldn't go back. And so by himself, without any intermediary, he changed teachers many times and with some (as he later told his wife) he would make a bargain and get a promise not to be beaten. If the bargain was kept he stayed, if not, he departed.[215]

But even education in the harsh day schools of the commune did not mean total separation of the boy from his parents, sisters and brothers.[216] That generally came with the next stage, apprenticeship to a merchant, banker, sculptor, painter, goldsmith, or in rarer cases entrance into a grammar school for training as a notary or in preparation for entrance into a university.[217] This phase of development, from about ten or twelve years, marks the beginning of a new life for the child, one which led to early maturity and independence.

In summary, the life of the ordinary urban middle-class child in the period of the Renaissance seems to have been marked by a series of severe adjustments, both physical and emotional. The first and most significant of these was the almost immediate displacement of the infant from its mother's bosom to that of a *balia;* the second was the return of the young child, after some two years of absence, to a strange mother and an unknown home; the third was the projection of the boy of about seven into the classroom, and later the shop, and of the young girl at nine or ten into a nunnery or, often before sixteen, into marriage. These major displacements of the child might be supplemented by minor ones, of flight with one's family from the plague into another house, to

the country or to another city, or departure from the native city with
one's exiled father. Disturbing as these changes might be they did not
require separation of the child from the mother as did the first displacement or as the remarriage of the mother might do.

In the first period of its life the child, handed over to a surrogate,
was deprived of the love and care of both parents; in the next period he
was probably drawn most closely under the mother's wing; in the next
the boy came under the tutelage of the father and his surrogate, the
master, while the girl remained under the mother's close supervision until her fate was determined. The first stage seems to me the most crucial
and the least recognized or understood. It poses an historical question
of absorbing interest: how could the deprived and neglected infants of
the middle classes develop into the architects of a vigorous, productive
and creative era which we call "the Renaissance"? The enigma will
probably remain with us but at least we are asking new questions and
devising new methods of inquiry. It seems likely to me that the approach of the psychologist and psychoanalyst will prove most fruitful
in illuminating the long-range consequences of emotional deprivation.

For the social historian the best focus of attention may be the second stage, the young child's life from about two to about seven years
when circumstances forced upon him an extraordinary adjustment to a
strange environment. For this period a greater volume of positive evidence can be found through the use of unpublished materials and the
critical re-examination of what we already have at hand. Although the
walls of the *balia's* house will stand forever between us and the swaddled infant, perhaps we can learn how to look more sharply through the
doors and windows of the urban home and see the child in his intimate
activities and relationships. In our efforts we can make fuller use, among
other materials, of the vast resources left to us by Italian architects,
painters, sculptors and craftsmen whose work has rarely been subjected
to psychohistorical analysis.

REFERENCES

I wish to express my deep appreciation of the invaluable aid I have received from
Dr. Gino Corti of Florence in finding, transcribing and interpreting unpublished
materials in the libraries and archives of Tuscany, and also of the hospitality I received in September, 1972, at the Villa I Tatti, the Harvard University Center for
Italian Renaissance Studies in Florence, from the Director, Prof. Myron P. Gilmore, his wife, the Fellows and the staff.

1. See standard authorities, including George F. Still, *The History of Paediatrics*
   (London, 1931); Abt-Garrison, *History of Pediatrics* (Philadelphia, 1965);
   and Albrecht Peiper, *Chronik der Kinderheilkunde* (Leipzig, 1966).
2. *Soranus' Gynecology,* tr. Oswei Temkin (Baltimore, 1956); this is seldom if
   ever named but it is obviously a major source. See M. McLaughlin, "Survivors and Surrogates", in this volume, n. 42.

3. *Ibid.*, p. 90.
4. Francesco da Barberino (1264-1348), *Reggimento e costumi di donna*, ed. G. E. Sansoni (Turin, 1957), pp. 189-191 (here translated in prose).
5. According to Soranus (*Gynecology*, pp. 89-90), "for twenty days the maternal milk is in most cases unwholesome".
6. Paolo da Certaldo, *Libro di buoni costumi*, ed. A. Schiaffini (Florence, 1945), p. 233.
7. Soranus, *Gynecology*, p. 93.
8. San Bernardino of Siena (1380-1444), *Sermons*, selected and ed. Don N. Orlandi, tr. H. J. Robbins (Siena, 1920), pp. 89-90. There is no complete translation of the works of the saint. The best work in English is by Iris Origo, *The World of San Bernardino* (New York, 1962) rich in quotations from the sources and equipped with extensive bibliography.
9. *Maphei Vegii laudensis De educatione liberorum et eorum claris moribus libri sex*, ed. Sister M. W. Fanning and Sister A. S. Sullivan (Washington, D.C., 1933-1936), p. 23. No translation exists but for a study with copious paraphrasing, see Vincent J. Horkan, *Educational Theories and Principles of Maffeo Vegio* (Wash., D.C., 1953).
10. The influence of Plutarch's treatise on education, translated by Guarino of Verona in 1411, and of the recovery of the complete text of Quintilian's works a few years later, is discussed in the classic account of W. H. Woodward, *Vittorino da Feltre and Other Humanist Educators* (Cambridge, England, 1897; reprinted with an introduction by E. F. Rice, New York, 1970), pp. 25-27 and *passim*. Plutarch stresses the emotional benefits of maternal nursing, saying, "this fellowship in feeding is a bond that knits kindliness together"; see *Moralia*, with English translation by F. C. Babbitt (Loeb Classical Library, Cambridge, 1927), I, 15-17.
11. Leon Battista Alberti (1404-1472), *I libri della famiglia*, tr. by R. N. Watkins as *The Family in Renaissance Florence* (Columbia, South Carolina, 1969), pp. 51-54; Matteo Palmieri (1405-1475), *Della vita civile*, ed. F. Battaglia (Bologna, 1944), p. 13, who explicitly mentions "custom"; and, echoing them, the merchant-humanist Giovanni Rucellai (d. 1481), *Il Zibaldone Quaresimale*, ed. A. Perosa (London, 1960), I, 13.
12. This is clearly stated in an early life of the philosopher Marsiglio Ficino where it is said of his father that although he was poor "we must believe that he lived decently since he sent his children out of the house to be brought up by a *balia*"; quoted by Raymond Marcell, *Marsile Ficin (1433-1499)* (Paris, 1958), Appendix II, p. 694.
13. See Still, *Paediatrics*, Chapters IX-XVIII.
14. The most famous example is Alberti's treatise on the family. Among studies of Renaissance society see the various works of Gene Brucker of which the most recent is *Renaissance Florence* (New York, 1969); Lauro Martines, *The Social World of the Italian Humanists, 1390-1460* (Princeton, 1963) and *Violence and Civil Disorder in Italian Cities, 1200-1500*, ed. L. Martines (Berkeley, 1973), John Gage, *Life in Italy at the Time of the Medici* (London, 1968); and several works in the English series "Studies in Cultural History", ed. J. R. Hale, published by Batsford: John Larner, *Culture and Society in Italy, 1290-1420* (London, 1971), Peter Burke, *Culture and Society in Renaissance Italy, 1420-1540* (London, 1972), and Oliver Logan, *Culture and Society in Venice, 1470-1790* (London, 1972).
15. It is both explicit and implicit in many of the sources used in this essay, for example in Paolo da Certaldo's *Libro di buoni costumi*, in Donato Velluti, *La cronica domestica (1367-1370)*, ed. I. del Lungo and G. Volpi (Florence,

1914), and Giovanni di Pagolo Morelli (1371-1444), *Ricordi,* ed. Vittore Branca (2nd ed., Florence, 1969).

16. See, for example, the petition for tax relief in *The Society of Renaissance Florence: a Documentary Study,* ed. Gene Brucker (Harper Torchbooks, 1971), p. 19: "This is the cause of my family's poverty: the taxes and the babies which we have every year. My wife has no milk and we must hire a wet-nurse."

17. Paolo da Certaldo, *Libro,* p. 234.

18. Barberino, *Reggimento,* p. 195 (in these few lines I have preserved the "poetic" form).

19. "Life of Perino del Vaga". (See any complete text of *Le Vite* of Giorgio Vasari of which there are many editions and versions; no complete critical edition in English translation exists but for a good selection with fresh translation, see George Bull, *The Lives of the Artists,* Penguin Classics, 1965.)

20. Vegio, *De educatione,* p. 23.

21. Paolo, *Libro,* p. 234.

22. Barberino, *Reggimento,* p. 182.

23. Alberti, *The Family,* pp. 51-54.

24. On the problem of the use of domestic space, see Richard A. Goldthwaite, "The Florentine Palace as Domestic Architecture", *American Historical Review,* LXXII (1972), 977-1012; see also his *Private Wealth in Renaissance Florence: a Study of Four Families* (Princeton, 1968).

25. The diary of Antonio di Bernardo Rustichi (1412-1436), Florence, State Archives, *Carte Strozziane,* series II, vol. 11, folios 11 *recto* to 71 *verso passim.*

26. "Ricordi di Cristofano Guidini", *Archivio Storico Italiano,* tome IV (1843), vol. I, pp. 25-48, especially 40-47. The mother and six children died in the plague of 1390.

27. "Ricordi di Guido dell' Antella", *Archivio,* IV (1843), I, 15-18, concerning the years 1375-1380.

28. The diary of Messer Virgilio Adriani (1463-1492), Florence, State Archives, *Carte Strozziane,* series II, volume 21, folios 4 *recto,* 7 *verso,* 70 *recto.*

29. Guidini, "Ricordi", p. 40.

30. The diary of Giovanni di Messer Bernardo Buongirolamo, (1492-1507), Florence, State Archives, *Carte Strozziane,* series II, volume 23, folio 179 *verso.*

31. Vegio, *De educatione,* pp. 25-26.

32. Vasari, *Lives of the Artists,* tr. George Bull, pp. 285 and 326.

33. See the documents from various *ospedali* included by Ridolfo Livi in *La schiavitù domestica nei tempi di mezzo e nei moderni* (Padua, 1928), pp. 218 ff. For a unique account in English of slavery and its social implications see Iris Origo, "The Domestic Enemy: The Eastern Slaves in Tuscany in the Fourteenth and Fifteenth Centuries", *Speculum,* XXX (1955), 321-366; concerning the use of slaves as wet-nurses, especially pp. 346-348. The famous Ospedale degli Innocenti in Florence, designed by Brunelleschi (1377-1446), with medallions of swaddled babies on the loggia façade by Andrea della Robbia (1463), contains in its archives a detailed record of "Wet-nurses and babies" from 1445. It was founded by the silk guild in 1421 to receive "those who, against natural law, have been deserted by their fathers or their mothers, that is, infants, who in the vernacular are called *gittatelli"* (literally "castaways"); from a petition of 1421 quoted in Brucker, *Society,* pp. 92-93. See the valuable statistical study of Richard C. Trexler, "The Foundlings of Florence, 1395-1455", *History of Childhood Quarterly,* I (1973), 259-284, published too late to be made use of in this essay.

34. I have been unable to find evidence concerning the process of birth and the initial rites of bathing and salting. Barberino, like Soranus, emphasizes the shaping or molding of the infant's features and limbs in the interest of beauty; and he seems to imply that the *balia* is or may be identical with the midwife (pp. 183-186). The routine of bathing, in a round basin, is usually shown in Italian pictures of the Nativity in the fourteenth century (in which the child is also shown swaddled, in the crib in the background) but persists, I believe, only in the more elaborate scenes of the birth of the Virgin and of St. John in the fifteenth century. One of the most realistic scenes is that by Giovanni Pisano, a detail from the cathedral pulpit at Pisa, in the early fourteenth century, where the bathing is done by simply clad women, and the smiling young mother peeks at the swaddled infant.
35. Prato, State Archives, Datini 329 (*Carteggio di Prato: Lettere da Firenze,* 1390), 20 Jan. 1391.
36. Prato, State Archives, Datini 699 (Firenze, *Lettere da Prato,* 1395-1396), 4, 5, 8 August, 1396.
37. Alberti, *The Family,* p. 51.
38. Quoted from the Datini Archives by Iris Origo, *The Merchant of Prato* (London, 1957), pp. 200-201. Some 150,000 letters of Datini have survived.
39. Prato, State Archives, Datini 702 (Firenze, *Carteggio da Prato,* 1404-1408), 10, 16 May, 1407.
40. Barberino, *Reggimento,* pp. 191-192 (translated into prose).
41. "Canzona delle balie," no. XXIX of "Trionfi e canzone anonimi", *Canti carnascialeschi del Rinascimento,* ed. C. S. Singleton (Bari, 1936), p. 39.
42. Paolo da Certaldo, *Libro,* p. 234.
43. Quoted by Origo, *Merchant of Prato,* p. 213, from *Lettere di un notaro a un mercante del secolo XIV,* ed. C. Guasti (2 vols; Florence, 1880).
44. Guidini, "Ricordi", p. 44. Brucker, *Society* (p. 2) estimates the gold florin as worth about 75 *soldi* or 3¾ *lire* in 1400: "unskilled laborers earned 7-10 *soldi* per day; skilled craftsmen might receive as much as one *lira* for a day's work." The silver pound or *lira* was a money of account, not a coin; one *lira* = 20 *soldi;* one *soldo* = 12 *denari.*
45. *Memoirs of Benvenuto Cellini, a Florentine Artist, Written by Himself* (Everyman edition, 1907), p. 393.
46. Alberti, *The Family,* p. 123.
47. These are taken *passim* from his unpublished diary (see n. 25), folio 8 *recto* to folio 71 *verso,*
48. See "The Diary of Gregorio Dati" (1362-1435), ed. G. Brucker in *Two Memoirs of Renaissance Florence,* tr. J. Martines (Harper Torchbooks, 1967), pp. 107-141 *passim.* Brucker (p. 9) estimates the existence in Florence of over one hundred such private diaries written between the fourteenth and sixteenth centuries.
49. Guidini, "Ricordi", pp. 40-45.
50. *Jerome Cardan, The Book of My Life,* tr. from the Latin by Jean Stoner (New York, 1930), p. 9. "Isidore" was a friend of his father who was at that time engaged in burying three children dead of the plague in 1501; see Henry Morley, *Jerome Cardan: The Life of Girolamo Cardano of Milan* (2 vols; London, 1854), I, 1-16, which is based upon all of Cardan's works.
51. *Canti carnascialeschi,* no. XXIX, pp. 39-40.
52. The meaning is not clear.
53. The following excerpts are from *Canti,* no. XCIV, pp. 125-126. I am grateful to Dr. Gino Corti for helping me translate this difficult vernacular; any mistakes are my own.
54. A fine example of a wholly swaddled infant is the Christ Child held by the

Virgin in Mantegna's "Presentation in the Temple" (Berlin-Dahlem, Picture Gallery). Such a cloth is visible in all of the medallions by Andrea della Robbia on the façade of the loggia of the Ospedale degli Innocenti in Florence in which the babies drop their bands in successive stages.

55. Paolo, *Libro*, p. 126.
56. San Bernardino, *Sermons*, p. 122.
57. *Ibid.*, p. 47.
58. Barberino, *Reggimento*, pp. 183-184.
59. Prato, State Archives, Datini 1091 (Bellandi to Datini, 29 July 1390). No indication of the child's age is given.
60. As directed by Barberino, *Reggimento*, pp. 193-194.
61. As seen in Fra Angelico's "Flight into Egypt" (Florence, Museo San Marco) where a long red cloak lined with white fur is held around the swaddled child upright in Mary's arms.
62. Barberino, *Reggimento*, p. 192.
63. The diary of Paolo Sassetti (1365-1400), Florence, State Archives, *Carte Strozziane*, series II, vol. 4, folio 22 *verso*, 7 Sept. 1370.
64. Prato, State Archives, Datini 1109 (*Lettere di diversi*), 8 August 1395.
65. Morelli, *Ricordi*, pp. 144-146.
66. The diary of Virgilio Adriani (1463-1492), folio 70 *recto* (see n. 28).
67. A case has come to my attention, in the diary of Luca Panzano (Florence, State Archives, *Strozziane*, series II, volume 9, folio 22 *recto*) where he notes the birth of a male child to him by a servant of his brother, born 5 February 1423, baptized 7 February, given to a *balia* the same day, died 9 November at the *balia*'s; this child, however, lived nine months.
68. Barberino, *Reggimento*, p. 195, repeating the warning of Soranus, "lest unawares she roll over and cause it to be bruised or suffocated" (Soranus, *Gynecology*, p. 110). A child who slept by the side of his *balia* is noted by Velluti; *Cronica*, p. 310.
69. A rectangular cloth cradle suspended by four ropes from the ceiling over a bed is shown by Simone Martini of Siena (1284-1344) in a panel from a triptich in the Church of Sant' Agostino, Siena; an infant, pushed too violently in the cradle by a woman to the left, has been ejected onto the floor at the right, breaking one rope as he shot out. He was saved by the Blessed Agostino Novello.
70. Morelli, *Ricordi*, p. 452.
71. Marcel, *Marsile Ficin*, p. 128, n. 1.
72. Cellini, *Memoirs*, p. 393.
73. Francesca of Pistoia, pregnant by Jacopo, married Cecco; when she secretly gave birth to a healthy male child she threw him into the river. She confessed, was condemned as "a most cruel woman and murderess", was led through the streets with her dead child tied to her neck and burned to death in 1407 (Brucker, *Society*, pp. 146-147). See Richard C. Trexler, "Infanticide in Florence: New Sources and First Results," *History of Childhood Quarterly*, I (1973), 98-116, which appeared after this essay was completed.
74. The problem of defining accurately "the family", its size and composition in town and country, and its changing character in Italy at this time is part of the larger historical problem treated in *Household and Family in Past Time*, ed. Peter Laslett and Richard Wall (Cambridge, England, 1972). For Italy the great Florentine *catasto* of 1427, a complete census of persons and goods, has been subjected to analysis by computers and its social significance is now being examined in demographic studies. Of these only a few can be noted here: David Herlihy, "Vieillir à Florence au Quattrocento",

Annales: E.S.C., XXLV (1969), 1338-1352, and "Mapping Households in Medieval Italy", *Catholic Historical Review*, LVIII (1972), 1-24; Christiane Klapisch, "Household and Family in Tuscany in 1427", in *Household and Family*, ed. Laslett, pp. 267-281, and "La Famille rurale toscane au début du XV siècle", *Annales*, XXVII (1972), 873-901. It is clear that one must distinguish between "the household" and the "family nuclei" within it. Dr. Klapisch stresses the distinction between simple and multiple households, and notes that "in urban surrounding, at least in Florence, the proportion of multiple households increases markedly with wealth" ("Household", pp. 278-279). The standard work of Nino Tamassia, *La famiglia italiana nei secoli decimoquinto e decimosesto* (Milan, 1911), is still valuable though outdated.

75. Alberti, *The Family*, p. 80.
76. *Il libro di commercio dei Peruzzi*, ed. A. Sapori (Milan, 1934), p. 463.
77. Brucker, *Society*, p. 17.
78. Velluti, *Cronica*, p. 307.
79. Goldthwaite, *Private Wealth*, p. 123.
80. Ginevra Niccolini di Camugliano, *The Chronicles of a Florentine Family, 1200-1470* (London, 1933), pp. 110-138.
81. San Bernardino, *Sermons*, pp. 224-225.
82. Morelli, *Ricordi*, pp. 180-181
83. Dati, "Diary", ed. Brucker, p. 112.
84. Velluti, *Cronica*, pp. 147-150.
85. See Origo, "The Domestic Enemy", especially pp. 332-336; *Merchant of Prato*, pp. 192-199.
86. Origo, "The Domestic Enemy", pp. 337-340.
87. Alessandra Macinghi-Strozzi, *Lettere di una gentildonna fiorentina nel secolo XV ai figliuoli esuli*, ed. G. Guasti (Florence, 1877), pp. 443-445.
88. See Janet Ross, tr. and ed., *Lives of the Early Medici as Told in Their Correspondence* (London, 1910); Yvonne Maguire, *The Women of the Medici* (London, 1927), *passim*.
89. "Portrait of an Old Man and a Boy" by Domenico Ghirlandaio (1449-1494) (Paris, the Louvre).
90. See Raymond S. Stites with M. E. Stites and P Castiglione, *The Sublimations of Leonardo da Vinci* with a translation of the Codex Trivulzianus (Washington, D.C., 1970), chapter I, "Images from the Family Constellation." The authors tentatively identify the profiles with persons who formed the successive "families" of Leonardo, that of the mother who bore him out of wedlock, her husband and their children, with whom he lived until five; that of his paternal grandfather to whom he was transferred at five, including a young uncle, a grandmother and aunt; and that of his father in Florence, whose two young wives were known to him. The profiles by size and expression seem to reveal the boy's feelings towards the persons represented, ranging from love to hatred; they show his high evaluation of his own beauty and worth.
91. Morelli, *Ricordi*, pp. 142-160.
92. *Ibid.*, pp. 155, 202-203, 496-497.
93. *Ibid.*, pp. 167-172.
94. *Ibid.*, pp. 177-183.
95. *Ibid.*, pp. 203-205, 267-270.
96. *Ibid.*, pp. 217-218.
97. *Ibid.*, pp. 500-502.
98. *Ibid.*, pp. 513-516. For an illuminating study of Morelli as a writer see Christian Bec, *Les Marchands écrivains à Florence, 1375-1434* (Paris, 1967), pp. 53-75.

99. Goldthwaite, "The Florentine Palace", *A.H.R.*, 77 (1972), 1009.

100. *Ibid., passim.*

101. The origins and transmission from east to west of the iconography of these representations have been studied in many learned works, such as that of Victor Lazareff, "Studies in the Iconography of the Virgin", *The Art Bulletin*, XX (1938), 26-65, and Gertrude Schiller, *Iconography of Christian Art*, tr. Janet Seligman, vol. I (New York, 1971). Lasareff traces the Italian transformation of traditional Byzantine forms of "the Madonna nursing", "the Madonna playing with the Child" and other types, from conventionalized icon images into realistic genre-like pictures, especially from the time of Ambrogio Lorenzetti of Siena (d. 1348); see pp. 36, 42, 46, 64-65. From an anatomical point of view Thomas E. Cone has studied "Emerging Awareness of the Artist in the Proportions of the Human Infant", *Clinical Pediatrics*, I (1962), 176-184; he considers Fra Fillippo Lippi (c. 1406-1469) as the first to give accurate proportions to the infant Christ, with the head about one-quarter of the body length, rather than one-sixth as was customary (pp. 180-181). The significance of "the intimacy between the Virgin and Child in the Madonna of Humility" which "effects a like intimacy between the figures and the spectator" is examined by Millard Meiss in *Painting in Florence and Siena After the Black Death* (Princeton, 1951; Harper Torchbooks, 1964), pp. 143-156; he stresses the influence of Simone Martini (1284-1344). The erotic symbolism, at first latent and "innocent", in the postures and gestures of the Madonna and Child, which became increasingly overt in the early sixteenth century, has been analyzed by Leo Steinberg in several articles; see especially "The Metaphors of Life and Death in Michelangelo's *Pietà's*", in *Studies in Erotic Art*, ed. T. Bowie and C. Christensen (New York, 1970), pp. 231-285.

102. No single painter represented a greater variety of intimate mother-child relationships than the Venetian Giovanni Bellini (c. 1430-1516). Of perhaps comparable range are the sculptured reliefs in terra cotta of the della Robbias, Luca (c. 1400-1482) and Andrea (1435-1525), and the low reliefs in marble of Desiderio da Settignano (c. 1430-1464) and his peers. One of the most playful and joyous young mothers is seen in the Benois Madonna of Leonardo da Vinci (Leningrad, the Hermitage); her pleasure might be compared to a rare verbal expression of maternal delight in a new-born babe, that of Niccolò Machiavelli's wife in a letter of 1503 to her husband; see the Italian version in *'The Gentlest Art' in Renaissance Italy; an Anthology of Italian Letters, 1459-1600* (Cambridge, 1954), p. 36. The most joyous child I have found is in a terra cotta statue of Antonio Rossellino (1427-1478), "The Virgin with the Laughing Child" (London, Victoria and Albert Museum); the infant is chuckling all over with glee.

103. Alberti, *The Family*, p. 50.

104. *Ibid.*, p. 45.

105. *Ibid.*, pp. 114, 207.

106. See especially Herlihy, "Vieillir", *Annales*, XXIV, 1338-1352; also Klapisch, "Household", in *Household and Family*, p. 272; "The difference in age between spouses, which had a mean as high as thirteen years for all married persons, reached almost fifteen years amongst the most affluent."

107. San Bernardino, *Sermons*, pp. 134-135.

108. Vespasiano Bisticci (1421-1498), "Notizie di alcune illustri donne del secolo XV", *Archivio Storico Italiano*, tome IV (1843), volume I, pp. 439-451, *passim*. See also *The Vespasiano Memoirs*, tr. W. G. and E. Waters (London, 1926), issued as *Renaissance Princes, Popes and Prelates*, introd. by Myron P. Gilmore, in Harper Torchbooks, 1963, *passim*, especially pp. 439-462

concerning Alessandra de' Bardi.

109. Girolamo Savonarola, *Vita viduale* (Florence, 1496), chapter II, unpaginated. There is a French translation in *Oeuvres spirituelles,* ed. E. C. Bayonne (Paris, 1879-1880), vol. II, pp. 5-51, which I have not seen.
110. San Antonino of Florence (1389-1459), *Lettere,* ed. T. Corsetto (Florence, 1859), pp. 125-126.
111. San Bernardino, *Sermons,* p. 92.
112. Paolo, *Libro,* pp. 239-240.
113. See examples in Brucker, *Society,* pp. 49-52, 56-59.
114. Morelli, *Ricordi,* pp. 213-218.
115. Guidini, "Ricordi", p. 31. He obeyed her.
116. Rucellai, *Il Zibaldone,* p. 118.
117. Alessandra Strozzi, *Lettere,* pp. 85-86.
118. *Ibid.,* pp. 45-46.
119. As in the case of Morelli and his siblings.
120. Barberino, *Reggimento,* pp. 193-194.
121. Omnibonus Ferrarius, *De arte medica infantium* (Verona, 1577), selections translated by Still, *Paediatrics,* p. 151.
122. *Ibid.,* plates on pp. 152-153. Such a walker, without wheels, is shown in a picture, "The Holy Family" by Vincenzo Catena, Venetian (1470-1531), Dresden, Picture Gallery. One of the clearest pictures of an infant trying to walk, sustained by his mother, is in Luca Signorelli's "Madonna with St. John the Baptist and Prophets" (Florence, Uffizi).
123. There are many evidences of this fact in the *ricordi* of the merchants, for example of Rucellai, noted above. But Cellini makes almost no reference to his mother, and Cardan, an illegitimate child, suffered from a callous and cruel mother.
124. Alberti, *The Family,* p. 50.
125. San Bernardino, *Sermons,* p. 90.
126. *Ibid.,* p. 213.
127. Giovanni Dominici, *Regola del governo di cura familiare parte quarta,* tr. by A. B. Coté as *On the Education of Children* (Washington, D.C., 1927), p. 44. The lady's husband was in exile.
128. *Ibid.,* p. 34: He also suggests pictures of the Slaughter of the Innocents to inspire "fear of weapons and of armed men" and of Holy Virgins to inspire a love of virginity in the little girls.
129. *Ibid.,* p. 37. 41. Cardan as a young child slept between his mother and his cruel aunt, and had to be held down when he cried out in misery (*Life,* p. 24).
130. Dominici, *Regola,* p. 41.
131. *Ibid.,* p. 43.
132. *Ibid.,* p. 67.
133. *Ibid.,* p. 66.
134. *Ibid.,* p. 45. Concerning "bogies", Vegio warns against telling children horror stories which implanted great fears in him (*De educatione,* p. 32).
135. It can be observed more frequently in genre scenes, incidents in the lives of saints, scenes of accident and terror, and so on, than in formal portraits.
136. Morelli, *Ricordi,* p. 342.
137. The diary of Bartolomeo di Filippo . . . Valori, Florence, Bib. Naz., *MSS Panciatichi,* 134, folio 5 *recto.*
138. Ross, *Lives of the Early Medici,* p. 220.
139. Dominici, *Regola,* p. 45. But Datini "out of love" ordered a special tamborine made for the little girls in his house; see Prato, State Archives, Datini 329 (*Carteggio di Prato,* Lettere da Firenze), 20 Jan. 1391.
140. Of innumerable examples one with a lamb by Titian (c. 1477-1570) is es-

pecially natural, "Madonna and Child and the Infant Saint John in a Land-scape" (Wash., D.C., National Gallery of Art). A study of the transformation of the aged hermit of tradition into a child contemporary with the Christ Child, its iconographical origins and significance, has been made by Marilyn A. Lavin, "Giovanni Battista: a Study in Renaissance Symbolism", *The Art Bulletin* XXXVII (1955), pp. 85-101, supplemented by "Notes", *ibid.*, XLIII (1961), 319-326.

141. For an introduction to this artistic phenomenon see J. Kunstmann, *The Transformation of Eros,* tr. M. von Herzfeld and R. Gaze (Philadelphia, 1965).

142. In the "Capella dei Putti Giocanti", Tempio Malatestiano, Rimini, in panels of low marble relief.

143. *Old Master Drawings from Christ Church, Oxford,* ed. J. B. Shaw (Oxford, 1972), no. 60. c. 1507-08.

144. Both of these *cantorie* are now in the museum of the cathedral in Florence. For interpretations see Charles Seymour, *Sculpture in Italy, 1400-1500* (Pelican History of Art, Penguin Books, 1966), pp. 93-95; H. W. Janson, *The Sculpture of Donatello* (Princeton, 1963), pp. 119-129; Kunstmann, *Eros,* pp. 21-22.

145. On special occasions, however, such as the Lenten observances of 1495 and 1496, under the aegis of Savonarola, the choirs of boys, five to fifteen in age, clad in white, moved the on-lookers to tears because it seemed that "truly the choir was full of angels"; see Luca Landucci, *A Florentine Diary from 1450-1516,* tr. A. Jervis (London, 1927; reprint, New York, 1969), pp. 101-111. These children could also be used for direct action against sinners as in the bon-fires of vanities, inspired by Savonarola in 1497 (*ibid.,* pp. 130-131) or in anti-semitic acts inspired by a Franciscan preacher in 1488-1493 (see Brucker, *Society,* pp. 248-250).

146. See Goldthwaite, "The Florentine Palace", *A.H.R.,* 77 (1972), 1006-1009, who urges further study of inventories and decorative arts since surviving domestic architecture reveals little about the actual use of rooms. Genre scenes have been used effectively for this purpose by Iris Origo in *The Merchant of Prato,* Part II, chapters 4-7, and illustrations *passim.*

147. Paolo, *Libro,* p. 127.

148. Dominici, *Regola,* p. 66.

149. *Filarete's Treatise on Architecture,* tr. with introd. and notes by John R. Spencer (2 vols; Yale, 1965), I, 236-238.

150. Pictorial recognition of the small child as a distinct individual emerges in the fifteenth and sixteenth centuries and reaches its culmination in the work of Titian in the 1540's, most notably in the portrait of a little girl, age two, full-length, alone except for her dog ("Clarice Strozzi", Berlin, State Museum); the portrait of a twelve year old boy, alone, three-quarters length ("Ranuccio Farnese", Washington, D.C., National Gallery); and the recently discovered (1971) dual portrait of two little brothers, half-length, about seven and eight ("Princes of the Pesaro Family", England, private collection). "The passionate intensity of personality" displayed in the last is noted by its discoverer, Michael Jaffé, "Pesaro Family Portraits: Pordenone, Lotto and Titian", *Burlington Magazine,* CXIII (1971), 688. In personality these children appear more sharply defined than do the children in the great family portraits (by Titian, Veronese and others) of the age or in the dual portraits of mother and son, father and daughter, and other pairs, in which both in size and posture the children seem to be largely appurtenances of their parents. Interesting religious prototypes of the secular single portrait is the full-length sturdy and grave "Christ Child Blessing" by Mantegna (Washing-

ton, National Gallery), and the marble "Head of the Christ Child" by Desiderio da Settignano (Washington, National Gallery). A realistic secular portrait bust in terra cotta, "The Bust of a Boy" by Andrea della Robbia (Florence, National Museum), suggests a young Morelli, inquiring and wary. Perhaps the most elegant single portraits of children are those by Bronzino (1503-1572), of both sexes, mostly of noble families, including one of a smiling baby of less than two, deliberately shown to reveal two lower front teeth ("Don Garzia de' Medici with a gold-finch", Florence, Uffizi). See Michael Levey, *Painting at Court* (London, 1971), p. 105. In general, children in portraits are shown in a grave mood or only slightly smiling.

151. Woodward, *Humanist Educators*, pp. 179-250. The best modern collection of humanistic texts, whole or in part, with the original Latin and Italian translation, is that edited by Eugenio Garin, *Il pensiero pedagogico dell' umanesimo* (Florence, 1958), vol. II of *I classici della pedagogia italiana*.

152. Garin, *Pensiero*, includes contemporary letters and other testimonials which illuminate Vittorino's aims, methods and fears. See also the list of sources for his life in Woodward, *Humanist Educators*, pp. XXVII-XXVIII.

153. See the demographic study of Richard C. Trexler, "Le Célibat à la fin du Moyen Age: Les religieuses de Florence", *Annales, E.S.C.*, XXVII (1972), 1329-1350; the evidence reveals a great increase in the numbers of nuns in Florence in the fifteenth and early sixteenth centuries, coming largely from middle-class families of modest wealth. The fate of the girl child was apparently decided at about six years, largely on the basis of health and charm; at about nine the less favored entered the nunnery, at about thirteen she took the vows, and thus the transference of the child was effected before puberty (see especially pp. 1340-1344).

154. "Canzona della monache", No. XXXIII, in *Canti*, pp. 44-45.

155. Prato, State Archives, Datini 337 (Prato, *Lettere da Firenze*, 1398).

156. *Ibid.*, Datini 329 (Prato, *Lettere da Firenze*), 7 June 1390.

157. *Ibid.*, Datini 702 (Firenze, *Carteggio da Prato*, 1404-1408), 10 May 1407.

158. *Ibid.*, Datini 1098 (Letters . . . from Avignon), 12 Sept. 1395.

159. Rucellai, *Il Zibaldone*, p. 118.

160. Letters of Aretino, 1537 and 1348, in Butler, *The Gentlest Art*, pp. 48-50, in Italian.

161. Paolo, *Libro*, pp. 127-128.

162. San Bernardino, *Sermons*, p. 150.

163. *Ibid.*, p. 92.

164. Alberti, *The Family*, p. 217.

165. Vespasiano, *Renaissance Princes*, p. 449.

166. Paolo, *Libro*, pp. 126-127. It is clear, however, that many girls did learn to read and not always in nunneries.

167. See the lively account in Origo, *Merchant of Prato*, pp. 186-191.

168. Prato, State Archives, Datini 1103 (Letters of Niccolo Tecchini to Datini), 1392, 1393, 1395, *passim*.

169. Dominici, *Regola*, p. 45. Perhaps the sumptuary laws affecting women and girls above ten, in effect in Tuscany from 1373, encouraged this indulgence. A girl of ten was fined 14 lire in 1378 for "wearing a dress made of two pieces of silk with tassels and bound with various pieces of black leather" (Brucker, *Society*, pp. 179-181).

170. The presentation of the Virgin at the Temple is a favorite theme from Giotto to Titian and Tintoretto.

171. The notary Lapo Mazzei (*Lettere*, I, 206) sums up his plight in 1398: "I find myself with eight children to dress and to shoe and discipline without any servant, male or female, with a wife who is certainly carrying two in her

body and in poor health." He seems to have made shoes for the children (I, 202) and to have read to the little boys in the evening from "the book of St. Francis" (I, 233).

172. Alberti, *The Family*, p. 52.
173. Morelli, *Ricordi*, pp. 495-497.
174. *Ibid.*, p. 455.
175. Prato, State Archives, Datini, 695 (Firenze, *Lettere da Prato*), 6 letters from March 4-6, 1378.
176. Mazzei, *Lettere*, I, 433.
177. Cardan, *Life*, pp. 24, 147, 196. More material about his childhood is to be found in his *Opera omnia* (10 vols; Lyons, 1663).
178. See Morley, *Cardan*, II, 202-203, drawing from Cardan's *Uses of Adversity*.
179. Still, *Paediatrics*, pp. 58-66. The first such treatise to make its original appearance in print was by Paolo Bagellardo, in 1472.
180. *Ibid.*, pp. 179-180.
181. Dean P. Lockwood, *Ugo Benzi: Medieval Philosopher and Physician, 1376-1439* (Chicago, 1951), pp. 105-106, 309.
182. Cardan, *Life*, pp. 135-137, 173-176.
183. For a brief up-to-date account of the Black Death with good bibliography see Philip Ziegler, *The Black Death* (Penguin Books, 1970), especially chapter 3, "Italy". The mortality of children was greater than that of any group.
184. Morelli, *Ricordi*, pp. 293-302, a notable example of conscious effort to maintain an atmosphere of normal family life.
185. Alberti, *The Family*, pp. 126-127.
186. Origo, *Merchant of Prato*, pp. 317-324.
187. Rustichi, Diary, folio 11, *recto*.
188. Dati, "Diary", ed. Brucker, p. 132.
189. Mazzei, *Lettere*, I, 247-250. Antonia survived. Another moving incident is found in frescoes in the church of the small Tuscan town of San Giovanni Valdarno where a pious woman of seventy-five, Monna Tancia, saved her grandchild, whose parents had both died of the plague, by praying God to send milk to her breasts to nourish the infant girl; her prayers were answered and she suckled the child for many months.
190. Boccaccio, *The Decameron*, in "The First Day". See, for example, "The Flight into Egypt" of Vittore Carpaccio, Venetian (c. 1465-c. 1526) (Wash., D.C., National Gallery of Art) in which the haste of the father and the anxiety of the mother are apparent.
191. Fra Angelico (1400-c.1455), "The Slaughter of the Innocents" (Florence, Museo di San Marco). Behind her another mother tries to repel a soldier while a third screams as she recoils clutching her swaddled and dazed infant. San Antonino in a letter to a mourning mother says: "Who ever forbade a mother to bewail her child? She speaks according to the natural and sensual instinct"; he also urges concern for the soul of the child (*Lettere*, pp. 153-154).
192. Occasionally one sees expressions of fear and terror on the faces of children. In many scenes of the circumcision the child seems anxious and shrinking. In "The Feast of Herod" (Donatello, gilt bronze relief for the font of the Baptistry, Siena) two terrified children rushing from the scene turn their heads convulsively toward the head on the platter; in "The Profanation of the Host" (Paolo Ucello, 1397-1475, Urbino, Ducal Palace), detail of a predella, a small child looks but clings to his mother, while an older child puts his right hand to his eyes; in the vast scene of "Redeemer and Heresies" (Lorenzo Lotto, c. 1480-1556, Trescore, Bergamo, Oratorio Suardi) a terrified child in flight falls face downward but saves himself on his hands, next

to another running; in "The Liberation of a Child from the Devil" (Ambrogio Lorenzetti, altar panel of the miracles of San Nicola, Florence, Uffizi) the child is shown in terror as the Devil seizes him by the throat. Lotto is regarded by Bernard Berenson as a painter of profound psychological insight (*Lorenzo Lotto*, Phaidon, 1956, Introduction, pp. ix-xiii, p. 159).

193. Alberti, *The Family*, p. 68.
194. Palmieri, *Vita civile*, pp. 18-19; Rucellai, *Il Zibaldone*, p. 14.
195. Dominici, *Regola*, p. 35.
196. Vegio, *De educatione*, pp. 57-58.
197. Villani's statistics in 1338 are the basis of all later studies: in a population of c. 90,000 in Florence, about 8,000-10,000 children were being taught to read, about 1,000 to 1,200 were studying abacus and algorism in six schools, and c. 550 to 600 grammar and logic in four big schools; see Giovanni, Matteo and Filippo Villani, *Croniche*, lib. XI, cap. 94 (2 vols; Trieste, 1857-1858). See Bec, *Les Marchands écrivains*, pp. 383-415; this is a work of exceptional interest, drawing from many unpublished sources.
198. Dominici, *Regola*, p. 35; he adds that "you will place a boy in great danger if you send him to learn with religious or clerics", and warns also against having tutors.
199. Vegio, *De educatione*, pp. 54-62.
200. The diary of Bartolomeo di Nicolo ... Valori, Florence, Bib. Naz., *MSS Panciatichi*, 134, no. 1, 1380, folio 1 *recto*.
201. Morelli, *Ricordi*, pp. 195 196.
202. *Ibid.*, pp. 457, 505.
203. *Ibid.*, p. 501.
204. The diary of Rustichi, folios 32 *verso*-53 *recto passim*. Many contracts of fathers with teachers for the instruction of Venetian children are included in *Maestri, scuole e scolari in Venezia fino al 1500*, ed. Enrico Bertanza and G. della Santa (Venice, 1907).
205. Vegio, *De educatione*, p. 69. As an adolescent he received another kind of education when he and his school-mates were sent to witness an execution. At the warning words of the young thief on the scaffold, he trembled and shook as if in a violent storm; he could never forget the horror of the occasion (p. 116).
206. Cardan, *Life*, p. 142. "Arcana" refers to magic.
207. *Ibid.*, pp. 8-10. His contemporary, Cellini, was also taught by his father but only to play the flute which he detested (*Memoirs*, pp. 8-11).
208. In the church of Sant' Agostino, San Gimignano, one of a series devoted to the life of the saint. Rucellai, *Il Zibaldone*, p. 14, tells parents to order their sons to obey and follow the master, learning according to his will, not theirs, "for the master takes the place of the father for them, not in body, but in mind and manners."
209. From his treatise, *De ordine docendi et studendi*, tr. Woodward, *Humanist Educators*, p. 163. For similar opinions see *ibid.*, pp. 34, 103, 137, and Woodward's summary, pp. 204-207.
210. Dominici, *Regola*, pp. 48-49. He urges parents to induce their children to confess their faults to them. "When they are very small it would be wise to give them for penance a few nuts or figs or other fruit, so that they may willingly tell their faults ... afterwards change the fruit into real penance". From six to fourteen "ask them every day about the sins into which they may have fallen, as lies, swearing, deceit, and such like" so they will become accustomed to confess (p. 59).
211. Paolo da Certaldo, *Libro*, pp. 171-172, 177-178.
212. See Bec, *Les Marchands écrivains*, especially pp. 279-299. Even Dominici

recommends following the inclinations of the boy in choosing a vocation (p. 65).

213. Lapo Mazzei, *Lettere,* I, 225.

214. Petrarch's letter written to persuade a teacher to leave his task stresses the horrors of the classroom, the dust and noise, the screams, prayers and tears under the rod; *Le familiari,* Book XII, letter 3, ed. V. Rossi (4 vols: Florence, 1968), vol. III. A graphic enumeration of what naughty boys could do in the schoolroom is found in a curious sixteenth-century work by Tomaso Garzone, *La piazza universale di tutte le professioni del mondo* (Venice, 1616), folio 315 *recto.* The ideal scene, "grammar", is on a marble hexagonal relief made for the bell-tower of the cathedral in Florence, now in the Museo del Duomo. A convincing scene of instruction in arithmetic forms one of a vivid series of miniatures propounding problems in arithmetic, designed to present the subject in a pleasing as well as practical fashion, in a famous manuscript of 1492, *Trattato di aritmetica* by Filippo Calandri (Codice 2669, sec. XV, Biblioteca Riccardiana, Florence). In this problem, which concerns the master's income, he is seated, his rod with barbed thongs raised on high, teaching eight very small boys, all in colored jerkins and hose, seated on hard benches to right and left, calculating on their fingers, while a ninth sits alone in front, perhaps the object of recent punishment. This beautiful manuscript, dedicated to the twelve-year old Giuliano de' Medici, was issued in facsimile edition with introduction, transcription and glossary by Dr. Gino Arrighi in 1969, by the Cassa di Risparmio of Florence to which I express my appreciation for their generous gift of a copy of the two volumes.

215. Morelli, *Ricordi,* pp. 146-147; Morelli in general throws more responsibility upon the child for his own development than the humanist-educators do; see especially pp. 270-285.

216. Resident tutors, like resident *balie,* were sometimes used, especially in richer families, but seem to have often proved unsatisfactory to the parents if perhaps more humane to the children. In the family of Lorenzo de' Medici his humanist friend, Angelo Poliziano, tutor to the children, was ousted by his wife (see Ross, *Letters, passim*); in the Niccolini family the tutor of the younger children absconded with the breviary (see *The Chronicles of a Florentine Family,* pp. 330-331); in the Rustichi household the tutor went off to Pisa to study.

217. Material concerning mercantile apprenticeships can be found in the *ricordi* and in correspondence like that of Datini (see Origo, *Merchant of Prato,* especially in Part I). Vasari's *Lives* afford considerable evidence about the artist-apprentice.

CHAPTER 5

The Child as Beginning and End:[1] Fifteenth and Sixteenth Century English Childhood

M. J. TUCKER

"The child whom the father loves most dear
he does punish most tenderly in fear."

The medieval idea that children were not terribly important persisted into the fifteenth and sixteenth centuries. Nowhere is this attitude more evident than in the household proverbs on the lips of princes,
parsons, and poets. Children were equated to senile old men, foolish
women, and doddering drunks.[2] One proverb said: "For children and
women naturally are hard to keep counsel of that thing a man would
have kept secret (1525)."[3] To the sixteenth century children were no
better than churls, aged men, or women, for "all is lost that one gives
to four sorts of people. the first is a villain or churl, for again you shall
him prove unkind, the second a child, for his forgetful mind expells
kindness, the third a man in age, the fourth a woman variable as the
wind, being of her love unstable and fickle (1509)."[4] Even the Pastons
in their famous correspondence repeated the old saw that children
were about as trustworthy as a broken sword. Their language is picar-
esque: "A man should not trust on a broken sword, nor on a fool, nor
on a child, nor on a wraith, nor on a drunkard (1460)."[5] Again: "He is
a fool that agrees to the counsel of a child (1533)."[6]

Constant repetition of such notions must have added to the child's
feeling that it counted for little and that childhood was a state to be

endured rather than enjoyed. As parents and others measured them in their early years, hardly a kind word was spoken of them. Some placed them in the same unproductive categories as sad-eyed drunks, jabbering women, and foolish old men. Others said "Who sees a child sees nothing."[7] Such a view is best illustrated in Pynson's *The Kalendar of Shepherdes* where the ages of man are divided into twelve six-year periods corresponding to the twelve months of the year. The first period likened to January consists of man's first six years where he is "without wit, strength or cunning and may do nothing that profits (1506)."[8]

Before demonstrating that this view was in the process of being changed by new attitudes, let me define the limits of my inquiry. First, children will be considered from birth to age seven, Piaget's threshold of abstract reasoning. Second, chronologically speaking, the fifteenth and sixteenth centuries will be taken as 1399-1603 because these dates coincide with great dynastic changes in English history. Third, geographically and linguistically speaking, the inquiry will be confined to England; the continent, especially France, will be used only for comparison with England.

The sources used are primarily early printed books which deal with children, education, pediatrics, and parental attitudes.[9] The discussion divides naturally into the categories of physical care, education, religion, witchcraft, work and play. One must emphasize, however, before considering physical care, that the men and women of early modern times thought about children, if at all, in hierarchical terms. Children were at the bottom of the social scale. That children were human beings with human needs seldom entered their minds. If the child was noble, gender was the central focus. When the king, as in the case of Henry VIII, sought a son as a legitimate male heir, having a daughter was a national disaster, the frustration of a nation doomed to bend the knee to a woman. Henry VIII was so disappointed on the birth of Elizabeth, he didn't attend her christening. Moreover, he never had himself painted with her in a portrait, although one finds several portraits of him with his son Edward. Edward brought joy; Elizabeth grief. When her mother could not produce a healthy baby boy, Henry had her executed.

Even Elizabeth, succeeding her ill-fated sister Mary to the English throne, faced opposition because of her sex. With the failure of Mary before them, the wisest Englishmen recommended marriage. Woman, the weaker vessel, should be joined to the stronger, man. With what contemporaries thought good reason, the Scottish religious reformer, John Knox, thundered against *The Thieving and Monstrous Regiment of Women*. The Scots, of course, had beautiful, vain, capricious Mary Stuart, Elizabeth's second cousin, for a queen.[10] That Elizabeth did not end as her cousin, defeated, deposed, and deported, is a testament to her capacities and a triumph over her gender.[11]

What was perhaps worse than a woman for a ruler was a child. The childhood reigns of Richard II (d. 1399), Henry VI (d. 1471), and Edward V (d. 1483) proved disastrous. To the credulous they were confirmation of the biblical warning contained in Ecclesiastes 10:15: "Woe be unto thee, O thou land, whose King is but a child." Shakespeare used the theme in writing about Henry VI who inherited his crown at the age of nine months.[12] In a way, governance concentrated in a child's hands was an acceptable reason for subverting or challenging the normal line of succession. As Englishmen well knew, the long minority of a child king led to a situation where factions fought to see who would rule while the king was a child and to additional fighting when the king tried to wrest power from his council when he came into his majority.

Even kings, however, ultimately found themselves on the Day of Judgment held accountable before God for their life on Earth. They shared a common Christianity with their people, and if looked upon in life as a *pater patriae* to their people, they finally had a greater accountability because of their greater responsibility. Yet all were equal before the throne of God. Thomas More, Henry VIII's Chancellor, retells the episode where King David replies to his wife Mical who was criticizing him for dancing before the Ark of the Lord. "Thrice does More echo the blame David administered to his 'haughty and stupid wife' for not realizing that he danced 'before Yahweh,' in whose sight a crowned king is no greater than a child or a clown."[13]

While children were at the bottom of this scale there was a very real ambivalence about them. There was a tendency to treat them as neuter in some contexts, such as not recording sex in child burials in 14th century Italy.[14] The ambiguity extended to whether or not children were good or evil, and when to include or exclude them from adult society.

With the Christ child as the model, how could children be anything but innocent? They had no sexual desire; they did not know evil in adult ways. Scripture said that one must become as a child to enter the Kingdom of God. Even the depiction of the central drama in the Christian liturgy, Christ's passion, began with Christ's birth which became Prime, the first office in the *Opus Dei*. The fifteenth and sixteenth centuries were fascinated with the relationship of the child Jesus to His mother Mary.[15]

To be childlike was to be Christ-like. Christ with His sacrifice purchased paradise for His followers who were called the children of God. Christian believers were the children of light who warred against the children of darkness. The way of the child was the Way. As the prophet in Ecclesiastes observed, "better is a wise child than a foolish king." (Ecclesiastes 4:13). There was a certain innocence and perfection about all children. On the one hand, baptized children who died soon after the ceremony went immediately to Heaven; even the unbaptized only suffered a relatively mild imprisonment in Limbo. On the other hand, the most heinous crime in Christian history was King Herod's slaying of all the Bethlehem children up to the age of two as he ruthlessly attempted to slay the king of kings who would be greater than he and his seed.[16] Ever after, his crime was commemorated by the Christian Festival of Holy Innocents Day (December 28).

The folklore of the period recognized the innocence of children. The medieval bestiarist tells us that lions, unlike immoral men, do not attack innocents, including children.[17] White, the signification for innocence and purity, was most often appropriated by the child. When children died, white predominated at the funeral. The dead child was clothed in white, the casket was white, and the attendants were dressed in white. For example, in Cheshire "up to the middle of the last century, a child's coffin was carried by women dressed all in white who supported it by white napkins slung through the handles."[18] If the child were less than a month old, however, he was buried in the chrisom cloth, that is the cloth used at his baptism, and this was entwined with his swaddling bands.

Surprisingly, children were included in funeral processions. There was not the modern reluctance to shield children from death, and there was a stronger family solidarity in which it would have been inappropriate for them not to attend. Perhaps the most bizarre attendance of children at a funeral occurred "when in 1575 a woman was buried a month after giving birth to quadruplets, the four baby survivors were born to church after her."[20] The adult practice of embalming might sometimes be accorded an infant. The twenty-month old daughter of James VI of Scotland and his wife Anne of Denmark was embalmed in 1599.[21] Children even wore mourning clothes to funerals as late as 1686 and occasionally performed the role of chief mourner as did the eleven-year-old Lady Jane Grey at the funeral of Catherine Parr, Henry VIII's sixth wife.[22]

Children, in fact, were included in most ceremonies. The distinctions between adult and child were not made as today. Clearly there were certain activities denied them by their size, experience, and maturation. Until they reached puberty it was assumed that they were innocents without sexual appetite. I have not yet found any English equivalents to the sexual activities surrounding little Louis XIII (1599-1643) which Héroard records. Certainly fifteenth and sixteenth century English people recognized physical functions. Perhaps they thought it unimportant to report on such matters as childhood masturbation. Nonetheless, they sometimes saw children, if mostly asexual, as agents of evil. For example, they probably shared with Burgundian artists the notion that children stoned Christ as he bore his cross to Calvary.[23] What an ultimate insult to the Savior, that he should be rejected by children, who occupied the lowest rung on the social ladder.

Children, of course, were considered unclean before Baptism. Should they die before Baptism they could never enter into Christ's Kingdom. Common folklore likened new-born children to the offspring of animals and birds. The bestiarist saw that:

> The children of all birds are called 'Pulli' or poults. However, the offspring of four-footed beasts are also called 'pulli' and a baby boy is called 'pullus' too. In fact, all recently born creatures are called 'pulli,' because they are born dirty or polluted. Whence our dirty clothes are also called 'pulla.'[24]

But children increasingly were becoming a delight. Child angels often decorated the fringes of frescoes. When wretched, despondent Queen Mary (d. 1558) lay on her death bed; she comforted her attendants by telling them "what good dreams she had, seeing many little children like Angels play before her, singing pleasing notes. Music and little children—she had loved both during her life, and now, instead of anxieties, sorrows, and uncertainties, her dreams were full of these."[25]

Indeed, children to some became a sign of good luck. F. R. H. Du Boulay cites the example of Reynold Peckham, a childless widower, who wanted images of children placed on his gravestone. Before his death in 1523 he instructed in his will "that mine executors shall provide a fair stone with the pictures of a man and of a woman and of children therein set of latten, and it to be laid over and upon my grave within the space of six weeks next immediately after my decease."[26]

Du Boulay cites this evidence to infer that the sixteenth-century English placed a high value on children.[27] Furthermore, he sets his view of children in the historical context of later medieval England. He argues from economic evidence that the economics of an English recovery stimulated an interest in children.[28] Further he suggests that changed economics was at the heart of changed attitudes. With more money in the purse, men and women cast about for ways to spend it. They invested it in larger homes,[29] with additional rooms for privacy, in portraits of themselves and their families, and in their children via education and clothing. The surplus of money made it possible to use children as objects of conspicuous consumption. Noting these changed circumstances, let us turn to the physical care which early modern children received.

PHYSICAL CARE OF CHILDREN

Ever since Eve women have risked their lives to have children. Truly, as John Donne, the 17th century Dean of St. Paul's, said, the woman's womb was the "house of death." Death could strike the mother as easily as the child. Mortality for infants and women in labor was extremely high. Yet, propelled by a primitive urge and enjoined by the Biblical "Be fruitful and multiply," women have stoically accepted their lot. In fact, many like Rachel wept for children never born and told their husbands as she did Jacob, "Give me children, or else I die."[30]

Biblical mothers like Rachel, the Virgin Mary, and the Holy Elizabeth became models in an age saturated with belief in the Christmas story. The artist's madonna and child conveyed the message of Mary's love for her Son and His love for her. Even in His torment on the cross, Christ remembered His mother. Seeing His mother and the disciple whom He loved, "He saith unto His mother, 'Woman behold thy son'! Then saith He to the disciple. 'Behold thy mother!' And from that hour that disciple took her unto his own home." (John, 19:26-27).

Though the emphasis in this period may seem to be more on the child's obligation to his parents than on the parent's responsibility to the child, a child's survival then, as now, depended on the kind of physical care which he or she received. This section deals with physical care and continues the exploration of the biblical, pro9verial, and hierarchical context set forth in the introduction.

My intention is to treat the changing view of children and then to examine in detail pregnant women, deliveries, swaddling, feeding, and growth. As is usually the case, the evidence is over-weighted towards royalty and aristocracy. Most of what is said applies only to them. They were the ones who read the new manuals about child care, for only they could afford them. For the most part, how the cottar's son or weaver's daughter entered the world has not been recorded, and so we may only speculate on the differences between attendances at lyings-in at tapestry-hanged palaces and dirt-stained hovels.

Clearly children were becoming important enough to write about. The observation of physiological change in children, as in adults, became more scientific as doctors actually looked at their patients. The first English book on pediatrics was published in 1545. The author, the physician Thomas Phayre (variously spelt Phayer and Phayr) titled his work *The Regiment of Life, whereunto is added a treatise of pestilence, with the boke of children* (London, 1545).[31] Phayre's work was not entirely original. He drew on such continental authors as Jehan Goeurot and cited the ancient guides of Galen and Pliny. He treated such childhood diseases as colic, canker, and bleeding teeth. His attitude may

roughly be characterized as pseudoscientific and he partook of that enthusiasm for systematization that had resulted in the creation in 1518
of the Royal College of Physicians in London sponsored by Henry
VIII's personal physician Thomas Linacre.[32]

Of course, Phayre's book was not the first European work on pediatrics. One earlier book was Paolo Bagellardo's *De egritudinibus et
remediis infantium*, Patavia, 1498 and the first poem on pediatrics occurred in Heinrich von Louffenberg *Versehung des Liebs*, Augsburg,
1458. The first European notice of jaundice in newborn was found in
Bartholomaeus Metlinger, *Regiment der jungen Kinder*, Augsburg, 1473.
His work, like Bagellardo's was derived from Arabian physicians. In fact,
the work of Rhazes who lived during the ninth and tenth centuries
(850-923) was printed in Latin in 1481. (*De curis puerorum in prima
aetate*, Mediolani, 1481). Rhazes' work is generally considered to be
the first devoted entirely to children's diseases.[33]

One detects an interesting attitude in Dr. Phayre. He announced his
purpose as "here to do them good that have most need, that is to say
children." Further, he wanted to make available to the unlearned, un-
sophisticated medical practitioners "part of the treasure that is in other
languages." Hence his reliance on the ancients, the Arabians, and contemporary European medical works. To this lore he added the benefit
of his own experience.[34] Although Phayre did not explain his motivations it is evident that he thought pediatrics a fertile new medical field
and that children seemed deserving enough to receive careful medical
attention.

Treatises such as *The Byrth of Mankynde* substantiate the latter in-
ference. The work, a translation of Eucharius Roesslin from the Latin by
Richard Jonas, was dedicated to Henry VIII's ill-fated fifth wife Katherine Howard and in a more universal sense to all women "which sustain
for the time so great dolor and pain for the birth of mankind and deliverance of the same into the world."[35] A later edition contained illustrations of the various fetal positions and also the famous three-
legged birthing stool akin to a milking stool with a horseshoe sitting surface and straps to contain the woman in labor.[36]

Despite the birth of modern pediatrics, superstition was not dead.
For example, pregnant women sought charms such as eagle stones to
insure a safe delivery. Eagle stones, which sometimes varied in color,
were hollow stones with pieces inside that rattled; the Greeks originally
named them for the eagle who brought them to her nest to help her lay
her eggs. Pliny spoke of them as early as 79 A.D. The 17th century
canon of Canterbury, Dr. John Bargrave, wrote a description of one
in 1662:[37]

This is a kind of rough, dark, sandy colour and about the bigness of [a] good walnut. It is rare and of good value, because of its excellent qualities and use, which is, by applying it to childbearing women, and to keep them from miscarriage... It is so useful that my wife can seldom keep it at home, and therefore she has sewed the strings to the knit purse in which the stone is, for the convenience of the tying of it to the patient on occasion; and has a box she has to put the purse and stone in.[38]

Henry VIII's second wife Anne Boleyn wore one during her confinement; her solicitous and superstitious spouse provided it. Generally it was tied to the left wrist for the term of pregnancy. Medieval women also believed that if they wore a lace girdle similar to the smock worn by the Blessed Virgin that they would have an easy delivery. Generally they wore current fashions somewhat more loosely.[39]

Naturally, pregnant women had to take special precautions in their condition. For example, the pregnant Anne Boleyn did not take part in the impromptu festivities decreed by Henry VIII on the death of his first wife Catherine of Aragon in January 1536. Anne dared not risk dancing. Her precautions were for nought, however; she miscarried of a boy baby on January 29. Six days earlier she had swooned on learning that Henry's mailed horse had fallen on top of him. Though she was put to bed immediately, she could not keep her baby. The baby's death sealed hers, and she was executed in May.[40]

If Anne Boleyn avoided exercise to no avail, the usual regimen was to advise it. For example, Plato was approvingly cited by Peter de la Primadaye, gentleman of the chamber to the French king Henry III (d. 1589). Primadaye saw Plato as advising "that the husband and wife that are desirous of children should keep themselves from drunkenness, and from entering into the bed when they are choleric and full of trouble, because that many times is the cause of vices in children. Next he requires that great bellied women should give themselves to walking, and beware of living either too delicately, or too sparingly: that they should have quiet minds, with many other things, which he alleges to that purpose. He says also, that children being in their mother's womb, receive good and ill, as the fruits of the earth do."[41]

As the lying-in approached, women braced themselves for their bout with destiny. If no mischance happened at the birth, the dreaded puerperal fever or septicemia still might carry them off. Three Tudor queens succumbed to the latter. Nine days after being delivered of a baby girl, Henry VII's wife Elizabeth Plantagenet died. So did the child. Jane Seymour, Henry VIII's third wife, fell fictim to it twelve days after successfully delivering a male heir, Edward, the future Edward VI. Henry's sixth wife, Catherine Parr, died in childbed delivering a baby girl.

Erasmus (d. 1536), the noted humanist, tells in his *Seven Dialogues Both 'Pithie and Profitable* about a superstitious custom concerning the lying-in. His two characters Entrapilus and Fabulla are talking about a woman in childbed. Entrapilus, walking by several houses, saw one with "the crow on the ring of the door bound about with a white linen cloth, and I marvelled what the reason of it should be." To which Fabulla replied: "It is a sign that there is a woman lying-in where that is."[42] White, the symbol of purity, innocence, holiness—perhaps protection too.

Consolation was found in the example of Christ's birth. He became Man, and His mother bore Him in exactly the same manner in which all children were born. As Frances Quarles noted in his sentimental seventeenth-century poem, Christ inhabited four houses:

> His first house was the blessed Virgin's *Wombe;* The next, a *Cratch;* the third, a *Cross;* the fourth, a *Tomb.*[43]

Christ became the epitome for the journey of life from womb to tomb. Quarles continued his observations in his poem "On the Infancy of Our Saviour":

> Hail blessed *Virgin,* full of heavenly *Grace,*
> Blest above all that sprang from human race;
> Whose Heav'n saluted *Womb* brought forth in *One,*
> A blessed *Saviour,* and a blessed *Son:*
> O! what a ravishmen't had been, to see
> Thy little *Saviour* perking on thy Knee!
> To see him nuzzle in thy *Virgin* Breast;
> His milk white body all unclad, undressed!
> To see thy busy fingers clothe and wrap
> His spradling Limbs in thy indulgent *Lap!*
> To see his desp'rate *Eyes,* with Childish grace,
> Smiling upon his smiling Mother's face!
> And, when his forward strength began to bloom,
> To see him *dlddle* up and down the Room!
> O, who would think so sweet a *Babe* as this,
> Should ere be slain by a false hearted *Kiss!*
> Had I a *Rag,* if sure thy body wore it,
> Pardon sweet *Babe,* I think I should adore it;
> Till then, O grant this Boon, (a boon far dearer)
> The *Weed* not being, I may adore the *Wearer.*[44]

Christ's mother Mary bore him in a stable with few preparations. Generally there were elaborate arrangements made for the birth of royal children. For example, when in September 1486 Elizabeth Plantagenet, Henry VII's wife, awaited the birth of her first child, Arthur, her chamber was hung with rich tapestry, but this must not have "imagery," which was considered unsuitable for women in childbirth.[45] She may have worn velvet and ermine, for there is a reference in the household accounts to apparel "For the Queen . . . 1 round Mantle, velvet plain, furred through with fine ermine . . . for the Queen to wear about her in her closet and all other things necessary for the same."[46] On the other hand, Queen Jane Seymour is described at her lying-in as "She reclined, propped up with fair cushions of crimson damask with gold, and was wrapped about with a round mantle of crimson velvet furred with ermine."[47] Ermine, of course, was much favored by royalty and affected by Queen Elizabeth I who associated it with purity and virginity.

No male attendants were allowed at a lying-in. When Margaret of Anjou, Henry VI's Queen, had her confinement in 1442, all men were excluded. The order was set that ". . . in the second chamber, (a secret oratory for divers matters) must be a traverse which shall never be but drawn until she be purified. . . . After that traverse there may not openly no man officer or other come there nearer than the outer chamber. . . . Instead of men officers must be gentlewomen. . . ."[48]

Not until mid-sixteenth century did men make their way into the delivery room. Until then there were severe penalties for any male who attempted to view a birth. Perhaps the most celebrated example is that of Dr. Wertt of Hamburg.

> Wertt realized that he could only study the process of birth at an actual labour, and knew that as a man he would never be admitted to a lying-in room. He dressed himself as a woman and went boldly in to the next confinement in the district. This was in 1522. For a brief while all went well, then somehow or other one of the midwives realized that he was a man masquerading in a woman's garments. The mere idea of a male being present at a confinement raised a storm of protest. Punishment was swift and salutary. Wertt was burned to death. Other physicians watched him die and realized then, if they had not done so before, that midwifery was a woman's art still protected by every possible taboo. The only men who dared even discuss the subject were cloistered and celibate clerics, for their motives only could be deemed pure. Only one other group of men had been known to enter a lying-in chamber. Martin Luther told the story of an Empress of Germany whose labour was slow and protracted. It was still generally accepted that any procedure which frightened the mother might accelerate labour. Some authorities held that whipping the mother would cause fear and distress and so promote the expulsion of the foetus. Whipping the Empress was out of the question. The alternative was simple. Twenty-four men were brought in succession into the imperial lying-in chamber and flogged. Two of them died as a result and the labour continued still slow and protracted.[49]

Nonetheless, male astrologers were sometimes in attendance for the express purpose of casting the new born babe's horoscope.[50]

As the medical advances of such men as the German Eucharius Rösslin and the Frenchman Ambroise Paré became more widely disseminated, the taboo against male midwives was relaxed. Both assisted at deliveries.[51] The work of Rösslin was made available to the English through the verbatim translation by Richard Jones, and became a sixteenth-century bestseller. Paré's work, of course, would be available to the educated English who read French.[52] Undoubtedly the invention of forceps and their use by the Chamberlain family in the seventeenth century sped the process by which males were allowed to assist at births.[53]

Medieval women were usually delivered on a straw mattress, naked.[54] Sometimes a birthing stool was used, depending on the difficulty of delivery. The first English midwife of record was Margaret Cobbe, the midwife to Queen Elizabeth Woodville at her delivery of Edward V. Most women had midwives who took a special oath and were licensed by the local bishop. Edmund Bonner, the Bishop of London, is supposed to have been the first bishop to require such licensing. The reason was obvious; sometimes it was urgently necessary to baptize a failing child. The Archbishop of York ordered: *"Item:* All curates must openly in the Church teach and instruct the midwives of the very words and form of baptism."[55]

Baptism, however, was generally a solemn occasion ordinarily occurring two or three days after birth. Salt would be put into the child's mouth to signify the gift of heavenly wisdom from the Holy Ghost. The child would also be annointed with oil on the forehead, ears, and nose. This symbolizes the Holy Ghost's protection and recalled Christ's healing of the deaf.[56]

Babies were given popular saints' names and sometimes such holy names as Pentecost and Baptist.[57] The tendency was to repeat such names as John, Thomas, William, Edward, Anne, Elizabeth, and Margaret. If one examines the names of the royal family in this period, one sees the popularity of Edward and Henry for males. Two kings, Edward IV and Edward V had that name and three Henrys: Henry VI, Henry VII, and Henry VIII. The most popular woman's name was Elizabeth, with Margaret, Mary and Catherine also favored. Henry's first born son was named Henry, but the child lived less than two months. His bastard son by Elizabeth Blount was also named Henry, but he died at the age of 17 in 1536. Perhaps to change his luck Henry named his son by Jane Seymour Edward, after his Plantagenet grandfather Edward IV.[58] Edward's birth was at Hampton Court via natural delivery, not Caesarian as sometimes erroneously reported;[59] it quickened the pulse of both Henry VIII and his nation. The child was indisputably legitimate and there was now no bastard son to challenge his right. His two sisters yielded to his superior male right of inheritance.

The news of the birth of a prince was received with great rejoicing and festivities throughout the realm, but particularly in London where the bells were rung, 2000 salvos were fired from the Tower, and a high mass was sung at St. Paul's, while ale and wine flowed in the streets for all to take. Plans were at once drawn, in which the King played an active role, for the christening of the infant on the third day after birth, a proclamation being issued dated October 12th, which sternly forbad access to the court on the baptismal date because of the plague still epidemic in London.... The protocols established for such functions by Margaret Beaufort were followed, requiring the Queen to receive perhaps as many as 400 guests while she was seated with the King on a state pallet, and then to observe the procession of the great clergy, the Council, and the nobels, in that order, as the company moved into the chapel where Cranmer performed the baptism. Edward was carried by the Marchioness of Exeter and the train of his robe by the Earl of Arundel, while Cranmer and Norfolk were godfathers at the font and Suffolk at the confirmation. Queen Jane, through this long ordeal, appeared reasonably well, but three days later she was ill with a very high fever, delirium, and a state of collapse which were the certain symptoms of almost invariable fatal puerperal fever.... At just before midnight on October 24th the Queen was dead.[60]

The King, shaken by the death of the Prince's mother, personally prescribed almost clinical orders for the protection of the child in his various nurseries. Scrupulous cleanliness was to be observed; the premises were to be scrubbed and swept twice daily; no outsider was to have physical contact with the baby; and every article used by him was to be washed immediately. Henry lavished an almost pathetic personal affection on the child, visiting him at Hampton Court, bringing him to Greenwich for his first Christmas, and then in May, 1538, to the royal hunting lodge at Royston, playing with "much mirth and joy, dallying with him in his arms a long space, and so holding him in a window to the sight and great comfort" of the townspeople who had gathered round to see their sovereign and their prince.[61]

Edward was considered to be the "realm's most precious Jewel... and foresee that all dangers and adversaries of malicious persons and casual harms (if any be) shall be vigilantly foreseen and avoided. They [his attendants] alone were to have access to the person of the Prince, and no one under the degree of knight was to be admitted, and then only under supervision. None of his household was to visit London or any other place in the summer months, when there was danger of plague, and any sick person in the household was to be withdrawn at once."[62] Henry had been so frightened of the plague that he had not been with Jane at her delivery. Edward's birth filled him with joy.

Bishop Latimer best summed up the feelings of Henry and his grateful nation "We all hungered after a prince so long that there was so much rejoicing as at the birth of John the Baptist."[63] Had it not been blasphemous he might have said Christ.

Present at the birth scene were midwives and their helpers. They were dressed in their everyday clothes with the possible addition of an apron.[64] A late sixteenth-century list of the midwife's necessities is found in Thomas Delaney's *The Gentle Craft* (1597-1600): "Soap and candles, beds, shirts, biggins, wastcoats, headbands, swaddlebands, crossclothes, bibs, tailclouts, mantles, hose, shoes, coats, petticoats, cradle and crickets."[65] Soap to cleanse mother and child; an assortment of clothes for the baby, including the tailclout—his diaper and biggin-bonnet; a crosscloth to tie about the mother's forehead to prevent wrinkles; and the cricket-low stool for the attendant midwife.[66] The midwives' duties included cutting the umbilical cord, washing mother and baby, annointing and dressing the baby, and seeing to any other immediate needs.

According to Jonas' 1540 translation of Roesslin, called *The Byrth of Mankynde*, the cord should be cut "three fingers breadth from the belly and so knit up." Attendants were advised to look closely at the child's navel, for if it had no wrinkles it indicated future barrenness. The child's body should then be annointed with oil of acorns as a protection against smoke and cold. Then the child should be thoroughly washed in warm water; the child's nostrils should be opened with the midwife's finger and oil dropped in to the eyes. Furthermore, mother or nurse should handle the child's sitting place with the intent of purging the belly. When the stub of the navel skin falls off after three days, the midwife should apply powder of burnt calves' ashes or "of snail shells, or the powder of lead, called red lead tempered with wine."

> Furthermore when the infant is swaddled and laid in cradle, the nurse must give all diligence and heed that she bind every part right and in his due place and order, and that with all tenderness and gentle entreating and not crookedly and confusedly, the which also must be done oftentimes in the day: for in this it is as it is in young and tender imps, plants, and twigs, the which even as you bow them in their youth so will they evermore remain unto age. And even so the infant if it be bound and swaddled, the members lying right and straight, then shall it grow straight and upright, if it be crookedly handled it will grow likewise, and to the ill 'negligence of many nurses may be imputed the crookedness and deformity of many a man and woman which otherwise might seem well favored as any other.

The nurse is also advised to often wash the baby in hot water in winter and in luke warm water in summer. She should stroke the child's belly "to provoke the child to the making of water, and when you lay it in the cradle to sleep set the cradle in such a place that neither the beams of the sun by day neither of the moon by night come on the infant: but rather set it in a dark and shadow place: laying also the head higher than the rest of the body."[67]

Dr. John Jones, who also wrote on child care, agreed that: "The place for children to rest or sleep in best, is a cradle, because that thereof may grow a threefold commodity that is sleep sooner obtained, the parts through rocking better exercised, and the infant safer from such hurt preserved, as by having it in bed often happens." However, he agrees with Eucharius Roesslin that "immediately after sucking: violent rocking to be hurtful, lest that thereby the child should be provoked to cast up his milk again."[68]

Swaddling was *de rigeur*. Even the portraits of Christ's birth showed him swaddled lying in the manger. Swaddling included arms as well as feet; it was done to insure that the child grow straight. A seventeenth-century account advises that all the infant's

> parts be bound up in their due place and order gently without any crookedness or rugged foldings; for infants are tender twigs and as you use them, so they will grow straight or crooked. . . . lay the arms right down by the sides, that they may grow right. . . .
>
> After four months let loose the arms but still roll the breast and belly and feet to keep out cold air for a year, till the child have gained more strength. Shift the child's clouts often, for the Piss and Dung. . .
>
> When the child is seven months old you may (if you please) wash the body of it twice a week with warm water till it be weaned. . .[69]

A tender example from 1568 which shows a mother's care for her child is the following dialogue between her and the child's nurse.

> How now, how does the child? . . . Unswaddle him, undo his swaddling bands . . . wash him, before me . . . Pull off his shirt, thou art pretty and fat my little darling . . .
>
> Now swaddle him again, But first put on his biggin and his little band [collar] with an edge, where is his little petticoat? Give him his coat of changeable [shot] taffeta and his satin sleeves.
>
> Where is his bib? Let him have his gathered apron with strings, and hang a Muckinder [handkerchief] to it.
>
> You need not yet to give him his coral with the small golden chain, for I believe it is better to let him sleep until the afternoon.[70]

Coral was a good luck charm and was supposed magically to protect the child. Reginald Scot in *Discoverie of Witchcraft* (1584) noted:

The coral preserves such as bear it from fascination or bewitching and in this respect they are hanged about children's necks. But from whence this superstition is derived, or who invented the lie, I know not, but I see how ready the people are to give credit thereunto, by the multitude of corals that are employed.

It was thought to be good for teething as well.[71]

Selection of the nurse, in view of the possibility of her over-laying her charge, might be a life and death matter. Much attention was devoted to her selection and to whether a mother should nurse her own child. Most sixteenth-century authors agreed that mothers' milk was best.[72] *The Byrth of Mankynd* advised: "it shall be best, if the mother give her child suck herself, for the mother's milk is more convenient and agreeable to the infant than any other woman's and more doth it nourish it, for because that in the mother's belly it was wont to the same and fed with it and therefore also it doth more desirously covet the same as that with the which it is best acquainted, and to be short, the mother's milk is most wholesome for the child."[73]

If, however, the mother is sick, or did not want to nurse her baby, a wholesome nurse should be selected. She should be carefully examined for bulk and complexion. A recent mother would be a good candidate; her milk should be examined "that it be not blackish, bluish, grey, or reddish, neither sour, sharp, salty, or brackish."[74] Dr. Jones advised that the nurse's breasts be examined for "great pappes or teats hurt the gums, and the small jaws, because that through the one they are constrained to open the mouth too wide, over-stretching the sinews, causing grief, much like to the cramp. Through the other, in that they can not easily of the Infant be catched, making it wide mouthed, over wayward and angry, and as I have often noted, to weep very much."[75]

Some children would be nursed at home. Others, especially if their parents were wealthy, would be sent to nurse in the country. Long after, they might remember with pleasure their stay in the country.[76] Once a nurse was selected, other affairs such as the christening of the baby and churching of the mother could be attended to.

Both were important ceremonies. The baby was christened in a white chrisom cloth which signified innocence. Usually the infant wore the cloth for a month after the ceremony. The child was dipped naked into the Font unless he was sickly. A lighted taper, probably to symbolize God's light, was placed in the hand of the Godfather. Before an illegitimate child could be baptized, the mother had to do penance in the church or market clothed in a white sheet.[77]

Churching may seem a barbarous custom to a generation that fully believes in the liberation of women. Following the ancient Hebrew custom, however, Christians believed that a woman should be purified after the birth of her child. Royalty, as usual, made an elaborate ceremonial of it. After the birth of her son Prince Arthur in 1486, Queen Eliza-beth, Henry VII's wife, was to be dressed in rich laces; she was to be led from her bed by a Duchess or Countess and led to her chamber door; then a Duke would lead her to the church.[78]

Children subsisted mostly on their mother or nurse's milk. Gradu-ally they ate other foods as they were able when their teeth came. The general rule for this period was to nourish on milk until four front teeth came in; then feed on breadcrusts and milk, gradually introducing other foods such as butter, capons in small quantities.[79] The time of weaning varied. The Arabian Avicenna recommended two years, how-ever, *The Byrth of Mankynde* notes "how be it among us most com-monly they suck but one year. And when you will wean them, then not to do it suddenly, but a little and little, and to make for it little piles of bread and sugar to eat and accustom it so, till it be able to eat all manner of meat."[80] A good case in point is the little Elizabeth who became Elizabeth I. The decision to wean her was taken on October 9, 1534; she was a little over a year old.

Some children, of course, did not survive to be weaned: ill health, plague, a poor diet, or nurse whose milk dried up, or in some cases in-fanticide accounted for their death. Dr. Emmison has an interesting analysis of infanticide as it appeared in the Essex Quarter Sessions Records.

Infanticide was woefully common, and there were probably many other violent deaths by smothering or bruising which were concealed from the coroner. The Essex records disclose at least thirty unwanted babies whose brief lives were cut short by their mothers. Except for three, they were all apparently unmarried. One spinster, on 21 October 1570 between 12 and 1 a.m. at the house of William Fytche gentleman, her master, at Little Canfield (Hall), gave birth to a dead infant in the backhouse and threw it into his horse pond; no verdict given. Another, in the house of John Perrye yeoman, her master, at Standord-le-Hope, secretly gave birth at night, after which she cut the baby's throat and threw him into the nearby stream, weighted with stones; guilty. A baby was born in Cludens Close in Copy Hall Park, Epping, and thrown into the 'mud or slud' of the ditch; not guilty, but John Stile did it. Another, born in a field on a December night, was drowned. Another was left to die in the cold of January. A servant of Richard Harte of St. Mary's, Maldon, yeoman, bore a daughter without a midwife's aid and put her naked into a chest in the bedroom. Next day she took the infant, then dead, and by advice of her master, the putative father, buried it in a heap of horse dung in the garden; 'not in prison' (refers presumably to the mother). Another infant, born 'without the help of any woman', was strangled. Only in one other case is the father or putative father specifically named. The mother of a stillborn infant took him to a pond full of water, and tying a weight to his neck threw him in.

Analysis of the causes of death in the thirty infanticide cases, including those already referred to, gives: strangled, five; smothered, two; suffocated—by pillow, one, in oven, one, in ditch, three; in haystack, one; drowned—in pond, four (one stillborn), in well, one; buried in a hole, one; broken or twisted neck, three; put in chest and then in dung heap, one; cut throat, two (one then drowned); struck against bedpost, one; struck by a man, one; cause not stated, three. The verdicts, etc., were: guilty, seventeen (three women were remanded because they were pregnant again); not guilty, five; John a Style guilty, one; guilty of homicide but not of murder, one; not proved that child was alive, one; killed by a man, one; inquests without verdict, three; 'abortion,' one.[81]

EDUCATION OF CHILDREN

Though education in these centuries ceased to be the exclusive preserve of the clergy, it had a religious base and was Christ-centered. Christ had been the child who taught the wise men in the temple. On being rebuked by His mother for remaining there without her permission, Christ lectured her on having to be about His Father's business. Ostensibly education was the Lord's business, for it trained the child's reason to be the servant of faith with the intent that the child ultimately win salvation. Content-wise religion formed the base, and the little children learned Christian moral precepts as they learned their A B C's and Latin syntax.[82] It could not be otherwise in such a religious age in which men were prepared to burn or hang those of opposite religious beliefs.

If one looks at early modern education, one may safely make several generalizations. First, education was becoming more important; parents put a higher premium on having their children obtain it. Increasingly, it became an avenue to upward social mobility and to securing important government posts.[83] To meet the need to supply a growing population's children with education, more grammar schools were created, the most famous being St. Paul's.[84] More Elizabethan members of parliament were university-educated than those of the fifteenth and early sixteenth centuries. Of course, those getting the education were the aristocrats. Society was still dominated by its hierarchies.

Second, the mania for the ancients insured that a rigorous classical scholarship would become a part of the educational curriculum. The early sixteenth-century English leaders in this movement were John Colet, William Lily, and Thomas More. By imitating antiquity, it was thought one could learn all that was necessary to control oneself and to advance in the world of affairs.

Third, education became necessary to develop a person into a gentleman or gentlewoman. No more was it to be solely administered by the clergy. The English Reformation, of course, intensified this development. The abandonment of clerical celibacy by Elizabethen parsons insured that their genes would not be lost to the service of Church, University, or State. What I would like to do in this section is briefly to focus on discipline as manifested in education, for it demonstrates prevailing attitudes in the treatment of children, and then to consider the education of such figures as Edward VI and More's children as symptomatic, even if special cases, of what happened educationally to children.

The base of educational discipline was the biblical adage: "Spare the rod and spoil the child." At the turn of the fifteenth century this became the proverb: "He that spares the Yard hates his child,"[85] which survived in later parental admonitions such as: "The child whom the father loves most dear he does most punish tenderly in fear."[86] Psychologically speaking, parents recognized that acceptance of their authority depended on instilling respect and reverence for themselves and the hierarchical system. They hoped for obedience based on a rational acceptance of their position as natural in the hierarchical system where the king was the *pater patriae* for his people, in the same way a father had dominion over wife and children. Legally wives and children held a subordinate position; they were merely things to be used as a father saw fit. Whether he obtained obedience by love and affection rather than through pain and fear by frequently administered beatings mattered little; legally he had the right. Some fathers may even have taken pleasure in beating spouse and children and derived satisfaction from the contemplation of the old say that: "As a sharp spur makes a horse run, so a rod makes a child learn (1475)."[87]

Most aristocratic children were sent to grammar school at six or seven years of age. In the seventh year children entered the second stage of man's twelve ages. *The Shepherdes Calendar* compared this period to February when the child, like the earth, turned green and began to learn in school.[88] Most students began their schooling much earlier. If the boy or girl were a prince or princess, education commenced at the age of three or four. Edward VI began his formal education at three as did James VI of Scotland; Edward's sister Mary began hers at four. Even Edward was not exempt from corporal punishment. When he refused to memorize long passages from *Proverbs,* his tutor Dr. Richard Cox beat him. The results, he felt, were highly gratifying; fear spurred Edward on to new industry.[89]

The education of Edward illustrates both the nature of discipline and the nature of the new humanistic studies. The discipline harkened back to that of his fifteenth-century predecessor Henry VI of whom it was said that when he was two years old his nurse, Dame Alice Butler, was

given "license to chastise" him "from time to time."[90] Edward's father
Henry VIII may not have been punished as a student. At least I can find
no reference to his having been.[91]

Perhaps the best way to get insight into the process of Edward VI's
education is to consider the evaluations made in December 1544 by
Edward's tutor, Dr. Richard Cox. The seven-year-old Edward had then
been at his studies for three years. Cox noted that his young charge had:

> "expunged and utterly conquered a great number of the captains
> of ignorance. The eight parts of speech he hath made them his
> subjects and servants, and can decline any manner Latin noun
> and conjugate a verb perfectly unless it be *anomalum*. These parts
> thus beaten down and conquered he beginneth to build them up
> again and frame them after his purpose with due order of con-
> struction, like as the King's Majesty framed up Bullayn [Boulogne]
> when he had beaten it down. He understandeth and can frame
> well his iij concords of grammar and hath made already xl. or l.
> pretty Lattins and can answer well favouredly to the parts, and is
> now ready to enter into Cato, to some proper and profitable
> fables of Æsope, and other wholesome and godly lessons that
> shall be devised for him. Every day in the mass time he readeth a
> portion of Solomon's proverbs for the exercise of his reading,
> wherein he delighteth much and learneth there how good it is to
> give ear unto discipline, to fear God, to keep God's command-
> ments, to beware of strange and wanton women, to be obedient
> to father and mother, to be thankful to them that telleth him of
> his faults, &c." Describes, similarly, how, before they left Sutton,
> he obtained the victory over Captain Will and now trusts by exer-
> cise to chase away Captain Oblivion. The Prince is "a vessel apt to
> receive all goodness and learning, witty, sharp and pleasant."[92]

In addition to his studies in languages and religion, he learned to play
the lute. He, like other children, was treated like an adult. His schooling
was a somewhat arid no-nonsense achievement-oriented process. In order that he gain experience in dealing with other people, well-born
youths were selected to study with him. To his death Edward kept a
strong feeling for one of these boys, Barnaby Fitzpatrick, but apparently made strong attachments to no others. This was strange, for
athletic and attractive Robert Dudley who became so close to Elizabeth
I was one of the group.[93]

Girls, of course, were often denied education, but increasingly
princesses and aristocratic girls received it. The education of Elizabeth I
and Lady Jane Grey was equally as rigorous and comprehensive as that
of Edward I. Each became scholars in their own right. Apparently discipline was as severe for girls as boys. Lady Jane Grey had no quarrel
with her tutor Roger Ascham, instead she ruefully reflected on the contrast between his gentleness and her parent's severity. She thought that

"One of the greatest benefits that God ever gave me is that he sent me so sharp and severe parents . . . For when I am in presence either of father or mother, whether I speak, keep silence, sit, stand, or go, eat, drink, be merry or sad, be sewing, playing, dancing, or doing any thing else, I must do it, as it were, in such weight, measure, and number, even so perfectly as God made the world, else I am so sharply taunted, so cruelly threatened, yea presently sometimes with pinches, nippes, and bobs, and some ways which I will not name for the honour I bear them, so without measure misordered, that I think myself in hell."[94]

Jane's parents were typical. Over and over again the biblical adage, spare the rod and spoil the child, finds its way into daily relations between parent and child. Common usage decreed that parents who love their children will beat them. The thought is that beating is natural. It proceeds from affection and instills regard for the parent's place in the natural order. Little girls, like Lady Jane Grey, never doubted that her beatings issued from parental concern and blessed herself that her parents took their responsibilities so seriously.

Other women who were educated included Thomas More's three daughters. Perhaps the most educationally gifted of them was Margaret, his favorite daughter. She may even have been tutored by Erasmus. She translated Erasmus' *Precatio dominica* which became the Treatise on the *Pater Noster* and composed a work titled *The Four Last Things* which More preferred to his own study of the same subject. When the time came, she educated her own three daughters.[95]

More's treatment of his three daughters and son is in marked contrast to that of Lady Jane Grey. More didn't believe in beatings. When chastisement was required, he said that he beat his children with a peacock feather. The context in which More said this is of interest because it shows More as perhaps the most loving father of his generation. The remark occurs in a letter to his children where he declares his love for them:

It is not so strange that I love you with my whole heart, for being a father is not a tie which can be ignored. Nature in her wisdom has attached the parent to the child and bound them spiritually together with a Herculean knot. This tie is the source of my consideration for your immature minds, a consideration which causes me to take you often into my arms. This tie is the reason why I regularly fed you cake and gave you ripe apples and fancy pears. This tie is the reason why I used to dress you in silken garments and why I never could endure to hear you cry. You know, for example, how often I kissed you, how seldom I whipped you. My whip was invariably a *peacock's tail*. Even this I wielded hesitantly and gently so that sorry welts might not disfigure your tender seats. Brutal and unworthy to be called father is he who does not himself weep at the tears of his child. How other fathers act I do not know, but you know well how gentle and devoted is my manner toward you, for I have always profoundly loved my own children and I have always been an indulgent parent—as every father ought to be. But at this moment my love has increased so much that it seems to me I used not to love you at all.[96]

Yet others in the sixteenth century believed that discipline was necessary for both boys and girls. Princess Mary's tutor Vives observed that "It was a wise man, who said, Never had the rod off a boy's back; specially the daughter should be handled without any cherishing. For cherishing marreth sons, but it utterly destroyeth daughters."[97]

CHILDREN'S WORK

A favorite medieval doctrine was *laborare est orare:* to work is to pray or more simply, work is worship. Everyone, even the littlest children, had work to do. There was much to do: bread to bake, beer to brew, fish to catch, animals to butcher, meat to roast, tables to set, houses to build, metal to mine, ships to sail, pots to peddle. Idleness was a sin—a sin against the individual in his pursuit of paradise. It was one of the seven deadly sins, sloth; it was also a sin against the community which was deprived of that individual's service. Besides, sloth might be the occasion of far worse sins, for everyone knew that the devil found his work for idle hands to do. Work was a virtue long before the birth of the Puritans.[98]

Children were not excluded from work. From the highest to the lowest they had their assigned tasks: for princes and princesses it was learning governance and statecraft; for aristocratic children, good manners and royal service; for children of lesser folk, agriculture, trade, industry. For the most part, they calmly accepted work's necessity. Nonetheless, there is the amusing example of the young Catherine Parr retorting to her mother who told her to sew: " 'My hands,' she said, 'are ordained to touch crowns and sceptres, not needles and spindles.' "[99] Her reluctance to sew must have been overcome, for later as Henry VIII's sixth wife she superintended the needlework of Henry's daughter Elizabeth.

While most aristocrats could not afford to set their children up in separate establishments as did royalty, they did send them away to learn good manners in the home of another aristocrat. In a sense this was merely a continuation of the older medieval practice of giving young boy's service as pages. Often they married into the families of their patrons. Later, however, the aristocrats abandoned this custom as the hiring of private tutors, the sending of sons to boarding grammar schools, and going abroad took its place.

In the lower reaches of society, children were not kept at home but apprenticed to learn a trade. Apprenticeship was so highly regarded it was an instrument of national policy. For example, in 1536 every parish was required to collect begging children between the ages of 5 and 14 and apprentice them in unskilled jobs. Under the Statute of Artificers of 1563, the system of apprenticeship was overhauled and systematized so that the term of apprenticeship became a standard seven years. Moreover, justices of the peace were given the power to oversee the whole process. Children's welfare was also looked after in the Poor Relief Act of (1598).[100] Parish overseers of the poor were empowered to set children of indigent parents to work. These were parents who were not ". . . . thought able to keep and maintain their children, and also such persons married or unmarried as, having no means to maintain them, use no ordinary and daily trade to get their living by. . . ."[101] In reality what this act did was to make each parish responsible for destitute orphan children. It remained on the books until 1834.

Obviously there were drawbacks to Poor Relief and to apprenticeship. There was no guarantee that parish officials would exercise compassion on their young charges who were costing the parish hard-earned money, nor was there any promise that a master would treat his apprentices with justice, kindness, or love. One of the most unflattering glimpses of fifteenth-century English apprenticeship, before the system became structured by statute, is offered by an Italian observer. He notes that:

> The want of affection in the English is strongly manifested towards their children; for after having kept them at home till they arrive at the age of 7 or 9 years at the utmost, they put them out, both males and females, to hard service in the houses of other people, binding them generally for another 7 or 9 years. And these are called apprentices, and during that time they perform all the most menial offices; and few are born who are exempted from this fate, for every one, however rich he may be, sends away his children into the houses of others, whilst he, in return, receives those of strangers into his own. And on inquiring the reason for this severity, they answered that they did it in order that their children might learn better manners. But I, for my part, believe that they do it because they like to enjoy all their comforts themselves, and that they are better served by strangers than they would be by their own children. Besides which the English being great epicures, and very avaricious by nature, indulge in the most delicate fare themselves and give their household the coarsest bread, and beer, and cold meat bakes on Sunday for the week. . . . That if they had their own children at home they would be obliged to give them the same food they made use of for themselves. That if the English sent their children away

from home to learn virtue and good manners, and took them back again when their apprenticeship was over, they might perhaps be excused; but they never return, for the girls are settled by their patrons, and the boys make the best marriages they can, and assisted by their patrons, not by their father, they also open a house and strive diligently by this means to make some fortune for themselves. . . .[102]

Deloney expressed this attitude best in his ballad of the wool trade where he observed young children picking and sorting wool for the spinners. He marveled that: " 'Poor people whom God lightly blessed with most children, did by means of this occupation so order them, that by the time they were come to be six or seven years of age they were able to get their own bread.' "[103]

CHILDREN'S PLAY

J. H. Plumb has noted: "Certainly there was no separate world of childhood. Children shared the same games with adults, the same toys, the same fairy stories. They lived their lives together, never apart. The coarse village festivals depicted by Bruegel, showing men and women besotted with drink, groping for each other with unbridled lust, have children eating and drinking with the adults. Even, in the soberer pictures of wedding feasts and dances the children are enjoying themselves alongside their elders, doing the same things.[104] Not even nursery rhymes belonged to children, for as Iona and Peter Opie maintain, "From before 1800, the only true nursery rhymes (i.e. rhymes composed especially for the nursery) are the rhyming alphabets, the infant amusements (verses which accompany a game), and the lullabies. Even the riddles were in the first place designed for adult perplexity."[105] The first nursery rhyme book for children was *Tommy Thumb's Pretty Song Book*, and it dates from 1744. *Mother Goose's Melody, or Sonnets for the Cradle* dates approximately twenty one or two years later.[106] Thus, if the child heard a rhyme, it was probably in the company of adults and meant to convey a political message, as were the sixpence jingles which dealt with the careers of Henry VII and Henry VIII.[107] Gradually when the characters and policies of the kings receded into the past, the jingles remained to enchant the children.

Thomas More was tremendously interested in childhood and the child's use of play. Nowhere is the idea better expressed than in his poem "Childhood."

I am called Childhood, in play is all my mind,
To cast a quoit, a cockshy, and a ball.
A top can I set, and drive it in his kind.

But would to god these hateful books all,
Were in a fire burnt to powder small.
Then might I lead my life always in play:
Which life god send me to mine ending day.[108]

He was fond of telling his children "to take" virtue and learning for their meat and play for their sauce.[109] Play had its place. The inculcation of virtue came first. Yet this good opinion of More as a father was confirmed by Nicholas Harpsfield, who reported that: "you should never see him in any chafe of fretting with his said wife, children or family. Master William Roper, his son, hath reported that in sixteen years and more, being in his house, he could never perceive much as once in any fume."[110]

Attitudes to children change considerably during the period from 1399-1603. For example, English parents viewed their children differently in 1603 than that view taken by the fourteenth-century poet Symon, who summed up contemporary attitudes to children in these lines:

A child were better to be unborn
Than be untaught to so be lorn.
The child that hath his will alway
Shall thrive late, I thee will say;
And therefore every good man's child
That is too wanton and too wild,
Learn well this lesson for certain,
That thou may be the better man.
Child, I warne thee in all wise
That thou tell truth and make no lies.
Child, be not forward, be not proud,
But hold up thy head and speak aloud.[111]

The attitude that the failure to maintain discipline ruins a child is consistently maintained during this period. The inculcation of respect and subservience to parents is also constant. If one can discern change, it is most seen in the area of physical care. A greater value is put on the child and a greater attempt is made to please him through attention to his physical welfare and happiness. More and more children were being recognized as human beings with different developmental problems than adults. In the best of fathers, like Thomas More, there is a genuine regard and concern and joy in children. As Ivy Pinchbeck and Margaret Hewit observe, "a new consciousness of childhood" was beginning.[112]

REFERENCES

I am grateful for the help of Lloyd deMause and Manuel Lopez for valuable advice and assistance.

1. Taken from C. G. Jung, *Psyche & Symbol*, edited by Violet S. de Laszlo (New York, 1958), p. 143.
2. Bartlett Jere Whiting with Helen Wescott Whiting, *Proverbs, Sentences, And Proverbial Phrases From English Writings Mainly Before 1500* (Cambridge, Mass., 1968), p. 372. Quotations have been modernized in capitalization, spelling, and word usage.
3. Whiting, p. 662.
4. Whiting, p. 8.
5. Whiting, p. 377.
6. Whiting, p. 198.
7. Whiting, p. 83.
8. Oscar H. Sommer, ed., *The Kalendar of Shepherdes* .... (London, 1892), p. 10. This idea of the ages of man is a common one, for example see the customary discussion in medieval bestiaries. T. H. White, ed., *The Bestiary: A Book of Beasts* (N.Y., 1965), pp. 219-226. Or see Jacques' speech on The Ages of Man in Shakespeare's *As You Like It*, Act II, Scene vii.
9. For these sources I have searched A. W. Pollard and G. R. Redgrave, *A Short-Title Catalogue of Books In England, Scotland and Ireland and of English Books Printed Abroad, 1475-1640* (London: The Bibliographical Society, 1926). Two important works for the historian of childhood are Philippe Aries, *Centuries of Childhood: A Social History of Family Life*, trans. by Robert Baldick (N.Y., 1962) and Lawrence Stone, *The Crisis of the Aristocracy, 1558-1641* (N.Y., 1967). Both works are valuable, but Aries' tendency to consider the age one to seven period as without discrete stages makes it less useful in my inquiry which focuses specifically on this time span. Stone, too, is less concerned with childhood itself and more with it as it relates to sociological structural changes. Stone acutely notes the scarcity of behavioralistic evidence, in a recent article on "Prosopography" he wonders whether the early modern historian will ever be able "to penetrate, the bedroom, bathroom, or nursery." In fact, Stone asserts that the historian is "unable" to do so. *Daedalus* Vol. 100 (Winter, 1971), p. 53.
10. The standard life of Elizabeth is John Neale, *Queen Elizabeth I* (London, 1934); that of Mary Queen of Scots, Antonia Fraser, *Mary Queen of Scots* (N.Y., 1969).
11. Consider also Shakespeare's sonnet 144 where man has two angels, the good being male, the evil female.
12. Richmond Noble, *Shakespeare's Biblical Knowledge And Use Of The Book Of Common Prayer* ... (N.Y., 1970), p. 112.
13. Germain Marc'hadour, *The Bible In The Works of St. Thomas More*, 5 vols. (Nieuwkoop, 1969-72) IV, 75. See also Vol. I, 78-79.
14. David Herlihy, "Life Expectancies For Women in Medieval Society," May 7, 1972 CEMER Conference, SUNY at Binghamton.
15. Marc'hadour, IV, 171.
16. See Alexander Cruden, *Cruden's Useful Concordance cf the Holy Scriptures* ... (N.Y., 1970), pp. 104-106 for a useful listing of scriptural references to children.
17. White, p. 9.
18. Phillis Cunnington and Catherine Lucas, *Costumes For Births, Marriages & Deaths* (London, 1972), p. 270.
19. *Ibid.*

20. *Ibid.,* p. 272.
21. *Ibid.,* p. 271.
22. *Ibid.,* pp. 272-73.
23. See for example, Hans Multscher (c. 1400-1467), *The Road to Calvary,* in Hans H. Hofstätter, *Art Of The Late Middle Ages* (N.Y. 1968), pp. 184-185.
24. White, p. 104.
25. H. M. F. Prescott, *Mary Tudor* (London, 1954), p. 390.
26. F. R. H. Du Boulay, *An Age Of Ambition: English Society In The Late Middle Ages* (N.Y., 1970), pp. 90-91.
27. *Ibid.,* p. 91.
28. *Ibid.,* p. 32.
29. Little is known about precisely where the additional income was spent.
30. Gen. XXX, 1 Quoted in Philip J. Greven, Jr., ed., *Child-Rearing Concepts, 1628-1861* (Itasca, Ill., 1973), p. 12.
31. STC 11970, Jehan Goeurot, *The Regiment of Life whereunto is added a treatise of the pestilence with the boke of children newly corrected and enlarged* by T. Phayre. E. Whitchurche 1550 (orig. pub. 1545).
32. Sir George Clark, *A History of the Royal College of Physicians of London* (Oxford: Clarendon Press, 1964), p. 59.
33. Fielding Hudson Garrison, *A Medical Bibliography* (N.Y.: Lippincott, 1970), p. 729; Louis K. Diamond, "A History of Jaundice in the Newborn," *Birth Defects,* Vol. 6 (June 1970) 3-6.
34. STC 11970. In his excellent paper "On the Longevity of 'Xistus Philosophus: An Exploration in the History of Memory," delivered at the Cheiron Meeting, Calgary, June 29, 1972. Prof. A. B. Laver (Psychology, Carleton Univ.) notes the English reliance on foreign works for its medical expertise.
35. STC 21153. Eucharius Roesslin, *The byrth of mankynde.* Newly tr. out of Latin by R. Jonas. T. R[aynald], 1540.
36. STC 21154 dated 1560.
37. Cunnington, p. 13.
38. *Ibid.,* pp. 13-14.
39. Cunnington, pp. 13-14.
40. Neville Williams, *Henry VIII And His Court* (N.Y. 1970), p. 140; J. J. Scarisbrick, *Henry VIII* (Berkeley, 1967), p. 348.
41. Peter de la Primavdaye, *The French Academie* . . . . trans. by T. B. (London, 1586), p. 552.
42. Erasmus, *Seven Dialogues Both Pithie and Profitable,* tr. W. Burton (London, 1606). Quotation modernized.
43. Francis Quarles, *Divine Fancies* (London, 1641), p. 5.
44. *Ibid.,* p. 3.
45. Cunnington, pp. 16-17.
46. *Ibid.,* p. 17.
47. *Ibid.*
48. Cunnington, p. 21.
49. Harvey Graham, *Eternal Eve* (London, 1950), p. 148.
50. *Ibid.,* p. 149.
51. *Ibid.,* pp. 142-143, 170.
52. *Ibid.,* p. 151.
53. *Ibid.,* p. 188.
54. Cunnington, p. 16.
55. Graham, pp. 174-176.
56. STC 4801. *A Cathechisme, or a Christian Doctrine Necessarie for Children* (Lawson, 1568), pp. 75-76.
57. Sylvia Thrupp, *The Merchant Class of Medieval London* [1300-1505] (Chi-

cago, 19   ), p. 180.

58. A. F. Pollard, *Henry VIII* (London, 1951), pp. 140- 147-49, 279, 288-89.
59. W. K. Jordan, *Edward VI: The Young King* (Cambridge, Mass., 1968), p. 36.
60. *Ibid.*, pp. 36-37
61. *Ibid.*, p. 38.
62. *Ibid.*, p. 39.
63. Williams, *Henry VIII And His Court* (N.Y. 1970), p. 162
64. Cunnington, p. 20.
65. *Ibid.*, p. 24.
66. *Ibid.*
67. STC 21153. *The Byrth of Mankynde*, fols. LIII-LVI.
68. John Jones, *The Arte and Science of Preserving Bodie and Soule in Health, Wisdom, and Catholihe Religion: Phisically, Philosophically, and Divinely*, p. 46. Jones, of course, is referring to nurses overlaying and smothering babies when they slept with them. It is difficult to know how many babies were overlaid since nurses would not normally be indicted. Scevole de St. Marthe, the 16th century physician, who dedicated his *Paedrophia* to Henry III (d. 1589) has a similar discussion of cutting the umbilical cord, washing the baby, and laxatives. The edition used here is the translation (London, 1797) by H. W. Tytler. See pp. 55-65, 138-141. Here is an example of Tytler's 18th century poetical translation. The subject is swaddling:

> Remember too, that only, by degrees,
> His tender skin endures the cooling breeze:
> Expose not recent from the womb, the child,
> Except to gentle heat, and seasons mild;
> Lest ills succeed, lest penetrating cold
> Benumb his limbs, and of his joints take hold.
> As when a Libyan traveller must defy
> Th' inclement seasons of an arctic sky,
> Unus'd to face the blust'ring North and West,
> He wraps his body in a woolen vest,
> Head, limbs, and feet, defends with cautious art,
> In double folds involving ev'ry part;
> So, from relaxing baths, still keep in mind
> That you more open ev'ry pore will find,
> And more unfit to bear the cooling air.
> For this, in powder, finest salt prepare,
> T'anoint his skin, and all his joints around,
> Constringing thus what bathing had unbound.
> Nor then forget that wrappers be at hand,
> Soft flannels, linen, and the swaddling band,
> T'enwrap the babe, by many a circling fold,
> In equal lines, and thus defend from cold. (pp. 66-67).

The story that the Germans plunged their children in the Rhine is repeated:

> The Germans us'd, a race inur'd to cold,
> To war, to labour from the cradle bred,
> And, like themselves, their infants far'd and fed.
> The new-born child, yet reeking from the womb,
> They took to what oft gave him to the tomb;
> Lest he should from his father's strength decline,
> They plung'd him shiv'ring in the freezing Rhine. (p. 62).

69. Cunnington, p. 31.
70. *Ibid.*, pp. 28, 30.
71. *Ibid.*, pp. 38-39.

72. Erasmus, *Seven Dialogues;* Primadaye, p. 552, *Byrth of Mankynde,* fol. lvi.
73. *Byrth of Mankynde,* fol. lvi.
74. *Byrth of Mankynde,* fol. lvii.
75. Jones, p. 12.
76. Thrupp, *The Medieval Merchant Class,* p. 226.
77. Cunnington, pp. 41-43.
78. *Ibid.,* pp. 18-19.
79. J. C. Drummond and Anne Wibraham, *The Englishman's Food* (London, n.d.) p. 79 ff.
80. *The Byrth of Mankynde,* fol. LIX. Jones cites Galen as recommending weaning at three years but says it can be conveniently accomplished at two years.
81. F. G. Emmison, *Elizabeth Life: Disorder* (Chelmsford, Essex, 1970).
82. STC 25874, John Withals, *A Shorte Dictionarie for Yonge Begynners.* T. Berthelet, 1553, I have examined a later edition, STC 25875, John Withals, *A Shorte Dictionarie for Yonge Beginners.* J. Kingston, J. Waley, A. Vele, 1556. Its aim is to familiarize children with Latin equivalents for common English words. Intriguingly the title which appears at the top of its pages is *A Littell Dictionarie for Children.* The age of the children is not specified, but it probably would have been four since this was the usual age for entry to the ABC or petty school which preceded entry to the grammar school at age six or seven. Students were expected to know their ABC's before acceptance at grammar school or being apprenticed. Withals' dictionary, like a medieval encyclopedia, has entries that range from parts of the world, fish, fowl, and beasts to articles of clothing. There is no individual entry for children's clothing but there are entries for both men and women's apparel. Most of the games listed, such as swimming, dancing, dicing, tennis are adult pastimes. The work is dedicated to the minor Tudor public figure and scholarly translator of Erasmus' *Praise of Folly,* Sir Thomas Charloner (d. 1565). Formerly Withals' work was attributed to Chaloner, Sir Thomas Chaloner, *The Praise of Folie,* ed. by Clarence H. Miller, Early English Text Society, vol. 157 (London, N.Y., Toronto: Oxford University Press, 1965), p. xxx. A useful pamphlet which discusses ABC schools and grammar schools is Craig R. Thompson, *Schools In Tudor England* (Washington: The Folger Shakespeare Library, 1958). The standard history of Tudor education is Joan Simon, *Education And Society In Tudor England* (Cambridge: C.U.P. 1966) which has an extensive bibliography.
83. See especially "The Education of the Aristocracy in the Renaissance" in J. H. Hexter *Reappraisals in History* (N.H., 1961) and Lawrence Stone, *The Crisis of the Aristocracy* (Oxford, 1964) which treats the subject in general as well as Stone's learned articles.
84. Simon, pp. 73-80, 306-308, 353-354.
85. Bartlett Jere Whiting with Helen Wescott Whiting, *Proverbs, Sentences, Proverbial Phrases from English Writings Mainly Before 1500* (Cambridge, Mass., 1968), p. 372. Dated 1440.
86. *Ibid.,* p. 662. Dated 1525.
87. *Ibid.,* p. 8. Dated 1509.
88. Sommer, p. 10.
89. Morris Marples, *Princes In The Making: A Study of Royal Education* (London, 1965), p. 26.
90. A. L. Rowse, *Bosworth Field* (London, 1966), pp. 134-135.
91. See my "Life At Henry VII's Court," *History Today* (May, 1969), 325-31.
92. L. P., XIX, no. 726.
93. Jordan, pp. 40-44. See also James K. McConica, *English Humanists and Reformation Politics Under Henry VIII and Edward VI* (Oxford, 1965), pp.

217-218.

94. Roger Ascham, *The Scholemaster,* ed. Edward Arber (London, 1870), p. 47.

95. Pearl Hogrefe, *The Sir Thomas More Circle: A Program of Ideas and Their Impact On Secular Drama* (Urbana, Ill., 1959), pp. 206-07. For other examples of educated women see *Ibid.* pp. 208-13.

96. Leicester Bradner and Charles Arthur Lynch, *The Latin Epigrams of Thomas More* (Chicago, 1953), pp. 230-231.

97. Prescott, p. 26. Apparently Vives was merely repeating the pattern of his own education, for he noted that his mother never "lightly laughed upon me, she never cockered me, and yet, when I had been three or four days out of the house, she wist not where, she was almost sure síck; and when I was come home, I could not perceive that ever she longed for me. Therefore there was nobody that I did more flee, or was more loath to come nigh, than my mother, when I was a child." *Ibid.*

98. Edward Surtz, *The Works And Days of John Fisher* (Cambridge, 1967), p. 397.

99. Prescott, p. 98.

100. For the text of this act and the statute of Artificers see Carl Stephenson and Frederick George Marcham, eds., *Sources of English Constitutional History* (New York, 1937), pp. 348-58.

101. *Ibid.,* p. 356.

102. Charlotte Augusta Sneyd, *A Relation Or Rather A True Account Of The Island of England* . . . Camden Society, No. XXXVII (for 1846-7) (London, 1847), pp. 24-26.

103. Eileen Power, *Medieval People,* 2nd ed. (N.Y., 1970), p. 167.

104. J. H. Plumb, "The Great Change in Children" *Horizon,* XIII (Winter 1971), p. 7. Of course, such toys as dolls, tops, windmills, etc., were usually given over to children. Lady Fraser says that "the Renaissance period appears to be singularly lacking in interest in the flowering of the child, apparently absorbed in the flowering of man." Antonia Fraser, *A History of Toys* (London, 1966), p. 72. See also her chapters, "The Nature of Toys" and (Mediaeval Childhood."

105. Iona and Peter Opie, "Nursery Rhymes," in William Tary, ed. *Bibliophile in the Nursery* (Cleveland and New York, 1957), p. 266.

106. *Ibid.,* pp. 305, 307.

107. "I love sixpence, pretty little sixpence, / I love sixpence better than my life," was meant to illustrate Henry VII's avarice. Katherine Elwes Thomas, *The Real Personages of Mother Goose* (London, 1930), pp. 42-43. "Sing a song of sixpence" told the story of Henry VIII's love for Anne Boleyn and the story of the English Reformation. *Ibid.,* pp. 68-69.

108. Reynolds, p. 47.

109. William Roper & Nicholas Harpsfield, *Lives of Saint Thomas More,* ed. by E. E. Reynolds (N.Y.: n.d.), p. 4. Taken from Roper's biography.

110. *Ibid.,* p. 96.

111. E. M. Field, "In The Cradle" in William Targ, ed., *Bibliophile in the Nursery,* pp. 59-62.

112. Ivy Pinchbek and Margaret Hewitt, *Children In English Society* (London, 1969), p. 41.

CHAPTER 6

Nature Versus Nurture: Patterns and Trends in Seventeenth-Century French Child-Rearing

ELIZABETH
WIRTH
MARVICK

Unless you give children all they ask for, they are peevish and cry, aye, and strike their parents sometimes; and all this they have from nature. Yet are they free from guilt, neither may we properly call them wicked . . . because wanting the free use of reason they are exempted from all duty. These when they come to riper years . . . if they shall continue to do the same things, then truly they . . . are properly accounted wicked. Insomuch as a wicked man is almost the same thing with a child grown strong and sturdy. . . . and malice the same with a defect of reason in that age when nature ought to be better governed through good education and experience.[1]

Not a Frenchman but Thomas Hobbes—a mid-seventeenth century Englishman for long a visitor in France—pronounced these conclusions on the nature of children and the hoped-for effects of their nurture. In this chapter we endeavor to draw upon a variety of documentary resources to clarify seventeenth-century beliefs and practices which characterized French child-rearing.

No French intellectual of the time would have disagreed with Hobbes. Children were by nature vexing and peevish. The biographer of a saintly Catholic reformer contrasted the childhood character of his subject ("sweet and agreeable") with that of "normal children who are usually irritating, stubborn and not serious." On Hobbes' second point, that a child was not responsible for its actions, there was wide concurrence. Even Boguet—an expert on sorcery and an implacable enemy of witches—acknowledged that children below the age of puberty are generally innocent of corruption by the devil. Satan only pursued "those above twelve or fourteen years of age" wrote this jurist; before this they were of little value to him "because of the lack of judgment and discretion." Thus, even if they should be enlisted, as children, in the service of the Evil One, they were not to be held responsible for their behavior.[2]

But where did "nature" leave off and "nurture" begin?[3] In seventeenth century French beliefs a child's nature—his *naturel*—began with his basic constitution (*complexion*). In medical terminology of the time this could be one of four types: aqueous, melancholic, choleric or sanguine. These labels described temperamental and intellectual as well as physical endowment: "Having judged Monseigneur the Dauphin to be basically sanguine but on the choleric side (giving him by his nature quickness) . . . while *sang* serves as a restraining moderating quality," wrote Jean Héroard, doctor of the child who was to become Louis XIII, "there follows from this a constitution promising a completely healthy body and a benevolent understanding. . . . a good and kind prince."[4]

Héroard's words were written in the early 1600s. If we stand in 1700 at the threshold of the Enlightenment and look back at the documentary accumulation of the previous century, there is a strong impression of important cultural change. The world of Jean Bodin and Henri IV at the end of the sixteenth century was vastly different than that of Louis XIV and Montesquieu in the first part of the eighteenth. Not only culture but also social structure and patterns of action presumably also changed—and child-rearing practices along with them. To identify changes in child-rearing correctly is difficult, because, like most other social patterns in traditional societies, far less changed than remained the same. And much that was taken for granted was not discussed in any document. Thus most of what we know about seventeenth century French child-rearing must be conjectured from peripheral indicators.

SOURCES: TRADITIONAL RESERVOIRS AND NEW ACCRETIONS

In seventeenth century France the world of the child from birth to the age of six or seven was for the most part the world of women. This means it was the world of customary practice governed by unwritten traditions—the world of *face-to-face* contacts and *spoken* words.

As long as communication is of this kind, the domain of woman and infant remains mostly closed for us. Indeed, because so much significant communication issued from the mouth and penetrated only the ear, even the most important mystery for children—"Where do babies come from?"—was sometimes solved for seventeenth-century children by the concept of insemination (and issue) through the ear. A striking example appears in Héroard's diary. Louis learned his nurse was pregnant and was asked where the baby was. He whispered, the doctor reported, "in a very low voice in his nurse's ear, 'He is in your stomach.' " Héroard then asked him, " 'How did he get in?' " " 'Through the ear,' " Louis answered. " 'How will he get out?' " " 'Through the ear.' "[5]

The seventeenth century witnessed an explosion of literary correspondence and diaries from erudite men. But these observers of the passing scene continued to overlook the lives of children around them. Ariès has found a newly realistic attention to babies in the plastic art of the seventeenth century.[6] No parallel exists in literary art. The classical renaissance in French imaginative literature ignored the infant and small child.

Three basic sources do exist. *Livres de raison*—family diaries, kept usually by the male household head—were a form of record which dates back as far as the fourteenth century. For the most part they changed their characteristics little, giving mere vital statistics. Details of births, baptisms and deaths, sales and purchases of property and services, were occasionally interspersed with more intimate comments on the course of a marriage or the vicissitudes of a child's life.[7]

Two sources on early childhood did expand significantly. First, a new type of report from educated women, mostly in the vanguard of the Catholic reform movement, reflected a new moral interest in children. Second, a new fund of information on children was furnished in works by physicians and medically-trained midwives.

Works by women which concerned children were mostly in the form of letters and reports to leaders of the Christian revival in France—leaders such as François de Sales, Vincent de Paul and Pierre Fourier. Many of these women had been mothers themselves; most were actually engaged in pioneering social or educational work among women and children. Occasionally the spirit of reform which took them into convent, hospital, orphanage and nursery allows us to enter the child's world through their eyes. Their purpose was innovative: it was the moral salvation of women and children. But it involved ministering to the practical as well as spiritual needs of its objects. By observing what they considered important we may sometimes glimpse an unknown aspect of what was ordinary practice in child-rearing. The pressures they applied show at least the directions in which they wished ordinary practice to change.

The spate of new works by doctors and midwives reflected new interests in nature which had appeared in the late sixteenth century. Even though the great discoveries in human physiology were not made until the middle of the seventeenth century (and took longer than that to be accepted by the French medical establishment), medical literature at the start of the century showed unprecedented interest in empirical description. The child came in for a share of this attention. This literature provides some new information on pregnancy, delivery and the early care of infants. For the most part, these sources do not follow the child much beyond his adjustment to a nursing figure. As a consequence our information on babies between three months and six years of age is usually not enlarged. But there are some exceptions to this generalization

The most notable exception is Jean Héroard's diary, which covers in detail the life of one individual from birth to the age of twenty-six. In the middle of the nineteenth century this physician's manuscript was found to be a unique source, and it began to be mined for information on seventeenth century child-rearing. However, the observations Héroard made cannot be uncritically generalized even to princely or aristocratic milieus of the time. This is because it is a biography of a very special subject—the dauphin of France—and much of the doctor's record is only meaningful in this narrow context. For example Héroard attributed —quite as a matter of fact—supernatural powers to the five week old prince:

> He listens very attentively . . . as I tell him that he must be good and just, that God gave him to the world for this purpose . . . that if he were then God would cherish him. He smiled at these words.

Héroard was serious in assuming that the baby understood what he was being told. Next he attributed articulate speech to the infant:

> His nurse was holding him in her lap. . . . She said to him: "Well, Monsieur, when I am old and go around with a cane, will you still love me?" He looked her straight in the face and then, as though having thought about it, replied, "No!" I was right there and was completely astonished as were all those who heard him.[8]

A further peculiarity of Louis' case derived from his unique position as the first legitimate heir in a new dynasty. This made his procreative potential a crucial issue to all who were associated with Bourbon rule. The result was that Héroard's diary shows an exaggerated attention to the prince's phallic development. The supposedly precocious genital interests and capacities of the baby and their encouragement by others comprise a leitmotiv of this unusual chronicle.

Members of the court amused themselves by training the one-year-old to offer his penis instead of his hand to be kissed.[9] Games sometimes used courtiers' fancies about a marriage between Louis and his age-mate the Spanish princess. (She did actually become his wife thirteen years later.) When he was fourteen months old Héroard participated in such play: "I ask him, 'Where is the Infanta's darling?' He puts his hand on his penis."[10]

Later the object of these phallic games became more explicit: Louis was in training for an important role. At the age of three as he was being prepared for bed he "crosses his legs, asking 'Will the Infanta do this?' " Héroard wrote, "A lady in waiting says, "Monsieur, when you go to bed together she will put her legs in that position.' " The doctor was proud that his little patient knew what to do in such a case: "He replies promptly and cheerfully, 'And I, I will put them like *that*' spreading his legs apart with his hands."[11]

We can scarcely draw conclusions about ordinary parents' attitudes towards autoerotic activities of French seventeenth-century children from the fact that Héroard reported with pride the penile erections of the dauphin, who was still at the breast:

> While nursing he scratches his 'merchandise', erect and hard as wood. He often took great pleasure in handling it and in playing with the tip of it with his fingers.[12]

A third reason for reservations about the generalizability of this unique child's history was the personal oddity of the doctor who recorded it. Héroard's obsessive passion for chronicling his ward's behavior was only one of his peculiarities. His persistent, intensely manipulative intervention in Louis' early life gave to his *Journal* a pathological character making it unrepresentative of patterns of child care of the time.[13]

But not all medical sources on seventeenth-century childhood showed the perverse preoccupations of the dauphin's first physician. Although none was as detailed or prolonged in its observations as Héroard's diary, a number of other treatises by doctors and midwives offer data useful in tracing patterns and trends in child-rearing of the period. For present purposes our interest in such accounts begins at the point where nature and nurture begin to interact—with the establishment of the nursing couple.

THE CHILD'S NATURE AND THE NURSING BOND

Common to all seventeenth-century French views of infancy was the assumption that survival in the first few months depended absolutely on the formation of a satisfactory nursing relationship with a woman. The possibility of artificial feeding—animals, feeders, concoctions—was not unknown. The *Journal des Scavans* described one mixture and solemnly assured its readers, "almost all *Bavarian* babies are nursed in this way."[14] But it was universally regarded as unsuitable for infants and undesirable and unsafe for the first year or two.[15]

The best assurance for forming a successful nursing bond was usually thought to be feeding by the mother. A statement by a noted obstetrician, François Mauriceau, was typical: "The first and good principle of all the qualities in a good nurse is that she be the own mother of a child ... because of the mutual agreement of tempers, as that having much more love for the child she will be much more careful."[16] Another doctor, Laurent Joubert, gave spirited and acute observations of the nursing relationship. Although he had actually been a professor of Héroard at the famous medical school of Montpellier, he showed none of the perversities of his pupil. His entrée into the world of the nursery was normal, as he told us, through being the father of eleven children all nursed by their mother, his wife. Joubert's appeal to mothers to nurse their own babies gives us an attractive picture of a model nursing couple:

> If women only knew the joys of nursing they would not only not forego it with their own—they would hire themselves out: nurses are usually so in love with and devoted to babies not their own.... Is there a better passtime than one with an infant who is endearing to his nurse and strokes her as he suckles while with one hand he uncovers and handles the other breast and with the other grasps her hair or her necklace, playing with them. When with his feet he kicks at those who want to divert him, at the same moment with his loving eyes he gives a thousand little smiling glances to his nurse. ... What a delight to see it![17]

The *nourrice du corps*—the breastfeeding figure—might be the child's generative mother or its "second mother" as Louise Bourgeois, the most illustrious midwife of the age, called her.[18] Whichever she was, the nursing relationship was seen as more profoundly influential on the developing nature of the child than the pre-natal experience. The threshold of birth was not the decisive one. Intrauterine gestation and extrauterine parasitism were regarded as one continuous process in the formation of the child's *naturel*. For a woman, suppression of her milk was like abortion of her foetus.[19] Indeed, until late in the century even medical authorities believed mother's milk literally to be menstrual blood—suppressed for nine months to nurse the embryo in the womb—diverted and purified for the infant's further nurture. If a baby was delivered to a hired nurse, "he has been engendered and partly nursed for nine months with one blood and then nursed two years more with another."[20] One danger in changing "bloods" was that they might be chemically incompatible. Jacques Guillemeau, a famous surgeon of the time, recounts the legend of Queen Blanche who made her infant son, Saint Louis, vomit the milk given him by another in her absence.[21]

The characteristics acquired by the child in the arms of his nurse were therefore truly as *innate* as those acquired *in utero*—and probably more significant in later life: "To give birth is nothing, to nurse is to give birth continually."[22] Like the experience in the womb, nursing experiences were indelibly imprinted: as the fancies (*imaginations*) of the women might affect the foetus she carried, so would the *mélancolie* of the nurse affect the child she held in her arms.[23] Just as the mother's experiences might cause her child to change sex in the womb, so if the nurse's milk was too hot for a boy or too cold for a girl, the result would be a "mannish" girl, an "effeminate" boy.[24]

Not only physical traits—including the dreaded syphilis—but also characteristics of temperament such as sloth, promiscuity, impiety, could be transferred pre-natally or from nurse to child. In a discourse giving advice on raising Louis XIV, selection of a nurse was to take into account "beauties of the soul . . . so that the prince receives impressions of good habits with the milk . . . and of goodness and wisdom."[25] Mme. de la Guette was grateful all her life to her mother for the lasting advantages she had obtained from her nursing: "good disposition and good health."[26]

A successful nursing bond was more than desirable. It was vital. In an era when the infant mortality rate rarely dipped much below 25% and in hard times frequently reached 75%, the life of a newborn hung by a slender thread. This was well recognized.[27] Survival to the age of one year was not something probable, providing only that no force actively prevented it, but rather an achievement reached—if at all—only by concerted and persistent efforts. And the establishment of a successful nursing relationship was almost the whole story.[28]

The signals of impending failure were familiar: the syndrome of infant attrition we know as marasmus was recognized by Héroard in his little patient at the age of ten weeks. Louis had as yet been unable to form a satisfactory nursing relationship and his doctor observed: "Everyone could see that his body was not being nourished: the chest muscles were all atrophied and the big fold around his neck was only skin."[29] Another prince had a similar problem. The dowager Duchess of Orléans wrote, "I find my grandson so delicate that I can't believe he'll survive very long. In truth he's big for his age but his whole organism is weak and frail."[30] Children who failed to thrive were sometimes thought to be the product of insemination by the devil. From such coupling, Uvier thought, "are born thin children who are rather smaller than the others who wear out three nurses without getting plumper and cry when one handles them."[31]

Since the best assurance for a successful nursing bond was nursing by the mother, a bourgeois father's will might make his wife's capacity to inherit contingent upon her personally nursing their son for a prolonged period.[32] The *livres de raison* told of various other expedients adopted to fill in for maternal failure. A father of the Froissard-Boissia family recorded that a son born to him in October was nursed jointly by the mother and a domestic servant until the following July, when the mother, finding herself feverish and pregnant, "gave up nursing her baby" and handed him over to two nurses outside the home. Later these women became ill (during a hot August) so the child was taken home and put in the charge of a "single nurse".[33] Apparently this baby survived these transfers. Such records usually describe prosperous, rapidly-growing families. As the children multiply in number the probability that the mother—occupied with a growing problem of family management—would personally nurse the new additions seems to have declined.

In some cases medical opinion held that nursing by the biological mother was counter-indicated. The best age for a nurse was 25 to 30, but according to some the range within which women were thought most likely to bear robust offspring with males in the majority was 17 to 25.[34] Successful procreation and optimal nurture might thus be incompatible. However this incongruity was less likely to be a problem for the laboring classes in which a later marriage age for women was more common than for the upper bourgeoisie and aristocracy. And although the practice of hiring wet-nurses seems to have spread from the topmost stratum to the upper-middle and even down to the artisan class during the course of the century,[35] most of the medical advice which refers to hired nurses was directed at a small minority of the population. In rural areas and in all but the affluent classes the babies that survived were still in the majority of cases nursed by their natural mothers.[36]

Medical advice on nursing techniques also varied by social class, although it is doubtful that many of the pediatric advisors had much professional contact with the lower orders. For aristocratic women who were "delicate" the best policy was to put the infant to the breast after a lapse of anywhere from a few days to several weeks.[37] More than one such author maintained that new milk from a new mother disagrees with a high-born child. This presented no problem for the child of well-to-do parents: it was assumed that substitute nurses were available. Attention was given to the mother: she might avoid discomfort—if she waited until engorgement passed—by putting small puppies (always at hand!) to her breasts or by expressing her milk into a receptable through a straw.[38] For these clients' babies colostrum was regarded as unhealthy food: viscous substances may have been suspect on account of the general concern with clearing the baby's passages of mucus.[39] Several counselors observed that such nice discrimination was lost upon the poor: "Poor people cannot observe so many precautions and such mothers are obliged to give their child such from the first day," said Mauriceau.[40] "As for the poor," wrote the countess of the great estate of Vaux-le-Vicomte, "they don't know what it is to follow a diet, being obliged to eat everything that they have."[41]

Various other obstacles to nursing adaptation were mentioned but one is of special interest: the membrane under the tongue. The fact that the need for cutting this *filet* remained unquestioned by physicians throughout the century gave the practice an aspect of ritual. Scévol⊇ de Sainte-Marthe, the "Dr. Spock" of the late sixteenth century, wrote that if the tongue were folded back "as if tied" clipping is necessary.[42] One of the most enlightened obstetricians of the early eighteenth century agreed.[43] Héroard wrote of his day-old patient, "Seeing that he had trouble nursing we looked into his mouth. It was seen that the tongue-string was the cause. At five in the evening it was cut in three places by M. Guillemeau, the king's surgeon."[44] "Freeing" the tongue was often done by a pinch of the nurse's fingernails in the case of less august infants—although surgeons advised professional intervention.[45] Sucking itself was not seen as a need of the baby. However it had a "chemical" function, "by the movement suction gives to the jaws it opens up the salivary vessels." Saliva, mixing with nutrients, aided digestion "marvelously."[46]

Advice on when to feed the baby was almost entirely lacking in the literature. Putting the child to the breast was the practice of first resort whenever the baby indicated discomfort; there seems to have been no notion that an infant—or his nurse—could be trained to a schedule.[47] Medical advice aimed at teaching the art of establishing this relationship, a difficult matter and an urgent one because of the extreme jeopardy of the newborn. Since most women had to depend on themselves to achieve it, the seventeenth-century Daniel Martin, author of a schoolbook to teach German speaking Alsatians French, imagined one housewife of Strasbourg saying:

> I pity my poor cousin if she has as much trouble as her sister in nursing her child. Her breasts became hard as stones—inflamed and ruptured to such an extent that when the baby suckled pure blood came out with extreme pain. So she was obliged to wean him and give him water in a baby feeder (*tuterolle*) in which were dissolved tablets of manus-Christi.[48]

These women must have known that artificial feeding was a death-warrant for infants. Physicians warned against the practice of feeding pap or *bouilie*—even as a supplement—prematurely: "Beasts show us that milk alone is sufficient to nourish an infant."[49] Any other than human nursing could only suit children who were already strong and ready for weaning.[50]

The importance of her function made the position of the nursing woman one of deference. Semi-magical properties were attributed to human milk;[51] to a great extent the producer of this irreplaceable substance shared the deference given to the product. It was usually reported of female saints that they had personally nursed their infants to "full

term."[52] Gratitude to the nurse—whether or not she was the biological
mother—was commensurate with the magnitude of her service. Although Mme. de la Guette reported a happy marriage and maternity of
her own, she "loved her mother more than my life." When her mother
died she had the rather bizarre notion of keeping her mother's head in
her room "in order to see her whenever I wanted."[53]

If the successful nurse was hired, to a great extent this esteem was
transferred to her. Coustel told of a son returning, as an adult, with
lavish gifts for his nurse. He made the following speech to his "real"
mother:

> I show more affection and gratitude to the one to whom I owe
> the most. When the time for your lying-in came you rid yourself
> of me as of a burden that was inconvenient . . . while instead my
> nurse continually caressed me, nourished me for two years with
> her own milk and by her care and trouble brought me to the
> vigorous manhood in which you see me at present.[54]

This was a morality tale, but one with much basis in reality. The value
and importance of the hired nurse let her share much of the esteem of
the mother. In her memoir of her husband Mme. de Duplessis-Mornay
noted his birthplace fifty years earlier, his noble parents, grandparents,
aunts and uncles and "Dame de Morvillier, his nurse, whom I don't wish
to forget . . . a woman of sweet disposition (*doulce humeur*)."[55] The
sharing between nurse and progenitive mother of the honors of motherhood was symbolized in many a portrait of the time showing the two
side by side or in a complementary pose.[56]

The century wore on, and the wages of wet-nurses rose steadily. The
ideal hired nurse became almost a jewel beyond price. When Mme. de
Sévigné finally found a satisfactory nurse for her granddaughter, she
put up with the most humiliating demands on the part of the woman's
husband for the sake of the baby's preservation.[57] *Livres de raison* tell
of the rehiring of wet-nurses for later children when they have succeeded
in seeing one family member through infancy. And in affluent families
the nurse became a permanent member of the household after her
nurturant function had been successfully filled. Louis XIII's nurse was
present on his wedding night. As a little boy he had given a number of
women the title of "Mama", including his nurse,[58] but he was not easily
able to show tender feelings towards any but the one who had nurtured
him. Héroard records the following expression of sentiment from the
four-year-old prince:

> Listening to his nurse complaining of the fact that her friends had
> been sent away when they came to see the Dauphin; he starts to
> cry saying, "I want them to go fetch them here." He had had his
> shoes removed while at table; his nurse wanted to put them back

on: "No, Mama Doun-doun, I don't want you to have to put my shoes on." "Why not, Monsieur?" "Because you suckled me (*m'avez donné a téter*) when I was little."[59]

HANDLING THE CHILD: CLOTHING, CLEANING, TRAINING

While seventeenth-century Western European swaddling techniques seem to have followed a common pattern, local variations must have been myriad. Thus Daniel Martin's eye-witness description of the equipment needed should not be taken as universal in seventeenth-century France. He reported one of his Strasbourgers saying that all was ready for the expected infant: "mattress filled with straw . . . cushions, swaddling clothes (*maillots*) and the *bandelette* with the *cercle*."[60] These last were narrower bandages for wrapping the child's head, held in place by a circle of cloth—the whole resembling a modern sheik's headdress looped under the chin, as in the touching infant portraits of Georges de la Tour who probably portrayed actual practices in the neighboring state of Lorraine.[61]

In wrapping up the baby, particular attention was given to the head, although here too practices seem to have been quite variable. Louise Bourgeois thought the custom of binding the infant's head tightly in order to narrow and elongate it was a very bad one; perhaps the practice was localized around the French capital for she condemns the "*bandelettes* which make their heads long and by which everyone recognizes them as children of Paris."[62] In some places a slat was bound within the swaddling clothes running along behind the head and neck of the newborn to make them even more secure.[63] Martin did not include in his list the *béguin*, an additional headdressing which consisted of several thicknesses of cloth crowning the head underneath the swaddling. This may have been used because the fontenelle or opening in the skull at the top of the baby's head was considered particularly vulnerable. A father in the family of Froissard-Boissia attributed the death of a two-month old son to cold on the brain, from being born with a "brain much open." "Insufficient care" had been taken, he added, "to protect him from the cold entering in said opening."[64] A doctor of the time recommended a little skullcap of furred stuff to protect from temperature change that might penetrate to the brain.[65]

Three chief rationales for swaddling are manifest in discussions of the time. First, it was necessary to insure that a human posture would be learned by the child. If the infant's arms were not rigidly bound along the side of his body, and if his legs were not extended and straightened, he might naturally walk on "all fours" like other animals.[66] Given the tendency of a sleeping infant to resume the foetal position, swaddling was a method of nurture designed to prevent reassertion of the child's "nature"—to wit, regression to a more animal state.

Concern with erect posture was exaggerated in the case of upper-class girls whose forms were thought to be especially vulnerable to getting out of shape. Marie de Medicis wrote her seven-year-old daughter in 1609 warning against too much horseback riding "which might in the long run spoil your figure (*taille*)."[67] The *corps,* a corset of whalebone stays, was applied to young girls (and certain boys) to "support the *taille* and prevent it from becoming deformed." Toward the close of the period we are considering, Buffon thus compared the corsetting device to swaddling bandages and condemned both practices.[68] Allegedly, the *corps* had been introduced by Catherine de Medicis in the latter half of the sixteenth century.[69] Its popularity reflected the belief that upright stance (at least in women) had to be achieved by design.

A second reason for swaddling was the weakness of the neonate. Since he was *faible* (weak) and uncoordinated, his random movements might dislocate a limb. Until he gained control, swaddling was necessary for his protection. Before he reached a stage when he could support his head and control his arms and legs, he was thought to be a danger to himself.[70]

A third reason for swaddling was prosaic and usually unspoken. This was the influence of the weather. Climate made it imperative for most French children to be wrapped warmly. In winter, only a place close to a fire permitted a baby to be unswaddled and cleaned without great haste.

There could have been little desire to prolong swaddling. It was costly both in time and human effort.[71] As soon as it was believed to be safe for the baby, swaddling was ended. Guillemeau assumed the arms would be released by the twentieth or thirtieth day.[72] Others indicated the wrapping would be continued as long as nine months or more.[73] It is not clear, however, whether this meant the "whole treatment." Very young babies were often painted nursing with arms free of swaddling clothes.[74] In an often-reproduced painting of M. de Montmort's seven children, one is a baby of eight months, sitting erect on a table in the ordinary loose bonnet and dress of an older child.[75]

From the age of four months or so a child was increasingly left unswaddled· during daylight hours. At night swaddling not only kept an older baby warm but also facilitated fastening him securely in his cradle so that rocking would not eject him. In contemporary advice, nurses are warned against shirking their duty to clean or feed a child by substituting too-violent rocking to soothe him—a practice only possible with a swaddled, strapped-in package.[76]

There were several reasons for getting the baby out of the *maillot* as soon as possible. For one thing, keeping the baby swaddled created a number of laundry problems. Not only the *langes,* or swaddling bands, but also *couches* or diapers underneath them had to be laundered by boiling and then dried.[77] For another, keeping the baby itself clean was an even more onerous task than cleaning its clothes. Mauriceau recommended a complete change two or three times daily and at night as well.[78] Only the upper classes (who of course comprised Mauriceau's practice) could manage this.

Soap was the cleaning agent for the baby's linens but not for the baby, on whom vinegar and wine solutions were used, sometimes with rosewater oil. These solutions were effective preventives for rashes due to excessive alkaline deposits on the skin perhaps more effective than soap could have been. Wine alone was a "natural" antiseptic and it was a universal remedy for childhood ills, applied both internally and externally from birth onward.

Despite what must have been heroic and continual effort, even the best-tended babies developed severe and extensive rashes. As an infant, Louis XIII was scarcely ever free of them [79] His son, the future Louis XIV, also developed ugly skin eruptions and scales (*crasses* and *gâle*) as a baby. The eruptions were so conspicuous that his worried parents had to be reassured. They were told that the king himself had experienced similar afflictions—a fact Héroard had carefully recorded at the time.[80] Other inconveniences of swaddling included chafing and skin abrasions (combatted by additional bolsters between limbs and body underneath the *maillot*), fleas and discomfort from pins.[81]

As the child emerged from the *langes* and gained muscular control, bowel and urinary autonomy became possible. The techniques used by adults in toilet training their children were rarely reported. Whether or not a child was trained to a pot at an early age and with what concern compliance was demanded must in part have depended on the size and status of the family, in part on the season. To support an infant on a pot required a considerable investment of time and effort. The royal family had an abundance of pots and "pierced chairs": At least as early as 16 months of age the Dauphin sat on such a "petit séant" for hours at a time with his games before him on a table.[82] If the climate permitted, even children of royalty relieved themselves in the courtyard or garden. In winter greater effort may have been made to induce defecating and urinating into a receptacle. Evidence leads us to believe, however, that at all levels of society "outdoors" and "indoors" were little distinguished. Pet animals wandered freely between yard and living quarters. Among the affluent, outdoor exercise took place on semi-enclosed balconies, when weather did not permit ranging farther afield. Tennis, shuffleboard and other such sports were played in corridors and halls of palaces or châteaux. When courtiers are reported urinating or defecating in corners of the house or on staircases it should be remembered that in the house and out of doors did not then suggest the contrast that those phrases now evoke.

As for persons lower on the social scale, particularly in the country, practices are still followed in rural France today which have their analogues in the seventeenth century. Consider a modern account:

> The child normally roams around without any ... knickers, to save washing. ... This solution is peculiar to country districts—it makes less work for the mother.[83]

Three hundred year old pictures and statues show use of the same expedient.[84]

How intensely did parental attention concentrate on the development of cleanliness and self-control in toilet matters? Unfortunately, consensus on what was done seems to have been so general that it was almost never discussed. It would be mistaken, however, to assume that indifference to *where* excrement was deposited extended to *whether* or not bowel control was developed by the child. Lack of concern about location is quite compatible with toilet training. Efforts to train the child were expected to be successful by the time he graduated from his cradle to a regular bed—in most cases a bed shared with adults or other children. The Dauphin acquired a bed of his own at the age of two and one half. When he made the big step from cradle to bed he had already been trained to the use of a pot for some time. During the first night however he was upset by having urinated in his sleep: "I've spoiled my beautiful bed!" he cried.[85] Six months later when he again wet his bed he projected the responsibility: "It's Neptune who pissed," he claimed. ("Neptune" was part of the palace fountain system.)[86]

Adults were hopeful and reassuring when Louis wet his bed. But we may surmise that lapses by less influential children were not so well received. More than one medical work warned against severe punishment for enuresis lest the child tie a cord around his penis to prevent accidents.[87]

Authorities differ on the need to induce evacuation in infants: Mauriceau advises purging the meconium; Guillemeau suggests that suppositories need only be used in ill infants;[88] Dionis condemns such tactics as a frequent practice. He writes, "I consider a poor baby extremely unfortunate when he falls into the hands of people who subject him to such remédies at such an early age and who force him to submit to them with so little need."[89] But his enlightened denunciation—coming as it does at the century's end—suggests that the practice of applying suppositories had been widespread.

Louis XIII's case was certainly exceptional in many respects, but the information it gives on his early anal experiences should be noted. As an infant he was constantly given suppositories at Héroard's direction. The struggle between this child and his doctor over his bowel products was particularly intense. Cathartic preparations of mounting potency were administered to him from the age of three. Horrible black preparations were intensely feared by the child; he was much relieved whenever he was told he could take a milder, white preparation of almond oil.[90]

Nor was Louis XIII entirely alone in receiving such treatment. Marie de Medicis reported of her third son, Gaston, that "it took five or six people to hold him down" while his medicine was forced into him because "not for the pleas nor commands nor promises nor threats that I made to him" would he agree to cooperate.[91]

Enemas were frequently administered in the royal household. This practice gave rise to much anxiety for Louis XIII. At the age of eleven we find him praying fervently before he is given an enema in hopes that it "will not do me harm."[92] The practice of syringe-administered enemas for children must have been widely diffused among the upper classes. The childhood experience of Jean-Jacques Bouchard (around 1610) was recalled in the following terms:

> He was scarcely eight years old when he started to clamber up on little girls. . . . Instead of sticking little sticks up their [rectums] as children do, pretending to give each other enemas, he lustily screwed them without knowing what he was doing.[93]

In Louis' history a number of conversations and night-time anxieties show the importance of his preoccupations with anal controls. On one occasion the four-year-old prince woke thinking he had defecated in his nightshirt. "Was this his imagination?" asks Héroard, "There was nothing there."[94] As a seven-year old he showed more complex attitudes. While paying a visit to his father he refused to use the king's *chaise percée* despite his need. Returning to his own home he and Héroard gave much attention to his soiled shirt. Héroard noted that "he had made a little diarrhaeic fart on his shirt."[95]

"TAKING OFF": WALKING AND OTHER MOTOR SKILLS

It is now generally understood that the child's growing control over internal processes is physiologically related to his capacity for increased mobility in space. This connection was by no means obvious to seventeenth-century French adults. The development of gross motor controls was not taken for granted as "natural". In the same way that the infant had been swaddled to encourage his development into an erect biped, so also deliberate training efforts were used to control and further the style of walking.

Louis XIII, with many attendants, was often "walked" before he could walk.[96] When the child seemed ready to acquire this skill—in the dauphin's case at the age of about ten months—*lisières* or apron strings were attached to his garments. These were designed more to indicate the limits to permitted freedom than actually physically to restrain him. Their removal would accompany change to an adult costume.[97]

Ryerson has reported some of the reasons for thinking that children were prevented from crawling.[98] From the portraiture of the time we learn that when children left the swaddling bonds they were induced by one means or another to sit or stand in an erect posture. Engravings of the time show children standing in basketwork "barrels"—stationary walkers in which pre-toddlers were held in an upright position.[99] Children of poor families were pictured in paintings by LeNain sitting on the floor at the feet of the elders; portraitists of aristocratic children typically depicted their subjects standing.

In accounting for these apparent restrictions we may recall the physical environment in which the seventeenth century French child lived. Some floors were of dirt, sometimes covered with straw; animal excrement was often to be found on them. In houses of the more affluent, the floors were of cold stone. At all levels of society, animals inside and outside the house were not necessarily household pets that could be trusted with babies. Despite precautions apparently aimed at preventing contact of well-to-do children with the floor, worms, transmitted from animals to children, were a common affliction.[100] The ubiquity of pets and their excrement was no doubt responsible for the prevalence of these parasites in children.

Whatever the reasons for the restrictions on motility, the danger of childhood infection from adults and other children was clearly understood and provided an additional motive for circumscribing the child's area of freedom. When some of the royal children had smallpox Marie de Medicis wrote Louis' governess, "I certainly think that my son should be lodged in the new building and that care should be taken to see that those who serve the others never come near him."[101] Royal children were isolated completely when contagious diseases appeared in the household of one of them.

"HATCHING": WEANING AND AFTER

The appearance of the first tooth was for many a sign that the child was ready for solid food. The eruption of the last baby tooth was a signal for weaning.[102] Like weaning, the acquisition of each tooth was understood to be a painful and significant event in the child's life: Héroard noted the appearance of each of the dauphin's teeth by number in his *Journal*. Like other aspects of growth, producing teeth was partly the result of effort. Mauriceau spoke of "budding" teeth.[103] One father wrote to his wife comparing her child-delivery to the travail of their baby daughter in teething: "Be as brave in bringing your little one into the world as our Thérèse is in bringing forth (*enfanter*) her teeth.[104]

Thus twenty-four months (more or less) was considered the appropriate age for weaning. A mother in the Mairot family nursed a son, her first to survive infancy, to the age of eighteen months. She then separated him from the breast but he became so ill it was necessary to hire a nurse who fed him for four months, then another whom he used for three.[105]

It has been suggested that the French child's loss of the breast through weaning represented the loss of a loved object. Sainte-Marthe's description of the event seemed to confirm this interpretation: he wrote that the child cries at weaning "like a bride whose husband is snatched away to war."[106]

However, the timing of this event in the seventeenth century suggests that another interpretation is more plausible. If the mother was also the nurse, or if the nurse remained in the home—and these two cases together still did comprise the vast majority of seventeenth century French childhood experiences—the "true" object, that is, the mother who is just beginning to be individuated for the child, is not lost, and the "hatching" process continues after weaning as before.[107] Whatever its importance for the child, the event of weaning was known to be a crisis. Sometimes it was avoided for fear that the child would become ill; Marie de Medicis sent an order postponing her daughter's weaning on this account. The decision was an affair of state, made after consultation with three physicians "and on their advice I consent . . . until Easter if between now and then nothing happens to change the decision," she had her secretary write the children's governess.[108]

Héroard's diary entry on Marcy 3, 1605, relates the implementation of the Queen's decision:

> Madame [the princess Elisabeth] weaned this morning at eight o'clock. She nursed, then her nurse said, "Madame, you will nurse no more. You must be weaned." Whereupon [Elisabeth] said decisively, pulling the breasts to her, "Goodbye, dear breast, I shall no longer nurse." And from that time on she no longer wished to nurse.

Had Elisabeth been less malleable, her brother observed what preparations were ready to discourage her further. On the same day, Héroard recorded, "Monsieur le Dauphin saw the mustard in a sauceboat, went over to say in a low voice to Madame, "See the mustard over there to put on your '*tétoun*'."[109]

Although Guillemeau advised gradual weaning, leaving night feedings till last, most seventeenth-century French medical advice assumed it was a sudden event.[110] The separation was achieved by putting mustard, aloe or other distasteful substances on the nipples. After that the breast was not offered again. Like his sister, Louis had been weaned abruptly. In his case the supplementary deterrents had been necessary.[111]

By contrast, it is probable that lower-class nursing was terminated more gradually and extended for a longer period except in cases of new pregnancies. "So long as there is milk," says Joubert of the poor, "they will give it, to the very last drop."[112] It seems likely that this contrast in practice between upper and lower classes had significant effects that it would be profitable to explore farther.

When weaning was accomplished, the child was watched with concern for adverse effects from the severance from his chief sustenance. Marie de Medicis wrote to Louis' governess soon after his separation. "I would be grateful to be often informed on the state of my son's health after they have deprived him of milk."[113] There were likely to be nutritional problems for some children when the supply of human milk was cut off. Guillemeau describes the cases of *ventre grand*—enlarged abdomen—in which may be recognized the symptoms of malnourished children.[114]

FEAR, SHAME, GUILT AND PUNISHMENT

Weaning left the child newly vulnerable in another respect: it made him eligible for corporal punishment. The traditional form of such punishment—at least for boys—is illustrated by the many surviving caricatures of the child, held by his hands over the shoulders of another, while a third person administers a whipping with *verges*—a bundle of switches tied to a handle—applied either to bare or covered buttocks.[115] No doubt more violent and impromptu methods were also common. Elisabeth Charlotte, Duchess of Orleans, a woman notable for her practical common sense, implied as much:

> In my whole life, I've never given a blow (*soufflet*) to my son, but I had the *verge* administered to him as it should be; he still remembers it. Blows are dangerous; they can damage the head.[116]

Henri IV's rustic upbringing placed him in the "spare the rod and spoil the child" tradition. He recommended frequent whippings for his son the dauphin and was not above administering *soufflets* in person. But the child's mother countermanded the king's orders whenever she could—secretly on occasion—and took the position that whipping was a last resort, signifying failure of those in charge. Whippings, she wrote, must be applied "with such circumspection as to make sure that the anger he might feel as a result will not make him ill."[117]

Marie de Medicis reflected the "modern" view that coercion was counter-productive to securing compliance from children. "Kindness gets more results than harshness," wrote Jeanne Frémyot, the leading educator, "one gets used to *that* kind of noise the way children do to the whip."[118] Another seventeenth century saint, Jean-Baptiste de la Salle, gave a like warning: "Of all the affronts," he wrote, "a blow is the most wounding; it is the result of wild anger.[119]

Manipulation rather than domination was the key to a newly popular strategy: more flies could be caught with honey than with vinegar. But the sanctions used to insure its effectiveness were not necessarily novel. One of these was fear. Elaborate methods were needed in court circles in order to control the willful Louis XIII without direct personal intervention which would incur his wrath, dangerous for a hired servant. Various figures around the palace grounds of whom the child was frightened were used as bogymen. One was a gigantic mason (who no doubt carried formidable tools); another was a one-eyed warrior-colleague of the king (the *borgne*) who represented barely concealed castration threats.[120] Sometimes the castration danger was openly mentioned: Louis' nurse told him never to let anyone touch his penis for fear they would cut it off.[121]

Other forms of manipulation using fear were more subtle. The tutor of Louis' little brother Gaston carried switches on his belt, "but this was only for very infrequent use, as whenever he fell into some fault or other he got [Gaston] to behave most often by a meaningful glance or by force of reasoning."[122] Ornano, an ardently devout figure who took over Gaston's education in 1619, went through the pretense of threatening to whip his charge, then had his wife intervene in the boy's behalf on the child's promise that he would henceforward behave.[123]

Shame also played a part in the manipulation of conformity. Héroard expressed the acceptable view:

> One has to ... teach them by means of kindness and patience rather than by rigor and impetuosity ... punishing misdeeds in such a way as to give them a little honest shame to have committed them rather than too much fear of punishment.[124]

More refined were the tactics used at Port-Royal, a convent and school for girls that was center of a new and more puritanical morality. Shame had a part in achieving compliance but the aim was to substitute inner motivations for good behavior as soon as possible:

> One can make the little and middle ones placards which describe their fault in large letters—one or two words is enough, such as "lazy", "negligent", or "liar".

As for the older ones, continued Jacqueline Pascal, the headmistress, they could be made ready to act directly from a love of God except on a few occasions when it was suitable to impose humiliating penitences on them "as one does on the younger ones, such as to make them go without a veil or ask the prayers of the sisters in the refectory."[125] Her warning to take care that "this will not harm them through embittering them" was echoed by another member of the Catholic vanguard, Isaac-Louis le Maistre de Sacy, who reminded the readers of his "Advice on the Guidance of Children" that love of God was better inspired by kindness and gentleness than harshness; prayers rather than whippings were the effective means of control.[126]

The revival of religious asceticism worked its influence powerfully upon educated men and women of the early seventeenth century. It caused a change in educational approach. A deliberate effort was made to replace the traditional external threats and sanctions with inner controls established by the child himself. The new tactics were designed to heighten guilt rather than induce shame. This called for energetic and patient attention to children's behavior beyond anything that had been asked of adults before. Jacqueline Pascal's intensely puritanical regimen for little girls at Port-Royal was so demanding in this respect that her publisher thought it necessary to add a preface with a "wise and useful" caveat that would excuse readers from feeling obligated to institute like measures:

> Even though these regulations . . . have been drawn up on the basis of . . . actual practice at Port-Royal . . . it is necessary to admit that for those outside it would not always be easy nor even useful to apply them in all details. Because . . . all children are not capable of . . . so demanding (*tendu*) a life without falling into depression (*abattement*) . . . and all mistresses cannot enforce such an exacting discipline and win at the same time their devotion and love. . . .[127]

At Port-Royal little girls as young as four were taught to follow a schedule wholly dedicated to putting individual consciences in the service of God. From their first awakening every rule was considered for its relevance to this purpose. For example, hair-combing and dressing were to be achieved speedily "in order to give as little time as possible to decorating a body that is to serve as pasture for worms."[128]

The new attention to the inner life of children in convent, monastery and school was totalitarian in design: body language as well as the spoken word were censored by the pedagogue. The child should strive to keep still, but not insultingly stiff or langorous, and not jiggle or make gestures of the head. Nor should he show emotions "by motions of his forehead, eyebrows or cheeks." These rules for boys by J.-B. de la Salle extended to the manner in which the child should lie in bed, so that "those who come near . . . cannot see the form of the body."[129]

At Port-Royal, "perfect watchfulness over the children is necessary, never allowing them to be alone no matter where it may be. . . ." The regime was all-hearing as well as all-seeing: "Everything that they say must be heard by their mistress . . . lest they learn to use deception to hide faults that they wish one not to know of."[130]

FANTASY

Aspirations such as those just described may well have been too demanding for wide adoption. Among the restricted group for whom the Catholic reform was an immediate influence, however, this intensified concern with the inner life probably modified the content of childhood fantasies by weighting the characteristic balance of sanctions for childhood misbehavior away from fear of external retribution and in the direction of internally-generated guilt.

To test such a proposition systematically would be difficult. What can be offered here are representative samples of different styles of fantasy. The "old style" played heavily on threats of the devil, fears of hellfire and imaginings of possession. Students of Charcot have analyzed the hallucinations of Jeanne des Anges which resulted in the accusation and condemnation of Urbain Grandier. They were classic hysterical fantasies in which unpermitted sexual wishes were attributed to external agents (Grandier and the devil)[131] Louis XIII himself seems to have hallucinated the devil from early childhood.[132] When he met Jeanne des Anges in 1638 she showed him the stigma on her hand and he told her "My faith is fortified."[133]

In contrast with this imagery of external dangers, the "new style" of fantasy showed the effects of an aim to reform conscience and character *within* the child rather than to achieve mere formal compliance with adult demands. Discipline by adults was designed to inspire guilty feelings rather than intensify the child's terror. The schoolteacher's objective was to show children

> one loves them for God and that it is that affection which makes their faults so painfully affecting to bear. . . We are impelled only by . . . the desire to render them such as God wishes them.[134]

No encouragement here to strike out at the devil. The new model was the inward-looking, self-abnegating man or woman. Aggression was to be turned against the self: "One must bear the lashes of the whip which our good Lord gives us, and kiss the *verges* tenderly, for he strikes us out of love," said Saint Chantal.[135]

Marie-Marguerite Acarie, daughter of the founder of the first Carmelite order in France, underwent rigorous training in self-abnegation and humiliation at the hands of her mother. At the age of four, her biographer reports, she was found rigid in bed, arms extended, crying "with admirable sweetness, 'Ah, my God, don't nail me down!' "[136]

In this "new style" forbidden desires are not projected onto devils nor converted into symptoms. They are offered to God for his greater glory. The renewal of religious ardor offered a channel for the sublimation—for example—of incestuous wishes. A passionate correspondence between Angélique Arnauld and her father took place on the occasion of her profession as a nun at Port-Royal. Her father expressed his delight at her marriage to Christ: "May it unite us one day in heaven by a stronger bond than the one that links us on earth."[137] Her aunt and namesake, first reform abbess of Port-Royal had welcomed her own mother to the cloister, where daughter, as Mère Angélique, thus became "mother" to her parent.

LeRoy Ladurie has called attention to the cannibalistic content of fantasies associated with public orgies in which animal totems were prominent. Public executions such as the ceremonial disembowelment and dismemberment of Ravaillac, assassin of Henri IV, suggested anthropophagic rituals.[138] Children were witnesses at such events. They also watched the frequent struggles to the death between bears and dogs or other wild animals which were arranged for public amusement. Louis XIII's childhood was heavily populated with animals. Reports of his dreams and fantasies reveal that his mental life typically contained animals and humans in dramatic situations. At the age of five, Louis had already witnessed the killing of wild animals. Like many of his countrymen, he became a passionate hunter.

The close proximity to animals in which humans lived seems to have meant that barriers to sodomy were lower than in modern times. Animal sodomy, one jurist notes, was a capital crime punishable by execution by fire. It was also necessary to burn the animal partner, lest the notion of a like offense arise in the minds of others seeing it. By contrast, masturbation (*corruption de soi-meme*) was punishable only by banishment or fines, unless it occurred during dreams in which case it was innocuous. But, he concluded, this offense was never discovered anyway; thus it was a matter for God rather than the civil authority.[139]

THE CHILD IN A DEMOGRAPHIC CONTEXT

The evidence so far examined on child-rearing attitudes and practices has been primarily literary. However another kind of documentary evidence—population data—offers additional insight into the position of the seventeenth-century French child. Recent studies of demographic material, particularly of family patterns of natality and mortality, will be briefly considered here for their bearing on the topic at hand.

At the top of the social ladder, among the royal family and great nobility, early marriages and short intergenesic periods were the rule. In much of the upper bourgeoisie too the desire to perpetuate the line often resulted in marriages arranged before puberty followed by the earliest possible impregnation of the bride.[140] For all but women with great independent fortunes, marriage became more difficult after the age of twenty. After that age, as Estienne Pasquier wrote of his grand-daughter, "the older she grows the more her price will be marked down."[141] One consequence of this pattern was that many upper class women had produced several children before they issued from adolescence themselves.[142] For such families fertility was apparently only rarely allowed to be interrupted by the mother's lactation; with a high rate of infant mortality in all classes the affluent could count on a supply of women ready to nurse their children.

The death of the mother in such well-to-do families did not necessarily interrupt the pattern of childbearing, Baulant observes. The disadvantaged position of women in marriage bargaining meant that even very old men could command wives in continuous succession: "The rapidity of remarriages is often such that the rhythm of childbirth in the family is scarcely altered by the change of partner."[143]

However, as one descended the social ladder, seemingly the pattern of marriage and natality changed. What has been called the "European marriage pattern" characterized by late marriages and a small family size was the more general rule—at least in central and western France.[144]

A number of circumstances operated to make large-sized families uneconomic among the poor. Goubert has shown that the average income of a seventeenth century Beauvais laborer was in a normal year about sufficient to support a wife and two children at subsistence levels.[145] For the impoverished strata paid nurses were not in the picture. Support of a nursing mother meant relinquishing some part of her other services—resources were diverted to the nurture of an infant who might not survive in any case. In short it was a large investment with high risk.

Large family size among the poor also was discouraged by the inheritance laws in some regions. Laws permitting the unequal division of property (and therefore the possibility of passing estates along intact despite a large number of children) were applicable chiefly to the noble class. Lower class inheritance laws generally required more equal division. For the peasant or artisan operating near the subsistence level this was a disincentive to producing more children than those necessary to carry on the economic activity.[146]

Regional differences introduce a wealth of variations. In fact cultural patterns seem frequently to have differed from village to neighboring village sufficiently to introduce important differences in natality.[147]

Recent French research has sought to discover the factors which were most important in seventeenth-century France in effecting controls on population size. Differentially "adaptive" practices have been briefly sketched. Much attention has focussed on the extent to which contraception was practiced and on the influence of the physical environment on fertility.[148] Death rates of various population subgroups during famines and epidemics have also been investigated.[149] In the present discussion, however, our chief interest in population control lies in the more or less conscious practices by which parents affected their children's conditions of survival.

At the start of the seventeenth century the legal power of a father over his household was virtually absolute. Jean Bodin had described the dominant rationale that legitimatized a paternal authority extending even to the power of life or death over his offspring.[150] A 1611 review of the criminal code enumerates the conditions under which a father has the right to kill an adult son or daughter.[151] His rights over younger children may not have needed to be formally defined. In the late sixteenth century Estienne Pasquier, a humane and intelligent lawyer, took it for granted that his son had the power "as you write me" to "suppress" a new child, although he questioned the wisdom of such a move. "How can you think of it? After having lost the first one, to be parricide of the second? No. . . ."[152]

What method Nicolas Pasquier would have used to "suppress" his unwanted child is not specified. The midwife Lapère, we are assured, knew well the terrible effect of a drop of laudanum on the tongue of a newborn baby.[153] There are many reasons to suppose that outright infanticide of legitimate infants was uncommon.[154] A more blameless method of controlling family size was available; it was the simple failure to provide active and purposeful nurture calculated to maximize chances of survival. Lebrun cites a case record from a *livre de raison* which illustrates well a "failure of nurture":

> At eight in the evening my wife delivered a girl who didn't seem capable of surviving. The . . . midwife baptised her in the presence of eyewitnesses as she did have signs of life. It was more than an hour before she cried. . . . The next day she was baptized . . . in the church . . . and on the following day sent away *en nourrice* at a distance of six leagues and died on the fifth day of life.[155]

Lebrun observes that since the *ondoiement* or baptism in the home had been perfectly adequate to prevent risking the loss of an infant soul to limbo, it would seem that dragging the weak two-day old off to church, not to mention sending it far away to nurse, should have been avoided. He considers that the parents would have been "well-advised to wait for several weeks."[156] However, the frequency of similar reports in many bourgeois diaries suggests that this case is not simply one of "poor judgment." Rather, a process of rejection is at work. When a child seemed less than usually viable or was perhaps for any reason unwanted, policies not calculated to be life-saving were sometimes adopted. Unproved, inadequate or unsupervised nurses were assigned or the infant was otherwise exposed to unusual risks. Even under the best conditions, the probability of a child surviving to maturity was around fifty percent. Infant mortality rates were in the order of twenty to thirty percent in most regions, even in normal years. Under the circumstances "for a child to reach the red letter day of a first birthday is a major victory over death."[157] Heroic and life-saving tactics adopted in the care of some infants show us that this victory, when it occurred, was scarcely a matter of accident.

WHO SURVIVED? SEX, CLASS AND OTHER INFLUENCES ON INFANT MORTALITY

Seventeenth-century vital statistics are incomplete and unreliable. Although curates in every parish were supposed to record the deaths of newborn children, Mousnier finds that before 1667 this practice was not conscientiously followed.[158] Thus seventeenth-century French historians have devised supplementary approaches to the problem of identifying demographic patterns. These, together with evidence on cultural patterns, can be appraised in weighing the relative importance of variables affecting the chances of infant survival.[159]

Of these variables, probably none was more influential than attitudes towards the sex of the child. Marriage patterns, family fertility and infant care were subject to many influences—among these class, regional and urban-rural variations, trends in religious organization—but any one of these must be considered as modified by the extent to which male children were desired and female children negatively valued.

At the upper levels of society the desire for children was rather usually the desire for male children. Women did not wish each other happy deliveries—they hoped for "un beau fils." Mme. de Grignan's intense wish for children was described as "barbarous" by a friend but events showed that it was not the desire for "children" but for male offspring which pressed this daughter of Mme. de Sévigné on to seven deliveries in about the same number of years. At birth her first child was mistakenly thought to be a boy. When closer inspection revealed the awful truth the mother simply discarded the infant completely. The grandmother rescued and cared for the baby girl until, at the age of about nine, she was incarcerated in a convent—"a burnt offering to the future of her brother." This younger brother, though born frail, had been the object of every possible parental solicitude.[160]

When children were orphaned, relatives responsible for their future arranged for their guardianship and some were disposed of "at a knocked-down price" as Micheline Baulant reports.[161] Girls were apparently more heavily discounted. When an orphaned nephew and several nieces were left homeless Jeanne du Laurens had first choice: "My husband, whom I had to put first, took the boy.[162]

Martin's French schoolbook of the time has some Strasbourg gossips say of an aged burger whose new young wife is pregnant:

Oh how the good old man would be delighted if she was a boy!

For he had treated his first wife "like a princess" in all her lying-ins

even though she never produced her "masterpiece" but only girls which they call in France "pissers" or "split pals" (*compagnons fendus*).[163]

Few illegitimate babies reached the baptismal fonts and recent secondary analyses do not usually record the sex distribution of these. Bouchet, a contemporary observer, took it for granted that bastards were far more likely to be boys than girls.[164] If this was accurate it is not likely to have been determined pre-natally!

A threat to the survival of the daughters of the poor is implied by the belief that the milk of women who had delivered girls was the best kind for newborn boys.[165] This would seem to be an incentive to the abandonment of girls.

Indeed, as the century wore on, countrywomen increasingly abandoned their infants in search of employment as nurses.[166] This accounts in part for the "curious" fact noted by Mols. He comments on a universal surplus of "births" of boys over girls in Europe between 1450 and 1750 (exceeding considerably the slight biological superiority in numbers of boys born). Observing that in 23 of 30 cities the masculinity ratio was lower than in the corresponding rural area he concludes (rather naively) "Urban life would thus seem to favor the birth of girls."[167] In modern non-industrialized countries, as in early modern Europe a differential survival rate, not birth rate, favors boys in the rural areas and tends to disappear with urbanization. Cultural differences between town and country account in part for the improved survival chances of newborn girls in an urban setting. In seventeenth-century France, too, cultural changes were taking place affecting family patterns. These changes were naturally first felt in the urban centers and especially in Paris.

Consider the case of abandoned children. A feature of the French Catholic reform movement of the seventeenth century was a deepened concern with the salvation of *all* souls—including those of women and infants. Intensified supervision of midwives and clerical policing of parental practices were designed to this end: to the extent that they were effective it seems obvious that these measures had a life-saving effect in which girls benefitted disproportionately.[168]

Law enforcement was enlisted on behalf of the safety of the neonates; penalties were strengthened against concealed pregnancies and abortion. That these changes were effective in reducing infanticides of illegitimate children seems confirmed by a rapid increase, throughout the century, in the numbers of children abandoned—especially in Paris and other urban centers.[169]

The difference between Parisian norms and those in the provinces is also illustrated by Fléchier, an observer of special grand jury proceedings in the Auvergne in 1635. He marvels at the lightness of penalties short of death for three girls who have concealed their pregnancies and murdered their newborn babies. "Even the judges were surprised at their own leniency" in condemning one merely to be flogged, branded and banished, he thought. (The judges were Parisian jurists sent down for the assizes.) Of the two others, "both were sentenced to every penalty except death. This verdict would not have been satisfactory at the Tournelle," (the criminal court of the Parlement of Paris).[170]

The religious revival preached the virtues of the large family—"real riches are in mortal souls"—and a morality of sexual parity—if not equality. A difference in good conduct, wrote Coustel, is the only legitimate ground for preferring one child to another. Mauriceau reproached his clientele for wishing so much for sons, "inquietudes not becoming ordinary people, although excusable and permitted to great monarchs and illustrious men."[172] The ascetic nuns of Port-Royal did not permit such sentiments even to the great. Mère Angélique congratulated Marie de Gonzague, Queen of Poland, for her declaration that she was as happy to have given birth to a daughter as to a son.[173] Indeed at Port-Royal the ardent attention given to the moral welfare of young girls was unprecedented. At the start of the century the monasteries had been depositories for "supernumerary children or those physically poorly endowed as many parents did not hesitate to say quite crudely."[174] Now Bourdaloue, the most popular preacher of the last years of the century denounced upper class parents for dragging their young daughters off to convents "feet and hands tied, not daring to complain for fear of unleashing the rage of the father and the obstinacy of the mother."[175] A champion of the Carmelite nuns in France—leaders of one branch of the Catholic reform in France—understood the radical nature of the new morality. "The world is astonished," he wrote, "to see us seek so eagerly for what the world recks so little of"—the souls of females.[176] And in Paris one further innovation testified to some influence of the equalitarian ethic of the Christian reformers: orphanages, formerly provided only for boys, were established for girls as well.[177]

Beyond an apparent improvement in the survival rate of urban female children, there is little to confirm an impression that life chances
for French seventeenth-century children were bettered as a result of the
Catholic reform movement. Undoubtedly, underlying patterns for the
vast majority of families were unchanged.

The heavy toll of children's lives exacted by Malthusian forces operated more heavily upon the poor than upon the rich. Goubert has
shown that in Beauvais and its surroundings when a time of food
scarcity began infant- and child-mortality rose more steeply for classes
near the subsistence margin than for the *bourgeoisie*.[178] Famine imposed
its penalty on the infant through the nursing mother; when food resources were in short supply the lower class infant was entirely dependent on his natural mother.

In Paris, in time of crisis destitute mothers without milk herded in
the Hotel de Ville in hope of help. In 1597 according to Félibien,
hungry *lansquenets* went so far as to eat some of the unlucky babies,
but this story (repeated at the time of the *Fronde* in the mid-seventeenth century) is unconfirmed.[179] Again *enfants trouvés,* abandoned
children of the poor—sometimes in the latter half of the century the
legitimate children of the poor—rarely survived when found in infancy.
Early in the century such infants were taken to the Hôtel Dieu, a general hospital and poorhouse, "where being neither cleaned, cared for
nor bedded as their young age requires . . . not a single one was found
to have survived to adulthood."[180] Vincent de Paul, soliciting help for
their care from the Dames de Charité in 1638, assured the ladies that
scarcely any of the infants so abandoned had survived in the past fifty
years. By this time such children, when they were found in the streets
of Paris and retrieved by the police, were taken to the *Couche* in the
rue Saint-Landry before they could be sold to beggars (*gueux*) for
"three sous each who broke their arms and legs to excite the public to
pity and alms giving, and let them die of hunger.[181]

The *Couche* was a nursery supported by the parishes of the community (St. Germain subscribed 150 *livres* per cradle per year).[182]
Nurses were employed and attempts made to find homes for the children, although (according to Vincent) they were often allowed to die
of hunger. The two facts are not inconsistent since there was always a
shortage of nurses at the *Couche*. Vincent's biographer may exaggerate,
although he claims authentication in the saint's papers, when he writes
that at the *Couche* "the dreadful hag who is charged with receiving the
children . . . in order to diminish their crying . . . gave them laudanum
pills to make them sleep . . . and with those that survive . . . engages in
an abominable traffic. She sells them . . . to women who . . . make

them such a milk corrupt with deadly maladies." But even Chantelauze is skeptical of a colleague who claims that "a certain number of these children were sold to people with a mad passion for life who disemboweled them in order to plunge themselves in bloodbaths, imagining . . . an infallible remedy for all their ills.[183]

Louise de Marillac (Mlle. le Gras), worked arduously to implement Vincent's designs to save a certain number of these discarded children. Organizing and directing the Daughters of Charity she nevertheless found innumerable obstacles to providing services more-life-saving than those of the *Couche*. In spite of efforts to sustain a home for a few dozen foundlings outside of Paris, she reported her dismay at the death of "so many of these little creatures."[184] Her letters to Vincent were a chronicle of the difficulties of getting adequate nurses. In 1638, as she is unable to find a nurse in the country where the children had been located in unhealthful quarters, he advised her to take the one "who is so good" offered by the Hôtel-Dieu.[185] A plan to use a cow and some goats for the older children seems to have failed.[186]

A decade later the struggle to provide for the children was equally acute; in mid-century their funding became inadequate to cope with the upsurge of children abandoned during the civil war. St. Louise reported that nurses were threatening to bring back the babies assigned to them for lack of pay.[187]

Exposure to infection from crowding and immobility was another class-associated variable which showed its effects in a heightened mortality rate for children of the poor. When possible, caring for foundlings in nurses' homes was always preferred to institutional lodging where the children formed a large group. While the seventeenth-century bourgeois parents in Paris and other towns most often brought nurses into the household—a placement agency or *sage-femme* found healthy country types—they were also freer than the poor in times of epidemic or civil strife to locate their children away from likely dangers.

Contagion could also better be avoided within the households of the well-to-do. In spite of an ordinance requiring separate cradles for newborn infants there is little doubt that small babies in poor families were often nursed and allowed to sleep—for warmth or lack of alternative furnishings—in beds of their parents with the dangers of suffocation as well as infection that this comported.[188] As for the spread of infection, few children seem to have had a bed to themselves. The educators of the Catholic reform often counselled isolating children in bed at nighttime, but then followed this advice by the more realistic plea for segregation of the sexes when beds were shared.[189]

SEVENTEENTH CENTURY FRENCH CHILDREN IN THE CONTEXT OF FAMILY AND SOCIETY

A high mortality and remarriage rate introduced a complex kinship relationship into the households of many French seventeenth century children. Marc Bloch has drawn attention to a pattern of rural child-rearing in which grandparents are the decisive influences on a young child's life while his parents are absent in the fields.[190] Often, in three-generation families, the authority of a grandparent may have been an effective one for the child's own parents. Many a will left grown children accommodation in the parental home provided they deferred to a widowed mother. A remarried father might be producing a new family at the same time and under the same roof as his son; the special danger of such an arrangement is reflected by the provision in French law of the time that a father may kill his son if he finds him to have committed adultery with his stepmother.[191]

The high rate of mortality meant that roles within the family were frequently exchanged and reassigned. This is most noteworthy in the case of the roles of "mother" and "father"—roles which seem as often to be *formally designated* as to be *ascribed* on the basis of kinship. The role of mother was often, in the case of a woman's death, reassigned to another. When the male head of the household died a conclave of male relatives assigned the guardianship (*tutelle*) to some other person, most often the natural mother if she was the widow. Her role was as formally defined by the decision as though she were the actual male head of the family: Arnauld d'Andilly wrote of Mme. de Fontenay-Mareuil, "Widowed she served as father to her children and as mother to the poor."[193]

In this context it is not surprising that while *performances* of special kinds were expected in specific roles, particular kinds of *affect* were not inherent in them. Maternal affection towards children was not taken for granted. Goussault exhorts the bourgeois mother to show the same charity to her children as to her servants.[194] On the child's side respect for the role of mother was required, but the affect had to be earned: "You did honor to her as much through esteem of her merit," writes Arnauld to the son of the late Mme. de Fontenay-Mareuil, "as through obligation of birth."[195] The mother of Louis XIII, a historian of the time reported, had failed to earn his affection, for she had not once kissed him during the first four years of her regency. Finally a courtier warned her of the need to take pains to "win his attachment." By contrast, Balzac said, Anne of Austria was entirely different toward her son, "tender and caressing and has won his heart."[196]

Affection or *tendresse* for a child is as frequently attributed to a father as to a mother. In La Hoguette's view the tie between fathers and children was the strongest parental bond because it was of a higher nature than any other—a link between souls rather than bodies.[197] The steadfast love of a father for his son is recounted by Boguet. Accused of witchcraft by his twelve-year-old son a father remained loyal though the boy was willing to be the cause of his being burnt alive. Manacled hands and feet, the father fell to the earth in lamentation, yet continued to speak affectionate words to his son telling him he "would always cherish him as his child."[198]

Maternal rejection or failure to feel affection is reported quite matter-of-factly. Few seem to have been as puzzled as Mme. de Sévigné at the inability of a mother to feel affection for a child (her own daughter's rejection of her first-born.)[199] Antoinette Bourignon leading Catholic educator and devotional writer, recalled how her mother "was not able to love me as she did the other children, but my father loved me more than all the other children put together."[200] Bussy-Rabutin was the beneficiary of his mother's rejection of his brothers: "I was raised with more affection, particularly on the part of my mother, than my other brothers." He was the third born of five boys, all of whom died young except for him "and it seemed as though, in view of the care she gave me—greater than the others—that she might have had some presentiment that I would be the sole support of our house."[201] A note from Marie-Antoinette to her mother, the Empress Marie-Thérèse reports on her pleasure that her little daughter recognized her in a roomful of people: "I believe that I like her much better since that time."[202]

THE CHILD AND THE NEW MORALITY

Both the growth of state absolutism, fostered by an authoritarian monarchy, and the strengthening of puritanical individualism, fostered by religious zeal, were to diminish the force and authority of the father in his home. But for the family of the seventeenth century, individualism was probably the more important influence. The state intruded where ground could be taken by default, that is, by taking over the protection of destitute and abandoned children and by seeking to restrict the exploitation of the helpless. Conversely, Catholic reformers marched in where the ground was already occupied; in some respects their challenge to parental authority was a more radical confrontation.

For the reformers themselves this confrontation sometimes took the form of open revolt against paternal power. Angélique Arnauld recalls her conversion to the inward life in adolescence. New aspirations to saintliness caused her to "think seriously of satisfying God rather than my father."[203] When her father accepted her ascetic goals she went farther: in renouncing the world she endeavored to exclude her father from her convent as well. Many a Catholic reform leader, by encouraging others in the contemplative life and other-worldliness, also challenged the legitimacy of family demands in the present life.[204]

In no area was the Catholic reform more important in diminishing the power of parents over children than in the field of education. Everywhere the missionary movement penetrated, educational opportunity for children was enhanced, institutions were founded to perform functions for children that had formerly been performed, if at all, within the home. The seventeenth century was a period of sudden expansion of secondary education for boys—largely led by the Jesuits—and of the village primary school for children of modest circumstances.[205] The elementary education of girls was for the first time an object of general interest and schools for *jeunes filles,* mostly under the auspices of the new Catholic teaching orders, multiplied all over France.[206]

The Catholic reformers and educators emphasized inner controls for the discipline of the child. Building conscience and character were stressed. The earlier morality had been simple: parents were surrogates in this world for the authority of God in the next. "The father and mother being like images of God for children," one legalist wrote, it was necessary for conformity to be unquestioning. Defiance was treason.[207] Under the new regime of Sister Euphémie (Jacqueline Pascal) at Port-Royal, simple compliance with adult authority was no solution to the child's problems, for the adults were trying to make them self-directing: "We assure them that no matter how we act," she wrote, "we are only impelled by the desire to render them such as God wishes them."[208]

In the archaic world of Louis XIII's childhood, willfulness, and stubbornness had been the cardinal sins, *"Je veux"*—I *want*—were impermissible words uttered by the dauphin, with occasionally painful results. In the view of the new reformers the strong will of the child is not to be suppressed but instead transformed into an offering to God. Of a thirteen-year old niece Mère Angélique wrote, "she has too forward, too great a spirit which will do much harm if it is not led to do good."[209] The self-mortification practiced at Port-Royal was not designed to kill the spirit but to convert it into the service of God.

A more secular version of this objective appears in a letter of Jean Racine, himself a partisan of Port-Royal. Exhorting his daughters to serve God well he writes to his son, "and you above all, that he may support you in this year of study of rhetoric and give you grace to advance."[210] The "Protestant" flavor of this message is echoed even more strongly in the opinions of Liselotte, the Lutheran-raised German princess, who found child-rearing patterns at court old-fashioned and unsympathetic. She wrote her aunt, the Electress of Hanover, "I prefer children a little willful—it shows they are intelligent."[211] In her words we seem already to be hearing the voices of the Enlightenment and Jean-Jacques Rousseau.

CONCLUSION

The thrust of a brief survey like the one presented here is to call attention to trends and to emphasize transformation. Yet in seventeenth-century child-rearing, far less changed than remained the same. The general features of the social and economic structure, too, were by modern standards much more noteworthy for their stability than for their propensity to change. Patterns of population growth and contraction were basically unchanging as well. Long periods of gradually growing population and rising prices were followed by shortages, famine and epidemic. A suddenly increased death rate, particularly among small children, readjusted the number of inhabitants to what the virtually stable level of production would support.

A sense of what this demographic pattern meant for the families who were a part of it directed Ariès' attention to the feelings adults must have had towards little children, so few of whom were likely to reach adulthood. His view that a feeling for childhood as a separate state warranting special treatment was largely absent in seventeenth century France and before is partly based on the notion that such high rates of infant and child mortality imposed a kind of "tenderness taboo" preventing parents from becoming excessively attached to offspring whom they had no better than an even change of preserving.[212]

Another recent writer on attitudes towards life, death and children concludes that fatalism was a natural response to this inexorable toll: "How could one see so many children disappear while still in the cradle," LeBrun asks, "without regarding the happening. . . . as an event as ineluctable as the return of the seasons?" But he observes that the *livres de raison* which seemingly record imperturbably so many early deaths of children are, for the most part, the work of fathers. He asks, "How is it for the mother, whose reactions one cannot know. . . .?"[213]

The poignant questions raised by Ariès and LeBrun cannot be answered here. But a few examples of how the "new morality" may have influenced the attitudes of parents, particularly mothers, may be considered.

Throughout the century biographies, memoirs and *livres de raison* give evidence of efforts to ward off the threats to childhood by propitiatory acts. When parents had lost several children in infancy, a new arrival in the family was the occasion for offering a sign of humility, such as inviting two beggars to be godparents to the child, promising to raise it for religion, dress it always in white, and so on. The ceremony of baptism was an occasion for giving presents to the nurse in whose hands the child's safety rested. Catherine de la Guette on the occasion of her son's baptism was so grateful to the leading local noblewoman for her liberality with nurse and midwife that she remembered to record it in her memoirs many years later.[214] Babies were consecrated *in utero* in hopes this would protect them against the malign forces that snatched away so many in infancy. "My mother had consecrated me before I came into the world," Marie-Marguerite Acarie reported.[215]

When the Catholic reformers came upon the scene they found not an absence but an excess of parental tenderness for children. M. Vincent cautioned Louise de Marillac about her maternal solicitude. In exasperation he asked, "But what shall we do with too-great affection?"[216] It is to be offered to God, like all the strongest passions—not suppressed but put into useful service. Another saint, Mme. de Chantal, took similar instruction from François de Sales. As her family was struck by one blow after another she learned the hard lesson he was trying to teach her: "It is a very powerful offering to God—the total resignation of a maternal heart in such an affecting situation," she wrote to a princess whose baby son was ill.[217] Attempting to master her own feelings, she wrote de Sales of her efforts to control her grief at the loss of her young daughter—but then expressed it: "Truly this girl was the child of our heart, most perfectly beloved, because deserving it."[218]

It could be suggested that *propitiation* was the traditional mode of coping with anxieties and longings that concerned children; *sublimation* was required by the new morality. But in neither case was there a denial of the tender feelings felt for children in spite of the cultural overlay that half disguised them.

A new interest in applying conceptual frameworks from sociology, anthropology and psychoanalysis to traditional objects of historical research has led recent historians of childhood to raise novel questions about families of earlier eras. The methods that have been brought into use direct attention to aspects of family life unnoticed in the past and lead to the hope of illuminating discoveries. These new approaches have tended to focus on the *quality* of relationships between parent and child rather than, as before, on the outward forms of family life. Typically emphasis has been put on *contrasts* between belief and attitude patterns of distant cultures and those of contemporary society.

Nevertheless one assumption is necessarily basic to all social and historical research. This is that subjective understanding of human social and cultural relationships is possible, however remote from our own culture and society they may be in time or space. For the historian of childhood this means that the investigator, as father, mother, or child is linked to the objects he investigates by human characteristics he shares with those objects.[219] A twentieth century French political philosopher, Bertrand de Jouvenel, points to the fundamentally similar conditions for the survival of all human families—the protective response of the parents to the total dependence of the infant:

At all times, in all societies, parents attend to and provide for their children, feed protect and cherish them; any exception arouses scandal. . . .

There are of course huge differences in parental attitudes towards children, a matter of social fashion as well as of individual character. . . . But even where parental attitudes are far more repressive than we now like them to be, the Great Powers at whose feet the child plays are primarily helpful and beneficient. . . . Indeed the very fact that the child survives and develops testifies to the protective efficiency of the Great Powers.[220]

What Jouvenel has found true of "all societies" was no less true of the family in seventeenth-century France. In this essay we have suggested that the parental sentiments he describes as universal came into play in France once the nature of the child had begun to be modified by nurture. Birth alone did not qualify the infant for protection that would maximize its chances for survival, but once a bond between child and outside world had been forged the adults brought their powerful forces to bear on its behalf.

REFERENCES

1. Thomas Hobbes, "The Citizen," in T. S. K. Scott-Craig and Bernard Gert, eds., *Man and Citizen by Thomas Hobbes* (New York: 1972), p. 100. (First edition, 1642.)
2. H. Boguet, *Discours des sorciers* (Lyon: 1610), pp. 376f.; 400f.
3. The French word *nourriture*, like its English cognate, has the sense of rearing as well as that of sustenance or food.
4. Jean Héroard, *Journal sur l'enfance et la jeunesse de Louis XIII,* Eud. Soulié and E. de Barthélemy, eds., (Paris: 1868), II, 323. This edition is hereafter cited as *S. & B.*
5. *Ibid.,* I, 152-153. The editors note the same conceit in Molière's *Ecole des femmes.*
6. Philippe Ariès, *L'enfant et la vie familiale sous l'ancien régime* (Paris: 1960), p. 38 and *passim.*
7. For a discussion of these sources see Maurice Dumoulin, "Figures du temps passé: les livres de raisons," in *En pays roannais* (Paris: 1892), pp. 1-38.
8. *S. & B.,* I, 14
9. *Ibid.,* pp. 34; 36.
10. *Ibid.,* p. 38.
11. *Ibid.,* p. 100.
12. *Ibid.,* p. 50.
13. See my "The Character of Louis XIII: the Role of his Physician in its Formation," *Journal of Interdisciplinary History,* IV (1974), pp. 347-74.
14. "La manière d'élever les enfans sans nourrice: extrait d'une lettre à M. Justel," *Journal des scavans* (1680), p. 45.
15. *Journal des scavans* (1681), pp. 66f. A proposal to raise foundlings in the city hospitals "without nurses" was made to the Parlement of Paris in 1679 but vetoed by a committee of doctors and midwives. See Michel Félibien,

Histoire de la ville de Paris (1725), II, 1511.

16. François Mauriceau, *Diseases of Women with Child and in Child-Bed* (London: 1727), p. 368. (First edition Paris, 1668.)

17. Laurent Joubert, *Traité des erreurs populaires* (Lyon: 1608), pp. 418 f. (First edition, 1578.)

18. Louise Bourgeois, *Observations diverses sur la stérilité, perte de fruict, fécondité, accouchements et maladies des femmes et enfans nouveau naiz* (Paris: 1626), p. 163.

19. Joubert, *Erreurs*, p. 404.

20. Bourgeois, *Observations*, p. 164.

21. Jacques Guillemeau, *Oeuvres de chirurgie* (Paris: 1612), p. 390.

22. Quoted from J-L. G. de Balzac (1597-1654), "Mémoires de deux jeunes mariées," in preface to *Les caquets de l'accouchée* (Paris: 1888), pp. xxix-xx.

23. Bourgeois, *Observations*, p. 226.

24. Joubert, *Erreurs*, p. 515.

25. *Ibid.*, p. 416.

26. Catherine Meurdrac, *Mémoires* (Paris: 1856), p. 8. (First edition, 1681.)

27. Mauriceau wrote, "we see daily about half of the young children die before they are two or three years old." *Diseases of Women*, p. 317.

28. An English physician traveling in seventeenth century France remarked that the water was exceptionally bad in Paris and dysentery the most common disease there. Martin Lister, *A Journey to Paris in the Year 1698*, R. P. Stearns, ed., (Urbana, Ill.: 1967), p. 235.

29. *S. & B.*, I, pp. 14f.

30. *Correspondance de Madame, Duchesse d'Orléans*, E. Jaeglé, ed., (Paris, 1880), II, 48.

31. Boguet, *Discours*, p. 80.

32. For citations of two such wills in the fifteenth century see Charles de Ribbe, *La société provençale à la fin du moyen âge* (Paris: 1898), pp. 233f. Joubert speaks of the practice as an "Asian" custom. *Erreurs*, p. 425. An eighteenth century will admonishes that the duty of mothers is "personally to nurse their children and I recommend it expressly to my daughters." Charles de Ribbe, *La vie domestique: ses modèles et ses règles* (Paris: 1878), I, 185.

33. "Livre de raison de la famille Froissard-Boissia (1532-1701)," *Mémoires de la Société d'Emulation du Jura*, 4eme série, II (1886), 44. This work contains accounts of several nursing problems. Another *livre de raison* tells the occupation of the husbands of nurses assigned to seven children. All but one was from the artisan class. *Journal de Samuel Robert*, G. Tortat, ed., (Pons: 1883), pp. 13-15.

34. Gustave Fagniez, *La femme et la société francaise dans la première moitié du XVIIe siècle* (Paris: 1929), pp. 7; 60.

35. Pierre Coustel, *Les règles de l'éducation des enfans* (Paris: 1687), I, 66.

36. New documentary studies have shown a trend to hired nurses between the seventeenth and eighteenth centuries. See Michel Bouvet and Pierre-Marie Bourdin, *A travers la Normandie des XVIIe et XVIIIe siècles* (Caen: 1968), pp. 80f.; 254.

37. Mauriceau, *Diseases of Women*, p. 311. For an "early starter" see Marguerite la Marche, *Instruction familière et très-facile . . . touchant toutes les choses principales qu'une sage-femme doit scavoir. . . .* (Paris: 1677), pp. 93f.

38. Joubert, *Erreurs*, pp. 46f.

39. Joubert cites the "excrementous" nature of humans compared with animals. *Ibid.*, pp. 439-441.

40. Mauriceau, *Diseases of Women*, p. 311.

41. Marie Fouquet, *Suite du recueil des remèdes avec . . . un traité du lait*

(Dijon: 1687), p. 419. This work contradicts medical consensus on a number of points and should not be taken as representative.

42. Scévole de Sainte-Marthe, *La manière de nourrir les enfans à la mammelle* (Paris: 1698), p. 95. This work, like Joubert's *Erreurs*, was several times reprinted early in the seventeenth century. (First edition, 1584.)

43. Pierre Dionis, *Traité général des accouchements, qui instruit ce qu'il faut pour être habile accoucheur* (Paris: 1718), pp. 374-376.

44. *S. & B.*, I, 7.

45. Mauriceau, *Diseases of Women*, pp. 329f.

46. *Journal des scavans* (1681), p. 66.

47. In fact after the first few days the exhortation to feed the child when it cries was so general that one is encouraged to speculate that there was much over-feeding.

48. Daniel Martin, *La vie à Strasbourg au commencement du XVIIe siècle (Le parlement nouveau)*, Ch. Nerlinger, ed., (Belfort: 1899), p. 178.

49. Mauriceau, *Diseases of Women*, p. 311.

50. *Journal des scavans* (1681), p. 66.

51. Fouquet, *Suite du recueil*, p. 409. Also see Bourgeois, *Observations*, pp. 217-221.

52. Louis-Emile Bougaud, *Histoire de Sainte Chantal et des origines de la Visitation* (Paris: 1861), I, 8.

53. Meurdrac, *Mémoires*, pp. 47f.

54. Coustel, *Règles des enfants*, I, 68.

55. Philippe de Duplessis-Mornay, *Mémoires et Correspondence* (Paris: 1824), I, 10. This is the first edition of Mme. de Mornay's seventeenth century biography of Duplessis-Mornay. Other examples of undying devotion are given by de Ribbe in *Société provencale*, p. 232.

56. See the portrait of Gabrielle d'Estrées, mistress of Henri IV (Musée Condé, Chantilly), in which she is shown in her bath, one child standing beside her, a nurse feeding another at her right elbow and another nurse—apparently for relief of the first—in a room beyond. Absolute parity is depicted by a frontispiece to *Les caquets de l'accouchée*, 1623 edition.

57. Guillaume Gérard-Gailly, *Les sept couches de Mme. de Grignan* (Abbéville: 1926), pp. 3-15.

58. The division of mothering functions is illustrated in an extreme form when he thanks his father's first wife, "Maman ma fille" on behalf of his nurse "Maman Doundoun". *S. & B.*, I, 145.

59. *Ibid.*, 131.

60. Martin, *Strasbourg*, pp. 476f.

61. Georges de la Tour (1593-1652), "Le Nouveau-né," Rennes, Musée des Beaux Arts. The Louvre has a similar painting by this artist.

62. Bourgeois, *Observations*, p. 156.

63. For an eighteenth century list of swaddling equipment see Alfred Franklin, *La vie privée d'autrefois: L'enfant, la layette, la nourrice* (Paris: 1896), XIX, 21f.

64. "Livre de raison Froissard-Boissia," p. 89.

65. Nicolas A. de la Framboisière, *Advis utile et nécessaire pour la conservation de la santé* (Paris: 1639), p. 7.

66. Mauriceau, *Diseases of Women*, pp. 308f.

67. Bibliothèque nationale (BN), manuscrits, Fds. frçs., 3649.

68. G.-L. L. Buffon, *Oeuvres complètes* (Paris: 1824), XIII ("Histoire naturelle de l'homme"), 32. When the dauphin was less than one month old "a compress was put between his knees for fear he would turn them inward." BN, N. a., 13008, Nov. 28, 1601. This manuscript, a contemporary abridgment

by Simon Courtaud of his uncle's diary for which the original is missing for the years 1601-1605, gives a fuller account than the published version of Héroard's record. It is cited hereafter as *Courtaud*.

69. E. Littré, *Dictionnaire de la langue française* (Paris: 1863), I, 1817. It was held to be a sign of the feminine rearing experienced by Philippe, brother of Louis XIV, that he was made to wear the *corps* as a child. Philippe Erlanger, *Monsieur, frère de Louis XIV* (Paris: 1953), p. 38.

70. P. Fortin de la Hoguette, *Testament ou conseils fidèles d'un bon père a ses enfants* (Paris: 1648), 393.

71. The dauphin appears to have been completely unswaddled whenever he was fed. (See p. 000, above.) But he was furnished with a *remueuse* or full time dresser.

72. Jacques Guillemeau, *Child-birth or the Happy Delivery of Women* (London: 1635), p. 21. Elsewhere he recommends one month of swaddling. *Oeuvres,* p. 397.

73. In 1689 the Comtesse de Rochefort reported her nine-month old son was "still in swaddling clothes." Charles de Ribbe, *Une grande dame dans son ménage au temps de Louis XIV* (Paris: 1890), p. 82.

74. See the ceramic, "La nourrice," an illustration of Lucy Crump, *Nursery Life 300 Years Ago* (New York: 1930), p. 24.

75. See Ariès, *L'Enfant,* p. 84. The portrait, "Les enfants de Henri-Louis Hubert de Montmort, (1649)," is by Philippe de Champaigne, Musée de Reims. An inscription identifies and gives the ages of all the children, including twin boys of nearly five years, a seventeenth century rarity.

76. Buffon, *Oeuvres,* XIII, 35. The death of babies through a "magically overturned cradle"—said to be cause for husbands' recriminations of careless wives—is recounted in Etienne Delcambre, *Le concept de la sorcellerie dans le duché de Lorraine au XVIᵉ et au XVIIᵉ siècle* (Nancy: 1948-1951), II, 80.

77. Martin, *Strasbourg,* p. 87f.

78. Mauriceau, *Diseases of Women,* p. 315.

79. The published version of Héroard's journal omits much of the documentation on Louis' skin eruptions. See *Courtaud,* entries for December 1601 and January 1602.

80. Paul Guillon, *La mort de Louis XIII* (Paris: 1897), p. 70.

81. Nursing was said to be necessary to soothe the baby whenever "a pin . . . sticks him . . . a flea . . . bites him." Joubert, *Erreurs,* pp. 546f.

82. *Courtaud,* fols. 45; 98; 108.

83. Juliette Favez-Boutonier, "*Child Development Patterns in France* (1)," in *Mental Health and Infant Development,* Kenneth Soddy, ed., (New York: 1956), I, 18.

84. See the ceramic, "Boy with Puppies," an illustration in Crump, *Nursery Life,* p. 124. Also the painting by Jan Steen (1626-1674), "Twelfth Night," Los Angeles County Museum.

85. *Courtaud,* fol. III Vo.

86. BN, Fds, frçs., 4022, fol. 12 Vo. This is Héroard's original manuscript. It begins on January 1, 1605 and is cited hereafter as *Héroard*.

87. Guillemeau, *Childbirth,* p. 80.

88. Mauriceau, *Diseases of Women,* pp. 310f; Guillemeau *Oeuvres,* p. 45 and *Childbirth,* p. 53.

89. Dionis, *Traité des accouchements,* p. 373. At the other extreme was Jean Devaux whose universal and constant remedy was purging of the large bowel. *Le Médecin de soi-même* (Leyden: 1682), pp. 52-80.

90. At the age of 29 he was still fearful of these remedies. P. Suffren, "Véritable récit de ce qui s'est passe en la maladie du Roy à la ville de Lyon," in F.

Danjou, *Archives curieuses de l'histoire de l'histoire de France*, 2e série (Paris: 1838), III, 368.

91. BN, Fds. frçs., 10241, fol. 55.
92. *S. & B.*, II, 110.
93. Jean-Jacques Bouchard, *Confessions* (Paris: 1930), pp. 30f.
94. *Héroard*, 4022, fol. 137.
95. *Ibid.*, 4023, fol. 110.
96. *Ibid.*, p. 30.
97. See Ariès' discussion of children's dress. *L'enfant*, pp. 42-55.
98. Alice Ryerson, "Medical Advice on Childrearing Practices, 1550-1900," Unpublished Ph.D. dissertation (Harvard: 1960), p. 110.
99. See, for example, Bouzonnet-Stella, *Plaisirs*, p. 1.
100. But the connection between worms and animal excrement seems not to have been recognized. See Buffon, *Oeuvres*, XIII, p. 45. A medical authority reported worms to be among the three most common afflictions for which drugs were in demand. Jean Duret, *Discours sur l'origine des moeurs, fraudes et impostures* (Paris: 1622), pp. 9f.
101. BN, Fds. frçs., 3649.
102. Guillemeau, *Childbirth*, p. 27.
103. Mauriceau, *Diseases of Women*, p. 344.
104. Jules Gauthier, ed., *Le Ménage d'un ambassadeur d'Espagne au milieu du XVIIe siècle* (Besançon: s. d.), pp. 4f.
105. Jules Feuvrier, ed., "Feuillets de garde: les Mairot (1535-1769)," *Mémoires de la Société d'Emulation du Jura*, 7e Série, I (1901), 192.
106. Sainte-Marthe, *La manière de nourrir*, p. 76.
107. See Margaret Mahler, *On Human Symbiosis and the Vicissitudes of Individuation* (New York: 1968), I, 20ff. Compare D. W. Winnicott, *The Child, the Family and the Outside World* (Harmonsworth, Middlesex, England: 1964), pp. 80-89 in which weaning from the breast is assumed to be at about nine months with the same author's "Transitional Objects and Transitional Phenomena," in *Collected Papers: through Pediatrics to Psychoanalysis* (London: 1958), pp. 229-242.
108. BN, Cinq-cents Colbert 86, fol. 230.
109. *Héroard*, 4022, fol. 30 Vo.
110. Guillemeau, *Childbirth*, p. 27.
111. *Courtaud*, 13008, November 7, 1603.
112. Joubert, *Erreurs*, p. 437. This author suggests the possibility of an earlier (by about six months) weaning time for girls. *Ibid.*, p. 570. If this practice was general it gives additional reason to expect greater probability of bone deformities in young women.
113. BN, Cinq-cents Colbert, 86, fol. 175.
114. Guillemeau, *Oeuvres*, p. 451.
115. This method goes back at least to Roman times. See G. Boissier, *La fin du paganisme* (Paris: 1891), II, 182. A series of comic strips—Exhibition 'Le dessin d'humour," Bibliothèque nationale, 1971—illustrated the method "turned upside down" (le monde à renvers) for the sixteenth, seventeenth and eighteenth centuries. In these reversals the child whips while the father is held over the back of the mother.
116. *Correspondance de Madame*, II, 48.
117. BN Cinq-cents Colbert, 86, fol. 275.
118. Jeanne Frémyot (Sainte Chantal), *Lettres*, Ed. de Barthélemy, ed., (Paris: 1860), p. 237.
119. J.-B. de LaSalle, *Règles de la Bienséance*, p. 26.
120. For examples see *S. & B.*, I, pp. 108; 113.

121. *Ibid.*, p. 76. The dauphin defended himself accordingly: he threatened to cut off the penis of his nurse's husband. *Ibid.*, p. 108.
122. St. Calgay de Martignac, *Mémoires de Monsieur* (Paris: 1685), pp. 16f.
123. *Ibid.*, p. 26.
124. *S. & B.*, II, 325.
125. Victor Cousin, *Jacqueline Pascal* (Paris: 1862), p. 409. The *règlement* was drawn up in 1657.
126. BN, N. a. frçs., 1702, fol. 270.
127. Cousin, *J. Pascal*, pp. 360ff.
128. *Ibid.*, p. 363.
129. J.-B. de LaSalle, *Règles de la bienséance*, pp. 18; 43.
130. Cousin, *J. Pascal*, pp. 399; 374.
131. Soeur Jeanne des Anges, *Autobiographie d'une hystérique possédée*, annotated by G. Legué and G. de la Tourette (Paris: 1886), pp. 321ff.
132. *S. & B.*, I, 254.
133. Jeanne des Anges, *Autobiographie*, pp. 233f.
134. Cousin, *J. Pascal*, p. 404. The introspection encouraged was extreme: "One must strongly encourage the children to know themselves . . . and to plumb to the bottom of their faults." P. 402.
135. Frémyot, *Lettres*, p. 66.
136. Tronson de Chenevière, *Vie de Marie-Marguerite du Saint-Sacrement* (Paris: 1690), p. 11.
137. Robert Arnauld d'Andilly, *Lettres* (Lyon: 1665), p. 396.
138. Emmanuel LeRoy Ladurie, *Les Paysans de Languedoc* (Paris: 1966), I, 397.
139. C. LeBrun de la Rochette, *Le procès criminel* (Rouen: 1647), pp. 13; 20.
140. On legal and moral restrictions affecting marriage age see Fagniez, *La femme dans le XVIIe siècle*, pp. 58-61.
141. Estienne Pasquier, *Oeuvres* (Amsterdam: 1723), II, 674.
142. Jean-Jacques Boileau, *Vie inédite de la Duchesse de Luynes (1624-1651)* (Paris: 1880), pp. 34-43. For a comparable Protestant example see Samuel Robert, *Journal.* Robert married on the day in 1639 that his bride reached the age of sixteen. Nine years later she had borne seven children. Pp. 13-15.
143. Micheline Baulant, "La famille en miettes: sur un aspect de la démographie du XVIIe siècle," *Annales, ESC*, XXVII (1972), 967.
144. J. Hajnal, "European Marriage Patterns in Perspective," in *Population in History*, D. V. Glass and D. C. Eversley, eds., (London: 1965), pp. 101-143. But recent work seems to show that a small average family size does not depend on this pattern. See Christiane Klapisch and Michel Demonet, " 'A uno pane e uno vino': la famille rurale toscane au début du XVe siècle," *Annales, ESC*, XXVII (1972), 873-901.
145. Pierre Goubert, *Beauvais et la Beauvaisis de 1600 à 1730* (Paris: 1960), I, 299.
146. Emmanuel LeRoy Ladurie, "Système de la coutume: structures familiales et coutume d'héritage en France au XVIe siècle," *Annales, ESC*, XXVII (1972), 825-846.
147. Pierre Goubert, "Legitimate Fecundity and Infant Mortality in France During the Eighteenth Century: A Comparison," in Glass and Eversley, *Population*, pp. 593-603.
148. J. L. Flandrin, "Contraception, mariage et relations amoureuses dans l'occident chrétien," *Annales, ESC*, XXIV (1969), 1370-1390. For a useful compilation see also Orest and Patricia Ranum, eds., *Popular Attitudes toward Birth Control in Pre-industrial France and England* (New York: 1972), pp. 1-52.

149. Goubert, *Beauvais,* I, 78-149.
150. Henri Baudrillart, *Jean Bodin et son Temps* (Paris: 1853), pp. 249f.
151. LeBrun de la Rochette, *Le Procès criminel,* pp. 64f.
152. E. Pasquier, *Oeuvres,* II, 297.
153. P. E. LeMaguet, *Le monde médical parisien sous le grand roi suivi du porte Feuille de Vallant* (Paris: 1889), p. 305.
154. Other methods were readily available. Putting the child out to nurse with several others is mentioned in A. Corre and P. Aubry, *Documents de criminologie rétrospective: Bretagne XVIIe et XVIIIe siècles* (Paris: 1895), pp. 517ff.
155. Francois Lebrun, *Les hommes et la mort en Anjou aux XVIIe et XVIIIe siècles* (Paris: 1971), p. 424.
156. *Ibid.,* p. 424n.
157. *Ibid.,* p. 187.
158. Roland Mousnier, "Etudes sur la population de la France au XVIIe siècle," *Le dix-septième siècle,* XVI (1952), 527-530.
159. For an example of the method of reconstitution of families see Etienne Gautier et Louis Henry, *La population de Crulai, paroisse normande* (Paris: 1958), 47-194.
160. Gérard-Gailly, *Les couches de Mme de Grignan,* pp. 1-15.
161. Baulant, "Famille en miettes," p. 963.
162. Jeanne du Laurens, *Une famille au XVIe siècle,* Charles de Ribbe, éd., (Paris: 1867), p. 104.
163. Martin, *Strasbourg,* pp. 178f.
164. Guillaume Bouchet, *Sérées* (Paris: 1873), IV, 10.
165. Joubert, *Erreurs,* p. 515.
166. See Pierre-Marie Bourdin, "La plaine d'Alençon," in *A travers la Normandie des XVIIe et XVIIIe siècles,* Michel Bouvet and P.-M. Bourdin, eds. (Caen: 1968). Although babies put out to nurse were rare in this Norman countryside for most of the seventeenth century he finds that by the eighteenth century even small craftsmen were engaging nurses. One nurse had borne a child every two years for the past twenty and taken a nursling each time at high wages "never mind her own child." One family listed as "infertile" proved to have had three infant deaths. P. 254.

 In 1687 Coustel wrote "formerly it was a universal custom practiced by all mothers to nurse their babies themselves but the delicacy of those who have a little bit of wealth has now become so great that this good custom has almost entirely been abolished." *Règles des enfants,* I, 66.
167. Roger Mols, *Introduction à la démographie historique des villes d'Europe du XIVe au XVIIe siècle* (Louvain: 1955), p. 290.
168. Ernest Semichon, *Histoire des enfants abandonnés* (Paris: 1888), pp. 95-134.
169. L. Lallemand, *Histoire des enfants abandonnés et délaissés* (Paris: 1885), *passim.* See also the interpretation in Francois Lebrun, "Naissances illégitimes et abandons d'enfants en Anjou au XVIIIe siècle," *Annales, ESC,* XXVII (1972), 1183-1189.
170. E.-V. Fléchier, *The Clermont Assizes of 1665,* W. W. Comfort, trs. (Philadelphia: 1937), pp. 131f.
171. F. de Grenaille, *L'honneste mariage* (Paris: 1640), pp. 81-83. An increased papal tolerance at the beginning of the seventeenth century for illegitimacy (in contrast with infanticide) is indicated in R. Genestal, *Histoire de la légitimation des enfants naturels en droit canonique* (Paris: 1905), pp. 83-84.
172. Coustel, *Règles des enfants,* II, 330-331. Mauriceau, *Diseases of Women,* p. 5. This view was echoed by the canon, R. Dognon, *Le modelle du mesnage heureux* (Paris: 1633), p. 190.
173. Angélique Arnauld, *Lettres* (Utrecht: 1742), I, 496-497.

174. Louis Cognet, *La spiritualité française au XVIIe siècle* (Paris: 1949), pp. 20f.
175. E. Griselle, *La vénérable mère Marie de l'Incarnation* (Paris: 1909), pp. 9f.
176. Henri Brémond, *A Literary History of Religious Thought in France* (London: 1930), II, 215.
177. Jacques Brousse, *Tableau de l'homme juste: François de Montholon* (s. 1.: 1626), p. 100. Also see G. Hector Quignon, *L'assistance dans l'ancienne France* (Paris: 1904), pp. 10-12.
178. Goubert, *Beauvais*, I, pp. 299-302.
179. M. Félibien, *Histoire de Paris*, II, 1197.
180. Jacques du Breul, *Le Théâtre des antiquités de Paris* (Paris: 1639), p. 744.
181. R. Chantelauze, *Saint Vincent de Paul et les Gondi* (Paris: 1882), pp. 259f.
182. Breul, *Théâtre*, pp. 27f. The regimens of older children in some of the Paris orphanages are described in Laurens Bouchel, *Thresor . . . de droit français* (Paris: 1647), I, 1213-1215.
183. Chantelauze, *Vincent*, p. 260n.
184. Vincent de Paul, *Lettres* (Paris: 1880), I, 185.
185. *Ibid.*, p. 242.
186. *Ibid.*, p. 168.
187. La vénérable Louise de Marillac, *Lettres* (Paris: 1898), p. 443.
188. For this reason an ordinance requiring a separate cradle for infants was passed for Anjou in 1615 according to Lebrun, *La Mort en Anjou*, p. 422.
189. J.-B. LaSalle, *Règles de bienséance*, p. 48. Separate beds were required for each child at Port-Royal "without exception no matter what the pretext may be," said Jacqueline Pascal. Cousin, *J. Pascal*, p. 381.
190. For a review of recent literature on varieties of Western European family structure see "Under the Same Roof-tree," *Times Literary Supplement*, 3713 (May 4, 1973), 485-487.
191. LeBrun de la Rochette, *Procès criminel*, pp. 64f.
192. Fagniez, *La Femme du XVII siècle*, p. 182.
193. R. Arnauld d'Andilly, *Lettres*, p. 125.
194. L. Goussault, *Le portrait d'une honnête femme* (Paris: 1693), pp. 25f.
195. R. Arnauld d'Andilly, *Lettres*, p. 124.
196. J.-L. Guez de Balzac, *Les Entretiens* (Paris: 1660), p. 374.
197. La Hoguette, *Conseils d'un bon père*, p. 388.
198. Boguet, *Sorciers*, pp. 384-388.
199. Gérard-Gailly, *Les couches de Mme. de Grignan*, p. 11.
200. Antoinette Bourignon, *La parole de Dieu* (Paris: 1682), p. 143.
201. Roger de Rabutin, *Mémoires du Comte de Bussy-Rabutin* (Paris: 1882), I, 5.
202. Edmond Pilon, *La vie de famille au dix-huitième siècle* (Paris: 1928), p. 97.
203. Marie-Angélique Arnauld, *Relations* (s. 1.: 1716), p. 20.
204. Jeanne Frémyot defied a son, Antoinette Bourignon a father.
205. François de Dainville, "Collèges et fréquentation scolaire au XVIIe siècle," *Population* (1955), 455-488.
206. These are described by Fagniez, *La femme du XVIIe siècle*, pp. 13-48.
207. Le Brun de la Rochette, *Le procès criminel*, p. 64.
208. Cousin, *J. Pascal*, p. 404.
209. Guillaume Dall, *La mère Angélique d'après sa correspondance* (Paris: 1893), pp. 116f.
210. Louis Racine, *Oeuvres* (Amsterdam: 1750), II, 191.
211. *Lettres de Madame*, II, 48.
212. Ariès, *L'enfant*, pp. 134-142. The question of such inhibition of feeling in a modern country with an "old" demographic pattern is discussed in Arthur Geddes, "The Social and Psychological Significance of Variability in Population Change: with Examples from India, 1871-1941," *Human Relations*,

I (1947), 181-205.
213. Lebrun, *La Mort en Anjou,* p. 424*n.*
214. Meurdrac, *Mémoires,* p. 47.
215. Chenevière, *M. -M. Acarie du Saint-Sacrement,* p. 38.
216. Vincent de Paul, *Lettres,* I, 26.
217. Sainte Chantal, *Lettres,* p. 25.
218. *Ibid.,* p. 8.
219. See the discussion of this point by Marc Bloch, *Apologie pour l'histoire ou Métier d'historien* (Paris: 1949), p. 13.
220. Bertrand de Jouvenel, *The Pure Theory of Politics* (New Haven: 1963), pp. 48-50.

CHAPTER 7

Child-Rearing in Seventeenth-Century England and America

JOSEPH E.
ILLICK

". . . to reign over every wrong Thing in ourselves, and also in others, but especially in our Children."

An Account of the Life of John Richardson[1]

A careful student of pre-modern England, the demographer Peter Laslett, has recently reminded us that "we know very little indeed about child nurture in pre-industrial times, and no confident promise can be made of knowledge yet to come."[2] Anyone examining the materials extant from seventeenth-century England and America will hasten to agree with Laslett. The surviving data is scant—yet there is a story to be told.

That story must be concerned not only with the conditions of child-rearing, which would include attitudes as well as behavior, but also with the possibility that these conditions were altered between 1600 and 1700. Certainly there were changes taking place in related areas. It appears that life expectation dropped during the seventeenth century in England, and the fertility rate declined, due in part (probably) to contraception.[3] It has been claimed that the seventeenth century witnessed "new methods of child-rearing, based on the small, nuclear family, and designed to instil a strong sense of personal responsibility in the growing child."[4] Also, the patriarchal family of the early seventeenth century was said to have been superseded by a unit based on contractual relations.[5] A narrative of childhood, from pre-natal care through adolescence, cannot ignore these assertions concerning change.

Pregnancy, at least among the class of women able to profit from the recorded advice of physicians, midwives and other commentators, was a time for emotional and physical preparation for childbirth. Rules were to be followed and signs were to be noticed. Shunning rigorous exercise (even riding in coaches might cause premature delivery), blood letting, dieting and avoidance of bad smells and salted meats, foregoing a corset ("for feare lest the child be mishapen or crooked") but in the third or fourth month wearing "a Swathe . . . to support her belly," were among the prescriptions given prospective mothers. A woman whose color was good and body temperature comfortably warm might expect a boy, while if she were carrying a girl she would be distinguished by "a pale, heavy, and swarth countenance, a melancolique eye: she is wayward, fretful, and sad . . . her face is spotted with red. . . ."[6] Surely these admonitions added to the anxieties attendant on childbirth and even to later feelings of guilt. After Lady Frances Hatton was safely delivered of her third daughter, she wrote her husband: "I am sure you will love it though it be a Girle and I trust in God I may live to bring you boys."[7]

Giving birth was not an event to be anticipated with confidence. A female reader of Francis Mauriceau's *The Disease of Women with Child . . . With fit Remedies for the several Indispositions of New-Born Babes* might be slightly reassured by the charge to save the mother's life before the child's. But the many complications chronicled under "Of natural, and unnatural Deliveries" must have frightened novice and veteran alike, if only because of the unpredictability involved.

> It is an undoubted truth, and well known to all such as lay Women, that the several unnatural Postures, wherein Children present themselves at their Birth, are the cause of most of the bad Labours and ill Accidents there met with, for which usually recourse is had to Chirurgeons.

Mauriceau knew but did not approve of "that cruelty and barbarousness of the *Caesarean* Section." He regarded it as sure death to the mother.[8]

Less sophisticated practitioners might save neither party. Elizabeth Tufton wrote to her sister-in-law Cecilie, Lady Hatton, about the labor of Frances Drax:

> on munday my Sister was pleased to send for mee, I since am told that she had paines a Saterday, & Sunday, but Mrs. Baker beleeved it was not her labor, and soe made nothing of it, when I came a Munday morning I found her in greate paine, which continued till night when her water broke, and the midwif said the

Child came wrong; I had prevaild with Mr Drax to send to Canterbury, for Doctor Peters, whoe is very famous for his skill, and he was in the house ready, if there were occasion, but wee were desirous if possible to save the life of the Childe by not using forcible meanes till it needes must, but her paines continuing all munday nights, without any profit to her labor, and the midwif finding by some tokens that the Child was deade, she desired Doctor Peters would maeke use of his skill, for it was past hers, my poore Sister seemed content that he should, only desired him to put her to as little paine as hee could, and seemed very little discouraged. but prayed as shee had done all allong, that god would enable her,: in the afternoon the Docter began to makc use of his meanes, and we prayed either in the same roome, or the next to it, all the while: hee continued his endeavours till 10 a Clock at night, and we were forced to give her Cordialls almost every minuit, but at last noe pasage being made for her delivery, though the man protested hee tryed all the wayes hee could imagine, though in vaine, and shee growing faint and light headed, begd of the Docter for Christs sake, to lett her dye at rest, and her condition being desparate wee got her to bed, where shee continued all that night without any rest, her spirits being spent by the floud of those, that came from her, as well after the Doctor left handling her, as before, and the child deade within her made her never lye still one moment, on wensday morning the Doctor having told me that all hopes of her life was gone, I desird the minister to advertise her of her end, which hee discoursed to her in a very pious manner, she told him shee was very willing to dy and hoped god would receive her, the day after she died shee was opened, and the Child lay right at the birth, but the Docter saide hee had forced it to that place, but when she was opened her Back bone was soe bowed, as he said it was impossible to make passage so much as for a limbe of the Childe[9]

How many mothers died in childbirth is not known, but it is estimated that infant mortality rates varied from 126 to 158 per thousand in the first half of the seventeenth century and from 118 to 147 in the second half of the century.[10]

As the preceding description suggests, children were delivered at home, usually in bed—though a chair might be recommended for "strong and lusty women." Seldom was a physician in attendance. Midwives were responsible for deliveries, and they often bore the onus for the high mortality rate. As one of their number, Elizabeth Cellier, pointed out in 1687:

... within the space of twenty years last past, above six-thousand women have died in childbed, more than thirteen-thousand children have been abortive and about five-thousand *chrysome* infants [those in their first month of life] have been buried within

the weekly bills of mortality; above two-thirds of which, amount-
ing to sixteen thousand souls, have in all probability perished, for
want of the due skill and care, in those women who practice the
art of midwivery.[11]

There had been ecclesiastical licencing of midwives since the early sixteenth century, but only for two decades (1642-1662) had there been a
system where "Midwives were licenced at Chirurgion's Hall, but not till
they had passed three Examinations, before six skilful Midwives, and as
many Chirurgions expert in the Art of Midwifery"—a practice which, it
was claimed, substantially reduced mortality rates. After 1662 the midwives went "back to Doctors Commons, where they pay their money,
(take an Oath which is impossible for them to keep) and return home
as skilful as they went thither."[12]

The oath was certainly demanding. It showed, among other things,
the dangers to which a new born infant was exposed, both from the
midwife and others. Yet it put the burden of protection on the midwife.
She was to swear:

I will not destroy the child born of any woman, nor cut, nor pull
off the head thereof, or otherwise dismember or hurt the same, or
suffer it to be so hurt or dismembered.

The midwife was constrained from using abortifacients, or delivering
secretly, or clandestinely burying a stillborn child. Nor was she to practice witchcraft in her trade; rather, she was to see that baptism was administered only under the laws of the Church of England. Also, she was
expected to obtain the name of the true father of the child.[13] Clearly, the
midwife was indispensable, if not always considered trustworthy. She
engendered both respect and fear, as did the act of childbirth over which
she presided. Probably the anxiety concerning the event was projected
onto the person associated with it.[14]

Such adages as "For nature surpatteth all; and in that she doth, is
wiser than either Art, or the Midwife" appear to have been a sort of
conventional wisdom which was not heeded. Jacques Guillemeau, surgeon and author of the homily, confessed that a child usually could not
come into the world by himself but that delivery should be attended by
a midwife and four other women to restrain the mother in labor. When
it was necessary to summon a surgeon, he might find his work hindered
by the fact that the women were "constrained to hide" the womb from
him, a bit of modesty that obviously hindered his task.[15]

The surgeon did not arrive prepared to let nature take its course.
Though he recognized that the "naturall disposition" of a woman, such
as fear of pain, could hinder delivery just as physical attributes such as
size, age or vaginal obstructions could pose problems, he brought his
tools: the crochet, an instrument shaped similarly to our crocheting

needle, used to deliver a dead child; a smaller, hooked knife, used in the eventuality that the child was alive but swollen, to "cut the part where the wind and water shall be inclosed, (whether it bee the head, breast, or belly). . . ." Indeed, at least some people thought nature might be aided: the navel string having been cut, if it were tied long for boys, the length of the tongue and the penis would be increased; conversely, it should be tied short for girls.[16]

While Guillemeau himself was faintly skeptical of such practices, he asserted in a second treatise—an essay on child-rearing rather than child-birth—that: "Nurture prevailes more than nature." This admonition was attached to a warning against putting a child out to wet-nurse (milk has as much power as the parents' seed; the child will imitate the nurse), but its implicit message was widely applied.[17] The newborn baby was to be molded to his parents' desires. Notice was first to be taken of the infant's head which, if ill-formed, should be shaped like a bowl, a little flat on both sides, using "head-clothes," stroking without crushing. The ears should be cleaned and "wrapped about with fine linnen clouts." Eyes, nose and mouth were to be cleansed, but "not onely his face, but his whole body," using fresh butter, oil of roses or oil of nuts. Even the stomach was to be purged of its "clammy Phlegm" through feeding the infant a bit of sugared wine.[18]

"As for the armes and legges, if they be either crooked or stand awry, they must bee set straight with little swaths, & fit boulsters, made for the purpose; as likewise if eyther the back bone, or the belly, do stand out"—in which case a surgeon should be consulted. When a child cannot "keepe his hands swathed in, and hid any longer," probably after twenty or thirty days, he must have sleeves, though in the middle of the seventeenth century a midwife warned against releasing the arms before four months, while wrapping the "breast, belly, and feet to keep out cold air for a year."[19] Francis Mauriceau, who pointed out that his directions for swaddling were unnecessary "because it is so common, there is scarce a Woman but knows it," proceeded to give a rationale for the practice: "He must be thus swadled, to give his little Body a streight Figure, which is most decent and convenient for a Man, and to accustom him to keep upon the Feet, for else he would go down upon all four, as most other Animals do."[20] Perhaps swaddling served to quell fear of a more proximate form of degeneracy as well—masterbation. One anonymous writer warned that "when their knees are too strictly tied and bound up, and their thighs left at liberty, they are lamed."[21]

. Other controls were also exercised. In his cradle, the baby was to be laid on his back for the first month, afterwards on his right or left side, "having his head a little raised up, that the excrements of his braine may the more easily flow and pass through the emunctoryes thereof: And he must be bound and tied in with strings, lest in rocking him, he fall out of his cradle." Extremes were to be avoided. The child's room must be neither too hot nor too cold, too dark nor too light (in fact, he should be removed from sources of light so as not to become squint-eyed). Until he was two, he might sleep whenever he wanted; until he was three or four he should be more often asleep than awake.[22]

Considering the possibility of injuries inflicted on the child at delivery (bruises, especially of the head, and broken limbs; as to premature birth, "these Children are not usually long-liv'd") and the apparent ubiquity of defects and infant diseases, prolonged sleep may have been more the wishful thought of the mother than the actual condition of the child.[23] Actually, the fussing, crying child was not necessarily the charge of the mother, since putting the child out to wet-nurse was a practice engaged in by most of those who could afford it. It was also a practice condemned by virtually everyone who gave counsel on early child-rearing, which is of course to say men (Mrs. Jane Sharp, a midwife for over thirty years, only frowned on the practice). Condemnation was followed by detailed advice on how to choose a wet-nurse.

Thomas Phaer, whose *Boke of Children* was the first original treatise in English on childhood diseases, warned women that "it is agreeing to nature so is it also necessary & comly for the own mother to nource the own child. . . . if not, they must be well advised on taking of a nource, not of vil complexion and of worse manners. . . ."[24] The milk of the nurse must be tested (white, sweet, thick enough for droplet to cling to the inverted fingernail), of course, but her character was more important, since it was roundly conceded that through her milk she could communicate her own "bad conditions or inclinations" or even some "imperfections of her body." Given the emphasis on control of animal passion, it is not surprising to find that red-haired nurses, known to be of fiery temperament, were definitely not recommended.

The fear that a wet-nurse, almost inevitably of inferior quality to the mother in that status-conscious society, would adversely influence a child might have been reason enough to refrain from the practice. But there was a stronger argument against it. Guillemeau, though he followed conventional thought in recommending a nurse, darkly observed that there was "no difference between a woman that refuses to nurse her own childe, and one that kills her child as soon as she has been conceived. . . ." Mauriceau warned against the nurse sleeping in the same bed with the child "lest she overlay it; as I knew one that did and killed her Child, whether wickedly to be free from it, or innocently, she alone knoweth. . . ." It has since been argued that wet-nursing was a form of infanticide, and the fact that "overlaid and starved at nurse" was the stated cause of 529 child deaths in the London Bills of Mortality, 1639-1659, gives credence to the point.[25]

Probably superintendance of the nurse was a critical factor. Guille-meau assumed that the nurse would take the child to the country where neglect could go unnoticed; if the baby died, the nurse might substitute another. If the child did not get along with the parent, "the Proverbe goes, That they are chaunged at Nurse...." The Countess of Lincoln, though she had eighteen children and nursed none of them, claimed that it was "the express ordinance of God that mothers should nurse their own children." Her reason for writing may be explained by her observation: "I fear the death of one or two of my little babes came by the default of their nurses." On the other hand, the nurse employed by Mrs. Alice Thornton, resident in the house, was found asleep on top of little Alice and awakened before the child smothered.[26]

Still, the risk was there, and the reasons to endanger the child must have been strong. Guillemeau lists two—the sickness of the mother and the protests of the father against his wife's nursing—to which might be added a third, obviously related to the first two—nursing was physically and emotionally demanding. In addition to the likelihood of the child being sick, and therefore fussing, in the early part of the century it was recommended that the baby be fed on demand—as often as he cried. It was also suggested that the child be changed after each feeding—"unswath and shift him drie. If he be foule, she may wash him"—though it was conceded that this was "not commonly done," hardly surprising in terms of the time and effort but, no doubt, leaving the infant uncomfortable. This routine would have to be maintained a long time, since milk was to be the only nourishment until the upper and lower foreteeth came (probably at a year), when he would be introduced to gruel, chicken bones and, gradually, meat. Weaning would often not take place until the age of two, at which time such prescriptions as mustard on the nipple were allowed to make the breast loathsome. Although the mother was warned to guard against greediness in the child, the approach to nursing must be called permissive.[27]

Later in the century, Mauriceau—though observing that "some good People [mistakenly] affirm it necessary a Child should sometimes cry to discharge its Brain: the two best ways to quiet him when he Cries, is to give him suck, and lay him clean and dry"—provided for supplementing the breast with pap ("made of Flower and Milk") as early as two or three months of age. And Mrs. Jane Sharp, though also cautioning against letting the child cry too much, expressed the opinion that children should be weaned at the age of one, that they certainly should not be nursing after two and that if they were sucking at three or four, no good would come of them.[28] The tendency in the latter seventeenth century was to be less permissive concerning feeding.

If nursing became less demanding physically, its emotional impact could well have increased. At least the potential was there. Guillemeau noted that if a woman has nursed, bathed and tended her own child, "he endevours to show her a thousand delights.... Hee plays a number of apish trickes about her, he kisseth her, strokes her hair, nose and eares: he flatters her, he counterfeits anger, and other passions, and as he groweth bigger, hee finds other sports with her. . . ." The husband who had been denied his wife's body in late pregnancy might well resent the intrusion of an infant in his bed, especially if Mrs. Sharp's observation, based on thirty years of midwivery, was correct: procreation was followed by a diminished desire to copulate. Indeed, since one of the strictures in choosing a nurse was her total abstinence, this might have included nursing mothers. Even when Mauriceau noted that a nursing woman need not "totally abstain from [copulation], if her nature require it," he seemed to give his conditional "if" a class orientation by adding that such liberty was "founded upon the experience of all poor Women, who bring up their children very well, notwithstanding the[y] lie every Night with their Husbands. . . ."[29]

Employing a wet nurse was a practice of the upper class. Mauriceau, who advised that the mother not suckle her child until the eighth day, observed that "poor People cannot observe so many Precautions" but must begin the first day. Mrs. Sharp noted that the "usual way for rich people is to put forth their children to nurse. . . ." Sir Simonds D'Ewes was farmed out after his mother breast fed him for twenty weeks because his father demanded her company; the wife of a tradesman took over the nursing. Otherwise, circumstances might demand a nurse. Lady Frances Hatton wrote her husband that "there was but two things in the world that I set my hart upon one the first was to sucke my poor child myself but my soar nipples would not give me leave . . . I am resolved if ever I should have a nother I must try again everybody is against it. . . ." In Lady Hatton's circle of friends, putting out to nurse must have been not only acceptable but expected.[30]

Yet there was a story, dating from the late sixteenth century and appearing in different versions in later conduct books, which could not have been without impact. A child told his mother:

> You bore me but nine months in your womb, but my nurse kept me with her teats the space of two years; that which I hold of you is my body, which you gave me scarce honestly, but that which I have of her proceedeth of hur affection. And moreover as soon as I was born, you deprived me of your company, and banished me your presence; but she graciously received me . . . between her arms and used me so well, that she has brought me to this you see.[31]

Yet the denial of affection may have been the mother's very object. Certainly one response to (and, given the negligence of the nurse and the absence of mothering, one cause of) child death was putting the infant out to nurse. The absent baby's passing could not evoke the same maternal response as the death of a suckling infant. Even fathers would react differently. "I have lost two or three at nurse," said Montaigne, "not without regret but without grief."[32]

To connect this attitude of apparent indifference to infanticide would be a mistake. Although infants "died at nurse," there is only indirect proof that such was the parents' deliberate intent, while there is much to indicate that parents mourned the passing of their children. There *is* evidence that child abandonment and child murder occurred in instances of bastardy, which by the seventeenth century was considered a matter of social disgrace.[33] In the case of Marie Cambers, considerable testimony was taken to establish that she had given birth to and abandoned an illegitimate child. Two other cases of illegitimacy and neglect, one leading to the infant's death, took place in the same county within a decade.[34] Laws concerning bastardy usually showed no concern for the child involved, excepting the Act of 1623, "to prevent the Murthering of Bastard Children," which was not always executed [35]

Assuming that the child survived infancy, his training after that point cannot be described with certainty. There is, for example, practically no mention of toilet training in the early seventeenth century. Guillemeau did note precautions to be taken against bed wetting, including getting children up during the night, as well as threatening and shaming them, but he warned against harsh treatment. Other writers assumed that infants would dirty their swaddling cloths, which must mean that bowel training did not begin until after the age of one—and perhaps much later, given the indulgent attitude toward crying and its association with soiled clothes.[36] Indeed, the reader of *The Child-Bearer's Cabinet* would assume a long and protected infancy, followed by a permissive approach to early childhood.

> From three years of age until the seventh, they are to be educated gently and kindly, not to be severely reprehended, chidden, or beaten, for by that means they may be made throughout their whole life after too timorous, or too much terrified, astonished, and sotted.
>
> Being yet in their first years, they are not to be compelled to going [walking], for seeing all their bones are soft as Wax, and the body fall the heavier, they either become lame or universally resolved in their feet. . . .
>
> In the sixth or seventh year of their age, they are to be sent to schoole, and committed to the breeding and introduction of courteous and temperate Schoolmasters, who may not terrifie them.
>
> Before these yeares they are not to be compelled or forced to harder labours; otherwise they will not thrive well, but stand at a stay, and keep little, or become Dwarfes.[37]

Yet, despite this homely advice, it is clear that children were being beaten in the early seventeenth century; frequently by their mothers and seemingly without regard to sex.[38] (Indeed, there were apparently few exceptions, at least in the upper class, to John Aubrey's observation that "in those dayes, fathers were not acquainted with their children.")[39] In school, beating was the generally accepted way of maintaining order and ensuring learning, "spare the rod and spoil the child" having Biblical sanction—though there were dissenters from this strict regimen.[40]

Far from discouraging a child from early walking, domestic scenes painted in the seventeenth century give testimony to the use of contraptions with wheels which accommodate toddlers learning the rudiments of ambulation. Leading strings were attached to clothing, the purpose also being to steady youngsters attempting to walk. The portrait of a nine-month-old child standing up must testify to an adult's aspiration if not to a child's competence.[41] Precocity was of concern to the parent in physical development as well as in the mental realm.

The diarist John Evelyn, writing in mid-century, certainly pushed his child to "harder labours." He taught his son to pray as soon as he could speak. At age three the boy was reading and, soon afterward, writing. Before he was five he could recognize Greek and Latin words; simultaneously his mother was teaching him French. Evelyn's motives were clear enough. He thought the mind of the child was vulnerable, making it imperative that he be guarded from bad thoughts, that learning serve as a bulwark against the world as well as a determinant of future growth. To strengthen the child's resistance, manliness must be nurtured: his locks should be sheared in the cradle and, thereafter, a Spartan regime followed, though physical punishment was to be more a threat than a reality. Only occasionally was the child to be soothed and flattered, a concession which would not have been granted by Evelyn's contemporary, Ezekias Woodward, who asserted: "Indulgence is the very *engine* of the Devill. . . ."[42]

Evelyn might well have emphasized the vulnerability of children and, consequently, the need for discipline. His personal tragedy was the death of this cherished son at the age of five. The ubiquity of illness, the not unlikely possibility of death—for the life expectancy of children (ages 1-14) declined from 42.5 to 34 in England in the seventeenth century—was a constant source of anxiety to parents. Children, though infrequently mentioned in personal correspondence, were most commonly depicted in the setting of a sick room. Thus, Sarah Meade kept her mother informed about her son for two years after his delivery.

> He has been a little froward [peevish] this day and last night, but I hope it is but wind. . . . We are well and the child thrives. . . . I hope the child has not taken cold. . . . Nathaniel had a looseness for above 2 weeks, which wee thought did him good, & carried of

his flegme & stoppage at his stomacke; & I was in hope, when hee came into the country, it might have abated, but it yett continues upon him; having 4: or 5: stooles in a day & night, which keeps him pretty weake and low; & his stomacke is weake; we are fearfull to give him things to stopp it least hee should be worse; for we suppose he is A breeding some more great teeth; and several have told mee that many children breeds their teeth with A Looseness, which many Reckons best:—I am a little fearful of him about it. . . . our little boy is now fine & well & his looseness is much abated, & I think has noe more now fine than doth him good, goeinge to stoole but about 3 or 4 times in a day & a night; his teeth troubled him much; & wee gott James Wass to come & cutt his gumms in 2 places, since which he has been much better.[43]

In addition to the explicitness and the constant undertone of worry evident in these letters, it is notable that Sarah was aware of information to be found in books on child care. Mrs. Sharp pointed to loose bowels as a consequence of the "breeding of teeth," while Robert Pemell was the first English physician to advocate gum-lancing during teething.[44] It seems probable that child care manuals were reaching more people in the later seventeenth century, and that children were receiving more attention.

Sarah Meade's concern with teething might be the least of a parent's worries. Lady Hatton wrote her husband: "my daughter Nancy presents her duty to you she is very well Susana is not very well she has a nother tooth just ready to cut little Betty has had the chiking pox but they are now beginning to dry away & I hope the worst is past with her never any poor child has been so ill that lived. . . ." To comfort Lord Hatton at the time of his wife's miscarriage, Lady Manchester pointed to the misfortune of "Sir Robert Cotton [who] lost this year 5 daughters which was all the children he then had in three days time," while Lady Hatton heard from her brother that "upon my telling [Lady Northumberland] some remedies for her child's convulsions, we all wish it well in heaven, to be no more a disturbance to us here . . . for once a week we are all troubled with it, either loosing balls or some other diverting appointments through it. . . ."[45] There are three reactions to disease involved here, in addition to the earlier one of concern: identifying it and, presumably, attempting to control it; affecting a callous or disinterested attitude toward it; declaring it out of human hands and, thus, a religious matter.

Insofar as identification and control of disease were concerned, the claim has been made that the "middle period of the seventeenth century witnessed the awakening of medicine from its age-long sleep of well-nigh 2,000 years." At the end of the Tudor period, the study of children's disease was a combination of "crude theories and meager observations" based on classic and contemporary writings, hardly separate from pedagogical considerations. During the Stuart era, the names of William Harvey, Francis Glisson, Thomas Sydenham and many lesser but important pioneers appeared, not to mention such luminaries as Bacon and Locke.[46] Yet despite efforts to raise the level of medical therapy (most obviously in the areas of pharmacology and epidemiology) and the attention paid to preventative medicine (especially regarding the plague), effective techniques were slow in coming. "The change which occurred in the seventeenth century was thus not so much technological as mental. In many different spheres of life the period saw the emergence of a new faith in the potentialities of human initiative."[47]

Guillemeau, Mauriceau, Mrs. Sharp and others confronted the diseases of childhood through an explicit description of symptoms and detailed instructions about the preparation of remedies. The earlier fascination with magic was still sometimes present, though concern with religion could also be noted, as well as a new analytical spirit. Mrs. Sharp, having discussed the problems of "flegme," "Codds be swoln," "Fundament slip forth," "loose-bellyed" or "cannot go to stool," "worms," "breeding of their teeth," and other ailments, noted:

> Some children grow lean, and pine away, and the cause is not known; if it be from Witchcraft, good prayers to God are the best remedy: yet some hang Amber, and Coral about the child neck, as a Sovereign Amulet. But leanness may proceed from a dry distemper of the whole body, then it is bath it in a decoction of Mallows, Marshmallows, Branc-Ursine, Sheeps heads and anoint with oil of sweet Almonds, if it be hot and dry add Roses, Violets, Lettice, Poppey-heads, and afterwards anoint with oils of Violets, and Roses. The Child may be lean from want of milk, or bad milk from the nurse . . . . sometimes worms in the body draw away the nourishment.[48]

Hygiene was also discussed.[49]

Surgical operations, as well as medicinal cures, were recommended. It was not unusual to recommend for the "Tongue-tyed" that "the Ligament be cut that is too short and hinders speech." If urination was a problem, "hold down the child fast" and insert a long rod, slightly curved at the end, into the penis to remove the impeding stone from the bladder. If the penis pointed downward rather than straight, the ligament which, being too short, aimed it badly was to be cut when the member was stiff.[50] Surely there were some advantages to being female in the seventeenth century!

Analyzing and treating human ailments proceeded from an attitude different from but not inconsistent with religious rationalization of disease and death, or even recovery. Alice Thornton's daughter Naly was so terrified by the celebration of Charles II's triumphal return ("she never having had seene any such things as soldiers, or guns, or drums, or noyses, and shouting") that she fell into convulsive fits and was brought, "halfe dead," to her mother. "But I gave her all medicins for it, and oyle of amber and pieony and other things, which by the Lord's great and infinitt mercy to me, did at length preserve and restore her from them. O Lord God of mercy, what glory shall I give to Thee the God of heaven and earth, which hast delivered my sweet infant and saved her life again."[51]

But what good was medicine if divine intervention was purposeful? Lady Warwick's first child was a girl, "whom God was pleased to take from me by death." During her second confinement, with a son, her father died—"but I, being young and inconsiderate, grief did not long stick with me." She learned to grieve, and to accept. She felt she sought too much comfort in the world, and claimed to have had

> some inward persuasion that God would, in some way or other, punish me for my doing so. And, at last, it pleased God to send a sudden sickness on my only son, which I then doated on with great fondness. I was beyond expression struck at it; not only because of my kindness for him, but because my conscience told me it was for my back-sliding. Upon this conviction I presently retired to God; and by earnest prayer begged of Him to restore my child; and did then solemnly promise to God, if he would hear my prayer I would become a new creature. This prayer of mine God was so gracious as to grant; and of a sudden began to restore my child; which made the doctor himself wonder at the sudden amendment he saw in him.

At the time of her husband's unexpected inheritance of his title, due to the deaths of his elder brothers, Lady Warwick feared she might be drawn "to love the glory of the world too well." Her only surviving son contracted small pox and died. She was prepared but her spouse was not.

> I did endeavour to comfort my sad and afflicted husband, who, at the news of his death . . . cried out so terribly that his cry was heard a great way; and he was the saddest afflicted person could possibly be. I confess that I loved him at a rate, that if my heart do not deceive me, I would, with all the willingness in the world, have died either for him or with him, if God had only seen it fit; yet I was dumb and held my peace, because God did it.[52]

This incident was not isolated and discreet. The reaction of Lady Warwick, like that of Alice Thornton, suggests that girls were taught to sublimate anger or aggression through religion. A recent literary study claims that reading between the lines of seventeenth-century women's prayer books, one finds a concern with childbirth and sickness, just as the readers of these books were admonished to be silent, chaste and obedient.[53] Repression and religion were complementary.

Significantly, the men who invoked the Almighty at times of illness or death were usually ministers.[54] Many fathers, as already noted, chose not to know their children. Most men, unlike Lord Warwick, chose

silence, aloofness, a cold civility rather than showing emotion out-
wardly. The Dutchess of Newcastle's encomium for her husband—"My
Lord always being a great master of his passions"—was a common term
of praise, at least to the upper class.[55]

The Dutchess also noted that "both My Lord's parents, and his aunt
and uncle in law, shewed always a great and fond love to My Lord, endeavouring, when he was but a child, to please him with what he most
delighted in." But such indulgence was probably as unusual as Clarendon's companionship with his father. Moralists inveighed against it. John
Donne observed with pride: "Children Kneel to ask blessing of parents
in England, and where else." Thomas Cobbett, a mid-century Puritan
writer, warned children to "Present your Parents so to your minds, as
bearing the image of God's Father-hood, and that also will help your
filiall awe and Reverence to them." Parents were cautioned against un-
dermining their authority "by being too fond of your children and too
familiar with them at sometimes at least, and not keeping constantly
your due distance: such fondness and familiarity breed contempt and ir-
reverency in children." Even child-rearing books warned against "cockering" children.[56]

Yet it seems clear that the drive to love children was strong, and
Roger North demonstrated how the tendency to be lenient could serve
the ends of authority:

> great use may be made of that fondness which disposeth parents
> to gratifie children's litle craving appetites, by doing it with an
> adjunct of precept, as a reward of obedience and vertue, such as
> they are capable of, and at the same time being kind, and tender in
> Gratifiing them. This makes yong Creatures thinck that their will
> is not enough, without other means, to obtein their desires, and
> knowing that, they will Conforme, which breeds an habit of order
> in them and lasts to the end. The Contrary is seen, when fondness
> makes parents Indulg all things to children.[57]

In this manner, parents could succumb to children without feeling
guilty at having totally sacrificed personal restraint. Emotional display
would be disciplined.

Self-control appears to have been the crucial issue in this situation.
Projected onto the child, the obverse of self-control was seen in willfullness, a quality which North clearly opposed. His attitude was hardly
novel; it could be seen in depictions of the child dating at least to the
beginning of the century. In *A Godly Form of Household Government*
(1621) the Puritans Robert Cleaver and John Dod wrote:

> The young child which lieth in the cradle is both wayward and
> full of affections; and though his body be but small, yet he hath
> a reat [wrong-doing] heart, and is altogether inclined to evil. . . .
> If this sparkle be suffered to increase, it will rage over and burn

> down the whole house. For we are changed and become good not
> by birth but by education. . . . Therefore parents must be wary
> and circumspect . . . they must correct and sharply reprove their
> children for saying or doing ill.

Education, then, was necessary to protect a child against his own self-destruction. The attitude to be fostered in a child would have to be one of constantly questioning himself, making himself feel inadequate, engendering self-doubt.[58]

There was a quite opposite view on the nature of the child, that of total innocence, which was succinctly announced by John Earle in *Microcosmography* (1628):

> A child is a man in a small letter, yet the best copy of Adam before he tasted of Eve or the apple. . . . His soul is yet a white paper unscribbled with observations of the world . . . . he knows no evil. . . .[59]

Again, the antidote to the world's corrupting influence was education, as John Evelyn's regimen for his son made clear. A child nurtured on languages and the classics might not be so prone to self doubt as one whose diet was the Scriptures. But in either case precocity was at least a denial of self-expression, the forcing of adult values on the defenseless child.

This aggressive response to infant vulnerability may seem ironic until it is recognized that concepts of childhood innocence or depravity were themselves parental projections, either of helplessness or of rage, in the face of death that could not be controlled. The child learned his lesson, coming to understand his own mortality, as did women and clergymen, through religion. Alice Thornton recalled the passing of her daughter, Elizabeth.

> That deare, sweet angell grew worse, and indured it with infinitt patience, and when Mr. Thornton and I came to pray for her, she held up those sweete eyes and hands to her deare Father in heaven, looked up, and cryed in her language, 'Dad, dad, dad' with such vehemency as if inspired by her holy Father in heaven to deliver her sweet soule into her heavenly Father's hands, and at which time we allso did with great zeale deliver up my deare infant's soule into the hand of my heavenly Father, and then she sweetly fell asleepe and went out of this miserable world like a lamb.[60]

Indeed, a children's literature concerned with impending death emerged in the seventeenth century: sermons preached at the passings of young people, memorials, warnings, tokens, looking-glasses, messages, confessions, exhortations, testimonies, admonitions.[61]

Probably the most well read of these many books was James Janeway's *A Token for Children* (1671), a compendium of case histories of youngsters who experienced dramatic conversions and, in the course of dying shortly thereafter, exhorted sinful adults to lead virtuous lives. The death-bed admonitions to parents—"Oh Mother," said he, "did you but know what joy I feel, you would not weep but rejoice"—allowed adults to absolve themselves of guilt felt for bringing vulnerable children into the world.[62] Youngsters themselves might be called upon to shoulder the burden of mortality, as demonstrated in John Norris' *Spiritual Counsel: A Father's Advice to his Children*.

> be much in the Contemplation of the last four thyngs, Heaven, Hell, Death and Judgment. Place yourselves frequently on your death beds, in your Coffins, and in your Graves. Act over frequently in your Minds, the Solemnity of your own Funerals; and entertain your Imaginations with all the lively scenes of Mortality; Meditate much upon the places, and upon the Days of Darkness, and upon the fewness of those that shall be saved; and be always with your Hourglass in your hands, measuring out your own little Span and comparing it with the endless Circle of Eternity.[63]

However, the development of this sort of religious precocity was extreme, while the aristocratic ideal of the seventeenth century was moderation, which hinged on self-control. No man better articulated this goal than John Locke, whose stream of ideas on child rearing carried some sediment from the earlier part of the century as well as the distillate of his observations as scholar and physician. In the latter category may be placed his thoughts on pregnancy and early child care. When confronted with an expectant mother who was breathless following a fright, he raised questions meant to determine whether the woman suffered from cardiac failure, toxaemia of pregnancy or hysterical overbreathing. During childbirth, if the infant could not be put into a natural position, "surgery must be at once applied to bring forth the foetus while the mother still has strength."[64] He did not approve of swaddling, noting that Spartan nurses had brought up children "admirably" without it. He also observed that infants on the Gold Coast at seven or eight months were left "on the ground so that you see them dragging themselves like kittens on four paws; this is also the reason why they walk earlier than European infants."[65] Unlike some of his predecessors, Locks was unworried that these children would develop animalistic qualities.

He was concerned, though, that thought and care be given to raising children, believing that "little, or almost insensible impressions of our tender infancies, have very important or lasting consequences." He stood somewhere between advocates of infant innocence and infant depravity, arguing that few of "Adam's children" were born without "some byass in their natural temper." No childhood determinist, he believed that

"Men's happiness or misery is most part of their own making," and his advice was generally aimed at strengthening character toward the end of self-sufficiency.[66]

If the parent were to accomplish this task, he must from the cradle not give in to the child's will but, rather, "distinguish between the wants of fancy and the wants of nature." Locke recognized "cockering and tenderness," indulgent and corrupting practices, as an upper class phenomenon and exhorted gentlemen to imitate the discipline of "honest farmers and substantial yeomen." To harden the children, for example, their feet should be accustomed to cold water (poor people's children went barefoot, after all). Open air and a minimum of clothing, always loose-fitting, were essential to good health. Locke claimed that "the body may be made to bear almost anything."[67]

A simple diet, without permissive feeding, was recommended.[68] Crying was not to be indulged. Long hours of sleep were to be tolerated, but on a hard bed. "The great thing to be minded in education," Locke observed, was "what habits you settle." Most striking among these was "going to stool regularly," to be accomplished by enforced sitting. No previous commentator had ever mentioned toilet training. The purpose of this regimen was to cultivate the strength and vigor of the body "so that it may be able to obey and execute the orders of the *mind.*"[69]

It follows logically that the virtue of the mind would be "that a man is able to *deny himself* his own desires . . . and purely follow what reason directs as best." Locke called for a change in current disciplinary practices: "What vice can be nam'd, which parents, and those about children, do not season them with . . . .violence, revenge and cruelty. *Give me a blow that I may beat him,* is a lesson that most children hear every day." As parents should not be too tender, neither should they be too hard. The rod should be avoided, as well as rewards.[70] Shame should be the instrument used to motivate children.

> *Esteem* and *disgrace* are, of all others, the most powerful incentives to the mind, when once it is brought to relish them. If you can get into children a love of credit, and an apprehension of shame and disgrace you have to put into 'em the true principle.

Praise and commendation for accomplishment were to be counter-balanced by a "cold and neglectful countenance" for failure.[71]

Locke recognized the limits of rules (and, especially, of rote learning), saw the possibilities of play ("nothing appears to me to give children so much becoming confidence and behaviour . . . as *dancing*")[72] and emphasized the importance of parental example and a growing friendship between father and son as the boy gradually became a man ("The only fence against the world is, a thorough knowledge of it, into which a young gentleman should be entered by degrees. . . .").[73] Not only would children be watching their parents for the proper examples of behavior, but to carry out Locke's plan parents (or tutors) would have to spend a good deal of time surveilling their children.[74]

Nor would supervision account for all the time spent, since the stricture that all children be dealt with as rational creatures could only lead to hours of explanation and persuasion. But the energy might be better used than formerly, since Locke took an honest (and refreshingly realistic) view of educational approaches to children. He realized that reading first had to be encouraged for its entertainment value, strongly recommending *Aesop's Fables*[75] but remaining traditional enough to advocate learning the Lord's Prayer, the Creeds and the Ten Commandments. A chapter-by-chapter approach to the Bible, he noted, could only convey "an odd jumble of thoughts." He approved learning foreign languages ("*Latin* I look upon as absolutely necessary to a gentleman") but was not convinced of the worth of studying English grammar ("persons of the softer sex . . . without the least study or knowledge of *grammar,* can carry them to a great degree of elegancy and politeness in their language").[76]

Locke disclaimed having made a comprehensive and definitive statement on child rearing, and he made it clear that each parent must finally consult his own reason for the proper education of his child.[77] Locke himself deviated from conventional wisdom in child-rearing by changing the conditions of infancy: swaddling clothes would be discarded, crawling might be tolerated and, though crying would not be indulged nor feeding be so much a matter of demand, the mother would probably be present (how else would the nurse be surveilled?). The early years of childhood would witness the introduction of toilet training and the discarding of corporal punishment for the inducement of shame. (Engendering doubt, "the brother of shame" in Erik Erikson's words, was not a novelty, of course.)[78] More attention would be paid to children and to the nature of their education.

Interest in school learning, notably in the middle class, had been strikingly evident since the middle of the sixteenth century. It has been claimed that the "English in 1640 were infinitely better educated than they had been before," as they moved through the educational complex of petty schools (basic literacy), free schools (mathematics, English composition and rhetoric), grammar schools (free school curriculum plus classical linguistics and English grammar), universities and Inns of Court. The expansion of education owed to the impetus of the bourgeoisie, who were moved to mimic the bookishness of the gentry; humanists, who viewed schooling as the road to universal moral improvement (which might render unnecessary the protection of the innocent child against the corrupt world); and Puritans, who viewed ignorance as the root of evil (and, as a corollary, infant depravity as remediable).[79]

Another way of viewing this transformation would be from a changing perspective on childhood: in art, costume, leisure activities and literature, it can be seen that a separate world was being created for children in the seventeenth century.[80]

Perhaps the most interesting change in this regard had to do with the English practice of sending children out of the home at six or seven years to a school or an apprenticeship.[81] By the middle of the seventeenth century, parents were hanging onto their children a few years longer. The Reverend Ralph Josselin's children, born in the mid-seventeenth century, left home to be educated or become servants and apprentices between the ages of ten and fifteen. Nor was this a middle class pattern only. The gentry on one end of the social scale, the yeomen and poor on the other, kept adolescent children at home more often, but it still was exceptional to do so.[82]

A foreign observer in the early sixteenth century had attributed the putting out of children to the "want of affection in the English," while more recently an American historian of the Puritan movement has suggested that parents "did not trust themselves with their own children, that they were afraid of spoiling them by too great affection."[83] The many strictures against overfondness, against cockering and tenderness, suggest that affection was a crucial issue—Ralph Josselin valued his children "above gold and jewels." Possibly it was *the* crucial issue, despite the fact that financial burdens and educational aims motivated parents to send older children out of the home.[84]

In the middle of the seventeenth century there were only two counties in England where there was not a grammar school (offering a possibility of free tuition) within twelve miles of any family, a fact which suggests that other than pedagogical motives were involved in pushing children out to learn. The educator John Brinsley wrote: "If any are sent to school so early, they are rather sent to the school from troubling the house at home, and from danger, and shrewd turns, than from any great hope and desire that their friends should learn anything in effect."[85]

The troubles, dangers and shrewd turns must have included the unwholesome influence of servants,[86] seemingly inevitable confrontations with step-parents (the likelihood of both natural parents surviving until a child reached his majority was not high),[87] and a matter that involved servants, house guests and parents—the intimacy of sleeping arrangements.[88] Sexual attractions and rivalries in the family were, at most, alluded to and disguised.[89] Thus, Lord Halifax addressed his daughter:

> *You* are at present the chief Object of my *care,* as well as my *kindness,* which sometimes throweth me into *Visions* of your being happy in the World, that are better suited to my partial *Wishes,* than my reasonable *Hopes* for you. At other times, when my *Fears* prevail, I shrink as if I were struck, at the Prospect of

> *Danger,* to which a young Woman must be expos'd.... Your
> *Husband's* Kindness will have so much advantage of ours, that we
> shall yield up all *Competition,* and as well as we love you, be very
> well contented to surrender to such a *Rival.*

Halifax tried—not obtrusively, perhaps not consciously—to develop a
conspiracy between himself and his daughter toward other women,
which must have undermined the authority of Lady Halifax.[90] Moralists
encouraged mothers to establish close relationships with their daughters,
while they recommended modesty, chastity and piety in young girls.[91]

Conflict of authority in domestic relations was usually between
father and son (unless it involved step-parents, when the matter of inheritance often took precedence over sex). The fact that these conflicts were frequently religious in nature (almost any journal kept by a
male Quaker gives testimony to this observation) is significant when it
is recalled that the typical seventeenth-century father was apt to be a
secularist while his wife was inclined to religiosity and inculcated these
values in her children. Note the testimony of Reverend Oliver Heywood:

> But tho my parents were godly [it later appears the father did
> not attend church] yet my birth and my nativity was in sin, and
> so was my conception, for they were instruments to bring me
> into the world not as saints but as man and woman . . . of Adam
> by natural generation. . . . I am by nature a child of wrath, a limb
> of satan . . . and that not too fruitful root began to sprout in
> infancy. . . .
> I have observed from my childhood and youth my natural
> constitution exceedingly inclined to lust, which hath discovered
> itselfe betimes, and many times assaulted me both waking and
> sleeping. . . . tho I may take much paines in mortifying dutys to
> crucify the flesh and beat down my body. . . .
> I doe with thankfulness to god remember, that many a time
> my dear mother did zealously and famililarly presse upon me
> truths of the greatest concernment . . . I confesse I took much de-
> light in waiting upon her abroad, but what my ends were I cannot
> tel, yet this I beleeve, that god disposed of it for much good to
> my poore soul, yea I am sometimes thinking it may be god that
> made that time a time of love. . . .[92]

It could not be expected, however, that sexual attraction could always
be sublimated since this would not prepare most males for their careers.
The alternative was a strict discipline, the control of sexuality through
a different sort of religious sublimation—preparation for the "Calling."[93]
Certainly the school provided discipline. John Brinsley, the Puritan
divine and educator, put forth the regimen. School would begin at six,
with punishment for tardiness (virtually every picture of the classroom
showed the master with a birch in one hand). Homework in Latin was

presented and other studies pursued until nine, when there was a quarter-hour break. The work resumed until eleven, when there was a two-hour hiatus. From one to five-thirty students were again at their desks, with a quarter-hour break at three thirty. The purpose of education was divine, "God having ordained schools of learning to be a principall means to reduce a barbarous people to civilitie" and Christianity. The challenge was to gain "the veric savage amonst them unto Jesus Christ, whether Irish or Indian. . . ." Or, Brinsley might have added, "Child."[94]

The punctuality demanded of the student, the restraint needed to remain sitting almost all day at a desk would foster the self-discipline which was the object of earlier controls. As to apprenticeship it has been observed that the guilds attempted "to instil self-discipline and respect for the social code into those for whose industrial training they were responsible." The Shoemakers of Carlisle forbid apprentices and journeymen to play football without the consent of their masters; the Merchant Adventurers of Newcastle forbid "daunce dice cards mum or use any musick" and inveighed against extravagant dress and long hair, even establishing a prison to jail offenders against these rules. There are instances of masters imposing fines for missing prayer, "toying with the maids," teaching children "bawdy words" or even wearing "a foul shirt on Sunday." Working conditions were apparently as exacting as school situations, though in the seventeenth century apprentices were protected by law.[95]

There is no denying that parents in seventeenth-century England were interested in their children, but that interest took the form of controlling youngsters—just as adults restrained themselves—rather than allowing autonomous development. Before discussing the meaning of changes that took place in child-rearing during the course of the seventeenth century in England, it would be well to consider the situation across the Atlantic for comparative purposes.

America, though but a tiny offshoot of England in the seventeenth century, was to be a better place, a "city upon a hill" or a "holy experiment" where the godly would serve as an example to the rest of the world. Would children receive better, or at least different, treatment? Two theories about the colonial world suggest that a transformation would occur. One scholar asserts that "no one becomes a real colonial who is not impelled by infantile complexes which were not properly resolved in adolescence."[96] This suggests that as parents, colonials might be less adequate than those who stayed at home. The second hypothesis is complementary to the first, though it is based on the assumption that the environment rather than its inhabitants forms society: "American development has exhibited not merely advance along a single line, but a return to primitive conditions on a continually advancing frontier line. . . ."[97] Again, the emphasis is on a less mature stage of growth.

The abundance of propaganda literature depicting America as a place healthy for children suggests the importance of projection in the decision to emigrate.[98] Furthermore, if the true colonial is characteristically "anti-social," with a youth's escapist desires, the pilgrims who valued America's isolation might be seen in a new and different light.[99] The imagery of the departing colonists might also be appropriate to a child, as illustrated by the words of the Massachusetts Bay Company members:

> [we] esteem it our honor to call the Church of England, from whence we rise, our dear mother; and cannot part from our native country, where she specially resideth, without much sadness of heart and many tears in our eyes, ever acknowledging that such hope and part as we have obtained in the common salvation, we have received in her bosom and sucked it from her breasts. We leave it not therefore as loathing that milk wherewith we were nourished there; but blessing God for the parentage and education. . . .[100]

The discovery of America might be summarized in Anne Bradstreet's words "To my Dear Children," where she noted: "I found a new world and new manners, at which my heart rose. But after I was convinced it was the way of God, I submitted to it and joined the Church at Boston."[101] Innovation would be kept within the bounds of cultural inheritance.

The simple act of naming children testified to this observation. While the *Mayflower* was at sea Elizabeth Hopkins gave birth to her fourth child, called Oceanus. In a somewhat later migration, a son delivered to John and Sarah Cotton was labeled Seaborn. Children were named not only after the conditions of their births but with regard to their parents' expectations. These names might be of Biblical origin (Samuel Sewall named his son Joseph, "in hopes of the accomplishment of the Prophecy, Ezek. 37th") or of the parents' own invention. Roger Clapp's children were named Experience, Waitstill, Preserved, Hopestill, Wait, Thanks, Desire, Unite and Supply. Other appellations included Rich Grace, More Mercy, Relieve, Believe, Reform, Deliverance and Strange.[102] The exotic quality of these names seems to demonstrate a special recognition of the child, no doubt related to expectations applied to the New World.

But even the more prosaic names given to children are revelatory, since there is a necronymic pattern to the past. In the Middle Ages identical names might be applied to siblings, who were then distinguished by birth-order labels. By the early modern period this practice was no longer in use, but a dead child's name could be applied to a sibling born later. (Today, of course, no two siblings are given the same name because a name is seen as intrinsic to the irreplaceable person.) Moreover, in a seventeenth-century New England town over five-eighths of first sons and over three-quarters of first daughters bore the same forename as their parents. (By the nineteenth century these figures had markedly declined, much more for girls than boys). A study of this situation concludes that the "shift away from parental naming . . . [helps to] illustrate the movement from a traditional lineal orientation to a modern individuated conception of children." Furthermore, "the use of necronyms for the successor of a dead sibling [and] name-sharing among brothers' daughters suggests that 'pre-modern' New Englanders saw children as ultimate adults and not as persons inherently individuated as children."[103] A review of child-rearing practices might test this hypothesis.

In the pre-natal period the expectant mother was to curtail her activities, but there is no record that she sat pensive and worried about the sex of her forthcoming child.[104] Delivery was in the home, with the assistance of a midwife. Surely colonial women in childbirth must have shared the anxieties of their English counterparts, and sometimes they accused midwives of such heinous crimes as "familiarity with the devil." But midwivery was also a respectable profession, as testified to by the presence in its ranks of wives of eminent Puritan divines.[105] The mortality rate of newborn babies has been estimated at one in ten, though it was certainly higher in some families. Both Samuel Sewall and Cotton Mather had fourteen children. One of Sewall's was stillborn, several died as infants, several more as young adults. Seven Mather babies died shortly after delivery, one died at two years and six survived to adulthood, five of whom died in their twenties. Only two Sewall children outlived their father, while Samuel Mather was the only child to survive Cotton.[106]

There exists no evidence that infants were swaddled in the seventeenth century, although there can be no doubt that it was the practice later.[107] Babies were breast fed, usually by their mothers. Circumstances might require the services of a wet-nurse, as in the case of Reverend Thomas Shepard who sailed to Massachusetts with his wife and infant son. Once arrived, he later told the boy, "the mother fell sick of a consumption & thou my child wert put to nurse. . . ." Two generations later the merchant Samuel Sewall recorded matter-of-factly: "Joseph Brisco's wife gives my son suck."[108] Migrants from England to Massachusetts were drawn from the middle elements of society.[109] They may not have participated in the aristocratic practice of putting children out to nurse, but it is possible that the acquisition of wealth led later generations to imitate the English upper class.[110]

Sewall mentioned the weaning of two of his children, one at fourteen months (because the nurse was sick) and the second at eighteen months.

Weaning at one year appears to have been the practice earlier in the century.[111] The spacing of children in families suggests that lactation served a contraceptive function, though it is possible that there was a taboo on intercourse while a mother was nursing.[112] If so, however, there is no literature which documents a father's jealousy of his new-born child.

There is ample testimony to anxiety over illness and sorrow at death. Thomas Shepard described his own feeling of helplessness at his infant son's second affliction: "then the humour fell into his eyes; which grew so sore that partly by the humour and ptly by the ill handling and ap-plying medicines to them, his eyes grew starke blind with pearles upon both eyes and a white filme; insomuch as it was a most dreadfull sight unto all beholders of him & very pittiful which was such a misery that me thought now I had rather that the Lord would take away my child by death than let it live a blind & a miserable life." But once Shepard was resolved to bear his sorrow, the Lord intervened to restore the baby's sight "by a poore weake meanes, vizt the oyle of white pasec . . . almost miraculously."[113] Increase Mather, who sat up all night with his ill son Nathaniel, observed: "Little doe children think, wt affection is in ye Heart of a Father." A few days later he was praying and fasting for the health of Nathaniel and another son, Samuel.[114] Cotton Mather, soon after the birth of his son Samuel, recorded his "continual Appre-hension that the Child, (tho' a lusty and hearty infant) will dy in its In-fancy." Less than a month later young Samuel suffered convulsions. But Mather was by this time reconciled: "The Convulsions of my own Mind, were all this while, happily composed and quieted; and with much Composure of Mind, I often and often in Prayers resigned the Child unto the Lord."[115]

This was clearly not parental indifference but self-control. That re-ligion served the very necessary function of rationalization, a means to dealing with feelings of helplessness and consequent outrage, is almost too obvious an observation to need stating. Yet the apparent conflict in the minds of New Englanders, from whom most of the evidence comes, must be explained. The examples are frequent. At the death of her year-and-a-half grand daughter, the poet Anne Bradstreet wrote:

> Farewel dear babe, my hearts too much content,
> Farewel sweet babe, the pleasure of mine eye,
> Farewel fair flower that for a space was lent,
> Then ta'en away unto Eternity.

Yet the same woman could pen her "Contemplations":

> Here sits our Grandame in retired place
> And in her lap, her bloody Cain new-born.[116]

In the catechism he prepared for the young of Massachusetts Bay colony in 1646, John Cotton taught his charges to say: "I was conceived in sin, and born in iniquity. . . . Adam's sin imputed to me and a corrupt nature dwells in me." When, three years later, his eldest daughter and youngest son died of small pox he wrote:

Christ gave them both, and he takes them both again
To live with him; blest be his holy name.

His grandson, Cotton Mather, expressed the same sentiments at the death of his daughter, though he preached otherwise: "Don't you know that your Children are the Children of Death, and the Children of Hell and the Children of Wrath, by Nature?" But the retreat to theology was not always achieved with ease, as an unknown author (1710) made clear at the passing of a six-year-old:

Great Jesus claim'd his own; never begrutch
Your Jewells rare into the Hands of Such . . .
It is a lesson hard, I must confess
For our Proud Wills with Heav'ns to acquiesce.[117]

In *Day of Doom* Michael Wigglesworth would only concede "the easiest room in hell" to children who died, but the bodiless heads with wings on New England tombstones, in the judgment of one scholar, "probably stood for purity, innocence and the childlike character the soul was supposed to have." The time and care given to making christening gowns, small coverlets, children's furniture and the like is further testimony to the affection felt for the young.[118] Infanticide was the lot of bastards only.[119]

Consequently, it is not surprising that in America as in England, the self-control managed by adults was passed on to children. Although there exists no record of swaddling in America (or surgical operations on infants) and little evidence of wet-nursing—all manifestations of parental control—and there is no literature on such a subject as toilet training, where the child would himself be expected to show restraint, yet it is clear that American parents were admonished to take a strong stand against self-assertion, or willfullness, in children.[120] Breaking the will of the child was based on the supposition that the parents' will could be substituted. The child would doubt his own abilities, repress his strivings and look to a higher authority. Self-control and Divine guidance were complementary. Indeed, it might be speculated that the very absence of certain physical controls found in England made more necessary the ideological controls of New England. The phrase "swaddled in Calvinism" seems appropriate.

For Puritans, at least, the seeming chaos of England was replaced in America by the godly community whose rules were explicit and repressive.[121] The Massachusetts Bay Company instructions to settlers included the maintenance of family discipline: "we have divided the servants belonging to the Company into several families, as we desire and intend they should live together . . . take special care, in settling these families, that the chief of these families, at least some of them, be grounded in religion; whereby morning and evening family duties may be duly performed, and a watchful eye held over all in each family, by one or more in each family to be appointed thereto. . . ." In Connecticut and New Hampshire, as well as Massachusetts, it was a capital crime for a "child" over sixteen to "curse or smite his natural father or mother."[122]

The years between infancy and early adulthood (late adolescence) were, of course, successful in teaching children Christian behavior; deviant activity never characterizes more than a small segment of the population. Corporal punishment was a means to this end, as Samuel Sewall demonstrated when his four-year-old son misbehaved. "Joseph threw a knop of Brass and hit his Sister Betty on the forehead so as to make it bleed and swell; upon which, and for his playing at Prayer-time, and eating when Return Thanks, I whipd him pretty smartly." It was a form of punishment sanctioned by the *New England Primer:*

F   The Idle *Fool*
    Is Whipt at school.
J   *Job* feels the Rod
    Yet blesses GOD.

And, as in England, women were not exempt from applying it. As John Eliot noted in *The Harmony of the Gospels* (1678): "The gentle rod of the mother is a very soft and gentle thing; it will break neither bone nore skin; yet by the blessing of God with it, and upon the wise application of it, it would break the bond that bindeth up corruption in the heart. . . . *Withhold not correction from the child, for if thou beatest him with the rod he shall not die, thou shalt beat him with the rod and deliver his soul from hell.*"[123]

Yet there is no mention of such treatment of children in Cotton Mather's diary. On the contrary, there is evidence of indulgence on the fiery preacher's part, as when he denied his son candy for being cross with his sister. "I had no sooner turn'd my back, but the Good-condition'd creature fell into Tears, at this Punishment of her little Brother, and gave to him a Part of what I had bestowed upon her."[124] But Mather had other methods of discipline than the rod.

I took my little [eight-year-old] daughter, Katy, into my Study; and there I told my Child, that I am to *dy* shortly, and shee must, When I am *Dead,* Remember every Thing that I said unto her.

I sett before her, the sinful and woful Condition of her *Nature,* and I charg'd her, *to pray in secret Places,* every Day, without ceasing, that God for the Sake of Jesus Christ would give her a New Heart, and *pardon* Her Sins, and make her a *Servant* of His.

I gave her to understand, that when I am taken from her shee must look to meet with more humbling *Afflictions* than shee does, now shee has a careful and a tender *Father* to provide for her; but, is shee would *pray* constantly, God in the Lord Jesus Christ, would bee a Father to her, and make all *Afflictions* work together for her Good.

I signified unto her, That the People of God, would much observe how shee carried herself, and that I had written a Book, about, *Ungodly Children,* in the Conclusion whereof I say, that this Book will bee a terrible Witness against my own Children, if any of them would not bee *Godly.*

At length, with many Tears, both on my Part, and hers, I told my Child, that God had from Heaven assured mee, and the good Angels of God had satisfied mee, *that shee shall bee brought Home unto the Lord Jesus Christ, and bee one of His forever.*[125]

This was a heavy emotional burden, even for a Mather, and one which might be shared by the community.[126] This was most obviously done in the church, where sermons about childhood and youth were preached.[127] It was accomplished also in the school, as revealed in the *New England Primer:*

A In *Adam's* Fall
  We sinned all.
G As runs the *Glass*
  Man's life doth pass.
R *Rachel* doth mourn
  For her first born.
T *Time* cuts down all
  Both great and small.
Y *Youth* forward slips
  Death soonest nips.[128]

And it was achieved through the institutions of apprenticeship and service, which took children out of the household of the parents as early as the age of six but as late as fourteen. Still, it must be noted that most education took place in the home rather than in a school.[129]

It was also at the tender age of six that children began to dress as adults, though it is less clear that they were regarded as spiritually mature and, as already noted, legal adulthood came many years later.[130] Putting children out of the house was surely not felt to be a callous act nor, probably, was it due so much to a fear of spoiling children as to a worry among adults that they might become too attached to these vulnerable youngsters. And, as in England, the practice was probably related to domestic problems. Houses did not provide internal privacy:

they were neither soundproof nor always partitioned (and from the roofbeams every room might be visible), quarters were cramped and unmarried people of opposite sexes often slept in the same rooms or even the same beds. There is ample testimony to the primal scene having been witnessed.[131] Parents no doubt sensed the wisdom of removing from such a situation their own adolescent children, thus dampening familial sexual rivalries.

It is significant that the solution to this domestic problem was invested with religious meaning. Cotton Mather exhorted his congregation:

> See to it, O parents, that when you choose callings for your children, you wisely consult their capacities and their inclinations, lest you ruin them. And, O! cry mightily to God by prayer, yea, with fasting and prayer, for his direction when you are to resolve upon a matter of such considerable consequence.[132]

Just as the community shared the burden of disciplining the child, so the man at work contributed to the community. As Mather's grandfather, John Cotton, observed: "If thou beest a man that lives without a calling, though thou has two thousands to spend, yet if thou hast no calling, tending to public good, thou art an uncleane beast."[133]

The label "uncleane beast" has a hyperbolic ring unless it is remembered what the Calling diverts man from. John Calvin, who steered Protestants away from the Catholic concept of the Calling as a summons to the priesthood to a newer notion of the Calling as the "use of the gifts of God," articulated the idea of vocation as the sublimation of sexuality.

> Let us discard, therefore, that inhuman philosophy which, allowing no use of the creatures but what is absolutely necessary, not only malignantly deprives us of the lawful enjoyment of the Divine beneficence, but which cannot be embraced till it has despoiled man of all his senses, and reduced him to a senseless block. But, on the other hand, we must, with equal diligence, oppose the licentiousness of the flesh; which, unless it be rigidly restrained, transgresses every bound. . . .
> Lastly, it is to be remarked that the Lord commands every one of us, in all the actions of life, to regard his vocation. For he knows with what great inquietude the human mind is inflamed. . . .[134]

Discovering one's vocation was more than finding the best means to a profitable life; it was provided the method for regulating that life. It was the publically sanctioned way of self-control. Laws in Massachusetts in 1642 and 1643 charged "parents and masters" to "breed and bring up their children and apprentices in some honest calling, labor or employment" and communities of over one-hundred people to set up grammar schools for the "training of youths."

If study and vocational training were to provide necessary discipline, play ought to be discouraged. Cotton Mather never used play as a reward, attempting instead to have his children expect further teaching as recompence for success (though he remarked several times on "*Sammy's* inordinate Love of Play").[135] An apprentice's contract specified:

> ... he shall not commit Fornication, nor contract Matrimony with the said terms; at Cards, dice, or any inlawful game he shall not play ... nor haunt Ale house or Tavern.... And the said Master shall use the utmost of his endeavour, to teach or cause to be taught or instructed, his said Apprentice in the Trade or mystery that he followeth....[136]

Nor would young scholars be likely to fall into the lax habits of play, since school began at seven or eight and lasted until four or five (though with two hours for lunch), six days a week.[137]

There is a striking correspondence between the child-rearing patterns of seventeenth-century Americans and the advice given by John Locke: external physical controls such as swaddling were abandoned for internal mental restraints, namely, breaking the will, hardening the emotions, disciplining the intellect. Locke, it will be recalled, several times cited the good example of the yeoman in domestic relations; the class origins of Americans partially explain the correspondence noted. On the other hand, the characterization of colonials as "infantile" and living in "primitive" conditions would not seem to explain their child-rearing practices.

The meaning of these practices was related to demographic and domestic conditions of the seventeenth century. An increasing child mortality rate and a nuclear family whose relationships were increasingly contractual suggests a situation in which parents would show greater interest in children yet find means to cope with frequent death through aloofness, religiosity or putting the emotional burden on children and cautioning restraint. The discipline which yielded self-control also produced a heightened sense of self, the implication for the Anglo-American being an augmented rationality which would alter the conditions responsible for the high child mortality rate and, indeed, the conditions of childhood itself.

REFERENCES

I would like to thank Dr. Jules Weiss of the San Francisco Psychoanalytic Institute for his thoughtful comments on my work, as well as Dr. Isabel Kenrick of London and Robert Messer of the University of California, Berkeley, for their research efforts and helpful suggestions.

1. Published in London, 1774 (3rd edition), p. 26.
2. *The World We Have Lost. England Before the Industrial Age* (New York, 1965), 104.
3. E. A. Wrigley, "Family Limitation in Pre-Industrial England," *Economic History Review*, 2nd Ser., 19 (1966), 82-109; "Mortality in Pre-Industrial England: The Example of Colyton, Devon, Over Three Centuries," *Daedalus*, 97 (Spring 1968), 546-580.
4. Keith Thomas, *Religion and the Decline of Magic* (New York, 1971), 111. Ivy Pinchbeck and Margaret Hewitt, in *Children in English Society*, Volume I, "From Tudor Times to the Eighteenth Century" (London and Toronto, 1969), argue that during the seventeenth century the family contracted from an extended to a nuclear unit, so that "ties between parent and child were necessarily strengthened in a family reduced to parents and children." (p. 69). But Peter Laslett, in *Household and Family in Past Time* (Cambridge, 1972), pp. 1-89, has proved pretty conclusively that the nuclear family existed throughout the century.
5. Edwin G. Burrows and Michael Wallace, "The American Revolution: The Ideology and Psychology of National Liberation," *Perspectives in American History*, 6 (1972), 169-189.
6. *Anon., A Rich Closet of Physical Secrets . . . The Child-Bearers Cabinet . . .* (London, 1652). Caius and Gonville College, Cambridge Univ., Inner Library, K.30.1; Jacques Guillemeau, *Childbirth or, the Happy Delivery of Women. To which is added, a treatise on the diseases of infants, and young children* (London, 1612; 2nd ed., 1635) pp. 1-78, but especially 27-31. There is a discussion of magical attempts to control and astrological forecasts about the conception of children and the sex of the fetus in Thomas, *Religion and the Decline of Magic*, 188-189, 316-317. Methods of inducing conception were the topic of discussion at a bibilous luncheon given by the childless diarist Samuel Pepys; see *The Diary of Samuel Pepys* (London, 1894), p. 199.
7. Lady Frances Hatton to Lord Hatton, June 3, 1678. Finch-Hatton MSS 4322, Northamptonshire Record Office, Delapre Abbey. After three sons and the arrival of a sixth daughter William Blundell wrote: "My wife has much disappointed my hopes in bringing forth a Daughter which, finding herself not so welcome in this world as a Son, hath made already a discrete choice of a better. . . ." Reporting on the birth of his ninth daughter ("7 whereof, besides my three sons, are still living"), he noted his "great disability," while when his tenth daughter arrived he simply observed "the thing is called Bridget," *Cavalier-Letters of William Blundell to his Friends 1620-1698,* ed. by Margaret Blundell (London, 1933), pp. 44, 68, 79. The Dutchess of Newcastle wrote of her husband that he was "so desirous of male-issue, that I have heard him say, he cared not (so God would be pleased to give him many sons), although they came to be persons of the meanest fortunes." Ernest Rhys, ed., *The Life of the First Duke of Newcastle . . . by Margaret Dutchess* (London, 1916), 63-64. Lucy Hutchinson wrote about her parents: "The first year of their marriage was crowned with a son. . . . After my mother had had three sons, she was very desirous of a daughter. . . ." This fact, abetted by a dream Mrs. Hutchinson had during her pregnancy forecasting something extraordinary, and the unusual beauty of the child, was

responsible for Lucy's rich education. *Memoirs of Colonel Hutchinson* (New York, 1965), 10-15. Henry Newcome also notes that after seven sons his parents wanted a daughter. Richard Parkinson, ed., *The Autobiography of Henry Newcome,* Chetham Society, v. 26-27 (Manchester, 1852), I, 4. But Lady Hatton loved her daughters, worried about their illnesses and, on the eve of the delivery here noted, wrote: "If I should dye shew particular kindness to that child [Susanna] for if I have ten thousand sons I can not love them so well. . . ." Same to same, April 20, 1678 and also March, 6, 1676/7 and March 23 [n.y.], British Museum, Add. MSS. 29571, f. 377, 445, 460.

8. Published in Paris, it was translated into English by Hugh Chamberlen, M. D. Caius and Gonville College, Cambridge Univ., Inner Library, K.30.6. The illustrations are graphic, as are many of the passages, e.g., dismembering an infant to allow delivery.

9. n.d. (between 1664-1672), Finch-Hatton MSS 4412, Northamptonshire R. O. See also the description in Charles Jackson, ed., *The Autobiography of Mrs. Alice Thornton* (London, 1875), p. 95. Sir John Bramston description of his wife's death after the premature delivery appears in his *Autobiography.* Camden Society, v. 32 (London, 1845), pp. 109-111.

10. Wrigley, "Mortality," 570. Wrigley explains why the infant mortality rate for the aristocracy, whose literary evidence will make an inordinate appearance in the following pages, could have been higher than that of the population as a whole. (pp. 570-572). I have not found figures for death rates of mothers in childbirth.

11. Quoted in Thomas R. Forbes, "The Regulation of English Midwives in The Sixteenth and Seventeenth Centuries," *Medical History,* 8 (1964), pp. 235-236.

12. Again the argument is Elizabeth Cellier's. *Ibid.,* p. 241.

13. *Ibid.,* 237-238. Copies of some licenses issued and oaths administered appear in Thomas R. Forbes, *The Midwife and the Witch* (New Haven, 1966), 144-147. In the *Autobiography* of Sir Simonds D'Ewes (J. O. Halliwell, ed., 2 vols. London, 1845), the protagonist recalls how his mother's reaction to the physical oddity of her midwife so offended the attendant that she "whether maliciously or casually I know not, exceedingly bruised and hurt my right eye in her assisting at my birth, . . ." (vol. I, p. 5)

14. For example, though the midwife was warned against practicing sorcery, there were some generally accepted magical practices designed to protect a woman in child-bed. Thomas, *Religion and the Decline of Magic,* p. 188.

15. Guillemeau, *Childbirth,* preface, 81. Guillemeau cited this situation to explain why he was passing on forty years' experience to young surgeons. He had been official surgeon at the courts of three French kings, but the popularity of his work in early seventeenth-century England suggests his relevance there, as well.

16. *Ibid.,* pp. 99, 137, 141.

17. *The Nursing of Children. Wherein is set the ordering and government of them, from their birth. Together: with the means to helpe and free them, from all such diseases as may happen unto them* (London, 1612; 2nd ed., 1635), Preface. If the nurse could transmit her character, it is interesting to speculate as to Guillemeau's rationalization of his advice that: "If you cannot find a nurse that will venter to give the childe sucke, insteede thereof you shall cause him to sucke a goate, which I have caused some to do."

18. *Ibid.,* pp. 90-96; Mauriceau, *Disease of Women,* pp. 363-65; Edward Poeton, *The midwife's deputy . . . whereunto is added, a book concerning the ordering of young children* (n.p., n.d.) Sloane Coll. 1954.1, Manuscripts Rm., British Museum.

19. Guillemeau, *Nursing,* pp. 13-14; Mrs. Jane Sharp, *The Midwives Book. On the whole ART of Midwifery Discovered. Directing Childbearing Women how to behave themselves* (London, 1671), Caius and Gonville College, Cambridge Univ., Inner Library K.30.17. The Countess of Derby, French by birth, was appalled by the manner in which English children were swaddled. Mary C. Rowsell, *The Life Story of Charlotte de la Tremoille Countess of Derby* (London, 1905), pp. 35-36. The sense of helplessness which led to these practices is evident in a letter from Ralph Verney to his wife: "I must give you an account of our own babyes heare. For Jack his leggs are most miserable, crooked as evor I saw any child's and yett thank god he goes very strongly, and is very strayte in his body as any child can bee; and is a very fine child all but his legges .... he hath an imperfection in his speech ... he is a very ready witted Child and is very good company...." Quoted in Elizabeth Godfrey, *Home Life Under the Stuarts, 1603-1649* (London, 1925), pp. 4-5. But parents did not give up. Little Lady Margaret Clifford, between 2½ and 3½ years old (she had eighteen teeth), was put into "a whalebone bodice," G. C. Williamson, *Lady Anne Clifford* (2nd ed.; Buntingford, 1967), p. 111.

20. Mauriceau, *Disease of Women.* At the end of the century the physician John Pechey argued: "Do we not see that Young Lyons and Bears When they are Young can be made so tame as to obey the very nod of the Keepers, whereas if you let them alone till they are grown up they will forever after remain Fierce and Wild; why then should not the mind of a child be so trained as to obey Reason and harken to advice?" Quoted in George Still, *The History of Pediatrics* (London, 1965), p. 302.

21. *Rich Closet,* p. 20. Such references are veiled and, of course, ambiguous. But when Lady Margaret Hoby wrote that her mother told her "to doe nothing in secret whereof our conscience might accuse us, and by any means to avoyd the company of serving men," the sexual connotations were clear enough. D. M. Meads, ed., *Diary of Lady Margaret Hoby, 1599-1605* (London, 1930), pp. 49-50.

22. Guillemeau, *Nursing,* pp. 17-18.

23. These effects are given in graphic detail in all the above books and will be dealt with later. Isaac Newton was born prematurely and lived, a fact which he apparently viewed as miraculous. Frank E. Manuel, *A Portrait of Sir Isaac Newton* (Cambridge, Mass., 1968), 23-24.

24. *The Boke of Children* was published in London in 1545 and went through seven editions before the end of the century. See also Robert Burton, *The Anatomy of Melancholy* (1621; Floyd Dell and Paul Jordan-Smith, eds., New York, 1927), 282-284. Edward, Lord Herbert of Cherbury, whose youth was sickly, to whom speech came very late, and whose parents were practically never present, reached a different (but in view of his circumstances, not so surprising) conclusion: given the proper medicines, the nurse through her milk can cure inherited diseases. *Autobiography,* edited by Sidney Lee (London, 1886), pp. 29-30, 37, 45. Robert Boyle thanked his "Country nurse" for accustoming him "to a coarse but cleanly diet, and to the usual passions of the air"—both made him healthy and a stranger to convenience. Thomas Birch, *The Life of Robert Boyle* (London, 1734), 20.

25. Guillemeau, *Nursing,* Preface; Mauriceau, *Disease of Women,* p. 369; Morwenna and John Rendle-Short, *The Father of Child Care: Life of William Cadogan* (Bristol, 1966), p. 26. The Shorts judge the figure 529 to be a conservative statement. Two cases of neglect are cited in Pinchbeck and Hewitt, *Children in English Society,* pp. 218-219. Sir John Bramston recorded the death of his son John: "his nurse, had let him catch the itch of his children,

or had some other way negligently tended him that he brake out, and she, to cure it hastilie that we might not know it, applied, as she sayd, burnt or fried butter, on browne paper, whereby grew a great soare on the brest, and a core came out (soe that one might see the very heart pant). I had a very good surgeon, but he could not cure him, nor save his life. He was a very lovelie child." *Bramston Autobiography,* 104.

26. Guillemeau, *Nursing,* Preface. *Lincoln's Nursurie* (Oxford, 1622). The Countess of Derby's daughter was suffocated by her nurse. Rowsell, *Derby,* p. 58. *Thornton Autobiography,* 91. Mrs. Thornton nursed her next daughter herself. *Ibid.,* 92. And when her son William, her sixth child, was born, she noted: "my pretty babe was in good health, suckeing his poore mother, to whom my good God had given the blessing of the breast as well as the wombe," suggesting that her decision to nurse was based simply on whether she had milk, *Ibid.,* 124.

Henry Newcome, a parson, recorded that his first child "was inconsiderately nursed out [1649] ... we were sensible of the neglect of duty in not having nursed her at home, which made her mother resolved to endeavour to nurse. . . ." Apparently this was the case until the fifth child arrived, when the mother "was hardly put to it to nurse him" and brought a wet-nurse into the house with the family. *Newcome Autobiography,* I, 13, 69. John Locke mentioned the problem of a negligent nurse in a letter to his friend Edward Clarke, February 22, 1682/3, in Benjamin Rand, ed., *The Correspondence of John Locke and Edward Clarke.* John Dee noted that when his daughter was sent home from an ill nurse in another town, she was put out to a second nurse for a week, then a third nurse in a nearby village where her mother carried her in the midst of a rain.

27. If nursing did not terminate the child's crying, it was recommended that he be sung to or rocked. Guillemeau, *Nursing,* p. 17. Alice Ryerson, in "Medical Advice on Child-Rearing Practices, 1550-1900" (Unpublished doctoral dissertation, Harvard University, 1960), concludes that "the advice in the period from 1750-1900 seems to be considerably less permissive [compared to the period 1555-1790] than the cross-cultural average in the oral, anal, sexual and dependence categories and more permissive in aggression training." (p. 149) The evidence Ryerson draws on for the earlier period is, however, sometimes negative and often scanty. She does point out, interestingly, that a swaddled child could not suck his thumb. But as early as 1596 John Dee's daughter was weaned at nine months, his son in 1599 at a year and a half. *Diary of Dee,* 53, 55.

28. "An old child sucks hard" was a popular adage, according to John Manningham, *Diary,* Camden Society, v. 99 (Westminster, 1868), 12. Mauriceau, *Disease of Women,* 368, 372. Pap was apparently spoon fed. Ryerson, in "Medical Advice," claims there were no sucking bottles (p. 143); but Elizabeth Godfrey shows that there were (pp. 6n, 27). The "sucking bottle" is also mentioned in *The Life of Marmaduke Rawdon of Yorke,* Camden Society, v. 85 (Westminster, 1863), p. 3. Sharp, *Midwives Book,* Chapter VI. Sir Robert Sibbald was weaned by his nurse at two years and two months in 1643. *Memoirs* (London, 1932), pp. 50-51. Alice Thornton's daughter was weaned at one year in 1655. *Thornton Autobiography,* p. 91.

29. Guillemeau, *Nursing,* Preface; Sharp, *Midwives Book,* Chapter II; Mauriceau, *Disease of Women.* The matter of sexual rivalry is not far-fetched. Endymion Porter wrote to his wife from Spain (April 17, 1623): "Your two little babes . . . serve to entertain you and it teaches you to forget me." Dorothea Townshend, ed., *Life and Letters of Mr. Endymion Porter* (London, 1897), p. 51. Or, consider the Countess of Rutland's letter to John Locke (March 7,

[1671]) about her grandson, droll but meaningful: "so hopefull an heire, that early accosts ladies in bed and manages a weapon at 3 days olde. . . ." Public Records Office, London. SP 30/24, bdle. 47, no. 11.

30. Mauriceau, *Disease of Women,* p. 366; Sharp, *Midwives Book,* Chapter VI; *D'Ewes Autobiography,* I, pp. 24-25; Lady Frances Hatton to Lord Hatton, June 3, 1678. Finch-Hatton MSS 4322, Northamptonshire R.O., Delapre Abbey. But Anthony Ashley Cooper was "nursed at Cranborne by an Persce, a tanner's wife." W. D. Christie, *A Life of Anthony Ashley Cooper, First Earl of Shaftesbury* (2 vols.; London, 1871), Appendix II, xxv. Ten years earlier, Lady Frances was, in fact, nursing her own child. Anne, Countess of Pembroke to Frances Hatton, Dec. 10, 1668. Finch-Hatton MSS 4313, Northamptonshire R.O., Delapre Abbey. G. R. Taylor, in *The Angel-Makers. A Study of the Psychological Origins of Historical Change, 1750-1850* (London, 1958), has discovered that in the eighteenth century "the upperclass group of self-indulgent parents tended to farm children out to wetnurses, while the Puritan group pressed emphatically for breast-feeding." (p. 327). Thus, it is unsurprising to read in Reverend Ralph Josselin's *Diary* (ed. by E. Hockliffe, Camden Society, 3rd Ser., XV [London, 1908]): "God blessed my wife to be a nurse." In a narrative of his conversion, Thomas Goodwin recalled "when I hung upon my Mother's Breasts." *Works* (5 vols.; London, 1704), I, v. And Samuel Clarke, a minister, wrote about Mrs. Katherine Clark and her nine children: "she nursed them all with her own breasts." *The Lives of Sundry Eminent Persons* (1683), p. 155. Sarah Meade, a Quaker, wrote her mother, Margaret Fox (May 17, 1684): "I am fine and well and endeavouring to make a nurse, if the Lord gives me milk and ability to do it." Miller MSS no. 77 (transcript no. 7), Friends House Library, London. But only two years later she reported to her mother (April 2, 1686): "Many chuses hearawayes rather to bring children up by the spoon, than suckle them (unless they either sucke their own Mothers, or have very good Nurses). . . ." Abraham MSS, XXX, Friends House Library. London.

31. From Stefano Guazzo's *The Civil Conversation* (1581), quoted in Lu Emily Pearson, *Elizabethans at Home* (Stanford, 1957), p. 87. And consider the statement about wet-nursing from Mauriceau, *Disease of Women,* 373: "we see daily above half the children die, before they are two or three years old."

32. Quoted in Philippe Ariès, *Centuries of Childhood. A Social History of Family Life* (New York, 1962), p. 29. On the other hand, so far was Lady Anne Clifford from expressing affection for her children that her husband took her one-year-old infant from her to manipulate her into turning property over to him. Williamson, *Clifford,* 91, 157.

33. Pinchbeck and Hewitt, *Children in English Society,* 201. The Duke of Buckingham wrote that, having conceived legitimate children by his third wife, he wished he had never owned his bastards, "it being in private families an ill example." John Sheffield, Duke of Buckingham, "Memoirs" in *Works* (1723), II, 21.

34. Depositions at the High Sheriff's Assizes, MSS. H. L. 1668 S, nos. 44-48; MSS H. L. 1671, no. 74; MSS H. L. 1678, no. 72, Bedford Record Office.

35. Law cited in Pinchbeck and Hewitt, *Children in English Society,* 201. Thomas Raymond records in his *Autobiography* (ed. by G. Davies, Camden Society, 1917) that the unmarried mother of a buried but discovered child, "not withstanding contrary to law and expectation, escaped hanging." (p. 20) John Marshall gives two instances of women being executed in Massachusetts in the late seventeenth century as a consequence of murdering bastard children. August 8, 1698 and August 1700. Diary, Massachusetts Historical Society. Pinchbeck and Hewitt claim that "until the end of the eighteenth century, and to a less extent in the nineteenth century, it was a com-

mon practice to expose unwanted children, either the children of unmarried mothers, or those who considered their family already overlarge, in the streets and lanes of the cities or in the country." (p. 302) No citation is given. I would question whether this was "common practice."

36. Guillemeau, *Nursing, Anon., Child-Bearers Cabinet,* 20; Sharp, *Midwives Book.* There is evidence of concern for constipation, however, Roger North told of his mother accustoming her children to rhubarb, "which saved the ungratefull Importunity and Reluctance between parents and children about phisick, which generally is extream odious to them. . . ." *North Autobiography,* 3. ("What rhubarb, cyme, or what purgative drug/Would scour these English hence?" *Macbeth,* Act 5, Sc. 3, l. 55-56.) The importance of the practice was testified to by William Stout, who wrote of his father: "He was never inclined to make use of doctors or phisick, but, as he had lived temperatly, to resign himself to the will of God." *Autobiography,* Chetham Society, 3rd Ser., v. 14 (Manchester, 1967), 74.

37. Anon., *Child-Bearers Cabinet,* pp. 20-21.

38. Lady Falkland, regarded as "much governed by her nursery" (i.e., indulgant), relented from her vow to whip her quick-tempered son into obedience, whereupon he begged her not to break her vow, "nor was there any other way to satisfy the child but by whipping him." Quoted in Godfrey, *Home Life,* p. 11. A doting grandmother wrote her son about her grandson: "Let me beg of you and his mother that nobody whip him but Mr. Parrye," his tutor. *Ibid.,* p. 12. Endymion Porter's letters to his wife, full of fondness for his children, cautions her about son George "not to beat him overmuch." *Life and letters of Porter,* p. 68. Roger North wrote: "Wee were taught to Reverence our father, whose care of us then consisted chiefly in the Gravity and decorum of his comportment, order and sobriety of life. . . ." His mother did the birching. *Autobiography of Roger North* (ed. by A. Jessopp, London, 1887), pp. 1-4. At the end of the century, when John Richards beat his son, his wife interfered. "Diary," *Retrospective Review,* n.s., 1 (1853). Richards was not an aristocrat. Pinchbeck and Hewitt, in *Children in English Society* (p. 16), claim both boys and girls were beaten. In a dialogue composed by William Blundell for his daughters and himself, one of the children recalls "how often she has been whipt and penanced, and has promised and broke again and been whipt again"—largely for deportment: "How oft have I told you of that rolling untidy gait of yours? And the wild carriage of your head?" At one point a daughter observed: "Pray and mend, yes, by the grace of God I will pray and mend. I never came off thus in all my life when my father was so angry. I expected no less than to have been shut up in a dark room for a week or a fortnight together and to have dined or supped upon birchen rods. . . ." *Cavalier-Letters of Blundell,* pp. 45-46; John Dee recorded that "a blow on the eare given by her mother" caused his daughter's nose to bleed. *Dee Diary,* pp. 30-31. Samuel Clarke wrote about Mrs. Katherine Clarke's attitude toward her children: "She loved them dearly without fondness; was careful to give them Nurture as well as Nourishment, not sparing the Rod when there was just occasion." *Sundry Eminent Persons,* p. 155.

39. *Brief Lives,* ed., Oliver L. Dick (London, 1950) XXXIV. One of these exceptions was Edward Hyde, Lord Clarendon, who claimed that his father was "the best Friend and the best Companion He ever had or could have." *An Account of the Life of Lord Clarendon* (Oxford, 1759), p. 4. Ralph Thorsby expressed great remorse at the death of his father. *Diary* (London, 1830), p. 32. Thomas Raymond's father also paid him attention, much to Thomas' regret: "upon all occasions (though I was not above twelve years old at his

death) felt the effects of his cholor, which was of great mischiefe unto me, being of a softe and tymorous complexion. And indeed thus soon began the unhappy breaches made upon my spirit, which hath followed me in all the variations and course of my life, and proved a great obstacle to the advancement of my fortuntes. So mischevous is the nipping the bud of a tender mascuylyne spiritte. . . ." *Raymond Autobiography*, p. 19.

40. See the brief discussion of this matter in R. E. Helfer and C. Henry Kempe, *The Battered Child* (Chicago, 1968).

41. Pinchbeck and Hewitt, *Children in English Society*, facing p. 36.

42. John Evelyn, *"The Golden Book of St. John Chrysostom Concerning the Education of Children"* (1659), in William Upcott, ed., *Miscellaneous Writings of John Evelyn* (London, 1825), pp. 107-11; Ezekias Woodward, *Childes Patrimony* (1640).

43. Sarah Meade to Margaret Fox, May 17, 1684; July 10, 1684; Mar. 20, 1684/5; April 7, 1686; May 5, 1686; Miller MSS, no. 77; James Dix MSS no. 23, 24; Abraham MSS, no. 27, 30, Friends House Library, London. Sarah was fortunate with her only child, Nathaniel. Her sister-in-law gave birth to four children: one was still-born, another lived only three months, a third died as a child. Child mortality rates for 17th century England can be found in Wrigley, "Mortality," 557-560.

44. Sharp, *Midwives Book*, p. 380; Pemell's *DeMorbis Querorum, or a Treatise of the Diseases of Children* (London, 1653) was the first treatise in English on children's problems since Thomas Phaire's.

45. Lady Frances Hatton to Lord Hatton, June 8, 1678; Anne, Lady Manchester to Lord Hatton, June 19; Finch-Hatton MSS 4288, 4290, 4377, Northamptonshire R. O., Delapre Abbey. The Dutchess of Newcastle expressed surprise that of the eight children her mother bore, none had physical defects. *Life of Newcastle*, p. 164.

46. Still, *History of Paediatrics*, chaps. 19-33. Glisson's work on rickets, not the first but the most important, appeared in 1650; Alice Thornton refers to the disease in an incident involving one of her daughters in 1660. *Thornton Autobiography*, 129. Sydenham was the first to describe chorea ("a sort of Convulsion which chiefly invades Boys and Girls from ten years of age to Puberty"), gave the most careful details on measles to appear until that time and was first to account for scarlet fever under that name. Convulsions and measles appear in *Ibid.*, 6, 129. I have found no mention of scarlet fever or its symptoms. Small pox, which in the seventeenth century "was regarded as almost an inevitable incident of childhood" (Still, *Paediatrics*, 324), is mentioned in *Thornton Autobiography*, 6; *Newcome Autobiography*, 43, and many other accounts.

47. Thomas, *Religion and the Decline of Magic*, pp. 656-661.

48. *The Midwives Book*, p. 415.

49. Mrs. Sharp, who argued "Shift the childs clouts often, for the Piss and Dung, if they lie long on it, will fetch off the skin," favored washing the baby only twice a week, and then only after seven months (till weaning). *Ibid.*

50. *Ibid.*, 377; Guillemeau, *Nursing*, pp. 45-46, 76-78.

51. *Thornton Autobiography*, p. 129.

52. Lady Warwick, now thirty eight, was unable to conceive again, which left the family heirless—again interpreted as a heavenly judgment on her earlier attitude of not wanting to have many children because married to a younger brother (quite possibly the couple practiced *coitus interruptus*). *Warwick Autobiography*, pp. 17-18, 26-33.

53. Suzanne White Hall, "Books for Women Printed in English, 1475-1640" (unpub. M.A. thesis, Univ. of Southern California, 1967), p. 55. Jonathan

Priestley said of his mother: I do believe few Christians attain to that height of knowledge, and to such a measure of grace in this world as my mother. The wisdom of God saw that she had both more to do and to suffer than some other good women; so his goodness gave her more faith and more patience. Let it be considered what sorrow the breeding and bearing ten children was; and to see six of them laid in the dust; which was more grief and sorrow to her, and went worse with her, as she would say, than bringing them into the world. The streights my father was put to must needs trouble her ... she patiently, by Divine help, went through all; was clothed with humility, and adorned with the ornament of a meek and quiet spirit.... Prayers were her daily exercise; if I say her daily food, I believe I speak not amiss. "Some memories Concerning the Family of the Priestleys," (1696), Surtees Society, *Yorkshire Diaries and Autobiographies,* 77 (London), pp. 28-29. See also Joseph Hall's description of his "saintlike" mother in *The Shaking of the Olive Tree* (London, 1660).

54. God was approached in a variety of ways. Reverend Owen Stockton noted on April 5 [1665]: "I set apt yt day for fasting & prayer on behalf of my daughter Elianor yt had been so long sick ... my faith renewed from Isa. 44.3 I will pour my spt upon thy soul. MSS Dr. William's Library, Gordon Square, London. Reverend Ralph Josselin recorded, on June 15, 1673: "About one a clock in the morning my eldest sonne Thomas and my most deare child ascended early hence to keep his everlasting Sabbath with his heavenly Father, and Savior with the church above...." Quoted in Alan Macfarlane, *The Family Life of Ralph Josselin. A Seventeenth Century Clergyman* (Cambridge, Eng., 1970), p. 166. Something of a reversal of the relationship between child mortality, parental projection and religion was achieved in Francis Quarles' "On the Infancy of Our Saviour":

Oh! what a ravishment 't had been to see
Thy little Saviour perking on thy knee!
To see him nuzzle in thy virgin breast,
His milk-white body all unclad, undressed!
To see thy busy finger clothe and wrap
His spradling limbs in thy indulgent lap!
To see his desparate eyes, with childish grace,
Smiling upon his smiling mother's face!
And, when his forward strength began to bloom,
To see him diddle up and down the room!
Oh, who would think so sweet a babe as this
Should e'er be slain by a false-hearted kiss!
Oxford Book of Christian Verse, p. 136.

55. *Life of Newcastle,* p. 64. Robert Boyle said his father had "a perfect aversion for [his children's] fondness." *Life of Boyle,* p. 18. See also *The Diary of John Hervey* [1st Earl of Bristol] (Wells, 1894), where more resignation than remorse is expressed: "Tis good not to be born; but if we must/The next good is, soon to return to dust." Also the Private Diary of Mark Brownell, Surtees Society, v. 124 (London, 1914), pp. 176-189; "Autobiography and Diary of Elias Pledger," MSS Dr. William's Library, Gordon Square, London.

56. *Life of Newcastle,* 22. John Donne, "Sermon on Genesis, I, 26" in Evelyn M. Simson and George R. Potter, eds., *Sermons of John Donne* (10 vols.), (Berkeley, 1953-1962), v. 9, pp. 68-91. Thomas Cobbett, *A Fruitful and Usefull Discourse touching the Honour due from Children to Parents and the Duty of Parents to their Children* (1656), as quoted in Pinchbeck and Hewitt, *Children in English Society,* pp. 19-20. Sharp, *Midwives Book.* In contrast to

Cobbett, George Herbert wrote:
    Throw away Thy rod,
    Throw away Thy wrath;
        O My God,
    Take the gentle path.
"Discipline," in *Oxford Book of Christian Verse*, p. 152.

57. *North Autobiography*, 2. Recall that North's father was grave, distant and condescending, a man who apparently never erred toward fondness. His mother was the disciplinarian, yet North warned that "the more these methods [of strict control of children] are neglected, or borne doune by Feminine vanity and fondness, the more profligate and debach't the age prooves." *Ibid.*, pp. 5-6.

58. Cleaver and Dod are quoted in Michael Walzer, *The Revolution of the Saints. A Study in the Origins of Radical Politics* (Cambridge, Mass., 1965), p. 190. The consequence of this training was expressed by Reverend Oliver Heywood: "I have often wondered what the design of God might be in casting me upon the ways of preparation for the ministry, whence I am conscious of more dulnes and weaknes in my intellectuals than I think most are. . . ." *His Autobiography* (ed. by J. H. Turner, Brighouse, 1882), p. 158.

59. *Microcosmography, or a Piece of the World Discovered in Essays and Characters* (London, 1934), pp. 5-6. See also Henry Vaughan's "Childhood":
    Since all that age doth teach, is ill,
    Why should I not love childhood still?

                    *   *   *

    Dear harmless age! the short, swift span,
    Where weeping virtue parts with man;
    Where love without lust dwells, and bends
    What way we please, without self-ends.
Oxford Book of Christian Verse, p. 230.

60. *Thornton Autobiography*, 94. At the death of a son, Mrs. Thornton was "instructed by the mouth of one of my oune children" that the boy was happily in Heaven, and that God would give her another son. The incident was repeated when her husband died. *Ibid.*, pp. 126-127, 262-263.

61. This literature is discussed in William Sloane's *Children's Books in England & America in the Seventeenth Century* (New York, 1955), which contains a "Checklist" in its back pages, listing published books. The varieties of children's literature on death is listed by its number in the Checklist: funeral sermons, 39, 161, 164, 207, 211; memorials, 42, 81; warnings, 45, 136, 143; tokens, 102; looking-glasses, 106, 197; messages, 120; confessions, 129, 247; exhortations, 150; testimonies, 167; admonitions, 184.

62. *A Token for Children* was published again in 1672 and 1676. In 1700 an edition appeared in Boston with a token for the children of New England written by Cotton Mather. Feelings of guilt might well be reversed. William Lilly recalled that at age sixteen he was "exceedingly troubled in my Dreams concetning my Salvation and Damnation, and also concerning the Safety and Destruction of the Souls of my Father and Mother. . . ." *Mr. Lilly's History of His Life and Times* (London, 1721), p. 6.

63. Published in London, 1694. Quoted from Pinchbeck and Hewitt, *Children in English Society*, pp. 269-270. John Dunton recalled his "servile fear of Hell . . . a place full of the blackest and most frightful terrors" and his thoughts of "*Death* . . . a walking skeleton, with a dart in his right, and an hour glass in his left hand." If these mental images were not unpleasant enough, he appears to have tempted Death several times, only to be fortuitously saved. *John Dunton's Life and Errors* (London, 1705), pp. 22-26.

Adam Martindale noted that his daughter Mary, by her own desire, was buried next to her brother: "She was a very wittie child, (for her age.) but after his death she seemed utterly to despise life, and would frequently talke of heaven and being buried by him." *Life of Adam Martindale,* Camden Society, v. 4 (Manchester, 1845), p. 109.

64. His awareness of the psychological aspect of disease was also evident in his advice to an ailing friend that she have "more exercise and less thoughtfulness." Kenneth Dewhurst, *John Locke (1632-1704), Physician and Philosopher* (London, 1963), pp. 296, 299.

65. *Ibid.,* 83, 141. Locke's explicit disapproval of swaddling occurs in "Some Thoughts Concerning Education," [1693] *The Harvard Classics* (ed. by Charles W. Eliot, New York, 1910), vol. 37, p. 15.

66. *Ibid.,* pp. 9, 126. He thought examples of "natural genius" were few.

67. *Ibid.,* 10-16, 29, 91-92. However, Locke had no special sympathy for the poor. In his *Report for the Reform of the Poor Law* (1697) he proposed that "working schools" be set up for poor children between the ages of three and fourteen so that "from their infancy [they] be inured to work. . . ." This, of course, is another version of the hardening process. (Quoted in Pinchbeck and Hewitt, *Children in English Society,* p. 309.) Half a century earlier Sir William Petty had proposed that every child, rich or poor, should have an education. (His program is quoted in Still, *History of Paediatrics,* pp. 314-317.)

68. Although Locke never disapproved of the upper-class practice of wet-nursing, and did not mention the subject in "Some Thoughts," it is clear from his letters to Edward Clarke and his wife (which, in revised form, make up "Some Thoughts") that he considered surveillance of the nurse necessary. See Locke to Clarke, Feb. 22, 1682/3; Locke to Mrs. Clarke, [Dec. 1683]; Locke to Clarke, Feb. 8, 1686, *Correspondence of Locke,* pp. 90, 101-102, 142-143. In 1684 John Tillotson, Archbishop of Canterbury, preached against the practice of putting children out to nurse. See *The Works of John Tillotson* (10 vols.; London, 1820), III, pp. 487-492. Tillotson's sermons—"Concerning Family Religion" and "Of the Education of Children" (III, 464-551)—notwithstanding their religious emphasis, echo some important refrains of Locke on restraint of passion, shaming children and educating them.

69. "Some Thoughts," pp. 16-28. Locke wrote to Clarke [Dec. 1684] that: "after my first eating, which was seldom till noon, I constantly went to the stool, whether I had any motion or no, and there stayed so long that most commonly I [attained] my errand; and by this constant practice in a short time the habit was so settled, that I usually feel a motion; if not I, however, go to the place as if I had, and there seldom fail (not once in a month) to do the business I came for. This is one of the greatest secrets I know in physic for the preservation of health, and I doubt not but it will succeed in you and your son, if with constancy you put it into practice." *Correspondence of Locke,* p. 116. There does seem to have been concern with toilet training by the end of the century. In the following letter, unfortunately, the age of the trained child is unknown: "tho Master is very well, lest it should be a forerunner of some illness I must tell you the little indisposition of body that he has. He has very frequent motions to stool 'sits long upon it by his good will tho neither bound, nore loose, very little comes from him at a Time. Last night he slept very well as soon as he waked he called & I left him at it, Susan says he goes at least a dozen times in the day time. . . . Mary Cook will have it only to be a habit he has got." Joseph Hammer to Mrs. Boteler, April 12, 1692. Trevor Wingfield. MSS, County Hall, Bedford.

70. "Some Thoughts," 28-31. Nevertheless, *"stubbornness, and obstinate disobedience,* must be master'd with force and blows; for there is no other remedy." *Ibid.,* 64. Decades earlier Locke seemed to approve of swaddling *and* whipping, though this cannot be asserted with certainty because the mention of both occurs in a humorous letter—one whose puns, significantly enough, are built on amusement at defecation and its smell. See Locke to Mrs. Sarah Edwards, July 21, 1659. Locke MSS, c. 24, ff. pp. 39-40. Bodelian Library, Oxford Univ.

71. "Shame in children has the same place that modesty has in women, which cannot be kept and often transgress'd against." "Some Thoughts," pp. 38-43. This sort of balance was admired at the end of the century by John Dunton, who described one Mrs. Green as "a good Mother to her Children, whom she brings up with that sweetness and facility as is admirable, not keeping them at too great a distance, as some do, thereby discouraging their good parts; nor by an *overfondness* (a fault most Mothers are guilty of) betraying them into a thousand inconveniences, which oftentimes proves fatal to them." *Dunton's Life,* p. 106.

72. Earlier in the seventeenth century, games had the sanction of the upper class (e.g., Henry Peacham, in the *Compleat Gentleman,* 1622, pictured physical education as a means of establishing communication between master and student) but were roundly condemned by Puritans, who viewed games and sport as part of a misspent youth. See Dennis Brailsford, *Sport and Society. Elizabeth to Anne* (London and Toronto, 1969), pp. 79, 131. The physician John Pechey wrote in 1697: "Play must be allowed to [children] to moderate their affections, and indeed this age can scarce do anything seriously, only you must take care that play does not injure their bodies. . . ." Quoted in Still, *History of Paediatrics,* p. 302.

73. Locke had earlier pointed out that "the principle aim of my discourse is, how a young gentleman should be brought up from his infancy, which in all things will not so perfectly suit the education of *daughters;* though where the difference of sex requires different treatment, 'twill be no hard matter to distinguish." "Some Thoughts," p. 11.

74. *Ibid.,* pp. 45-62, 78-89. ". . . you must watch him at play, when he is out of his place and time of study. . . ." *Ibid.,* p. 115.

75. In the introduction to the 1692 edition of *Aesop's Fables* Robert L'Estrange wrote: "Children are but Blank Paper," an idea often attributed to Locke but actually having a history that dates back at least to the sixteenth century. In "The Seventeenth Century in Search of 'Being'," a paper demonstrating how adults confronted the issue of childhood through the medium of education, Ruth Moffatt, a graduate student at California State University, San Francisco, shows that L'Estrange rewrote *Aesop's Fables* to make the tales more appealing to children.

76. "Some Thoughts," 141-153. Recognizing his own debt to the past, Locke asserted: "As nothing teaches, so nothing delights more than history." *Ibid.,* p. 168.

77. "Each man's mind has some peculiarity, as well as his face, that distinguishes him from all others. . . ." *Ibid.,* 195. Possibly Locke was passing upper-class conventional wisdom to the middle class. The Dutchess of Newcastle said that her husband's education was according to his genteel birth. When his father found that he was not inclined to education he "suffered him to follow his own genius" and encouraged the education of his younger brother. *Life of Newcastle,* p. 133.

78. Erikson, *Childhood and Society* (2nd ed., New York, 1963), p. 253.

79. L. B. Wright, *Middle Class Culture in Elizabethan England* (Chapel Hill,

1935), pp. 43-80. Godfrey Davies, in *The Early Stuarts* (Oxford, 1937), claims that the middle class contributed more money to education from 1560 to 1660 than in any other century (p. 349). Lawrence Stone, in "The Educational Revolutional Revolution in England, 1560-1640," *Past and Present,* 28 (July 1964), points to a decline in education in the late seventeenth century. (p. 68). See also Stone's "Literacy and Education in England, 1640-1900," *Past and Present,* 42 (February 1969), p. 90. It must be recognized that educational expansion applied to men. As Keith Thomas points out: "Women at this time were denied access to any of the normal means of expression afforded by Church, State or University...." *Religion and the Decline of Magic,* p. 138. A dissent from this position appears in E. S. Bier, "The Education of women under the Stuarts, 1603-1715" (M.A. thesis, Univ. of California, Berkeley, 1926), p. 157. Philippe Ariès, who devotes half of *Centuries of Childhood* to the subject of education in France, attributes expansion and reform to the work of "moralists and pedagogues," who wanted to lengthen childhood through prolonged and disciplined schooling so as to separate youth from a corrupt adult world.

80. Child portraiture began to appear in the late sixteenth and early seventeenth centuries. Clothing for children was altered at approximately age seven, a process that was particularly meaningful for boys since "breeching" was symbolic of young manhood. Phillis Cunnington and Anne Buck, *Children's Costume in England* ... (London, 1965), pp. 35-38, 52, 54, 71. On games see Brailsford, *Sport and Society,* and Joseph Strutt, *The Sports and Pastimes of the People of England* (Detroit, 1968). Certain popular stories by the end of the seventeenth century were considered "exclusively the property of children," while a whole new children's literature emerged, largely moralistic in content. Sloane's *Children's Books* is crammed with material, but see also Iona and Peter Opie, *The Oxford Book of Nursery Rhymes* (Oxford, 1952) and Harvey Darton, *Children's Books in England* (Cambridge, Eng., 1932).

81. Sir Thomas Wilson, *The State of England Anno Dom. 1600.* Robert Boyle, whose mother had died, wrote that his father sent him away at age eight because "great men's children at home tempts them to nicety, to pride, and idleness, and contributes more to give them a good opinion of themselves, than to make them observe it. . . ." *Life of Boyle,* p. 23.

82. This is the judgment of Alan Macfarlane (*Family Life of Josselin,* p. 210), who has made a thorough study of the matter. Children left wealthier homes for boarding school at about 10. In families of Josselin's status, the age of learning was between 7 and 13. It is not known how far down the social ladder this age pattern pertained. Of course, exceptions can be found. Mary Woodforde sent her youngest son out to board at age four. ("Private Diary, 1684-1690," in *Woodforde Papers and Diaries,* ed. by Dorothy H. Woodforde, London, 1932.) pp. 10, 15. The Dutchess of Newcastle wrote that most of her brothers and sisters never did leave home, even after marriage. (*Life of Newcastle,* p. 160.) Pegg Verney, boarding her spoiled ten-year-old Betty, wrote to an older sister: "I thenck hur past being so very a baby to do this ought of childishness. . . ." Godfrey, *Home Life,* p. 5.

83. *A Relation or Rather a True Account of the Island of England ... about the year 1500,* quoted in E. M. Field, *The Child and His Book* (2nd ed., London, 1892). Also E. S. Morgan, *The Puritan Family* (rev. ed., New York, 1966), p. 77. A passage from *The Office of Christian Parents* (1616) shows how parental reaction was not necessarily a true guide to feeling: "the father is over-hastie, and the mother is over-fond: some mothers have no other discipline but severe correction, some fathers cannot abide to hear their children

crie. . . ." Quoted in Sloane, *Children's Books,* p. 84.

84. The cost of maintaining children is calculated in Macfarlane, *Family Life of Josselin,* pp. 44-51.

85. W. K. Jordan, *Philanthropy in England, 1480-1660* (London, 1959), pp. 290-291; Brinsley, *The Grammar School* (1632).

86. Ben Jonson warned the Earl of Newcastle that his sons were "in more danger in your own family, among ill servants (allowing they be safe in their Schoolmaster), than amongst a thousand boys however immodest." "Timber, Or Discoveries Made Upon Men and Matter," in William Gifford, ed., *Works of Ben Jonson* (Boston, 1860), p. 880. Obadiah Walton, in *Of Education* (1673), also saw danger in "indiscreet, impertinent, unmanaged servants." Reprinted in Menston, Yorkshire, 1970, no. 229, p. 22. Locke himself mentioned the "indiscretion of servants." "Some Thoughts," p. 124.

87. The apparent inevitability of clashes between children and their step-parents easily accounts for the popularity of such tales as *Cinderella.* For some examples see W. G. Perrin, ed., *Autobiography of Phineas Pett* (London, 1918), pp. 2-3; *An Account of the Life of John Richardson* (3rd ed.; London, 1774), pp. 5, 16-22; *Josselin Diary,* p. 5; *Life of D'Ewes,* p. 227; "Pledger Autobiography."

88. Thus, Lady Frances Hatton wrote to Lord Hatton: "My daughter Nancy lyes with me constantly Shee has never lies with her Frenchwoman this last yeare." (Jan. 26, 1678); "My daughter Nancy is a very good bedfellow." (July 27, 1678). Finch-Hatton MSS, 4315, 4321. Lady Anne Clifford's daughter moved into bed with her at about age two. Williamson, *Clifford,* 110. Bedforshire R. O., Lucy Hutchinson told of her husband's plight as a boy at home: "he met there continual solicitations to sin by the travelled gentleman, who, living in all seeming sobriety before his father, was in his own chamber not only vicious himself, but full of endeavour to corrupt Mr. Hutchinson. . . ." *Memoirs of Hutchinson,* p. 49. Certainly incest is more likely to occur where there is a lack of privacy. Also, children probably will witness, or at least be aware of, the primal scene.

89. Macfarlane says of the practice of sending children away to be educated or to serve as apprentices or servants: "At the level of family life it would be a mechanism for separating the generations at a time when there might otherwise have been considerable difficulty. Both men and women had to wait roughly ten years, on average, between puberty and marriage in seventeenth century Europe; we might well have expected that such a delay would lead to sexual competition within families." *Family Life of Josselin,* p. 205. Adam Martindale recounts an incident in which his three-and-half-year-old daughter was allowed to give testimony against a man accused of seducing a neighbor girl, almost six. *Life of Martindale,* pp. 206-207. These seem very young ages to be able to testify to the occurrence of sexual intercourse.

90. *The Lady's New Year Gift or Advice to a Daughter* (Stamford, Conn., 1934), pp. 1, 42. (This interpretation of Halifax's book was derived from "The Changing Role of Women: Puritan Women in Seventeenth-Century England," a paper by Gloria Stoft, a graduate student at California State University, San Francisco.) Lady Warwick, whose mother died when she was three, leaving her to the care of "my indulgent father," developed an "aversion to marriage." "Some Specialties in the Life of M. Warwick," *English Poetry, Ballads and Popular Literature of the Middle Ages,* v. 22 (London, 1848), pp. 2-4. Admittedly, a reluctance to marry could be the consequence of two indulgent parents. (See *Thornton Autobiography,* pp. 9, 75) or a large, closely-knit family (see *Life of Newcastle,* pp. 157-165).

91. " 'Tis . . . a very useful part of the mothers care, to make her self company to her daughter to prevent the dangers of a more unequal and infectious converse. . . .," Richard Allestree, *The Ladies Calling* (London, 1693), p. 216. Lucy Hutchinson's father "would not endure the least immodest behaviour or dress in any woman under his roof." *Life of Hutchinson*, p. 11.

92. Heywood *Autobiography*, pp. 153-156. Testimonies to the piety and strong influence of a mother occur in "Observations of some Specialties of Divine Providence in the Life of Joseph Hall, Bishop of Nowich," *The Remaining Works of . . . Joseph Hall*, D. D. (Oxford, 1863), xx-xxi; "Dr. [John] Wallis's Account of some Passages of his own Life," *Peter Langtoft's Chronicle* (Thomas Hearne, ed., Oxford, 1725), pp. 143-145; "Memoirs of William Veitch," *Lives of the Scottish Reformers* (Thomas McGrie, ed., Cincinnati, 1846), 427; *Life of D'Ewes*, p. 117.

93. Compare Richard Allestree's table of contents in *The Gentleman's Calling* (London, 1696) to the same in his *The Lady's Calling*. The first focuses on the "calling" and the advantages of education, wealth, time, authority and reputation. The second treats the qualities of modesty, meekness, compassion, affability and piety, as well as the roles of virgin, wife and widow.

94. *A Consolation for our grammar schooles* (1612), preface. Brinsley's description of the school schedule can be found in *The Grammar School* (1632). Both W. D. Jordan, in *White Over Black* (Chapel Hill, 1968), and R. H. Pearce, in *Savagism and Civilization* (Baltimore, 1967), argue that the aim of seventeenth-century Englishmen was to subdue the savagery in other men and the wildness in nature, a repression of the bawdy Elizabethan (who might sail into foreign seas in search of adventure) by the austere Puritan (who would tame the new land and its people) In "Puritanism as a Revolutionary Ideology," *History and Theory*, 3 (1963), Michael Walzer argues: "Puritanism appears to be a response to disorder and fear, a way of organizing men to overcome the acute sense of chaos. . . . The study of the Puritans is best begun with the idea of discipline, and all the tension and strain that underlies it, both in their writing and what is known of their experience." (pp. 77, 79) The poet clearly saw the connection: "Can he that loves be man,/When his Captain's but a Child?/for he that leads is wilde. . . ." John P. Cutts, ed., *Seventeenth Century Songs and Lyrics* (Columbia, Mo., 1959), p. 45.

95. Hewitt and Pinchbeck, *Children in English Society*, pp. 224-234, 259. The attention paid to the complaints of an apprentice (in this case, Sarah Mosse) is evident in H. L. 1669 S., nos. 64-70, Bedford R. O. In *The Relation of Sydnam Poyntz*, 1624-36, Camden Society (London, 1908) Poyntz wrote: "To bee bound an apprentice I deemed little better than a dogs life and base." So he left England for 16 or 17 years as a soldier of fortune—the triumph of the bawdy Elizabethan! In *Newcome's Autobiography* there is an account of his son, Daniel, who failed to fulfil the terms of his apprenticeship. The best way to deal with the situation, Newcome thought, "was to send him beyond seas." (pp. 171-184)

96. O. Mannoni, *Prospero and Caliban. The Psychology of Colonization* (2nd ed., New York, 1964), p. 104.

97. Frederick Jackson Turner, *The Frontier in American History* (New York, 1921), p. 2.

98. See for example, John Smith's "A Description of New England," in R. H. Pearce, *Colonial American Writing* (New York, 1956), pp. 5-22. Images of childhood, the family and posterity abound in this essay. My thinking about childhood in America—actually, New England, as will be seen—has profited greatly from papers presented by two graduate students at California State University, San Francisco: Carol Adair's "The New England Child" and Joan

Mibach's "Parent-Child Relations in Puritan New England."
99. The quote is from Mannoni, *Prospero*, p. 101. William Bradford wrote (in *Of Plymouth Plantation, 1620-1647*, ed. by S. E. Morrison, New York 1967) that in Holland parents were forced to become taskmasters, burdening children as well as servants. Worse, under the Dutch influence "posterity would be in danger to degenerate and be corrupted." (Bradford also referred to the Leyden colony as "orphans.") The New World offered an antidote to these conditions. (pp. 19, 24-27.) Among John Winthrop's motives for immigrating to Massachusetts where he served as governor, was his concern about the spiritual degeneration of his son, Henry. E. S. Morgan, *The Puritan Dilemma* (Boston, 1958), p. 36.
100. "The Humble Request . . .," in Alexander Young, ed., *Chronicles of the First Planters of the Colony of Massachusetts Bay, from 1623- to 1636* (Boston, 1846), p. 296. Reverend John Robinson and Elder William Brewster of the Pilgrim congregation wrote of Holland: "We are well weaned from the delicate milke of our mother countrie. . . ." Elizabeth D. Hanscom, ed., *The Heart of the Puritan. Selections from Letters and Journals* (New York, 1917), p. 3.
101. *World of Anne Bradstreet*, ed. by J. H. Ellis (2nd ed., New York, 1932), p. 5. Anne Bradstreet also discussed how very much she wanted to have children. "Parents perpetuate their lives in their posterity," she noted sometime later. *Ibid.*, pp. 5, 49.
102. G. F. Willison, *Saints and Strangers* (New York, 1943), p. 133; *The Diary of Samuel Sewall*, ed. and abr. by Harvey Wish (New York, 1967), p. 57; Alice M. Earle, *Child Life in Colonial Days* (New York, 1926), p. 16; "Records of the First Church in Boston," Colonial Society of Massachusetts, *Publications*, 39 (Boston, 1961), p. 287. Although it was conventional for diarists to record the day and even the hour of a child's birth, the event was not usually celebrated. A young lady wrote in 1675: "I am fifteen years old today. . . . My mother hath bid me this day put on a fresh kirtle and wimple, though it be not the Lord's day, and my Aunt Alice coming in did chide me and say that to pay attention to a birthday was putting myself with the world's people." "A Puritan Maiden's Diary," *New England Magazine*, Ser. 2, 11 (1894-1895), p. 20.
103. Daniel Scott Smith, "Child-Naming Patterns and Family Structure Change: Hingham, Massachusetts 1640-1880," Paper prepared for the Clark University Conference on The Family and Social Structure (April 27-29, 1972), pp. 8-9, 11, 17, 20. Cited by permission of the author.
104. When a Massachusetts woman gave birth to a "monstrous child," Reverend John Cotton attributed it, in part, to a situation where "the rest of the women, which were coming and going in the time of her travail, would then be absent." John Winthrop, *Journal*, ed. by J. K. Hosmer (2 vols.; New York, 1908), I, p. 267. Not surprisingly, the magic associated with fertility persisted. Winthrop wrote of a midwife who "used to give young women oil of mandrake and other stuff to cause conception and she grew into great suspicion to be a witch." *Ibid.*, p. 268.
105. The wives of Thomas Thacher, pastor at the Old South Church in Boston, and John Eliot, minister to the Indians, were midwives. At the death of Ann Eliot Roxbury erected a monument with the inscription: ."She was thus honored for the great service she has done this town." Kate Campbell Hurd-Mead, *A History of Women in Medicine* (Haddam, Conn.) pp. 409-410. The problem of getting this information is suggested by Anne Bradstreet's writing on childhood ("Whose mean beginning blushing can't reveal") and childbearing ("To tell those pangs which can't be told by tongue"). *Works of Brad-*

street, p. 149.

106. The estimate of the infant mortality rate occurs in John Demos, *A Little Commonwealth. Family Life in Plymouth Colony* (New York, 1970), 131-132. Note that it is lower than the estimates for England in the seventeenth century. The information on Sewall and Mather was culled from *Sewall Diary* and *Diary of Cotton Mather* (2 vols.; New York, c. 1957).

107. For example, Elizabeth Cady Stanton wrote in the nineteenth century: "it is cruel to bandage an infant from hip to armpit, as is usually done in America." *Eighty Years and More; reminiscences, 1815-1897* (New York, 1971), 116. John Demos, who has searched widely for evidence of swaddling and found many other odd and intimate details of domestic life, wonders why—if the practice was used—there is *no* reference to it. Demos, *A Little Commonwealth*, pp. 132-133, and a letter to the author, December 9, 1972. Perhaps the only proof of the absence of swaddling will be found in attitudes, as Anne Bradstreet's observation may suggest: "A Prudent mother will not cloth her little childe with a long and cumbersome garment she easily foresees what events it is likely to produce, at the best but falls and bruises, or perhaps somewhat worse, much more will the alwise God proportion is dispensations according to the stature and strength of the person he bestowes them on." Could this not mean that the infant was in God's hands, not to be molded by man's desires, i.e., swaddling cloths? *Works of Bradstreet*, pp. 56-57.

108. *Ibid*, p. 133; "Autobiography of Thomas Shepard," Colonial Society of Massachusetts, *Transactions*, 27 (1927-1930), p. 355; *Sewall Diary*, p. 48. There is a reference in the *Records of the Courts of Quarter Sessions and Common Pleas*, Bucks Co., Pa., pp. 391-392, regarding default of payment for services which included nursing a child, whose mother may have been dead.

109. In "Moving to the New World: The Character of Early Massachusetts Immigration," *William and Mary Quarterly*, 30 (1973), p. 197, T. H. Breen and Stephen Foster report that most of the immigrants were urban artisans, with a few farmers. An earlier study, dealing with indentured servants who left Bristol and London in the middle and late seventeenth century, discovered a preponderance of husbandmen and yeomen among immigrants. See Mildred Campbell, "Social Origins of Some Early Americans," in J. M. Smith, ed., *Seventeenth Century America: Essays in Colonial History* (Chapel Hill, 1959), pp. 71-73.

110. The grandsons of John Winthrop, Sewall's contemporaries, certainly showed this tendency. See R. S. Dunn, *Puritans and Yankees. The Winthrop Dynasty in New England, 1630-1717* (Princeton, 1962), Chapter 9. A first-generation merchant, unlike Sewall, observed that his wife was nursing. "Diary of John Hull," American Antiquarian Society, *Transactions*, 3, (1857), 148. In England, Anne Bradstreet nursed at her mother's breast. *Works of Bradstreet*, p. 150.

111. *Sewall Diary*. Thomas Shepard's statement that at twelve months his son's mouth was so sore that "he could eat no meat, only suck the breast" suggests that the child ought to have been weaned by then. "Shepard Autobiography," p. 355. But John Hull, Shepard's contemporary, noted that his daughter was weaned at 14 months. "Hull Diary," p. 149. Anne Bradstreet wrote: "Some Children are hardly weaned, although the teat be rub'd with wormwood or mustard, they wil either wipe it off, or else suck down sweet and bitter together. . . ." *Works of Bradstreet*, p. 56.

112. Demos, *A Little Commonwealth*, pp. 133-134. Recall that in English child-rearing literature there was a concern that nurses shouldn't copulate, though

it was conceded that they would. And Ralph Josselin's wife thought she was pregnant before she weaned, meaning that sexual intercourse occurred during suckling. Macfarlane, *Family Life of Josselin,* p. 83.

113. "Shepard Autobiography," pp. 355-356. Illness always meant an encounter with God for Shepard. See also pp. 381-382.

114. "Diary of Increase Mather," Massachusetts Historical Society, *Proceedings,* 2nd Ser., 13 (1899, 1900), pp. 341-342.

115. *Mather Diary,* I, pp. 380-382. For more information on recurrent illnesses, see Ernest Caulfield, "Some Common Diseases of Colonial Children," The Colonial Society of Massachusetts, *Transactions,* 35 (1942-46), pp. 4-47. Most of the information concerns the eighteenth century, as do the entries in Mather's diary.

116. *Works of Bradstreet,* 50, p. 404.

117. John Cotton, *Spiritual Milk for Boston's Babes* (1656), 2; Bert Roller, *Children in American Poetry, 1610-1900* (Nashville, 1930), pp. 17, 21-22.

118. Wigglesworth, *Day of Doom* (1662) ed. by K. B. Murdock (New York, 1966); Allan Ludwig, *Graven Images* (Middletown, Conn., 1966); Earle, *Child Life,* p. 10.

119. "Journal of the Reverend John Pike," Massachusetts Historical Society, *Proceedings,* 1st Ser., 14 (1875-1876), p. 134; "John Marshall's Diary," *Ibid.,* 2nd Ser., 1 (1884-1885), p. 153.

120. The Pilgrim preacher John Robinson spoke of "a subborness, and stoutness of mind arising from natural pride" as inherent to children. The parents' duty with regard to the child's will was to restrain and repress, beat and keep down, break and destroy it. "Children should now know, if it could be kept from them, that they have a will of their own." Quoted in Demos, *A Little Commonwealth,* 135, from *The Works of John Robinson,* ed. by Robert Ashton (Boston, 1851), I, pp. 246-247. Demos' hypothesis, based on the premise that childhood assertiveness was crushed in the second year (a year bounded by weaning at its beginning and the arrival of a sibling at its close), derives from the developmental theory of Erik Erikson, who asserts that denial of autonomy at this age may lead to lasting shame and doubt (the negative side of autonomy) and an obsession with law and order (institutionalization of "face-saving," the obverse of shame). *Ibid.,* pp. 135-139. I have found no letters to document that this was done. Samuel Sewall's mother, temporarily in charge of his two-and-a-half-year-old son, was concerned with his physical development and comfort: "your Son Sam can goe about ye Roome prety strongly And would goe better had he a paire of shoes fitt for him, those you sent last are too long by an Inch or more. . . . I pray you send Sam: a cap for every day this winter. faile not to send Sam: a Robe. . . . Send[?] Sam 6 Course Bibes for hee Drincks much[?] hee hath 2 eye teth above what more wee well know not." Jane Sewall to Samuel Sewall, Nov. 1, 1680, Robie-Sewall Family Papers, Massachusetts Historical Society.

121. See footnote 94 for the English Puritan's response to chaos. Alan Simpson, in *Puritanism in Old and New England* (Chicago, 1955), and Kai T. Erikson, in *Wayward Puritans* (New York, 1966), discuss the repressive climate of Massachusetts as compared to England.

122. Young, *Chronicles of the First Planters,* 167, 177; Nathaniel Shrutleff, ed. *Records of the Governor and Company of Massachusetts Bay, 1628-1686* (5 vols.; Boston, 1853-1854), III, p. 101; J. H. Trumbull and C. J. Hoadley, eds., *Public Records of the Colony of Connecticut (1636-1776)* (15 vols.; Hartford, 1850-1890), I, p. 515; Nathaniel Burton, et al., eds., *Documents and Records Relating to the Province of New Hampshire (1623-1800)* (40 vols.; Concord, 1867-1943), I, p. 384. In no other colonies have I found a

similar law except in New York, put into effect by the proprietary government under the Duke of York. See Staughton George, et al., *Charter to
William Penn . . . preceded by the Duke of York's Laws . . .* (Harrisburg,
1879), p. 15. The limits of parental dominion were, needless to say, drawn
at sexual encounter. In a case of incest tried in Connecticut in 1672, the
daughter was whipped but the father was executed, after which time the
General Court declared incest a capital crime. Trumbull, *Pub. Recs. of
Connecticut,* II, pp. 184, 189. Implicit in these laws, quite obviously, was
the recognition that even for several years after puberty the child was not
held fully responsible for his behavior. That his responsibility was defined
differently from adults' is evident in an act for preventing theft, which specified that "if any person, whether Children, Servants or others, shall bee
taken or knowne to Robb any orchyards or garden, . . . he shall forfeitt treble
damage to the owners there of, and such severe punishment as the Courte
shall think meete." *Ibid.,* I, p. 514. Presumably this means that in other instances, children and servants were not responsible parties.

123. *Sewall Diary,* p. 74. The illustrated alphabet from the *New England Primer*
can be found in Robert H. Bremner, et al., *Children and Youth in America.
A Documentary History, 1600-1835* (Cambridge, Mass., 1970), which also
contains the warning from Eliot (p. 4, 33). Anne Bradstreet gave her usual
thoughtful view on the subject: "Diverse children have their different na-
tures; some are like flesh which nothing but salt will keep from putrefaction;
some again like tender fruits which are best preserved with sugar: those
parents are wise that can fit their nurture according to their Nature." *Works
of Bradstreet,* p. 50.

124. *Mather Diary,* II, p. 44. Mather also interceded in his son's behalf when the
boy was scolded by his grandfather, Increase. *Ibid.,* I, p. 583.

125. *Ibid.,* p. 239-240. Whether Mather's catechetical discipline succeeded is open
to dispute. He frequently reflected on children and the problems of raising
them, of which he had many as his own youngsters grew up—and did not
fulfil his hopes. He mourned his condition: "How little *Comfort,* yea, how
much contrary to it, have I seen in my *Children?*" *Mather Diary,* II, p. 706.
Samuel Sewall found his fourteen-year-old daughter Betty very upset as a
result of his reading "a Sermon of Mr. Norton's . . . Text June 7. 34. You
shall seek me and shall not find me." and her reading "out of Mr. Cotton
Mather—Why hath Satan filled thy heart, which increas'd her Fear." Hanscom, *Heart of the Puritan,* pp. 85-86.

126. And the child would reciprocally recognize the community. In John Cotton's
Spiritual Milk for Boston Babes the question was raised in connection with
the Fifth Commandment, "Who are here meant by Father and Mother?," to
which the orthodox answer was: "All our Superiours, whether in Family,
School, Church, and Common-Wealth."

127. Some representative sermons, catalogued in Charles Evans, ed., *American
Bibliography: a Chronological Dictionary of All Books, Pamphlets and Peri-
odical Publications Printed in the United States . . . 1639 . . . 1820* (12 vols.;
Chicago, 1903-34), are: Increase Mather, "Pray for the rising generation"
(1678), no. 255, and "Solemn Advice to young men, not to walk in the
wayes of their heart" (1695), no. 728; Thomas Bray, "The Necessity of an
early religion" (1700), no. 904; Cotton Mather, "Things that young people
should think upon" (1700), no. 934, and "The best ornaments of youth"
(1707), no. 1308.

128. Bremner, *Children and Youth in America,* p. 4.

129. Edmund Morgan, in *The Puritan Family,* notes that usually a boy entered
apprenticeship between the ages of ten and fourteen, while a girl might begin

as much as four or five years earlier since it was unlikely she would pursue any career but that of housewife (pp. 67-68). John Demos, in *A Little Commonwealth,* supposes that apprenticeship began between the ages of six and eight, but he points to boys and girls working with their fathers and mothers, only suggesting that some children entered apprenticeship or service at this age (pp. 140-142; on education in the home, p. 144). There were apparently several different arrangements. A child could live and work (or study) at home, live at home and work abroad (see *Sewall Diary,* pp. 77-78), live outside the home with relatives (see Thomas Hungerford to "Loving Sister," November 2, 1657, Lee Family Papers, Massachusetts Historical Society; also H. Saltonstall to Rowland Cotton, October 23, 1702, Mass. Hist. Soc.) or in the home of an unrelated family.

130. John Demos regards the age of six to eight as a major turning point for children, after which time development to maturity was gradual but straightforward (*A Little Commonwealth,* pp. 140-143). Ross Beales ("In Search of the Historical Child," a paper written at the University of California, Davis, in 1970 and given to me by the author) doubts that the change was so clear cut. Where Demos asserts that "many Puritan conversions seem to have occurred well before puberty," Beales points to Thomas Hooker's belief that a child of ten or twelve, "living the life of a beast," would find it almost impossible "to consider the mysteries of life and salvation." Whereas at middle age, probably between twenty and forty, "Understanding begins to shew itself in her operations." Anne Bradstreet observed: "A wise father will not lay a burden on a child of seven years old, which he knows is enough for one of twice his strength, much less will our heavenly father (who knows our mould), lay such afflictions upon his weak children as will crush them to the dust. . . ." *Works of Bradstreet,* p. 57.

131. David H. Flaherty, "Privacy in Colonial New England, 1630-1776," (doctoral dissertation, Columbia Univ., 1967), pp. 62-64, 66, 71, 89, 95-96, 120-121, 124-127. Certainly people valued privacy and believed in modesty; they could not always achieve it. But Cotton Mather mentioned that his wife had "her own chamber," and Samuel Sewall recorded an incident when his daughter knocked before entering the bedroom he and his wife occupied. *Mather Diary,* II, 9; *Sewall Diary,* p. 136. Furthermore, there are instances early in the century of an infant being overlaid by one of the two other children sharing a bed with him (cited in Demos, *A Little Commonwealth,* p. 132) and of a nursing mother having to share a room with her other child, who was dying of a fever ("Hull Diary," p. 148).

132. "A Christian at His Calling" (1701) in Evans, *American Bibliography,* no. 990.

133. "The Way of Life," as quoted in Perry Miller, *The New England Mind: From Colony to Province* Cambridge, Mass., 1953), p. 41.

134. John Calvin, *Institutes of the Christian Religion,* ed. by B. B. Warfield (2 vols.; Philadelphia, 1936), I, pp. 786-787, 790.

135. John Cotton, asked to judge the propriety of "toys they use at the time, which they say they celebrate in remembrance of Christ's birth . . . viz. carding, dancing, & c" as well as drawing Valentines out of a hat, condemned carding and choosing Valentines as a lottery, but approved "mixt Dancing"—though his son-in-law, Increase Mather, spoke against it. Hanscom, *Heart of the Puritan,* pp. 88-90, 176-179.

136. Quoted from the Boston Almanack of 1693 in Morgan, *Puritan Family,* p. 121.

137. This description is based on the model set up in Dorchester in 1645. G. E. Littlefield, *Early Schools and School-Books of New England* (New York, 1965), pp. 82-84.

CHAPTER 8

A Period of Ambivalence: Eighteenth-Century American Childhood

JOHN F.
WALZER

"Here is a land to employ them in to exercise their bodies, and keep them from idleness. . . . Here are none of the temptations to debauch their tender minds, which are common to more populous countries. . . ."[1]

George Whitefield, 1748

It may be that the most important contribution that psychology will make to the study of history will be to shake historians loose from some working assumptions they make about human motivation. It is commonplace for the historian to assume, for example, that men normally want to succeed and to be free, and that nations want to win wars. The contrary possibilities are not often considered. This chapter on the attitudes of eighteenth-century American parents toward their children, and the practices used to rear them, is based firmly on the notion that parents often entertain diametrically opposed attitudes toward their children and act on them at more or less the same time.

The initial set of contradictory wishes parents entertain is in regard to the value of having children at all. In eighteenth-century America, there were distinct economic advantages in having many children, and the classic problem of inheritance was greatly diminished where there was so much land, movement, and opportunity. Moreover, the public attitude was enthusiastically pro-procreation, so much so that newspapers frequently carried humorous stories about the "laudable accomplishments" of aging males who helped to populate the expanded empire.[2] Finally, there was not much one could do, anyway, or so it appears to have been assumed. A bachelor calculating the cost of the married state presumed that child-bearing would be an expense incurred every two years.[3] Samuel Sewall hoped uncertainly that "my dear wife may now leave off bearing" upon the arrival of his thirteenth child in twenty-seven years.[4]

While we today accept the idea of an initial ambivalence toward children as normal, we ordinarily attribute the more extreme manifestations of continued ambivalence to the realm of the abnormal, the unhealthy, and the bizarre. Good and proper parents love their children, if not for every waking minute, then at least in a basic way. They could not really want to kill or abandon them, much less badly harm them. And yet such behaviour was neither wholly fantastic nor unusual in the past. Quite normal parents harbored unconscious wishes of such an extreme nature that they could not be admitted to the conscious mind. In colonial America, the attitudes of parents toward their children were shaped by the basic ambivalent wishes to retain and to reject their offspring, to hold on to them forever, and to be rid of the noisome creatures, at one and the same time. When these contradictory wishes were restrained and balanced, they can be said to have disappeared. When not so well integrated, the results were less happy.

REJECTION

By the eighteenth century, the practice of abandoning new-born children where they were likely to be found, so common in London as to be institutionalized, was almost non-existent in America. In 1775, Dixon and Hunter reported in the *Virginia Gazette* that a post rider carrying the mail between Newcastle and Richmond found "a young child" in the road, "carefully placed in a box, with £10 cash," together with a letter saying that there would be more money forthcoming should the finder take care of the child; whereupon the post-rider carrying the mail promptly took it up and became the foster father.[5] Other such incidents, if they took place, were not frequently mentioned in the press.

Cases of infanticide were more commonly recorded, though they can hardly be said to have been frequent. The murderers were usually though not exclusively the mothers of the victims, and the murdered children illegitimate, although again, not always. The willful act often took place immediately after birth, a kind of late abortion.[6]

Unconscious infanticide is even more difficult for the historian to evaluate. Who can say whether or not Esther Burr, wife of the president of Princeton College, was entirely free from destructive motives when she took her little baby, Aaron, age about 11 months, on a long and dangerous trip to Stockbridge, Massachusetts, from which he nearly died?[7] Certainly she knew there was a good possibility he would be exposed to inclement weather. Esther's stated reason for taking Aaron along on a visit to her parents was that she could not bear to leave him at home. But for all her declared adoration, she does not say one word about how the baby fared in the drubbing rain she caused them both to endure by insisting that the wagon-master drive on as they neared the end of their journey, and this despite the fact that she saw the bad weather coming up. Admittedly, it was an exceedingly dangerous time to be near Stockbridge, for the woods were so full of Indians that Esther Burr told her diary again and again she could not sleep for fear "they will get me."[8] But if this helps explain the urge to drive on, it also causes one to wonder how a young mother could take a tiny baby into such a dangerous situation. She does not appear to have been troubled for the babe, however, or at least she never makes note of the danger he was in. She sincerely feared for his life only when he became very sick as a result of all the exposure. Parents often dangled their children before the maw of death in the eighteenth century. Numerous accidents occurred in which children were killed while "playing alone near a Cyder Tubb," or when their clothes caught fire when left alone.[9]

If cases of outright infanticide were rare in colonial America, the reverse was true of "putting out." Eighteenth-century American infants and small children were readily and frequently "put to" a nurse, a school, or a relative, and, as older children, to a master. The situation might be said to have been closer to that which exists in a primitive tribe where the child is seen as a child of the tribe as much as a child of a particular couple. It is impossible to determine what percentage of children were put out of their natural parents' home, either temporarily or permanently. Of those women who have left some record of themselves (almost always from the upper classes) many used outside nurses in the eighteenth century. Esther Burr nursed her own two babes, but Mrs. Robert Carter, of Nomini Hall, relied on outside wet-nurses for at least some of her numerous progeny.[10] "Your sister Fanny lies in with a daughter," Anne Tucker of Bermuda wrote to her son, St. George Tucker, of Virginia, in 1780: "she is too weakly to suckle her little girl, and is obliged to put it out to nurse."[11] Similarly, Gabriel Ludlow recorded the birth of his little girl on April 3, 1700, who "was put to nurse the 19th Instant in New York at 12 per annum and 12 weight of sugar, and dyed at 6 weeks old, buried in Trinity Church Yard."[12]

The *New York Mercury* featured an article in 1754 on "the Inconvenience of Hired Nurses" (first printed in an English newspaper) without any indication that this was some evil English practice from which the Americans were mercifully free.[13] The common argument that infants sucked in the physical disorders and crude passions of the far-from-tender nurses was often aired in the press, with examples drawn from ancient history. Later in the century, the nurse often came to the baby rather than the baby being taken completely away from the mother. In 1786, for example, Philadelphia merchant Thomas Leaming, Jr., wrote to a relative that one Abagail Williams, a widow, could come down to keep house. "She is recommended as a good nurse and if she don't go to keep house for you expects to go out a Nursing in Philadelphia at much higher wages, but in that case can't take her child with her."[14]

Perhaps we can learn something about the matter from an examination of the putting to nurse of Henry Drinker, Jr.[15] In July, 1771, his mother, Elizabeth, complained in her diary of ill-health, and said of her four-month-old son, "Dr. D____ says I must wean my little Henry or get a nurse for him. Either seems hard," she added, "but I must submit."[16] If this were all that the historian had to go on, one might be tempted to mistrust Elizabeth. "If a woman knows her husband can spare three to six shillings per week," a newspaper reported in 1754, "she . . . will persuade the good man to get a nurse, by pretending indisposition."[17] But Elizabeth Drinker truly seems to have agonized over the problem. A few days after receiving the doctor's advice she recorded that her side and breast were "painful," and that she went to one Sally Oates' house and "agreed with her to take my sweet, little Henry to nurse."[18] She stayed for an hour or two and then went back again in the afternoon to see her child. "I seem lost without my little dear," she confided to her diary that evening.[19] The next morning, before breakfast, she was off with her husband to see "our little dear." In the evening there was "no going out," but she sent one Johnny Foulk to see how her son was. Johnny brought back "pleasing accounts." The next day she was off to Sally's house bright and early again.

On Sunday, the whole family went to Oates', not once but twice.[20] In fact, from July 22, when she gave up the babe, to August 22, the only time she does not record a trip to Oates was when she made no entry whatsoever, one rainy day excepted. Occasionally she took the baby for a little ride while visiting. During the next three months, the impression one gets from the fewer entries is that she and her husband continued to visit the child, if not so regularly. On February 1, 1772, Elizabeth ordered Sally Oates to begin to wean Henry. On March 8, Sally brought the baby back to Drinkers to stay. She had had him approximately seven and one-half months, and he was just over a year old when she brought him back to his natural mother.

It is evident that Elizabeth harbored some genuine reservations about putting her baby out to nurse. It also seems that she got used to the situation. She undoubtedly could have hired a wet-nurse to live in. The powerful possessiveness toward tiny babies that we sometimes take for granted has not always existed undiluted. It was not the standard attitude in the world of Elizabeth Drinker; but neither did she abandon it, or send it to a baby farm, as some still did in 1771. Clearly Elizabeth cared a lot, and did not get rid of the baby casually. At the same time she was able to go off for a month, enjoy herself, and dismiss the infant from her mind, or at least not lament his absence in her diary.

One way "to be rid of them at home" after they were back from the wet-nurse was to send children away to school at an early age.[21] Where there were public-subsidized nursery schools, parents sometimes sent their children soon after they were weaned.[22] In Georgia, "a great many poor people that could not maintain their children . . . [sent] their little ones for a month or two, or more, as they could spare them. . . ."[23] In Philadelphia, the Swedish traveler Per Kalm alleged that children a little over three were sent to school both morning and afternoon although it was realized that they would not be able to read much.[24] In Virginia, there were instances of quite young children sent far from home to school.[25] Indeed, distance was considered by some as essential. "I hope it will be for the boys' advantage to be placed at school at a distance from home," Mary Norris wrote to her daughter.[26]

Parents sometimes openly expressed their ambivalent feelings. Richard Smith of Pennsylvania sent his young son away to school, but put him under the care of his grown son, with instructions that the older boy should take a fatherly care of the young one. "He seems to affectionate to me that it goes a little hard to me to part with him. . .", he added, "but I apprehend it is for his good to get a little more schooling. . . ."[27] Similarly, Thomas Frame wrote to John Penn: "You seem to think my fondness for my child will be his ruin. I hope not, for I do assure you I had rather see him dead than to have him when he is grown up, a blockhead."[28]

Sending one's child away to school often involved sending him to live with a relative. Putting a child out to a relative was also the result of one or the other parent dying. But often children young and old were sent to stay for a while, or to live permanently, with a relative in any case.[29] There is no way of knowing what percentage of children were put out in this way, but it does appear to have been taken for granted as a healthy and standard practice. "I have a little pratler, your namesake," Pamela Sedgwick wrote from western New England to a close girlhood friend and cousin in Boston, "If you do not burden yourself with a family before [she] is old enough to leave her mama I intend to send her to your care. . . . So you see my dear," she wrote, "you must not expect to get rid of trouble by living single.[30] Yet Mrs. Sedgwick did not send little Betsy to Miss Mayhew for another six years, at which time she was twelve. Miss Mayhew was not eager to have her, either, for she soon passed her along. Mrs. Sedgwick, usually self-effacing, let her annoyance show at this, and worried about her daughter being "removed from all her natural connection."[31] Nevertheless, she did not summon Betsy back to her home.

Littleton Waller Tazewell, of Virginia,[32] whose mother died when he was two, was sent to live with his maternal grandparents, and from there, when British armies threatened, to one Fanning, who probably was a distant relative. Fanning sent him in turn to a boarding school, but when Fanning then died, "my father was obliged to find another home for me," and back he went to his Grandfather. There does not appear to have been any obstacle to his living with his father, however, for when Grandfather Waller died, Littleton Waller Tazewell returned to his father's home, only to find a boy his own age living there. The father could hardly have been entirely insensitive to the plight of being shuffled from home to home as a child, for he, too, was sent to live with his maternal grandfather at age two, and then on to another relative. Indeed, according to family tradition, Henry's father was scheduled to be sent to England to a relative who had no sons, and was saved this fate by the death of his father, and the protection of his mother, who kept the father's wish a secret. Finally, Tazewell's maternal grandfather, Benjamin Waller, was also sent away from home when he was a boy.

On the peninsula between the James and the York Rivers, north of Jamestown, in early Plymouth, the straying of young children must have been something of a problem. "H.D. and John Drinker gone this morning toward Trenton," Elizabeth Drinker wrote in her diary for December 24, 1771, "in search of H.D., J.D.'s son, who's been missing several days."[33] Although the problem of lost children is not recorded nearly as often as one might expect,[34] an old English story became very popular in the last decade of the eighteenth century, and was printed and reprinted in America, enlarged and embellished in plays, and cheaply printed for sale by the "flying stationers", or chapmen.[35] *The Children in the Woods, Being a True Relation of the Inhuman Murder of Two Children,* was in some editions clearly intended for young readers.[36] Other editions called on parents to ponder the fate of *The Two Babes in the Wood,* and a Salem broadside was aimed specifically at executors and overseers of children that are fatherless, and "infants mild and meek."[37] The story involved an English family who were blessed with two beautiful children of "inexpressible sweetness."[38] Renditions vary, but either the parents sensed that their own death was near, or they had to go away, and they entrusted their dear children with an uncle and bequeathed to them a large sum of money. The bequest was arranged so that the money would go automatically to the uncle upon the death of the children.[39] No sooner were the parents removed from the scene than the uncle hires two ruffians to take the children to a distant wood and murder them and gives out the story that the children were sent to London to be properly educated. Along the way, the "youthful prattle" of the children causes one of the desperados to soften and protect the three-year-old boy and his sweet sister, but the other man, more hardened and resolute, insists on completing the task because they will be well paid.[40] The two men duel, and the more tender-hearted rogue wins. He then abandons the children rather than slaughtering them, and they eventually die of exposure. Two robins then come along and cover them up with leaves, "with the tenderness of two affectionate parents."[41] The wicked uncle receives his retribution: his house is consumed by fire, his cattle die in the fields, and "his two sons were so disobedient that they would not pay the least attention to his commands . . . and were continually destroying his peace of mind by head-strong passions."[42]

In this eighteenth-century rendition, the fearful parental wish to get rid of his children, who are nevertheless "inexpressibly" dear to him, is separated from the parent by dramatic device. Rejection gives way to renewed ambivalence, which is also personified and dramatized. Parental affection is reasserted at the end, and guilt is properly punished, while that behavior which heightens parental hostility, and threatened the late eighteenth-century world as nothing else, *disobedience,* is separated from the dear, sweet children. If it is true that people deal with their anxieties through reading fiction as well as by dreaming, this particular story seems an appropriate one for eighteenth-century parents to have responded to, as they "put out" their children less and less often, and chose, instead, to hold on to them.

RETENTION

While parents in eighteenth-century America resorted to the various methods described in the foregoing section to "be rid of them", as Per Kalm cynically remarked, at the same time they strove mightily to hold on to them—even when grown—and gave signs that they were genuinely interested in them. They noted the birth of their children, and, while they did not really celebrate their birthdays, they did sometimes express their delight upon the occasion. They also grieved at the death of their infants, and even more so when older children died. There is occasional evidence of fathers playing with their children, and some parents exchanged letters with their children. There was also a clear but more self-serving concern. Children were hailed as carriers of the father's true religion, as perpetrators of the one life style God smiled on. Children were said to "exonerate" their parents. They became a way of proving one's own worthiness in the world, of attaining salvation. As John Barnard pointed out to his New England congregation in 1737, "are not your children a part of yourselves?"[43]

The institution of the children's birthday celebration did not exist in eighteenth-century America. The birth of a child was mentioned only briefly;[44] the anniversary of the birth was seldom noted, and when it was, it was done in a morbid way: "this day being my brother Hugh's birthday, who if alive enters [sic] the 28th year of his age."[45] Upper or middle class parents did sometimes give their children presents, however. Father's return after a long absence sometimes provided the occasion, significantly. If a father could not come home, he sometimes wrote to his children. The letters of St. George Tucker to his stepsons, although they contain the standard stilted expressions of love and duty, illustrate that these children were not just incidental waifs who happened to be standing around in the wings of a busy man's life.[46] Indeed, he scolded his wife for forgetting to mention one of his several children specifically. Mrs. Tucker made amends in her next letter with a multitude of details about the children. "I have not been guilty of the omission in any other" letter, she pointed out.[47] The mention of children in letters, while frequent, was often a formality, or an after-thought.[48] One is often struck by how infrequent, brief, casual, and sometimes hardhearted are the references made to children by eighteenth-century Americans. Yet they did take a definite interest in what those children were up to, and, above all, in what they would become.

The evidence suggests that the American mother of the eighteenth century was in closer and more constant contact with her children, and interacted more often and more deeply than her counterpart in Europe. Servants were certainly less available. It is true that in *Virginians at Home*, Edmund S. Morgan could characterize the relationship between parent and child in Virginia as "pleasant," because the tutor or governess often had the unpleasant task of punishing the children.[49] But Mdmes. Drinker, Burr, Sedgwick, and Tucker had a regular, close contact with their little ones. Mrs. Burr's only servant was a twelve-year-old girl, whom the good woman attempted to educate, and nursed when she fell ill.[50]

Fathers, when they were home and available, on occasion played with the kiddies. "I suppose you twert yourself very often in play with your little sons when you are able," Anne Tucker wrote to her son, St. George in 1780.[51] Pamela Sedgwick told her husband that the children missed him and wished for his company, "that they may hang around [your] neck...."[52] On one occasion, Samuel Shoemaker was made physically ill by nine-year-old Edward's return to school.[53] The Virginia planter William Byrd was a similarly intense father.[54]

Just as there were sometimes genuine if brief expressions of "a great deal of joy" at the birth of son or daughter, so occasionally one finds heart-felt sorrow at the death of an infant, toddler, or older child. One Mrs. Brown, an Englishwoman considering emigration to America, and on visit there, did not return to England at the death of her child, Charlotte, but she definitely felt a sharp and lasting sorrow, sense of loss, and depression when she heard of Charlotte's death. For a week or so she lamented to her diary that she could not go on.[55] Esther Burr likewise spoke of real anxiety when Aaron almost died.[56] Other parents recorded genuine grief and despair in their letters and diaries, although such records also contain passages that may be paraphrased, "he died, God's will be done, did the pickles get there without spoiling?" Mrs. James Burd wrote to her husband in 1764 with a casualness hard to believe that no doubt he had already heard of the death of one of their children.[57]

On May 12, 1710, William Byrd recorded in the secret diary he kept, in code, that his son, Parke, age about twenty-two months, was very sick of a fever.[58] The child continued unwell, and on the 17th Byrd sent "an express" for a Mr. Anderson. Anderson was not a doctor, but a person with some medical skill. On the next day the boy was a bit better, "thank God," but on the 21st, Evie, Byrd's two-year-old daughter, came down with the fever. Byrd therefore sent excuses to Colonel Harrison, with whom he was scheduled to dine. On the 24th Byrd and his wife stayed up until midnight with the children, and then turned the job over to an apprentice to the secretary at Westover plantation, who was followed in turn by the overseer.[59]

On June 3, Byrd "rose at 6 o'clock, and as soon as I came out news was brought that the child was very ill. We went out and found him just ready to die and he died about 8 o'clock in the morning. God gives and God takes away; blessed be the name of God."[60] The most charitable way to read this evidence is that Parke suddenly became a lot sicker than he had been; yet these parents do seem different from those who might have taken turns sitting up each night with the child, or given orders to wake them if the child took a turn for the worse.

The entry for June 3 continues:

> Mrs. Harrison and Mr. Anderson and his wife and some other company came to see us in our affliction. My wife was much afflicted but I submitted to His Judgment better, notwithstanding I was very sensible to my loss, but God's will be done. Mr. Anderson and his wife with Mrs B-k-r dined here. I ate roast mutton. In the afternoon I was griped in my belly very much but it grew better towards the night. In the afternoon it rained.

Byrd is "very sensible of his loss," but he does not spend the space and energy remaining for the diary entry on enlarging upon it. Rather, he recorded what he ate, as he usually did. Also, on this day and several of the following days, he has a stomach ache, and does not know why, or says he does not. Twice he says he is suffering "for no thing". It did not occur to him that it might be because the death of his infant son had upset him. On the contrary, it is as if it was especially important to him to consciously deny this. Although he never again refers to the boy, it seems evident that his death upset him more than he wanted to admit.[61]

Mrs. Byrd, by Mr. Byrd's account, was not as stoical. It may be that Mr. Byrd dealt with the grief which, according to the accepted attitudes of his day, he was supposed to minimize, by attributing it to Mrs. Byrd. "My wife had several fits of tears for our dear son," Byrd recorded in his entry for the next day, but "kept within the bounds of submission. I ate hashed mutton for dinner." The next day "my wife continued very melancholy, notwithstanding I comforted her as well as I could."[62] This probably was the first child that Mrs. Byrd had lost. After the funeral, Byrd wrote, "my wife continued to be exceedingly afflicted for the loss of her child, notwithstanding I comforted her as well as I could. I ate calf's head for dinner." He did take note that his wife was melancholy for a week or two thereafter. Then he appears to forget why she should be depressed, for in subsequent entries he mentions her headaches, and melancholy, and wonders what could be troubling her.[63]

When the Puritan experiment began to fail in New England in the 1660's and '70s, owing to the lack of zeal of the new generation, the saints occasionally lapsed into the familiar lament of frustrated parents: "but we did it all for you!"[64] In saying this they were momentarily being a little dishonest about means and ends. Usually, Puritans admitted rather openly that their children were a means to an end: namely, the perpetuation of the parents' life-style, or ideology. Indeed, when they published anything on the subject of children, it usually dealt with this particular aspect of the subject. Of course they did not stress their selfish interest; perhaps they did not even see it. They brought up their children, they said, for "the honor and interest of God." For "how should the interest of God be promoted" if they were not careful to "hand religion down in the truth and purity of it, to their posterity?" Children were "a Holy Seed" to serve God when the present generation of saints was rotting and consumed by worms.[65] They would be replaced by a "rising generation" which was again and again referred to as a godly or visible seed, "the seed of the blessed of the lord."[66] As such they were superior to "a new ingrafting," whereby the true way might also be preserved.[67]

The character of the child was seen to reflect on the "credit and reputation" of the parent.[68] "Verily, we may often guess at the parent from the manners of his children," New England parents were warned, as they no doubt point out to their children to this day. But what was involved in the "seed of the blessed" idea was something more serious than credit and reputation. Puritan parents were not supposed to think themselves to be in a position to decide whether they cared or not what people thought of them because of their children's behavior. For if God's charge "perish at last through your default," parents were threatened, God would not be merciful. "Unnatural wretch, you neglectful parent, how will it sting you to hear your children roar out against you from the place of eternal torment?"[69]

Parents who did not give their children the wherewithal to perpetuate the true word of God, who did not shape their children so that they would *not* reshape the word (or the world), were worse than cruel sea monsters.[70] That "a perfect subordination" or "a hearty submission," at least in ideological matters, was wanted, is very clear, although the Puritans were actually ambivalent on this crucial matter.[71] The oft-quoted text, "know ye Solomon, the God of thy Fathers, and follow him with a perfect heart," best sums up the attitude and purpose.[72] God, it seems, knows one's thoughts so absolutely no deviation is allowed. "God's eye is *ever* upon them," parents were admonished to remind their children. "He sees and inspects them day and night in all their youthful prophaneness and dissolute courses."[73] What was in store for those children who forgot about the omniscient eye of the omnipotent parental figure, and who forsook the way of the Lord in any thing? The eighteenth-century parent was not yet merciful, or at least not supposed to be, when it came to ideological soundness. "If indeed there should happen to be any Shimei, or Rabshekah in the family, one that reproaches the living God, and mocks and reviles you, and your offerings, it were better that you should turn such an one out of your doors, than that you should shut God out of your house."[74]

Such complete submission, such an effort to subdue the individuality of the child, to hold on so completely, when actually accomplished, could manifest itself in a way that the opposite form which rejection sometimes took: infanticide by smothering. James Janeway, a Puritan Mrs. Hennyfalcon, who "dearly loved children," delighted in reciting the strange cases of children who succumbed to heavy doses of "omniscient eye," and wasted away at an early age.[75] Of one four-year-old he wrote, she was often in "one Hole or another," in tears upon her knees.[76] Another "sweet" five-year-old "buried himself" in praying, reading the Bible, and saying his catechism. Both were actually buried soon enough.[77] In other words, many parents in colonial America wished to hold on to their children completely, wherein they saw their own interests bound up. While parents were doubtless sensitive to the notion that "the sooner they are made acquainted with the world the better," they were at one and the same time eager to establish their children "in the knowledge and [perfect] service of the true God."[78] These two quotations could stand as symbols for two opposing conditions which parents wished to impose on their children: independence and dependence.

Having children also involved a more immediate compensation which was frankly admitted and even stressed. Proper upbringing "makes your children an honor and a comfort to you," was the promise.[79] "A wise son maketh a glad father." Conversely, "a foolish son is the heaviness of his mother."[80] Children properly tied to their parents would care for them in their old age, in unfavorable comparison to "some of the old pagans," whose "children [were] under no obligation to do anything for . . . parents when a needy old age might overtake them."[81] The self-interested and manipulative quality of parental love for children was further revealed by an occasional unveiled threat that it would be withheld if undeserved. "I send Edward my love," Rebecca Shoemaker wrote to her husband in 1784, "which he may always be assured of while he continues so worthy of it."[82] "I . . . send my love and a kiss to Mopsey," wrote another parent at approximately the same time. "If she ceases crying in the night you may do her that courtesy, but otherwise I hardly think her entitled to it."[83]

It is abundantly clear that parents did not always succeed in imposing a hearty submission, a perfect subordination. Even when one takes with a large dose of salt the eternal complaint of parents that their children are not behaving as they should, one is struck by the repeated assertion that children in eighteenth-century America were unusually recalcitrant.[84] In New York, at the beginning of the eighteenth century, Dutch children were blamed for having "played at their unusual games" outside the doors of the churches on the sabbath. Moreover, the children even of rich Dutch parents were "usually without shoes or stockings," a sure sign that they were not under proper, civilized restraints.[85] Lists of "don'ts" for children give us some idea of a few of the omissions of the time, and what was feared from "the wild asses."[86] "Don't gnaw on bones," one New Yorker admonished, don't dip your sleeves in sauces when you reach for them, don't run about wildly on the streets, don't go on the ice, don't snowball, don't go sledding with disorderly boys, don't join hands with other children, and, as a general rule, "learn to curb thy affections."[87]

But for all the failure, the written evidence left to us suggests there was a large measure of success in the efforts of colonial parents to "hold on" to their children. One way in which this success might be measured is by the salutations and closings employed in such correspondence.

"Honored Sir," "I am your dutiful son," "your ever dutiful son," "Honored Parent," "I am in all respects your dutiful son," "I am, dear Sir, your Humble Dutiful [sic] Son," "My duty to Papa," "My love and duty to Papa"—these are what one finds, with far fewer "My dear Sir," "Dear Father," or similar, more modern salutations.[88] Further, the obligation that "gratitude to your parents demands," was often mentioned by children writing to their parents.[89] "I am very sensible of the many obligations I am under to you," John R. Coombe wrote to his grandparents who had brought him up.[90] "I hope I shall . . . in some measure, dear Papa, repay the obligation that I am under by paying constant and diligent attention to my studies," Theodore Sedgwick, Jr. wrote to his father.[91]

The assiduousness by which adults urged proper attention to their aging parents is further testimony to the degree to which parents succeeded in obtaining a sense of duty from their children.[92] In fact the impression one gets from the sources is that the concern of such adults for their aging parents was greater than that exhibited by parents for their young children. Pamela Sedgwick wrote to Boston after her mother's death to ask for a lock of her mother's hair, just as in our time a young mother often preserves a lock of her baby's golden tresses.[93] Mrs. Sedgwick, who could not go to Boston when her mother died, spoke glowingly of her stand-in sister-in-law's behavior. She "could not have possibly attended one of her natural parents with more tenderness and unwearied kindness than she has my mother," Pamela told her husband.[94] But the clearest re-kindling of the dependence relationship, which has the added interesting feature of a reversal of roles, can be found in Mrs. Morris' letter to her son, penned on November 28, 1793. "May heaven preserve thee," she tells him in closing, "to 'rock the cradle of reposing age.' This is the fervent and affectionate prayer of thy tender mother."[95] The child, held on to properly, becomes the parent, and the aging parent can return to the comfortable encapsulation of childish dependency, and be "draw[n] towards her long desired home," and "gathered into the fold of rest."

Just as there is a long history of child abuse, of child abandonment, of the murder and exposure of children, so there is no doubt a long history of spontaneous love and self interested concern for children. Sixteenth- and seventeenth-century Puritans were also very much concerned about the future, and saw their children as the obvious inhabitants of that future. For a millennium and one-half, Christians called their children "seeds," and regarded them as the perpetuators of their way of life. It has been argued that the Jews were the first people to emphasize this idea, although it would be surprising if they really were.[96] It was this tradition of children as carriers of the true word of the true

God that early modern Europeans and American Puritans revived and re-emphasized. Winthrop Jordan draws a neat analogy between two aggressive, wandering peoples, the Jews and the Elizabethan Englishmen who went to America, and who felt that they had sinned against God, especially in connection with their eagerness to inherit the fruits of the earth.[97] The analogy is an important one. I do not think it an accident that both these peoples had a strong linear sense of time, and of history, a great interest in the past and the future, in their lines of descent, and in their "visible seed." The feeling of insecurity on the part of Americans, coupled with the early modern European growth of the importance of the individual, lies at the bottom of what we might call "the rise of the child."

GOVERNMENT OF CHILDREN

"Parents should be very careful to uphold a prudent Government of their Children. A steady, mild, yet close and taut Government is the best."

John Barnard, 1737[98]

For all their eagerness to reject their children on the one hand, and hold on to them so completely on the other, eighteenth-century American parents did of course allow children to survive and even thrive. It may be that for reasons yet to be explored Americans resisted the extremes of these two opposing wishes to an extent their ancestors in England did not. The surviving children, if properly "governed," were subjected to a regime which protected them within the fold of the family until they had arrived "to a capacity of choosing for themselves," at which time it was hoped they would choose the life-style of their parents, but at the same time, somehow, be independent.[99] Above all, whether they were raised by their natural parents, a relative, or a master, children in America were subjected to a regime designed to civilize and tame them, to restrain their natural tendency to "run wild." Seventeenth-century children were regarded as both inherently wicked and as totally innocent, angels, not yet corrupted by the wickedness of the temporal scene. Eighteenth-century Americans had similar notions. Infants, though seldom called angels by their parents, were sometimes referred to as "strangers," not immediately accepted as full-fledged human beings.[100] Having passed beyond this stage, children were regarded as highly malleable rather than inherently wicked. It was believed, however, that they could be easily and quickly drawn into wickedness.[101] In the correspondence of the upper classes, small children were most often referred to in an optimistic way, as "fine" and "lusty." They were also called "sweet" and "tender," little "lambs," and in one case "a fat little pig."[102] Similies were drawn from the vegetable as well as the animal world. As "tender plants," "my choicest plants," "my little vineyard," children were to be carefully cared for, protected, and, most of all, "cultivated."[103] "Were your children idiots, you might be excused," but "God has given you children that are . . . capable of learning [and] you should cultivate them."[104] As young plants, children could be shaped, and brought up in the way that they should grow.[105]

But the positive aspect of their "susceptibility" was more than outweighed by the danger of their going wrong if they were not properly instructed, governed, or curbed. Like the plants they were compared to, they would go wild if not cultivated. It was this natural tendency to go wild which was most often emphasized by those eighteenth-century Americans who held forth on the nature of children. A child, being a child, and born without discipline, was subject to "unbridled appetites and passions."[106] Such a "wild Asses' colt" had to have "the reins . . . laid upon the neck" of his appetites.[107] Children had to be broken, or "there will be the utmost danger of their breaking their parents' spirit, and hearts too."[108] "Parents should carefully subdue the wills of their children," argued one relatively liberal American, "and accustom them to obedience and submission."[109]

The actual experience of being a child in eighteenth-century America is a great deal more difficult to assess than the ideas of parents and preachers about the nature of children. We can learn far more about the cultivation of flax in the colonies than how mothers raised children. How-to-do-it manuals, when they were forthcoming in the second half of the century, were all English in origin, as were a large percentage of the newspaper articles which bore on the subject. A picture of childhood based on the feelings and experiences of those who were experiencing it is so far beyond our reach. Even the basic fears of children can be known only by circumstantial evidence, and second-hand accounts, such as the account of Dan Bradley, aged 3, who reportedly feared he would die and be eaten by worms, and who asked how heaven could be such a wonderful place if his parents were not there.[110] At best our picture is heavily slanted toward "good" children and not those who filled out the ranks of the "bad company" so often warned against. "Childhood and youth is naturally full of warmth and heat, . . . indecencies and enormities," according to Barnard, but how much can we know of these?[111]

Infants were probably almost all breast-fed. Dry-nursing, condemned by English manuals in America, does not appear to have been "in fashion," although we do not really know that poor women, especially those who hired out as wet-nurses, did not practice it.[112] And what about the one-fifth of the population that was black? The question of how frequently children were put out to nurse has not yet been analyzed. "In America, there are comparatively few mothers so un-natural as of choice to put their children out to nurse," an aristocratic English-woman proclaimed in 1790, but this is hardly trustworthy evidence.[113] By 1790, Americans should certainly have been receptive to the "natural" argument, but earlier in the century they are known to have eagerly sought to follow "the latest fashions from London and the continent."

The age at which a child was weaned can occasionally be ascertained, as in the case of little Henry Drinker (13 months).[114] Weaning according to superstition was on the way out, but was still practiced in 1793, according to *Poulson's Town and Country Almanac*.[115] "Even Aunt Deborah [some sort of fictional character, presumably], though she yet has her notions, forgets to look for the sign when her advice is asked about . . . the weaning of a child." Old ladies still advised mothers to begin weaning according to the dictates of the constellations, even though the sign might appear in the midst of dog-days, or while the child was cutting its teeth." As a consequence "a sacrifice of helpless innocence" was made.[116]

Of toilet training I have found narry a word, but then it would be difficult to prove that eighteenth-century Americans ever urinated and defecated from the existing source material. Recognition of adults, teething, walking, and talking, the accomplishments of developing infants, were welcomed and noted by colonial parents. "St. George [Jr.] is a sweet, little fellow," Frances Bland Randolph Tucker wrote to her husband. He "begins to know me." (He was approximately four months old.)[117] "Robert can walk tolerably well and is desirous to show everyone, and how smart he can run," his mother reported.[118] "Mopsy . . . talks *prodigiously*. She will walk in a fortnight."[119] But "even before they can speak," children would "discover the strength of the appetites and violence of their will."[120] Young Esther Burr, a new mother, took steps to meet the problem. "I had almost forgot to tell you," she wrote to a friend in 1755,

> I have begun to govern Sally. She has been whipped once on *Old Adams'* account, and she knows the difference between a smile and a frown as well as I do. When she has done anything that she suspects is wrong [she] will look with concern to see what Momma says, and if I only knit my brow she will cry till I smile, and although she is not quite ten months old, yet when she knows so much I think 'tis time she should be taught.[121]

Esther Burr was not acting prematurely by the standards of her time. Parents ought properly to institute a government over their children as soon as "the first glimmerings of reason and understanding" made their appearance, and "while they are scarce weaned from the milk or drawn from the Breast."[122] Every opportunity must be taken to curb their willfulness and teach them to respect and obey. The admonition to be eternally vigilant applied to parenthood: be always dropping them a little lesson, "when thou sittest in thy house, and when thou walkest by the way, when thou lyest down, and when thou riseth up."[123] Cotton Mather was always admonishing himself to pay more attention to "educating" his children.[124]

A proper government included not only constant lessons in obedience, manners, and religion, but also in diligence. When children were too young for hard labor, parents should "keep them within doors at their book, and at some little service, that they may be capable of any business rather than let them be idle."[125] Such an admonition fell heaviest on mothers without nursemaids. Esther Burr, who had some young help complained: "You can not conceive how my time is taken up. Sometimes I never sit down a whole day unless to vittles."[126] Pamela Sedgwick made a similar but more poignant complaint to her "lucky" spinster pen-pal: "I snatch a moment from a crying infant, and the noise of two or three ungoverned children, which is as distracting to the brain as a confused din of arms to a timid soldier."[127] To her absent husband she wrote: "I am tired of living a widow and being at the same time a nurse."[128] A year earlier she told her husband that if she could "still a squaling infant and settle a matter of great contention among a company of unruly boys, I feel myself as happy and as great as an Empress."[129] A Virginia Lady, Margaret Lynn Lewis, found it difficult to retire to her private withdrawing room to shut out "my noisy little ones," but this was because she was living in smaller quarters than she was used to, temporarily.[130] In a rare reference to children, the Marquis de Chastellux complained that American women did little more than take care of their children and clean house, hardly enough, he complained innocently, to keep a woman busy.[131]

Child-care was even more demanding on such well-to-do, middle class mothers as Mrs. Sedgwick, Mrs. Burr, and Mrs. Tucker, when one or more of their children was sick, which was frequently the case. "Last night up almost the whole night," Esther Burr complained in January, 1757, and the next night, "very little sleep." The third night she was "up the whole night" again.[132] When Sally was a little better her mother found her "extremely cross, crying all day, *Mam, Mam* If I hav't her in my arms." She was "more troublesome than when she was sicker."[133] "I begin to feel almost worried out, for she will go to nobody but me," a tired Mrs. Burr complained after Sally had been ill for six months. "I am afraid this illness will cause another whipping spell," she admitted.[134]

In all likelihood, not all mothers were as attentive as Esther Burr, although few houses in America were spacious enough to allow the parents much distance to separate themselves from sick or squalling infants. Even the wealthy planter, William Byrd, got up quite late on one oc- cation "because the child had disturbed me in the night."[135] And a re- view of eighteenth-century parental correspondence leaves one with the very strong impression that there was always at least one child ill in the colonial home.

Some of the pressure of parental duties spilled over on to American fathers, and there is some evidence that it was not entirely unwanted. Although Fanny Tucker and Pamela Sedgwick complained that their politically active husbands were too often gone from home, the impli- cation of their complaints, and of the apologies offered by their hus- bands in return, was that they were fond parents when at home.[136] The busy William Byrd and the merchant Henry Drinker took time to in- volve themselves in the problems relating to their small children, and Byrd seems to have been especially fond of his little three-year-old daughter. Children were taught to stand in awe of their fathers, but the distance appears to have broken down in some cases. The example of David, who would himself be a teacher of his child, was held up to colonial fathers to emulate.[137] Robert Carter, in contrast, clearly turned over his duties as father to tutor Phillip Vickers Fithian. When Fithian could not cope with the rambunctious second son, Ben, he handed the duty of chastisement by the rod back to the great man in the big house. Ben was duly frightened and behaved himself, for a few days.[138]

The symbol of the government of children was the book. Children must be always "kept at their book." The book symbolized civilized re- finement. Book-learning might be conveyed at home by a parent with time and ability. "The schools here are not such as I choose so that I have not sent either of my girls to them," Isaac Morris confessed in 1748.[139] A few parents could afford a tutor. But the emphasis on books, reading, and especially on "a good hand," certainly encouraged the spread of schooling. Fathers had little leisure to look after such matters, and few mothers felt much confidence, especially in spelling and pen- manship.

It has already been seen that early "putting their children . . . to school" was a form of abandonment. But schools were also a means of holding on, an important part of inculcating the proper attitudes and ideals, and at the same time a place of confinement and protection. Pro- tection, "by removing the hindrances of an unfavorable environment," dovetailed nicely with confinement and restraint.[140] What children in school were protected from was a world which offered too much free- dom. Upon examining the home for orphans in Georgia (which was also open to children with parents), George Whitefield remarked, "here are none of the temptations to debauch their tender minds."[141] An early advocate of compulsory, public-supported schools in New Jersey and

Pennsylvania pointed out that at such schools "our children will be hindered of running into that excess of riot and wickedness that youth is incident to. . . ."[142]

Protection from the wickedness of the world could not be complete, naturally. When the child was led astray it was essential that he be speedily corrected. As of old, the rod was the great symbol of such correction. We have already seen that bodily chastisement could be applied early. Even little Sally Burr's serious illness did not grant her immunity. One mother, whose youngster was temporarily out of reach, summed up the position concisely: "tell Tommy I will have him whipped for I will have him very good," she wrote.[143]

At school as well as at home, direct action was often the course taken. Catching a boy in a lie, a school teacher recorded, "I took my ruler," which was "a large, round ruler, made of cherry wood," and "repeated the operation of the ruler against his hand till I made him confess the crime."[144] The boy's hand turned black and swelled up a good deal, whereupon an irate father threatened court action. Schoolmaster Felton therefore sought the support of the selectmen. "Colonel Barnes told me the law was very favorable to schoolmasters," he reassured himself. Robert G. Livingston recorded in his diary that he had flogged James Powers and given him a black eye.[145] William Byrd never took a stick to his "little Evie," but he did flog his niece Sue Brayne, and on one occasion used a different and unusual physical punishment on a dependent.[146] "Made Eugene drink a pint of piss," he recorded in his diary entry for December 3, 1709. But Eugene did not stop wetting his bed, so Byrd gave him another dosage a week later.[147] That may have stopped the lad, for on the 16th Byrd noted that he whipped Eugene "for nothing."[148] Such irresponsibility in his wife, however, the well-to-do Virginian could not tolerate, and he questioned her closely when she caused her maid to be burned for some small mis-step which Byrd did not think warranted corporal punishment.[149] If one were to broaden the definition of children to all wholly dependent persons, which should in truth be done, then it is clear that the rod and the whip found widespread application, indeed, in the eighteenth century.

We delicate people of today may cringe at the idea of drinking urine, but many colonial medicines forced down the throats of infants and small children were not much lovelier. Without giving it too much emphasis, it is worth considering that foul-tasting medicines are sometimes a form of physical punishment. Of course, other painful forms of healing, such as bleeding, and "the blisters," were regularly imposed on children.[150]

On the more subtle side, parents increasingly employed shame in order to keep their children on the straight and narrow path. "My dearest sweet child," Theodore Sedgwick wrote to his first son, Theodore, Jr., in 1790, "do you love to have me write to you? I know you do. How much more am I pleased when my children write to me? . . . Besides, my dear fellow, by writing to me you will learn and will be ashamed to write in a slovenly manner."[151] The relatively enlightened Puritan ministers Josiah Smith and John Barnard joined with their much more old-fashioned colleagues to suggest that shaming children was a legitimate and effective way to obtain desirable behavior in them.[152] Even the still more liberal *Advice on Children,* published by Pennsylvania Quakers, called the inculcation of "a sense of shame" a "benevolent art in instruction.[153]

In addition to shaming, parents resorted to playing on a child's greatest fears as an effective way to force him to behave properly. The dark closet, together with "tying to the bedposts," rough-handling, and the rod were begun to be banned from the nursery in the more sensitive days of the early nineteenth century, so one may guess that they were earlier techniques. The closet was a favorite place to send children to pray. There is some unusual direct evidence that at least one child in eighteenth-century America had the sort of fears associated with dark places. In 1780, St. George Tucker wrote to his wife that he hoped his stepson Theodore had "overcome his dread of the double-backed monster."[154]

It is significant that while early nineteenth-century how-to-do-it manuals for parents warned against the dangers of "telling frightening stories to children," the eighteenth-century guidebooks read in America did not.[155] The old-fashioned frightening techniques of the morbid James Janeway were repeated by such later preachers as Samuel Phillips. Phillips warned naughty children who "had rather spend their time in play than to learn their book" that God knew where all such children lived and what their names were.[156] Even Josiah Smith, generally very "enlightened" compared to other would-be advisers to parents, reminded children of their closeness to death.[157] The technique of scaring children by waving the scepter of death at them seems all but unforgiveable in our times, but parents found it impossible to deal with their own anxieties without this technique. As late as 1790, the good Mrs. Sedgwick sent her fourteen-year-old daughter to attend the funeral of a girl who was soon to be married but had died instead. "I hope this afflicting providence will make a good and lasting impression on her tender mind," the mother wrote without conscious cruelty. "There is surely something . . . uncommonly striking in the death of a young person cut off in the bloom of youth. . . ."[158] Warnings to children issued early in the century were the most extreme in delighting to threaten children with their imminent demise in order that they might mind. James Janeway's little Mary A. went as joyfully to death as to school, happy that she was dying for her mother's "reproofs and corrections, too."[159] But it was Benjamin Bass, writing in the 1740s, who pointed out the further danger of going to "a dark place" forever.[160] Janeway offered instead the comfort that if they were good, children who died suddenly would go to a place where "they shall never be beat anymore."[161]

As early as 1727, the advocation of a careful and considered "prudent government," attuned to the needs of individual children, could be detected in Massachusetts Bay, in Pennsylvania, and in South Carolina. Moreover, there were signs that parents were listening. Certainly there were those who felt that children were "running away with their parents."[162]

"Be not over-rigorous in your Government," "temper . . . your family government with a suitable degree of mildness," "be very careful to uphold a prudent government of . . . children"—these were the phrases used by John Barnard, minister at Marblehead, in Massachusetts in 1737.[163] They characterize what was perhaps a new attitude toward children beginning to be held about this time. Children should be "managed mildly, in love, without brow-beating, or striking terror," Pennsylvanians were advised in 1732.[164] "Ye Father, provoke not your children to wrath," Josiah Smith told his Carolina audience in 1727.[165] "With patience, curb your passions." Be not too hasty to discover your resentments. Wait patiently upon their weakness. Teach by example,

> they have eyes to see as well as ears to hear, and are very much governed by the life and behaviour of their parents.[166]

A prudent government was more demanding of parents than a more severe government. It was also less tolerant of their "using" their children. Especially, the rod must be used discreetly. Where a gentle reproof and admonition will answer, use that, "for a reproof entereth more into a wise man than a hundred stripes into a fool."[167] Some children are stubborn, and must be used with severity. Some "discover a temper more soft and generous, and a word to these is more than a rod to the other."[168] They should be encouraged rather than reproved. Parents should use discretion with regard to age, capacity, and temper of their individual children. They were not all exactly the same, after all, like the offspring of brutes.[169]

Moreover, all must be done "with calmness." The great error of parents was in "giving correction rather from their own passion than the importance or consequence of the fault."[170] Very few things in children required bodily correction.[171] Even the more old-fashioned Samuel Phillips agreed in 1739 that "it is hazardous for any to be abusive toward them. . . . Children . . . are tender and we must lead them as they are able to endure."[172]

"Gentleness" was the recommendation of Thomas Coombe to his son, when the latter received his little Johnny back in 1781. The boy had "a mild and gentle disposition," the grandfather explained, and "severity of discipline" would be a great mistake. "Suffer me to remind you that tenderness in every shape must be attended to" in the management of the little boy.[173] Esther Burr, after she had disciplined Sally, confessed to her friend, "none but a parent can conceive how hard it is to chastise your most tender self. I confess I never had a right idea of the mother's heart at such a time before."[174] The gleeful schoolteacher, Silas Felton, who "caught" a boy in a lie, "examined witnesses carefully," and "made him confess," himself confessed "I took a wrong way to punish him."[175] William Byrd showed strong signs of doubt and ambivalence about whipping.

If punishment was to be adjusted to the child, so also was education, particularly reading material. In 1727, Josiah Smith advised parents to use language which children could understand when instructing them, language that was "free and easy," but not "mean."[176] Throughout the second half of the eighteenth century, books adjusted to children in size, language, and format began to pour from American presses. This adjustment was relatively new to both England and America. 1744 is said by one historian to be a watershed year.[177] One of the earliest such works, A Child's New Plaything, was "intended to make the learning to read a diversion instead of a task."[178] "Young people will have language, pathos, and picturesque images, or they will not read," one author rationalized. "Some little condescension is due to their weakness."[179]

Books adjusted to the supposed "capacity of children," such as The Protestant Tutor for Children, although simplified in language, did not show much real understanding of children.[180] A heavy dose of sugar sweetness was no substitute for real empathy.[181] In contrast, one child-advocate associated with early Pennsylvania history did succeed in putting himself "in the place of the child." Count Zinzendorf, who underwrote the Moravian experiment at Bethlehem, believed in free development where "rules are for the most part unnecessary."[182] A less empathetic European visitor to the colonies complained that it was whispered of him "that I cannot talk to children."[183] Such a remark at least suggests that this was considered undesirable. The Englishman in question, for his part, was not eager to be "pestered with the petulances of ludicrous prattle," and was quite sure that Americans had no more sense than his hostess, who assumed that others "can be as interested in her own children as herself." He warned: "early licentiousness will, at last, mock that paternal affection from whose mistaken indulgence it arose."[184]

There is further evidence that a new indulgence toward children was already well underway in America in the eighteenth century. The various pamphlets offering Advice and Caution to parents all spoke of a "growing degeneracy" among the young, noted also by Peter the Hermit in 1274. One man warned against "too great remissness in parents and governors of families," and concluded that "most of the evils that abound among us proceed from the defects [of] family government."[185] Little Edward Shoemaker, temporarily in England with his Loyalist father, was indulged with "thy favorite Lobsters, sweet oranges, etc."[186] The willfulness of small children in Virginia was attested to by Morgan in his *Virginians at Home.*[187] Edward Shippen, Jr., of Lancaster and Philadelphia, Pennsylvania, was unable to follow the advice to "accustom them to submission" offered by most experts. "I sometime ago gave my little Betsy a half promise to take her to Lancaster," he admitted to his father in 1748.[188] "She now so strenuously presses me to keep my word that if the weather should be fitting I have thoughts of setting off with her. . . ."[189] Henry Tucker, Jr. admitted to his brother that Nan, "the saucy Baggage, runs some risque of being spoilt." In 1774, Phillip Vickers Fithian observed that his charges were all "in remarkable subjection to their parents," which was a gross exaggeration, perhaps the result of a comparison with his own failure to keep the Carter children under control.[190]

We turn now to one final aspect of eighteenth-century childhood: play. A detailed description of the games and sports of colonial children can be found in Jane Carson's book on the subject.[191] In the eighteenth century, play was still extremely suspect. "Of idleness comes no good, but in all labor there is some profit," the liberal John Barnard told his congregation in 1737. "Keep them within doors at their book, at some little service," rather than allowing them to go out to play.[192] Play, which it was admitted children delighted in, was connected with sin, and the demands of the flesh.[193] Especially was play wicked when it took place while children should be listening, or on Sunday.[194] At the same time, the eighteenth century in America saw a definite recognition of the idea that "there is a time for all things under the sun, and that children have their times of instruction, which parents and teachers must be cautious not to exceed. Time must be allowed for recreation and innocent diversions, to unbend the mind and preserve the health," according to Josiah Smith.[195] Sam Moody said good children "play sometimes, a little, and there is no hurt in it, but they are often thinking of Christ, while they are at their play."[196]

CONCLUSIONS

This chapter has been built around the premise that parents entertain a basic ambivalence toward their offspring. It is now time to argue that children are motivated by a basic ambivalence which is comple-

mentary to their parents' ambivalence toward them: namely, to be rejected and be retained. Or, to put it more precisely, children, as they
are raised by their parents and become adults, want both to become independent and to remain dependent. Perhaps the latter wish exists first,
and remains the stronger of the two. But it does seem as if, beginning in
the eighteenth century Western men and women have been less ready to
accept a continued dependent state and more eager to assert independence and mastery.

This shift in attitudes toward independence was probably caused by
a shift in parental attitudes toward children, and at the same time caused
a significant change in these. A great deal of unnecessary disagreement
sometimes arises over the question of which of such inter-related phenomena brought about the other. In this case, one may have preceeded
the other in a significant way, but very quickly the two developments
became what might be characterized as "causally reciprocal." By the
eighteenth century it would seem that the shift in parents' attitudes
toward their children and the shift in children's attitudes toward dependence and independence had surfaced and probably had a great deal
to do with the Atlantic revolutions which occurred at the end of the
century. Both were also clearly related to two of the most central developments of modern Western history: the growth in the importance of the
individual as an increasingly independent and responsible entity who was
no longer primarily a member of a corporate body and the replacement
of hierarchical relationships by egalitarian relationships as an ideal.

What could possibly have affected early modern men and women so,
altering the forms of their basic wishes relating to rejection and reten-
tion of his children and leaving the fabric of eighteenth-century American society wrenched by these adjustments? Any attempt to answer this
basic question at this time must be highly tentative and hypothetical.
And yet, one is tempted to put forward a grand theory, if only because
it is in the character of this study: that is, psychological and sweeping.
Melanie Klein once supposed that in pre-Hellenic times there was no
super-ego. Although this assertion may or may not have merit, it gives
rise to the speculation that this faculty, however defined, is something
that at some time or another must have evolved in the human species.
This, in turn, suggests the idea of psychological evolution. If man has
evolved biologically, does it not follow that he must have evolved
psychologically? And is it not possible that this evolution has been slow?

A sense of the past and a linear view of history involve an anticipation of the future. Any scheme of psychological evolution places us
now in a period where an especially possessive attitude toward our
natural offspring, coupled with the seemingly opposite wish for their
independence, continues to be predominant. But it may well give way
to a new state characterized by inter-dependence, or the recognition of

the mature dependence of equal and fully developed individuals on one another. It is to be recognized, however, that this scheme is itself predicated upon some of the ideas which affected eighteenth-century American attitudes of parents toward their children. That is to say it is itself shaped by a linear sense of time and history.

REFERENCES

1. George Whitefield (1714-1770), *A Brief Account of the Orphan House in Georgia* (Philadelphia, 1746), p. 61.
2. *New York Mercury*, 4 Aug 1775, sister of woman who has had triplets "doubts not but that with as active an husband she might do the same"; 4 Feb 1754, laudatory notice of 4 women in one neighborhood producing 10 children; 31 Aug 1752, humorous notice of woman of Plymouth, age 50, swearing a child upon a man aged between 70 and 80; 12 Nov 1739, announcement of birth of triplets and prediction of discontent among married women "that their husbands can't perform the same piece of manhood", 7 Jun 1754, widower with 132 living descendants marries again, and "from the vigor and activity which he displayed at the wedding and afterwards", more predicted.
3. *New York Mercury*, 7 Jan 1754, "as for children . . . we may reasonably expect one in every two years, if not oftener. . . ."; *Virginia Gazette*, 12 Mar 1767, of a Virginia woman, "she preserves the prerogative of being often pregnant and is perpetually breeding"; William and Avis Andrews, of Bristol Parish, Virginia, had a child on 14 Jan 1723, on 1 Jun 1724, 7 Dec 1727, 7 Jul 1729, and 9 Sep 1731, or at intervals of 17 months, 3½ years, 19 months, and 26 months, Vestry Book of Bristol Parish, Colonial Williamsburg, Incorporated.
4. See entry for 2 Jan 1702, "The Diary of Samuel Sewall," Massachusetts Historical Society *Collections*, 5th Series, 4(1879), p 49.
5. *Virginia Gazette*, 4 Mar 1775.
6. 11 Sep 1710, "Sewall Diary", p. 288; *Boston Gazette*, 30 Apr 1722; buried in orchard, *Boston Evening Post*, 8 Sep 1734; *New York Mercury*, 24 Dec 1753; thrown in well, *New York Mercury*, 21 Apr 1755; "for the murder of her husband's child", *New York Mercury*, 9 May 1757; father seizes baby from mother's arms and throws in river, *New York Mercury*, 22 Jul 1754, 6 Oct 1755, 1 Oct 1753, and 17 Jun 1754; *Boston Evening Post*, 19 Aug 1765; *Boston Gazette*, 10 Mar 1740; *Virginia Gazette*, 25 Jun 1752.
7. See entries from 16 Aug to Oct 1756, in the *Journal of Esther Burr*, The Beinecke Rare Book and Manuscript Library, New Haven, Connecticut.
8. *Ibid.*, 13 Sep 1756.
9. A number of fatal accidents involved infants "being left alone": clothes caught fire, *Boston Evening Post*, 8 Mar 1736; similar incident, *New York Mercury*, 25 Feb 1754; 18 month old into tub of cider, *Boston Evening Post*, 20 Oct 1735; similar incident, *New York Mercury*, 28 Jun 1756; similar incident, *New York Mercury*, 17 Jul 1710; "Sewall Diary," p. 284.
10. 24 Dec 1773, *The Journal and Letters of Philip Vickers Fithian, 1773-1774* (Williamsburg, Va. 1943), p. 52.
11. Anne Tucker to her son, St. George Tucker, 13 Apr 1780, Tucker-Coleman Collection, Earle Gregg Swem Memorial Library, College of William and Mary.
12. 3 Apr 1700, *Grabriel Ludlow Memorandum Book 1693-1745*, New York Historical Society.

13. *New York Mercury,* 6 May 1754.
14. Thomas Leaming, Jr. to unidentified kinsman, 1 Mar 1786, Spicer-Leaming Papers, Historical Society of Pennsylvania. Advertisements, such as one in the *Virginia Gazette,* 25 Feb 1773, "any lady in want of a wet-nurse", were to be seen. In 1793, wet-nurses were found for 16 infants orphaned by the small pox epidemic in Philadelphia, Margaret Morris to Richard Morris, 12 Oct 1793, Copybook of Margaret Morris, 1737-1793, Quaker Collection, Haverford College Library, Haverford, Pa.
15. This account is based exclusively on *Elizabeth Drinker's Journal,* entries for June, 1771 to March, 1772.
16. *Drinker Journal,* 13 Jul 1771.
17. *New York Mercury,* 6 May 1754.
18. *Drinker Journal,* 17 Jul 1771.
19. *Ibid.,* 22 Jul 1771.
20. *Ibid.,* 28 Jul 1771.
21. The phrase is Per Kalm's, ed. Adolph Benson, *Travels into North America* (2 vols., New York, 1937), vol. 1, p. 204, Fall, 1748.
22. Gillian L. Gollin, *Moravians in Two Worlds* (New York, 1967), p. 81.
23. George Whitefield, *Orphan House,* p. 52.
24. Kalm, *Travels,* vol. 1, p. 204.
25. Edmund S. Morgan, *Virginians at Home: Family Life in the Eighteenth Century* (Charlottesville, Va., 1952), pp. 9-11.
26. Mary Norris to Deborah Norris Logan, 16 Sep 1799, Logan Collection, Hist. Soc. Pa.
27. Richard Smith to John Smith, John Smith Correspondence, 1740-1770, Hist. Soc. Pa. Isaac Norris, of Philadelphia, apologized to his uncle Charles for keeping his daughters at home, but explained "our schools here do not satisfy me," and furthermore, the youngest had been very sick. If peace instead of war prevailed, he would "willingly take a voyage to England" to see that they got proper schooling, Isaac Norris to Charles Norris, 25 Mar 1748, Isaac Norris Letterbook, 1735-1755, Logan Collection, Hist. Soc. Pa.
28. Thomas Frame to John Penn, 19 Aug 1737, *Penn Papers,* Hist. Soc. Pa.
29. "Mother was in town yesterday and brought out dear little girl to see us," John Smith to James Logan, Jr., 2 Feb 1751, Logan Collection. Smith speaks of his wife in this letter, so we know she is living. "Mr. William Reat of Fredericksburgh called this morning to request we would take a daughter of his for three years," John Boyce Diary, Huntington Library, San Marino, Ca. "What is become of our dear brother Tommy? If he is with . . . you, tell him his children . . . are well," Elizabeth Tucker to St. George Tucker, Tucker-Coleman Collection. Thomas was widowed.
30. Pamela Sedgwick to Betsy Mayhew, 25 May 1782. Sedgwick Papers.
31. Pamela Sedgwick to Betsy Mayhew, 25 Dec 1788.
32. This account is based on an unpublished mss., Sketches of his own Family, by Littleton Waller Tazewell, Norfolk, Virginia, 1823, pages not numbered, Tazewell Papers, Colonial Williamsburg. Instances of European children being sold into slavery were occasionally reported, *Virginia Gazette,* 24 Sep 1767, "to go to America"; 18 Aug 1774, "into abject slavery in the East Indies." The *Boston Gazette,* 10 Jul 1750, announced a proclamation forvidding the taking of any more Indian children as pledges for debts. Black children were bought and sold, of course, and poor children (and adults) were "rented" or leased out of towns, see, for example, Townbook of Dover, New Jersey, 1794, New York Historical Society.
33. *Drinker Journal,* 24 Dec 1771.
34. Near Reading, Pa., two young children, sent out to bring home some sheep,

"lost their way in the woods" and were found the next day, frozen to death, *New York Mercury,* 4 Feb 1754; the *Boston Evening Post,* 23 Feb 1736, carried a long account of two little girls lost in the woods. The girls were sent out to pick berries. 500 men on horseback searched the woods for them. The youngest was found "under a bush, carefully wrapped up, head, hands, and feet, with her own and the eldest's riding hood." This account was carried in another Boston paper, but did not show up in the New York or Philadelphia press.

35. The story was first published, possibly in 1640. Clifford Shipton, *National Index of American Imprints Through 1800: The Short-Title Evans* (2 vols., Worcester, Mass., 1969), vol. 1, pp. 146-7, lists 20 American printings. The earliest is tentatively dated 1768, a second in 177? (sic). A Boston printing for 1785 is the first definite dating. Beginning in 1790, there was at least one printing per year, with the height of popularity coming in 1795 (5 different imprints, 3 of them "musical pieces," and one "for the Flying Stationers.") The story was printed in Albany, Poughkeepsie, Newport, Hartford, and Salem, as well as Boston and New York.

36. *Children in the Wood* (Hartford, 1796). This edition was approximately 4" by 6" in size.

37. *Children in the Wood* (Salem, 1792), a broadside.

38. *The Affecting History of the Children in the Wood* (Hartford, 1796), p. 7.

39. *Ibid.,* p. 8.

40. *Ibid.,* pp. 12-13.

41. *Ibid.,* p. 15.

42. *Ibid.,* p. 18.

43. John Barnard (1681-1770), *A Call to Parents and Children* (Boston, 1737), p. 38.

44. Elizabeth Drinker failed to make note of the birth of baby Henry, *Drinker Journal,* entries, Jan, Feb, Mar 1771. Dr. Samuel Adams noted in his diary for 20 Jun 1764, "we had a daughter born this afternoon," and 5 Sep 1764, "our child died this morning with Hooping cough which brought on convulsions, being 11 weeks old, and was interred the 6th in the afternoon." That was the extent of his remarks, see *Diary,* New York Public Library. The sole comment of Alexander Coventry was "to me a girl is born this day, it is a fact, I am a father," 28 Sep 1788, Journal of Dr. Alexander Coventry, New York Historical Society. Robert G. Livingston wrote to his brother, Henry Livingston, 22 Jun 1745, "am very sorry to hear of the loss of your three babies, but am glad your wife is like to do well. . . ." Half an hour after Robert received his brother's bad news, he lost a son of his own, which brought "very great grief", but it was God's will. "Tea is 9/." Journal of Robert G. Livingston, New York Hist. Soc. Charles Carter wrote his brother, Landon, 4 Aug 1766, Carter Papers, Earle Gregg Swem Memorial Library, Coll. of Wm. & Mary, Williamsburg, Va., if your daughter Judy dies "I dare say you have too much good to repine long at the dispensation of Providence" and will silently acquiesce, and cheerfully submit. I admit I am myself "too apt to complain upon every trifling occasion. . . ." Also see Anne Tucker to St. George Tucker, date unknown, perhaps Jan, 1780, Tucker-Coleman Collection; Robert Smith, Jr., to John Smith, 26 Dec 1750, John Smith Correspondence; Henry Livingston to William Alexander, 28 Apr 1747, William Alexander Papers, N. Y. Hist. Soc. Henry Livingston's congratulations were accompanied by the wish that his sister would thereafter "beget a more masculine breed and not spoil the family with such Liliputians as your daughter."

45. 17 May 1748, Diary of Rev. Robert Rose, Huntington Library. Mrs. Sedg-wick does mention Christmas and New Years, Pamela Sedgwick to Theo-dore Sedgwick, 25 Dec 1794, 1 Jan 1794, but no birthdays. Rev. Rose notes his son Patrick's birthday, 11 Jul 1747, Rose Diary.

46. John Randolph to his stepfather, St. George Tucker, 9 Jul 1781, Tucker-Coleman Collection; Theodore Sedgwick to Theodore Sedgwick, Jr., 20 Feb 1790; Theodore Sedgwick, Jr., to Theodore Sedgwick, 9 Mar 1794; apolo-gizes for not writing to daughters, Theodore Sedgwick to Mr. Williams, 29 Apr 1794: Pamela Sedgwick discusses children writing to their father, to Theodore, 15 Dec 1793; "the children were very much elevated with joy at the reception of your letters," Pamela Sedgwick to Theodore Sedgwick, 25 Dec 1794. Sedgwick's second eldest daughter was grieved when her father wrote less to her than to his eldest daughter, Pamela Sedgwick to Theodore Sedgwick, 5 Mar 1790.

47. Frances Tucker to St. George Tucker, 22 Mar 1781.

48. Robert G. Livingston to father, Gilbert Livingston, mentions children and sundry family members in closing, or in post scripts, see, for example, letter to Gilbert, 9 Dec 1742, Robert G. Livingston Journal. But family letters do seem to have represented a centripetal force to counteract the centrifugal ef-fect that mobility in the 18th century exerted on families. "What a blessing is the art of writing," Rebecca Shoemaker told her husband in 1784, "to be able . . . to converse with dearest friends," and her letters, like those of the Sedgwicks, Tuckers, and others, were filled with family news, and occasional laments at being separated. "Heaven grant that we may all meet where we are never to be separated," Anne Tucker wrote to her son in Virginia from Bermuda, Anne to St. George Tucker, 8 May 1778.

49. Morgan, *Virginians at Home*, pp. 20-21. The Carters ate together, or at least on one occasion, "there was at table, Mrs. Carter and her five daughters that are at school with me," *Journal of Fithian*, 25 Dec 1773.

50. Both Esther Burr and Pamela Sedgwick complained rather regularly that car-ing for their children and infants took up most of their time, Burr Diary, pp. 86, 131, 132; Pamela Sedgwick to Betsy Mayhew, 31 Jan 1789. There was a "Nursery" in the home of Mr. Thomas Duncan, merchant in New York. Four children sick with small pox perished there in a fire, *New York Mercury*, 7 Feb 1757.

51. .Anne Tucker to St. George Tucker, 13 Apr 1780.

52. Pamela Sedgwick to Theodore Sedgwick, 12 Nov 1791.

53. 5 Oct 1784, Samuel Shoemaker Diary, 1784-1785, Shoemaker Letters and Diaries, Hist. Soc. Pa. Samuel walked part way back to school with his son, lamented his leaving, and 6 Oct, had a headache all day, 8 Oct, noted that he had had bowel trouble for 3 days.

54. A judgment based on the whole of Byrd's 1709-17-12 diary, but see, for example, entries for 6 Jul, 30 Aug 1710, relationship with nephew Billy Brayne, eds. Louis B. Wright and Marion Tinling, *The Secret Diary of William Byrd of Westover, 1709-1712* (Richmond, 1941).

55. 11, 12, 14 Aug 1755, Journal of Mrs. Browne, 1754-1757, New York Hist. Soc.

56. 8 Oct 1756, Burr Diary, Beinecke Library.

57. Sarah Shippen Burd to James Burd, 28 Aug 1760, Shippen-Burd Family Letters.

58. 12 May 1710, *William Byrd Diary*.

59. *Ibid.*, 17, 18, 21, 24 May 1710.

60. *Ibid.*, 3 Jun 1710.

61. Byrd was "a little griped" on the 4th, "and so indisposed that I could not settle anything." Nevertheless, he had "good thoughts and good humor." Parke's death caused little change in the routine diary entries. On the 7th,

"my gripes returned again and made me uneasy." He did not attribute this to the death of his son, whom he never made reference to again. He never once referred to him by his given name in the diary. In August, his two-year-old daughter, whom he did refer to by not only a given name, but even an endearing nickname, grew ill, and a doctor as well as Mr. Anderson was sent for, see entry for 4 Aug 1710. The doctor was not sent for in May and June, when Parke died, judging from the diary. On Aug 6, Evie was "much better", and the doctor was given four pieces of gold.

62. *Wm Byrd Diary*, 4 Jun 1710.
63. See, for example, the entry for 24 Jul 1710, *Wm Byrd Diary*.
64. Edmund S. Morgan, *The Puritan Family* (New York, 1944), pp. 168-9.
65. Barnard, *Call to Parents*, p. 37.
66. *Ibid.*, p. 6; Peter Clark, *The Scripture–Grounds of the Baptism of Christian Infants* (Boston, 1735), pp. v-vi.
67. Clark, *Baptism of Infants*, p. viii. Morgan, *Puritan Family*, Chapter 7, "Puritan Tribalism", makes it clear that perpetuation of the system by the children of the saints was preferred over a new ingrafting in the seventeenth century as well.
68. Smith *Duty of Parents*, p. 16.
69. Barnard, *Call to Parents*, p. 41.
70. Cotton Mather, *Cares about the Nurseries* (Boston, 1702), p. 33.
71. Barnard, *Call to Parents*, pp. 26-28, preaching in 1737, is typical of the necessity to "subdue their wills," and he was in other ways not overly severe. But the basic way in which Puritan ideas *limited* power and authority made itself manifest in the pronouncements of Josiah Smith, dissenting minister of South Carolina. The limits of parental power over children "ought to be clear, some have stretched it beyond its bounds." It must not extend over the consciences of children, lest "they live and act by implicit faith, and make ignorance the mother of devotion," Smith, *Duty of Parents*, p. 18. This is an extremely important point. When Smith pointed out that "everyone of us must give account to God for him*self*" (italics mine), and that therefore children must eventually see with their own eyes and make their own choice, most Puritan parents would have agreed heartily, all the while they attempted to do everything they could to hold on to their children's minds.
72. I Chronicles 28:9; Barnard, *Call to Parents*, p. 1; Benjamin Bass, *Parents and Children Advised and Exhorted to their Duty* (Newport, 1730), preface.
73. Smith, *Duty of Parents*, p. 6; Samuel Moody, *Discourse to Little Children* (New London, 1769), taken from a sermon originally preached in 1721), pp. 3, 6, and 8.
74. Barnard, *Call to Parents*, 17.
75. James Janeway, *A Token for Children* (Philadelphia, 1749). This was apparently an oft-reprinted tract. Janeway lived from 1636 to 1674. Mrs. Hennyfalcon is a fictional nanny whose name explains her attitudes toward children. She succeeds in killing one of her brood in a powerful short story by Graham Greene, the Party, by forcing a particularly timid child to play hide-and-seek in the dark.
76. Janeway, *Token for Children*, p. 14.
77. *Ibid.*, pp. 61-66.
78. Margaret Penn Frame to John Penn, Penn Manuscripts, Hist. Soc. Pa.; Barnard, *Call to Parents*, p. 3.
79. Smith, *Duty of Parents*, p. 32.
80. Barnard, *Call to Parents*, p. 41. (Proverbs, 10:1.)
81. Mather, *Cares abt. Nurseries*, p. 11.
82. Rebecca to Samuel Shoemaker, 29 Dec 1784, Shoemaker Letters.
83. St. George Tucker to Frances Tucker, 28 Feb 1780.

84. See, for example, preamble to Connecticut statute of 1702, *Acts and Laws, 1702*, p. 15; Barnard, *Call*, pp. 28-29; Bass, *Parents and Children*, p. 3; *Advice and Caution from Our Monthly Meeting*, pp. 3-4; Burr Diary, p. 205.
85. *The Life and Works of Christopher Dock*, (Philadelphia, 1908), p. 103.
86. Mather, *Cares abt. Nurseries*, p. 32; *Christopher Dock*, p. 104.
87. *Dock*, p. 104.
88. See correspondence cited throughout this study, and especially Isaac Norris, Jr., to father, Norris of Fairhill Mss., Family Letters, Hist. Soc. Pa.; and letters of Ebenezer Huntington to his father, Jabez Huntington, 1775, 1776, Huntington Collection, Huntington Library.
89. Josiah Smith, *Duty*, p. 43, uses this phrase.
90. John R. Coombe to Thomas Coombe, Sr., 19 Feb 1793, Coombe Papers, Hist. Soc. Pa.
91. Theodore Sedgwick, Jr. to Theodore Sedgwick, 27 Nov 1791.
92. Anna to Rebecca Shoemaker, 7, 30 Jun, 29 Jul 1780, Shoemaker Letters; Deborah Norris to brother Isaac Norris, Jr., 3 Nov 1733, Norris of Fairhill Mss.; Benjamin Smith to John Smith, 10 Nov, 12 Nov 1793, Margaret Morris Copybook.
93. Pamela Sedgwick to Betsy Mayhew, 13 Feb 1791.
94. Pamela Sedgwick to Theodore Sedgwick, 13 Feb 1791.
95. Margaret Morris to Richar Morris, 28 Nov 1793.
96. Page Smith, *The Historian and History* (New York, 1960), p. 5.
97. W. D. Jordan, *White Over Black*, pp. 42-43.
98. Barnard, *Call*, p. 26.
99. *Ibid.;* Smith, *Duty*, pp. 17-19.
100. Rebecca Shoemaker to Edward Shoemaker, 29 Sep, 26 Oct 1784, Shoemaker Letters. It is almost as if new-born infants were unconsciously regarded like the embryos of marsupials rather than full-fledged human beings: out of the womb, but not really "born". This would help explain Byrd's attitudes toward Parke compared with Evie, and also the reuse of names of infants who died quite young.
101. Smith, *Duty*, p. 9; Barnard, *Call*, p. 29.
102. Dr. James to St. George Tucker, 4 Mar 1780; Francis Tucker to St. George Tucker, 22 March 1781; Pamela Sedgwick to Theodore Sedgwick, 14 Mar 1792; Phillips, *Children Well Employed*, p. 36; Janeway, *Token*, pp. iv and ix; Barnard, *Call*, p. 38.
103. Margaret Morris to Richard Morris, 22 Dec 1793; Barnard, *Call*, p. 26.
104. Smith, *Duty of Parents*, p. 39.
105. After "Know Ye, Solomon, the God of thy Father" the favorite text of the advice-to-parents preachers was "Train up the child in the way that he shall go, and he will not depart from it" (Proverbs 22:4), Mather, *Cares*, p. 26; Barnard, *Call*, p. 1; Bass, *Parents and Children*, preface.
106. Barnard, *Call*, p. 27.
107. *Ibid.*, Mather, *Cares*, p. 4.
108. Barnard, *Call*, p. 28.
109. *Ibid.* Barnard is called "relatively liberal" because he develops the idea of "prudent government," which represents the modification of the severity of the 17th century Janeway approach, although no doubt late 17th century authorities, like Locke, did say the same thing. Barnard seems less severe, too, than his contemporaries, Samuel Moody and Samuel Phillips.
110. Janeway, *Token*, p. 96.
111. Barnard, *Call*, p. 29.
112. Cadogan, *Nursing and Management*, pp. 16-18; Hugh Smith, *Letters to Married Women* (1st American edit., Philadelphia, 1792), pp. v-viii.
113. Enos Hitchcock, *Memoirs of the Bloomsgrove Family* (Boston, 1790), p. 82.

114. Drinker Diary, 1 Feb 1772.
115. *Poulson's Town and Country Almanac,* 1793, contained in Hannah Thompson's Memorandum Book, Hist. Soc. Pa.
116. *Ibid.*
117. Frances Tucker to St. George Tucker, 22 Mar 1781.
118. Pamela Sedgwick to Theodore Sedgwick, 16 Jul 1790.
119. Frances Tucker to St. George Tucker, 22 Mar 1781.
120. Barnard, *Call,* p. 28.
121. 28 Feb 1755, Burr Journal,
122. Barnard, *Call,* p. 22.
123. *Ibid.* (Deut. 11:19.)
124. 12 Feb 1711, Wm. R. Manierre, ed., *The Diary of Cotton Mather for the Year 1712* (Charlottesville, 1964).
125. Barnard, *Call,* p. 28.
126. Burr Journal, p. 132, circa 1 Jun 1756.
127. Pamela Sedgwick to Betsy Mayhew, 31 Jan 1789.
128. Pamela Sedgwick to Theodore Sedgwick, 28 May 1790.
129. *Ibid.,* 26 Feb 1790.
130. Diary of Margaret Lynn Lewis, Virginia, Augusta Box, N.Y. Hist. Soc.
131. Francois Jean Chastellus, Travels in North America (Chapel Hill, N.C., 1963), vol. 1, p. 81.
132. Burr Journal, 9 Jan 1757.
133. Burr Journal, p. 95, c. 30 Apr 1757.
134. *Ibid.,* p. 85, 7 Apr 1755.
135. Wright, ed., *Byrd Diary,* 1 May 1711, p. 338.
136. Pamela Sedgwick to Theodore Sedgwick 20 Jan 1791, 20 Nov 1794, 26 Jun 1790.
137. Mather, *Cares,* p. 5
138. *Fithian Journal,* 5 Jan 1774.
139. Isaac Norris to uncle, 17 Nov 1758, Isaac Norris Letterbook, 1735-1755, Logan Collection.
140. Quote from German authority interested in schools, Henry E. Meyer, *Child Nature and Nurture, According to Nicolaus Ludwig von Zinzendorf* (New York, 1928), p. 104.
141. George Whitefield, *Orphan House,* p. 61.
142. Thomas Budd, *Good Order Established in Pennsylvania and New Jersey in America* (Philadelphia, 1685), p. 16.
143. prob Penn, see tape R7/1/c. 15.
144. Rena L. Vassar, ed., *The Life or Biography of Silas Felton, Written by Himself* (Worcester, Mass., 1960), p. 27.
145. 23 Mar 1783, Robert G. Livingston Journal, N.Y. Hist. Soc.
146. 8 Oct 1710, *Wm Byrd Diary.*
147. *Ibid.,* 3, 10 Dec 1710.
148. *Ibid.,* 16 Dec 1710. Other whippings, of nephew, dependents, 6 Jul, 30 (nephew whipped by someone else, Byrd scolds whipper), 31 Aug, 8 Oct 1710 (2 dependents and niece whipped, by Byrd).
149. *Ibid.,* 15 Jul 1710.
150. "The blisters" were laid on Robert Sedgwick, Pamela Sedgwick to Theodore Sedgwick, 13 May 1790.
151. Theodore Sedgwick to Theodore Sedgwick, Jr., 19 Jun 1790.
152. Barnard, *Call,* p. 27.
153. *Advice and Caution,* p. 7.
154. St. George Tucker to Frances Tucker, 7 Feb 1780.
155. Parent Lawrence Growden ran into an unusual problem in 1747, when, after his wife died, he wanted his daughters to come to Pennsylvania. The girls

had "imbibed strange notions of Pennsylvania" from stories "told you when you were children to frighten you," Lawrence Growden to Elizabeth Growden, 1747, Growden Family Papers.

156. Samuel Phillips, *Children Well Employed* (Boston, 1739), p. 34.
157. Smith, Duty, p. 7.
158. Pamela Sedgwick to Theodore Sedgwick, 28 Dec 1794.
159. Janeway, *Token*, p. 18
160. Bass, *Parents and Children*, p. 8.
161. Janeway, *Token*, p. vii.
162. Barnard, *Call*, p. 28.
163. *Ibid.*, pp. 33-34.
164. *Advice and Caution*, p. 5.
165. Smith, *Duty*, p. 11.
166. *Ibid.*
167. Barnard, *Call*, p. 32.
168. Smith, *Duty*, p. 10.
169. *Ibid.*, "a child of 10 years must be distinguished from one of 7, and that from one of 5."
170. *Advice and Caution*, p. 6.
171. *Ibid.*
172. Phillips, *Children Well Employed*, p. 37.
173. Thomas Coombe to his son, 16 Nov 1781, contained inside a letter, Sarah Combe to Thomas Combe, undated, Combe Family Papers.
174. Burr Journal, p. 114, c. 15 Apr 1756.
175. Vassar, ed., *Life of Felton*, p. 27.
176. Smith, *Duty*, p. 15,
177. Rosalie V. Halsey, *Forgotten Books of the American Nursery* (Boston, 1911), p. 51. As early as 1702, Cotton Mather asserted that teaching had to be adjusted to the capacity of children, "even as nurses cut small bits for little children," Mather, *Cares*, p. 28.
178. *The Child's New Play Thing* (London, 1743; Boston, 1750), title page.
179. John Bennett, *Letters to a Young Lady* (2 vols., London, 1716; American edit., 1796), vol. 1, p. 29.
180. *The Protestant Tutor for Children* (Boston, 1685), was supposedly "designed for children," see title page.
181. Janeway, *Token*, was especially guilty of feigned sweetness.
182. Meyer, *Child Nature According to Zinzendorf*, pp. 98, 102-4. The "rules" quote is from the Hernhutt Archives, 20 Jun 1758. Zinzendorf is also quoted as writing "we do not presume to require of a son that he should follow the same maxims as his father" in 1740, p. 102. I believe Meyer is a bit uncritical of Zinzendorf, and exaggerates the extent to which the man succeeded in his empathy.
183. *Virginia Gazette*, 12 Mar 1767.
184. *Ibid.*
185. Clark, *Baptism of Infants*, p. xxxi.
186. Rebecca to Edward Shoemaker, 19 Sep 1784.
187. Morgan, *Virginians at Home*, pp. 7-8.
188. Edward Shippen, Jr. to Edward Shippen, 30 Apr 1761.
189. *Ibid.*
190. *Fithian Journal*, 4 Jan 1774.
191. Jane Carson, *Colonial Virginians at Play* (Charlottesville, Va., 1911), p. 51.
192. Barnard, *Call*, p. 28.
193. Phillips, *Children*, p. 22.
194. Samuel Moody, *Discourse to Little Children* (New London, 1769), p. 2.
195. Smith, *Duty*, pp. 11-12.
196. Moody, *Discourse*, p. 9.

CHAPTER 9

"That Enemy Is the Baby": Childhood in Imperial Russia

PATRICK P.
DUNN

"And in this present moment the younger generation particularly interests me, and, as akin to it, the question of Russian family life, which, to my thinking, is today quite a different thing from what it was twenty years ago."

Dostoevskii, 1876

Historians of Russia acknowledge the importance of childhood. Almost without fail biographers of "great men" devote a few pages to their subject's father, family, or "early influences." Synthesizers of broad periods of Russian history include sections on the education of the younger generation, the development of foundling homes, or the evolution of the family. It is inferred that a harsh father, a friendly teacher, a protective mother, or the lack thereof, influenced the behavior of a person in adulthood; it is inferred that a governmental policy or an alteration in the family structure made a difference. Yet one is hard pressed to find literature on Russian childhood, literature which would serve as a baseline to which the childhood of biographical subjects could be compared, or with which it would be possible to measure the influence of governmental actions or cultural movements. The following chapter is an effort both to delineate the major features of childhood in Russia in the eighteenth and nineteenth centuries and to specify how the childhood experiences of Russians influenced their behavior as adults. The inferences made admit to alteration either through the correction of factual errors or the addition of new facts. Even then, however, the process of clarifying the nature of childhood in Russia has begun, but just begun.

It is difficult to place clear chronological limits on this chapter. Initially the period 1760-1860 seemed a natural focus. In the 1760's Russians, under the influence of Western writings and appalled by the staggering rate of infant mortality, began examining the nature of childhood. The noted scientist, Michael Lomonosov, for example, estimated that one-half of the 500,000 infants born annually in Russia died before the age of three. In letters replying to inquiries from Ivan Shuvalov, one of the chief advisors of Catherine the Great, he suggested a series of actions the government might take in order to reduce the mortality rate by up to ninety percent. Included in his suggestions were the establishment of homes for orphaned and illegitimate children, the publication of a manual for midwives, and releasing nursing mothers and children from the severe fasts prescribed by the Orthodox Church. In 1761 Lomonosov published his ideas and suggestions in an essay *Concerning the Reproduction and Preservation of the Russian People.*[1] In the same decade Catherine's favorite, I. I. Betskoi, published books and pamphlets explaining in detail the ideas of Locke and Rousseau concerning the rearing of children. The 1760's, then, marked a clear beginning of the awareness of the importance of childrearing practices; yet to understand that awareness I have found it necessary to delve back into earlier periods of history to uncover the practices against which Lomonosov and Betskoi reacted.

On the other hand, the reforms of the 1860's, which were designed to drastically alter Russian society, seemed initially to mark another clear break. Yet the desired changes did not occur rapidly, in terms of childhood; for example, the traditional authority of the head of a peasant household was actually strengthened in the statutes of 1861 which were designed to emancipate the serfs.[2] And indeed childrearing practices such as swaddling persisted well into the twentieth century.[3] Thus, although I am concentrating on the period 1760-1860, the practices and attitudes I shall describe and analyze began well before the 1760's and ended well beyond the 1860's.

A second point I must make is that this essay is restricted in the most part to the "Great Russians," who, at the close of the nineteenth century, constituted perhaps forty-five percent of the 120 million people living in the Russian Empire.[4] It would be nearly impossible to describe the variations in childhood among the many peoples of the Empire, but the differences were significant. Full-immersion baptism, for example, was not practiced by the Ukrainians in the Empire.[5]

Childhood in Russia in the period from 1760 to 1860 was an ordeal, a precarious existence fraught with obstacles to both physical and psychological development. Perhaps fewer than half of the children born survived to adulthood. In the 1760's Lomonosov estimated that fully one-half of Russia's children died by the age of three. Of 4600 male children born in Moscow in 1832, 1300 died in their first year. In 1884 E. A. Pokrovskii estimated that one-third of Russian children did not live to celebrate their first birthday.[6] Few of those who did survive physically reached adulthood as commonly understood today—an autonomous, self-directing person.

Of course the high rate of infant mortality can be explained in part by such things as poor diet, climate, rudimentary medical care, the grip of tradition itself. But these factors are insufficient to account for the death rate; in Norway in the nineteenth century, for example, the infant mortality rate was one-third that of Russia, although the climate was more severe.[7] What is more important, in my opinion, is that parents in Russia considered children and childrearing unimportant; children had to be cared for, but underlying that care was parental neglect, even hostility toward the children. The convenience of the parents had priority over the well-being of the child. To develop this interpretation I will consider four aspects of the problem: the details of physical care, a description of parental attitudes toward children, an analysis of the underlying psychological theme of childhood in Russia, and an analysis of forces working to alter the nature of that childhood.

SURVIVING THE EARLY YEARS

Although the majority of Russian children were born amidst the moist, enveloping warmth of the steam bath, an infant might also have been born in a cattle shed, back pantry, or even outdoors. If born into an aristocratic family, the birth might have occurred in a special room, the family's private bathhouse. But for the peasants, the vast majority of Russians, the public bathhouse served as delivery room. The peasants even called the prayer said by the priest shortly after the birth the "bath prayer" (*bannaia molitva*). In villages without a bathhouse mothers gave birth in a variety of places: sheds, pantries, store rooms, even fields and woods. The primary criterion was that the place of birth afforded privacy, and even in areas where there were bathhouses expectant mothers might, for the sake of privacy, prefer a cattle shed or store room.[8]

The art of midwifery had received increasing attention in the eighteenth and nineteenth centuries. Lomonosov recommended formal training for midwives and the preparation of a manual compiled by consulting those experienced in birth practices.[9] In 1776, the first schools which taught obstetrics were founded. The following year the government issued instructions to the medical boards which were supposed to exist in the major towns of each province, saying that at least one of their staff should be trained in obstetrics.[10] By the early nineteenth century interested parents could purchase Maksimovich-Ambodik's *Physiology, or the Natural History of Man*[11] or the Russian translation (1790) of *Domestic Medicine* by the English physician, William Buchan; or one might consult a physician who studied at the Medical-Surgical Academy under S. F. Khotovitskii, Professor of Midwifery and the Diseases of Women and Children. While evidence is scanty, one might assume that portions of the literate and wealthy classes took advantage of these opportunities;[12] but late in the nineteenth century the peasant mothers still preferred the assistance of the *babka povitvkha*, an experienced old woman, over the trained, district *akusherka.*[13]

The midwife was usually summoned two to three hours before the birth. The mother walked about during her labor, but might sit on her husband's knees during severe contractions. When the birth appeared imminent the mother returned to the bath, a separate room, or the cattle shed. The desire for privacy or secrecy during childbirth was so strong that it was not uncommon for women to retire alone, even when the midwife was available. Although among the gentry and middle class the women gave birth lying on a bed on the floor, the peasantry seemed to favor a kneeling position, with support for the arms in the form of a rope tied across the room or a table.

Once the newborn arrived the midwife assumed primary responsibility. If the infant appeared to be weak, the midwife would administer the slap to the buttocks, and blow into the child's ears, mouth and nose. The midwife would almost immediately give the baby a bath, generally accomplished in the heat of the bathhouse. Immediately after the first bath the midwife swaddled the child. Russians swaddled their children with three separate cloths; soft linen was used if available, but more often cotton and other scraps were sewn together. The *izgolovnik* or head band was a three cornered cloth in which the head was tightly wrapped, and the two ends of the cloth were drawn down and crossed over the chest of the infant, then brought under the arms and secured behind the child's back. The headband was usually discarded after six months when they thought the child could hold up its own head. The pelvis was wrapped in another three-cornered cloth called a *podguznik;* placed under the child's buttocks, two corners were brought around the child's waist and then down into the inguinal fold. The third corner was brought up under the buttocks between the child's legs, to the naval. Finally the trunk was wrapped with arms at the side in a cloth called a *pelenka*. There were, of course, variations. In a few areas children reportedly were by custom not swaddled, but simply loosely wrapped in a large cloth. In other cases the *izgolovnik* was not used, and the child's head was simply wrapped with part of the *pelenka*. In theory the swaddling might be changed three or four times a day, usually coinciding with bathing or feeding, and the usual duration of swaddling was six to twelve months.[14]

Throughout the period both journalists and medical men criticized swaddling. In the 1760's Betskoi wrote that swaddling was beneficial only in the case of an injured limb and should be "rejected entirely" in the case of healthy children.[15] In 1783 the publicist Nikolai Novikov pleaded for the end of this practice; not only did swaddling deform the body of the child, but, wrote Novikov, "it even has an influence on the morals of the child, since his first impression of himself proceeds from the feeling of illness or suffering, which, joined to the feeling of obstruction of his movements, sows in him the seeds of anger."[16] The theme was continued by writers throughout the first half of the nineteenth century; but as late as 1884 Pokrovskii, conceding the persistence of the practice, found it necessary to warn that tight swaddling often caused welts, bruises, and ulcerations. Parents defended swaddling on several grounds: the unswaddled child might injure himself or herself, the swaddled child is less likely to be startled or to frighten itself by its own sudden movement. Yet Maksimovich-Ambodik seems to have summed up the opinion of most students of the subject when he wrote that "newborn children are swaddled more by reason of habit than by necessity," despite the fact that the habit was hazardous to the infant's health.[17]

Well into the late nineteenth century, the great majority of Russian infants were nursed at the breast. In the late 1870's, for example, a survey in St. Petersburg revealed that of 8,000 children visiting the Oldenburg Hospital for Children only one-third were bottle fed. Among the peasantry mothers nursed their own children, while the use of wet-nurses was prevalent among the nobility. From the first day, however, a pacifier made of food tied in a small bag was utilized. By the fifth week the child was expected to stomach pieces of bread and a gruel made from buckwheat or barley. A peasant infant born near harvest when the mother's labor in the fields was essential might be fed cow's milk and expected to tolerate solid foods almost immediately. Within twelve to sixteen months after birth it was customary to expect the child to eat the same food as the parents.[18]

The feeding of children, like swaddling, had long been an object of criticism by medical men and journalists. In the 1760's Lomonosov argued for the release of nursing mothers and children from the strict religious fasts required by Orthodoxy,[19] while Betskoi urged his readers to obtain a good wet-nurse and to avoid giving the child coarse food in his or her first year.[20] In the 1780's Maksimovich-Ambodik urged that the use of gruel be delayed until the sixth month,[21] while Novikov published detailed advice on nursing—including smearing the mother's or wet-nurse's breast with garlic to facilitate weaning.[22] In 1837 Mark Nechaev, a graduate of the Medical-Surgical Academy, published in St. Petersburg a work *Concerning the Ways of Averting the Deaths of Children in Their First Year of Life in the Customs of the Peasants.* He denounced the practice of feeding bread to newborns, the use of a nursing bottle unless the mother was ill, and the custom of putting coarse foods in the baby's pacifier because these were known to break, forcing the child to swallow the contents. In 1874 Katherine Blanch Guthrie was told that among the peasants "the average number of children in a family being seventeen, of whom one-half perish in infancy—some from cold, others from the use of the *saska,* a milk poultice, tied up in a long bag, at which the infants, left alone for hours, suck away, "often so effectually that they draw the saska down into the throat, and are suffocated."[23] As late as 1888 the Petersburg Society of Children's Doctors cited the "striking" lack of knowledge concerning the dietary and health needs of children as a major cause of infant deaths in both the city and countryside.[24] In the same year, Pokrovskii, explaining statistics indicating that infant mortality was greater in the last nine months of the first year than in the first three, argued that the practice of replacing mother's milk with coarse solids was a major factor in infant mortality.[25] This after over a hundred years of effort by doctors and publicists!

In addition to the dangers of the birth process, swaddling, and feeding, not to mention disease and other outside factors, a Russian infant might be subjected by his parents to extreme heat or cold either as part of traditional "hardening" practices or in order to conform to old rituals. A mid-eighteenth century traveler wrote that:

> The *Muscovites* too are inur'd to hardships even from the womb. They use their children to endure the extremities of heat and cold, hunger, thirst, and labour. They wash their new-born infants in cold water, and roll them upon ice, and amongst snow, which if they out-live not, their mothers think them not worth a tear.[26]

In his 1761 work on childhood Lomonosov protested the custom of baptizing children in winter in unheated churches, immersing the newborn the required three times in water in its "natural" state. This ritual Lomonosov related to the custom of cold-water baths in winter and he called priests who continued the customs "executioners." But Robert Pinkerton, reporting on the practice in the early nineteenth century, said that "such are the superstitious opinions of the people, that were the chill taken off the water, they would probably doubt the validity of the ordinance."[27] By the mid-nineteenth century cold-water baptisms were uncommon; yet in January, 1883, Pokrovskii had occasion to witness such a christening, and its fatal results.

> ... in an old fashioned family a fully healthy child was born of wealthy, young, and completely healthy parents. Shortly after birth he was given over to a healthy wet-nurse, at whose breasts he passed his first days peacefully. Within a few days it was decided that the child should be baptized according to the old-fashioned rituals—hence it was done in the manner: outside the temperature was near $-10°F.$, never-the-less at the directions of the old-fashioned priest the large stone hall of the parent's house in which the baptism would occur was not heated for twenty-four hours since, in the opinion of the priest, only in this manner would it be possible to recreate the atmosphere of an old church for the baptism of the child. At the date determined for the baptism water was taken directly from the well and not warmed in any manner. When the infant, lightly swaddled, was carried into the hall, he, according to the wet-nurse, quickly began to feel chilly, to shiver, and become restless. The baptismal ceremony according to the old ritual was very long—more than an hour according to the wet-nurse. When the priest, with his cold hands, began to unwrap the infant, the child cried out furiously and did not cease screaming with his whole strength except for short spells of breathing after complete immersion in the water. Each immersion, according to old traditions, was completed slowly, with attention to the full respect due the holy ceremony. When the child was placed in the swaddling clothes upon completion of the baptismal ceremony the child fell into an unconscious state, would not take the breast of his wet-nurse, and by the following morning had developed convulsions and fever. The next day the spasms and fever continued ...

Three days after the baptism Pokrovskii was called, but the child died the following day.[28]

Another traditional practice, especially among the peasants of Northern and Central Russia, was that of subjecting the newborn to the heat and rigors of the steam bath. Birch twigs softened by steam were used to gently beat the body in order to open the pores to the cleansing steam. The temperature of the baths reached $120°$ or $130°F.$ (or higher) as pails of water were thrown onto heated stones to produce the billowing steam. Pokrovskii warned that subjecting infants to such intense heat could result in severe rashes and even death; yet observers well into the nineteenth century reported the presence of birch leaves on the body of infants being christened.[29]

The first years of life for a child admitted to state foundling homes were more precarious than those years of children cared for by their families. Tooke was told that in the period 1766-1786 some 37,600 children were admitted to the foundling home in Moscow; of that number 1,000 were eventually sent out and some 6,100 were still housed there in 1786. This meant that some 30,000 children were lost! Of course Tooke rightly qualifies this staggering estimate by noting that it is impossible to determine how many of these deaths occurred as the result of a pre-admittance disease or defect. Still, one hundred years later a visitor accidentally entered a room at the foundling home in Moscow and there encountered a "strange sight": "At the end was a stack, composed of the naked bodies of a couple of hundred babies packed like sardines biding their time for internment in spring." One can only guess what went on in the state-run homes for infants.[30]

There is little detailed information on the physical aspects of the later stages of childhood. Encouraged by parents, older children, and a variety of devices ranging from benches with holes cut in them to wooden, wheeled walkers, Russian children were usually walking by the age of eleven to thirteen months, perhaps as early as nine or ten.[31] By then the children had left their cribs, which were constructed in a variety of styles, most being suspended from tensile board or poles which could be bent to rock the cradle; John Quincy Adams, observing Russian cradles in 1810, wrote that the Russian cradle "is a very clumsy contrivance, and the child must be always in danger of falling to the floor, an accident which four times in five must prove fatal."[32] By the end of the first year the child also was out of swaddling clothes; although among the nobility there may have been some variation, Russian children generally were dressed in loose shirts and perhaps pantaloons. Pokrovskii, however, did note that "a few stupid nurses" did dress children in narrow trousers that rubbed against the genitals, and that this was done deliberately with the intention of "affording pleasure to the children or stimulating good dreams for them."[33] Beyond these few generalizations, however, little can be said about physical care of children, especially concerning such critical topics as toilet-training and parental handling of childhood sexuality. The manuals did not consider these topics, and memoir and letter traces are rare.[34]

PARENTAL ATTITUDES TOWARD CHILDREN

"Between parents and children there reigned a spirit of slavery..."
                                                        Kostomarov

At least until 1890 Russia was predominately a "traditional" society, and although this is not the place for a long description of what "traditional" means an understanding of some features of the social context might be conducive to understanding adult-child relationships. In the first place, traditional Russia was based on an agriculture which, mired in centuries-old routines and lacking the modern application of science, yielded a constant or declining return per acre. Additional population, therefore, did not mean increased production, but it did mean that there were additional mouths to be fed from the same fixed or declining amount of food. Furthermore, lacking knowledge of an effective means of birth control, Russian parents had little if any control over the arrival of new mouths to feed. Also, in traditional Russia the emphasis was not on the individual and the position one achieved, but on the family and position ascribed to one by virtue of his or her birth into that family. The good of the family superceded that of any of its members. Finally, the authority structure of traditional Russia was patriarchal. According to Wilson R. Augustine:

> For a Russian nobleman, 'good authority' (on the throne and elsewhere) was a duplication of the 'good father'—stern, loving, extending his patriarchal power over a numerous family. In such a system a man's worth and standing were not judged by his success or failure in living up to abstract rules of behaviour (as in the Western model), but by the internal test of his family relationships with his superiors. Finally, it should be noted that the native model applied not just to politics, but to all social relations. Just as the nobility were subjects of the monarch, they were masters over their serfs, and the nature of authority in each case was the same. Whatever individual lords might in fact do to their peasants, the social ideal of a landlord was that of a stern and wise father of his people, exercising his unlimited authority for their benefit.[35]

Within peasant families, the eldest male held similar authority over members of the household.[36]

Russian parents in general in the eighteenth and nineteenth centuries can be described as detached rather than involved with their children, hostile rather than warm in interaction with them, and restrictive rather than permissive in handling the spontaneous behavior of the child. Life for the child was dominated by a detached, hostile, sometimes violent father who determined the course of his child's life, and by the lack of a warm relationship with mother.

The detachment of Russian parents is reflected in the details of infant care. The use of wet-nurses and later of older children, old women, and, in the case of the nobility, serfs, as supervisors and playmates for children limited maternal involvement with the child. Because of this pattern of physical care, according to Ruth Benedict, "there is consequently a much more diffuse relationship during the first year of life than in societies where the child's contact is more limited to that with

its own mother."[37] The grueling labor of peasant mothers both in the
field and home was not conducive to parent-child interaction; but even
among educated and noble Russians maternal involvement was minimal.
The supervision of serf nursemaids, tutors, and servants was part of the
home life of the pre-school nobleman in the eighteenth century.[38] Indeed, in the 1780's when the mother of Sergei Aksakov personally put
her infant daughter to the breast of the nurse and personally rocked her
child to sleep a relative warned that "such exaggerated love was a crime
against God, and he would surely punish it." That the infant subsequently died could only reinforce the prediction, and the mother did
not personally care for the children she bore after that.[39] In 1833 the
young Nikolai Gogol wrote his mother pleading with her to change the
way she raised her children and asking especially that she keep the children in her personal company.[40] Sonia Kovalevsky, born in 1850, recalled how she and her brother and sister slept, breakfasted, and dined
in their quarters with their nurse; the most frequent occasion on which
they were with their mother was when some guest wished to see the
children.[41] In 1850 Aksakov wrote that "the first objects still preserved
in the faded picture of the distant past . . . are my wet nurse, my little
sister, and my mother."[42] The order is significant; Russian children developed deep bonds of affection with their nurses and with the other
children in the household, while mothers remained in the background.[43]
Fathers also were detached from their children. The *Domostroi*, a traditional guide to household management compiled by churchmen in the
sixteenth century, counseled fathers that in interaction with their sons,
"do not smile at him, do not play with him, for having been weak in
little things, you will suffer in great ones, ..."[44] The eighteenth-
century nobility "continued to live by the traditional precepts of the
Domostroi,"[45] and Vladimir Polunin recalled that in Kursk in the
1840's "the rules laid down in the *Domostroi* were regarded in those
days as containing the essence of married happiness, and any departure
from them led to family strife—a grievous sin."[46] In 1849 Gogol recommended this traditional guide as one book which could "acquaint one
with what is best in the Russian man."[47] Novikov, writing in 1783,
pleaded with fathers to try to spend at least one hour a day in the company of their children.[48] But Kovalevsky recalls that in her nineteenth-
century childhood, "our father's relations to us were confined to his
asking nurse, when he happened to meet us, whether we were well . . .
and sometimes taking us in his hands and tossing us up in the air."[49]
The great Count Witte summed up the theme of parental detachment
when he recalled that "speaking of my early upbringing I must say that
while my parents hired for us boys, governesses, and tutors without
stinting money, they failed to give us enough of their personal attention."[50]

The second characteristic of Russian parents in the eighteenth and nineteenth centuries is that they tended to be hostile toward their children, to use power-assertive discipline rather than warmth, understanding, and love-oriented disciplinary techniques. Again this characteristic is reflected in the details of physical care; sociological studies have linked parental disinclination to personally care for their children to parental hostility toward their offspring.[51] Russian parents tended to use physical punishment to correct and direct their children. This, too, was consistent with the *Domostroi* which counseled fathers to:

> Punish your son in his early years and he will comfort you in your old age and be the ornament of your soul. Do not spare your child any beating, for the stick will not kill him, but will do him good; when you strike the body, you save the soul from death.... If you love your son, punish him often so that he may later gladden your spirit. Punish your son in his youth, and when he is a man he will be your comfort and you will be praised among the wicked, and your enemies will envy you. Raise your child in fear and you will find peace and blessing in him.[52]

Novikov warned fathers in 1783 that if they relied on "harsh words, strict rules, severe punishments, commands, morose behavior, and angry deeds" to control their children, the children might fear their parents, but would have contempt rather than respect for them.[53] Alexander Herzen's memories of his childhood in the first quarter of the nineteenth century vindicate Novikov:

> Mockery, irony, cold, caustic, utter contempt, were the tools which he [his father] wielded like an artist; he employed them equally against us and against the servants.... until I went to prison I was actually estranged from my father, and joined with the maids and man-servants in waging a little war against him.[54]

Baron Wrangel, raised in the mid-nineteenth century, believed that the harsh discipline, including whippings, used by his father was but a reflection of a society where "harshness had become a moral principle. To shew benevolence was to be weak, to be cruel was to be strong."[55] Power-assertive discipline, like the disinclination to care for one's own children, correlates highly with parental hostility toward their offspring.[56]

The incidence of child murder is also an indicator of adult hostility toward children. Tolstoi's play, *The Power of Darkness*, which revolved around the grisly murder of a new-born child was based on the 1880 trial of a peasant for having committed such a crime. In *The Diary of a Writer* Dostoevskii recorded the details gleaned from newspaper accounts concerning the trial of a father for "too cruelly" flogging his seven-year-old daughter, and the conviction of a stepmother who threw her six-year-old stepdaughter out of a fourth-story window.[57] Most revealing, however, is Anton Chekhov's short story, "Sleepy," which centers upon a thirteen-year-old girl hired to care for a baby. Wracked by memories of her own painful childhood, she seeks escape in sleep. But the baby's crying, at times, keeps her awake; and when the baby is quiet, and she does doze off, the master or mistress invariably wake her with angry words or blows. Then she concludes that the enemy interfering with her life is not her master, or the society, or her memories, but "that enemy is the baby."

> Laughing, winking at the green patch, and shaking her fingers at it, Varka steals up to the cradle and bends over the baby. Having strangled it, she quickly lies down on the floor, laughing with joy now that she can sleep, and a minute later is already sleeping as soundly as if she were dead. . . ."[58]

Although these may be fictionalized or spectacular incidents, they were by no means rare. Statistics on child murder in Russia are scattered and questions can be raised concerning the thoroughness of the data; still they do give us a general indication of the phenomenon. One study by a physician in Poltavskaia province recorded 343 instances of child murder in the province in the period 1855-64. There were 28,000 births in the same period, or about one out of every eighty children was murdered; this accounted for a quarter of all the violent deaths in the province. Pokrovskii noted that the Medical Department recorded about 400 child murders annually in Russia in the 1870's.[59] But these figures represent only cases that had been processed through the courts, and it is unclear to what percentage of the population the statistics apply. The law reforms of 1864, which established the Russian court system, were only gradually extended throughout European Russia. If the data was collected in all of European Russia, but only there, then the rate of child murder was about one per every 200,000 people. It is also interesting to note that two of the greatest Tsars in Russian history, Ivan the Awesome and Peter the Great, both murdered their eldest son.

The third characteristic of Russian parents is that they were restrictive in dealing with the spontaneous behavior of their children, seeming not to understand that the child might have problems and feelings that were more important than adult rules. It is true that children of noblemen were often said to have been raised in a permissive atmosphere while under the care of tutors and servants. One eighteenth-century nobleman wrote, for example, that

> [serf-nurses] accustom the child to believe that his will must be executed without question; he gets used to this, and when he grows up this passion increases and the consequence is that the child entrusted to their care often becomes a slave to his passions, for without the approval of the nurse he could not have let passions manifest themselves so easily and with such success.[60]

In 1833 Gogol complained of the "wildness children who stay in the maids' room get,"[61] while Herzen recalled of his childhood a generation earlier:

> The servants' hall and the maids' room provided the only keen enjoyment left me. There I had complete liberty; I took the side of one party against another, discussed their business with my friends, and gave my opinion upon them, knew all their intimate affairs, and never dropped a word in the drawing-room about the secrets of the servants' hall.[62]

Yet in interaction with parents strict enforcement of discipline was the general rule. For the children of the nobility the eighteenth-century pattern of "almost anarchial freedom and shorter periods of very strict discipline and control" continued well into the nineteenth century.[63] Further, a recurrent theme in nineteenth-century memoir material is that parents, especially fathers, conceived of children as objects to be nourished and directed, but not understood. In 1783 Novikov decried the fact that "parents generally imagine the physical upbringing of children requires nothing more than feeding their children well", it is ironic that one hundred years later, as noted above, Pokrovskii believed feeding practices to be a major cause of infant mortality.[64] Kovalevsky was convinced that her father did not even suspect "what a complicated inner world" his daughter had developed and hence he never understood her behavior; when told of her "misconduct" he responded by telling her "what a horrid little girl" she was.[65] Wrangel concluded from his childhood experiences that children were believed to scarcely possess a soul, and therefore his father "could feel pity only for physical ills and probably did not even suspect the existence of other suffering."[66] Herzen described his childhood as "oppressive," with innumerable restrictions imposed for his physical and moral health; he preferred the company of serf-servants because they treated him like a person.[67] It is consistent with parents' inability to understand that their offspring had personal feelings and needs that, when noble children matured, their parents generally chose their career and their spouse; this was also true among the peasantry—unless the owner intervened.

THE BATTLE FOR AUTONOMY

So far I have sketched the details of the early physical care of children and have attempted to describe parental attitudes. In analyzing the nature of Russian childhood I am persuaded by historian David Hunt's argument that the second psychosocial stage of Erik Erikson's model is of most value to historians.[68] Focused in this stage is the child's need to delineate his own sense of autonomy as he or she develops motor control, verbalization, and the power to discriminate among objects. The question of parental control is crucial; children must learn to regulate their own actions if they are to develop a sense of pride and autonomy. Too much parental control will leave the child with a lasting sense of doubt in self; but the parent must protect the child from overestimating his or her yet untrained powers, lest the child fail repeatedly and be left with a lasting sense of shame. In modern societies it may be that toilet training is the central event in this stage; but Russians were indifferent to bowel training.[69] The "battle for autonomy," as Erikson calls it, took place rather in the broad context of all childhood actions.

Russian childhood can be analyzed in terms of the parents' efforts to block their children's delineation of autonomy. Traditional child-rearing practices limited the intrusion of children into the lives of adults; but since they must sometimes intrude, their behavior must be strictly controlled and their autonomy repressed. Personal autonomy was not traditionally valued in Russian society, and it was in the family that the personal autonomy of future citizens was repressed. To break the autonomy of a son the fifteenth-century *Domostroi* counseled a father: "Do not give him his will in his youth, but crush his ribs while he is not yet grown, or else he will harden and cease to obey you, and then there will be grief and vexation for your soul. . . ."[70] This attitude was reinforced by such folk sayings as "If God gives you sons, don't be lazy, teach them and beat them," and "if he did not obey his father, he will obey the whip."[71] The historian Kostomarov wrote that in the seventeenth century "between parents and children reigned a spirit of slavery, covered by the cloak of holy, patriarchal relations. . . . the obedience of children was more that of a slave than a child, and parental power turned into blind despotism, lacking any moral force."[72]

Additional power over their sons was one of the requests made by the aristocracy at the Great Commission of Nobility convened by Catherine II in 1767. An analysis of one set of requests calling for freedom of bequest reveals that "apparently no thought of economic improvement is present, only the desire to empower fathers to reward obedience and gratitude and to punish unworthy sons."[73] The decree of 1775 ordering the establishment of poor houses in each province included among possible residents of such houses "individuals of both sexes who are useless or shiftless, such as sons and daughters who disobeyed their parents or led base lives. . . ."[74] Among the peasantry parental authority seemed to be nearly without limits. Several travelers noted how peasant fathers, for example, married their son to some girl in the village, then sent the new husband to work in the city or fields, leaving the dauther-in-law to the whims of her father-in-law:

> Fathers marry their sons to some blooming girl in the village at a very early age, and then send the young men either to Mosco or St. Petersburg to seek employment, leaving their brides of a few days after their marriage to the care of their parents. At the expiration of some years, when the son returns to his cottage, he finds himself the nominal father of several children, the offspring of his own parent who had deemed it his duty thus to supply the place of a husband to the young wife. This is done all over Russia, and is never considered a hardship by the parties. . . .[75]

A nineteenth-century traveler, Leroy-Beaulieu, observed an older peasant showering abuse and blows upon a younger man; when efforts were made to separate the two, the younger peasant objected, saying "leave us; he is my father."[76] One nineteenth-century legal authority noted that "the duty of submission to one's parents is ended only by the death of the latter. . . . Thus, the acceptance of domestic correction (such as whippings with rods) would apply to grown-up children, even to married ones."[77] A folk saying, however, summed it up more eloquently: "When the earth receives the parents, the children receive their freedom."[78] Both governmental action and custom, therefore, reinforced parental, especially paternal, authority among both peasants and nobles.

Many noble children realized that in terms of personal autonomy they were as subject to their parents' will as the serfs; and they sympathized with and acted like the serfs. In the home of the future novelist Turgenev the children conspired with the serfs to thwart the order of the mistress of the house that the children of her maid be sent to an orphanage.[79] Herzen waged "a little war" with the serf-servants against his own father.[80] The young Wrangel and his sister pledged that when they grew up "all our serfs will be emancipated, and we shall never treat them, or our children, unjustly."[81]

The blocking of autonomy in childhood, however, was functional in a traditional society where the image of a good authority was the Tsar, a stern, awesome "little father" extending his patriarchal authority over his family of subjects, a society that tended to discourage individual initiative and ignore personal rights. And in many cases the child's resentment of his father and sympathy for the serfs were translated on an adult level into anti-government activity.[82]

But to say, as Hunt does,[83] that fathers blocked the autonomy of their sons because society restricted adult autonomy explains little. The question as to why society developed in this manner remains. I suggest that the explanation may be found in the defense mechanisms the ego might employ in the conflict between the impulse for autonomy and crushing parental overcontrol. Might, for example, the exaggerated acquiescence shown by sons to fathers, serfs to masters, and nobles to the

"little father," be a reaction formation in the service of the ego's repression of the impulse for autonomy? On the other hand, might the
"blind despotism," to use Kostomarov's term, exercised by parents over
children and by nobles over serfs be the heightened and direct expression of the original impulse for autonomy exercised in restricted areas
of activity? Such an interpretation might help define society as an out-
growth of childhood, not the reverse. For purposes of this chapter,
however, the main point is that the child's delineation of autonomy was
blocked and that the social and political environment was consistent
with such blockage.

CHANGING PATTERNS OF RUSSIAN CHILDHOOD

> If I took better care of you than many do, I simply followed the
> dictates of my heart.
>
> Radishchev

In the eighteenth and nineteenth centuries significant changes were
occurring within the traditional pattern of Russian childhood. The attempt of nobles attending Catherine's assembly to obtain the right to
freely determine in their wills how their estates would be divided, a right
they wished to use to control their sons, indicated some problem in the
exercise of traditional paternal authority. In his memoirs Polunin saw
parental despotism as the cornerstone of family life in the home of his
grandfather, a mid-nineteenth-century merchant, yet thirty years later
his own father was a gentle and affectionate man who tolerated his son's
right to disagree with him.[84] In his explosive volume, *A Journey from
Petersburg to Moscow* (1790), Alexander Radishchev depicted several
scenes consistent with the traditional customs of childrearing. In describing the sale of a group of serfs, for example, he wrote:

> The forty-year-old woman is a widow, the young master's wet-
> nurse. To this very day she feels a certain tenderness for him. Her
> blood flows in his veins. She is his second mother, and he owes
> his life more to her than to his natural mother. The latter con-
> ceived him in lust and did not take care of him in his childhood.
> His nurse really brought him up.[85]

But in another section of the book Radishchev provided a literary portrait of an untraditional father bidding farewell to his two grown sons
who were entering state service. The old nobleman explains to his sons
that they were not raised by nurses and tutors, but grew up under the
eyes of their father, eyes described by the author as those "of kindly
reasonableness." Then the nobleman tells his sons:

> From your childhood on you have never experienced any compulsion. I did not want timidity or abject obedience to make you feel so much as the weight of its finger. . . . If in your childhood I found that, diverted by some accidental force, you departed from the path I had prepared for you, I stopped you, or, better, imperceptibly led you back into the old path, even as a stream that breaks through its dikes is turned back by a skillful hand.[86]

The analogy itself connotes not blockage, but the free flow of development under skillful guidance but within broadly defined limits.

The question remains: how could a person whose autonomy was blocked in childhood by traditional practices grow up either to challenge the authority of the father (as apparently the sons of noblemen were doing in the 1760's), or become a parent who tolerated his children's delineation of autonomy? The adult who in his or her lifetime had little experience of autonomy could hardly be expected to tolerate children's efforts to act autonomously. Further, such a child challenged the parent in the family, the one area in which any parent might be free to exercise authority. The basic need of the child for his or her autonomy was a threat to what little autonomy adults possessed, and it had to be repressed. When the child became parent, he or she experienced the same restricted sense of autonomy, and the same threat to it posed by children. So the cycle went on and on. It appears to me that the key to change in the parent-child relationship had to be some force external to the family that allowed the individual, be it parent or child, to begin to delineate autonomy outside the family.

In the traditional Russian family, as well as in the society itself, where the dominant values included obedience and the suppression of individual autonomy, individual egos had little choice but to repress and defend against the drive for autonomy. Yet repressed drives can surface if social conditions allow their expression. This, I suggest, is what happened in the eighteenth and nineteenth centuries to individual Russians who were, either as a result of change or a governmental action, thrust into new situations. They were then able to experience the autonomy blocked in childhood. Yet if, due to some sudden change in cultural conditions, a father could first feel his own autonomy, then one would expect that he might more easily tolerate his children's own autonomy One would then expect severe conflicts with his or her parents, as well as with traditional social values.

The influence of chance events can be seen in the families of Vladimir Polunin and the noted literary critic Nikolai Chernyshevskii. Polunin's grandfather, Akim, a prosperous fish wholesaler in Kursk in the mid-nineteenth century, kept tight reins on his household, even following the *Domostroi*. He trained his son Yasha in the family business and even chose whom his son was to marry (for business advantage, of course). But when the fish supplier died, disaster struck the family business. Akim's creditors refused to pay their bills, claiming that by doing so they would only be sending money to the heirs of the dead man, heirs who would surely waste the money. Yet Akim felt morally bound to settle his accounts with the estate of the deceased, which drove the family into bankruptcy. Yasha was forced to become a tea merchant, eventually moving to Moscow to take an administrative post in the tea firm of the Perlov Brothers.[87] Chernyshevskii's father, Gavriil, was the son of a village Deacon and, as was traditional, was sent to the local seminary to be trained for the same career as his father. "Then in 1818 an unusual circumstance brought about a sudden change in his career."[88] A priest attached to one of the best situated churches in Saratov died, leaving a fifteen-year-old daughter. The Bishop of Penza decided to send young Gavriil to Saratov to both marry the girl and assume clerical duties. In these two cases, then, a chance event removed the son from the traditional pattern of his family and forced him into a situation in which he was on his own and for which his traditional up-bringing was inappropriate. The new situation allowed, if not forced, each to develop behavior patterns other than those developed under parental direction; in short, Polunin and Chernyshevskii could develop the autonomy blocked in childhood by their upbringing. And both be-came untraditional fathers; Polunin was a kind, affectionate man who tolerated his son's disagreements with him, and Chernyshevskii has been described as a "wisely permissive guide for his son's self-education," a man who instilled values in young Nikolai by example rather than physical punishment.[89]

The actions of the Tsarist government represented another force for change in parent-child relationships. Most significant, of course, was the removal for education of noble children from the influence and en-vironment of the family. Peter I (1689-1725) had decreed compulsory education for all sons of noblemen to begin at age ten, but had to rescind the order in 1716. In 1722 state service was made compulsory for all sons of nobles, and gradually, as education became the key to a good career in state service, leaving home around the age of ten or twelve to attend school and enter state service became the common pattern among the nobility. Like Peter I, Catherine II (1762-1796) recognized that the family was the source of the traditions that held back Russia's development as an "enlightened" state, and part of her motivation in developing and expanding the school system was the de-sire to create "a new breed of men" through educational institutions. Catherine had planned to remove children from the family as early as five years of age,[90] but never carried through her intention. The effect on the parent-child relationship of separation from the family for pur-poses of education is hard to assess. The extent to which the young

Russian was able to delineate his autonomy in school would depend upon the attitudes of his superiors and his own ability and experiences. Peter Kropotkin might be cited as the model of what school might mean. In 1862, at the age of twenty, Kropotkin finished his five years in the Corps of Pages in which his father had enrolled him and chose to take his military service in Siberia. His father forbade it; but the Grand Duke Michael intervened and Kropotkin got his wish.[91] Here, then, is an example of how school and service might combine to break a nobleman's authority over the future of his son and allow that son to make decisions affecting and directing his own life.

The life of Grigorii Belinskii, father of the noted critic Vissarion, offers a clear example of the effect state service could have on an individual. Grigorii Belinskii was born in 1784, the son of a poor village priest. Following the tradition that sons inherited the vocation of their father, in 1798 Grigorii Belinskii was enrolled in the seminary at Tambov. In that same year Tsar Paul, facing an increasing need for military doctors, issued a decree encouraging seminarians with a good knowledge of Latin to enroll in the newly-opened Medical-Surgical Academy in Petersburg. If accepted into the Academy the new student would be exempted from all clerical obligations and would receive a stipend in return for a period of military service following graduation. In 1804 the name of Grigorii Belinskii was added to the Academy's roster. This was the decisive break with tradition; the social demands of the war had created an opportunity for a conflict-free choice that broke traditional patterns of life. Left behind was not only the traditional career of the Belinskii family, but also the paternal authority which traditionally dominated the life of a young Russian. Little is known of Grigorii Belinskii's medical training or his subsequent military career; but what is known points clearly to an ever-widening exercise of personal autonomy. He, for example, married in Petersburg the girl of his choice and in battle won medals for personal valor. When reassigned to medical duties in the provincial city of Chembar, he soon became isolated and bitter. As a father, however, Grigorii Belinskii was highly interactive with his son, educating him at home and allowing him to choose his own career while at the university in Moscow.

In short, then, it appears that the keys to changes in parent-child relationships in Russia in the eighteenth and nineteenth-century Russian family were the chance events and governmental actions which put individuals into situations that allowed them, to some extent, to delineate their own personal autonomy outside the family. Given the opportunity, individuals who did develop some sense of autonomy were often alienated from and in conflict with their society and its values. Perhaps this was behind the effort of Catherine's nobles to obtain additional controls over their heirs; perhaps these sons, experiencing the pattern of school and service, no longer accepted the absolute authority of their fathers. The conflict with traditional values is clearer in the case of Kropotkin, who became an anarchist, and both Grigorii Belinskii and Gavriil Chernyshevskii who soon became alienated from the society in which they lived.[92] Further, as fathers, Belinskii and Chernyshevskii, having experienced their own autonomy, interacted warmly with their sons and encouraged their autonomy. Finally both sons, Vissarion Belinskii and Nikolai Chernyshevskii, like their fathers, were alienated from and in conflict with the traditional values of the Russian autocracy.

Changes in the nature of childhood had, I suggest, deep implications for Russian society. Beginning in the eighteenth and extending into the nineteenth century the Russian *intelligentsia* dominated culture and spawned revolutionary movements. This *intelligentsia* can be defined as a group of educated individuals who stressed personal values over traditional values. When one begins to carefully examine the early lives of members of the *intelligentsia,* the dominant pattern is one of an untraditional childhood. Conflicts between parent and child existed, as they must, but more striking is the warm interaction of parent and child, the concern shown and support given to the child by the adult. In the case of men that adult was most often their father; we have seen this in the case of Chernyshevskii and Belinskii, but it even holds true for the anarchist Michael Bakunin whose father "lavished on his children a wise and far-seeing affection, and was, on the testimony of his eldest son, unalterably indulgent and kind."[93] Among women the mother usually took the role of the warm adult. In a recent paper dealing with Vera Figner, Sof'ya Perovskaia, and other women prominent in the revolutionary movements of the 1870's, Barbara Engel has noted that "when we seek a generational conflict between these daughters and their mothers . . . we find that, by and large, it did not exist." Rather, what is striking is "the degree of support, either overt or tacit, which these and other women received from their mothers."[94]

The origins, then, of at least one large segment of the *intelligentsia* seem to lie in changes in the nature of childhood. Raised in an untraditional manner with warm adult support and encouragement, and having delineated their autonomy in childhood, these young men and women found traditional Russian society and its values intolerable. And they sought to change that society either through cultural change—or revolution. Thus it was that Lenin's father "taught his children the art of the game of chess and constantly played with his sons."[95]

REFERENCES

1. *O razmnozhenii i sokhranenii rossiiskogo naroda.* On Lomonosov's pediatric interests see E. M. Konius, *Istoki russkoi pediatrii* (Moscow, 1946), pp. 73-76, and V. S. Vail', *Ocherki po istorii russkoi pediatrii vtoroi poloviny XIX veka* (Stalinbad, 1959), pp. 3-5.

2. William T. Shinn, Jr., "The Law of the Russian Peasant Household," *Slavic Review,* XX, 4(1961), p. 605.

3. Geoffrey Gorer and John Rickman, *The People of Great Russia* (New York, 1962), p. 98.

4. Richard Pipes, *The Formation of the Soviet Union. Communism and Nationalism, 1917-23* (rev. ed.; New York, 1968), p. 2.

5. Aleksandr V. Tereshchenko, *Byt russkago naroda* (7 vols. in 2; St. Petersburg, 1848), III, 46.

6. The study is reported in Vail', *Ocherki,* p. 67. [E. A. Pokrovskii, *Pervonachal'noe fizicheskoi vospitanie detei* (Moscow, 1888), p. 3.]

7. *Ibid.* In his earlier work, *Fizicheskoe vospitanie detei u raznykh narodov preimyshchestvenno Rossii* (Moscow, 1884), p. 272, Pokrovskii gives, for purposes of comparison, the rate of infant mortality in several European countries including: Norway–10.4 deaths per hundred births, Denmark–14.4, England–15.4, France–17.3, and Russia–32.6.

8. *Ibid.,* pp. 41-48.

9. Konius, *Istoki,* p. 73.

10. Gavriil P. Uspenskii, *Opyt' povestvovaniia o drevnostiiakh ruskikh* (2 vols. in 1; Kharkov, 1818), I, 129.

11. Nestor Maksimovich-Ambodik, *Fiziologiia, ili estestvennaia istoriia o cheloveke* (St. Petersburg, 1787).

12. On the use of Buchan, for example, see Sergei Aksakov, *Years of Childhood,* trans. by Alec Brown (New York, 1960), p. 10.

13. Pokrovskii, *Fizicheskoe vospitanie,* p. 41.

14. Last two paragraphs based on *ibid.,* pp. 42-48, 135-36. See also Robert Pinkerton, *Russia, or Miscellaneous Observations,* (London, 1833), pp. 153-56.

15. Konius, *Istoki,* p. 97.

16. Nikolai I. Novikov, "O vospitanii i nastavlenii detei," *Izbrannye pedagogicheskie sochineniia,* ed. by M. F. Shabaeva (Moscow, 1959), p. 111.

17. Maksimovich-Ambodnik, *Fiziologiia,* p. xx.

18. Pokrovskii, *Fizicheskoe vospitanie,* p. 41.

19. Konius, *Istoki,* pp. 73-74.

20. *Ibid.,* pp. 97-98.

21. Maksimovich-Ambodik, *Fiziologiia,* p. xxiv.

22. Novikov, "O vospitanii," p. 114.

23. "O sposobakh otvrashchat' smertnost' mladentsev na pervom godu zhizni v bytu krest'ianskom," in Vail', *Istoki,* p. 238; Guthrie, *Through Russia* (2 vols. in one; New York, 1970), I, 259-60.

24. "Otvet peterburgskogo obshchestva detskikh vrachei na zapros S. P. Botkina o prichinakh vysokoi detskoi smertnosti," in E. M. Konius, "Ocherki po istorii russkoi pediatrii," *Puti razvitiia sovetskoi okhrany materinstva i mladenchestva* (Moscow, 1954), p. 18.

25. Pokrovskii, *Fizicheskoe vospitanie,* pp. 271-72.

26. Anon.: *The Common Errors in the Education of Children and their Consequences* (London, 1744), p. 10.

27. Vail', *Ocherki,* p. 4; Konius, *Istoki,* pp. 73-74 (there is also a painting depicting a cold-water bath on p. 29); Pinkerton, p. 153.

28. Pokrovskii, *Fizicheskoe vospitanie*, p. 100.
29. *Ibid.*, pp. 77-78.
30. Guthrie, p. 57.
31. Pokrovskii, *Fizicheskoe vospitanie*, p. 244.
32. From his memoirs, in *Russia Under Western Eyes*, ed. by Anthony Cross (New York, 1971), p. 290
33. Pokrovskii, *Pervonachal'noe fizicheskoe vospitanie*, p. 255.
34. Some data on customs as they persisted into the twentieth century is available. in Gorer, *Great Russia*, pp. 106-07, 142.
35. Wilson R. Augustine, "Notes Toward a Portrait of the Eighteenth Century Russian Nobility," *Canadian Slavic Studies*, IV (Fall, 1970), 384,
36. Shinn, "Russian Peasant," pp. 601-05; Dinko Tomasic, *The Impact of Russian Culture on Soviet Communism* (Glencoe, 1953), pp. 82-85.
37. "Child Rearing in Certain European Countries," *American Journal of Orthopsychiatry*, XIX(1949), 345.
38. Marc Raeff, "Home, School, and Service in the Life of the Eighteenth-Century Russian Nobleman," *The Structure of Russian History*, ed. by Michael Cherniavsky (New York, 1970), p. 215.
39. Sergei T. Aksakov, *Chronicles of a Russian Family*, trans. by M. C. Beverly (London and New York, [1924]), p. 205.
40. *Letters of Nikolai Gogol*, trans. and ed. by Carl R. Proffer (Ann Arbor, 1967), pp. 44-45.
41. *Sonya Kovalevsky. Her Recollections of Childhood*, trans. by Isabel F. Hapgood (New York, 1895), pp. 3-8.
42. Aksakov, *Years*, p. 3.
43. See, for example, *My Past and Thoughts. The Memoirs of Alexander Herzen*, trans. by Constance Garnett, rev. by Humphrey Higgins (New York, 1968), I, 23.
44. Quoted in Marthe Blinoff, *Life and Thought in Old Russia* (University Park, Pennsylvania, 1961), p. 35.
45. Raeff, *The Origins of the Russian Intelligentsia. The Eighteenth-Century Nobility* (New York, 1966), p. 123.
46. Vladimir Polunin, *Three Generations, Family Life in Russia, 1845-1902*, trans. by A. F. Birch-Jones (London, 1957), p. 5.
47. *Letters*, p. 199.
48. Novikov, "O vospitanii," p. 95.
49. Kovalevsky, *Recollections*, p. 34.
50. Sergei I. Witte, *The Memoirs of Count Witte*, trans. by Abraham Yarmolinsky (Garden City, 1921), p. 10.
51. Bettye Caldwell, "The Effects of Infant Care," *Review of Child Development Research*, ed. by M. L. and Lois W. Hoffman, I (New York, 1964), 61-62.
52. Blinoff, *Old Russia*, p. 35.
53. Novikov, "O vospitanii," pp. 169-70.
54. Herzen, *My Past and Thoughts*, I, 77-78.
55. Nikolai E. Wrangel, *Memoirs of Baron N. Wrangel, 1847-1920*, trans. by Brian and Beatrice Lunn (Philadelphia, 1927), p. 14.
56. Wesley C. Becker, "Consequences of Different Kinds of Parental Discipline," *Review of Child Development Research*, I, 176-77.
57. Fedor Dostoevskii, *The Diary of a Writer*, trans. by Boris Brasol (New York, 1949), I, 211, 459.
58. Anton Chekhov, "Sleepy," *Russian Stories*, ed. by Gleb Struve (New York, 1961), p. 235.
59. Pokrovskii, *Fizicheskoe vospitanie*, p. 36.
60. Quoted in Raeff, "Home, School, and Service," p. 215.

61. Gogol, *Letters,* p. 46.
62. Herzen, *My Past and Thoughts,* p. 23.
63. Raeff, "Home, School, and Service," p. 213.
64. Novikov, "O vospitanie," p. 95.
65. Kovalevsky, *Recollections,* pp. 47-49.
66. Wrangel, *Memoirs,* pp. 14-15.
67. Herzen, *My Past and Thoughts,* pp. 37, 27.
68. David Hunt, *Parents and Children in History* (New York, 1970), p. 191.
69. Gorer, *Great Russia,* p. 100.
70. Quoted in Blinoff, *Old Russia,* p. 35.
71. Tomasic, *Impact of Russian Culture,* p. 81.
72. N. I. Kostomarov, *Ocherk domashnei zhizni i nravov velikorusskago naroda* (St. Petersburg, 1860), p. 109.
73. Augustine, "Notes," p. 408.
74. I. Gurevich, *Roditeli i deti* (St. Petersburg, 1896), p. 44.
75. Robert Ker Porter, *Travelling Sketches in Russia and Sweden, 1805-08,* in *Seven Britons in Imperial Russia, 1698-1812,* ed. by Peter Putnam (Princeton, 1952), pp. 327-28. See also Tomasic, *Impact of Russian Culture,* p. 82; Georg Brandes, *Impressions of Russia* (New York, 1966), p. 44.
76. Anatole Leroy-Beaulieu, *The Empire of the Tsars and the Russians,* trans. by Zenaide Ragozin (New York, 1893), I, 489.
77. Gurevich, *Roditeli,* p. 44.
78. Tomasic, *Impact of Russian Culture,* p. 93.
79. V. Zhitova, *The Turgenev Family,* trans. by A. S. Mills (London, 1947), pp. 42-43.
80. Herzen, *My Past and Thoughts,* pp. 77-78.
81. Wrangel, *Memoirs,* p. 44.
82. See, for example, Martin Malia, *Alexander Herzen and the Birth of Russian Socialism* (Cambridge, 1961), p. 32; Peter Kropotkin, *Memoirs of a Revolutionist* (Garden City, 1962), pp. 38-39, 204-07.
83. Hunt, *Parents and Children,* p. 153.
84. Polunin, *Three Generations,* pp. 141-42.
85. Alexander Radishchev, *A Journey from St. Petersburg to Moscow,* trans. by Leo Wiener (Cambridge, 1958), pp. 188-89.
86. *Ibid.,* p. 113.
87. Polunin, *Three Generations,* pp. 141-42.
88. William F. Woehrlin, *Chernyshevskii. The Man and the Journalist* (Cambridge, 1971), p. 13.
89. *Ibid.,* pp. 18-19.
90. Konius, *Istoki,* p. 91; see also Elaine Elnett, *Historic Origin and Social Development of Family Life in Russia* (2nd ed.; New York, 1927), p. 54.
91. Kropotkin, *Memoirs,* pp. 124-28.
92. On Chernyshevskii see Woehrlin, *Chernyshevskii,* pp. 23-25; on Belinskii see Patrick P. Dunn, "V. G. Belinskii: The Road to Reality, 1811-41" (Unpublished Ph.D. Dissertation, Duke University, 1969), pp. 4-6, and "Perepiska Belinskago s rodnymi," ed by A. Akskariats, *et al., Literaturnoe nasledstvo,* vol. 57: *V. G. Belinskii,* III (Moscow, 1959), pp. 30, 60-62.
93. E. H. Carr, *Michael Bakunin* (New York, 1961), p. 7.
94. Barbara Engel, "Mothers and Daughters. A Model for Feminine Solidarity in the Revolutionary Movement of the 1870's" (an unpublished paper read before the 1973 convention of the American Association for the Advancement of Slavic Studies), pp. 1, 3.
95. Nikolai Valentinov [N. V. Volski], *The Early Years of Lenin,* trans. by Rolf H. W. Theen (Ann Arbor, 1969), p. 33.

CHAPTER 10

Home As a Nest: Middle Class Childhood in Nineteenth-Century Europe

PRISCILLA
ROBERTSON

"Christopher Columbus only discovered America:
I have discovered the Child."

Victor Hugo

If the philosophy of the Enlightenment brought to eighteenth-century Europe a new confidence in the possibility of human happiness, special credit must go to Rousseau for calling attention to the needs of children. For the first time in history, he made a large group of people believe that childhood was worth the attention of intelligent adults, encouraging an interest in the process of growing up rather than just the product. Education of children was part of the interest in progress which was so prominent in the intellectual trends of the time.

The rate at which children died in the eighteenth century was shocking to a generation noted for its interest in human welfare and confident in rational means of attaining it. Since the best thinking of the period supported individual enterprise, the first approach to child-rearing was to direct the attention of parents to their own young. Mothers were summoned from their social pleasures to seek the joys of running a nursery, while fathers were encouraged to feel it not beneath their dignity to romp with infants and to keep a close eye upon their development.

This ideal of domesticity was reinforced on the continent by various conditions following the French Revolution and the Napoleonic Wars. In France, the revolutionary turmoil made public life so insecure that many persons were driven indoors, so to speak, while at the same time many of the institutions, mostly religious, that had previously had a near monopoly on educating the young, and of giving care to orphaned and abandoned infants, were closed. In the observation of Mary Berry, this led to a "regeneration" in upper-class French life, since children were no longer separated from parents at birth and no longer had to return as strangers to their father's house in adolescence.[1] In Germany, under the Napoleonic domination, when the various princely governments disappeared and the national mood was one of intense humiliation, the regrouping of forces took place first of all inside the family. At the hearth were reborn patriotism, loyalty, and the determination to recreate their own nation which would enable them to drive the French invaders out. No political revolution or foreign invasion occurred in England, but the industrial revolution there drew increasing numbers of men from their homes to work elsewhere. A flood of religious and sentimental propaganda was then directed to the women left alone at home to persuade them that their work could be just as useful to society and even more "sacred" than the men's, and they were not to fret at narrow walls, since they could make a heaven inside them.

Much of the child care in the nineteenth century was, of course, in the hands of parents and servants who trusted conventional wisdom, habit, and superstition. But a new intellectual underpinning and a new sense of commitment was creating a kind of childhood among middle-class Europeans that was thoroughly new in spirit and effect.

PHYSICAL CARE OF BABIES

Childbirth itself remained dangerous and painful throughout the century, even though chloroform came in the middle of the period to ease the worst pain for those mothers whose doctors would administer it—"the sweetest smell you ever smelt," as my mother-in-law once told me.

The practice of using male obstetricians, adopted among the higher classes on the continent during the eighteenth century, spread very slowly to England, and to the poor. William Cobbett deplored this change, and felt he had made a mistake, in the 1790's, to have summoned a male *accoucheur* after his second child was stillborn.[2]

By the 1860's, in Paris, doctors delivered 35 per cent of the babies, mostly for the rich; 12 per cent arrived in hospitals, and 53 per cent had midwives.[3] Midwives were also the chief practitioners of abortion, and the waiting rooms of those willing to perform this operation were always full.[4] Mme. Millet-Robinet, whose books of advice were widely popular in France, recommended medical doctors by 1889, but noted that *sages-femmes* too had to have medical licensing. The advantage of a man, she thought, would be his greater composure.[5]

In England, childbirth was usually concealed, and was rarely described in literature. Siblings were whisked away and were expected to be astonished when they filed in to see the new baby the next day. In France there was less concealment, and one account of birth in a middle class home deserves to be a classic. It appeared in a popular book by Gustav Droz, called *Monsieur, Madame, et Bébé,*[6] and it was apparently written with the aim of interesting men in the process of becoming fathers—and possibly thereby increasing the falling birth rate.

Everything was in his picture: the young wife on the bed crying, "Oh, doctor, *mon dieu,* doctor" with increasing intensity until her husband got cold chills and was certain something must be wrong; the good doctor smiling calmly and borrowing a robe and slippers to make himself comfortable for the long night; the young woman's mother fighting back tears as she called, "Courage my darling, we have to pay for our happiness"; the nurse dozing stiffly in the anteroom beside the waiting crib; the two maiden aunts in the parlor, one reading Voltaire, the other telling her rosary, murmuring "frightful" to each other at intervals. At one of the worst cries the doctor put in a little joke. "The little girl," he opined, "will be here in half an hour." This upsets the husband almost more than his wife's pains. "Don't joke with me, doctor," he begs, "you know it has got to be a boy." And of course it is, for if M. Droz was anxious to encourage fatherhood, he seemed interested only in male offspring.

The baby's first cry produced a mood of triumph as everyone streamed into the chamber. The new mother squeezed her husband's hand and whispered, "Are you pleased with me? I did the very best I could for you," while the doctor dressed the slippery infant in diaper and bonnet, giving the nurse precise instructions to follow in the future.

At every stage, in every country, however subtly, boys continued to be favored over girls. In England this was often disguised, and with their larger families it didn't seem to matter if a particular child was male or female; yet Mme. de Ségur, visiting her married daughter in London, was shocked that the *accoucheur* charged fifteen pounds for a girl and twenty for a boy.[7] In Germany the village pastor asked four kreutzer for a Thanksgiving service, but the father would happily pay ten for a boy while scraping his pockets for small change for a girl.[8] In France, the preference for boys was related to the pressing need for a big army. "Another new defender for the country," the mayor would declare to the witnesses who registered the birth of a boy, and French peasants were known to declare, "I have no children, monsieur, I have only girls." Frances Power Cobbe, in 1862, reported that "until recently" it had been customary in Naples to hang out a small black flag when a girl was born to save neighbors the painful embarrassment of inquiring about it.

Rousseau is best known for his plea to mothers to nurse their own babies. At the time he wrote, it was the near-universal custom in France to send children born in cities out to be nursed in the country. Over eighty per cent of the 21,000 babies born in Paris in the 1780's were shipped out to professional wet-nurses. In the course of the next hundred years the practice nearly ceased, being limited in the 1870's to children of small tradesmen and artisans where the wife was needed in the shop. Instead there grew up the custom of importing wet-nurses by families that could afford them, married ones commanding a higher price than the unwed because of their supposedly higher moral standards.

Following Rousseau, most books for mothers recommended that they should nurse their own children if possible, and it was no longer considered in bad taste to do so. Mme. de Rémusat in 1824 said it might be hard on an upper-class girl to suckle, but she should at least take care of the baby herself and use the wet-nurse merely as an instrument for her own purposes.[9] To their homely counsels Michelet added the striking observation that a nursing baby experiences the dawn of tenderness when he tries to offer himself entire to his mother by contracting his small body.[10] A midwife, Mme. Breton, invented a popular kind of artificial nipples and bottles, which she sold in Paris. They were in great demand by the thirties and forties, but unfortunately were only available in the city, so some of the mothers' manuals described the process of making one's own by cooking a cow's or goat's tit in limewater.[11]

Affluence and women's independence gave wet-nursing another boom at the end of the century, and an unsavory trade in girls for this purpose grew up, exposed, among other places, by Brieux's drama, *Les Remplaçantes,* which contains in its title a pun on the male use of military substitutes (*remplaçants*). For both sexes, Brieux suggests, the Third Republic demanded that each should do his own duty, and he added punch to his play by suggesting the hard fate of the nurses' own infants, left to artificial feeding back in the provinces, and caricatured the modish life of the Parisian mothers with their teas, their bicycling around in culottes, and their attending lectures at the *Collège de France.*

In England, wet-nurses had nowhere near the vogue they had on the continent, and in our period middle and upper-class women were advised to nurse their own and most of them made a serious effort to do so. Mrs. Beeton's well-known *Handbook of Domestic Management* assumed her readers would suckle their infants from nine to fifteen months. Lady Auckland, Emily Eden's mother, was proud to have suckled thirteen of her fourteen children. That nursing is good for mothers, which doctors had long known, was supplemented by the thought that milk from a "coarse" woman could not be a fitting diet for an upper-class child.[12] Yet when bottles came in they became popular. Mrs. Panton, a baby-hater who wrote a manual for mothers on how to cope with their bad situation, informed her readers that nursing a child, besides being painful, led to a middle age of despair and an early death—and might even drive its practitioners to drink. She pointed out how much easier it is to train a young child in good habits from a bottle.[13]

In German middle and upper classes in this period, wet-nurses were used very freely and it was rare to see a mother nursing her own.[14] In Italy, the custom of sending children out lasted far longer than in France, and even at home they seemed to be left largely to the care of servants-in-general rather than with someone specially responsible for them.

Another custom attacked by Rousseau was swaddling, nevertheless the habit died so slowly in France that in 1891 a book on child care could express amazement that a century after Rousseau it was necessary to caution against the practice.[15] Many books of parental advice actually hedged although almost never recommending the old tight swaddling which confined the arms, many gave mothers a choice between modified swaddling bands or clothing in the "English" manner, which involved fastenings in the crotch and was called *culottes*. An advantage to this method was that it made potty training easier. The tight swaddle had often left the baby so stuck up that it was painful to change him, and this led in a vicious circle to the nurse's unwillingness to do so.[16]

German babies were wrapped up tighter and longer than French ones, and were called *Wickelkinder*.[17] In 1877 *Fraser's Magazine* described a German baby as "a piteous object", pinioned and bound like a mummy in yards of bandages that were unfolded once, or at most twice, a day. The child was rarely bathed. They were kept in swaddling clothes until about six months old, then often allowed to crawl on the floor with a cold potato in their fist to keep them from crying. The English author made the point that it is hard to hug a swaddled child, and that it is impossible for him to wind his arms about his mother. Even in adulthood a German girl's posture was said to be different from an English girl's because of the early swaddling.[18] About 1908 an English visitor described the *Steckkissen*, a comparatively recent successor to the swaddling bands—a long bag that confined the legs and body but not the arms. It was lined with wadding, and nurses were told that it was dangerous to pick up a baby outside of one while his bones were still soft, so the infant lay in it day and night for eight weeks. Air, sunlight and soap were all considered equally dangerous to a child, and sleeping out of doors was not allowed.

In Italy, Lady Morgan reported babies being wrapped up so tightly that the pressure forced blood to their heads and made their little faces purple, and she reported that when members of the enlightened middle classes questioned the practice, they were opposed by the clergy. She smugly remarked that swaddling had been unheard of in England for many years.[19]

Washing was a severe problem, especially on the continent where nursemaids had long indulged the labor-saving superstition that it was dangerous, and in some cases that even to comb the child's hair before two was bad. In England on the other hand, cold water was considered bracing. William Cobbett, a great do-it-yourself father, urged washing each child well each day—an hour's good tight work, indeed, but as the child kicked, *you* sang. Singing, talking and rolling children around were very good for them, he thought, and believed that rickets come from a dull environment.[20] Even grown-up English people favored cold bathing, to be sure, but for children it could be a torture. The routine in Elizabeth Grant's London home was that the lightly-clad children were brought down from their nursery at the top of the house to the kitchen courtyard, where the tub of water might have a coat of ice. She screamed, begged, prayed to be saved from immersion, but to no avail. After the dip she was put into a cotton frock with short sleeves, no flannel underwear, and was served a stone-cold breakfast. Her father stood over her and if she complained would cut her with his whip.[21]

Sea bathing was considered a fine health builder, so Augustus Hare was dipped in the waves before he was able to speak clearly,[22] and it became "necessary" for Marianne Gaskell to "bathe" at the age of two. Mrs. Gaskell dreaded it for her, but her Aunt Anne was "a capital bather" and took charge.

Despite Elizabeth Grant's light wardrobe, many Victorian children had too much rather than too little clothing. Few parents noticed what Charles Kingsley pointed out, the instinct of children to get rid of clothes and to cuddle to flesh.[23] Instead they were trained from infancy never to expose themselves. When little girls began to walk they were put into a vest, a chemise—without which it was not "nice" to go—and stays. Both sexes wore stays, boys till about seven, girls for a lifetime. There were buttons to hold up garters, drawers, the flannel petticoat, the white petticoat with its bodice, black stockings, a frock and pinafore. Boys began with the same set of dresses, but it was a great day when one got his first breeches (though the experience was supposed to be a trauma for his mother.)

Joy to Philip! he this day
Has his long coats cast away,
And, (the childish season gone)
Puts the manly breeches on. . . .
Sashes, frocks to those that need 'em,
Philip's limbs have got their freedom.
He can run, or he can ride,
And do twenty things beside
Which his petticoats forbad:
Is he not a happy lad?[24]

One cannot help wondering if girls ever had such a moment of joy.

The best account I have found of how an enlightened mother felt about, and took care of, an actual baby was the diary that Mrs. Gaskell, the novelist, kept of her daughter Marianne's first years.[25] Marianne was born in September, 1834, and the journal starts a few months later.

At the age of six months, the baby smiled and kicked when her father came in, showing that she recognized him. The parents tried to train her attention span by encouraging her to look as long as possible at objects in view, and they were pleased that her sense of distance was improving so she no longer tried to catch sunbeams. They were troubled by her little bursts of impatience, "obstinacy, really, only that is so harsh a word to apply to one so dear." At this age she liked to hear singing, but was afraid of the piano. She was suspicious of strangers. She lay on the floor and kicked a lot, which did her worlds of good, but her mother was determined that she should learn to walk by herself, when she was ready for it, and was neither going to help her herself, nor allow the servants to do it.

Five months later her fond mother fancied she heard the child say "Mama". By this time she could stand steadily, by taking hold of something. She clapped hands, shook hands, and understood sentences like, "Where are the cows?" They did not, however, like to let her show off for strangers. Mrs. Gaskell determined that she would never promise anything to Marianne without performing it, and never distract her by calling attention to things that are not there.

Two months later, when Marianne was thirteen months old, the mother had read in Combe's *Physiology*, that bodily conditions like hunger and fatigue can make a person cross. She wished to gratify all Marianne's legitimate wishes, but speculated on the best way to handle "sensibilities"—since these could be so beautiful when healthy, so distressing when morbid. At this time the child's accomplishments included barking like a dog, mewing, kissing, and pointing to various articles

At sixteen months Marianne still did not scramble after toys which rolled away, so that Mrs. Gaskell worried about her weakness of limb;

but by February, 1836, she was at last walking with the assistance of chairs, her little legs were getting stronger, and her teething was comparatively easy.

Although Mrs. Gaskell wanted her child to "mind", and complained of her little disobediences, she was capable on the very same page of writing "she is not so independent as she should be and as I intended her to be." This at eighteen months. Marianne was, however, very fond of other children, a taste the mother was eager to gratify.

Only at twenty-two months, with her eye teeth safely through, did Marianne suddenly begin to walk. She loved stories and was quite a chatterbox, but since the Gaskells had been told by a medical man that up to the age of three a child's brain is constantly on the verge of "inflammation", they did not try to teach her anything. They planned to start lessons at four, and until that time to encourage her observation, attention and perseverence.

When she was three a new sister was born, and Marianne was removed to the house of an Aunt Lamb for the occasion. One night Aunt Lamb had a paralytic stroke and could not respond when the infant begged to be taken into bed with her. Still she was kept on at Aunt Lamb's for eight weeks, a trying experience.

Home again, she became most useful and independent (at last) and used to think of such little services as fetching Papa's slippers. With considerable hesitation, they decided to send her to an infant school at three-and-a-half. They supposed it would perfect her sense of obedience and perseverence, but that it might weaken her pleasure in her home, and that she might meet children who would tell her of things which they wished her to be ignorant of. They compromised that Marianne should attend for half a day only, and that Mrs. Gaskell would fetch her, herself, to prevent her playing loosely around, and that she should spend her afternoons with the family. Mrs. Gaskell also hoped that on walks home, she would hear "what happened"—including, no doubt, any confessions of undesirable communications from the other children.

DISCIPLINE OF CHILDREN

Dr. George Moberly, an English clergyman, said in 1840 that a child should know by three that if it chooses to be disobedient it is entering on a losing game.[26] He considered he had proved his point when his little daughter got scarlet fever. Although swallowing was agony to her, she took her medicine when they said, "Now, Alice,"—and this, he believed, saved her life.

This study is interesting partly because it duplicates a story from Dr. Daniel Gottlieb Moritz Schreber, a prominent German doctor who had set himself up as an authority on child psychology just a bit earlier.[27] Dr. Schreber believed in total control of a child's mind and actions. He didn't believe that beating was the best method to achieve this state, but rather that a well-trained child could be controlled by the eye of the parent, since a good child would not want to behave differently from what the parent wished. The child was meant to feel genuine love and freedom, and if he *were* beaten, he was to shake hands with a friendly smile afterwards just to prove there were no hard feelings. The result of this discipline was that Dr. Schreber's son became one of the most famous mental patients in the nineteenth century—he wrote an autobiography about his mental disease and had the honor of a paper on his case by Freud, who analyzed him at a distance.

Most cases of child control were less sophisticated. When Augustus Hare was three, his mother noted in her journal that he kept asking *why*, but she made a point of never giving any reason except that it was her will that he should do so.[28] At five, little Augustus was shut up in his room for two days on bread and water explicitly to break his spirit, by an aunt whose little boy had bit and slapped him, which he was not allowed to retaliate. Later on in boyhood he was severely punished for expressing the wish that he might invite some children to play on his birthday.

Although this sort of brutality was clearly an exception, even the most enlightened philosophers were convinced that the important thing for children to do was "to mind". Their spirits must be curbed, wrote Ann Taylor although she specifically added they need not be broken, and there might arise situations when they could be allowed to dictate to their parents without at all "endangering" parental authority. Thus to Mrs. Gaskell, the initial confrontation with discipline came when Marianne was still in her cradle. If the baby cried, and if it turned out that what she wanted was good for her to have, then Mrs. Gaskell gave it to her right away, even if it meant interfering with her own convenience. A mother should give up a good deal to keep her child from unnecessary irritation. But if it turned out the baby wanted something she should not have, then never give it to her, and the child will soon lose the habit of crying.

Few parents were as observant as Mrs. Gaskell was about what was really going on in her child's mind, and few were as persistent in their own fantasies as Mrs. Hare. When nurses were in charge, naturally, mothers were likely to be less noticing and less interfering. The nurse's greater emotional distance may have slowed the children's emotional development.

C. W. Cunnington[29] places the changeover from physical to mental punishment during the 1840's, but I have not discovered good evidence for such a change. Caning has never ceased to be used in the British public schools, and it was late in the nineteenth century before birching at home was abandoned by the most enlightened parents. After all, they took the Bible a great deal more literally than we do, and felt its injunction about sparing the rod simply could not be erroneous. Edmund Gosse, when he was six (around 1855), was caned by his father for disobedience. Ruminating later, he said he supposed that some children might be smartened up by a whipping, but in his case it provoked only murderous rage. "It is largely a matter of convention, the exercise being endured (I am told) with pride by the infants of our aristocracy, but not tolerated by the lower classes."[30] Augustus Hare was punished, at the request of his adoptive mother, by his uncle, a clergyman of the Church of England, who wrote a book entitled "The Mission of the Comforter". The instrument was a riding whip. When Augustus, grown up, wrote a frank account of his painful childhood, he was bitterly criticized for his lack of the usual pieties. When he wrote his uncle's life for the *Dictionary of National Biography*, however, he succumbed to custom and wrote a flattering account.

J. A. Froude's first recollection of being whipped was at two, for dirtying his frock;[31] while Ann Taylor was whipped for not being able to remember what T-H-Y spelt. She was imputed with wilful perversity. Ruskin was whipped if he cried, or disobeyed, or tumbled down the stairs, so he soon learned "serene and secure methods of life and motion", and he learned to enjoy "staring at things", even though his later emotional life was crippled.[32]

Mrs. Gaskell, who did pay attention to her daughter's moods, was "obliged", when the child was three and a half to give her "a slight whipping, sorrowfully and gently". Such treatment never failed to make Marianne more obedient without resentment, she discovered.

The whole subject of corporal punishment of girls in the home was thoroughly aired in the correspondence columns of the *Englishwoman's Domestic Magazine* during the years 1867 to 1869. Half the parents who wrote in, seeking and giving advice on the subject, were appalled at the very idea, and felt it unnecessary, misguided, and likely to have very bad results for the girls' modesty and sense of shame. But the more dramatic letters came from those who, always with great satisfaction, reported beneficial results. They debated whether to start in infancy or wait till the child was five or six; whether to continue it up to fourteen or fifteen; whether to do it on the unclothed buttocks; what instrument was best—a slipper (ineffective), a birch (most favored), or specially constructed leather thongs (most painful). Some felt that a quick whipping was cleanly done and soon over with, and actually created less resentment than prolonged isolation or bread-and-water. Others were certain whipping was a sure way to alienate children not only from their parents, but from their own sense of personal dignity and identity.

When it came to punishments other than beating, favorite methods were often connected with food. English children's food was at best extremely simple and monotonous—the customary nursery supper was dry bread and milk, and it was held that fancy food was bad for children's digestions and morals. An almost universal tenet was that children should never be allowed to ask for anything, or to express a preference, but simply to eat what was set before them.[33] So Elizabeth Grant's sister, who had an aversion to spinach, found it reappearing at every meal, until, after thirty hours, she was starved into eating it.[34] Mrs. Hare punished Augustus for sucking a lollipop by giving him a huge dose of rhubarb and soda with a forcing spoon. Even where the punishment did not fit the crime, deprivation of food was often used. James Mill condemned both his two younger children—who made an error in one word on their lessons—and John Stuart—who allowed it to pass—to miss their dinner.[35]

One of the hard features was that English children were permitted, at a certain age, to come down for dessert—to appear in the dining room when their parents were finishing off their doubtless bounteous meals. Sometimes the children actually shared the same rich dessert as the grown-ups, but more often they were given a section of an orange or an apple, or, like Ruskin, were forced to crack nuts for the guests without getting any for themselves. The first time Ruskin tasted custard was when he was given his father's unfinished dish.[36] Charlotte Yonge stressed the point that her mother trained her not to feel it a hardship to watch others consume food she was not allowed,[37] but once again the acme of torture was reached in Augustus Hare's young life. His mother and aunt deliberately had wonderful fancy cakes and puddings made and presented to the boy as if he could eat them, then whisked them away untouched, saying that they were intended for the village poor.

Another common means of punishment was psychological. Although the story in *The Fairchild Family* of the two children who were taken to the gibbet and made to look at the hanged criminals was fictional, and was even removed from later editions because of public protest, lesser forms of fear and shaming were believed efficacious.[38] For example, Milly Acland's little brother had to wear a card saying, "Georgina, she kicks," which he hated, and which confirmed Milly in her view that there was never any rational connection between an offense and its punishment.[39]

An occasional clever child, like Fanny Kemble, was unreachable. "I never cried, I never sulked, I never resented, lamented, or repented either my ill doings or their consequences, but accepted them alike with a philosophical buoyancy of spirit which was the despair of my poor bewildered trainers." Once, at four, she was given a fool's cap to wear at home, but she danced down the driveway and called on passers-by to admire it. Fed on bread and water, she declared that she was now like those poor French prisoners everyone pitied so. And when a friend of her aunt, Mrs. Siddons, asked her, "Fanny, why don't you pray to God to make you better?" she answered, "So I do, but he makes me worse and worse."[40]

Sometimes parents were the ones who were ashamed. In a poem, *The Toys,* Coventry Patmore wrote how he struck his child and sent him to bed unkissed for seven times disobedience, but when he went in to look at him in bed, he noticed the wet lashes and the way the child had collected toys around himself for comfort. It was the father whose *sang froid* broke down.[41]

There are always a few who brought up their families without any corporal punishment. Having been jailed for protesting the flogging of some British soldiers, William Cobbett handled his children without scolding, "without even command".[42] He gave them no schools, no teachers, but all kinds of opportunities, books, pencils, paper. He called the child who was first down in the morning "the lark" for the day. To rear children this way, he insisted, you must make them feel that you prefer this to any other thing you could possibly be doing, and perhaps that was why it was rare, although later in the century Charles Kingsley and Charles Darwin worked exclusively on the good feelings of their children and found conventional discipline unneeded.

Corporal punishment seems to have been used much less in France than in England. Philip Hamerton reported that beatings were never used in the middle classes, whose customary punishment was confinement or putting children on dry bread.[43] Among peasants, he admitted, beatings were common and a kind of patriarchal obedience required. (But my French informant, a postmaster's daughter, born in 1900, tells me she was spanked from time to time and considered it entirely normal.)

French books of advice bear out the impression of mildness. The semi-official *Manuel des Jeunes Méres* (1884) by Mme. Millet-Robinet, urges parents never to hit children, though bad habits should be broken up early, the child should know there is "a will stronger than his own". Her recommended methods of persuading him of that fact were deprivation of a toy, or of dessert—never confinement, nor bread-and-water.[44] The popular *Livre de Famille,* where the view of life and discipline is much harsher, recommends whipping, but only for children over five or six. Even this author points out, however, that you can ruin children as easily through harshness as through weakness.[45]

A predictable result was that foreign observers found middle-class French children spoiled. Miss Betham says that the wet-nurses were told never to let them cry, and that later they were given whatever they asked for. When they were old enough to eat with the family they were always served first, and discipline in the home was, by German and English standards, lacking. But the French themselves felt that children gained immeasurably by eating with their parents, both in taste for good food and in conversational ability.[46]

For their part, the French who studied German life were astonished at the precocious disciplined quality of German children. Henri Didon, admittedly a Germanophobe, felt that violence and brutality, which would only disgust a French child, were successful in dominating German ones. Otto Corvin tells of losing consciousness several times under his father's lash and believed that his brother was permanently damaged in the process.[47] When Corvin reached Cadet School, it is interesting that he knew of two suicides among students who could not brook the shame of a whipping for discipline, quite in contrast to the universal acceptance of the practice in English public schools. When she was well grown up, Adelheid Mommsen asked her father, Theodor Mommsen, the great historian of Rome, why children could never speak first, and never criticize either their parents or older siblings. This custom, she said, made them shy and maladroit, and her father conceded she might be right.[48]

On two subjects, at least, the Victorians tended to be both obsessional and reticent—constipation and masturbation. They hated to put on paper what they considered to be dirty words, so that otherwise comprehensive manuals of child care usually omit the entire subject of toilet training. Nevertheless regularity of the bowels was almost the first rule of health in the nineteenth century, and it was the first subject asked about by a doctor called to a case of illness. The actual handling of a baby in this area was left to folk wisdom and oral tradition. The author of *The Rise and Fall of the British Nanny* deduced from talking to survivors of the nanny system that the nurses often began pot training at one month, and when the child grew older they would leave him alone on his pot to "try" each morning. Failure usually led to some nasty laxative.[49]

A little French tale of 1895, *Carrots*, in the form of the autobiography of a bad boy, tells how one night the young hero decided it was too cold to go out into the back yard where the facility was, and decided it would be easier to defecate in the fireplace. His mother had forgotten to give him a chamber pot, she said, but in the morning she cooked up a special soup, containing a bit of his own waste product, and made him eat it.[50] From this story, to be sure, we learn more about French lack of inhibition about bodily processes and their strict sense of logic than about ordinary toilet training.

If constipation led to all kinds of bad bodily conditions, masturbation was assumed to lead directly to insanity, which made it seem necessary for parents to do everything possible to curb the practice. Their efforts were bizarre, harsh, and ineffective.

Although their heaviest batteries were often directed toward self-abuse among boys at puberty, there was much subtle pressure to keep younger children from starting—often so subtle that it misfired. Thus Gathorne-Hardy reports people who remembered being simply mystified at the exhortation not to "touch themselves." The cold baths so urgently advised may have been part of the campaign, too, since they were often consciously recommended to the adolescents eager to control the bad habit, although cold bathing had other merits in Victorian eyes.

More severe measures involved tying children's hands in bed, so that, for example, Dr. Maeve Marwick, an Edinburgh physician, remembered her piano teacher's questioning why her wrists were so scarred. Most drastic of all were efforts at surgical intervention, so that circumcision was usually recommended for boys caught in the act, and at least one doctor in mid-century advocated clitoridectomy for girls—but happily he was almost immediately expelled from the British Medical Association.

The ineffable Dr. Schreber never mentioned masturbation in his exposition of total control over the child, but many of the measures he recommended, from cold baths exclusively from the age of four or five on, to his elaborate system of harnesses and braces, ostensibly to keep the child growing straight, suggest that he might have had the practice in mind.

Persistent whispered rumors circulated, especially in Germany, that nurses masturbated their children to keep them quiet,—and these broke out afresh whenever any child turned out autistic or mentally unsound. (I have heard of the same attributions in Louisville, Kentucky dating back to about the turn of the century.)

Fortunately some people could see things straight, and one wholesome influence was Dr. Albert Moll, whose *The Sexual Life of the Child* appeared in the early years of the twentieth century, based on a lifetime of research and sympathetic observation.[51] Although he says he began as a young doctor with the beliefs he had been taught concerning the immense harm masturbation could do, he noticed that practically all boys and a large proportion of girls engaged in it without apparent ill effect. He mentioned particularly an eight-year-old boy, brought to his office by his mother and nurse who believed that he masturbated every night. It happened that the doctor was able to check up on the same patient at the age of 24, and found him to be perfectly sound and of absolutely normal sexual capacity. In his book he warned parents not to regard an oscillatory motion by a baby or young child as in itself evidence of masturbation—the infant may just be expressing his general good feeling.

THE IDEAL OF CHILDHOOD, HOME AND FAMILY LIFE

Rousseau—although many perceived him as the eighteenth century's *enfant terrible*—provided rationale for the view that children are born good, with a capacity for reason, and that their natural virtues need only to be brought out. The opposite attitude, that children are born troublesome if not corrupt, implies that the remedy is *force majeure*. In the early 1800's Rousseau's ideas had the bloom of fashion, and several books of practical advice by popular women writers passed his theories along. Many are delightful, like Maria Edgeworth's *Practical Education,* which can still be read with profit because of her respect for the child's mind, and with pleasure for its beguiling examples. Maria, who with her father, Richard Lovell Edgeworth, brought up her sixteen younger brothers and sisters, was once asked how she knew so much about children. "Why, I don't know," she said, "I lie down and let them crawl all over me." She was influenced by one of her stepmothers, Honoria Edgeworth, who believed that education is "an experimental science" and who kept notebooks on her children's behavior.[52] One of Maria's best conclusions was that we should not prejudice either by our wisdom, or by our folly, children's assertion of their own values.

In Germany, representative of the same epoch and principle, Karoline Rudolphi wrote a series of letters, addressed as if by an experienced mother to a younger one,[53] following in lightly fictionalized form the experiences and how to handle them of a little girl from eight days old until her marriage. This writer urges at every stage gentleness, rationality, encouragement of natural impulses in a constructive way. Mme. Guizot, wife of the French statesman, did the same thing for French mothers with "letters" from a mother who sought to keep her husband informed about their children's progress while he was in the diplomatic service.[54] These writers stress the education of girls more than of boys, since it is assumed that the mother will be in charge of her daughters until they marry, while the boys will go off to school—but each one of them also gives precepts and examples about little boys, with comment on the necessary differences between the sexes.

The best example of the opposing theory is Hannah More, who, though slightly older than Maria Edgeworth, overtook her in popularity around the 1820's. To her, children were born bad, and before they could become acceptable adults their will needed to be broken. "Is it not a fundamental error to consider children as innocent beings, whose little weaknesses may, perhaps, want some correction, rather than as beings who bring into the world a corrupt nature and evil dispositions, which it should be the great end of education to rectify?"[55] A philosophic character in one of her didactic pieces of fiction was pleased that his only son had died as a child, because he would have inherited a large fortune, and it was obvious God was protecting his soul by not letting him be tempted.

In France the pejorative view of childhood, though less common, found expression from time to time. The *Livre de Famille,* a cheap paperback handbook available late in the century, described the child as cruelty and egoism personified—an angel only when he sleeps. Waking, he had to be brought into absolute submission.

In spite of harsh sentiments like these, it was still true that childhood had become both interesting and serious, and the standardized indifference or brutality of earlier centuries were mitigated in the nineteenth by greater understanding. Hannah More, even though she sounds uncompromising, was not a cruel woman. Though she upheld the old Christian idea of man's corrupt nature, she still believed it could best be coped with by mildness and a steady gentle insistence on obedience.

These two attitudes run in counterpoint throughout the nineteenth century—those who like children against those who do not; those who trust nature versus those who fear God; those who discipline lightly opposed to those who believe that pain is good for the young; the Age of Reason confronting the Puritan Ethic. If the afterglow of the Enlightenment gave a certain freedom to the period until about 1820, the reaction toward conventionality and respectability gave the edge to publications restressing Miss More's way during the thirties, forties and fifties. Yet at the end of the century again came a new movement toward freedom, when Ellen Key predicted the twentieth century would be "The Century of the Child". In France Rousseau's influence weakened but was never lost. In Germany theoretical interest in childhood seemed less evident until the eighties when it manifested itself with scientific thoroughness in the starting up of laboratories for experimental work in child psychology and journals to disseminate the results.

Babies, of course, had to be brought up without waiting for the issues to be settled, but whether consciously or not, mothers fell into one or the other of these two patterns and had to balance their natural feelings against the great sense of Duty which loomed so large. There were always those who find children a pleasure, and those who consider them an appalling responsibility. Literature provided a rationalization for either emotion.

Early in the century a remarkable English family, the Taylors of Ongar, set a new family style and wrote about it with considerable impact. Home, they declared, is the grand nursery of virtue. Do not put children off in separate quarters, but let parents and children form one large compact circle in the parlors of the house and the kitchen. By reading aloud—a practice they did much to make popular—by educating the children themselves, by letting the children help in family decisions, and by encouraging hand work (the girls were taught engraving) they hoped to bring up uncorrupted young people. One of their particular tenets was the mutuality of family relationships. To them, "the child begins to bestow when it has nothing to give but affection". There was, however, a notable lack of our modern feeling that it is good for children from other homes and different classes to play together, since in the Taylors' opinion the poor were ignorant and corrupt, the rich, dissolute and cruel. Hence children should be kept from bad company and false notions by isolation.

Mrs. Taylor insisted that mothers are meant to be the teachers of their own children, and that this job "is one of the most rational and pleasing employments in which the human mind can engage."[56] Later on, Mrs. Beeton, whose book of household management was a universal reference work for more than one generation of English housekeepers, wrote, "It ought . . . to enter into the domestic policy of every parent to make her child feel that home is the happiest place in the world; that to imbue them with this precious home-feeling is one of the choicest gifts a parent can bestow."[57] Likewise Mrs. Ellis, who rivalled Mrs. Beeton in popularity, told mothers that a happy childhood is the best preparation possible for the realities and hardships of later life.[58]

In spite of the reams of good advice, there is much direct testimony that English mothers, in practice, tended to be cool and distant. Flora Tristan, a French traveler of the thirties, found that English children did not know what it was to be petted by their mothers, so their loving faculties remained inert, she thought, and the young girls became incapable of intimacy.[59] In an early draft of his *Autobiography* John Stuart Mill referred to "that rarity in England, a really warm-hearted mother"—but this passage was subsequently expunged.[60] Harriet Martineau remembered that caresses from her mother were so rare that when she was petted by a stranger one day, she burst into tears, while Mrs. Asquith said it was almost impossible to describe the gulf she felt between herself as a child and the grown-ups, her first emotional impression being that she should have been effaced, that she should not have been born at all. When her mother started to teach her to read and write the lessons always ended in punishment, and she never got a word of praise.[61]

E. E. Kellett, analyzing his own childhood, figured out that many Victorian families so hid their despotism, by emphasizing the duty of love as well as the love of duty—that the children were not really aware of it; and he attributed part of this feeling to the fact that mothers were seen so seldom that they seemed like special guests to their children.[62]

For English children were commonly raised in a special nursery, under the charge of a special person, the nurse, the British Nanny, who was usually unmarried, very proper, and by no means a wet-nurse. She was a bathing, dressing and supervising nurse. The difference in custom here and on the continent was that, though the very definition of a middle class family was that it should keep at least one servant, in France and Germany the serving personnel were not specialized. They were hired to help wherever asked, and not to perform a particular, limited list of duties. French babies were not only much more in the presence of their parents, having no special nursery to retreat to, but when they went for an outing the mother and the *bonne* often took them together, so it was less easy for something to go drastically wrong with the child without the mother's being aware.

In England the custom of treating servants with considerable reserve, the feeling that they should be left alone to perform their duties, often led to bad situations for the children. After all, if the silver didn't shine, the mistress could see it and fire the housemaid, but if Nurse pinched a little boy black and blue, and threatened worse things unless he chanted to his mother, "I love Julia, I do, I do" (an actual example) the problem could exist undetected for years. Even Lady Amberley, Bertrand Russell's mother, an exceptionally conscientious and interested parent, had to be informed by the other servants that her first child (not Bertrand) was being starved, neglected and lied about—after which she dismissed the delinquent nurse within three hours.[63] Years after her nursery days, Milly Acland asked herself why her mother had never noticed that her nurse, Barley, had been a sort of evil genius throughout her childhood, and concluded that the nurseries were so separate that a child was seldom in the mother's and nurse's company simultaneously, and that intensive child study was not yet in vogue.[64]

At its best, of course, the English system created lifelong devotion— attested to in a hundred autobiographies—between children and their nurses and conferred a certain extra glamor on the parents who contributed to the higher pleasures of life. Beyond that, while the family structure and the nurse provided protection from danger and established the routines of eating and bedtime, there seemed always to be plenty of time for pursuing individual interests, lots of afternoons and lots of siblings to play elaborate charades, run family newspapers, collect flowers or minerals. A certain number recalled boredom, but far more were grateful all their lives for this gift of unstructured time in their youth.

It is interesting that the early reformers did not differentiate so much as later ones between the roles of mother and father. Surely one of the most enthusiastic fathers ever was the journalist, William Cobbett, who declared he never knew a man who was good for much that had a dislike for little children. "How many days, how many hours, all put together, have I spent with babies in my arms! My time, when at home, and when babies were going on, was chiefly divided between the pen and the baby. I have fed and put them to sleep hundreds of times, though there were servants to whom the task might have been transferred." He said he had written many score papers amidst the noise of children and never once bade them be still.[65]

Although so much physical care was unusual in the middle class, the willingness of English fathers to be interrupted, to carry on work amid rumpus, was borne out in many families. John Stuart Mill learned Greek, in a day before bilingual dictionaries, at his father's worktable, and James Mill, the most impatient of men, would look up from his own writing to answer the little boy's questions. There is also a familiar description of Dr. Arnold at home in the evenings, reading and studying with all his brood around him; when they took a holiday in 1832, it was four weeks "of almost awful happiness, absolutely without a cloud, and we all enjoyed it equally,—mother, father, and fry."

Thackeray's daughter, Ann, used to be taken to see her father early in the mornings, where it was a privilege to watch him shave, better still to see him tearing up paper into processions of little pigs with curly tails, or drawing pictures.[66] Eleanor Farjeon's father, a novelist, took his children for long walks, with long stories in their course. The power of spinning tales out of one's head was widely shared in that generation, and seemingly is lost today. At that time, Lewis Carroll was only a genius in a field where talent abounded.

On the other hand, one confronts many examples of tyrannous and obtuse fathers. E. E. Kellett tells us that Victorian children hated their fathers even while paying ludicrous forms of deference, and that the fathers would have been astonished to know it.[67] The most famous example of the type is Theodore Pontifex, in The Way of All Flesh, which Samuel Butler modeled on his own parent, but he was bitterly criticized by other members of his family who knew the old man and perceived him differently. Still, it is probably true that most Victorian fathers hated to admit they did not know all the answers to all questions, and it was not for nothing they were commonly referred to as "the Governor".

This impression is deepened by foreign observers like Emile Boutmy, from France, who did not find in England the irreverence and lack of constraint he was accustomed to at home,[68] while Dr. Wiese, a German, felt there was no intimacy in an English home.[69] Even Dr. Arnold felt that family relations were more confidential on the continent.

The prettiest sight in Paris, according to nearly every visitor, was the crowds of children with their parents in the Tuileries or Luxembourg gardens on Sundays or holidays, and the extraordinary kindness and attentiveness of both parents.[70] Guizot, who studied examples of conjugal love throughout history, claimed that never before had parents lived on such affectionate terms with their children—[71] or, as Taine put it, in the French family every soul is open to the day.[72]

If this was true, it was closely related to the small size of French middle class families. The Parisian bourgeois wanted children, but usually stopped at two, and often proclaimed his intention to do so in his marriage contract. As Adeline Daumard pointed out, the conscious control of births enabled "love" to replace "authority" as the cement of family life.

It is hard to know how much French fathers physically cared for their children, but the literature on the subject advised them to do a lot. It was felt that the new concept of a people's state required a new sort of paternal feeling. In feudal society, they thought, fatherhood, through concentration on the oldest son, became unnatural, but the new French law of equal inheritance gave value to each child.

If boys were preferred before girls, it was because of France's desperate need of soldiers. Otherwise the equal inheritance laws and the smallness of most families made girls an object of financial and emotional concern like their brothers. Still, there was some latent prejudice. A writer who used the pen name of Gyp used to be walked by her grandfather at the age of three. He loved telling her about the Emperor. "I want to see the Emperor," she declared. "Little girls don't say, 'I want to'," she was told. She imagined war must be glorious, and asked if she could be a soldier, but was of course told it would be unsuitable. "What a misfortune I'm not a boy." "Yes, it is!" said Grandpa.[73]

In Germany there was a regular cult of the "organic" family, best described by Dr. W. H. Riehl in a sociological study, *Die Familie.*[74] Riehl wanted a strictly hierarchical set-up, with father at the top, and the rest of the members stationed according to what he felt were "natural" laws of submissiveness and group identification. The kind of simple healthy childhood celebrated by writers like Gustav Freytag left children with rosy cheeks, a lack of sophistication, but a thorough devotion to the ideals of duty—and to the state.[75]

CONCERN FOR CHILDREN NOT ONE'S OWN

The nineteenth century was the time when public responsibility for children not one's own greatly expanded. When, with the French Revolution, the state began to be considered as the organ of all its citizens, then its regulatory and exploitatory aspect was changed to include also a paternal interest. The nation itself then assumed the guise of the great Mother, or the great Father. "Allons, *enfants* de la patrie" became the rallying cry, or, "Lieb *Vaterland,* magst ruhig sein."

On the continent a large number of state-run orphanages were set up to take care of the war orphans, and this concern was soon broadened to include those who were parentless for other reasons: illegitimate and abandoned infants of whom, for example, there were said to be 117,000 in France in 1825. The first Factory Act in England, in 1802, applied only to orphan apprentices who were wards of the state, but it was still the first act of legislation intended to insure the well-being of a class of citizens solely because they were young. The British government then enlarged its concern to include the protection of children against abuse by their own parents and guardians—so it acted to stop the worst practices of child insurance (often used in Britain as an incentive to let a child die or even hasten the process) or of baby farming (where greedy individuals would offer to "adopt" children for a fee, but all too often kept their charges drugged with laudenum, filthy and underfed). In the same category are the various child labor laws which every European nation enacted to protect youngsters from overwork and from illiteracy.

Still later came the feeling that the state might have responsibilities even for children with good parents, by providing education and various health services.

It is clear the governmental interest was not exclusively humanitarian, for it became apparent to economists and especially military strategists that the prosperity and safety of the state depended on having a class of healthy citizens. Rousseau was now perceived as "giving citizens to the country, while he appeared only to think of giving mothers to their children!" The authoritarian *Livre de Famille* stressed both militarism and nationalism, while even Gustav Droz explained that enough families like the one he described in *Monsieur, Madame et Bébé* would "build a nation."

Sometimes even legislation not intended for child welfare at all had an effect on family structure and the well-being of children in it. Thus, the French revolutionary principle that all children in a family should receive equal inheritances was universally perceived as having the effect of making families smaller and organized intimately around the children, instead of around the fortune as had been the case in the old regime.

Parallel to the governments' growing interest in child welfare, or often, indeed, preceding it, came a great burst of private charity, an interest in children not their own by groups of private citizens. Long before the states felt it their duty to educate children, such groups had begun to set up infant schools for children of working mothers, or "ragged schools" where poor boys, and even girls, could learn to read and sometimes to write.

About the time that Victoria came to the throne, Flora Tristan attended a board meeting for an infant school in London, chaired by a peer.[76] She was much amused that the deliberations foundered because the upper-class board members seemed to be afraid that the school would be so beneficial that the children of the poor would overtake the rich; it did not occur to any of them, however, that they could ever send their own children to any sort of school. Flora supposed they were afraid of a mixture of classes, but in her socialistic view, this would have been a very good thing.

On the other hand, Florence Nightingale—a quarter of a century later—stated that if she had her way, no mother should bring up a child herself, there would be infant schools for everybody and if she had a child she would send him to one.[77]

When Laura Solera set up nurseries for children of factory workers in Italy, she ran into dreadful opposition because it seemed to sanction mothers' working outside the home—but later on Italian work with infants came to the forefront, as Maria Montessori developed her principles of free development, first for handicapped, later for normal children.

But private charity could never accomplish the task of reaching every child—only government could do that. So privately run schools were superseded by compulsory free schooling for all; private effort to mitigate cruelty to children was followed by laws for that purpose. In 1889 the British Parliament passed a law to protect children from cruelty only after the Society for the Prevention of Cruelty to Animals had received complaints and decided that it could hardly draw the line at protecting animals. In 1895 the Society for Prevention of Cruelty to Children received its royal charter.

The chief enemies of children were poverty and ignorance. So many children were abandoned, so many died in their mothers' arms, that Count Pellegrino Rossi was moved to declare in a lecture at the Collège de France that "the destruction of children is not official, with us, but it is perhaps more cruel" than in the exposure system of the ancient world.

Solicitude for infants seemed like a virtue of the modern period, it is true, but it could not, at first, be truly enlightened. At the very least, however, the nineteenth century was the time when public bodies began to think of children as children, with special needs because of their helplessness and vulnerability, rather than as small adults with the right to hire themselves out for sixteen hours a day, or as the chattels of their parents. The change in sentiment that began within the family had, before the century was over, grown to work great changes in society as a whole.

REFERENCES

1. Mary Berry, *Social Life in England and France, from the French Revolution in 1789 to that of July 1830* (London, 1831), p. 152.
2. William Cobbett, *Advice to Young Men and (Incidentally) to Young Women in the Middle and Higher Ranks of Life in a Series of Letters Addressed to a Youth, a Bachelor, a Lover, a Husband, a Father, a Citizen or a Subject,* originally published 1830 (London, 1926), p. 221.

3. Jeanne Daubié, *L'Emancipation de la Femme* (Paris, 1871), p. 362.
4. Madeleine Pelletier, *L'Emancipation Sexuelle de la Femme* (Paris, 1911), p. 44.
5. Cora Elisabeth Millet-Robinet and Dr. Emile Allix, *Le Livre des Jeunes Mères* (Paris, 1884), p. 64.
6. Gustav Droz, *Monsieur, Madame et Bébé*, 131st ed. (Paris, 1886), pp. 243 ff.
7. Marthe de Hédouville, *La Comtesse de Ségur et les Siens* (Paris, 1953), p. 182.
8. Theodor von Hippel, *Uber die Ehe, Sämmtliche Werke*, vol. V, Introduction.
9. Claire, Comtesse de Rémusat, *Essai sur l'Education des Femmes. Précédé d'une Etude par Octave Gréard*, originally published 1824 (Paris, 1903), p. xciii.
10. Jules Michelet, *Woman (La Femme)*, tr. J. W. Palmer (New York, 1867). p. 61.
11. See ad in *Gazette des Femmes* (May 28, 1842). Also, Mme. Celnart (Pseud. of Elisabeth Bayle-Mouillard), *Manuel Complet de la Maîtresse de Maison*, 3rd ed. (1834).
12. Sarah Ann Sewell, *Woman and the Times We Live In* (Manchester, 1869), p. 45.
13. Jane Ellen Panton, *The Way They Should Go: Hints to Young Parents* (London, 1896), *passim*.
14. Sabine Baring-Gould, *Germany: Present and Past* (2 vols; London, 1879), II, p. 274.
15. Millet-Robinet, *Jeunes Mères*, p. 17.
16. J. Sevrette, *La Jeune Ménagère: Soins Domestiques* (Paris, 1904), a text for primary schools, p. 180. See also Celnart, 37, and Sophie, Comtesse de Ségur, *La Santé des Enfants* (Paris, 1857).
17. Henry Mayhew, *German Life and Manners as Seen in Saxony at the Present Day: with an Account of Village Life, Town Life, Fashionable Life, Domestic Life, Married Life, School and University Life etc. of Germany at the Present Time*, 2nd ed. (London, 1865), p. 140.
18. William Howitt, *The Rural and Domestic Life of Germany* (Philadelphia, 1843), p. 30.
19. Lady Morgan, *Italy* (3 vol; London, 1821), II, p. 225.
20. Cobbett, *Advice*, p. 240.
21. Elizabeth Grant Smith, *Memoirs of a Highland Laby: the Autobiography of Elizabeth Grant of Rothiemurchus, afterwards Mrs. Smith of Baltiboys, 1797-1830*, ed. Lady Strachey (London, 1911).
22. Walter de la Mare, *Early One Morning in the Spring. Chapters on Children and on Childhood as it is Revealed in Particular in Early Memoirs and in Early Writings* (New York, 1935), p. 242.
23. Fanny E. Kingsley, *Charles Kingsley: His Letters and Memories of his Early Life*, original ed. 1877 (2 vols; Leipzig Tauchnitz, 1881), I, p. 260.
24. de la Mare, *Early One Morning*, p. 180.
25. Elizabeth Cleghorn Gaskell, *"My Diary"; the Early Years of my Daughter Marianne*, privately printed (London, 1923).
26. C. A. E. Moberly, *Dulce Domum: George Moberly, his Family and Friends* (London, 1916), pp. 71 ff.
27. Morton Schatzmann, *Soul Murder: Persecution in the Family* (New York, 1973).
28. Augustus Hare, *The Years with Mother: Being an Abridgment of the First Three Volumes of The Story of My Life*, ed. Malcolm Barnes (1952).
29. Cecil Willett Cunnington, *Feminine Attitudes in the Nineteenth Century* (New York, 1936), p. 129.
30. Edmund Gosse, *Father and Son: Biographical Reflections* (New York, 1908),

p. 50.

31. Waldo Hilary Dunn, *James Anthony Froude, a Biography: 1818-1856,* incorporates Froude's *Autobiography* (Oxford, 1961), p. 17.

32. John Ruskin, *Praeterita. Outlines of Scenes and Thoughts Perhaps Worthy of Memory in My Past Life,* with an introduction by Kenneth Clark (London, 1949), p. 12.

33. Ann Hinton Taylor, *Practical Hints to Young Females on the Duties of a Wife, and a Mother, and a Mistress of a Family,* 3rd ed. (London, 1815), p. 51.

34. de la Mare, *Early One Morning,* p. 232.

35. Graham Willas, *The Life of Francis Place, 1771-1854,* 3rd ed. (New York, 1919), p. 74.

36. Ruskin, *Praeterita,* p. 17.

37. de la Mare, *Early One Morning,* p. 231.

38. F. J. Harvey Darton, *Children's Books in England: Five Centuries of Social Life* (Cambridge, 1958), p. 177.

39. Eleanor Acland, *Good-bye for the Present: The Story of Two Childhoods: Milly, 1878-1888, and Ellen, 1913-1924* (New York, 1935), p. 31.

40. Frances Ann Kemble, *Records of a Girlhood* (New York, 1879), p. 9.

41. Derek Patmore, *Portrait of my Family, 1783-1896* (New York & London, 1935), p. 120.

42. Cobbett, *Advice,* pp. 275 ff.

43. Philip Hamerton, *Round My House: Notes of Rural Life in France in Peace and War,* 3rd ed. (London, 1876), p. 275.

44. Millet-Robinet, *Jeunes Mères,* p. 337.

45. *Livre de Famille,* p. 188.

46. Matilda Betham-Edwards, *Home Life in France,* 6th ed. (1913), p. 44.

47. Otto von Corvin, *Ein Leben voller Abenteuer, herausgegeben .. von Hermann Wendel* (Frankfurt, 1924), p. 36.

48. Adelheid Mommsen, *Theodor Mommsen im Kreise der Seinen* (Berlin, 1936), p. 48.

49. Jonathan Gathorne-Hardy, *The Rise and Fall of the British Nanny* (London, 1972).

50. Jules Renard, *Carrots,* tr. from the French by C. W. Stonier, original French ed. 1895 (London, 1946).

51. Dr. Albert Moll, *The Sexual Life of the Child,* tr. from German by Dr. Eden Paul, German ed. 1909 (New York, 1913).

52. Maria Edgeworth and Richard Lovell Edgeworth, *Practical Education,* American ed. (2 vols; New York, 1801), II, p. 301.

53. Karoline Rudolphi, *Gemälde Weiblicher Erziehung,* 4th ed. (Heidelberg & Leipzig, 1857).

54. Elisabeth Charlotte de Guizot, *Lettres de Famille sur l'Education,* 4th ed. (2 vols; Paris, 1852).

55. Hannah More, *Strictures on the Modern System of Female Education, in Works* (New York, 1835), vol. VI, p. 36.

56. Isaac Taylor of Ongar, *Advice to the Teens,* from 2nd London ed. (Boston, 1820), p. 64.

57. H. Montgomery Hyde, *Mr. and Mrs. Beeton* (London, 1951), p. 98.

58. Sara Ellis, *The Mothers of England: Their Influence and Responsibility* (New York, 1844).

59. Flora Tristan, *Promenades dans Londres* (Paris & London, 1840), p. 303.

60. Michael St. John Packe, *The Life of John Stuart Mill* (London, 1954), p. 33.

61. Margot Asquith, ed. *Myself When Young: By Famous Women of To-Day* (London, 1938), p. 45.

62. E. E. Kellett, *As I Remember* (London, 1936), p. 238.
63. Eleanor Farjeon, *A Nursery in the Nineties* (London, 1935), p. 183.
64. Acland, *Good-Bye*, pp. 25, 196.
65. Cobbett, *Advice*, p. 176.
66. Anne Ritchie, *Introduction to The Sketch Book by W. M. Thackeray in Works*, biographical edition (New York & London, 1899).
67. Kellett, *As I Remember*, p. 227.
68. Emile Boutmy, *The English People: A Study of their Political Psychology*, tr. from the French by E. English (New York & London, 1904).
69. Ludwig A. Wiese, *German Letters on English Education*, tr. by W. D. Arnold (London, 1854), p. 36.
70. Arnold Ruge, *Studien und Erinnerungen aus den Jahren 1843-45*. Also, Harriet Beecher Stowe, *Sunny Memories of Foreign Lands* (Boston, 1854) and Thackeray, *The Paris Sketch Book*, dated 1840.
71. Karl Hillebrand, *France and the French in the Second Half of the Nineteenth Century*, tr. from the 3rd German ed. (London, 1881).
72. Taine, *England*, p. 91.
73. Gyp (Sibylle Gabrielle Mirabeau), *Souvenirs d'une Petite Fille* (2 vols; Paris, 1927).
74. W. H. Riehl, *Die Familie* (Stuttgart, 1856).
75. Gustav Freytag, *Erinnerungen aus Meinem Leben* (Leipzig, 1887).
76. Tristan, *Londres*, p. 352.

Index